S. Hrg. 109–916

TUNE-UP ON CORPORATE TAX ISSUES: WHAT'S GOING ON UNDER THE HOOD?

HEARING

BEFORE THE

COMMITTEE ON FINANCE
UNITED STATES SENATE

ONE HUNDRED NINTH CONGRESS

SECOND SESSION

JUNE 13, 2006

Printed for the use of the Committee on Finance

U.S. GOVERNMENT PRINTING OFFICE

35–704—PDF WASHINGTON : 2006

For sale by the Superintendent of Documents, U.S. Government Printing Office
Internet: bookstore.gpo.gov Phone: toll free (866) 512–1800; DC area (202) 512–1800
Fax: (202) 512–2250 Mail: Stop SSOP, Washington, DC 20402–0001

COMMITTEE ON FINANCE

CHARLES E. GRASSLEY, Iowa, *Chairman*

ORRIN G. HATCH, Utah
TRENT LOTT, Mississippi
OLYMPIA J. SNOWE, Maine
JON KYL, Arizona
CRAIG THOMAS, Wyoming
RICK SANTORUM, Pennsylvania
BILL FRIST, Tennessee
GORDON SMITH, Oregon
JIM BUNNING, Kentucky
MIKE CRAPO, Idaho

MAX BAUCUS, Montana
JOHN D. ROCKEFELLER IV, West Virginia
KENT CONRAD, North Dakota
JAMES M. JEFFORDS (I), Vermont
JEFF BINGAMAN, New Mexico
JOHN F. KERRY, Massachusetts
BLANCHE L. LINCOLN, Arkansas
RON WYDEN, Oregon
CHARLES E. SCHUMER, New York

KOLAN DAVIS, *Staff Director and Chief Counsel*
RUSSELL SULLIVAN, *Democratic Staff Director*

CONTENTS

OPENING STATEMENTS

COMMUNICATIONS

TUNE-UP ON CORPORATE TAX ISSUES: WHAT'S GOING ON UNDER THE HOOD?

TUESDAY, JUNE 13, 2006

U.S. SENATE,
COMMITTEE ON FINANCE,
Washington, DC.

The hearing was convened, pursuant to notice, at 10:05 a.m., in Room SD–215, Dirksen Senate Office Building, Hon. Charles E. Grassley (chairman of the committee) presiding.

Present: Senators Hatch, Kyl, Thomas, Bunning, Crapo, Baucus, Bingaman, and Wyden.

OPENING STATEMENT OF HON. CHARLES E. GRASSLEY, A U.S. SENATOR FROM IOWA, CHAIRMAN, COMMITTEE ON FINANCE

The CHAIRMAN. Before I start, from the Kenya government's Committee on Finance, Planning, Trade, and Tourism, we have Dr. Oburu Oginga. And I am not going to pronounce this second name right, so I am not even going to try to pronounce it, but they are standing up there. We welcome you very much. Thank you.

[Applause.]

The CHAIRMAN. Today's hearing will be primarily focused on the current state of our corporate tax system, but we will also touch on basic issues to consider in the context of business tax reform—lowering rates and broadening the base.

The continued globalization of our economy, and of course the complexity of our business activity, presents significant challenges to our corporate tax system as a whole, but also to problems related to the administration of that system.

The complexity of the tax code itself creates burdens and inefficiencies for taxpayers, as well as for the Internal Revenue Service, although some taxpayers may view that complexity as creating opportunities for tax avoidance.

According to the Congressional Budget Office, corporate income tax receipts were a record $278 billion in 2005, up 47 percent over the prior year, representing, as a part of Gross Domestic Product, 2.3 percent. That is also the highest percentage since 1980.

The first 8 months of 2006 show the trend continuing, with corporate tax receipts up 30 percent over last year. The recent surge in corporate tax receipts is due in large part to the strong performance of our economy. Corporate tax receipts have gone up, along with rising corporate profits resulting from a growing economy.

Now, in addition to the growing economy, I think some of that increase is also because of continuing efforts to combat corporate tax abuse and improve corporate tax compliance.

As an example, in the year 2004, Congress enacted my package of legislation, cracking down on tax shelters and requiring companies to publicly disclose, in SEC filings, penalties for failing to report a tax shelter so investors will know whether a company is violating tax shelter laws.

These provisions provided the Internal Revenue Service with tools to combat tax abuse, and also to work to deter tax shelter activity. We need to do all we can to ensure tax compliance by corporations and individuals alike to maintain the fairness and integrity of our tax system.

To that end, I look forward to hearing from Mark Everson, Commissioner of IRS, and David Walker, Comptroller General of the Government Accountability Office, about the current state of play in corporate tax compliance and what is known about the corporate tax gap.

Tied into corporate profits is the taxation of appreciated investment in corporations. In May of 2005, Senator Baucus and I requested the Government Accountability Office to conduct a study on the capital gains tax gap. Today, Mr. Walker will also discuss his Agency's findings from that study and its recommendations as to how we can close that capital gains tax gap.

The Department of Justice also plays a key role in enforcing tax laws. Eileen O'Connor, the Assistant Attorney General, Tax Division, will help us and fill us in on the current issues in corporate tax from that division's perspective. She will also discuss some related matters, including the civil and criminal laws at issue with stock options being back-dated.

As promised earlier this year, we will examine the tax policy behind the LIFO method of inventory accounting with the help of Dr. Plesko, associate professor of accounting, University of Connecticut School of Business.

Dr. Plesko's scholarship in the area of bridging the reporting gap for the many differences between financial accounting standards and the tax code supports recent changes in the Internal Revenue Service's form Schedule M–3.

The IRS recently came out with a new Schedule M–3, which will provide examiners of that Agency much more detail regarding these differences.

One of the panelists, Mr. Edward Kleinbard, a New York partner at the law firm of Cleary, Gottlieb, Steen & Hamilton, has recommended public disclosure of the M–3 to promote transparency in financial reporting.

Confidentiality of tax returns, of course, is a fundamental part of our self-assessment system. It is important to balance taxpayers' interests and privacy with the need for tax law compliance.

Commissioner Everson has publicly stated that corporate tax return disclosure is something that merits serious debate. This hearing will provide a forum for that debate.

In addition to tax compliance and enforcement matters, we will also hear testimony on the basic aspects of our current corporate system, the tax rate, as well as the tax base, that we should consider revisiting in the context of business tax reform.

It is obvious that, in the global economy, tax policy is not so neatly put into domestic and international categories. Our corporate tax rate is typically thought of as domestic tax policy, but when it ranks at or near the top among OECD countries, it influences international business decisions like, obviously, where to build a plant, and it gives companies incentives to shift income offshore.

As this committee turns to tax reform, a key objective should be to make the system one that is fair and allows businesses to make decisions based more on economic merit and less on distortions generated by the tax code.

The recent global trend has been to lower corporate tax rates and to broaden the tax base. This is no longer an abstract idea. Our last panelist, then, Dr. Martin Sullivan, economist and contributing editor at Tax Analysts, will discuss this new era in corporate taxation that has arrived in many countries, particularly across Europe. I look forward to hearing our panelists discuss each of these important issues.

I now have the opportunity to turn to Senator Baucus, our Ranking Democrat.

OPENING STATEMENT OF HON. MAX BAUCUS, A U.S. SENATOR FROM MONTANA

Senator BAUCUS. Thank you, Mr. Chairman. Thank you very much.

Woodrow Wilson once said, "Every great man of business has got somewhere the touch of an idealist in him." Well, based on many Montana business owners whom I have met, I believe that is true. They take care of their workers, they pay their taxes, because it is the right thing to do.

Unfortunately, there are other people in business as well. The IRS estimates that, every year, taxpayers fail to pay $350 billion in taxes that they owe. That is every year.

That number is growing. About 40 percent of that tax gap is attributed to corporate and other business income, 40 percent of the $350 billion each year. The term "tax gap," I think, grossly understates the problem. We have gone far beyond a gap. That $350 billion a year is more like a tax gulf.

The tax gap is not just the IRS's problem; it is our problem. It is the problem of all taxpayers in America who pay their fair share.

Former IRS Commissioner Charles Rossotti called it the "free rider tax." Those who do not pay get a free ride on the backs of everyone who does.

On September 7, Treasury Secretary Snow testified before this committee, and I asked him about the administration's plan for closing the $350 billion annual tax gap. I did not get a satisfactory answer.

He said, "IRS continues to work on it. They are aware of it." He referred me to five legislative proposals in the President's budget. The Secretary argued that these five proposals were going to help close the gap.

Well, I have studied those proposals, and they are very modest, to give them the most credit. According to the administration's own projections, these proposals will raise $3.5 billion over 10 years.

The yearly tax gap is $350 billion. So over 10 years, that is $3.5 trillion. The gap is $3.5 trillion. The administration's proposals will raise $3.5 billion over the same period of time, so the administration is proposing a $3.5 billion fix for a $3.5 trillion problem.

Well, I told Secretary Snow at the hearing that I wanted results. I wanted a plan within 30 days. That deadline has come and gone, yet the tax gap—the tax gulf—keeps expanding.

The IRS says that it gets a 4 to 1 return on investment in tax enforcement. For every one dollar it spends, it gets four dollars back in additional taxes collected. So it makes sense for the administration to propose an IRS budget that would take advantage of the 4 to 1 return, but they have not, and the tax gulf just keeps growing.

Two years ago, I issued a challenge. I called on the IRS to achieve a 90 percent voluntary compliance rate by the year 2010. At the time, the tax gap was $311 billion a year. Two years later, we are looking at a gap of $350 billion a year. If we continue at this rate, by the year 2010 the tax gap will be more than $500 billion a year.

We need effective enforcement efforts to detect and stop abuse and fraud. It is critical that tax cheats know they are going to get caught. We need to stop winking at this problem.

This problem has been raised by me especially, and by others, many times. I have given challenges to the administration, to Secretaries, to IRS Commissioners. Nothing happens. Nothing of consequence happens.

So we need to stop winking at this problem and we need to stare it down, to solve it. We need to make sure that all taxpayers are on a level playing field. We need to ensure that some do not gain a competitive edge because they have gamed the tax system. Protecting taxpayers' rights, providing quality of service, and enforcing the law effectively are obligations this IRS should meet, and exceed.

So, Mr. Chairman, I am glad we are holding this hearing today to examine the corporate tax gap, and hope that these hearings will produce solid recommendations to close that gap.

I, for one, have about had it. I am not going to rest until this thing is solved. Maybe not every penny, but that we solve it so we know that, by and large, we have gotten the job done.

I am astounded, frankly, that the administration has not done more about it. I am embarrassed that the Congress has not done more about it, and, by gosh, if I have anything to do with it, we are going to do something about this.

The CHAIRMAN. Thank you very much, Senator Baucus.

We are going to now go to our witnesses in the way that you are lined at the table. For the benefit of our committee members, the three government witnesses will have 10 minutes each, contrary to our tradition of 5-minute turns. So Mr. Everson, Mr. Walker and Ms. O'Connor will have 10 minutes apiece.

Would you proceed?

STATEMENT OF HON. MARK EVERSON, COMMISSIONER, INTERNAL REVENUE SERVICE, WASHINGTON, DC

Mr. EVERSON. Good morning, Mr. Chairman, Ranking Member Baucus, other members of the Finance Committee. It is my pleasure to be with you this morning to discuss corporate compliance issues.

I want to thank the committee for its interest in the issues I am going to talk about today, and for the support you have provided for our efforts to rebuild IRS enforcement programs, including, in particular, some very helpful provisions that were contained in the American Jobs Creation Act, and subsequent tax legislation. As always, I also appreciate your efforts to secure adequate resources for the IRS.

Turning to today's subject, corporate compliance challenges, the IRS faces new and more challenging tax administration problems resulting from globalization, complexity of the code, complexity of business transactions, and the growing book tax gap.

Let me briefly outline these environmental factors.

Globalization. Globalization and cross-border activity continue to challenge tax administration. With multiple domestic and global tiered entities, it is often difficult to determine the full scope, and resulting tax impact, of a single transaction or series of transactions. Complexities of globalization and cross-border activity create opportunities for aggressive tax planning, demonstrated in several of the compliance issues mentioned in my letter to Chairman Grassley of May 19.

Complexity of the Internal Revenue Code. The code itself continues to expand, becoming more complex and challenging to administer. Large businesses utilize every available resource to explore opportunities to reduce their tax liability by entering into transactions which take advantage of the most intricate and complicated code provisions.

Complexity of transactions. Large businesses engage in sophisticated transactions that result in complex relationships with multiple filing requirements. The increasing volume and complexity of these transactions make it difficult for us to identify them and to effectively address them in a timely manner.

Growing book tax differences. Companies strive to reflect the highest possible after-tax profits in their financial statements, while at the same time they are incentivized to report the lowest possible taxable income and tax liability.

Research indicates that book tax differences sometimes indicate significant compliance risk. When the details of business transactions and book tax differences are not visible, the accurate determination of shareholder value, the efficiency of capital markets, and the correct determination of tax can be jeopardized.

Let me now turn to specific areas of concern.

Transfer of intangibles offshore and cost-sharing arrangements. Taxpayers, especially in the high-technology and pharmaceutical industries, are shifting profits offshore, often to low- or no-tax countries, through a variety of arrangements resulting from the transfer of valuable intangibles to related foreign entities for inadequate consideration. Cost-sharing arrangements are often the method of choice for this activity. The buy-in amount in cost-sharing arrangements is often understated, resulting in the improper shifting of income offshore.

Abusive foreign tax credit transactions. Taxpayers are manipulating the code to create and claim foreign tax credits, where the associated foreign-source income is not taxed in the United States. These structured financing transactions often result in the unintended realization and duplication of tax benefits through the use of certain structures designed to exploit inconsistencies between U.S. and foreign laws.

Abusive hybrid instrument transactions. Taxpayers can use hybrid instruments, hybrid entities, and similar structures to capitalize on differences between foreign and domestic tax laws because these structures are often treated differently for U.S. and foreign tax purposes. This leads to transactions with results that in many cases are unintended by Congress, though technically compliant.

Transfer pricing. Taxpayers are continuing to shift significant profits offshore. Taxpayers often manipulate the price of related transactions so that the income of an economic group is ostensibly earned in a low-tax jurisdiction, or in no jurisdiction at all, rather than the U.S., thus lowering the enterprise's world-wide tax burden with an unwarranted loss to the U.S. FSC.

R&E credit claims. Taxpayers are filing refund claims, often marketed to them on a contingency fee basis, to claim additional research credits. These claims are frequently based on insupportable amounts, non-qualified expenditures, or estimates for which the taxpayers do not have contemporaneous documentation.

The universal service fund. Federal and State governments impose taxes on telecommunications service consumers to fund subsidies to the telecommunications carriers for universal service programs. The issue is whether amounts received by telecommunications carriers from Federal and State universal service programs constitute non-shell older contributions to capital. Some telecom taxpayers are receiving significant subsidies and are not reporting them as income.

Mixed service costs. Some electric and gas utility companies have changed their method of accounting to allow them to consider certain large self-constructed assets "routine and repetitive" under the simplified service cost method, which allows a much faster, and on occasion even immediate, write-off.

Section 199 issues. This JOBS Act provision provides a deduction for certain manufacturing activities conducted in the United States. We are concerned that mass marketed contingency fee-based refund claims and other excessive deductions will become a problem under section 199.

Foreign earnings repatriation. This JOBS Act provision provided a limited opportunity for companies to repatriate foreign earnings to the U.S., provided they satisfied certain requirements and conditions. Audit issues are likely to include compliance and board-approved reinvestment plans and the compliance of repatriated funds with regulatory requirements.

Executive compensation. Section 409A of the JOBS Act provides that the executive or other service provider must include all deferred amounts under a non-qualified deferred compensation plan for all taxable years, to the extent that they are not subject to a substantial risk of forfeiture and not previously included in income, unless certain requirements are met.

The IRS is working actively on each of these issues. Some are being addressed through guidance, others by increased audit activities, and even enhanced cooperation with other national tax administrations.

Before closing, let me mention a few areas which I believe merit review by this committee. We think the Finance Committee should reexamine the increase in book tax differences in greater depth in order to fully understand its impact on compliance and to consider appropriate remedies.

The R&E credit should be made permanent. Record-keeping and substantiation requirements need to be more comprehensive to improve our ability to effectively administer the code for R&E credit refund claims.

These claims continue to have a substantial adverse effect on compliance and produce substantial administrative burdens. The temporary nature of the credit, its repeated renewals, and its incremental nature each contribute to these difficulties.

Penalties are needed for improper refund claims. The accuracy-related penalties in the code apply only in the case of an underpayment of tax and provide no disincentive to taxpayers who file frivolous or negligent claims for refund.

We believe this encourages promoters, including accounting firms, to market improper refund claim schemes with very limited down-side risks. The Finance Committee should consider how the accuracy-related penalty could be expanded to cover abusive refund claims.

Let me just close by showing you two charts on this point. This shows you the growth in the refund claims that we are examining for a 4-year period, from $10 billion to $15 billion.

This is what we are disallowing upon examination, and this is what we are allowing. This percentage has actually decreased, through resource constraints, to about 50 percent over time due to the growth, really, of what is being claimed.

This shows you what happens when we make the disallowance. In 85 percent of the cases, the taxpayer just rolls over; they do not fight it, because they knew what they did was bogus. There is no penalty for this action.

In contrast, there are complicated issues on a regular examination, and there is a reversal. About a third of the time or more the taxpayer agrees on the large corporate examination, but more often than not they slug it out through appeals or through the courts because they think they are right.

Clearly, what you have here is a case of ambulance-chasing by the big accounting firms, trying to get contingent fees, because there is no consequence when they make a claim.

Thank you.

The CHAIRMAN. Thank you very much, Mr. Everson.

[The prepared statement of Mr. Everson appears in the appendix.]

The CHAIRMAN. Now, General Walker?

STATEMENT OF HON. DAVID WALKER, COMPTROLLER GENERAL, U.S. GOVERNMENT ACCOUNTABILITY OFFICE, WASHINGTON, DC

Mr. WALKER. Thank you, Mr. Chairman and members of the committee. I assume that my entire statement will be included in the record, Mr. Chairman, therefore, I will move to summarize.

I appreciate the opportunity to be before you to discuss corporate income tax compliance issues, as well as options for improving taxpayers' voluntary compliance in the reporting of capital gains or losses on their sales of securities.

The complexity of the corporate income tax generates opportunities for tax avoidance that can be categorized as either clearly legal, clearly illegal, or of uncertain legality.

Although bringing in less revenue than used to occur, the corporate income tax is one of the pillars of the Federal tax system. The $277 billion in estimated 2006 corporate tax revenues must be a part of the overall consideration in dealing with our Nation's large and growing long-term fiscal imbalance.

Determining corporate income tax liabilities and the extent of corporate tax avoidance is a challenge because of the complexity of the tax code, coupled with business transactions that are often extremely complex and involve multinational corporate structures. Frankly, in many regards, Mr. Chairman, the government is simply outgunned when it comes to corporate income tax compliance.

Since the early 1980s and through 2005, the corporate income tax has accounted for from 6 to 13 percent of total Federal revenues, or from 1 percent to 2.5 percent, approximately, of the economy during those same years. Consequently, while it is not the largest part of our Federal revenue, it is an important part of our Federal revenue.

Corporate tax expenditures serve to reduce the amount of revenue that otherwise would be raised through the corporate income tax. The sum of estimated foregone revenue for the Federal Government because of corporate tax expenditures was $80 billion for fiscal year 2005.

We reported, in September of 2005, that the effectiveness of many tax expenditures is not subject to the level of review similar to programs that spend money directly.

To a large extent, they are off the radar screen. They are not part of the budget process, they are not part of the appropriations process, and they are not subject to a periodic review and reexamination, as should be the case.

In our September, 2005 report we recommended that the Office of Management and Budget and the Treasury Department take steps to ensure regular reexamination of tax expenditures, including various corporate tax preferences.

As far back as 1994, we have also suggested that Congress should review these tax expenditures, considering such things as how well the corporate tax expenditures are achieving their stated purpose, who is benefitting from them, and whether they should remain, given the potential benefits of moving to a simpler corporate tax code, possibly with a broader base and reduced rates.

Ensuring corporate income tax compliance is challenging because much of the corporate tax avoidance is legal. Also, the true tax liability for large corporations is extremely difficult to determine, and often subject to negotiation. The amount of corporate tax avoidance, candidly, is unknown.

As noted, IRS's published estimate of the corporate tax gap, the difference between what corporations pay voluntarily on time in taxes and what they are required to pay under the law, was $32 billion for tax year 2001. That is compared to an overall gross tax gap of $345 billion for that year.

Under-reporting of income was the largest single component of the corporate tax gap, contributing an estimated $30 billion out of the $32 billion. Importantly, the IRS does not have an estimate for non-filing of corporate income tax returns for fiscal year 2001.

IRS has not systematically measured the level of compliance for large corporations, and the last measure of non-compliance for small corporations was in the 1980s.

In order to improve efforts to reduce the tax gap, we have recommended that IRS develop plans to periodically measure tax compliance for areas that have been measured and study ways to cost-effectively measure compliance for other components of the tax gap that have not been measured, such as excise taxes and corporate taxes. IRS has agreed with our recommendations.

IRS has recently increased the number of corporate audits and recommended tax assessments. These trends are both positive and promising. However, given the lack of reliable measures to assess the extent of corporate non-compliance and other factors, continued oversight of these efforts will be warranted in order for Congress to be able to make informed judgments on their overall effectiveness.

In addition to examinations, the IRS has taken a number of initiatives, some of which are new, to help ensure corporate tax compliance. IRS has also been revising the corporate tax examination process. For example, IRS reports that it has shortened the cycle time for examinations.

Future success in following through on these initiatives will require replenishment of IRS staff, which could be challenging given the increasing number of employees who are eligible to retire, and who are otherwise leaving key occupations within the IRS.

In part, because the IRS does not have a reliable measure of corporate tax compliance, it will be a challenge to demonstrate the effectiveness of increased audits and various initiatives it has undertaken.

The effectiveness of IRS's efforts will depend on the extent to which the taxes recommended are actually collected, given past data showing that a relatively small portion of recommended assessments is ultimately collected.

For these reasons, as well as for human capital management and other reasons, IRS's increased compliance efforts will warrant continued oversight. Judicious use of technology has already helped the IRS to improve its productivity, and continued well-managed technology initiatives have the potential to further improve the use of its resources and to increase its productivity and effectiveness.

The IRS plans to gradually expand the number of firms that are required to electronically file. This effort and other opportunities to leverage modern technology can serve to help IRS deal with the complex issues in the corporate tax environment.

When any taxpayer is found to owe taxes—and these amounts are no longer in dispute—failure to collect the taxes sends an adverse compliance signal. In February of 2004, we reported that some Department of Defense contractors abused the Federal tax system with little consequence.

In June of 2005, we reported that many contractors of civilian agencies in the Federal Government also abused the Federal tax system. Our analysis showed that 33,000 Federal contractors received substantial Federal payments from civilian agencies during fiscal year 2004 but also owed more than $3 billion in unpaid Federal taxes.

In our reports on this issue we made numerous recommendations intended to improve the Federal payment levy program by expanding the amount and type of tax debt eligible for inclusion in the program, expanding the volume of Federal payments subject to levy, and correcting process and control deficiencies that hinder the program's ability to maximize the amount levied for payments to contractors with unpaid Federal taxes.

In our 2004 report, we also recommended that OMB develop options for prohibiting Federal contract awards to businesses and individuals that abuse the Federal tax system, including designating such tax abuse as a cause for government-wide debarment or suspension.

Consistent with our recommendation to OMB, I believe that Congress should consider suspending government business with contractors who are delinquent on their taxes as of a specific prospective effective date, with a provision for limited waivers in unique circumstances. The same concept could also be applied for Federal grantees where there are similar problems.

Finally, Mr. Chairman and members of the committee, you asked GAO to testify on a report, done at your request, that we are issuing here today on individual taxpayers' compliance in reporting capital gains income from the sale of securities.

For tax year 2001, an estimated 36 percent, or over 7 million, of individual taxpayers who sold securities misreported their capital gains or losses. Using the words "wrong cost basis for securities" was the primary type of non-compliance leading to this misreported income.

IRS's attempts to address misreported security sales income through enforcement and taxpayer service programs, which are to help taxpayers voluntarily comply, have had mixed success. Expanding information-reporting to taxpayers and IRS on security sales to include the cost basis has the potential to improve, not only taxpayer voluntary compliance, but also to help IRS enforcement.

Our new report includes several matters for Congressional consideration, including requiring brokers to report to both taxpayers and the IRS the adjusted basis of securities and to ensure that the IRS has sufficient authority to pursue actions in this area.

Furthermore, we recommend that the IRS modify the instructions for individual income tax returns to clarify the appropriate use of capital gains to offset capital gains or other income, and to provide guidance on resources available to taxpayers to determine their basis. IRS has agreed with our recommendations.

So in summary, Mr. Chairman, IRS is agreeing with most of our recommendations and is pursuing administrative implementation, but some of our recommendations require Congressional action.

Thank you very much, Mr. Chairman.

The CHAIRMAN. Thank you, General Walker.

[The prepared statement of Mr. Walker appears in the appendix.]

The CHAIRMAN. Now, Ms. O'Connor?

STATEMENT OF HON. EILEEN J. O'CONNOR, ASSISTANT ATTORNEY GENERAL, TAX DIVISION, U.S. DEPARTMENT OF JUSTICE, WASHINGTON, DC

Ms. O'CONNOR. Mr. Chairman, Ranking Member, members of the committee, thank you very much for your interest in these issues and for inviting me to be with you today. It is my honor to testify today on behalf of the more than 500 men and women of the Justice Department's Tax Division.

As you know, their mission is the fair and consistent enforcement of the laws that provide the funds our government needs to do what we ask of it. Your focus in today's hearing is corporate tax issues, by which I understand you to mean not only tax issues presented by large corporate taxpayers, but also large-dollar issues presented by the tax shelters many individuals have used to virtually eliminate their tax on large amounts of taxable income. You also suggested I might comment on recent developments concerning tax fraud scams.

It is appropriate to consider these together. Abusive tax shelters for corporations and wealthy individuals are at one end of the illegal tax avoidance spectrum. At the other end are the scams that cost the Federal Treasury less per person who uses them, but that can be used by many thousands of people.

Until 2001, the scamsters who sold these low-end tax fraud schemes often went for years without apparent government attention. They used the fact that they had been selling their schemes out in the open and the government had not sought to shut them down as proof of their legitimacy.

Likewise, the developers, peddlers, and enablers of the high-end tax schemes, the so-called sophisticated tax shelters, believed they too could evade detection, and failing that, they could use an attorney's opinion letter as a "get out of jail" or "get out of penalties free" card.

I am pleased to report that, as a result of the work the Tax Division has undertaken during the past 5 years, these expectations are changing. From the high end to the low end, these scams and shelters are major contributors to the $350-billion tax gap to which Ranking Member Baucus referred.

A quick peek under the hood of the Tax Division reveals that Federal refund litigation involving tax shelters has burgeoned in the last several years, and will continue to do so in the foreseeable future.

At this moment, the Tax Division has 80 to 100 attorneys, nearly one-third of our attorney workforce, working in various combinations on a great many trial teams engaged in more than 100 high-stakes cases in 23 Federal trial courts.

I hasten to add, they are excited and eager, these attorneys, about defending the integrity of our Federal tax laws and doing all they can to put a stop to the abusive tax shelter phenomenon that drains the Federal Treasury and shames the legal, accounting, and banking professions.

Let me mention just a few of the types of sophisticated tax shelters the Tax Division is presently litigating. Each of these shelters is used by corporations and wealthy individuals and carries with it, according to the best estimates, a cost to the Federal Treasury of approximately $5 billion.

You will recall the Tax Division's victory in the Long-Term Capital Holdings case in the District of Connecticut year before last. Last fall, the U.S. Court of Appeals for the Second Circuit upheld the IRS's application of the 40-percent penalty.

So in addition to the $40 million in taxes held to be due, the principals in this entity are subject to $16 million in penalties, this notwithstanding opinion letters vouching for the tax consequences of the deal. Forty percent penalties are significant; there should be harm in trying.

Similarly, notwithstanding the more-likely-than-not opinion letters from a Washington, DC law firm and a major accounting firm, Judge Rodriguez of the Western District of Texas recently ruled in one of the Trans-Capital Leasing Associates cases that "the 1991 mainframe investment was a transaction solely shaped by tax avoidance objectives and completely lacking in profit potential" and entered judgment in favor of the government. The court noted that, for a half-million-dollar fee, the taxpayer received $11 million in tax deductions, with no corresponding taxable income.

The U.S. Court of Appeals for the Sixth Circuit recently held that Dow Chemical's corporate-owned life insurance program had "no practicable economic effect, other than the creation of income tax losses," and it denied Dow Chemical the $33 million in deductions it had claimed from the plan.

Even people who do not watch tax developments closely sat up and took notice last year when a District Court in Maryland granted summary judgment for Black & Decker in a contingent liability tax shelter.

The Tax Division appealed that loss to the U.S. Court of Appeals for the Fourth Circuit in February and won a reversal. The Court of Appeals remanded that case to the District Court for a trial on the merits of the government's economic substance arguments. We expect that trial to take place next spring.

Finally, the Son-of-BOSS tax shelter cases. Proving the probable accuracy of the $5-billion estimate that is attached to these tax shelters is the fact that, of the two-thirds or so of the Son-of-BOSS participants—of whom there are approximately 1,800 identified through Tax Division's aggressive summons enforcement litigation—of the 1,200 or so who participated in the IRS settlement initiative, the IRS has already received about $3.7 billion from those 1,200, and last I heard the IRS was still counting.

The first of these cases to be tried, Jade Trading, that trial concluded in December in the U.S. Court of Claims, and the decision in that case is pending. The Tax Division presently has 45 other Son-of-BOSS cases in various stages of litigation, and we understand there are many, many more on their way. These are a few of the cases in which the United States, in a refund suit, is the defendant.

Let me now turn to some of the criminal prosecutions that have arisen from the development and sale of sophisticated tax shelters. The United States entered into a deferred prosecution agreement with KPMG LLP in which the firm admitted that it marketed and sold fraudulent tax shelters, and it agreed to pay $456 million in penalties.

Domenick DeGiorgio, a former HVB accountant, pleaded guilty to defrauding the United States by helping promoters of the so-called BLIPS shelter.

HVB Group itself, Germany's second-largest bank, agreed to pay $29.6 million in fines and restitution and entered into an 18-month deferred prosecution agreement in connection with its role in tax shelters.

Eighteen former KPMG partners, and Raymond Ruble, a former partner at the law firm Sidley Austin Brown & Wood, were indicted by a grand jury in the Southern District of New York on charges of conspiracy to defraud the United States in connection with their efforts to market, sell, and conceal a series of fraudulent tax shelters. That trial is scheduled for September of this year.

Former KPMG partner David Rivkin has pleaded guilty to charges of conspiracy and tax evasion and agreed to cooperate with prosecutors in the case against the 18 other defendants. Rivkin admitted that he conspired with the others to prepare and execute false documents so that clients could file false returns.

Let me now mention two brief examples of criminal prosecutions arising from what I referred to earlier as the low-end tax schemes. You might call them tax shelters for the less wealthy, and you might note some common features between these and the more sophisticated schemes.

Royal Lamarr Hardy was sentenced to 13 years in prison for promoting a scheme that cost the U.S. Treasury more than $8.5 million, and a Federal jury convicted Hardy and four co-defendants of conspiracy and other tax offenses for promoting what they called the Reliance Defense.

Perhaps taking a leaf from the opinion letters rendered by law and accounting firms in the more sophisticated deals I mentioned earlier, the Reliance Defense consisted of books and binders filled with materials purporting to show a studied conclusion that the purchaser had no duty to file a return or pay tax.

Daniel Fisher, a Dallas, TX resident, was sentenced to 20 years in prison and fined $1 million for preparing false returns for wealthy clients. His scheme created sham business entities and transactions—much like the sophisticated tax shelter transactions except less sophisticated—to give the appearance of losses. Fisher is believed to have caused a loss of approximately $10 million to the U.S. Treasury.

The increasing ease and invisibility with which money can flow from one jurisdiction to another increases the challenges to tax law enforcement. Tax Division attorneys actively participate in solutions to these challenges. We assist in the drafting and negotiation of Tax Information Exchange Agreements and Mutual Legal Assistance Treaties, we perform reciprocal evidence gathering to meet tax law enforcement needs, and we participate in international training programs to improve other countries' tax administration and enforcement programs. In these and other ways, we work to foster international cooperation of tax enforcement, money laundering, and counter-terrorist financing matters.

Finally, Mr. Chairman, in our view, justice must not only be done, it must be seen to be done. For our tax system to succeed, it must be enforced. The Tax Division and the Internal Revenue Service work hand-in-glove on matters requiring litigation, including summons enforcement, civil injunctions, criminal prosecution, and tax refund suit defense.

Since I last had the opportunity to address the committee, we have made significant progress. Also, since then, however, it has become apparent that our litigation challenges will continue to grow during the next few years. For the sake of the law-abiding taxpayer and the law-abiding tax advisor, as well as for the sake of the Federal Treasury, it is our obligation to rise to these challenges.

Thank you again for inviting me to be with you today. I look forward to responding to your questions.

The CHAIRMAN. Thank you, Ms. O'Connor.

[The prepared statement of Ms. O'Connor appears in the appendix.]

The CHAIRMAN. Now, Dr. Plesko?

STATEMENT OF DR. GEORGE A. PLESKO, ASSOCIATE PROFESSOR, DEPARTMENT OF ACCOUNTING, UNIVERSITY OF CONNECTICUT SCHOOL OF BUSINESS, STORRS, CT

Dr. PLESKO. Chairman Grassley, Ranking Member Baucus, members of the committee, thank you for inviting me to testify today.

My remarks will primarily deal with the Last In/First Out inventory method and touch on conformity in financial and tax accounting. My written testimony provides greater detail of these issues, as well as some figures and a table I will refer to in my presentation.

When discussing inventory accounting, it is important to keep in mind that inventory accounting methods are cost-flow assumptions and are not meant to reflect physical inventory.

Under LIFO, the costs of the most recent purchases are recognized first. If prices are rising over time, LIFO firms will report higher costs of sales and lower profit. To maximize reported profit, however, inventory choice seems straightforward: choose the method that allows the firm to recognize the least amount of cost. However, this decision is complicated by the tax code's allowance of LIFO, provided that the firm also uses LIFO for financial reporting.

Figure 1 on page 14 of my testimony shows the trend in the use of LIFO among the largest publicly traded firms. Firms are not required to use the same method for all of their inventories, so the solid line in Figure 1 shows firms using LIFO for at least part of their inventory, while the dashed line reports the percentage that use LIFO for a majority.

Both lines show the same pattern. The use of LIFO rose dramatically during the mid-1970s, a period of high inflation, peaked in the early 1980s, and has generally declined since. At the end of 2004, only 40 percent of these large firms used LIFO at all, and only 21 percent used it for a majority of their inventory.

Going beyond the largest firms, however, an analysis of all publicly traded firms shows that fewer than 10 percent with inventory report LIFO-related reserves. Treasury's 1984 tax reform study ("Treasury I") reported that 95 percent of all tax filings use First In/First Out or FIFO.

The primary advantage of LIFO is the tax benefit that LIFO provides firms experiencing increases in input prices. For electing firms, LIFO can provide an indefinite deferral of profits that would otherwise be reported.

Indeed, since the effect of LIFO conformity is to require companies to report lower earnings to their shareholders, the tax benefits to the firms that use LIFO must be larger than the sum of the administrative costs incurred to maintain LIFO records and any financial reporting costs they might incur through reporting lower profits.

Figure 2 provides some information on the magnitude of the tax benefits of deferral based on data from publicly traded firms. This data is taken from firms' LIFO reserve and represents the cumulative amount of additional costs that have been expensed by the firm because of a choice of LIFO.

Similar to the pattern in Figure 1, the dollar value of the LIFO reserve—the gray bars—has generally declined. For 2004, the last year for which data is readily available, the aggregate value of the reserve was nearly $60 billion, and I expect it was higher at the end of 2005.

This $60 billion represents the amount of additional net income publicly traded firms would report on their tax returns if a change required them to recognize this reserve as income, less any operating loss carried forwards to offset.

Assuming this income was to be taxed at an average rate of 30 percent, the implied potential revenue gain is approximately $18 billion before credits. By contrast, the Joint Committee estimated the revenue effects of the LIFO provision in H.R. 4297, affecting only oil companies, to be $4.3 billion.

The use of LIFO raises many concerns. Because a firm knows both the current costs of new inventory and the presumably lower cost of selling existing inventory, firms have a greater opportunity to manage the earnings they report to their shareholders.

If a firm wants to report higher earnings, it can choose to sell from older, lower-priced existing inventory rather than acquire new, or purchase additional inventory at the end of the year to avoid additional tax liabilities.

If the financial reporting benefits of LIFO were superior to any other available method, we would expect to see more widespread use of LIFO by both U.S. firms and in other countries.

However, international accounting standards generally prohibit the use of LIFO. Given the trend to harmonize accounting standards, it is not clear that LIFO will remain an acceptable method for U.S. reporting purposes, and, given the conformity requirement, for tax reporting purposes.

In these circumstances, Congress could repeal LIFO conformity and allow firms to continue to choose LIFO for tax reporting only. But doing so would only create additional administrative complexity, as well as increased book tax reporting differences. Such an action would appear to generate no benefit, other than provide a tax benefit to these firms.

The fundamental question, therefore, is whether the tax code should allow use of an inventory accounting method that would likely not be used in the absence of a tax preference.

Related to this, there has been substantial discussion on increasing book tax conformity, if not convergence. I do not agree that more book tax conformity is always desirable, and I advise careful study of these proposals.

Tax and financial accounting serve related, but distinct, functions, and the measure of income for one cannot be assumed to be an appropriate measure for the other. LIFO, as discussed above, does conform, but it may not yield the best financial reporting outcome.

Such a conclusion goes to the heart of the economic analysis of the tax system. If the tax system is to be neutral, firms should make the same decisions in the presence of the tax as they would make in its absence. LIFO appears to violate this.

Thank you again for the opportunity to be here today. I look forward to further discussion of these issues.

The CHAIRMAN. Yes. Thank you.

[The prepared statement of Dr. Plesko appears in the appendix.]

The CHAIRMAN. Mr. Kleinbard?

STATEMENT OF EDWARD D. KLEINBARD, PARTNER, CLEARY, GOTTLIEB, STEEN & HAMILTON, LLP, NEW YORK, NY

Mr. KLEINBARD. Chairman Grassley, Ranking Member Baucus, members of the committee, thank you for inviting me to testify on the advisability of public disclosure of U.S. corporate Federal income tax returns.

In brief, I believe that there are strong policy and practical reasons not to mandate the public disclosure of the entirety of corporate tax returns.

On the other hand, I believe that there is a completely persuasive case for requiring public companies to release to the public their consolidated Schedule M–3s, a new IRS schedule whose purpose is to reconcile a corporation's financial statement and taxable incomes.

So what exactly is this Schedule M–3? You can understand it as kind of a tax Rosetta Stone. It maps the relationship between a corporation's financial statement on the one hand, and its income tax return on the other.

It does so by dividing a company's income and deductions into 30 or so categories, and then requires the taxpayer to reconcile the amount in each category, for tax purposes, with a comparable amount available to that category for financial statement purposes.

My first observation is to urge that this committee not mandate the release of the entirety of corporate tax returns. A recent IRS news release revealed that General Electric's 2005 tax return was the electronic equivalent of a 24,000-page document. I hope that Commissioner Everson knows what to do with these 24,000 pages; I know that I would not, and I doubt very much that any public investor or securities analyst would either. Making returns of this kind of heft public thus would sacrifice the confidentiality of a taxpayer's commercial information for very little benefit to the public.

My second fundamental observation is that the Schedule M–3 is different from the entirety of the return. The M–3 is relatively short. It is unlikely to contain confidential commercial data, and its public release would convey useful information to investors and policymakers alike.

My first sub-point within that is simply that I believe that investors could directly benefit from the publication of M–3s. Investors today are conditioned to view the financial performance of publicly held companies solely through the prism of financial accounting conventions, and corporate managers, of course, manage with a view to achieving financial accounting targets.

In the absence of any other viewpoint, investors and managers alike often confuse a corporation's financial statements with the underlying economic reality that those accounting principles seek to model. That is, they treat the model as if it were reality.

By virtue of the M–3, the IRS now enjoys a stereoscopic insight into corporate economic performance through tax and financial accounting. Investors in public companies deserve the same. The public disclosure of Schedule M–3s would permit just that.

At the same time, the public release of M–3s should not expose companies to the risk of revealing proprietary commercial information to competitors, especially when compared to the information already available to the public in SEC filings.

The public release of the consolidated M–3 thus would not expose material proprietary commercial information to public scrutiny, but would still have direct and material financial benefits for investors.

In addition, investors today know shockingly little about the actual cash tax liabilities of public companies, because the financial statement current tax liability provision is not equivalent, and has only a casual relationship to, the cash taxes paid and payable in respect of a year.

To address this point, I recommend that the release of public corporation Schedule M–3s be accompanied by a simple reconciliation of the cash taxes actually paid and payable by a company to its financial tax provisions.

My second subpoint is that the public release of Schedule M–3s can be expected to have a modestly helpful impact on curbing corporate tax shelter activities.

The development of the M–3 was an enormously important step forward for the administration of the corporate tax system, but the direct beneficiary of this development, the IRS, does not need public disclosure in order to reap the benefits of using the M–3.

At the margin, however, public M–3 disclosure might dampen some corporate enthusiasm for tax shelter transactions by making plain to investors that the source of a company's enhanced after-tax earnings was the wholesale pursuit of aggressive tax trades.

My final subpoint is, simply, that public M–3s will improve the quality of tax and accounting systems as a whole. Many of you today are troubled by the fact that the gap between corporate pre-tax financial statement income and taxable income, as reported to the IRS, is said to have exceeded $200 billion in 2002.

The simple fact is, no one knows the source—all the sources—of this $200-billion book tax earnings gap. Some of the reasons are benign, others are possibly malignant, but we lack good data to distinguish between the two.

If the Schedule M–3s of publicly held companies were available to the public, the current collective uncertainties for the reason for this gap would dissipate, and we could replace wild suppositions with actual facts, susceptible of being catalogued and analyzed.

In sum, the combined public disclosure of the consolidated Schedule M–3 and company reconciliation schedule of taxes paid through the financial statement tax provisions would permit investors to bring stereoscopic vision to bear on corporate financial performance.

It would reduce any potential for corporate earnings management through the timing of additions to tax reserves, and it would permit a more pointed analysis of the quality of a company's tax expenses and appetite for tax risk.

The public release of the Schedule M–3 would modestly help tax administration, it would improve public dialogue on the corporate tax system, and it would encourage the recalibration of the tax or financial accounting model when either is seen to produce non-economic results. These are powerful reasons to proceed with the idea.

Thank you.

The CHAIRMAN. Thank you, Mr. Kleinbard.

[The prepared statement of Mr. Kleinbard appears in the appendix.]

The CHAIRMAN. Now, Dr. Sullivan?

STATEMENT OF DR. MARTIN A. SULLIVAN, CONTRIBUTING EDITOR, TAX ANALYSTS, FALLS CHURCH, VA

Dr. SULLIVAN. Mr. Chairman, Ranking Member Baucus, and members of the committee, thank you for the opportunity to appear before you today.

This morning I will discuss developments in international corporate taxation that truly mark a new era. I will explain their underlying causes and suggest how the United States should respond.

Mr. Chairman, the forces of globalization are reshaping corporate taxes around the world. Consider three basic facts about Europe, which is home to 5 of the world's 10 largest economies.

Fact number one. Over the last decade, statutory corporate tax rates in Europe have declined dramatically. The average top statutory corporate tax rate in the European Union fell from 43 percent in 1996 to 33 percent in 2006. And it is not just the newer members of the EU with their flat taxes and their low rates; over the last decade, 22 out of the 25 countries in the EU have cut their corporate tax rates.

Meanwhile, the top U.S. corporate tax rate has not budged. Taking into account State taxes, in order to make the U.S. data consistent with the EU data, the top rate in the U.S. is 39.5 percent, higher than the corporate tax rate in all 25 EU countries. Around the world, only Japan has a higher corporate tax rate, and it is only slightly higher.

Mr. Chairman, by standing still, we have fallen behind. Ten years ago, our corporate tax rate was 3.7 percent below the EU average. In 2004, it was 6.9 percent above the EU average.

Fact number two. Despite the large rate cuts, European corporate tax revenue has not declined. Corporate tax revenue should have fallen, for two reasons: first, the lower rates; second, because of the profit-shifting from high-tax to low-tax countries. Yet, revenue has not fallen, which leads me to my next point.

Fact number three. To offset the revenue costs of rate cuts, European governments have broadened their corporate tax bases. As the EU reported last month, corporate rate cuts in Austria, Belgium, Cyprus, France, Germany, Hungary, Portugal, Slovakia, and the United Kingdom, all these rate cuts coincided with cutbacks in corporate tax breaks. Depreciation schedules across Europe have become less generous. In fact, the United Kingdom and Ireland have both eliminated expensing.

Now, why is this happening? Tax reform that involves rate cutting and base broadening is always a big plus for competitiveness. It reduces government's role in the economy, it reduces economic distortions, it increases efficiency, productivity, and wages.

But it is more important now than ever, for three reasons. First, as the economy moves away from manufacturing, and intangible assets take the place of plant and equipment, rates play a larger role than conventional investment incentives in determining after-tax profits.

Second, as transportation and communication costs have dropped, there is more cross-border investment, so now the governments concentrate their efforts on trying to influence the location decisions of multinationals. In these decisions, tax rates, not investment credits or accelerated depreciation, matter.

Third, as mobile as capital may be, profits are more mobile. When multinationals are deciding where to channel profits, tax rate differentials are all-important, and conventional incentives do not matter at all.

Now, what should the United States do? We should reduce our corporate tax rate significantly—I would suggest from 35 to 25 percent—and offset the revenue loss by broadening the corporate tax base. This would boost economic growth, and that growth would raise revenues from all sources, not just the corporate tax.

Plant closings would decline. Inbound investment would increase, artificial profit-shifting out of the United States would slow, and we would create an incentive to begin shifting profits into the United States.

To broaden the tax base, I am going to make five concrete suggestions. First, reduce depreciation allowances. Bringing tax depreciation into conformity with true economic depreciation would raise tens of billions of dollars annually.

Second, eliminate the deduction for domestic production activities. That would save the Federal Government another $10 billion a year.

Third, tighten transfer pricing rules, particularly those pertaining to cost-sharing arrangements. The revenue gains here could be enormous. I have estimated that profit-shifting out of the United States to a single country—that is, Ireland—in a single year cost the U.S. Treasury at least $2 billion.

Fourth, eliminate profit-shifting to low-tax countries through related-party loans, through the hybrid entities that the Commissioner mentioned. These loans are not like real loans, but the tax code treats them that way. We could see significant revenue by disallowing deductions for interest from related-party loans.

Fifth, eliminate, or at least reduce, tax credits. Most tax credits are well-intentioned, but they are ineffective. We could eliminate energy credits and employment credits and cause no great harm to the national well-being. Even the venerable Research Credit could use a good trimming.

Mr. Chairman and members of the committee, that concludes my remarks.

The CHAIRMAN. Thank you, Dr. Sullivan.

[The prepared statement of Dr. Sullivan appears in the appendix.]

The CHAIRMAN. We will have 5-minute rounds. The first four or five people on the list would be: Grassley, Baucus, Hatch, Thomas, Bunning, Bingaman.

I am going to start with Commissioner Everson. One of the compliance issues you raised related to abusive hybrid instruments, financial instruments that may be characterized differently in the United States and foreign tax jurisdictions as either debt or equity.

You recommend that this committee examine the increase in book tax differences. I suppose the term "hybrid instrument" could also be used to describe financing structures that are characterized as debt for tax purposes, but equity for financial accounting purposes.

So, a two-part question. Dr. Sullivan, you might pay attention, because I might ask you a follow-up depending on what the Commissioner says.

Commissioner Everson, do you think that debt equity issues are a significant part of the book tax gap? And second, could you please comment on the significance of the distinction between debt and equity from a tax administration point of view?

Commissioner EVERSON. Sure. Let me make one broad point, if I might. What we are getting to now is a discussion of things that fall outside this tax gap. We are talking about things that are a manipulation of the code, and looking at comparison points between our system and the systems of other countries.

So it is not included, in many instances, in the strict non-compliance issues. So if you take a look at the problems that we talk about in the gap, $350 billion, this goes beyond that. It is changes in practices that involve, if you will, the coordinated work of investment banks, accounting firms, and commercial banks in terms of structuring transactions.

Oftentimes they are complicated financing, they are hard for us to find. Debt and equity is subject, in our system, to substantive tests; we make judgments depending on the circumstances. My understanding is, overseas it much more closely follows questions of form.

Therefore, this presents opportunities for the financial institutions to structure deals—and they are in the business of structuring deals so these are a small part of their volume, but this is very helpful for tax avoidance—where one instrument will be treated as debt here and equity overseas, or equity here and debt overseas.

The way they come together, they come together with no tax. I think it is fine if a company wants to go to a lower tax jurisdiction if they are really doing business there. But the idea that a company could be doing business here and in the U.K. and not paying tax in either place, I do not think that is what is intended. So this is an issue. I understand the Tax Reform Panel has highlighted this as something to look at.

I think the committee would be well-served to address this issue, and also what I talked about, Mr. Chairman, the foreign tax credit generators, which are much the same, in my view. They are, I would say, even more abusive, where you get circular financing streams and you are taking advantage of setting up the same sort of complicated hybrid instruments.

The CHAIRMAN. Dr. Sullivan, you proposed to prevent income shifting to low-tax countries through related-party loans. In a broader sense, what are your views on the economic implications of reducing the disparity and tax treatment between debt and equity?

Dr. SULLIVAN. Mr. Chairman, the corporate income tax is not a principled tax, it is an arbitrary tax. The distinction between debt and equity is an arbitrary distinction.

When the tax laws make that distinction, they create all types of economic distortions that are bad for the economy, and every economist would agree it is bad. I think the committee, as it continues its study of corporate issues, should look seriously at tax proposals that would treat debt and equity equally.

The 1992 Treasury comprehensive business income tax is one of those proposals. And recently, Belgium has enacted a proposal to neutralize the treatment of debt and equity that provides equity a notional interest deduction. These are very big changes. They would involve enormous transition costs and would be very controversial. In the meantime, I would suggest lowering the corporate tax rate as helping alleviate the problems caused by the distinction between debt and equity.

The CHAIRMAN. Commissioner Everson, do you think that basis reporting would reduce, or help to reduce, the tax gap?

Commissioner EVERSON. I certainly do think it would, sir. We want to look at this. I have to go back to Senator Baucus for a minute. I would disagree with your characterization as to the third-party reporting proposals that we have. I think that, while you are right, they are modest in the amount in terms of the revenue generated, I believe, in fact, some of them are probably understated, very conservatively stated.

They are the first third-party reporting proposals that have been made in 20 years, since 1986. If we can get these through—and some of them are quite controversial because of the impact on small businesses—I believe we can look at other issues like the basis reporting. That is about $11 billion a year, based on the 2001 statistics.

I do want to point out, though, we have to be very careful with transition issues because, as you all know, people change brokers, and some of the information on securities held for many years would be hard to retrieve, so we would want to make sure that we do this wisely and over a period of time going forward.

But I would be happy to take a look at this, but I would really ask the committee to take a good look at the administration's proposals. Let us get those done as a starting point, demonstrate that we can increase some of the third-party reporting, and then go forward, potentially, looking at these other issues.

The CHAIRMAN. Senator Baucus, it is your turn now.

Senator BAUCUS. Thank you, Mr. Chairman.

As you know, Mr. Everson, this committee—at least Senator Grassley and I—sent a letter to you asking about what appears to be the failure of the IRS to look at foreign-source information returns, or at least foreign-source information reports.

That is, IRS has asked for certain data that come from other countries be sent to the United States with respect to, I guess, American citizens or something that is relevant to the United States. It is my understanding that these were sent to a repository in Philadelphia, basically, since 1976. It is further my understanding that generally the IRS has not done much with this information.

Commissioner EVERSON. That is correct, sir.

Senator BAUCUS. And also it is my understanding that the paper reports have been destroyed and some of it has been uploaded—I do not know how much—electronically.

But when we asked in the letter why more had not been done about this, why did you not mention this, why are you not seeing what is going on here? The response we got back was, well, it is hard, it is difficult. There are currency issues, exchange rate issues, language issues.

In some cases, IRS did not know who the real "business owner" was. So it seems, therefore, that not much was done about this; that is, that the IRS did not assign somebody to try to solve this problem with the exchange rate issues, or currency, or language, et cetera. There are even computer problems there, too.

It is further my understanding that the Inspector General at Treasury has done a cost-benefit and figured that if these were looked at, just the information reports only, a lot of revenue could be discovered.

I am, frankly, kind of stunned that all this material, since 1976, has just sat there and nobody looked at it, or if they did it was just too difficult and did not do anything about it. I mean, how could that have happened?

Commissioner EVERSON. Well, I was just finishing college in 1976. I just went back to my 30th reunion. So, I do not want to take responsibility for 1976.

Senator BAUCUS. How about 2004, 2005, 2006?

Commissioner EVERSON. I am happy to take responsibility for the last 3 years. I think that the focus you provided on it, and the Chairman, is appropriate. I do think this is an area where we can, and need, to do more.

You list some of the problems. The problems are real. I gather that in something like 90 percent of the cases, the identifying information, the TINS, is not there. As you indicated, there are currency issues, there are timing issues, different fiscal years.

So I think the intervention that you have made is important. I give you my commitment, we are going to take a very strong look at this and do what we can to improve the use of this information.

A lot of this gets back to systems investment as well, though, I would point out. Some of it goes back to the funding issue, where in our base budget we have a lot of processing monies, about $1.6 billion, that sort of keep the system going. That money has not grown over a period of years.

The Congress actually brought that down a little tiny bit from the administration's request last year. We got all the money we requested overall, but a little was taken out of this. It is very important that we work on the technology elements of this to solve this as well.

Senator BAUCUS. But your own inspector at the Treasury, the Inspector General, says that you get $168 million in return for a few thousand dollars in investment.

Commissioner EVERSON. Well, if it is a few thousand, I did not see that ratio. But if it is only a few thousand to get $168 million, we will do that.

Senator BAUCUS. That raises a sort of deeper question for me. That is, it is astounding that we have this huge gap.

Commissioner EVERSON. Yes.

Senator BAUCUS. It is astounding to me that not a lot, really, has been done about it in the last several years, though we have known that this gap exists.

I sense that the failure to sufficiently address the gap is because of lack of resources, lack of intent, lack of sufficient computer technology, lack of matching. There are a lot of issues that I think the IRS is competent to address.

So, what stuns me, frankly, is that we have not heard a bigger hew and cry from IRS saying, my gosh, we have a problem here, we have to do something about this, and we need these extra resources and whatnot to get the job done.

We need to hire better personnel for the IRS because we need smarter people. We need more resources. There is too much inertia down there at the IRS. We have to do whatever it takes—whatever it takes—to solve this. I am just surprised that I have not heard more. Why have we not heard more in terms of urgency and getting this thing done?

Commissioner EVERSON. I have to, with all due respect, disagree entirely with that characterization. If we can go to the enforcement revenue chart, I think an awful lot has been done, in part through the actions of this committee. In the 1990s, the enforcement efforts of the IRS were drawn down. Everybody knows that.

When I got on the watch 3 years ago, I set out to rebuild the enforcement programs. Not at the expense of services; we have improved services along the way. But if you look at what we have done, the enforcement revenues have increased dramatically in just a few short years.

That does not capture the indirect effect. That is the monies that come in from collections, document matching, which you were talking about, and our examinations. Those have gone up steadily over the last few years, and quite dramatically, considering the investment that has been made. So I believe a lot is happening.

Now, I agree with you 100 percent, sir, that more needs to be done. We are doing that. If I could ask for your help on the funding side. The Budget Committee was helpful on the Senate side. They wanted to go beyond the administration's bill in enforcement. That will be helpful. But already in the House so far, we have received a cut of $100 million in our funding request. So, I am hopeful we will get our money.

Senator BAUCUS. But how much have you asked OMB for in this current go-around?

Commissioner EVERSON. I do not get into——

Senator BAUCUS. How much?

Commissioner EVERSON. I cannot comment on what I asked for from OMB, but you can safely assume that I asked for more than I got. That is the way the system works.

Senator BAUCUS. Are you stomping your feet, threatening to resign if you do not get it?

Commissioner EVERSON. No. [Laughter.] I need the job. [Laughter.]

Senator BAUCUS. I do not think you do need the job. You are doing a good job, and you have a lot of credibility. You have a lot of credibility in this town about how hard you have worked and so forth, and I think you have a lot of leverage that you could use to get the job done. My time has expired.

Commissioner EVERSON. All right. Thank you, sir. As always, it is a healthy exchange.

Senator BAUCUS. But I am serious about that.

Commissioner EVERSON. I know. I know.

The CHAIRMAN. I think you can conclude he likes you. [Laughter.]

Senator BAUCUS. But I want to get the problem solved.

Commissioner EVERSON. I agree. I agree.

The CHAIRMAN. Senator Hatch?

Senator HATCH. We all like you. [Laughter.] Except the people out there. [Laughter.]

Commissioner EVERSON. That is it.

Senator HATCH. Dr. Sullivan, let me just start with you. You discussed in your testimony the fact that the U.S. has a very high corporate tax rate compared with most developed economies.

What do you see as the societal and economic cost of this? That is number one. To what extent does it encourage firms to push certain income abroad, number two? And number three, specifically, how does our relatively high rate hurt the competitiveness of U.S. firms?

Dr. SULLIVAN. Senator Hatch, if I may, I'll take one and three and put them together in the same answer.

Senator HATCH. That is fine.

Dr. SULLIVAN. The societal cost is an economic cost. The corporate tax is a bad tax, from an economic point of view. It creates distortions between debt and equity and between corporate and non-corporate investment. It keeps government in the hair of businesses. It interferes with the free market.

The flow of investment is outward from the United States because we have the highest rates. This hurts us in terms of productivity, this hurts us in terms of competitiveness, and ultimately it hurts us in terms of wages and standard of living.

In addition to that, if that was not enough to incentivize lower tax rates, we lose quite a bit of revenue—Commissioner Everson mentioned this—through profit-shifting.

Multinational corporations are able, through transfer pricing, through cost-sharing arrangements, and through the use of hybrid entities, with the assistance of some very good accountants and attorneys, to shift profits across international borders.

So we see, for example, in Ireland, where the tax rate is 12.5 percent, a tremendous amount of profit—billions of dollars of revenue every year—is shifted easily into Ireland and out of the United States.

One way of attacking that problem is to try to tighten the transfer pricing rules. The other way is to lower the rates and provide incentive to bring some of that revenue back.

Senator HATCH. Thank you.

Mr. Walker, let me ask you a question. Why is our corporate tax revenue falling as a percentage of GDP, while corporate profits increase and the tax rate stays the same? Number two, how is our corporate tax base shrinking?

Number three, what role have corporate tax shelters had in this, and how much of this is due to lower tax rates abroad and the shifting of liabilities to other tax jurisdictions?

Mr. WALKER. First, Senator, my understanding is that the corporate tax revenues went up in 2005. Corporate taxes, as a percentage of the budget and as a percentage of the economy went up in recent years, especially 2005, in large part because of increased corporate profits.

There is absolutely no question, however, that I believe that if you really want to deal with the so-called tax gap, then one of the things that this Congress is going to have to do is to streamline and simplify the tax code in order to promote economic efficiency, enhance voluntary compliance, reduce administrative burdens, facilitate compliance and enforcement, and potentially, depending upon how you do it, enhance our international competitiveness.

You are correct in noting that this is not merely a domestic issue, it is also an issue of, how does it affect our economic growth and how does it affect our competitive posture with regard to other major countries? So, those would be my thoughts.

The other thing I would say, related to your questions, is the government is always going to be outgunned, in my opinion, with regard to major corporate tax filers. That is all the more reason why you need streamlining and simplification.

Senator HATCH. Well, thank you.

Dr. Plesko, I have heard some suggest that we could make our corporate tax system much simpler by having publicly traded corporations merely use the income they report to shareholders as the base for paying Federal income taxes rather than having income defined by the Internal Revenue Code. Why would this be a good, or not-so-good, idea? Would this not have the potential to save billions in tax compliance costs?

Dr. PLESKO. I think there are a couple of key issues we have to deal with as we address those proposals. Let me start by saying I am against them. I do not think that we want to move to a system where we only have one set of accounting rules, both for financial and for tax.

The data needs of financial statement users and of investors and the types of information they need is separate and distinct from the type of information that the tax authorities need in order to administer the tax code. Recognizing that the reporting and the use of that information is for different purposes, we should recognize that what gets reported should not necessarily be the same.

That said, one of the things that I think is important to recognize, as Mr. Kleinbard pointed out, is that the two systems reinforce each other. As I point out in my testimony, there may be times when conformity is the right thing to do.

To the extent that there is conformity between book and tax, if a company decides to do something for tax purposes, it will be transparent to investors. So, very aggressive decisions made by the firm on a tax basis would have to be reflected in lower profits reported to the shareholders.

But overall, because the users want to do different things with that data, I think that having one set of books does not serve either party effectively.

The other thing is administrative. Whose rules? I do not think that this committee would want to defer to the Financial Accounting Standards Board or any other non-legislative body the decision to set what the definition of income is by allowing someone else to say this is how we are going to measure income, nor, again, should it necessarily be the case that the best information for tax purposes is what investors need.

I think that conformity needs to be thought about on an issue-by-issue basis, but as a general rule, having the same rules is not going to be effective.

Senator HATCH. Well, thank you. My time is up.

The CHAIRMAN. Thank you.

Senator Thomas?

Senator THOMAS. Thank you, Mr. Chairman.

Ms. O'Connor, this is a very complicated issue, but, in general terms, what would you think are the most significant areas of the corporate tax gap and what do you think are the general enforcement changes that should be made?

Ms. O'CONNOR. The gist of your question was, what are the major areas that give rise to the corporate tax gap?

Senator THOMAS. What do you think are the most significant areas of the tax gap?

Ms. O'CONNOR. Well, the one that we see in the Tax Division is the use of tax shelters. As Commissioner Everson pointed out in his testimony, the elements of the corporate tax gap, ones that we see in the Tax Division, would be the items that are given rise to by the corporate tax shelters.

We do a lot of litigation on corporate tax issues in the Tax Division, but many of those cases involve legitimate questions of interpretation and application of the tax laws.

On the tax gap, I do not know whether the Commissioner's numbers include this, but I would imagine that the billions of dollars that are lost to tax shelters are an element of that.

I think, also, as the Commissioner alluded to, and I mentioned in my remarks, that the absence of meaningful penalties for promoting and using tax shelters cannot help but make the problem worse than it ought to be.

Senator THOMAS. Very good. Thank you.

Dr. Plesko, the LIFO method has been part of the Generally Accepted Accounting Principles, the GAAP principles, since the 1930s. As I understand it, the Financial Accounting Standards Board has no plans to disallow that. So why, at this point, when it has been acceptable practice for 75 years, or close to that, would we consider disallowing this method?

Dr. PLESKO. I think, again, if we want to consider the reasons for dealing with the appropriate measurement of inventory cost flow assumptions, the fundamental question is that, under the current system, in looking at the research, it appears that the only reason that companies choose this method is for its tax reporting benefit.

When we think about neutral tax policy, when we think about the idea of setting up a tax system that tries to neither encourage nor discourage any particular type of activity, absent the tax benefit, the evidence seems to be that no one would do this.

So the financial reporting or other benefits that are often argued to be out there as in favor of using LIFO are not there by the vote of companies. We do not see large numbers of companies choosing to use LIFO. We see companies using other methods.

The second issue is historical. It is not clear that all of the reasons that motivated the original use of LIFO and its increased growth during the 1970s, appear now. That is, a high inflationary period where LIFO was designed to try to mitigate the tax on the gain on profits that would otherwise arise because of the change in the value of the inventory.

Senator THOMAS. Yes. Of course, if there is not high inflation, then it does not make that much difference. It seems like the practical effect of repeal would be to immediately recognize the amounts of profit, along with the tax liability, that you passed along, completely divorced from the actual realization of the profit in a short time. In any event, I do not agree with your evaluation of this particular issue.

So, thank you, Mr. Chairman.

The CHAIRMAN. Thank you.

Mr. WALKER. Mr. Chairman, could I come back on that, real quickly, on the issue of LIFO? I think one of the issues that one has to consider in the broader context, with just-in-time inventory management and with a movement towards improving supply chain management, today corporations are trying to minimize their inventory.

That was not always the case in the past, where there were large accumulated inventories that were maintained, especially when we were primarily a manufacturing-based economy back in the 1930s and the 1940s.

So my understanding is, and having been in the private sector for over 20 years, including with two of the largest public accounting firms in the world, that LIFO is used primarily now for tax purposes, but that the whole way that management has changed means that it is less of an issue than it was back in the 1930s and 1940s.

The CHAIRMAN. Senator Bunning?

Senator BUNNING. Thank you, Mr. Chairman. I would also like to have my opening statement included in the record.

The CHAIRMAN. Without objection, yes.

Senator BUNNING. Thank you.

[The prepared statement of Senator Bunning appears in the appendix.]

Senator BUNNING. Dr. Plesko, there has been some discussion of the fact that international accounting standards generally do not recognize the LIFO method. I understand that FASB and the IASB are having a number of discussions about the possible convergence of U.S. and international accounting standards.

However, I understand that the issue of inventory accounting generally, and the LIFO particularly, is not on any current agenda. Is this true that inventory accounting is not on the FASB-IASB agenda?

Dr. PLESKO. Where it stands in line, on the specifics of the order in which they are discussing, I cannot attest to.

Senator BUNNING. You do not know, in other words?

Dr. PLESKO. Again, in listening to the general trend of what is going on, the long-term trend appears to be FASB and the IASB working towards one set of standards.

Senator BUNNING. Well, would it not be more reasonable or better for this committee to at least hold hearings on the two different methods that are used presently before we are considering legislation to do away with one of them?

Dr. PLESKO. Again, Senator, more information and more discussion on LIFO is——

Senator BUNNING. But as you well know, there are bills out to do away with that.

Dr. PLESKO. They are out there.

Senator BUNNING. Without any discussion on the Finance Committee or any discussion in any committee prior to us moving on these issues.

Dr. PLESKO. Senator, I would hope that my written statement and the testimony today at least helps initiate that discussion among the committee members and the rest.

Senator BUNNING. All right.

Dr. Sullivan, your discussion on the types of changes that the Europeans are making in their corporate tax system is very interesting. This year marks the 20th anniversary of the 1986 Act—

thank God I was not in the Congress at that time—which was an attempt in the USA to reach this same goal, lower rates with a broad base.

How successful was that change here in the United States? What was the general reaction of the business community to those reforms?

Dr. SULLIVAN. I think the 1986 Tax Reform Act was landmark legislation that was enormously successful. It is hard to imagine what our tax code would be like now with a 46-percent tax rate, investment tax credits, and more accelerated depreciation. We would be even further out of line with the rest of the world than we are now.

With respect to the reaction of the business community, it did not like tax reform when it started, and it hated it more after it was enacted. But may I respectfully suggest that, on the Hill, you are going to hear a lot more complaints from people who are not satisfied than compliments from those who are.

Senator BUNNING. But, sir, what has happened on rates since the 1986 tax code was enacted?

Dr. SULLIVAN. Since 1986, when the rate was lowered from 46 to 34 percent, the United States took a step backwards when the Clinton administration proposed raising rates from 34 to 36 percent in 1993, and the Congress only raised them to 35 percent.

Senator BUNNING. But, in fact, there are some people right now currently paying 39-plus percent?

Dr. SULLIVAN. Certainly. Yes.

Senator BUNNING. All right.

Dr. SULLIVAN. On the margin.

Senator BUNNING. On the margin.

Dr. SULLIVAN. On the margin.

Senator BUNNING. All right.

Mr. WALKER. Senator Bunning, if I might, for the record, based on your question: if you look on page 6 of my testimony, you will see that, since 1986, corporate income tax revenues, as a percentage of the economy and as a share of Federal income taxes, have generally gone up.

Senator BUNNING. That is because, thank God for our economy progressing and corporate profits being higher, and therefore paying more taxes into the treasury, even though the rates were reduced.

Mr. WALKER. I understand. But we also have to look at the overall fiscal situation. Just dealing with the corporate, the facts are the facts.

Senator BUNNING. But if we wait just a little bit, maybe with the current Federal Reserve reacting as they have reacted, maybe we will have the same problems that we had prior to 1986.

Mr. WALKER. Well, let us hope not. But let us also note that, while this hearing is on corporate taxes, we are short 3 percent of GDP as it relates to the overall Federal budget, and it is going to get worse when boomers start retiring.

Senator BUNNING. Well, let us give our Finance Committee credit for complicating the tax code also. Since I have been on Ways and Means and the Finance Committee, we have added a lot of pages to the code; rather than simplifying the code, we have made it more complicated.

My time has expired. Thank you.

The CHAIRMAN. I hope you are around when we try to make it less complicated and see how paralyzed we are.

Senator BUNNING. I will, Mr. Chairman.

The CHAIRMAN. Thank you.

Senator Bingaman?

Senator BINGAMAN. Thank you all very much for testifying. Let me ask about this issue about taxes that are owed but not collected. Everyone agrees, there is no continuing dispute about the payment of taxes.

Comptroller General, you have said that your recommendation is that we change the law by improving the Federal payment levy program, expand the amount and type of tax debt eligible for inclusion in the program, expand the volume of Federal payment subject to levy, and a variety of things.

I would like to ask the IRS Commissioner, is that your view of the solution to this problem? What do you think the solution to this is? It seems as though, from an investment point of view, this would be like shooting fish in a barrel. Once you got a determination that the tax is owed, it ought to be reasonably straightforward to go ahead and collect the tax. What is the problem there?

Commissioner EVERSON. If we can go to the tax gap map, to sort of just set the picture here. What you are speaking about—you will see when the map gets up there—the piece out at the right of the chart, the biggest portion of the tax gap, is under-reporting, which means under-reporting of income and overstatement of deductions. Out at the left, you have non-filing. Non-filing is less than 10 percent. The smaller piece, like that size, is what you are talking about, sir.

Senator BINGAMAN. Right.

Commissioner EVERSON. It is the underpayment when you agree you owe us $20,000, but you only send us $12,000, or you do not send us anything at all.

Senator BINGAMAN. Right.

Commissioner EVERSON. We are doing a variety of things to attack that. We are increasing our collection efforts rather significantly. We are modernizing our processes there. This takes investment. So our collection numbers are up. I showed before this enforcement revenue chart. The bulk of that increase is in the collections area, so we are making headway.

The other thing we are doing, which is somewhat controversial, particularly on your side of the aisle, is we have authority that we received a little over a year and a half ago or so to have private collection agencies assist us in the collection of certain kinds of debts. There are some things we do not get after. I try to run a balanced system. If you gave me all the money in the world, I would not put it all into collections.

As you say, it may be easier, relatively speaking, but we have to work on a whole series of issues, including tax-exempt organizations, where it is not about revenue generation at all, but it is consistent with our responsibilities. So we are using private collection agencies now to go after a portion of the debt. That should help us as well.

Senator BINGAMAN. Let me ask Mr. Walker, if you could expand on your comments here or respond to that.

Mr. WALKER. Well, Senator, one of the things that I added in my testimony today is the government, frankly, ought to be leading by example in not doing business with contractors and grantees who do not pay their taxes. There are billions of dollars involved.

I would respectfully suggest that the Congress may want to consider setting a prospective date to say that, as of X date, if you are not current on your taxes, possibly with narrow exceptions for national security or some unusual circumstances, we are not going to do business with you.

So, we have a situation now where we are providing taxpayer money to contractors and others where they have not discharged their obligation to the taxpayers.

Senator BINGAMAN. Let me just ask on that, I think that is a good suggestion, but could that not be done by executive order? Could the President not issue an executive order saying, effective the 1st of January, 2007, no Federal agency shall sign a contract with any corporation that is not up-to-date on its taxes?

Mr. WALKER. My understanding, Senator—and I will check with our counsel and provide something for the record—there may be some privacy issues here as to what type of taxpayer information can and cannot be shared with other agencies under current law. I will provide something for the record. If that is an impediment, that is what would require legislation.

[The information appears in the appendix on p. 371.]

Commissioner EVERSON. If I could comment, sir.

Senator BINGAMAN. Yes.

Commissioner EVERSON. There have been a series of hearings on this. Senators Coleman and Levin have chaired three over the period of several years with the government reform subcommittee, the Permanent Subcommittee on Investigations. This does get a little complex.

You want to be careful here because many individuals and companies have legitimate disputes with the government over the payment of taxes. The degree to which you say, if something is at issue that you cannot bid on government work, that could be a standard that would potentially be very burdensome and incorrect because the taxpayer can be in the right.

So we have talked about this with your colleagues, and we just need to be careful and consider, as the Comptroller General is saying, some of these privacy issues as well.

Senator BINGAMAN. I was trying to focus in on this area that the Comptroller General is talking about where the amounts are no longer in dispute. In those circumstances, it seems to me that either we should be legislating the prohibition on doing business with those companies—the government doing business with them—or we should be doing it by executive order.

Commissioner EVERSON. I do not disagree with that element.

Senator BINGAMAN. Thank you, Mr. Chairman.

The CHAIRMAN. Could I add something to this issue of contractors? That is that we, including this committee, plus the Senate, did pass, in a recent bill, withholding in this area so that we have some record of these people, to help our efforts to close this tax gap.

Senator Wyden?

Senator WYDEN. Thank you. Thank all of you.

To me, the reality is, for the last 20 years, Democratic Congresses and Republican Congresses, Democratic Presidents and Republican Presidents have just poured on more tax breaks, more rules and regulations, and produced more migraines for the American people who are trying to comply.

What I am trying to do—I have talked to both the Chairman and Senator Baucus about it—is to see if we can jump-start bipartisan tax reform once again. I have made a proposal called the Fair Flat Tax Act, and others have proposals. I think you have given us some good arguments for why we do need comprehensive reform.

Let me ask you about one area. The corporate tax, as far as I can tell, is just a roller coaster of seven different rates. The one that, to me, just defies logic is the rate is 35 percent for companies with income between $10 million and $15 million. Then it goes up to 38 percent for income between $15 and $18 million. So in effect, what has happened, again, in a bipartisan way, is that the country has said, we are going to sock it to the medium-sized businesses harder than the large businesses.

Do any of you think that this roller coaster of rates on the corporate side makes sense, or should we just try, on a bipartisan basis, to have a flat tax for business. Let us debate what the percentage ought to be, in other words, a lot of different points of view, but let us get away from the roller coaster.

Does anybody on this panel think that the roller coaster of corporate tax rates today is a defensible proposition? I will start with you, Mr. Commissioner.

Commissioner EVERSON. Senator, I make it a policy not to comment on rates. That gets into the responsibility of the Treasury Department and others in terms of pure policy. What I will say is, I am absolutely in agreement with you that simplification is essential to achieving better compliance.

That is because, as the Chairman indicated in his opening remarks, as the code gets more complex, individuals and corporations use that to find the pockets where they can escape detection. So I am very much in favor of looking at tax reform, and particularly tax reform and simplification.

Senator WYDEN. Mr. Walker? The roller coaster.

Mr. WALKER. It is illogical. I do think it is absolutely essential, in order to maximize economic efficiency, assure our competitiveness, promote voluntary compliance, and help enhance enforcement, for us to streamline and simplify the tax code across the board, including in the corporate area.

Senator WYDEN. Let us go right down.

Ms. O'CONNOR. I am here representing the Tax Division of the U.S. Department of Justice, and we defer to the Treasury Department for things like that.

Senator WYDEN. Very good. All right.

Dr. PLESKO. The fundamental principle of having as low a rate as possible on as broad a base as possible is one that I think is almost universally accepted. I am going to defer to Mr. Kleinbard on the rate structure, because I think we both have the same answer.

Mr. KLEINBARD. Yes. Let me give sort of a two-part answer, Senator, if you do not mind. The first part is, there is a logic to it. It may not be ultimately convincing, but the logic is that large companies should pay a flat rate of 35 percent on their incomes. Smaller companies should get a break so they have a lower rate than 35 percent.

How do you get back to a flat rate of 35 percent corporate income of large companies? Well, you have to capture in some fashion the lower rate on their first X million dollars of income. That is why the bump that you describe exists in the code. So there is a logic to it. But I completely appreciate your point, that it exposes mid-sized companies to higher tax rate.

Senator WYDEN. Let me just amplify on that. The rate is 35 percent for companies with income between $10 and $15 million. Then it goes up to 38 for income between $15 and $18 million. Finally, the rate drops down to 35 percent for income above $18 million.

Mr. KLEINBARD. Yes, sir.

Senator WYDEN. So we are sticking it to the middle-income company in a more extensive way than we are the high-income.

Mr. KLEINBARD. Yes. One can imagine moving the bump further up the income curve. But the idea of it—and I am not here to defend this particular structure—is that large companies should not get a benefit from the lowest rates. So maybe the bump should be at $100 million and not where it is now. That is a fair point.

Senator, if I could just add, it seems to me, when you move to the topic of corporate tax reform, the Chairman has emphasized the problems of debt versus equity characterization. We have all talked about the problems of high rates.

We have talked about the problems of burden neutrality, of making sure that when a business is going to decide to locate a plant, whether it locates that plant in Des Moines or Dublin should be based on commercial considerations and not tax considerations. We have talked about the problems of transfer pricing, which I think is the number-one issue in corporate tax compliance today. And we talk about keeping America competitive.

It is possible to imagine corporate tax reform that addresses all of those issues: debt equity, high rates, burden neutrality, transfer pricing. I had the pleasure of participating in the President's Advisory Panel on Tax Reform in that process. In fact, there was a proposal made that accomplished all of those results that I thought was very well-reasoned, but that was principally because it was my proposal. [Laughter.]

Senator WYDEN. Let me just, if we could, have Dr. Sullivan, since he was my biggest sympathizer, I think.

The CHAIRMAN. Then when Dr. Sullivan is done, Senator Baucus has some questions.

Senator WYDEN. Would it be possible then, Mr. Chairman—because I have some additional questions—after Senator Baucus has another round, can I have another round?

The CHAIRMAN. Yes. We will have another round.

Senator WYDEN. Great.

Dr. Sullivan?

Dr. SULLIVAN. Senator, because I am just a U.S. citizen, I can say whatever I want. [Laughter.] High corporate tax rates are strangling the business community, and that is becoming ever more apparent in this international environment.

As a regular citizen, I sort of resent that our tax system has gotten so convoluted. It provides special breaks for many different constituencies, and it makes our economy less efficient with the higher tax rates that are necessary to pay for that.

Senator WYDEN. I am going to come back on this. It just seems to me to go from 35 to 38 to 35 is just a portion of this roller coaster. I think David Walker, in calling it illogical, essentially hits the key point. There are no private sector entities that would make their strategy based on something like that roller coaster, and that is why I want to change it.

I look forward to our next round. Thank you.

The CHAIRMAN. Senator Baucus?

Senator BAUCUS. Thank you. It has been brought to my attention, Mr. Everson, that several States are utilizing data warehouses in order to make sure that they, the States, are collecting the revenue that is legally owed and paid.

The people I have talked to about this, of course, they have an axe to grind because they do not like doing this. I say that if we, the Federal Government, were to do the same, there are enormous opportunities here, again, to close this tax gap.

Commissioner EVERSON. Sure.

Senator BAUCUS. Basically it is getting data from driver's licenses, business, all kinds of data and normalizing it into one sort of format. There are not too sophisticated computer programs to do this. I wonder how much you know about these States' efforts, and the degree to which that could be utilized by the IRS.

Commissioner EVERSON. I am not familiar with particular State efforts. Let me make a comment, though, on the use of systems and technology that I think is an important one in the context——

Senator BAUCUS. I would just suggest——

Commissioner EVERSON. I will certainly take a look at that.

Senator BAUCUS. And look pretty aggressively on that.

Commissioner EVERSON. Yes.

Senator BAUCUS. Because I was impressed from what I heard in talking to these people.

Commissioner EVERSON. Sure. I would like to see whatever materials you have.

Senator BAUCUS. There are States that are doing this.

Commissioner EVERSON. I have a point that I think is directly related to this. One thing that was already referenced earlier today: we mandated at the end of 2004 the electronic filing of corporate tax returns and returns of the largest nonprofits.

This was over the objections of corporations who said that we could not get it done. We have gotten it done. As was indicated just several weeks ago, the largest corporate taxpayer, General Electric, filed their return electronically.

This will cut about a year and a half off the audit cycle, so we will bring the return examination process much more current. But it will do exactly what you are talking about.

You and the Chairman have raised questions about the oil industry. We will be able, instead of looking at just one return, to compare an array of data across an industry, and instead of looking at Exxon-Mobil every year, we might look at elements of the return based on things that are outliers from what BP is doing. This is exactly the capability you are talking about. We are aggressively moving on that. We can look and see what other applications——

Senator BAUCUS. Mr. Chairman, this might make some sense, that is, for the IRS to tell this committee, in a certain reasonable period of time, say by the end of this fiscal year, a plan, with benchmarks and so forth, as to what resources are needed and spent over what period of time to achieve what percent of our objective, that is, elimination of the tax gap.

What would you need to get the job done, either resources, or changing the law, or whatever is necessary? There are probably three or four leverage points, or five or six that, if utilized much more effectively, could help us address and solve this tax gap. Now, it will not be done immediately. It will probably take maybe a year or two, or something. But if you could give us a time line.

Commissioner EVERSON. Why do you not ask me to get it done by May 4 of 2008? That is when I am done.

Senator BAUCUS. All right. That is the deadline. I think it might make sense, Mr. Chairman, that we have a hearing on this proposal that you come up with, this plan that you come up with. After you give us the plan, we will have a hearing on it and help make it work. It is a partnership here, the executive branch and legislative. But we need to solve this.

Commissioner EVERSON. I agree, we do need to solve it.

Senator BAUCUS. And we need a plan to solve it. If you could give us the outlines of a plan, what it takes to solve it, and be aggressive—reasonable but aggressive—then we will have a hearing on that plan and just see how far along we are, what is good about it, and maybe people have some suggestions, and so forth.

Mr. Walker?

Mr. WALKER. Senator Baucus, I am somewhat familiar with some of those State efforts. As you know, GAO has previously recommended an area of opportunity for closing the tax gap, which is to pursue additional data matching and data mining. But in some cases, we have also noted that there is a need for enhanced transparency for certain information.

Two things I would like to note for the record there. One, what I said today and what is included in this report, is additional transparency with regard to the basis of securities transactions, and second, Schedule M–3. I think there is strong conceptual merit to providing public transparency with regard to Schedule M–3.

Senator BAUCUS. And that is a very good point. In fact, Commissioner Everson, I think items like this should be included in your plan. That is, M–3 made public, for example. The basis issue we discussed might be another example. It is, what needs to be done to solve this thing?

Mr. WALKER. Could I mention one other thing, Senator Baucus?

Senator BAUCUS. Yes.

Mr. WALKER. Sometimes the Congress, in its intent to do a positive thing, can place handcuffs or constraints on the ability of agencies to get their job done.

For example, Congress has placed certain constraints on the ability of the IRS to reallocate resources from taxpayer service to enhance enforcement activities.

I can understand that the Congress would be concerned not to reduce taxpayer services, but that inhibits the ability to leverage technology and engage in process improvements where you can still provide the same amount of service, but free up resources that can be focused on the tax gap.

I think that is something that the Commissioner should also think about as well, where you can leverage whatever dollars you get to maximum effectiveness, but also address some of the statutory constraints.

Senator BAUCUS. I am asking you to address that as well.

Mr. WALKER. Thank you, Senator.

Senator BAUCUS. You bet. Those are all very valid points, and I am sure there are others that we have not yet discussed. But the basic point is, what does it take to get the job done?

The CHAIRMAN. Thank you.

Senator BAUCUS. Thank you. Thank you, Mr. Chairman.

The CHAIRMAN. I think, if you just wanted 5 minutes more, I would rather have you take your 5 minutes now. Then I have a longer list of questions that I want to go probably longer than 5 minutes on, and I do not want to hold you up, Senator Wyden.

Senator WYDEN. Great. Thanks, Mr. Chairman.

Continuing again on this question of the clutter of the code and how it affects our country, it seems to me what you all have been able to spell out is that the current corporate code hurts our competitiveness in two ways.

First, it distorts business decisions in the marketplace. Second, with all the clutter in the code, all of these breaks, we are not driving the rates down as low as we possibly can. I think we have consensus on that.

I would like to go a little bit further and ask you, Mr. Walker, could giving special tax breaks for certain businesses and activities not potentially undermine competitiveness?

Because if somebody has a really good idea with great promise for the economy but no lobbyists, they do not get their break into the tax code; somebody with an idea that does not make as much sense for our long-term future has the good lobbyists, and off they go with their little break tucked away in the code.

Mr. WALKER. There are complexities and risks that occur when Congress tries to target tax preferences. You are, in effect, trying to pick winners and losers or you are trying to encourage certain types of activities. You may be right, you may be wrong.

But I think one of the other things we have to keep in mind here is, in the end, in addition to promoting economic efficiency, in addition to ensuring equity, in addition to maintaining our international competitiveness, we have to raise an adequate amount of revenue to pay our current bills and deliver on our future promises.

Senator WYDEN. We are going to have less revenue to honor our promises and our future obligations if we continue to reward foolish practices with breaks in the tax code.

Let me ask you one other area, Mr. Walker. The Congress has now decided to take action with respect to foolish spending, what are called these "earmarks" that get tucked into the tax code and items that you cannot possibly justify.

Do you think Congress should look at changes along those lines with respect to the tax code? The tax code is, again, the people's money. The money does not belong to the government, it belongs to the people.

So if the Congress fritters it away with foolish tax breaks, that is wasting the people's money. Should Congress take a look at cracking down on these breaks in the tax code along the lines of what is being done to crack down on foolish spending on pork barrel projects?

Mr. WALKER. Senator, my comments here have been clear and consistent: Congress needs to look at both the spending side and the tax side of the ledger. A vast majority of the Federal Government's spending programs and tax policies are based upon conditions that existed in the United States and the world from the 1940s to the 1970s. They need to be subject to a fundamental review, reexamination, and reprioritization. We have a tremendous amount of complexity, duplication, and inefficiency. The tax side, including tax preferences, needs to be on the table and under the microscope.

Senator WYDEN. Dr. Sullivan, I know you wanted to respond.

I will just say, Mr. Walker, to me, it is still the people's money. If the people's money is being wasted on spending projects that do not have a good cost-benefit analysis, that is something that ought to be stopped. The same is true on the tax side. I am interested in following this up with you because it is still the people's money any way you look at it, and it is being wasted.

Dr. Sullivan, did you want to add anything to that?

Dr. SULLIVAN. Thank you. Sometimes, but rarely, there is good economic justification for any tax incentive; most of the tax incentives in the law have no economic justification. They distort market decision-making and they hurt the economy.

Even when there is a good justification for them, there is very little economic evidence that they actually provide the incentive to increase the target of activity, so then all you are doing is giving a subsidy to a politically favored group. On top of that, because you have no money left over, the rates are high. So, for all those reasons, most tax incentives are not justified, and we should have lower rates.

Senator WYDEN. Mr. Chairman, you have been kind to give me a second round.

I want to close by saying, I was looking at the title of today's hearing, "A Tune-Up on Corporate Tax Issues." I just wanted to say in wrapping up, I am looking forward to working with you in a bipartisan way, and other colleagues on this committee, to do more than tune up a system that I think is broken.

I think we need to look at a big-time overhaul of this. This tax code needs major body work, folks. It needs more than a tune-up.

I am looking forward to working with you and Senator Baucus and our colleagues in a bipartisan way.

The CHAIRMAN. This is just the first of a series of hearings that we have planned. There will be more hearings in July.

Commissioner Everson, you noted the worldwide income reported by public companies to their shareholders, and then that on taxes, and I think the difference was $266 billion, up from $79 billion just 10 years ago.

Based on information that is currently available to the IRS, can you give this committee an idea of what the top three book tax differences would be in terms of the use of IRS resources?

Commissioner EVERSON. Certainly, Senator. What we are looking at is, generally, shelters. One of the biggest numbers that is in this reconciliation of the M–3, is reportable transactions. You are familiar with that. It is, in fact, over $40 billion, what is in that gap in terms of what has been produced so far.

Now, let me say this. The M–3 information we have asked for, we have not gotten all of it. We have gotten about 86 percent of the companies that have provided it. We have to figure out what we are going to do to pursue those who have not provided it.

Another big number that is in there is in the compensation area. Executive compensation is increasingly complex. That is a large number. We need to be looking at that as well.

Another piece that is in these gaps, the book gaps, is what we have been talking about earlier today: the difference between what is picked up in book earnings in the worldwide consolidation of the financial statements, but is excludable because it is from a foreign subsidiary.

This takes, in terms of the tax return, an awful lot of work in terms of looking at the comparison line there, and it starts to get into a lot of the issues we have been talking about this morning. So, those are three areas that are very important that we work on.

The CHAIRMAN. Mr. Kleinbard, in regard to your M–3 discussion that you have had, would a disclosure regime that applies only to U.S. corporations not put U.S. corporations at a disadvantage relative to foreign competitors?

Mr. KLEINBARD. Well, Senator, that is an excellent question. In a perfect world, we would have identical disclosures between U.S. and foreign firms because we do not want to disadvantage U.S. firms through more burdensome disclosure obligations.

But I have to conclude that that goal is probably unattainable in the world in which we live because foreign firms are subject to U.S. tax only in respect to a fraction of their operations, or not at all, and the foreign firms can sell securities in the United States, in appropriate circumstances, without preparing U.S. GAAP financial statements.

So the M–3 is designed to reconcile U.S. GAAP to tax, but we do not have U.S. GAAP financial statements, and we do not have the entirety of the parent company being subject to U.S. tax. We have a very difficult time figuring out what it is that, in fact, we could compare.

The purpose of the M–3 is to provide a line-by-line comparison between accounting items and tax items applied to the common base of the U.S. tax consolidated group, but, when the U.S. tax consolidated group is just one subsidiary of a multinational that is not based in the United States, the value of that public disclosure would be limited.

I do think it is fair, however, to demand that foreign firms that have access to the U.S. securities market comply with the cash tax reconciliation that we have discussed before, so that, in particular, tax cushions—that is, the hidden reserves for tax disputes—would be made more explicit so that we could get a better picture of the company's actual financial results.

The CHAIRMAN. Regarding your proposal to reconcile cash taxes to the company's book tax provisions, the main objective seems to be for companies to disclose more information about their tax reserves. What is your reaction to complaints by companies that they should not be required to give the IRS a road map to this issue?

Mr. KLEINBARD. Well, I guess I have two reactions to this question of providing a road map to the Internal Revenue Service by publishing an explicit cash tax reconciliation.

My first reaction is that the IRS, in fact, already has, by virtue of the M–3, all, or nearly all, of the information that would be provided by the cash tax reconciliation table that I described. It is investors who do not have the information.

My second reaction, frankly, is that it is completely fair that the IRS in fact be furnished with a road map. How else is the IRS supposed to navigate the 24,000-page return that we described earlier?

Companies can, and companies should, disagree with the IRS, it seems to me, as to the application of the law to their facts; after all, that is how I make my living. But I have no patience, frankly, with the view that hide-the-ball strategies should be encouraged, or even tolerated.

The CHAIRMAN. All right.

Ms. O'Connor, I wanted to discuss with you about corporate executives back-dating their stock options. Of course, this ought to be very troubling, about using this to maximize their profits.

I would like you to tell me what the Federal Government is doing to prosecute cases, the priority that these prosecutions have in the Federal Government, and, particularly, I would like to know what are the maximum civil and criminal tax and related penalties that these corporate executives could be facing who engage in these actions.

Ms. O'CONNOR. Certainly, Mr. Chairman. Thank you for that question. Stock options give employees the right to purchase shares later at the price of the stock on the date of the grant. The issue to which you refer is the highly suspicious award of stock options to executives at a low point in stock value.

In several districts around the country, the Department of Justice is investigating allegations that certain stock option grants were back-dated to provide the executive a lower price at which to exercise the option, or that other unfair—and perhaps illegal—practices were employed to price options at a low dollar amount, like awarding options based on insider information about a pending event that was going to send the stock price upwards. Such conduct would be a fraud on the market. It would boost the executive's compensation at the expense of other investors.

If investigations reveal criminal behavior, charges that might be brought would include securities fraud, mail fraud, wire fraud, and possibly various tax charges against both the individuals and the corporations.

Information more detailed than that I am not at liberty to disclose. I can tell you, however, that the Department considers allegations of this nature to be very serious.

The criminal penalties, if the crime occurred after July 30, 2002, would be: for mail fraud, 20 years incarceration and a $250,000 fine; for securities fraud, 25 years incarceration and a $250,000 fine; tax evasion would bring 5 years incarceration and a $250,000 fine; a conviction on filing a false return could bring 3 years incarceration and a $250,000 fine. Penalties under the Securities Act of 1934 would bring 20 years incarceration and a $5 million fine.

Successful prosecutions are going to require careful and detailed investigations. Until those investigations are concluded, it is difficult to assess whether, and what, charges will be brought.

The CHAIRMAN. All right.

Dr. Plesko and Mr. Kleinbard, in regard to LIFO, it has been discussed quite a bit this morning. Could you give us your opinion on whether there is a tax policy justification for retaining LIFO for tax purposes? A second question. If LIFO is repealed, what method would you suggest to replace it? To both of you.

Dr. PLESKO. My first reaction is, there better be, otherwise it should not be in the code and we should not have had it this long.

However, the fact that it has been in the code for a long period of time, by itself, does not mean that it is still good tax policy. Whatever the reasons were in the 1930s and 1940s, and its increased use, they do not necessarily fit, as General Walker has pointed out, the tax system we have in place right now.

It appears that the primary reason why firms choose this accounting method is the tax benefit and not any of the financial or other aspects that we care about when it comes to financial reporting.

In terms of alternatives to LIFO, I think this is a situation where the earlier questions Senator Hatch had on book tax conformity come into play. I would not think that we necessarily have to pick one particular method for tax accounting and say you must, for example, only use FIFO.

There are many other methods that are permitted: average cost, which would mitigate some of the recapture, as well as FIFO. The basic issue here should not be to say you must use one of these other methods, but rather that LIFO would not be permitted.

That said, the tax code should probably still maintain book tax conformity for inventory so that we would still get the benefits of having similar reporting for both tax and financial.

Mr. KLEINBARD. Mr. Chairman, I think that Dr. Plesko is convincing on the first point, which is that there is no policy justification for LIFO beyond the tax advantages that are obtained through it. It is quite interesting to see its selective use in the business community, which is consistent, I think, with the view that it is primarily driven by tax considerations.

Second, there are lots of outmoded ideas in the Internal Revenue Code. Because an idea has been there for decades does not necessarily mean that it is hallowed by age; it could just be a barnacle on the ship that needs removal. I think this is an example.

For example, in an area that I worked on, we had "lower of cost or market" accounting for securities inventories for many decades. In 1993, we came to the realization—this committee did—that that was not appropriate, and we went to mark-to-market systems for securities inventories. So we do need, from time to time, to review the methods applied to inventories.

A final thought on this question, coming back to the theme of book tax transparency. I find it quite ironic that corporations prepare disclosure of their tax liabilities in their financial statements that are impenetrable to me and to most securities analysts, but when it comes to this issue, where there is conformity that is required between tax and book as a way of sort of punishing the corporation for using LIFO accounting, in that case corporations that use LIFO accounting are pellucidly clear in their financial disclosure about what the income would have been had only they used FIFO, because they want, in fact, to make it very clear to investors that their real book income is the larger number.

So when it is in their interests, corporations know how to write crystal clear disclosure. I think you see that in the FIFO footnotes for those companies that do employ LIFO accounting.

Dr. PLESKO. Senator Grassley, if I could quickly add, again, looking at the literature, it appears that even the firms that use LIFO for tax and financial reporting do not use it for other decision-making.

The evidence suggests that they do not use it for internal compensation and bonuses, they do not use it for planning internally. The use of LIFO, based on the reading of the literature, appears to be solely to get its tax benefits and plays no other role in the design or the operation of the corporation.

Mr. KLEINBARD. If I could just add, this is a very good point that Dr. Plesko is making. One of the reasons why this committee and the Congress required the securities industry to go to mark-to-market accounting was because it was demonstrably true that for all decision-making purposes, for risk assessment purposes, for capital allocation purposes, firms operated in a mark-to-market environment. That was the world in which they lived as a commercial matter.

If you want to ask whether an inventory method is an appropriate method, Dr. Plesko's last observation is a very powerful one. You should ask, what are people doing for commercial and business purposes? If they are not using it for those purposes, then you have, I think, good evidence that it is an artifice of tax planning.

The CHAIRMAN. Senator Kyl?

Senator KYL. Thank you, Mr. Chairman.

Mr. Sullivan, I read with interest your statement. I would like to ask you to respond to a point that was just made: more than one thing can be true at the same time.

In other words, it is not necessarily the case that a particular method of tax accounting is appropriate in one context, and therefore must be appropriate in all other contexts, and that the converse would also be true.

The question I have about this method of accounting is whether it makes good tax policy to tax inflationary gain. We are looking at a time when we may be seeing inflationary pressures in our economy, and, if that occurs, the question is whether or not the effect of repealing LIFO on industries, especially those that are susceptible to inflationary gain on the inventory, what the effect of that would be, and in fact whether it would result in simply taxing them on the inflation.

Dr. SULLIVAN. Senator Kyl, you are exactly correct that inflation would have a detrimental impact. I am going to leave it up to Ed and George to provide details about how we should address the inflation problem with LIFO versus FIFO.

Senator KYL. Actually, the reason I was calling on you is because I wanted to ask you the next question. If we have time, I would be happy to do that.

The general issue of a manufacturing credit and changing the tax rate for manufacturing corporations vis-à-vis all others was one that troubled both Senator Nichols and me when that occurred.

What problems are you aware of that have resulted from this second method of taxation? Are there compliance problems? Is it more difficult to administer, from your experience?

Dr. SULLIVAN. As the Commissioner mentioned, there are massive compliance problems with the production activity credit. On top of that, it is either, you can say, unfair or inefficient from an economic point of view to give one part of the economy a tax break and not the other part. We should get government out of the business of picking winners and losers.

Senator KYL. Just a third question for you, then I would like to call on the other members of the panel. In your testimony, you note that the U.S. corporate rate, in effect by standing still, has lost ground vis-à-vis all of the 25 European Union countries, and that only Japan, fractionally, has a higher rate than the United States.

By doing nothing, we have fallen from the point of 3.7 percent below the EU average to a point of 6.9 percent above the EU average. But, interestingly enough, by lowering their rates they have not decreased revenue. Now, we have seen the same thing with dividends, we have seen the same thing with capital gains in this country. Why does the same thing not apply to corporate rates here, or does it?

Dr. SULLIVAN. It does apply. When we lower the rate, of course, by arithmetic we should expect less revenue, but by behavioral effects, through increased investment, which is real activity, through profit-shifting, which is more of a paper transaction, and through economic growth, that will partially offset the direct revenue losses from a rate cut. Yes.

Senator KYL. Does anybody on the panel have an observation on that that is contrary?

Mr. WALKER. Senator, I think it is very important to reinforce what was just said. Certain types of tax cuts can be stimulative and they can help to offset the amount of revenue that otherwise you would lose if you did not have the stimulation; however, very few tax cuts pay for themselves.

The idea that you have more revenues after the transaction than you would have otherwise had before the transaction is a whole different issue. I think there is a lot of confusion about that.

But, clearly, as has been said by this panel, efforts designed to minimize rates by broadening the base can serve to help enhance our competitive posture, improve compliance, and promote economic efficiency.

Senator KYL. Yes, Mr. Everson?

Commissioner EVERSON. Senator, I would just add that, beyond the economic impact, the economic impact presumably creates real value somewhere. That is a good thing. If it is not a good thing here, it is a good thing for people in another country.

What you really have, with all of these disparate rates and in the tax haven countries, is you have the parking of income in countries where nothing is happening. That is in nobody's interests, except to enrich those who are not really creating any additional value there.

Senator KYL. Just in the last 58 seconds or so, Mr. Kleinbard and Dr. Plesko, would you like to comment on the first question I asked?

Mr. KLEINBARD. Sure. On inflation, I believe, as a citizen, that inflation is a great evil. It is pernicious to the democracy.

But the question you have to ask yourselves is, is LIFO the way to deal with inflation? In effect, LIFO is a kind of ersatz indexation of some assets, but not all assets. Why would you choose, if you believe that indexation is a good idea, to index cost basis for inflation?

Why would you do it only in this case? Investors, for example, have to pay a tax on gains recognized from sales, even attributable solely to inflationary pressures. So if indexation is the right idea, then this kind of ersatz selective indexation seems to me simply to convey benefits to some parts of the economy and not to others.

Senator KYL. Could I just interrupt for one second? We have a few minutes left on a vote and my time is about to expire.

But the treatment should not be disparate for different segments of business. Is that a correct statement?

Mr. KLEINBARD. Yes, sir. The other is that LIFO, in particular, creates opportunities for earnings management. This is not a good thing, it is a bad thing. It is a way of massaging earnings results.

LIFO is like the layers of an onion. Your inventories are different layers, like an onion, and you decide how much income you want to report by deciding how big a bite of the onion you are going to take. By peeling down the layers you can increase or decrease the amount of taxable and financial profits you report. Earnings management like that is not a good idea.

Dr. PLESKO. I will steal a couple of seconds here before they are claimed by somebody else. One of the questions that has to be raised, especially with LIFO being around so long, is, if it has generated a substantial amount of deferral, it appears that much of this deferral is infinite.

If you look even during the low inflationary times of the 1990s, we did not see substantial reductions in the reserves. There is evidence that firms will manage their inventory purchases if they do not want to show increased earnings. If they are concerned about a tax loss of the LIFO reserve, they will buy additional inventory at the end of the year just to avoid that.

That is another situation where the tax code gets in the way—going back to General Walker's comment about just-in-time inventory or other types of business practices. This is an action that firms would not take but for the existence of a particular tax preference.

Senator KYL. Thank you, Mr. Chairman.

The CHAIRMAN. All right.

I have just three points that I want to make in closing. I will put a longer statement in the record.

One, of course, obviously, is to thank the very expert panel we have, and everybody, particularly on the government side, working hard to help us implement some of these things to close the tax gap.

I think we found some ideas today that need to be reviewed further, but we have also had lots of ideas—I think maybe a repeat of ideas we have already known—that need to be done, and I intend to take some action in those areas.

Lastly, I intend to have hearings further yet in July on individual tax reform—when I say "individual tax reform" I mean hearings on individual tax reform—and yet this fall, more detailed corporate tax reform hearings. So we are going to continue down this road. I think the admonition of Senator Wyden is well-taken by all of us, and that is what we intend to pursue.

Thank you all very much.

[The prepared statement of Senator Grassley appears in the appendix.]

[Whereupon, at 12:27 p.m., the hearing was concluded.]

APPENDIX

Additional Material Submitted for the Record

STATEMENT OF SENATOR BUNNING
SENATE COMMITTEE ON FINANCE
"A Tune-Up on Corporate Tax Issues"
13 June 2006

Thank you, Mr. Chairman.

I am very interested in the discussion of the LIFO method of accounting that we are expected to get into today.

While I am pleased that this committee is taking the time to have a look at this issue, I am concerned that this examination is taking place only after several provisions to repeal this accounting method have already been proposed.

The prospect of repealing an accounting method that has been in use for over 75 years is a serious proposal that could have a far-reaching impact on many businesses in this country.

Thus, an examination of any changes in the use of this method for tax accounting must be looked at, if at all, in the context of proposals for broad-based changes to the tax and tax-accounting systems.

I have not yet been convinced of the need for implementing a change to the methods for inventory accounting as large as the repeal of LIFO in isolation.

Additionally, if this proposal continues to be examined by the Committee, I hope that we will have an opportunity to hear from the business community that will be impacted by any changes to the acceptable accounting methods for inventory.

Another issue that we will discuss today is a proposal for expanded third-party reporting of basis information for capital assets.

The GAO's report, which will be presented today, identifies a number of potential challenges to the implementation of such a regime.

I am interested to hear the response of the panelists, particularly Commissioner Everson, to these challenges and to discuss whether these challenges can be overcome.

I thank the Chairman for holding this important hearing, and I look forward to the testimony and discussion today.

Thank you.

WRITTEN TESTIMONY OF COMMISSIONER OF INTERNAL REVENUE MARK EVERSON BEFORE SENATE COMMITTEE ON FINANCE ON COMPLIANCE CONCERNS RELATIVE TO LARGE AND MID-SIZE BUSINESSES JUNE 13, 2006

Good morning Mr. Chairman, ranking Member Baucus and members of the Senate Committee on Finance. It is my pleasure to be with you this morning to discuss compliance issues relative to large and mid size businesses. These types of issues are handled by our Large and Mid-Size Business Division (LMSB), one of four operating divisions at the IRS.

I want to thank you and all of the Members of the Committee for your interest in the issues I am going to talk about today. I also want to thank you for the support you have demonstrated in the past for our work to rebalance the IRS's enforcement efforts with our service improvements, including some very helpful provisions that were contained in the American Jobs Creation Act. A number of these provisions are directly relevant to LMSB's taxpayer base and to programs which are administered by LMSB, such as the tax shelter work performed by the Office of Tax Shelter Analysis.

LMSB's taxpayer base, though small in number relative to the overall taxpayer population, consists of the largest businesses in the United States, including corporations, sub-chapter S corporations, and partnerships with assets greater than $10 million, including over 6,100 publicly traded companies. LMSB taxpayers most recently filed approximately 176,000 income tax returns, and while the overall large business population base remains relatively stable in number, we continue to see an increase in complex business structures and pass-through return filings.

LMSB taxpayers are sophisticated, well-capitalized, well-organized, and adept at planning. Particularly in the case of public companies, they are driven to show high after-tax profitability to shareholders in a very competitive and complex economic environment. They have the resources and willingness to aggressively defend and contest tax positions.

Climate and Challenges for Large and Mid-Size Business

Those factors and others influence the results that appear when we attempt to capture the portion of the tax gap attributable to these businesses. The National Research Program (NRP) results provided last February estimate the underreporting non-compliance by larger corporations in 2001 to be $25 billion. The estimate for all corporations is $30 billion. This represents a voluntary compliance rate in 2001 of 83 percent. Please keep in mind that the NRP did not conduct new research on the corporate portion of the tax gap. As a result, these estimates are rough orders of magnitude.

While several factors could be offered to suggest that the corporate tax gap may in fact be larger than the implied figure, I will simply say that the corporate tax gap is significant, that I see no evidence to conclude that it has not grown in absolute size, and that this sector continues as one of the Service's and my top priorities.

As an aside, I would note that these estimates do not include refunds claimed subsequent to the filing of the original return. Disallowed claims are important, since they permit dollars to remain in the fisc that would otherwise be absent. In the large business environment, this is an important consideration as in FY 2005 our LMSB division disallowed $8 billion of $16 billion in taxpayer claims.

Turning now to the environment for large business taxpayers and corporate tax administration, it is clear that we face new and more challenging tax administration problems resulting from globalization, complexity of the Code, complexity of business transactions, and the growing book-tax gap.

First, tax administration is complicated by the rapid pace at which businesses are continuing to expand globally. A growing percentage of large and mid-size business tax filings are from multinational companies that have a myriad of subsidiaries and partnerships operating within an enterprise structure where the ultimate parent is as likely to be foreign as domestic. In addition, a growing number of U.S. businesses acquire raw materials, inventory, financing, products and services from foreign businesses. These events are natural outcomes of an increasingly global economy and businesses have the right to optimize their global structures. Nonetheless, the complexities of globalization and cross-border activity continue to challenge the Code and U.S. tax administration. With multiple domestic and global tiered entities, it is often difficult to determine the full scope and resulting tax impact of a single transaction or series of transactions. Complexities of globalization and cross-border activity create opportunities for aggressive tax planning demonstrated in several of the international/global current compliance issues mentioned in this letter.

Second, the Internal Revenue Code continues to expand, becoming more complex and challenging to administer. Large businesses are able to utilize every available resource to explore opportunities to reduce their tax liability by using the most intricate and complicated Code provisions. Every new tax law, even those that are simple on their face, creates additional complexity while providing taxpayers with further tax planning opportunities adding to our challenges to administer the federal tax system. Changes to the tax law make it more difficult for us to treat similarly situated taxpayers in a consistent manner. Three of the current specific compliance issues mentioned in this letter arise from new Code provisions enacted by the AJCA.

Third, large businesses increasingly engage in sophisticated transactions for both non-tax purposes and tax purposes, resulting in complex relationships with multiple filing requirements. Tax administration continues to be challenged by the increasing number of high value, sometimes cross-border, mergers, acquisitions and other multifaceted international and domestic tiered transactions. The increasing volume and complexity of these transactions make it difficult for us to identify them and to effectively address them in a timely manner.

Fourth, companies strive to reflect the highest possible after-tax profits on their financial statements while at the same time being incentivized to report the lowest possible taxable income and tax liability. The difference between income reported by public companies to their shareholders and taxable income reported on their tax returns to the IRS has grown dramatically in recent years, from $79.0 billion in 1995 to $203.8 billion in 2002 The climb slowed in the period 2000-2002 when the economy cooled down and the equity markets declined. After the economy returned to a period of expansion and the equity markets have recovered, the differential rose again to $266 billion in 2003.

Research indicates that book-tax differences sometimes indicate significant compliance risk, as is the case in many of the issues discussed in the compliance issues below. When the details of business transactions and book-tax differences are not visible to the IRS, the correct determination of tax can be jeopardized.

The IRS Addresses These Challenges

We have taken a proactive approach to dealing with the challenges of effective tax administration in the environment described above. Overall, our strategy depends on making compliance checks as much as possible on a real-time or near-real-time basis, being as current in our examinations as possible, and having as much transparency to book-tax differences and other indicators of risk as possible. To that end, we have initiated several programs that foster transparency, currency, pre-filing compliance opportunities, and improved efficiencies in issue and risk identification.

We are looking at various methods to better address issues involving cross-border/multi-national enterprise activities as well as the domestic items that are a subject of this letter. In general, we have found cross-functional Issue Management Teams (IMTs) to be successful when we employ them to provide executive oversight and focus upon areas of high risk. We have used IMTs to combat tax shelters, and have expanded their use to include other areas of high compliance risk. We have also used special teams of experienced personnel to assist with the examination of specific issues in the tax shelter arena, and plan to use similar teams to address other compliance issues. Additionally, we are working to enhance the use of internal web site information to better inform examiners of high risk areas and the steps they must take to ensure consistent application of the law. Let me mention some of our key efforts.

First, to improve transparency on corporate tax returns, we introduced a new Schedule M-3. The Schedule M-3 provides transaction-specific detail on book-tax differences, enabling us to identify and focus more quickly and precisely on those tax returns and issues that present the highest potential compliance risk.

Second, we introduced the Compliance Assurance Program (CAP), to improve both currency and transparency. CAP is a real-time approach to compliance review that allows us, working in conjunction with the taxpayer, to determine tax return accuracy prior to filing. We believe CAP is more efficient than a post-filing examination–we are currently piloting the model and will refine as necessary–as it provides corporations certainty about their tax liability for a given year within months, rather than years, of filing a tax return. This win-win program greatly reduces taxpayers' compliance burden and their need for contingent book tax reserves, while increasing currency and allowing for more efficient use of our resources.

Third, we are conducting the Pre-Filing Agreement (PFA) program to provide taxpayers an opportunity to request that revenue agents examine and resolve potential issues before tax returns are filed. We continue to explore ways to improve and create additional pre-filing compliance opportunities.

Fourth, working with Treasury and Chief Counsel, LMSB identifies emerging high risk issues as early as possible, issuing guidance to taxpayers and examiners on the proper treatment of these issues, and efficiently and vigorously examining those returns where taxpayers engage in that behavior.

Fifth, we are mandating, in stages, the electronic filing of large corporate returns *(E-Filing)* in order to improve issue identification and the selection for examination of high risk returns. Large corporations are required now to file their tax returns electronically and this mandate will expand in future tax years. *E-filing* will provide more consistent treatment and data analysis for efficient, near real time identification of high risk issues and taxpayers. *E-filing* and Schedule M-3 together also allow us to more efficiently identify and exclude lower risk taxpayers from consideration for examination.

The approaches described above better position us to more timely address the rapid change of business in the domestic and global arenas. The earlier we learn of emerging trends, the better positioned we will be to adjust resources to appropriately address compliance risks.

Finally, I would note that I told you early in my term that I believe corporate audits take too long. We have launched a number of initiatives in this area to improve our results including some of the items I have mentioned. I have seen improvement and I expect to see more as these processes increasingly take hold.

Specific Compliance Issues

The most significant compliance problems facing LMSB are issues that include one, several, or all of the following factors: significant impact on one or more industries; a large number of taxpayers; significant dollar risk; substantial compliance risk; and/or high visibility. In addition to these transactions that involve these general compliance issues, we continue to combat other tax shelters and abusive tax avoidance schemes.

To address these tax compliance challenges, to dissuade promoters and others from initiating new abusive schemes, and to achieve our key goal of tax compliance through service and enforcement, we are working to make our examination resources more efficient, using tools to increase taxpayer disclosure and transparency, leveraging technology, and reengineering our processes to identify and resolve emerging issues and potentially abusive transactions.

The volume of return examinations and the level of audit coverage have increased with a focus on returns where we have identified significant compliance issues. IMTs have been, or are in the process of being, established for all issues with significant compliance problems. We continue to work with Counsel to ensure written guidance is provided to examiners for addressing all significant compliance issues. Examiners are expected to consider penalties on all returns with examination adjustments and on promoters of abusive tax avoidance schemes. Below is a summary of our most significant compliance problems and the actions we are taking to address these areas of non-compliance.

International/Global Transactions

Transfer of Intangibles Offshore/Cost Sharing: Tax issues associated with the transfer of intangibles outside the United States have been a high risk compliance concern for us and have seen a significant increase in recent years. Taxpayers, especially in the high technology and pharmaceutical industries, are shifting profits offshore through a variety of arrangements that result in the transfer of valuable intangibles to related foreign entities for inadequate consideration. Cost sharing arrangements are often the method of choice for this activity. The buy-in amount in cost sharing arrangements is particularly troublesome. It is often understated, resulting in the improper shifting of income offshore.

As part of our response to these issues, we proposed a comprehensive set of cost sharing regulations in August 2005, that seek to ensure such arrangements do not facilitate a disguised transfer of intangible assets outside the United States in a manner inconsistent with the arm's length standard. We intend to finalize these regulations this year.

We have also established a cost sharing IMT to improve Service-wide coordination in the identification, development, and resolution of cost sharing issues. The IMT issued a cost sharing audit checklist in 2005 that provides guidance to field examiners for developing potential cost sharing audit issues and ensuring consistency. The team has completed its efforts to identify and review cases with a cost sharing issue to determine the impact and compliance risk. The team is developing a coordinated issue paper that will provide the basis and support for examining issues and to assist with potential Appeals Settlement Guidelines. In 2005, the LMSB Commissioner issued guidance to field examiners for requesting transfer pricing documentation.

Abusive Foreign Tax Credit Transactions

Some taxpayers are manipulating the Code to create and claim foreign tax credits (FTCs) where the associated foreign-source income is not taxed in the United States. One type of transaction involves the inappropriate separation of the FTCs from related foreign-source income. These transactions typically involve the acquisition of assets that generate an income stream or built-in gain that is subject to foreign taxes but not U.S. taxes; or, the use of partnerships, foreign consolidated regimes, or "check the box" reverse hybrid entities to obtain FTCs before the related foreign income is subject to U.S. tax. In addition, cross-border financing transactions are being structured to generate abusive FTC results. In the case of U.S. lender transactions, a U.S. person makes a loan to a foreign person in a transaction structured to shift a portion of the borrower's foreign tax liability to the U.S. lender. In the case of U.S. borrower transactions, a U.S. person borrows from a foreign person in a manner that allows the U.S. person to pay creditable foreign taxes in lieu of deductible interest. In both types of cases, the FTCs are used to shelter unrelated foreign source income. These structured financing transactions often result in the duplication of tax benefits through the use of certain structures designed to exploit inconsistencies between U.S. and foreign laws.

To address cross-border financing transactions that are designed to generate FTCs, LMSB has formed an IMT. The team will work to: identify and address all open cases with an abusive FTC issue; identify and explore all viable legal arguments to combat the abuses including the application of judicial doctrines such as economic substance, and/or step transaction arguments; provide guidance to the field; and pursue possible legislative and/or regulatory modifications. Due to the global aspects of this issue, we must consider tools available under international treaties and exchange of information agreements. In addition, the IRS and Treasury have several major regulatory projects underway that will address numerous issues involving the inappropriate separation of FTCs from related foreign-source income.

Abusive Hybrid Instrument Transactions: Taxpayers can use hybrid instruments, hybrid entities, and similar structures to capitalize on differences between foreign and domestic tax laws because these structures are often treated differently for U.S. and foreign tax purposes. This kind of arbitrage can be the natural outgrowth of global economies and disparate tax systems. Concern exists, however, that in some cases, hybrid instruments or entities might be used to avoid U.S. tax rules. For example, inappropriate FTCs can be generated. The use of these hybrid instrument transactions by U.S. multinational domestic corporations and foreign controlled domestic subsidiaries is a common practice. Indications are that the use of these types of transactions is on the rise.

In response, we recently formed an IMT to develop a Service-wide position on hybrid instruments. Due to the global aspects of this issue, we will consider international treaties and simultaneous examination processes. In addition, the IRS and Treasury have a number of guidance projects under way that would address some of the issues raised by hybrid instruments, hybrid entities, and similar structures.

Transfer Pricing: Taxpayers are continuing to shift significant profits offshore. Taxpayers often manipulate the price of related transactions so that the income of an economic group is ostensibly earned in low tax jurisdictions, or in no jurisdiction, rather than in the U.S., thus lowering the enterprise's worldwide tax burden. We apply the arms length principle to determine the appropriate allocation of income between related parties based upon the application of acceptable transfer pricing methodologies (section 482 of the Code).

In response to the significant compliance risks of transfer pricing issues, the LMSB Commissioner issued a Transfer Pricing Compliance Memorandum in January 2003 that provided instruction and guidance to all field examination personnel regarding potential transfer pricing issues. Additionally, the LMSB Commissioner issued a Transfer Pricing Documentation Memorandum that requires all field examination personnel to request and review taxpayer transfer pricing studies. As a subset of the transfer pricing issue category, a section 936 Termination Strategy issue has been identified for additional compliance coordination. Associated with the sunsetting of section 936, taxpayers have created structured transactions to transfer U.S. intangibles that were used in Puerto Rico to other low tax jurisdictions. An IMT has been established to identify, coordinate, and propose resolution alternatives for this issue. Field examiners and technical advisors will provide technical support to teams with the development of this tax issue.

Significant Domestic Issues

Research & Experimentation (R&E) Credit Claims: Taxpayers are filing refund claims, often marketed to them on a contingency fee basis, to claim additional research credit. These claims are frequently based on unsupportable amounts, nonqualified expenditures, or estimates for which the taxpayers do not have contemporaneous documentation. The Ogden Service Center has received 673 corporate tax year claims for more than $1.3 billion in additional R&E credits since we released Notice 2002-44 (July 8, 2002). This notice provides new guidance for claiming the research credit on an original return or claim for refund.

The increase in the number of research credit refund claims, often filed late in the examination cycle, has placed an enormous resource burden on many examination teams. In addition to the administrative burden created by the filing of these research credit claims, other significant issues need to be resolved, such as identifying the business entity within a consolidated group that is claiming the credit, prototype issues, re-computation (or computation for the first time) of base period historical information for the years 1984 through 1988, and start-up company issues. These issues are often exacerbated by a lack of contemporaneous records to support the amounts claimed.

To address improper research credit claims, we have a number of administrative actions in process. These include conducting training and providing expert guidance to examiners to assist with examining the issue, the issuance of a Research Credit Audit Technique Guide (ATG), and the issuance of four Coordinated Issue Papers providing guidance on the research credit.

The difficulties we have encountered in administering this credit are exacerbated by the temporary nature of the credit. In addition, the credit's structure raises a number of technical issues – defining what constitutes "qualified research," determining the proper treatment of section 174 depreciation expenses, defining "supplies" and "gross receipts" (as well as determining the treatment of foreign gross receipts), and defining the effects of the section 280C(c) reduced credit election, to name a few. Although the Treasury Department and the IRS are working to address many of these issues through the administrative guidance process, substantial noncompliance will likely continue in this area.

Universal Service Fund (USF): Federal and state governments impose taxes on telecommunication service consumers to fund subsidies to the telecommunication carriers for universal service programs. The issue is whether amounts received by telecommunications carriers from federal and state universal service programs constitute non-shareholder contributions to capital under section 118, or are taxable income under section 61. The funds are paid to reduce rates and are charged to customers so that certain customers in high cost areas or rural areas are not charged more than customers in urban areas where costs are lower. The total federal USF payments are in excess of $7 Billion annually. A complete dollar estimate for the state USF payments is not available now, but it is substantial. Approximately 1,500 carriers are receiving USF subsidies, and, combined with the expansion of the USF program, the number is likely to increase in the future along with the total amount of subsidies.

Some telecom taxpayers are receiving significant USF subsidies and not reporting them as income. The position of these carriers, that the USF subsidy is a non-shareholder capital contribution that is not taxable income under section 118, creates a competitive disadvantage for compliant taxpayers. Taxpayers are relying on the language in the Federal Telecommunication Act of 1996 that the funds are to be used for "the provision, maintenance, and upgrading of facilities and services for which the support is intended." The use of section 118 by businesses to exclude other governmental subsidies is spreading–benefits, such as local incentives for a business to relocate to or stay in its jurisdiction and for utility companies to continue to provide basic services, are being claimed as nontaxable contributions under section 118, while related expenses are being fully deducted.

We believe these positions often are without merit, and we have challenged them on audit. We have issued a Coordinated Issue Paper directing examiners to take specific audit positions which was followed by an Appeals Settlement Guideline allowing for minimal litigation hazards. We believe the courts will sustain our position under the current statute. Nevertheless, we are working on guidance to address the USF issue.

Mixed Service Costs: Some electric and gas utility companies have changed their method of accounting to allow them to consider certain large self-constructed assets "routine and repetitive" under the simplified service cost method (SSCM), which allows a much faster (on occasion it has been immediate) write off. The impact of this issue is substantial. Our position is that the classification as "routine and repetitive" is often flawed. We recently published a regulation that eliminates this issue as of August 2005. An IMT is currently examining 62 claims that pre-date the regulation changes. The IMT is partnering with other IRS functions and external stakeholders to develop a resolution strategy that will resolve open cases under Rev. Rule. 2005-53. No additional legislation or legal guidance is currently required. The new regulations remove the ambiguity for what qualifies as "self constructed assets" that led to the 62 taxpayer claims.

Issues Resulting From or Impacted by the American Jobs Creation Act

Section 199 Issues: This AJCA provision provides a deduction for certain manufacturing activities conducted in the United States. The section 199 deduction increases from 3% of qualified income during the first 2 years, to 6% for the next 3, and finally reaches 9% in 2010. Many difficult issues arise as a result of this complex section, some of which were addressed in final regulations published last month. We are concerned, however, that mass-marketed, contingency fee-based refund claims could become a problem under section 199.

We have formed an IMT has been formed to address the many potential issues which may arise and are paying special attention to the potential challenges posed by different business types and industries in which taxpayers operate. We have issued extensive guidance under section 199: Notice 2005-14 in January 2005; proposed regulations in October 2005; and final regulations in May 2006. With recently enacted changes to section 199, other guidance is forthcoming. The IMT has regular communications with external stakeholder organizations and the Multi-State Tax Commission. It will use information gathered on calendar year 2005 filings to determine audit selection and compliance risks and to create a Coordinated Issue Paper.

Foreign Earnings Repatriation (Sec. 965): This AJCA provision provides a limited window for companies to repatriate foreign earnings to the United States at a reduced tax rate provided they satisfy certain requirements and conditions. Audit issues are likely to include compliance with board approved reinvestment plans, and the compliance of repatriated funds with statutory requirements. Significant tax dollars are at stake. As of late 2005, 91 of the S & P 500 had repatriated or planned to repatriate funds under this provision.

To address this issue, we have established a process to capture tax return information from 2005 tax returns filed by taxpayers claiming the benefits of this provision. The IMT formed for this issue has developed initial administrative guidance for field examiners to use for compliance checks of taxpayers claiming the benefit to ensure compliance. In 2005, we issued three pieces of published guidance regarding section 965: Notice 2005-10; Notice 2005-38; and Notice 2005-64.

Executive Compensation (Sec. 409A): Section 409A was enacted as part of the AJCA. It provides that the executive or other service provider must include all deferred amounts under a nonqualified deferred compensation (NQDC) plan for all taxable years to the extent they are not subject to a substantial risk of forfeiture and not previously included in income, unless certain requirements are met. If the service provider does not meet these requirements, it will be taxed on the deferred amounts, and will owe an additional 20% tax and an additional tax based upon interest on the deferred tax. This issue crosses all industries. The Joint Committee on Taxation estimates that the revenue impact of this provision for all taxpayers is approximately $1 billion for tax years 2005-2014. This issue is reflected as a book-tax difference on Schedule M-3.

While section 409A is effective for taxable years beginning on or after January 1, 2005, we have issued guidance that extends certain transition relief until December 31, 2006. Other transition relief provides that information reporting for 2005 will not be required until further guidance is issued. We have formed an IMT and most, if not all, of its activity is focused upon issuing final guidance for both the transition and post-transition periods. Guidance issued to date includes: Notice 2005-1 – December 20, 2004 (revised January 6, 2005); Proposed Regulations – September 30, 2004.

Tax Shelters and Other Abusive Tax Avoidance Transactions

One of the most significant compliance challenges facing us is the early identification of abusive transactions. In an effort to address this challenge, the Office of Tax Shelter Analysis (OTSA) continues its effort to identify and combat abusive tax shelters through analysis of Forms 8886 – Reportable Transaction Disclosure Statement filed by investors, and Forms 8264 – Application for Registration of a Tax Shelter filed by material advisors. We assigned for examination listed transactions identified on Form 8886s. We evaluate non-listed transactions identified on Form 8886s for emerging issues and other enforcement action as appropriate.

To effectively use the strengthened material advisor rules enacted in the AJCA, we are focusing more heavily on Forms 8264 in order to identify promoted transactions as early as possible. Analysis of transactions at the time of implementation better enables us to develop a position and take preemptive measures to address any abuse.

To address abusive transactions more quickly, we have implemented a new emerging issue process. The new process, while still under refinement, will expedite the assembly of an IMT to more effectively develop our position with the goal of getting ahead of abusive transactions before returns are filed claiming inappropriate benefits.

LMSB continues to allocate resources to abusive transactions as a top priority. LMSB initiatives such as settlement agreements or Appeals Settlement

Guidelines have helped us address these transactions, resulting in billions of dollars in collected taxes, interest, and penalties. In addition to recapturing lost revenues, targeting abusive transactions produces favorable returns on investment relative to other populations of returns, and should reduce future non-compliance by deterring repetition. We do not believe this effort is over, and continue to look for ways to better leverage the enhanced reporting rules and penalties under AJCA to help us in identifying new transactions.

III. Tax Policy Issues and IRS Focus Areas for Discussion of Reform

To effectively address the compliance challenges of globalization, the complexity of the Code and modern business transactions, and the growing difference between income reported for book and tax purposes, we need support and perhaps new legislation that will improve our ability to effectively administer the Code. Several tax policy issues and focus areas are briefly described below.

Book-Tax Differences

We think the Senate Finance Committee should examine the increase in book-tax differences in greater depth in order to fully understand its impact on compliance. The Finance Committee might consider whether some reduction in the number of provisions in the tax law that create book-tax differences might help to improve compliance. Book-tax differences will require the use of a growing percentage our resources to enforce tax compliance.

Other Tax Policy Issues and IRS Focus Areas for Discussion of Reform

Tax Administration Support Needed for R&E Credit Claims: The R&E credit should be made permanent. Recordkeeping and substantiation requirements need to be more comprehensive to improve our ability to effectively administer the Code for R&E credit refund claims. These claims continue to have a substantial adverse effect on compliance and produce substantial administrative burdens. The temporary nature of the credit, its repeated renewals, and its incremental nature each contribute to these difficulties. In addition, the credit's structure raises a number of technical issues, such as, defining what is "qualified research" and the "costs" that qualify for the credit. While these problems may be alleviated to a degree by additional regulatory guidance or legislation to clarify or resolve some interpretative issues, we believe that absent substantial simplification in the structure of the credit itself and a targeted penalty provision aimed at frivolous or negligent assertions of qualified research expenditure credit claims, substantial non-compliance will continue in this area. Issues involving one aspect or another of the R&E credit constitute a high portion of Chief Counsel's significant case litigation inventory.

The IRS and Treasury are currently working on a number of guidance projects to improve application and administration of the R&E credit. These projects include: internal use software; gross receipts for purposes of the research credit computation; computation and allocation of the research credit for controlled groups; and section 174 depreciable property for purposes of the research credit.

Penalties are Needed for Improper Refund Claims: The accuracy related penalties in the Code apply only in the case of an underpayment of tax and provide no disincentive to taxpayers who file frivolous or negligent claims for refund. We believe this encourages promoters, including accounting firms, to market improper refund of claims schemes. The Finance Committee could consider how the accuracy-related penalty could be expanded to cover abusive refund claims.

Conclusion

Mr. Chairman, ranking Member Baucus and members of the Senate Committee on Finance, the increasing complexity of the tax code combined with the complex and dynamic business models of LMSB taxpayers have extremely complex tax implications with mixed results. Some are perfectly within the boundaries of the law, but this complexity creates opportunities for taxpayers and those who advise them to structure transactions and entities to minimize or avoid paying taxes in ways that were not intended by Congress. At the same time, the growing tension created by the desire of corporations on the one hand to maximize book-earnings, and on the other hand to minimize taxable earnings and increase cash flow, presents incentives which could drive non-compliant behavior. These dynamics create steep and growing challenges for tax administration.

We believe that the tax gap related to large corporate taxpayers is increasing. We have employed strategies to improve the currency and efficiency of our examinations, use the enforcement tools and information available to us, and enhance our ability to identify high risk issues and taxpayers through systems modernization. There is still more to be done.

The issues I have described are key examples of compliance challenges for us. Those taxpayers who choose to comply with the letter and spirit of the law should know that we are aggressively identifying and pursuing those who do not. I have described some of our strategies designed to prevent, identify and deal with noncompliance. I have also identified some examples of steps that Congress could take to assist us. While we have made significant progress in the past few years, more needs to be done to keep up with, if not ahead of, emerging trends and compliance issues. I welcome an opportunity to explore some of these options in more detail at a later date. I appreciate the opportunity to share these observations with you and would be pleased to answer any questions the Committee might have.

Thank you.

Tax Year 2001 FEDERAL TAX GAP

(in Billions of Dollars)

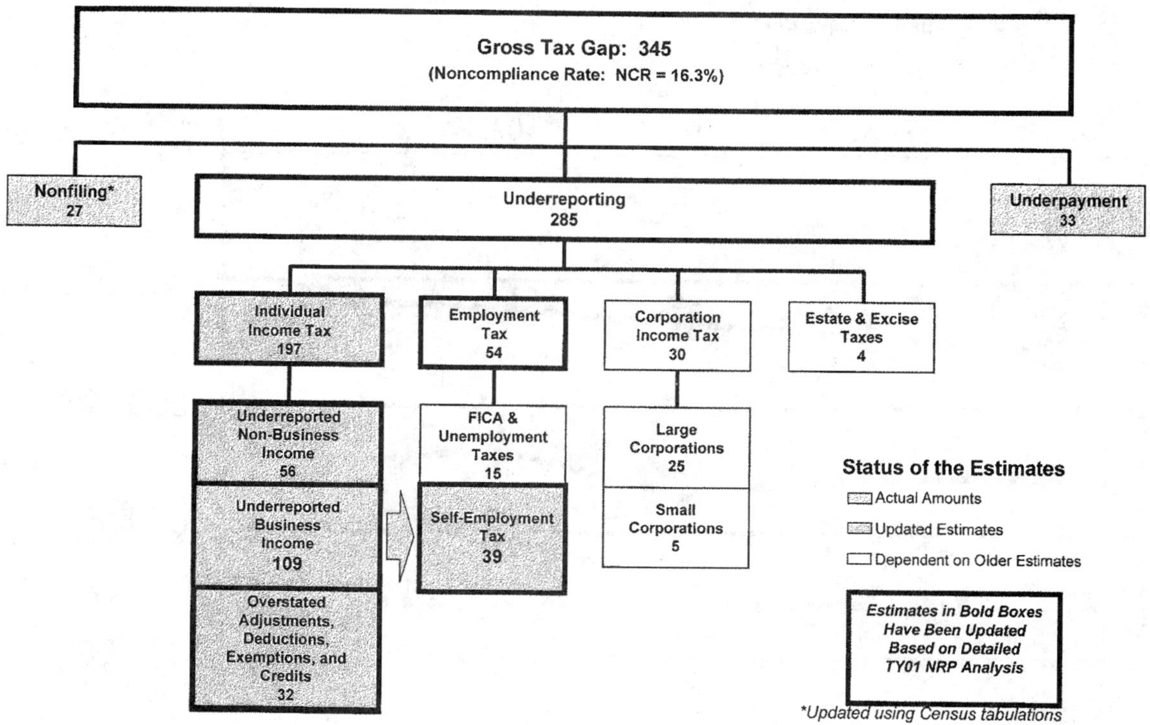

Growth in Large Business Returns

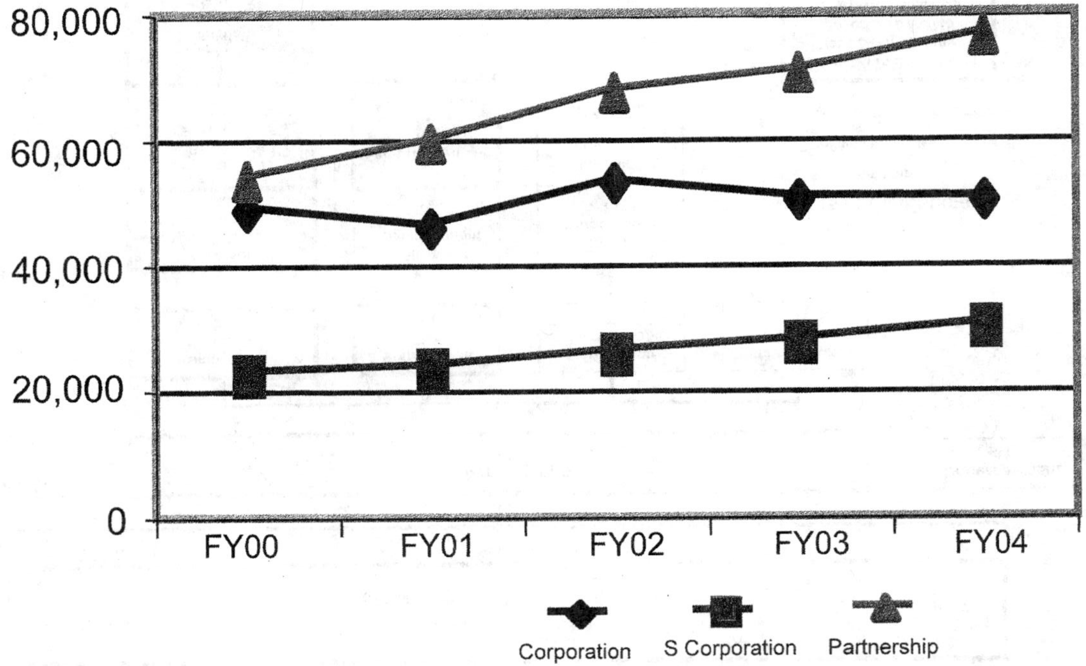

	Corporation	S Corporation	Partnership
Growth	+3%	+24%	+42%
05 Audit Coverage	18.4%	3.6%	2.2%

Selected IRS Coverage Rates – FY 2005

Corporate with Assets > $250M	44.06%
Estate Tax with Gross Estate > $5M	28.12%
Corporate with Assets $10M - $250M	13.86%
Individual with Income > $1M	5.23%
Large S Corporations	3.6%
Individual Business with Schedule C	3.07%
Individual with EITC	2.39%
Large Partnerships	2.2%
All Individuals	0.93%

Agreed & Unagreed Claim Amounts

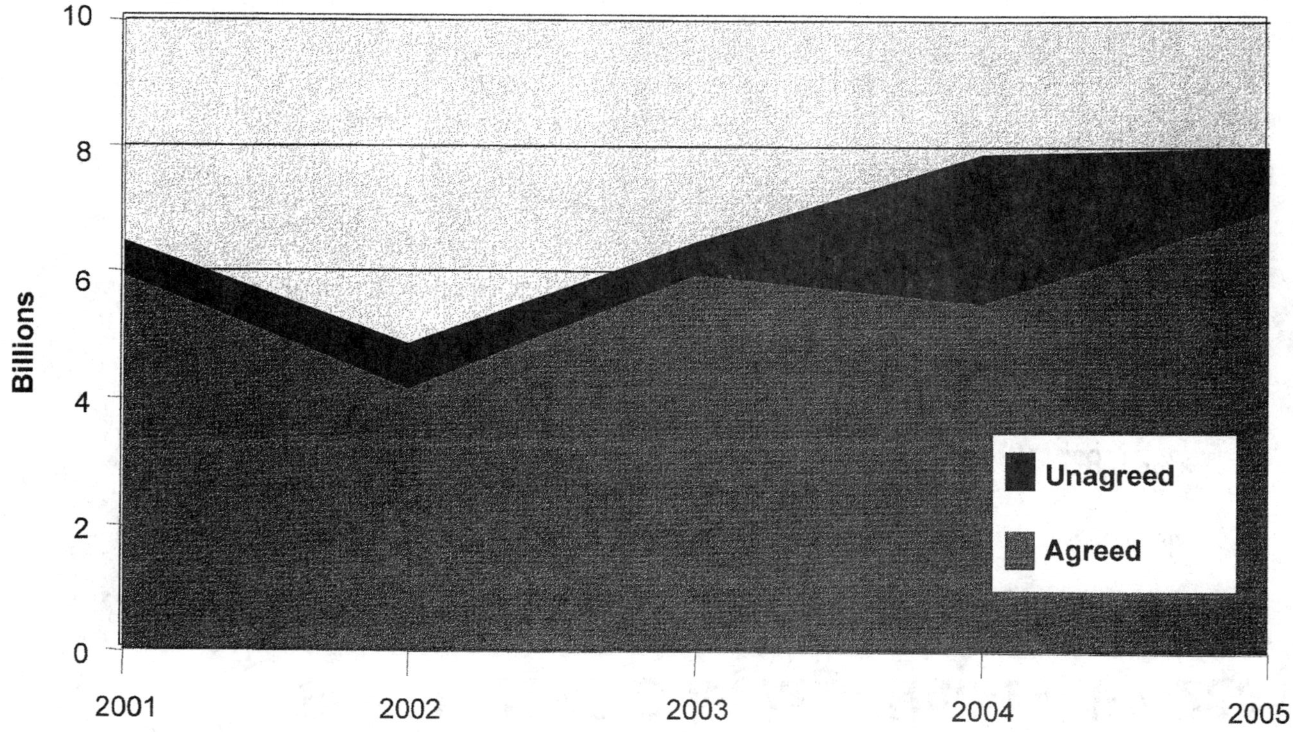

Growth in Refund Claims Examined

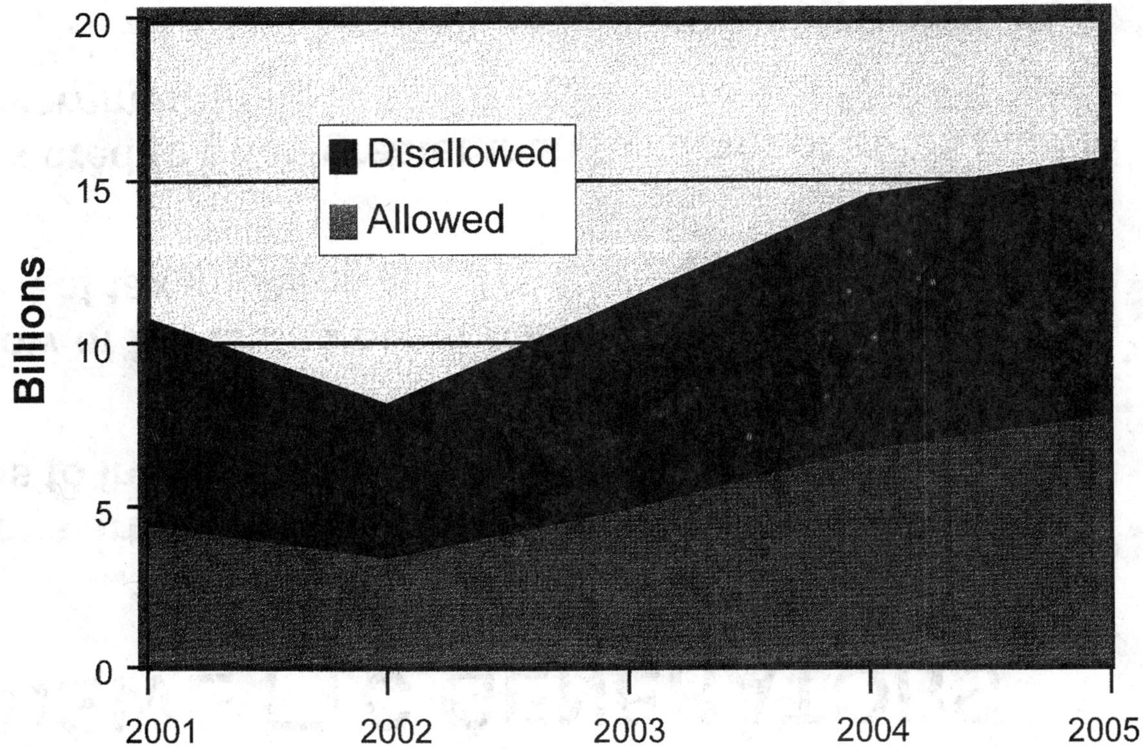

ABUSIVE FTC GENERATORS

- Transactions artificially structured by large financial institutions to inflate foreign tax credits.
- Circular flow of funds and economically needless steps reminiscent of tax shelters
- Foreign tax credits often greater than the amount of tax paid to foreign government.
- Eleven transactions generating $ 3.5 billion in foreign tax credits have been identified to date.

Growth In Book-To-Tax Differences

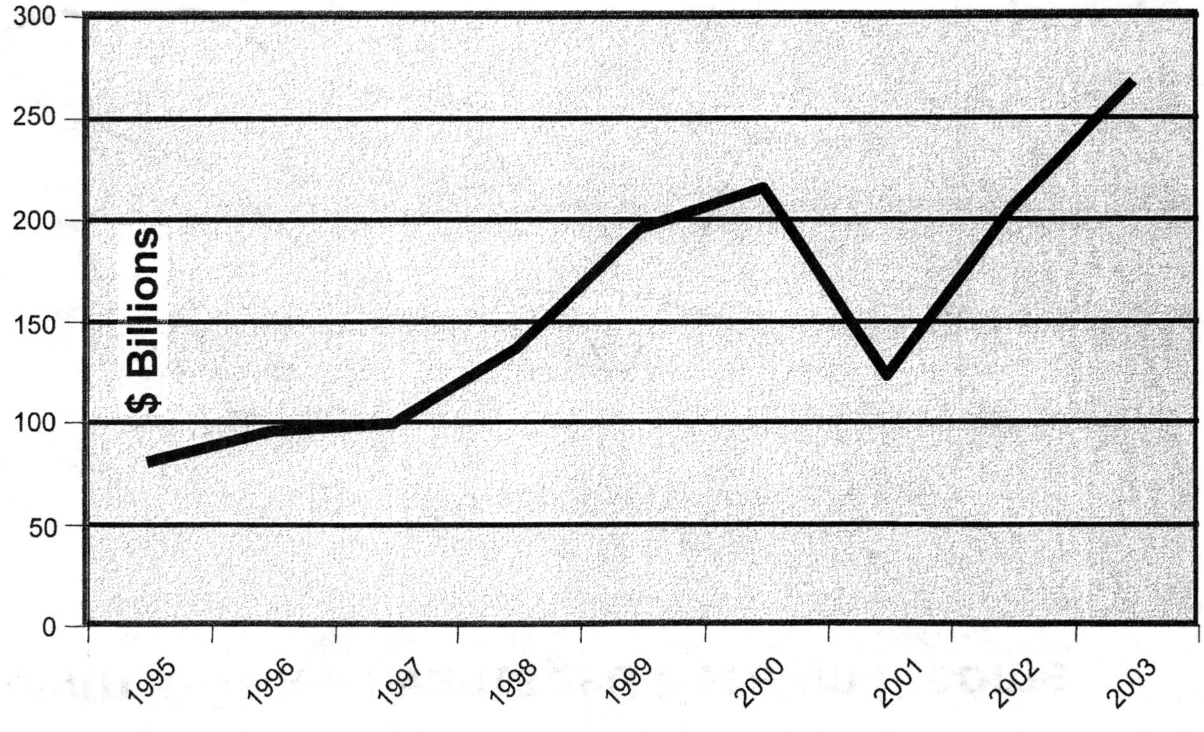

Growth in Tax Advantaged Foreign Income

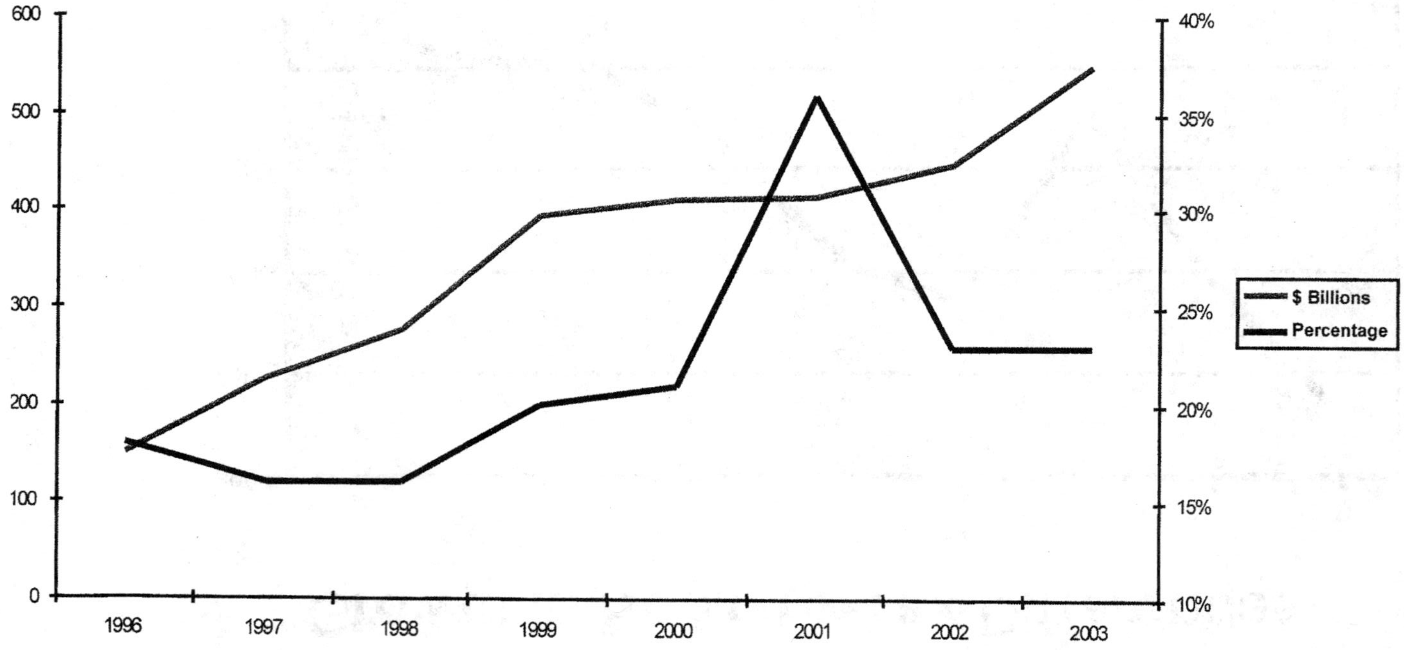

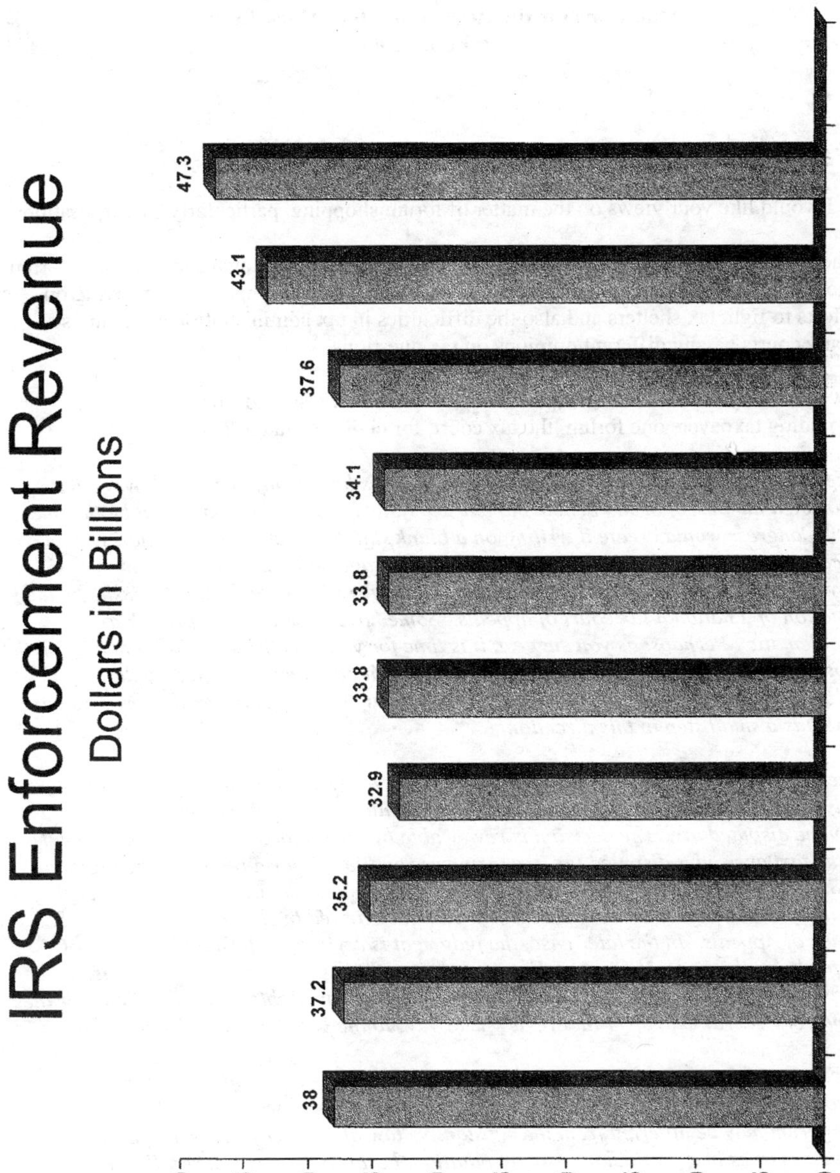
IRS Enforcement Revenue
Dollars in Billions
50
45
40
35
30
25
20
15
10
5
0
FY-96
FY-97
FY-98
FY-99
FY-00
FY-01
FY-02
FY-03
FY-04
FY-05
38
37.2
35.2
32.9
33.8
33.8
34.1
37.6
43.1
47.3

Questions for the Record for Hon. Mark Everson
June 13, 2006

From Senator Grassley:

1. I would like your views on the matter of forum shopping, particularly by corporations.

The Committee is hearing more and more that corporations are aggressively using forum shopping for purposes of litigation. I'm concerned about the impact this is having on efforts to fight tax shelters and also the difficulties in tax administration of having so many courts having different opinions on tax questions.

I would like your views on this problem and specifically, should Congress look at providing taxpayers one forum, the tax court, for civil tax matters?

The current tripartite civil tax litigation system goes back many years and, while it may provide a number of broad benefits to our tax system, it would probably not be the one that Congress would create if writing on a blank slate. The civil tax litigation system can create complexity and inconsistency that disadvantage both taxpayers and the government. Over the years, there have been suggestions to deal with this issue by the creation of a national tax court of appeals. Some have viewed this approach as problematic. Perhaps, as you suggest, it is time for you to consider a different approach. Notably, Congress recently enacted a provision that has been supported by the Administration to make the Tax Court the only venue for all collection due process cases, which is a small step in this direction.

The current structure of the tax system allows taxpayers a choice of forums. A taxpayer may petition the U.S. Tax Court for a redetermination of a deficiency without having to pay the disputed tax. The decision is reviewable by the regional U.S. Court of Appeals. If the taxpayer pays disputed tax, the taxpayer can file suit for a refund in the regional U.S. District Court. Alternatively, the taxpayer can sue in the U.S. Court of Federal Claims. In the former case, the judgment can be reviewed by the corresponding U.S. Court of Appeals. In the later case, the judgment is reviewable by the U.S. Court of Appeals for the Federal Circuit. For refund cases brought in the District Courts, taxpayers have the right to a trial by jury, which is not available in the Tax Court or the Court of Federal Claims. Final review is always to the U.S. Supreme Court.

Because of the trifurcated system of jurisdiction, there are many opportunities for inconsistent or divergent holdings. This leads to a system in which the substantive law in one forum may be different from the substantive law of another forum with respect an issue or issues in a particular case. In addition, because the Tax Court follows the substantive law of the Court of Appeals to which an appeal would be taken, taxpayers litigating the same issues in the Tax Court may be subject to different substantive law depending on where they live or where their principal place of business is located.

Moreover, there may be other significant differences between the courts, including rules of procedure, time frames for disposing of cases, expertise in tax matters, and the identity of those representing the government. Taxpayers who are able to pay the disputed tax have the opportunity to choose the most favorable forum by choosing between filing suit in Tax Court, in District Court, or in the Court of Federal Claims.

We believe that taxpayers do consider the legal authority and procedural rules from different courts when determining how to go forward with tax litigation. The law that applies will depend not only on the court the taxpayer chooses, but also the venue in which the taxpayer's case lies.

The venue for a tax case is generally based on where the taxpayer resides. For corporate taxpayers, U.S. District Court venue (and, consequently, appellate court venue upon appeal) generally is based on the taxpayer's principal place of business, principal office or principal agency. (28 U.S.C. §§1294(1) and 1402(a)). This is true also for appellate review of a Tax Court case (Code §7482(b)(1)(B)). Thus, the substantive law applied by the Tax Court and a District Court would generally be the same, provided that there was a judicial statement of the law by the relevant U.S. Court of Appeals.

Although we are aware of isolated instances involving taxpayers who appear to have taken steps to move or manipulate principal places of business, offices or agencies in order to access the law of a specific jurisdiction, we do not have systematic data, and we are unaware of any studies on the subject. Nonetheless, this remains an issue on which we are watchful, especially in tax shelter cases.

2. We appreciate your testimony and you should know that it has a real impact on our work.

A recent example of that is shown in the tax reconciliation bill just signed into law by President Bush. It contained legislation that addresses the problem of tax-exempt entities that serve as accommodating parties for tax shelter transactions.

Mr. Commissioner, you first raised this issue about tax-exempt entities involved in tax shelters in our first hearing about charities two years ago. I and other members of the committee were shocked to hear you state that approximately half of all corporate tax shelters could or did involve a tax-exempt entity – be it a public charity, a government entity or other organization that receives preferential tax treatment.

Since then, as I mentioned earlier, we've included legislation in the tax reconciliation bill that brings significant penalties on tax-exempt entities and managers who serve as accommodating parties for tax shelters. I think this is a very important new tool for IRS and Treasury in the fight against tax shelters and I want to make sure that you are aggressively taking full advantage of this new authority.

I would like your views on this new anti-shelter language and your plans for implementation.

Section 516 of the Tax Increase Prevention and Reconciliation Act of 2005 (TIPRA) imposes excise taxes on certain tax-exempt and governmental entities that are parties to listed and certain reportable transactions. Section 516 also imposes excise taxes on certain managers of tax exempt and governmental entities, and of many types of employee benefit plans, that approve the entity or plan becoming a party to such transactions. Finally, section 516 imposes related disclosure obligations and imposes penalties for failing to comply with those disclosure obligations.

We believe Congress has handed us a very important tool in the battle against tax shelters. Sec. 516 of the Act encourages transparency of tax shelters which we believe is a cornerstone of an effective system to discourage the use of abusive tax transactions. Sec. 516 in fact advances well established tax policy that both encourages disclosure and penalizes those who fail to comply.

Tax-exempt and government entities are essential parties in many tax shelter structures, but we have had few ways to deter them from acting as accommodating parties in transactions that typically have little to do with their tax exempt status. We intend to use the new provisions fully in order to discourage the involvement of tax exempt entities in transactions that we view as having no practical use, other than the tax savings generated.

Immediately upon enactment on May 17, we developed a multi-pronged effort to ensure compliance with section 516 of TIPRA:

o *Alerting taxpayers to their responsibilities under the statute: IRS and Treasury issued a notice to taxpayers explaining their obligations under the statute and requesting comments on issues to be addressed in guidance. (Notice 2006-65, issued July 11, 2006)*

o *Compiling a list of issues to be addressed in follow-up guidance and potential resolutions of those issues. Follow-up guidance will be issued shortly.*

o *Revising necessary forms (generally, Forms 4720 (Return of Certain Excise Taxes on Charities and Other Persons Under Chapters 41 and 42 of the IRC), 5330 (Return of Excise Taxes Related to employee Benefit Plans) and 8886, (Reportable Transaction Disclosure Statement)).*

o *Creating the necessary programming to accept and record payment of the IRC § 4965 tax, along with developing programming and procedures to ensure that, where required, the appropriate information is publicly disclosed.*

o *Working to more effectively identify tax-exempt entities that are acting as accommodation parties in tax shelter transactions. We are planning to capture the relevant data from filed disclosure forms and conduct any follow-up action we deem appropriate.*

IRS will soon begin a small scale compliance check project, using one particular shelter transaction, to gather information on why and how tax exempt entities enter into these transactions.

3. Commissioner Everson, part of this panel's discussion today is focused on the pros and cons of the use of LIFO for tax purposes as we consider possible changes in the area of tax inventory accounting. In the course of the discussion about LIFO a question has arisen about whether some companies that are currently using LIFO aren't really allowed to use LIFO under the current tax law.

First, I would like to know what the IRS is doing in the course of examinations to track LIFO conformity especially for those U.S. companies that are listed on foreign exchanges.

Second, I'd be glad to have your comments on whether LIFO presents an audit burden for the IRS given the fact that very old records continue to be relevant to tax returns that span decades of time.

With respect to the first part of your question, when Revenue Agents examine the LIFO conformity issue they review taxpayers' financial statements prepared in accordance with U.S. GAAP to determine whether or not there is a conformity violation. Although LIFO conformity violations have rarely been discovered in the course of an examination, when they are, Revenue Agents raise the issue. As of January 1, 2005 the International Accounting Standards Board (IASB) began requiring U.S.-headquartered companies and their subsidiaries to use a method other than LIFO. This is a recent development, and we have not encountered the issue on audit. We recognize the importance of the IASB requirement and are taking steps to inform our examiners.

Secondly, the examination of a LIFO inventory is complex, and requires analyses of old records. The review of old records is frequently made difficult because the information is not easily located and the personnel who prepared the records may no longer be available. The problems of old records are a burden to the IRS, and to taxpayers as their inability/failure to provide adequate books and records becomes an audit issue. The availability and widespread use of the Inventory Price Index Computation (IPIC) method, enabling taxpayers to use an external index for LIFO purposes, has somewhat alleviated the complexity of auditing LIFO issues.

4. I have had a long history in the area of whistleblowers. Whistleblowers are a huge part of my success in oversight and through the False Claims Act – legislation I updated and had enacted – whistleblowers recover billions of dollars for the taxpayers. One loophole in the False Claims Act is that it doesn't apply to tax matters.

While I think there are good reasons why we should be cautious about having the False Claims Act apply to whistleblowers in tax matters, it is clear that the federal government can benefit significantly from making good use of whistleblowers in tax cases.

The IRS already has clear legislative authority to have a broad based program to reward tax whistleblowers. What the IRS hasn't had is clear sighted management that has taken full advantage of the possibilities of tax whistleblowers.

The recent TIGTA report on this matter has only made it all the more clearer that there are great benefits to rewarding tax whistleblowers and that the IRS and Treasury have fallen down on the job.

As you can see from this chart, based on the TIGTA report, cases based on whistleblowers are far more productive for the IRS than others cases. The return to the Treasury for dollars per hour worked of cases from whistleblowers is $946 as compared to $548 for IRS' regular cases. The trend continues with the other table that shows that for Small Business cases, the IRS is having a return of $688 per hour worked on whistleblower cases as compared to $382 per hour for regular IRS cases – getting close to 2 -1 .

In addition, the no-change rate is about a third lower for whistleblower cases – meaning that whistleblower cases are more likely to target tax cheats and not bother honest tax payers as compared to regular IRS audits.

TIGTA recommends that there be a centralization of whistleblower work at the IRS and other points. But I would say to you, Mr. Commissioner, that is the tip of the iceberg, we need to have leadership committed to making this program a success.

Whistleblowers having to wait seven and half years for a reward is nonsense; having to wait till every last time is paid before they get any reward; 76 percent of the cases rejected TIGTA found no justification or rationale in the files; the IRS basically burying the whistleblower reward program – with no advertising or notice of the program. This has to stop. Whistleblowers are a vital tool to efforts to fight tax shelters and tax abuse.

What are the steps I can expect to see NOW from the IRS and Treasury to make the whistleblower program a success?

The IRS receives numerous leads from many sources, such as informants, hotline calls, etc. Before diverting our audit resources from Discriminant Index Function (DIF) and other identified work that has a proven yield, we carefully screen the leads to ensure that the information is credible and specific with respect to a violation of the tax laws. While the IRS does want to pursue quality leads, it is not effective or efficient for the IRS to initiate audits based on general statements of noncompliance from business competitors, disgruntled employees or acquaintances. The fact that the examinations involving informant information result in a higher yield than DIF reflects the quality of our screening process.

An informant does wait on average 7 ½ years from the filing of a claim to receive a payment when the IRS utilizes the information in an audit. By law, the IRS cannot pay a reward until the taxes, fines and penalties have been collected from taxpayers. One area that we continually focus on is taking all actions within our control to shorten the time to complete an audit; however, taxpayer actions also contribute to the time to complete the audit. Furthermore, the taxpayer has complete control over whether to exercise their appeal and litigation rights, as well as when the taxes are paid.

Before TIGTA performed their review of the Informants' Claims for Reward Program (ICRP), we had performed our own review. Below are the steps we have taken to improve the administration and management control of the ICRP:

- *All informant claims have been consolidated in the Ogden Campus. This will ensure closer tracking and monitoring of these claims.*
- *As of January 31, 2006, each Operating Division has a designated coordinator that is responsible for oversight, coordination, and management of the informant reward program in their division.*
- *We have established a National Oversight Committee made up of the Operating Division Coordinators and the Senior Advisor to the Deputy Commissioner to centralize management and oversight. The Committee held its first meeting June 13, 2006, and now meets monthly.*
- *The new nationwide web-based system to track, monitor, and control claims will be operational January 1, 2007. This will streamline claims processing from receipt of the claim through its processing, tracking, reporting, and completion.*

5. Commissioner Everson, confidentiality of tax return information is a fundamental part of our self-assessment tax system. You have publicly said that the merits of publicly disclosing corporate tax return information should be debated. Today, we are having that debate.

Whatever benefits there might be of publicly disclosing tax return information must be carefully balanced against taxpayers' interest in confidentiality of that information.

We heard Mr. Kleinbard offer his view that the schedule M-3's of publicly traded companies should be made public, primarily to promote transparency in financial reporting. According to Mr. Kleinbard, tax administration would be modestly helped, and the quality of tax and accounting systems would be improved. Mr. Kleinbard does not think that making M-3's public will unduly harm taxpayer confidentiality.

Mr. Commissioner, I'd like your views, as our chief tax administrator, on Mr. Kleinbard's proposal. Specifically, I have four questions:

First, in what ways would disclosure of the M-3's of public corporations enhance tax compliance?

Some commentators have argued that public disclosure of the Schedule M-3 "would promote important financial transparency goals for investors and analysts, and could reasonably be expected to dampen some corporate enthusiasm for dodgy Enron type 'off-balance-sheet' tax (or financial accounting) strategies." While it is difficult to measure the factors that lead corporations to enter into aggressive tax transactions, increased public disclosures of return information could have some deterrent effect.

Because we do not audit each and every corporate income tax return, compliance depends in large part on the decisions taken by, and the relative appetite for risk, of corporate managements and boards of directors. Simply stated, managements might be less likely to take inappropriately aggressive positions if they might be queried about those positions by shareholders, analysts, academics and other users of financial information. That same notion of transparency underlies our Federal securities regulatory regime as well as the Sarbanes-Oxley reforms that Congress enacted to improve corporate behavior in governance and financial disclosure integrity. This enhanced transparency could be more informative if an aggressive tax position could be seen to explain the difference in performance between one company and another. Right now the question of quality of earnings is one that rarely includes a discussion of tax practices, behavior and corporate appetite for tax risk.

Second, what tax administration concerns would be implicated by disclosure of M-3's? For example, would public disclosure have any impact on the quality of information that taxpayers report on their M-3's?

Tax administration would likely be impacted by the public disclosure of corporate return information. Depending on the nature and scope of the information disclosed, the relationship between the IRS and many taxpayers could become more contentious, since reporting an item on a tax return would result in it being disclosed to the public and competitors as well. Companies might be reluctant to provide the IRS with information they deem sensitive and might seek ways to obscure certain details from the IRS and, in turn, public scrutiny.

Third, what confidentiality concerns would be implicated by public disclosure of M-3's?

Confidentially of tax returns and return information is an important part of our self-assessment tax system. It is important to balance taxpayers' interest in privacy with the need for tax law compliance. I think that the impact on the self-assessment system needs to be carefully considered before any changes are made to the confidentiality rules. Tax returns include far more detail than is included in financial statements used by financial institutions and others to assess businesses. In fact, some corporate returns run into the thousands of pages. Clearly, if complete returns and supporting schedules were to be disclosed, there would be at least two potential issues. First would be the confusion that could be prompted by the introduction of the different presentation of business results as captured on the return, particularly where there are valid reasons for the discrepancy, as there frequently are with items such as depreciation and amortization. Users might draw improper or unintended inferences from the myriad of details included in the return, information in many instances not material to an overall understanding of the business. A second issue would be the potential disclosure of competitive information. The risks in both instances could arguably be mitigated if only selected portions of the return were publicly disclosed, although the Schedule M-3 does contain a nearly complete picture of a business' tax position.

Fourth, if M-3's were to be made public, how could confidentiality be adequately preserved?

The risks to confidentiality could arguably be mitigated if only selected portions of the return were publicly disclosed and if a process were adopted to redact sensitive business information.

6. Commissioner Everson, you identified abusive foreign tax credit transactions as one of the specific compliance issues facing LMSB. You mentioned that the IRS and Treasury have several major regulatory projects underway that will address numerous issues involving the inappropriate separation of foreign taxes from the related foreign income. However, you also mentioned a new breed of cross-border financing transactions the IRS considers abusive, but is still exploring the legal grounds to challenge them. I'd like to flesh this out a little. What it is that makes these transactions abusive in your view? How are these transactions similar to or different from those Congress or the IRS has already dealt with?

U.S. taxpayers are subject to U.S. tax on their worldwide income. Foreign tax credits are intended to prevent double taxation of foreign income. The foreign tax credit regime permits a U.S. taxpayer to claim a credit against U.S. tax liability for foreign taxes imposed on foreign income.

Transactions we call "Foreign Tax Credit Generators" turn this regime on its head. In these structured transactions, U.S. taxpayers generate foreign tax credits in instances where the underlying business transaction (e.g., a loan) would not ordinarily be subject to foreign tax. In the more egregious transactions, U.S. taxpayers claim foreign tax credits even though the U.S. taxpayer has little or no income from the transaction.

These transactions are particularly troubling because they are designed to generate foreign tax credits in the amounts desired by the parties. The basic transactions are loans which are then surrounded by elaborate structures built to generate credits. Interest rates are adjusted to share the U.S. foreign tax credit benefit; that is, the U.S. government effectively subsidizes the transaction through the foreign tax credit, and makes cross border borrowing/lending more profitable than comparable domestic-to-domestic transactions.

One of the newest versions of this type of transaction causes U.S. income to be subject to foreign tax, resulting in a foreign tax benefit for the foreign person and foreign tax credits for the U.S. taxpayer. The taxpayer's U.S. income is "converted" into foreign income, allowing the U.S. taxpayer to use foreign tax credits to eliminate U.S. tax due on the income. The transaction also gives rise to a foreign tax benefit (such as a credit or a loss) to the foreign person. The U.S. taxpayer is compensated by the foreign person through the pricing of the transaction. For example, U.S. borrowers have been able to obtain loans at a reduced interest rate by paying foreign taxes claimed as credits by the foreign lender and also claimed as foreign tax credits by the U.S. borrower. The U.S. government, through the credit, subsidizes these loan transactions. Actual financing is not even required for some of these transactions; in certain cases, U.S. taxpayers are simply paid a fee by the foreign person for the foreign tax benefit.

Addressing the second part of your question, Foreign Tax Credit Generators have some overlapping similarities and some differences from another group of tax-motivated transactions currently being addressed, those involving the inappropriate separation of foreign tax credits from related foreign source income ("FTC splitters"). As described above, foreign tax credits are generated (purchased or created) in the generator transactions. In the FTC splitters, foreign tax credits are separated from the related foreign income.

There are two general types of FTC splitters. The first may involve the acquisition of assets that generate income or built-in gain that is subject to foreign tax, but will never be subject to U.S. tax. The second involves transactions whereby taxpayers use partnerships, foreign consolidated regimes, and reverse hybrid entities to claim foreign tax credits while deferring the corresponding income for U.S. tax purposes.

The IRS and Treasury recently issued regulations that will address many of the second type of FTC splitter transactions (by associating the right to claim the foreign tax credit with the person who is required to take the related foreign income into account). While these regulations will address some of the FTC splitters, they will not address the problems inherent in the FTC generators.

Note that the IRS first became aware of a type of FTC splitter transaction known as the "ADR transaction" in the mid-1990s. The IRS disallowed the foreign tax credits in these transactions based on the economic substance doctrine. The government won two ADR cases at trial, but lost both on appeal. See Compaq Computer Corp. v. Commissioner, 277 F.3d 778 (5th Cir. 2001); IES Indus., Inc. v. United States, 253 F.3d 350 (8th Cir. 2001). While these cases were being litigated, Congress enacted section 901(k) in 1997, which effectively shut down ADR transactions prospectively.[1]

7. Commissioner Everson, you identified a concern that mass-marketed, contingency fee-based refund claims related to the manufacturing deduction will become a problem. Your concern with refund claims is apparent in other parts of your testimony. You noted that

---

[1] Section 901(k) disallows a foreign tax credit for withholding taxes on dividends where certain holding periods are not met or a related payment eliminates the dividend from taxable income. In 2004, Congress enacted section 901(l), which essentially expanded the scope of section 901(k) to disallow a foreign tax credit for withholding taxes on certain items of (non-dividend) income or gain. These provisions generally apply to disallow credits for withholding taxes, but not for foreign net income taxes that are imposed on income not subject to U.S. tax.

LMSB disallowed $8 billion worth of refund claims in 2005 alone. You also mentioned contingency fee based refund claims with respect to the research credit. Finally, you recommend enacting a penalty regime for improper refund claims.

Is your concern that unintended benefits would be claimed by aggressive interpretations of the tax code, which would imply tax shelter-like activity? Or are you concerned that intended but unsupported benefits might be claimed through complicated, after-the-fact analysis of corporate data, which I suppose raises a question of how effective an incentive a particular tax benefit might actually be? Would you please elaborate on your concern and the nature of the potential problem of mass marketed contingency fee based refund claims generally, and claims with respect to the manufacturing deduction and research credit in particular?

We are concerned by the impact on compliance of all returns filed including mass marketed, contingency fee based refund claims submitted by large and mid-sized business taxpayers. Your question incorporates key characteristics of this issue. Some claims contain overly aggressive interpretations of the Code and Treasury Regulations, and some may have tax shelter characteristics. The amended return or claim process is also being used to provide unsupported benefits through a post filing analysis of corporate accounts. This analysis is designed to find groupings of expenses that can be used to create additional deductions or credits, that can involve unusual or extreme interpretations of facts or law.

We believe that the Domestic Manufacturing Deduction under Code section 199, enacted by the American Jobs Creation Act of 2004, will be susceptible to mass-marketed claims. Tax professionals, once the deduction has risen to the 9% level, will be able to persuade taxpayers that they are entitled to a significant deduction they may not otherwise have claimed. While we do not know the form that the claims will take or the manner in which the service will be marketed, it is likely to follow the model of the R&E Credit, i.e., potential improper re-classification of activities to increase the deduction resulting in refund claims. While the legal theories underlying these claims are often consistent with Congressional intent, applying those issues on an after the fact basis often raises complex proof issues.

For example, accounting treatment of certain expenditures on the original return resulted in a determination that they were not eligible for an R&E Credit. A claim marketing team with little knowledge of the nature of these expenses conducts oral interviews with the taxpayer's personnel to determine additional pockets of expenses or a percentage of time that employees worked on "qualified research". The result is that additional expenses that the preparer and taxpayer originally classified as not being credit eligible are re-categorized as eligible for the credit. We believe that any subsequent reclassification of these items should require due diligence regarding specifically why the original determination should be changed.

We believe that the contingency fee charged for preparing a subsequent claim for refund impairs the independence of the party selling the refund claim to large and mid-sized business taxpayers and presents a "no lose" proposition to the taxpayer. Additionally, this retrospective, post return filing analysis of corporate accounts unfairly exploits the intent of these credits to increase domestic expenditures in furtherance of research and manufacturing.

While we cited mass-marketed contingency fee based claims as a basis for legislative action to enact a penalty for improper refund claims, we also believe the penalty would reduce other improper claims.

8. Commissioner Everson, as you know, the Financial Accounting Standards Board is about to change the rules regarding accounting for uncertain tax positions. Under the new rules, a company can book a tax benefit only if, based on the merits, it is "more likely than not" to be realized. Audit lottery will not be permitted to be taken into account. The FASB is also considering a rule that would require companies to disclose changes in tax contingency reserves from period to period. In the Arthur Young case, decided in 1984, the Supreme Court confirmed the IRS's right to obtain a company's tax accrual workpapers under its summons authority. In Announcement 2002-63, the IRS stated that "Despite the broad scope of authority recognized by the Supreme Court, the Service has historically acted with restraint, declining to request Tax Accrual Workpapers as a standard examination technique."

Mr. Commissioner, would you please explain the IRS's policy on requesting tax accrual workpapers, the IRS's experience with that policy, the rationale for the restraint inherent in that policy, and whether the proposed FASB rule changes might have any impact on that policy?

In 2002, the Internal Revenue Service revised its policy concerning when it will request and, if necessary, summons tax accrual and other financial audit workpapers relating to the tax reserve for deferred tax liabilities, and to footnotes disclosing contingent tax liabilities ("Tax Accrual Workpapers"), appearing on audited financial statements. This limited expansion of the policy was necessary to allow the Service to fulfill its obligation to the public to curb abusive tax avoidance transactions, and to ensure that taxpayers are in compliance with the tax laws. In all other respects, the Service's current policy of restraint regarding requests for Tax Accrual Workpapers (TAW) remains.

Under the revised policy, the Service may request TAW in the course of examining any return filed on or after July 1, 2002, that claims any tax benefit arising out of a transaction that the Service has determined to be a listed transaction at the time of the request within the meaning of Temp. Treas. Reg. § 1.6011-4T(b)(2) ("Listed Transaction"). Temp. Treas. Reg. § 1.6011-4T(b)(2) defines listed transactions to include substantially similar transactions. If the Listed Transaction was disclosed under Temp. Treas. Reg. § 1.6011-4T, the Service routinely requests the TAW pertaining only to the Listed Transaction. If the Listed Transaction was not disclosed, the Service routinely requests all TAW. In addition, if the Service determines that tax benefits from multiple investments in Listed Transactions are claimed on a return, regardless of whether the Listed Transactions were disclosed, the Service routinely requests all TAW.

Similarly, if, in connection with the examination of a return claiming tax benefits from a Listed Transaction that was disclosed, there are reported financial accounting irregularities, such as those requiring restatement of earnings, the Service will request all TAW. For a return filed prior to July 1, 2002, that claims any tax benefit arising out of a Listed Transaction, the Service requests TAW pertaining to the Listed Transaction, if the taxpayer had an obligation to disclose the transaction under Temp. Treas. Reg. § 1.6011-4T, and failed to do so (1) on the return; (2) under Rev. Proc. 94- 69, 1994-2 C.B. 804, if applicable; or (3) pursuant to Announcement 2002-2, 2002-2 I.R.B. 304 (Jan. 14, 2002).

The Supreme Court confirmed the Service's right to obtain TAW under its summons authority, United States v. Arthur Young & Co.*, 465 U.S. 805 (1984). Since TAW are not generated in connection with seeking legal or tax advice, but are developed to evaluate a taxpayer's deferred or contingent tax liabilities in connection with a taxpayer's disclosure to third parties of the taxpayer's financial condition, TAW are not privileged communications. Neither the attorney-client privilege nor the IRC § 7525 tax practitioner privilege (which is based upon, but is more limited than, the attorney-client privilege) protects TAW from production upon proper request by an authorized examining agent. See also Treasury Department Circular 230, 31 C.F.R. § 10.20 (duty of practitioner to submit information upon a proper and lawful request by the IRS). Despite the broad scope of authority recognized by the Supreme Court, the Service has historically acted with restraint, declining to request TAW as a standard examination technique. The Service continues to exercise its authority to request TAW with restraint.*

IRS Experience with Policy

To date, 92 requests for TAW have been made. Three (3) have resulted in summons enforcement letters. Two of the three are pending at the Department of Justice. The third taxpayer complied after receiving the Department of Justice summons enforcement letter. As agents start to gain more experience in this area, positive and useful information is being reported. To date we know of 6 incidents where one of the following has occurred: a) it has strengthened our ability to develop and sustain penalties; b) it has helped us to identify new issues; and c) it has allowed us to improve development of previously identified issues.

Rationale for Restraint

After the Supreme Court's decision in Arthur Young, and prior to Announcement 2002-63, the IRS maintained a policy of requesting TAW from taxpayers or their accountants only in unusual circumstances. In arriving at its holding in Arthur Young*, the Court itself considered it significant that the Service had, "Demonstrated administrative sensitivity to the concerns expressed by the accounting profession by tightening its internal requirements for the issuance of a request for tax accrual workpapers." This statement of 'administrative flexibility' 'reinforced [the Court's] decision not to reduce irrevocably the § 7602 summons power.' The 'internal requirements' referred to by the Court were the IRM policy articulating the 'unusual circumstances' standard for requesting tax* *accrual workpapers. The Court's holding coupled with concern over the effects on the financial markets resulted in the policy of restraint.*

<u>*FAS 109 Impact on Policy*</u>

Uncertainty in Income Taxes, an Interpretation of FASB Statement No. 109, does contain new disclosure rules. Among other disclosures concerning accruals for interest and penalties related to potential tax liabilities, a tabular reconciliation of the beginning and ending balances of unrecognized tax benefits (tax reserves) will be required. LMSB plans to maintain its self-imposed policy of not seeking TAW on examinations except in very restricted, defined circumstances. It is not currently anticipated that the new interpretation of FAS 109 and its new disclosure requirements will have a significant impact on LMSB's current policy of restraint covering TAW.

9. Commissioner Everson, I am very interested in the credit card reporting proposal in the President's budget. Could you provide additional details related to the proposal? For example, would payments related to the provision of both goods and services be covered? What types of information would be reported to the IRS? Which entities, specifically, would be obligated to do the reporting and how would you define those entities? Would payments to corporations be subject to reporting? How would the IRS utilize the information to reduce the tax gap?

The Administration's proposal would require information reporting on the total amount of payment card sale reimbursements made by a merchant. This would include all transactions where the merchant agrees to accept a payment card to pay for goods and services.

Generally, any bank with a relationship to a merchant (or the bank's affiliated card processor) would be required to report the payment card sales. Information reporting would be required from those entities that provide the mechanism to effectuate payment between the purchaser and a merchant, or those entities who accept payment cards as an intermediary for one or more merchants. These are often referred to in the industry as "merchant" or "acquiring" banks. Regulations would relieve multiple parties from reporting the same transaction and ensure that reporting is required from the entity that can provide the most accurate information at the lowest cost.

The merchant or acquiring bank would be required to report the name, address, and taxpayer identification number of the merchant along with the amount of gross reimbursements from payment card transactions. For this information to be useful, the bank would be required to obtain the merchant's taxpayer identification number in writing. All credit card payments would be reportable, whether for goods or services. Additional information as prescribed by regulations may also be required. No information about the identity of the purchaser, the amount of any specific purchase or the item or service purchased would be required. Like similar reporting statutes, the new statute would not specifically exclude specific payees; however, the IRS could provide appropriate exclusions in regulations.

The information received would allow the IRS to estimate the amount of gross receipts that any merchant accepting credit cards should report on its return. IRS matching programs could use the information to better identify those entities that may be underreporting their gross receipts and to target, by industry or otherwise, non-compliant taxpayers who report low amounts of total gross receipts relative to credit card receipts.

10. As we have heard from several witnesses, a significant portion of corporate income tax noncompliance involves multinational corporations. I would like your thoughts on a few points.

- Please describe the degree of interaction you have with law enforcement offices from other nations.

In February 1995, Criminal Investigation (CI) established a formal International Strategy. One of the goals of the strategy involved the placement of special agents as a foreign country Attaché to facilitate development and utilization of information obtained from host foreign nations. The information obtained supports criminal investigations into alleged financial crimes over which CI has enforcement responsibility. This strategy has now led to Attaché placement in eight U.S. Embassies around the world. Each Attaché focuses on all aspects of the CI mission.

Although CI has been working international investigations for many years, the explosion of international crime involving tax evasion, narcotics, terrorism, and money laundering requires unique approaches.

- *International investigative work related to CI cases has increased greatly in conjunction with the increased use of offshore bank havens and foreign trusts, and increased international commerce in general; including corporate fraud.*
- *CI Attaché overseas posts also increased our ability to obtain assistance and evidence from foreign sources, including law enforcement offices.*
- *Increased globalization and common threats has encouraged other countries to cooperate more with U.S. requests for foreign assistance.*

Corporate Fraud encompasses investigations involving tax and money laundering violations by executives of large publicly traded (or private) corporations. These cases are prominent because of the magnitude of the resulting negative consequences for communities, employees, lenders, and investors. Some of these frauds cross international lines, involve multinational corporations, and utilize offshore bank accounts.

In 2002, President George W. Bush established a Presidential Corporate Fraud Task Force. That task force is intended to provide direction for the investigation and prosecution of significant cases involving securities and accounting fraud, mail and wire fraud, money laundering and tax fraud. Most of the corporate fraud investigations are joint efforts involving many federal agencies; and at times requires assistance from law enforcement offices from other nations in the form of investigative interviews, document searches/production, extradition assistance, joint investigations and other relevant investigative matter.

As financial investigators, CI special agents fill a unique niche in the federal law enforcement community. Because of our financial investigative expertise, CI is involved in most of the regional corporate fraud task forces. CI has exclusive investigatory jurisdiction over criminal violations of the Internal Revenue Code (IRC). Corporate fraud frequently involves violations of the IRC through falsification of corporate and individual tax returns.

Additionally, CI is involved in investigating various Foreign Trust schemes, which include offshore credit card, brokerage houses, and employee leasing fraudulent schemes.

In conducting corporate and foreign trust/offshore fraud investigations, as well as any other criminal tax and/or money laundering investigation, CI obtains assistance from law enforcement offices from other nations on a regular basis, in the form of requests for investigative information. These requests can be secured by contact with the legal authorities from other nations, generally through the Director, LMSB International, who serves as the designated U.S. Competent Authority, under most bilateral agreements relating to tax information.

On tax-related investigations, bilateral agreements that can be used include a bilateral tax treaty or a tax information exchange agreement (TIEA). CI coordinates the contacts relating to a bilateral agreement through CI's Foreign Attaché. Upon obtaining permission from a foreign country, special agents are able to conduct record searches and interviews in foreign countries, accompanied by law enforcement officers of the host country.

It is possible to conduct a joint criminal tax investigation with agents from a foreign country pursuant to a tax treaty when it is alleged the subject of an investigation has committed substantial tax violations in both countries. This is known as the Simultaneous Criminal Investigation Program (SCIP). This process was enacted in order to expedite the investigation by allowing agents from each country to work together and exchange information informally. However, at the end of the investigation all evidence must be exchanged through the Competent Authority of each country. Currently this program is in effect with Canada, Italy, France and Mexico. However, if the investigation warrants, a SCIP generally can be initiated with any country with which the United States has a tax treaty. Grand juries can be used in an SCIP either at the request of the IRS or the U.S. Attorney, subject to Department of Justice approval.

Interaction between CI and foreign law enforcement offices from other nations takes place under another type of bilateral arrangement known as a Mutual Legal Assistance

Treaty (MLAT) request. In addition to requesting testimony and tangible evidence from foreign countries through the IRS, agents can request information through the Department of Justice pursuant to MLATs. These treaties offer a wide range of assistance from the judicial and executive authorities of the counties involved. An MLAT can be used for any criminal violation, including Title 26; it can be used for both grand jury and, depending on the terms of the treaty, those administrative investigations where criminal referral and prosecution is anticipated.

If the United States does not have a bilateral agreement with a country, it may be possible to use a letter rogatory to request the information. A letter rogatory is a formal request from a United States Federal Court, before which an action is pending, to the court of the foreign country in which the information/evidence is located. A letter rogatory may require contact and communication between an agent from the United States and the offices of a foreign law enforcement agency, in complying with the request.

CI (International) has a direct connection to INTERPOL, the International Criminal Police Organization. Approximately, 180 countries' law enforcement authorities participate in INTERPOL. INTERPOL provides assistance in obtaining leads, information, and evidence from foreign countries. INTERPOL assists in searching for, capturing and returning international fugitives to the United States, otherwise known as Red Notices.

Essentially, an INTERPOL request is an official request from the police or criminal law enforcement authorities of one country made directly to the police or criminal law enforcement authorities of another country seeking what is commonly known as police information or assistance. Police information or assistance is, generally, information that can be obtained, or assistance that can be provided, by law enforcement authorities without using subpoenas or another legal process. The request is pursued within the context and confines of each country's laws and policies. Cooperation by participating countries is voluntary.

The Financial Crimes Enforcement Network (FinCEN) is the financial intelligence unit (FIU) operating in the United States. It was created to facilitate the exchange of information between U.S. law enforcement agencies and international agencies to fight money laundering. FinCEN responds to appropriate requests from U.S. law enforcement agencies for the exchange of financial information. Such requests must be in support of a law enforcement activity. To assist in the retrieval of this information from foreign countries, FinCEN became a founding member of the Egmont Group ("Egmont"). Egmont is an informal working group of 101 financial intelligence units ("FIUs") that form an important network of government agencies that share financial intelligence and analysis to fight money laundering. A Senior Analyst is CI's representative at FinCEN, and provides guidance in the area of information exchange between the Criminal Investigation and international law enforcement agencies.

Overseas enforcement activities include extradition, search warrants in foreign countries, and international undercover operations. Extradition is a formal process, regulated by treaty, by which a prosecutor or agent, through DOJ, makes a request for a person found in a foreign country to be surrendered to the United States for trial or punishment.

Search warrants can and have been conducted in foreign countries based on probable cause developed domestically with the assistance of foreign law enforcement. The CI Attaché advises/assists with coordination of a search warrant request. Where a formal treaty is in place (e.g., a tax treaty, a TIEA, or an MLAT), a foreign search warrant ordinarily is initiated through the formal treaty. Where there is no treaty in place, there still may be ways to enlist the cooperation of the local law enforcement. In certain situations, it may be possible for a CI agent to accompany the foreign agency on the warrant in some capacity.

CI has been successful in conducting undercover operations overseas since the inception of CI International and, as their presence and contacts have grown overseas, they have been able to facilitate more and more undercover activity. In most cases, the cooperation and support of law enforcement in the host country is obtained, or at least their approval. All communication with foreign law enforcement agencies are done by the Attaché.

- Are there any changes in U.S. law that would facilitate your work with other nations' law enforcement officers?

Individuals' and companies' use of foreign countries to conceal taxable income and financial transactions from the IRS and other law enforcement agencies is increasing at a substantial pace. In years past, the criminal use of foreign facilities was generally restricted to the wealthy or sophisticated violator. The Internet has evolved to such a degree that the use of foreign facilities has become much more commonplace. The use of the Internet permits less than sophisticated tax evaders and money launderers ease of access to foreign accounts, facilities, or persons to perfect their financial crimes. As a result, U.S. law enforcement must now attempt to secure evidence and witness testimony located abroad in both complex and less-than-complex cases.

Criminal Investigation is involved in various fraudulent foreign trust schemes, which include offshore credit card, brokerage houses, and employee leasing. Historically, the Service's ability to gain access to detailed debit card transactional data was limited. Although it appears that the Small Business and Self-Employed Operating Division (SBSE) has recently identified some of the major U.S. companies that maintain the transactional data for offshore cards, the available information may not be complete.

As part of another popular tax-fraud scheme, a U.S. individual might establish an international business corporation (IBC) or a foreign trust, which then opens a brokerage account in the United States. The brokerage house requires the IBC or foreign trust to complete a form W-8 specifying that account holder (i.e., the IBC or foreign trust) is not a U.S. person. If the income from the brokerage account is of a sort that is not ordinarily subject to U.S. tax in the hands of a foreign person (e.g., capital gain or portfolio interest), the U.S. broker does not withhold. If the income is then deposited in an offshore bank account that the U.S. individual can access with a credit or debit card, the income effectively escapes U.S. tax. Efforts are underway by SBSE to conduct W-8 compliance checks on brokerage houses to identify abuses. Regardless of whether the owner of the account is an IBC or foreign trust, information listed on the W-8 may lead to the true owner. At a minimum, we should be able to identify specific foreign bank accounts from the W-8s.

Offshore employee leasing (OEL) usually involves a deferred compensation plan which entitles the corporation to deduct a large lump-sum payment for compensation to the corporate officer yet the corporate officer only claims the portion of the lump. The remainder of the income to the corporate officer is deferred and claimed proportionately over several years. This is a legal arrangement as long as the corporate officer does not have control of the deferred funds. The abuse comes when they add an offshore employee leasing company to transact the deal, thereby clouding the paper trail. Once offshore, the funds are transferred to a myriad of entities and eventually end up in the hands of the taxpayer.

On August 5, 1983, the Caribbean Basin Economic Recovery Act, often referred to as the Caribbean Basin Initiative (CBI), was enacted into law and became effective January 1, 1984. Under the terms of the Act, the U.S. provides tax-related economic benefits to any beneficiary country that enters into a Tax Information Exchange Agreement (TIEA) that meets specific statutory requirements. Initially, the Secretary of the Treasury was authorized to conclude agreements with countries in the Caribbean Basin, but later the authority was expanded to include agreements with any country. Approximately 24 countries that eligible for CBI benefits, but only 15 of those countries have elected to enter into a qualifying TIEA. These countries are Antigua and Barbuda, Aruba, Bahamas, Barbados, Bermuda, Costa Rica, Dominica, the Dominican Republic, Grenada, Guyana, Honduras, Jamaica, Mexico, Peru, and Trinidad and Tobago. The United States has negotiated TIEAs with other countries, both within and without the CBI, although some of those countries have not signed or ratified the agreements The continued negotiation and implementation of TIEA's would definitely facilitate IRS work with other nations' law enforcement officers.

In short, laws that allow the IRS to readily secure information from foreign offshore institutions involved in these fraudulent offshore credit card, brokerage houses, and employee leasing schemes, <u>for purposes of tax administration, are important</u> in facilitating our investigative work involving other nations' law enforcement offices.

- Are there any holes in our legal sanctions that are needed to ensure that noncompliance that spans more than just the U.S. is properly punished?

Although exchanging information under TIEAs and tax treaties has been relatively successful, there are a variety of problems that can affect this process. For example, some countries balk at executing requests for information in criminal tax investigations, especially those arising from grand jury investigations. This problem can be aggravated where non-tax offenses are also under investigation. A few countries provide treaty partners only with information that currently exists in their tax files regarding a given taxpayer and will not undertake efforts to gather information from other sources, including third parties. Also, some treaty partners, even if they will undertake to gather information from sources other than their tax files, they will not obtain and provide financial information such as bank records, because of bank secrecy laws.

These problem areas involving TIEAs and tax treaties should be addressed, in order to ensure that noncompliant individuals and/or entities that spans more than the U.S. is properly investigated and punished.

I would also appreciate any thoughts or comments you may have given your recent trip to China.

I recently traveled to China where I conducted a series of meetings with senior and regional officials from the Chinese State Tax Administration. I have concluded that it is critically important for the Internal Revenue Service and the Chinese to establish a strong relationship and firm foundation to administer the U.S.-PRC Income Tax Treaty. The significant investment by U.S. taxpayers in China in recent years further confirms the importance of our bilateral tax treaty to ensure U.S. taxpayers receive the appropriate tax treaty benefits and issues of double taxation are resolved in a fair and timely manner. As the economic importance of China grows, the IRS needs to establish the service and enforcement capabilities to deal with both individual and business tax issues resulting from taxpayers doing business in China. The IRS will continue to focus and improve our international tax administration program.

From Senator Hatch:

1. Mr. Commissioner, the U.S. has negotiated exchange of information agreements with most countries to share tax information. I haven't heard this tool cited as a weapon to combat the international tax gap. Would you comment on the effectiveness of this tool? Is there more that the IRS, as an agency, or we, as lawmakers, could do to obtain more access to foreign records?

At present, the United States has over 74 bilateral tax treaties and agreements that provide for exchange of tax information. A notable program under these treaties and agreements is the ability of the United States to obtain specific information from other countries upon request in order to prevent noncompliance with its tax laws. The United States frequently is able to prosecute taxpayers for tax evasion because of information obtained from other countries. Further, the mechanisms in place to obtain information from a foreign country help to deter taxpayers from attempting to evade tax through entities or accounts in that country. Several information-exchange agreements signed within the last 5 years did not come fully into force until this past spring, and so we are just beginning to explore their effectiveness. In order to effectively enforce our own tax laws, it is critical that we are able to obtain the cooperation we need from similar jurisdictions.

The following are two possible law changes that could assist us:

1. *Change the law to allow a Competent Authority (or other tax administration official) in another country to provide the evidence certification required to introduce foreign gathered information in court. The keeper of records (who is required to certify now) will not sign the certification in some countries and cannot be required to do so.*

2. *Change the law to provide for tolling of the statute of limitations to make an assessment when a request for information is made to another country and a response is not received within a reasonable period of time.*

We are exploring the pros and cons of these ideas.

2. How is the IRS doing in the war against abusive tax shelters? What further tools should Congress give to the IRS to combat these shelters, if any?

The IRS has made significant progress in addressing abusive tax shelter transactions through better identification of the abusive transactions and their participants, public notification through the listing process, examination of participants, including consistent consideration, and appropriate application on the income tax and penalty issues for taxpayers, and penalties for the promoters of abusive tax shelters. Through settlement initiatives and other efforts, many taxpayers have been able to resolve and pay the additional tax liabilities and penalties asserted as a result of their participation in abusive tax shelter transactions with a reduced use of scarce enforcement resources.

Our efforts to combat abusive tax shelters continue. At the forefront is the effort to identify new issues or trends. For example, the Joint International Tax Shelter Information Centre (JITSIC) facilitates exchanges of information on tax avoidance cross-border transactions. Following the American Jobs Creation Act of 2004, there was an increase in the number of disclosures. These disclosures by taxpayers and material advisors are being scrutinized and appropriate actions will be taken. We have also set up a team to review the information requested and to consider and recommend form revisions to enhance our ability to evaluate the transactions as early as possible. Additionally, we are utilizing the Issue Management Team process to act quickly to expedite and coordinate efforts as new transactions are identified.

IRS efforts and emphasis on criminal fraud referrals and case development is beginning to bear fruit with an increase in the number of fraud referrals and criminal investigations.

In many of the tax shelter transactions, judicial doctrines are applied as part of the challenge. The recent Federal Circuit decision on *Coltec Industries v. United States,* *#05-*

5111, Fed. Cir. 7/12/06, endorsed our application of the economic substance doctrine in a listed transaction referenced as a Contingent Liability Transaction (Notice 2001-17). The confirmation of this application of judicial doctrines in abusive tax shelter transactions enhances and supports our efforts to address these types of abusive transactions.

Our efforts, along with the efforts and impact of others outside the IRS (for example, Sarbanes-Oxley), have significantly reduced the promotion of, and mass marketing approach to, selling abusive technical tax shelters and the willingness of taxpayers to participate in these questionable transactions. We remain vigilant in our effort to identify new transactions or new trends and committed to take appropriate and timely actions.

Assessment of the enhanced disclosure and penalty provisions, the guidance to secure TAW, the M-3 filing requirements and Section 516 of TIPRA will determine their impact and whether additional tools should be requested. Any newly identified transactions may also influence the determination of whether additional assistance is needed.

From Senator Baucus:

1. An IRS employee checked his or her laptop computer as luggage before taking a flight. The computer contained confidential employee information including names, social security numbers, addresses and fingerprints. Unfortunately, when the flight arrived, the computer didn't. It has not been recovered.

    a. How often does the IRS experience a security breach?

    The IRS has a highly mobile workforce that needs to be out of the office, meeting with taxpayers, and other entities in conducting audits and related activities. The IRS agents maintain sensitive taxpayer and personally identifiable information on their laptops in conducting official business, but the IRS uses encryption technology to automatically encrypt the data on the laptops. The IRS has over 50,000 laptops. Although the IRS has experienced several incidents of stolen laptops, (which is a widespread problem across both government and private industry), since the data is encrypted in most all cases, the IRS experiences a security breach, (loss of sensitive information), very infrequently.

    b. What are the IRS procedures for the physical security of computers and computer disks? What is the policy on use of passwords and encryption?

    IRS security policies require that employees properly safeguard government owned computers and computer disks. These are to be used for official business only. IRS facilities have appropriate physical security controls in place to guard against equipment theft. IT equipment must be properly accounted for, and employees are required to formally account for any equipment that is removed from IRS facilities.

The IRS implements the required password controls, in accordance with guidance specified by the National Institute of Standards and Technology (NIST), for access to the IRS network and all applications. IRS IT security policy requires the use of encryption to protect all sensitive information in IRS computers.

c. Is it acceptable procedure to let a computer containing confidential information out of the employee's control by checking it as luggage? What are the rules when an employee takes a computer home?

The employee should not have checked in (as luggage), the laptop with the sensitive information. IRS annual computer security training specifically informs employees to not check in laptops with their airline luggage. The rules for when an employee takes a computer home specifically require that the individual properly safeguard the computer, and the policies also mandate the use of encryption to protect sensitive information.

d. What actions are being taken to protect the identity of the individuals whose confidential information has disappeared?

Background: The IRS identified 291 individuals affected by the laptop loss, all of whom had provided the data as job applicants. IRS managers attempted to contact all by telephone to advise them of their vulnerability. By June 5th, 260 affected individuals had been contacted directly, with messages to contact us left for another 18. We were unable to reach the remaining individuals by telephone. On June 7, IRS mailed letters to all affected individuals detailing the situation and providing guidance, access to resources, and points of contact in TIGTA and the Human Capital Office. As of July 26, IRS has awarded a contract to Experian to offer credit monitoring services to the affected individuals. Letters to all individuals will be mailed during the week of July 31 advising them of this opportunity and how to take advantage of it. IRS will be charged for each individual who decides to engage these services from Experian.

e. Have any disciplinary actions been taken against the employee?

Appropriate disciplinary action has been taken for the employees involved.

2. Recently, the IRS agreed to send letters on behalf of the VA to the 26.5 million veterans whose confidential information was stolen from a VA employee's home. The letters did not include a VA address. As a result, it is likely that veterans who want to write to the VA for information about their case will send their letters to the IRS PO box that appears on the envelope.

a. What procedures does IRS have in place to ensure that the privacy of the veterans who write to the IRS is protected from further violations?

We have established procedures within the IRS Philadelphia Service Center campus to safeguard the information of the veterans if they write to the IRS. To date, we have not received any correspondence that was intended for the IRS. We have received 2,293 letters addressed to the VA, which the VA contacts picked up personally from the IRS office. We have also received 902,805 undelivered letters as of July 14 from the U.S.PS which the IRS destroys. No social security numbers were contained on the letters.

b. Why did the IRS agree to send out letters that did not contain a mailing address to the VA, especially after the Finance Committee was assured that the address would be included?

The VA did not provide an address in its letter but did provide a telephone number in the letter for veterans to call if they needed assistance.

c. How is the IRS going to handle the extra workload generated as a result of veterans writing to the IRS address?

Under an agreement with the VA, the IRS will be reimbursed by the VA for the additional costs incurred.

3. The IRS Criminal Investigation Division has a program called the Electronic Fraud Detection System that is meant to detect fraudulent refunds at the time the tax return is filed, stopping these refunds from ever being sent out. The IRS has spent two years and $21 million to upgrade this system and it still is not up and running. The old system has been retired, so now the IRS doesn't have any program to detect fraudulent refunds.

a. Explain how the IRS could pay $21 million and have nothing to show for it.

The IRS recently had a third-party review conducted on the EFDS project to determine the reasons for project failure, identify corrective actions for the IRS and the contractor, and recommend actions to apply the lessons learned from the EFDS project across the information technology portfolio in order to avoid similar mistakes in the future.

How will you hold your management accountable for this failure?

The IRS is currently pursuing appropriate action against IRS employees who failed to act responsibly, up to and including dismissal. Also, the IRS added a project manager with more seniority as well as a Critical Pay Executive with IT experience to oversee the project.

b. Is there going to be any kind of fraud detection program for the 2006 filing season?

The EFDS is one of several tools used by the IRS's Criminal Investigation (CI) Division as part of its Questionable Refund Program (QRP). The EFDS is an automated system that improves the effectiveness of the manual screening process. EFDS is used to screen returns filed with the IRS requesting a refund.

In addition to EFDS, the IRS also uses numerous refund fraud detection tools that remain in place. Among the methods at the disposal of the IRS:

- *The IRS operates an extensive third-party reporting and matching program to verify accurate income and refunds. This program helps identify taxpayers who claim too little income or too much refund.*
- *IRS Fraud Detection Centers intercept questionable refund requests for Criminal Investigation review.*
- *The IRS matches prisoners' Social Security Numbers provided by states to identify inmates who file fake tax returns and fraudulent refunds.*
- *The IRS manually reviews refund requests if a refund was frozen for questionable reasons the previous year.*
- *Earned Income Tax Credit claims that include children are matched through a dependent database. This program helps curb EITC fraud by identifying taxpayers who are fraudulently claiming children as dependents.*
- *The IRS identity theft program helps identify inappropriate use of SSNs for tax refunds.*
- *The IRS monitors Social Security numbers of deceased taxpayers to ensure that their SSNs are not used on fraudulent tax returns to claim fraudulent refunds.*

In addition, the IRS conducts an extensive set of enforcement activities to protect revenue and safeguard against fraudulent refunds. In Fiscal Year 2005, the IRS audited more than 1.2 million individual tax returns. More than 3.2 million liens and levies were issued and 155 individuals were sentenced to prison for an average of 19 months for committing refund fraud.

c. How many fraudulent refunds have gone undetected during the 2006 filing season?

In PY 2005, more than 174 million individuals filed 132.8 million income tax returns and paid $1.1 trillion in taxes. Of the 132.8 million tax returns, 106.2 million tax returns sought a refund. The IRS issued $227.5 billion in refunds to individuals. EFDS electronically reviewed each of the 106.2 million tax refund claims. EFDS and the QRP program held for scrutiny less than ½ of 1 percent of the total refunds. The result was 500,000 refund claims were temporarily frozen. Fewer than 200,000 of those questionable refund claims were held for longer *than one week. In PY 2005, the CI Division stopped $412.2 million in fraudulent refunds.*

So far this year, from January through June, the IRS froze 84,000 questionable refunds using QRP tools other than EFDS. The IRS reported that, due to other leads, $99 million of the $134 million potentially fraudulent refunds claimed has been stopped as of June 2006, without the EFDS being operational.

4. During your confirmation hearing on March 18, 2003, you testified that you can't be "overly dependent on contractors" and you agreed that you personally would have to drive these kinds of projects.

    a. To what extent is the IRS still overly dependent on contractors?

    It is important to note that contractors can be and are at IRS an efficient means to deliver quality work at the lowest possible cost. However, it is critical to manage contractors effectively and to choose appropriate work for contractors and government employees.

    We are still dependent on contractors to maintain legacy and modernized systems, however we have taken steps to mitigate some of the dependency in cases where it makes sense to bring more control in-house.

    The IRS continues to make changes in CSC's original integrator model managing the PRIME Alliance. The PRIME contract has been modified and IRS is taking more of a leadership role in managing the Business Systems Modernization (BSM) program. Although CSC continues to perform in areas where they have demonstrated success and where it is advantageous and appropriate for them to continue their support, such as Enterprise Architecture and Customer Account Data Engine (CADE), they are no longer the BSM overall program integrator, and today CSC competes with other vendors for any new projects, follow-on work and other services needed to support the program.

    In addition, we have complemented IRS talent with recruitment of executives from private industry with proven leadership abilities and extensive experience and success in the management of large IT projects. This mix of government subject matter experts and outside talent has been powerful in helping us strike a balance with our contractors.

    And finally, like many other government agencies, the IRS senior staff is aged and nearing retirement. To keep us from continued dependence on contractor support to address our aging workforce, we have also taken steps to augment IRS talent with critical functional skills and programming languages which are needed in the organization. We will need consistent funding in order to renew our workforce with the modernized skills necessary to maintain and enhance what the contractors are developing now.

b. What is the IRS doing to avoid situations like EFDS in the future?

The Associate Chief Information Officer (ACIO), AD, and the ACIO, Enterprise Services (ES) have begun initial evaluations of other projects being managed in the new AD organization. During a two day meeting conducted in April 2006, AD projects were reviewed and those identified as high risk/high impact were assigned to either the Senior Manager Dashboard Review (SMDR) or the Project Health Assessment Review process and to the appropriate governance structure, e.g. Executive Steering Committee, for oversight. This first phase of evaluation was to discuss and apply management judgment to ensure high risk projects identified to date were assigned to the appropriate oversight process. EFDS began reporting to the Taxpayer Relationship Management (TRM) ESC on June 27, 2006 and is also included in the SMDR process.

All projects were asked to complete the Health Check Questionnaire by the end of July 2006. Responses to the questionnaire will be assessed and corrective actions taken as needed on at risk projects. Further, based on the results of these on-going reviews, formal Health Check reviews will be scheduled, as needed. It is anticipated we will have completed the first iteration of the review process for all major projects (over $5M per year or over $50M over ten years) in AD by November 1, 2006. Projects that are identified as having potentially high risk resulting from the Health Check reviews will be referred to the appropriate governance and program control body , e.g. ESC, SMDR, etc.

In addition to the Health Check reviews, MITS is establishing a Tiered Program Management Office (PMO) in order to institute consistent standards, practices, tools, roles to provide the transparency required for effective program control, governance, and release management. Once established, the Tiered PMO will fold in the Project Health Assessments. To supplement the Tiered PMO and Health Check reviews, ES is currently standing up Non-Major ESC Governance, which will establish the approach and criteria to identify and govern high-risk projects and ensure that critical risks and decisions are being addressed at the right level.

5. In September of 2002, IRS Commissioner Charles Rossotti reported on his assessment of the IRS and the tax system to the IRS Oversight Board. His report contained the following statistics.

- 60% of identified tax debts are not pursued
- 75% of taxpayers who did not file a tax return are not pursued
- 79% of identified taxpayers who use abusive devices (e.g., offshore accounts) to evade tax are not pursued
- 56% of identified taxpayers with income over $100,000 who underreport tax are not pursued
- 78% of document matching discrepancies are not pursued

a. Please provide the Committee with the updated statistics cited by former Commissioner Rossotti.
b. What kind of objective measures have you developed to determine your performance?

The referenced statistics were included in the September 2002 report to the IRS Oversight Board on the Assessment of the IRS and the Tax System by Commissioner Rossotti. The report included statistics on what Commissioner Rossotti considered the workload gap resulting from resource limitations. It is important to note that even in an unconstrained resource environment, it would not make sense to pursue all of these potential cases. Not all would yield solid return on investment. The table below attempts to duplicate the methodology used to compile the statistics for the 2002 report, however, we would also like to refer you to the 2005 IRS Databook for the most current and complete compilation of the IRS' accomplishments. The chart below provides updated statistics that closely mirror the methodology used in the 2002 report. They demonstrate that we are working a larger percentage of potential cases.

Program Area	*% Gap FY 2002 per Commissioner Rossotti Report*	*% Gap FY 2005*
Field and Phone Accounts Receivable (TDA)	*60%*	*37%*
Nonfiler Cases (TDI)	*75%*	*67%*
Cases of Abusive Devices to Hide Income	*79%*	*67%*
Individuals over $100,000 Who Underreport Tax	*56%*	*43%*
Document Matching Cases	*78%*	*72%*

The IRS currently utilizes metrics that are more comprehensive to gauge its performance in the collection area. For example, the Compliance Services Collection Operation (CSCO) was not included in the September 2002 report referenced above. This operation, which is located in our Service Centers throughout the country, has become an integral part of our non-filer program. In fact, using a similar methodology to that used in the September 2002 report, but including the CSCO operations, results in a decrease in the potential case gap for the nonfiler program of approximately 18% from 2002 to 2005. This represents a significant decrease in the nonfiler potential case gap.

The IRS has a number of objective measures in place to assess performance. For example, we measure cases closed per full-time equivalent (FTE); dollars collected per FTE; and dollars recommended per FTE. Additionally, we use a variety of scoring techniques to prioritize resources.

Furthermore, a measure of performance currently in use is the comparison of the number of resolved cases to the new cases coming into the system. An increase in this measure reflects a corresponding decrease in the inventory of cases accumulating, and a decrease in the potential case gap. From FY 2002 to FY 2005, there was an increase in productivity in both the non-filer, TDI (49% to 53%), and the field and phone accounts receivable, TDA (62% to 79%). We continue to use our scoring techniques and review our performance measures to ensure a balance of overall coverage and priorities in these areas to leverage the resources available most efficiently.

6. Some of the "most significant" issues that the IRS identified to the Committee have been under consideration for years, including cost sharing, transfer pricing and the universal service fund.

    a. These are tough issues, but once the facts patterns have been determined, does the passage of time make it any easier for the government to take a legal position?

    Delay is often an unfortunate, but unavoidable part of dealing with these issues. Usually there are no "silver bullet" solutions. Even if the issues are well understood, finding the proper legal and administrative approaches is usually a complex and time-consuming process. These issues often can only be addressed by a careful, thoughtful, systematic approach by a team of knowledgeable people, and this can take time.

    b. To what extent do you think it takes the IRS too long to decide its position on an issue?

    It is always better to act expeditiously. There are however, many factors that can cause delay. These issues we raised in the testimony are very complex and it may not only take time to understand them, but also to determine how best to address them and whether there would be any unintended consequences to our approach.

    Other things may also interfere with prompt action, including foreign law considerations, frequent changes in the tax law.

    c. What impact does the lack of guidance have on corporate compliance and the tax gap?

    A lack of guidance undoubtedly has a negative effect on corporate compliance and the tax gap, but it is difficult to determine with any certainly the extent of the effect. Nonetheless, we believe the tax system is enhanced by more and better guidance, both because it helps us insure that all taxpayers are paying what they owe, and because it helps taxpayers who want to comply to do so more easily and with greater certainty.

7. To leverage its resources and to become more current in its examinations, the IRS uses several expedited or abbreviated audit techniques, including the limited scope audit and the LIFE (limited issue focused exam) audit.

a. Do you think that audits designed to pick the "low hanging fruit" are good policy? How efficient is the IRS at finding Enron-type situations that are not apparent on the face of the tax return?

The decision to pursue a Limited Issue Focused Examination (LIFE) is based on the historical compliance behavior of the taxpayer and a rigorous risk analysis of the tax return using established materiality thresholds. Both the traditional limited scope and Limited Issue Focused Examinations are employed only where the examiner's assessment of the return indicates that a few distinct areas represent substantial compliance risk, and that the balance of the return being examined represents relatively low risk. This determination is made only after the examiner has conducted a risk analysis that encompasses a review of the return, publicly available information, and may include a very limited review of taxpayer records

Limited scope examinations inherently involve a reduced review of the taxpayer's books and records. Although limited scope examinations are conducted only in situations where the examiners deem the compliance risk to be relatively low, a reduced review of records may decrease the chances that less obvious issues or schemes will be detected However, we are confident that by freeing up resources that would otherwise be targeted to compliant taxpayers, limited issue examinations provide a significant benefit.

b. What impact do you think limited audits have on the tax gap? Have you sacrificed quality for currency?

Limited scope and Limited Issue Focused Examinations should have a positive impact on the tax gap. After risk assessment, the examiners' conclusion that the return is likely substantially correct except for the areas immediately identified, a reduction of the resources devoted to that examination can be realized.

The resource savings from limited examinations can be deployed in the conduct of other examinations that would not otherwise have been done. By effective use of resources in this way an expansion of coverage should serve to foster compliance and reduce the tax gap. Large and Midsize Quality Scores indicate that there is no diminution in the quality of LIFE examinations as opposed to regular examinations.

The scores are similar, and while some differences are present, an overall reduction in quality is not apparent.

	Std. 1	*Std. 2*	*Std. 3*	*Std. 4*	*Std.5 - 1*	*Std. 5 - 2*
IC - LIFE	*88%*	*88%*	*100%*	*88%*	*75%*	*73%*
IC- All	*75%*	*86%*	*100%*	*80%*	*71%*	*75%*
CIC - LIFE	*80%*	*100%*	*100%*	*100%*	*100%*	*96%*
CIC - ALL	*90%*	*100%*	*100%*	*99%*	*97%*	*97%*

c. Are there alternative ways the IRS could conduct fast, efficient audits that would not sacrifice quality?

The Compliance Assurance Process (CAP) is an initiative designed to allow some of the nation's largest companies to resolve audit issues before they file their returns. Under the program, large companies can participate in "real-time" audits in which a variety of issues are resolved in advance of filing deadlines. Benefits accrue to both taxpayers and the IRS. CAP cases are slated to close within a few months of being filed, as opposed to three to five years after filing under the traditional examination program. CAP greatly reduces taxpayers' compliance burden and their need for contingent book tax reserves, while increasing currency and allowing for more efficient use of IRS resources. Additionally, IRS is hoping to more quickly identify emerging issues, design treatments and issue guidance to non-CAP taxpayers on the proper accounting treatment.

8. During the hearing, you said that you would look into the data warehousing programs being used by several states as part of their tax administration. States are creating databases of publicly available data that can be compared to tax return information in order to detect indicia of unreported income or unwarranted deductions. The states report they are collecting hundreds of millions of dollars in tax revenues as a result of this tool.

a. To what extent is IRS/State coordination of data warehousing viable?

The IRS currently shares tax information with the states. The states in turn use this information to improve tax compliance by matching it against information they have on file and identifying potential non-filers and taxpayers who have underreported income. The IRS is testing a pilot initiative at the present time to reverse the information sharing with the states for the states to provide data to the IRS based on certain criteria, the State Reverse File Match Initiative (SRFMI). Four states (Arkansas, Iowa, Massachusetts, and New Jersey) are participating in Phase I of this pilot. For this phase, the states were to match various IRS extracts against their systems and to identify individuals and businesses where a state return had been filed but no federal return was filed as well as where amounts reported on a state return were greater than amounts reported on the federal return.

The IRS is testing this pilot to determine its viability. If Phase I of the pilot is successful, the IRS will expand the pilot to additional states on or about January 2007.

Private contractors currently provide states with data warehouses that identify by ranking instances of non-filing and underreporting of income. We are currently exploring the possibility of using data warehousing to further refine the state reverse filing information, SRFMI, referenced above.

b. How much would it cost to implement a pilot program?

The first phase of the SRFMI pilot program was conducted within the current budget of the IRS. Because we are still determining the viability of the SRFMI as well as any potential added benefit from using it together with data warehousing, it is not feasible to estimate the cost of a data warehousing pilot at this time.

c. How long would it take to set up the pilot?

As stated in response to 8(a) above, we are currently in a pilot phase for the SRFMI and exploring the viability of combining data warehousing with state reverse matching. Once the success of the current pilot is determined, we will be able to better assess the timing of a pilot program for data warehousing in addition to the SRFMI.

d. What impact would the use of data warehousing to detect noncompliance have on the tax gap?

A major portion of the tax gap is underreporting of income. We anticipate that the current pilot of the SRFMI will provide information for the IRS that would identify those individuals and businesses with potentially unreported income. The IRS can in turn use this information and contact the taxpayers to determine whether additional federal income tax is due. Furthermore, the information sharing with the states will identify potential non-filers, who are also a component of the tax gap. As the SRFMI pilot has not been tested in connection with data warehousing, at the present time, we are unable to quantify the extent to which data warehousing can detect noncompliance.

9. When does the IRS intend to conduct a corporate NRP study? How reliable do you believe the current corporate tax gap estimate is, since it relies on old TCMP data and the results of corporate audits that are becoming increasing limited in scope and span?

   We are currently conducting an NRP reporting compliance study of returns filed by S-corporations and expect to complete the data collection phase by the end of fiscal year 2007. S-Corporations now outnumber all other corporations. This study includes a random sample of two tax years – 2003 and 2004. We would like to develop updated estimates for all corporations, however it is not clear that the same random sample audit technique will be effective for complex corporate returns and the future schedule of reporting compliance studies has not been finalized.

Our estimate of the Tax Year 2001 corporation income tax gap is a projection forward to 2001 of estimates based on reporting compliance data from the 1980s. The underreporting gap associated with small corporations (those with assets under $10 million) is based on the small corporation TCMP study conducted for Tax Year 1980. The estimates for larger corporations are based on regular operational audits conducted in the mid-1980s. We have projected these estimates to 2001 in line with the growth in actual corporation income tax receipts, assuming that underlying compliance rates have remained constant. In both cases, since the compliance data are quite old, this assumption may not be very accurate. However, since we lack more recent comprehensive reporting compliance data, this is currently our best basis for making estimates.

10. On June 12, the IRS responded to the Finance Committee letter of May 16, 2006 concerning foreign source information reports.

    a. Has the IRS identified the business owner (Question 8) of the foreign source information report data? Explain why it is so difficult to determine who is responsible for the data.

    This information may be relevant to all Business Operating Divisions, but until recently the IRS did not have a comprehensive "Servicewide" strategy for international tax administration. To correct this, we have established the new Deputy Commissioner LMSB (International) organization. That office will be responsible for providing the leadership to focus on this important sector of tax administration. As such, that office will become the "owner" of the information but work with other parts of the IRS to ensure that the information is used in appropriate compliance activity.

    b. Please provide the *actual* Research Plan identified in Question 13 (not the explanation of what the plan is – we are requesting the plan documents). If not included in the plan, please provide the goals, timelines, benchmarks and measures to track its progress.

    See next page

SB/SE RESEARCH REQUEST

1. **Date Submitted:** 04/17/2006	2. **Project ID:** **Project #: TBD**

3. **Project Customer Executive** *(Name, Title, Phone)*:

Joni Troncoso, Chief. International Operations SBSE, 202-874-1324

4. **Customer Contact Point** *(Name, Title, Phone)*:

Karen Van Fossan, SBSE International Policy Office, 727-568-2475

5. **Research Objective(s)**

Determine if data from the Foreign Information Reporting Program (FIRP) can be used to identify noncompliance. Information returns are provided by participating countries in a standard format via compact disc. However, matching this information to other Federal U.S. tax return and information reporting data is not straight forward. In many cases the U.S. TIN is not included in the data. SB/SE International asked that SBSE Research help conduct a pilot of this concept by using Canadian FIRP data.

Steps in this project will include:

- Extract, process and house the FIRP data
- Develop a methodology to perfect the TINS for matching (International will perfect the TINS)
- Execute the matching and analyze the resulting data
- Assess the costs and benefits of using this data for compliance testing
- Help International form an opinion on whether this process will be useful on a larger scale

This will be a traditional project with a final report and customer briefing after the results are analyzed.

6. **Are you aware of any issues such as data needs, staffing, equipment needs, time constraints, etc. that could impact this project?** ☒ Yes ☐ *No*

Data on International's in-house FIRP program will be migrated to a destination server (HQ Research at NCFB). Programming issues have been discussed with International's resident

7. **Have you discussed this project with any SB/SE Research site?** ☒ Yes ☐ No

If yes, Research Site or Contact's name *HQ Research, Alex Turk*

8. Initiator:

Name: *Karen Van Fossan* — *Title:* *Senior Policy Analyst*

Signature: *Karen Van Fossan* — *Date:* *April 17, 2006*

9. Approval: *(Area Director, Operating Unit or Functional Director)*

Name: *Joni Troncoso* — *Title:* *Chief International Operations*

Signature: *Joni Troncoso* — *Date:* *May 2, 2006*

10. Approval: *(Director, SB/SE Research)*

Name: — *Title:*

Signature: — *Date:*

Revised: 12/16/05

c. Does the estimated $345 billion tax gap figure include any figures for unreported foreign source income?

The gross tax gap measurement of $345 billion includes all legal sources of unreported income, both foreign and domestic.

11. How much of a role will corporate taxes play in the IRS meeting its goal of an 85 percent compliance rate by 2009?

We estimate that the overall voluntary compliance rate in Tax Year 2001 was 83.7 percent. Corporation income taxes accounted for just 7.6 percent of all tax receipts in 2001 and had an estimated compliance rate of 81.6 percent. In contrast, individual income tax accounted for 49.9 percent of all tax receipts and had a compliance rate of 79.1 percent. This means that the overall voluntary compliance rate is much more sensitive to changes in the individual income tax compliance rate than it is to the corporation income tax compliance rate. For example, if compliance rates remained constant for all types of tax except for corporation income tax, the corporation compliance rate would have to increase by 9.4 percentage points by 2009 in order for the overall rate to reach 85 percent. In contrast, an increase of 2.0 percentage points in the individual income tax compliance rate would produce the same result, holding all other compliance rates constant. This suggests while improving corporation compliance is important, it will not likely be the primary source of the improvement needed to reach our goal.

12. Figure 4 of the GAO testimony shows that the amount of taxes that IRS recommended as a result of examinations performed grew from its recent low of $13.5 billion in fiscal year 2003 to $32 billion in fiscal year 2005.

a. Why was there such a large increase between these two years?

Dollars recommended increased because of a 22% increase in the number of returns audited, which were selected for examination through an improved methodology for predicting the presence of non-compliant behavior. Additionally, IRS changed the audit process to focus on the limited few highest risk issues on each return instead of examining every possible issue. The result of the improved inventory selection and limited issue audit process was an increase in the dollars recommended per hour from $2,874 in FY2003 to $5,714 in FY2005; combined with the increased returns examined, resulted in the large increase in recommended additional tax.

b. How much of the $32 billion in fiscal year 2005 was actually assessed and collected? Was this an increase or decrease from the previous years?

Of the $34.6 B total FY 2005 audit results, $9.4 B was assessed as agreed; $25.2 was proposed as adjustments but not agreed to by the taxpayers. Of the $9.4 Billion agreed, approximately 95% was collected – this is based upon historic collection rates of large and mid-sized business taxpayers. However, the $25.2 Billion proposed but unagreed is currently neither assessed nor collected, is indeterminable and will remain so until all taxpayer issues are resolved through administrative appeals and litigation.

This represents an increase from both FY2003 and FY2004.

From Senator Kerry:

1. Thank you for your response to my inquiry concerning the Questionable Refund Program (QRP). It appears the Service had made substantive progress in the QRP by informing taxpayers that their refunds are being frozen and in trying to speed-up resolution of refund freeze cases. What steps had the IRS been taking to ensure that low-income families receiving the earned income tax credit (EITC) are not unfairly targeted by QRP? Is the Service coordinating audits across divisions? For example, Wage and Investment Examinations audit EITC taxpayers and Criminal Investigation (CI) has frozen EITC refunds. Would it make sense for Wage and Investment Examinations to refer to CI cases in which they suspect fraud?

The IRS is constantly working to improve its fraud detection systems. The IRS recognizes the impact its fraud detection activities can have on compliant low-income taxpayers whose refunds may be temporarily suspended by its systems. The IRS is continually striving to eliminate burden on compliant taxpayers through strategic approaches involving systemic and procedural improvements designed to detect erroneous returns with minimal impact to legitimate refund returns.

Currently, the IRS is implementing improvements to the QRP. An Executive Steering Committee comprised of numerous functions within the Service is currently studying workflow processes to determine what efficiencies and potential workload migration changes can be made in the QRP. This is being accomplished through refining and streamlining the processing of questionable returns, modifying existing technology and utilizing sophisticated analytical tools to assist in the identification of false claims and improvement of our filtering systems through technological enhancements.

One such improvement is the timely movement of work between functions in the IRS. In particular, issues identified through the QRP that are determined to be civil in nature are now moved in a more timely fashion through the process. This improvement helps ensure that low-income taxpayers are not unfairly impacted by the QRP process.

To improve its filtering system, the IRS has recently contracted with the Department of Health and Human Services (HHS) to verify wages for taxpayers who claim the EITC. This HHS database contains salary data updated quarterly. This filter will help the IRS release legitimate refunds with the EITC faster because it automatically verifies the wages and withholding credits. This will greatly reduce the number of initial freezes on questionable refund requests that have an EITC component because the IRS will not need to contact employers to verify income.

2. I share your concerns about the tax gap. However, I am concerned that there is too much of a focus on auditing EITC taxpayers. In fiscal year 2004, the IRS conducted 48 percents of its audits on EITC taxpayers. EITC error represents a very small portion of the overall tax gap. Will the IRS continue to concentrate on EITC taxpayers?

The IRS is building a balanced compliance program that addresses each segment of the tax gap. IRS's EITC efforts are just one component of this program but they have roots in previous Congressional guidance. For five years, the IRS received special funding for EITC compliance initiatives aimed at reducing the credit's error rate. Since that separate funding ended, IRS's spending on EITC audits has been virtually flat and, for the past two years, the number of EITC audits has been held constant. As IRS continues to increase compliance activities in a variety of other areas, the EITC audits as a percent of total audits will fall.

It is also worth noting that IRS' EITC program has adopted a balanced approach to administering the credit – one that seeks to maximize participation among eligible taxpayers even as it takes steps to combat noncompliance. As a result, in addition to EITC compliance activities, IRS actively promotes the credit through its stakeholder relationship management organization – working with hundreds of community-based organizations across the country to educate taxpayers about the availability of the credit and the requirements that must be met to claim it.

3. On page 5 of your testimony, you discuss that "Taxpayers, especially in the high technology and pharmaceutical industries, are shifting profits offshore through a variety of arrangements that result in the transfer of valuable intangibles to related foreign entities for inadequate consideration." What provisions in our tax code do you think

encourage the transfer of costs offshore? Do you think deferral plays a factor? Should we revisit deferral in the context of a global economy?

- What provisions in our tax code do you think encourage the transfer of costs offshore?

  I interpret the question to mean transfer of "profits" offshore – rather than transfer of "costs" offshore. In general, the tax code does not encourage taxpayers to transfer profits offshore. The transfer pricing rules have flexibility built into them in order for taxpayers to reach reasonable transfer pricing conclusions based on the arms-length standard. Some taxpayers, and their advisors such as accounting and law firms, use this flexibility in an aggressive manner to create transfer pricing structures that result in the improper shifting of profits outside the U.S.

- Do you think deferral plays a factor?

  A shift in profits to a "low tax" or "no tax" jurisdiction is valuable to a company only if the company can defer the U.S. tax on that income. However, the primary problem in such a case is the improper shifts of profits – not deferral.

- Should we revisit deferral in the context of a global economy?

  This would be an issue of tax policy best answered by the Department of Treasury's Office of Tax Policy.

4. Comptroller General Walker mentioned that $11 billion of the tax gap can be attributed to individual taxpayers who misreported their income from capital gains or losses. I am cosponsor of S. 2556 legislation introduced by Senator Bayh that would require investment brokers to report the adjusted basis of securities of their customers. Do you think this legislation will help narrow the tax gap? Do you recommend other reporting requirements that would help reduce the tax gap?

We agree that requiring brokers to report adjusted basis to taxpayers and the IRS would improve compliance. However, such a requirement would raise some unique and potentially burdensome challenges for brokers.

Determining cost calculations for stocks or mutual funds can be very complex especially when purchased over a long time span, and where dividends and other distributions have been automatically reinvested. Calculations may also be complicated by a taxpayer's choice of accounting methods, stock splits, mergers, corporate reorganizations, wash sales, and the exercising of options. Any legislation must take into consideration these circumstances.

(In June we responded to a similar recommendation by GAO. See: "Capital Gains Tax Gap: Requiring Brokers to Report Securities Cost Basis Would Improve Compliance if Related Challenges Are Addressed" (GAO-06-603).)

Our Office of Taxpayer Burden Reduction is currently engaged in an effort to analyze and address issues related to the capital gains tax gap and the related tax burden. They will be working with industry stakeholders to mitigate reporting challenges that impact financial institutions, taxpayers, tax professionals, and tax software vendors.

Regarding other reporting requirements, the IRS is proactively soliciting suggestions to impact the tax gap, both internally from all employees and externally from stakeholders, such as practitioners and representatives from state Departments of Revenue.

From Senator Wyden:

Mr. Everson, you testified that 91 of the S&P 500 companies had repatriated or planned to repatriate funds under Section 965 of the American Jobs Creation Act. How will the IRS ensure that earnings repatriated under this provision will actually be used to create jobs here in the U.S.?

IRS will administer the provision as it was enacted by ensuring that taxpayers comply with the specific requirements regarding the repatriation of the earnings themselves and that they have invested the earnings in permitted investments in the U.S.. The only permitted investment that requires a taxpayer to show that jobs were created or retained is an investment intended for financial stabilization.

U.S. SENATE COMMITTEE ON

Finance

SENATOR CHUCK GRASSLEY, OF IOWA - CHAIRMAN

http://finance.senate.gov

Opening Statement of Chairman Grassley
Hearing, "A Tune-up on Corporate Tax Issues: What's Going on Under the Hood?"
Tuesday, June 13, 2006

In today's hearing, we will primarily focus on the current state of our corporate tax system. But we'll also touch on basic issues to consider in the context of business tax reform – lowering rates and broadening the base. The continued globalization of our economy and the complexity of business activity present significant challenges to our corporate tax system as a whole, and to the administration of that system. The complexity of the tax code itself creates burdens and inefficiencies for taxpayers and the IRS, although some taxpayers may view complexity as creating opportunities for tax avoidance.

According to the Congressional Budget Office, corporate income tax receipts were a record $278.3 billion in 2005, up 47 percent over the prior year and representing 2.3 percent of GDP – the highest percentage since 1980. The first 8 months of fiscal year 2006 show the trend continuing with corporate tax receipts up 30 percent over last year. The recent surge in corporate tax receipts is due in large part to the strong performance of our economy. Corporate tax receipts have gone up along with rising corporate profits resulting from a growing economy.

In addition to a growing economy, I think some of that increase is also because of continuing efforts to combat corporate tax abuse and improve corporate tax compliance. For example, in 2004, Congress enacted my package of legislation cracking down on tax shelters and requiring companies to publicly disclose in SEC filings penalties for failing to report a tax shelter, so investors will know whether a company is violating tax shelter laws. These provisions have provided the IRS with tools to combat tax abuse and also work to deter tax shelter activity.

We need to do all we can to ensure tax compliance by corporations and individuals alike to maintain the fairness and integrity of our tax system. To that end, I look forward to hearing from the Honorable Mark Everson, Commissioner of the Internal Revenue Service, and the Honorable David Walker, Comptroller General at the Government Accountability Office, about the current state of play in corporate tax compliance and what is known about the corporate tax gap. Tied in to corporate profits is the taxation of appreciated investments in corporations. In May of 2005, Senator Baucus and I requested the GAO to conduct a study on the capital gains tax gap. Today, Mr. Walker will also discuss the GAO's findings from that study and its recommendations as to how we can close the capital gains tax gap.

The Department of Justice plays a key role in enforcing the tax laws. Eileen O'Connor, Assistant Attorney General in the Tax Division of the Department of Justice will fill us in on the current issues in corporate tax from the Tax Division's perspective. She will also discuss some related matters, including the civil and criminal laws at issue with stock options being backdated for the benefit of executives.

As promised earlier this year, we will examine the tax policy behind the LIFO method of inventory accounting with the help of Dr. George Plesko, Associate Professor of Accounting at the University of Connecticut School of Business. Dr. Plesko's scholarship in the area of bridging the reporting gap for the many differences between financial accounting standards and the tax code supports recent changes in the IRS form schedule M-3. The IRS recently came out with the new schedule M-3, which will provide IRS examiners much more detail regarding these differences.

One of our panelists, Mr. Edward Kleinbard, a New York partner at the law firm of Cleary, Gottlieb, Steen & Hamilton, has recommended public disclosure of the M-3 to promote transparency in financial reporting. Confidentiality of tax return information is a fundamental part of our self-assessment tax system. It's important to balance taxpayers' interest in privacy with the need for tax law compliance. Commissioner Everson has publicly stated that corporate tax return disclosure is something that merits serious debate. This hearing will provide a forum for having that debate.

In addition to tax compliance and enforcement matters, we will also hear testimony on the basic aspects of our current corporate system – the tax rate and the tax base – that we should consider revisiting in the context of business tax reform. In the global economy, tax policy is not so neatly put into domestic and international categories. Our corporate tax rate is typically thought of as domestic tax policy. But when it ranks at or near the top among OECD countries, it influences international business decisions, like where to build a plant, and gives companies incentives to shift income offshore. As this committee turns to tax reform, a key objective should be to make the system one that is fair and allows businesses to make decisions based more on economic merit and less on distortions generated by the tax code. The recent global trend has been to lower the corporate tax rate and broaden the base. This is no longer an abstract idea. Our last panelist, Dr. Martin Sullivan, economist and contributing editor at Tax Analysts, will discuss this new era in corporate taxation that has arrived in many countries across Europe.

Closing Statement of Chairman Grassley

I just wanted to make a few brief closing comments. I appreciate all the witnesses' time here today. I think this has been very informative for the committee. We have learned about problems with today's tax system and have heard valuable suggestions for ways to improve the current tax code. Some of these may need further thinking but some we should act on sooner rather than later. Beyond trying to improve today's code, the discussion about issues such as tax expenditures and fundamental problems with the tax system point the way for thinking about tomorrow's tax code. The comments we have heard calling for lowering the rates, broadening the base, and simplifying the tax code are good goals that should guide our work as we consider corporate tax reform.

Achieving these goals of tax reform will not only make the code fairer and more efficient, but it will also provide fiscal benefits to the budget. But of perhaps greatest importance, we've heard today that a system of lower rates, broader base and simplification will increase our nation's competitiveness in attracting capital for new and better jobs. We have to recognize that we live in a global economy that requires us to be competitive in securing capital investment if we want to improve the standard of living for our children and grandchildren. This hearing has been a good beginning for exploring further the issues of tax reform. It is my hope to have a hearing on tax reform and simplification focusing on individuals later this summer and to explore in more detail corporate tax reform this fall.

JAY D. ADKISSON
P.O. BOX 7088, LAGUNA NIGUEL, CA 92677
PH: 949.322.5111 – FAX: 877.698.0678

27 October 2005

Sen. Charles D. Grassley
Sen. Max Baucus
United States Senate
Committee on Finance
Washington, DC 20510-6200

RE: Senate Finance Committee Hearings of April 5, 2001
"Taxpayer Schemes, Scams, and Cons"

Dear Senators Grassley and Baucus:

This letter responds to yours of September 21, 2005, relating to the April 5, 2001, hearings of the Senate Finance Committee entitled "Taxpayer Beware: Schemes, Scams & Cons" and the questions set forth in your letter, to wit:

> *"1) Have the various concerns you raised in 2001 been addressed by the Internal Revenue Service and other Federal agencies responsible for the administration and enforcement of the income tax?"*

The efforts of this Committee have been instrumental in causing the Internal Revenue Service and the U.S. Department of Justice's Tax Division to make substantially greater efforts to combat tax scams.

In particular, the Internal Revenue Service has shown a greater awareness for the problems caused by those who promote tax scams and encourage others to become so-called "tax protestors". Such persons cause a unnecessary and expensive enforcement burden, and then later drain the scarce resources of the courts with frivolous arguments.

Some of the best efforts of the IRS have been to publish various rulings and notices that directly address and debunk common tax protestor arguments. An example is the 56-page publication "The Truth About Frivolous Tax Arguments", which is published on the internet at *http://www.irs.gov/pub/irs-utl/frivolousarguments-3-14-2005.pdf* Such publications serve several important purposes. First, they have the effect of educating the public in general about tax protestors' bogus theories. Second, they provide a resource that a professional advisor may supply their inquisitive client with to show them that tax protestors' theories are bogus.

Third, and most importantly, the existence of these publications often make it easier for the IRS and prosecutors to try cases against tax protestors and tax fraud promoters, since the fact of these publications creates difficulty by the defendant in asserting a good faith or *Cheek*-type defense that their actions were not willful.

The U.S. Department of Justice has also made tremendous strides in shutting down the promoters of tax fraud schemes, both by civil injunctions and criminal prosecutions of promoters. The DOJ's aggressive pursuit of civil injunctions has borne significant fruit, as many tax scheme promoters have simply closed their business and moved on to other endeavors. An example is that of promoters Thurston Bell and Rick Haraka, who were two of the most prolific promoters of a tax scam known as the "861 theory". After civil injunctions were entered against them, both immediately ceased their marketing and promotional activities and have scarcely been heard of since.

The DOJ's dogged pursuit of criminal actions against the worst promoters has also borne significant fruit. The convictions of high-profile promoters Lynne Meredith, "Judge" John Rizzo, Larken Rose, and Irwin Schiff have not only given notice to their many thousands of supporters that their pet theories for avoiding the payment of tax do not work, but has also served to chill the marketing efforts of other tax scam promoters.

One could not begin to list all the persons responsible for the greater and more successful efforts to combat tax fraud, including many criminal investigators and prosecutors who have labored tirelessly in their pursuit of individual cases. Nonetheless, the efforts of two persons stand out for special recognition: The Hon. Eileen O'Connor, Assistant Attorney General, and Mr. Evan Davis, Prosecutor, U.S. Department of Justice. Their aggressive civil and criminal actions against the certain high-profile promoters of illegal tax schemes have slowed the proliferation of such schemes and created tangible examples for would-be purchasers that those schemes do not work.

"2) What is the current state of the tax scheme and scam marketplace?"

Despite the strong efforts of the IRS and DOJ, there still exists a significant and visible industry of those promoting tax schemes and scams. The continuing overt marketing efforts by some of the promoters provides an indication of the status of the de-tax scam industry:

Freedom Law School, run by Mr. Peymon Mottehedeh at 9582 Buttemere Road, Phelan, CA 92371, and hosts a website at *http://www.livefreenow.org*, sells de-tax kits ranging from $1,970 (the "Challenger Package") to $6,000 (the "Royal Freedom Package – For those who desire to live freely And be treated like royalty!"), and to bolster its credibility presents the following $300,000 reward:

> Freedom Law School is offering $100,000 to the first person who can demonstrate any of the three propositions listed below. The winner can collect up to $300,000 if he or she can prove all of the propositions below.
>
> 1. Show what statute written by the Congress of the United States, requires Americans to file an income tax "CONFESSION" (return) and pay an income tax.
>
> 2. How can Americans file an income tax "CONFESSION" (return) without giving up their 5th amendment right not to give any information to the government that may be used to prosecute them.
>
> 3. Prove that the 16th amendment to the United States Constitution, which, according to the IRS and modern American courts permitted the income tax to exist, was lawfully added to the United States Constitution.
>
> Freedom Law School declares that:
>
> There is no statute that makes any American Citizen who works and lives in the United States of America liable or responsible to pay an income tax. Individuals only become liable to pay the income tax when they "voluntarily" file a tax return and the IRS follows their assessment procedures as outlined in the Internal Revenue Code.
>
> The IRS, under the United States Constitution, cannot legally require information on 1040 returns from individuals. This is the reason the IRS continually refers to the income tax as "voluntary."

There is also a $3,000 referral program offered by Freedom Law School who those who refer new customers, which is paid "cash only – no W-2s, no 1099s" according to the representations on its nightly nationwide conference calls.

Freedom Radio, run by Mr. Brent Johnson and Ms. Lee Parker, address given as Freedom Bound International, c/o 3939 South Sixth Street #138, Klamath Falls, Oregon, hosts a daily radio show on contemporary freedom issues by which they sell so-called Pure Trusts (a form of trust routinely deemed to be a sham for tax purposes by the courts and abusive by the Department of the Treasury):

> **Pure Trust Organizations**
>
> Freedom Bound International can provide you with a trust structure to suit your specific needs. We can show you how to use this structure to your maximum benefit.
>
> The cost of a Freedom Bound International common law trust is only One Thousand Two Hundred (1200) dollars complete. Additional Trusts purchased at the same time are only Seven Hundred (700) dollars each. I am certain you will agree that this is a small price to pay to guarantee protection of your assets from attachment by the IRS, the federal government, etc. * * *
>
> We have a 100% track record: after six years, not one of our clients has had any negative repercussions whatsoever from the IRS, federal government, etc. I acknowledge you for claiming your rights by exploring ways to protect your property

> from the government, and I look forward to the opportunity to serve your trust and other sovereign needs. * * *
>
> A conduit is a chain of trusts that begins domestically and ends up off shore. Offshore trusts are being used with increasing frequency to protect American assets. However, most people do not realize that a direct transfer of assets from the uSA [spelling as in original] to an offshore location, sets up a dozen different red flags at the IRS, which is looking for and targeting these direct transfers.
>
> The Internal Revenue Service Revenue Ruling 69-70 says, "a United States citizen may be the recipient of a distribution from a Foreign Grantor trust, and bring the money into this country tax free."
>
> A properly erected trust conduit allows you to move funds offshore and then bring them back tax free. For example, you might have a house in trust. The trust sells the house and runs the proceeds through the conduit, ending up in a Foreign Grantor trust, which makes a tax free distribution to you. End result: no capital gains taxes!
>
> The conduit structure I prefer contains five trusts: two domestic and three foreign. I use Belize as the domicile for my foreign trusts, but Isle of Man is very good, as are a variety of locations around the globe. Andorra looks particularly interesting. I have specific reservations regarding Cayman Islands, Bahamas and Switzerland.
>
> In the conduit structure, trust two is the Holder of Beneficial Interest in trust one. Trust three is the Holder in trust two; trust four in trust three, trust five in trust four. You are the Holder in trust five. Each trust makes distributions to the next trust in the conduit, culminating with trust five (Foreign Grantor) which makes a distribution to you which the IRS admits is totally tax free.
>
> Additional Points
>
> - The Internal Revenue Service admits that they cannot tax property owned by a PTO.
> - Most attorneys will not advise you to create a PTO, since it would represent a direct conflict of interest on their part.
> - A PTO may be considered a "living" or "inter vivos" trust, since these terms apply to any trust established during the lifetime of the Exchanger.
> - A Common Law PTO is irrevocable.
> - A PTO is an "active" trust, because the trustees have actual duties to perform.
> - A trust can be either "complex" (able to accumulate income with distribution at its discretion) or "simple" (income is distributed currently, which means at least annually).
> - A Common Law PTO is considered to be a "foreign trust" as defined in 26 USC 7701(31) (Internal Revenue Code) and as such is exempt from the income tax.

NonTaxPayer.org, run by Dave Champion of 1031 West Avenue M14, Suite A, Palmdale, CA 93551, also promotes Pure Trusts on his weekly radio program and also offers his clients:

> If you are a nontaxpayer, or believe that under the law you should be a nontaxpayer, let Dave Champion assist you in structuring your private financial affairs to avoid being wrongfully ensnared into the "taxpayer" status by employers, banks, real estate firms, etc.
>
> Mr. Champion provides telephone and in-person consulting services to private Citizens and private firms that are nontaxpayers, as well as to those who believe that under the law they should be nontaxpayers. Mr. Champion is available for group presentations, public speaking, and media appearances.

We The People Foundation and **We The People Congress**, run by Robert Schulz at 2458 Ridge Road, Queensbury, NY 12804, with website at *http://www.givemeliberty.org* seems to be the largest and most aggressive of the tax scam groups, as well as the facilitators of many other tax scam promoters. Although qualified as a Section 501(c)(3) organization, but only masquerading as a charity, We The People uses a variety of bogus tax protestor theories to convince its followers to send in donations for a wide range of questionable activities, from a "Right to Petition" lawsuit filed in federal court in Washington D.C. (which was quickly dismissed for lack of merit), and other grandiose attempts to manufacture defenses for the use of the We The People donors in their own civil and criminal defenses. Mr. Schulz himself claims to pay no taxes, and the website declares: "Schulz Stopped Filing & Paying. Learn Why & How."

LostHorizons, run by Peter Hendrickson (who was convicted and spent a year in prison as the result of a bomb incident that wounded a U.S. Postal employee), at 232 Oriole Road, Commerce Twp., MI 48382, with website at *http://www.losthorizons.com* and the author of "Cracking the Code: The Fascinating Truth About Taxation in America", which falsely claims:

> What You Will Learn in 'Cracking the Code':
>
> - That the vast majority of the Internal Revenue Code (IRC) is not the law itself, but is only evidence-- a representation-- of the actual statutes in force, and like in the game of post-office, the real language has been a bit garbled in transmission.
> - That "income", "wages", "self-employment income", "employee", "employer" and "trade or business"-- as these and certain other terms are used within, and in regard to, the tax law-- have narrow legal meanings exclusively involving, and applying to, certain privileged activities, such as holding or administering a government office, or working in one.
> - That although the tax statutes make perfectly clear that, for instance, language describing the obligations of "employees"-- and the taxes to which "employees" are subject-- only apply to a small minority of American workers, the distinction is artfully concealed in the IRC representation of the law, and is never forthrightly acknowledged in any IRS publication (although it is obliquely acknowledged whenever necessary for the avoidance of legal jeopardy).
> - That an elaborate system has been created which causes some people to whom the tax laws do not otherwise apply (maybe including you) to

> inadvertently declare themselves to be among the persons to whom those laws do apply.

The *LostHorizons.com* website then goes on to post online a collection of photo scans of actual refund checks and statements which were obtained by those who followed Mr. Hendrickson's advice, at http://www.losthorizons.com/BulletinBoard.htm which such examples as "Larry Hawkin's 2004 federal refund has been posted", showing a statement with a credit to Mr. Hawkins resulting from the filing of a false return.

These are but a few examples that, despite the best efforts of the IRS and the DOJ, the garden-variety tax protestor scams continue to proliferate. As the case of Peter Hendrickson illustrates, it appears that extremists and persons otherwise on the fringes of society and prone to violence are increasingly entering the tax scam marketplace.

Additionally, we are now seeing the growth of tax scams that bear the disguise of religion or charity. The "Become a Church and Pay No Taxes" scam is beginning to recycle in the form of the corporation sole. As some of the promoters of the corporation sole state on the internet website at *http://www.corporationsole.com*:

> One feature of religious societies is that they can accept vows of poverty by their members [Re; monks, nuns, priests and Overseers]. The IRS recognizes these vows of poverty. For a small part of the IRS information on Vows of Poverty, look at pages 3 and 8 in IRS Publication 517. When one is under a vow of poverty, the physical objects in their possession are not their own, although it may be their job to look after and use those objects. Thus, when you see a Catholic Bishop being moved between a cathedral and a golf course, he may be carried in a stretch limousine, but he is still under a vow of poverty that is recognized by the IRS and he is not questioned or bothered by the IRS.

It appears that the next wave of tax scams will be those that have a healthy mix of religious or charitable coloring so that enforcement action is made more difficult under the First Amendment. For instance, the We The People organization mentioned above has used its charitable status to mask its activities, by itself promoting the idea of bogus tax schemes and then collecting money as a 501(c)(3) to bring frivolous lawsuits or to provide money for the civil and criminal defense of tax scam promoters with which they are affiliated. Thus do scam artists hold the shield of the First Amendment in one hand, while collecting money for promoting abusive tax schemes with the other.

"3) What additional recommendations can you make to improve the future identification and control of tax scams and related schemes?"

Only by closely coordinated action by the IRS and the DOJ, and by quickly going after new tax scams and schemes as they appear, will significant progress be made against this industry. An energetic but disjointed and uncoordinated piecemeal pursuit of promoters, as seems to be the present state of affairs, may make a significant temporary dent against tax schemes, but will not have the desired long term benefits.

Anecdotally, I have heard that there is still a significant degree of confusion and frustration in the coordination between the IRS and the DOJ in both formulating a long-term and comprehensive strategy against tax scams, and in the day-to-day referrals from the IRS to the DOJ for injunctive action or criminal prosecution. Both the IRS and the DOJ are taking significant actions against tax scam artists, but it does not appear from a distance (and on my admittedly secondhand information) that those agencies are as successfully combining their actions as might be hoped. Some of this lack of coordination or direction can be attributed to the fact that the office of the Assistant Secretary of Treasury for Tax Policy has remained unfilled since the resignation of the Hon. Pam Olsen. It should be a priority to fill that office.

My specific recommendations are as follows:

- The efforts to combat fraudulent tax schemes must be permanent and have long-range goals of both education and enforcement, and not mere temporary efforts that address these schemes *ad hoc* only at those times when they are running amok.

- The Treasury Department and the IRS should continue and expand their education of the general public by way of Notices and Revenue Rulings, etc., as to why particular frivolous theories are wrong, and also make a greater effort to ensure that each person who has asserted those defenses to avoid the payment of taxes are given a copy of the publication that relates to the particular theory as soon as such are identified. Even if the person ignores the publication, the mere fact that they have received it may later by itself preclude the successful assertion of the *Cheek* defense that they did not know the theory was wrong.

- The numerous Notices and Revenue Rulings relating to frivolous theories are well-known at the higher levels of the Internal Revenue Service, but seem to be little known and poorly understood by the average IRS caseworker and field personnel. Thus, the IRS should give a higher priority to educating caseworkers and field personnel about the existences and purposes of these publications, the need to disseminate them as early as possible during the case process to those who would assert these theories, and to timely and properly document that the taxpayer was given such a copy.

- As Congress looks to tighten the rules so as to combat the abuses involving public charities and donor-advised funds, Congress should look for opportunities to increase the enforcement capabilities against promoters who are attempting to hide behind the First Amendment to sell their snake oil, as opposed to *bona fide* religious or charitable organizations that benefit operate to benefit the public without any profit motive.

- Very slight and non-substantial wording changes to the existing Internal Revenue Code could have the effect of defeating many of the most popular tax protestor theories. For instance, if Section 1 were amended to read "Individuals who receive the income upon which the taxes in this section are imposed are liable for those taxes," this would eliminate one of the most popular arguments of many tens of thousands of tax protestors, who claim that while Section 1 "imposes" a tax on income, it is difficult to determine who liable for the tax. Although the courts have consistently rejected their theory as frivolous, the theory persists because the term "liable" is not found in Section 1. There are numerous other non-substantial changes that could and should be made in the Internal Revenue Code to eliminate to foreclose the possibility of those frivolous arguments being made. Upon request of the Committee, I would be glad to assemble a small group of interested tax professionals and other who are familiar with the most common tax protestor theories, and propose such changes.

- In the long run, the goal of simplification of the Internal Revenue Code as it relates to individual taxpayers is a must. The Code is highly confusing to those who are tax professionals, and utterly indecipherable to persons who are not tax professionals. Not only does the complex and stilted wording of the Internal Revenue Code allow the promoters of tax scams to proliferate, but it probably also causes quite legitimate due process of law concerns as to those taxpayers who in their heart very much desire to comply with the laws, but can't decipher the tax laws on their own and are forced to rely upon the representations of those who hold themselves out to be learned in the tax law but which later turn out to be a tax scam promoter. Many an honest citizens has had their life ruined because they held a bona fide belief in the tax position espoused to them by a tax scam artist, and did not discover until far too late that the position was invalid. This result occurs primarily because of the utterly indecipherable nature of the Internal Revenue Code, and to simplify that Code at least as it relates to the individual income taxation should be made a high priority.

As always, I very much appreciate the continued diligence of the Committee in taking an interest in this matter, which affects many thousands of our citizens who will get entangled with a promoter of abusive tax schemes, and the many millions of taxpayers who will unfairly carry the extra tax burden, as well as the cost of enforcement, caused by such schemes.

Yours most respectfully,

Jay D. Adkisson

Creator of http://www.quatloos.com, an educational website about financial and tax frauds and scams

JJ MacNab
Bethesda, MD
(301) 767-1085
www.deathandtaxes.com

March 15, 2006

Senator Charles E. Grassley, Chairman
Senator Max Baucus, Ranking Member
United States Senate Committee on Finance
Washington, DC 20510

Re: Supplemental report to the 2001 Committee Testimony

Dear Sirs:

The purpose of this letter is to respond to your recent request that I provide an update to my 2001 testimony before the Committee on the subject of "Taxpayer Beware: Schemes, Scams, & Cons."

Background

As you may recall, my 2001 written and oral testimony focused primarily on tax scams being mass marketed on the internet to a wide variety of consumers. Some online buyers are long term tax cheats who are simply looking for new excuses not to pay, but many others are hapless victims who believe that what they are buying is a legal tax avoidance technique.

Since 2001, the online tax scam market has gone through some dazzling highs and lows. As a result of well financed websites, active political discussion groups, professionally produced video materials, national conferences, and media exposure in such respected forums as C-Span, the "detax gurus" who peddle their products online found an enormous market of angry Americans who wanted to vent their frustrations at the US government by paying no income taxes at all.

By 2002, additional factors such as uncertain economic conditions, the war in Iraq, and lack of enforcement from the IRS, enabled the online anti-tax movement to grow significantly.

The label "Tax Protestor" isn't an accurate description.

While protesting taxes is certainly not new in this country, the internet movement differs considerably from the tax protest activities of prior generations. In past acts of protest, such as those who refused to pay taxes that supported the Vietnam War, the participants did so with an understanding of the consequences (you could go to prison), and recruited others to the cause with full disclosure of the negative things that might result. Such tax evasion was an act of civil disobedience.

This new generation of tax evaders is different. They want the benefits of withholding funds from government (personal enrichment, punishing government programs they don't like) without any of the negative consequences. They are not practicing civil disobedience; they are following a cult-like belief system made up of absurd pseudo-legal theories and wild-eyed conspiracy tales.

They concoct nonsensical schemes about how income taxes are unconstitutional, they take Supreme Court quotes out of context, and they twist the meaning of common words such as "employee," "includes," "citizen," or even the "United States" to try to prove that they are legally correct in paying no taxes at all. Even when their scheme loses in numerous courts of law, they simply accuse those judges and juries of participating in an anti-American conspiracy against them. Since the new generation of tax evaders denies that any income tax laws make them liable, the label "tax denier" is perhaps more accurate than "tax protester."

While it may seem absurd to most Americans that anyone could honestly believe in such tax denier schemes, the numbers nonetheless appear to be growing rapidly on the internet. In the past, tax deniers were generally found in closed groups in isolated communities such as Montana, Idaho, or Texas, but now they thrive in large groups online. While no formal studies have been done about who makes up the modern tax denier movement, and indeed the IRS is explicitly prohibited from monitoring the movement as a group, close observation of several hundred online participants in the anti-tax community reveals several common factors (see diagram below.)

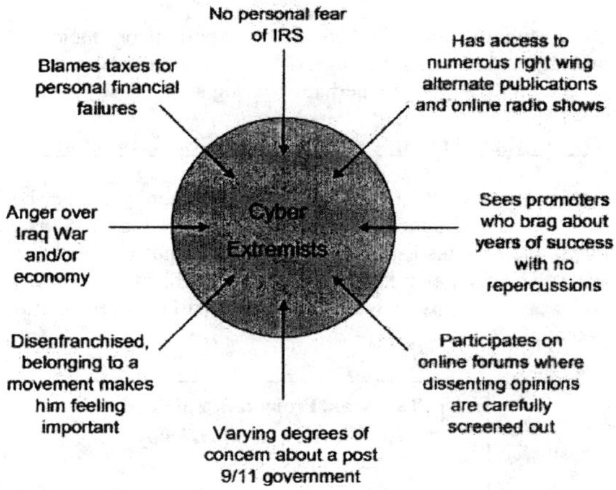

While several of these factors are political or personal issues that are beyond the jurisdiction of the IRS and Justice Department, the concerns on the right (in red) are items that can be and should be addressed by the government agencies in charge of enforcing the income tax laws:

1) The IRS needs to increase the number of tax deniers under audit, collection, and criminal investigation -- word of moth about such increased scrutiny will cause new potential members to rethink the choices they make;

2) The IRS and DOJ need to shut down promoters both civilly and criminally to send a clear message to their clients that their methods don't work;

3) The government needs to provide clearly written and easily understood fact sheets and websites to counter the myths and misconceptions being peddled by the promoters; and

4) All agencies need to communicate clearly and quickly with the press to ensure that the above efforts receive the maximum exposure, both online and in the traditional media.

The IRS Has Published Key Documents Online

Thanks to the attention brought to these issues by the Committee in the 2001 and later hearings, the Internal Revenue Service and the Department of Justice have made considerable headway into slowing down the tax denier movement.

The IRS, for example, has published numerous important guidelines and revenue rulings which not only counter the claims and promises made by the promoters, but serve to provide the followers with effective notice that these schemes don't work, an important issue if and when tax evaders end up in court.

The Truth about Frivolous Tax Arguments
http://www.irs.gov/pub/irs-utl/frivolousarguments-3-14-2005.pdf

Tax Scams and How to Recognize and Avoid Them
http://www.irs.gov/businesses/small/article/0,,id=106788,00.html

The Annual Announcement of the Dirty Dozen Tax Scams
http://www.irs.gov/newsroom/article/0,,id=154293,00.html

Recommendation: The IRS needs to continue producing such consumer education materials and targeted Revenue Rulings. They should, however, make such important information easier to find on their website, perhaps pooling all of these publications on a separate scam related site.

The turning of the tide in 2002 – The Civil Injunctions

By far the most effective strategy used in recent years has been the Justice Department's filing of civil injunctions against key promoters. More than 135 tax scam promoters have now been shut down, their clients lists (representing thousands of clients) turned over to the IRS, their websites gone. The campaign has been fast, thorough, and very well documented on the DOJ website so that search engines such as Google.com will pick up the crucial information for curious future potential victims.

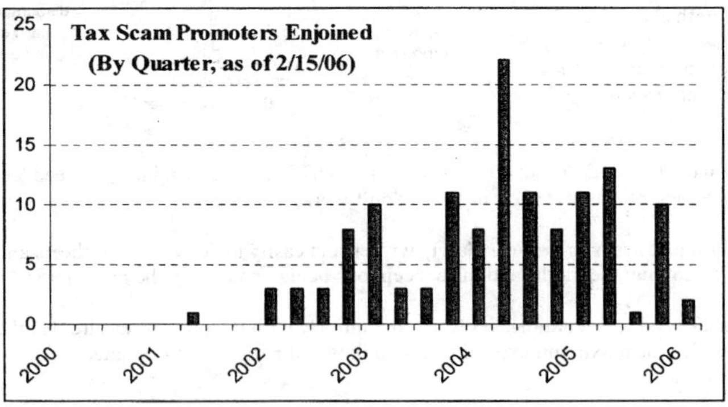

Recommendation: My only recommendation is that the DOJ continue this aggressive campaign, and that they focus on the detax industry leaders. The tax denier industry, while only loosely organized, is nonetheless a national movement, and targeting key promoters will be more effective than targeting a larger number of random promoters.

One step to aide the government's efforts to target key leaders in this movement is to amend existing laws to once again allow the IRS to label particular taxpayers as tax protestors or tax deniers. In order to provide meaningful statistics and plot an effective enforcement campaign, the Service needs to be able to track and analyze the people who aren't paying.

An Example

The most successful tax denial promoter in history is Irwin Schiff of Las Vegas, NV. Over the past thirty years, this colorful character has recruited an estimated minimum of 50,000 new members to the anti-tax movement, and the cost to the government in terms of collection efforts, due process hearings, tax court expenses, district court costs, and so on is monumental.

Irwin Schiff was convicted on multiple tax related felony counts last fall, and was recently sentenced to spend 163 months in a Federal prison. His 50,000+ followers are now scrambling to find a new leader. Many will end up with a promoter in Michigan named Peter E. Hendrickson; others have decided to hang their hats with a dozen or so other promoters. Still others will simply drop out of the tax system entirely.

Last year, Schiff followers filed "Schiff returns" which contained nothing but zeroes on every line of the 1040 with a two page attachment containing out of context quotes from unrelated court cases. This year, they could file dozens of different variations, or not file any forms at all. I can track where many of the Schiff followers are going through anecdotal evidence. The IRS can't track them at all.

Tax deniers move from promoter to promoter. By allowing the IRS to once again label tax deniers as what they are, the Service can have a better idea of who the real leaders in this movement are, and who to target for civil injunction and criminal prosecution.

Frivolous Filing penalties against non-promoters

Under current law, when a tax denier files frivolous arguments on or with his original or amended tax return in an attempt to evade taxes, the IRS has the ability to fine that person $500. In the past couple of years, Congress has considered various bills which would increase the frivolous filing penalty from $500 to $5,000 if the tax denier continues to rely on a frivolous argument which the IRS would place on a public list of schemes that don't work. Such legislation would also apply to frivolous arguments raised in collection due process hearings, offer in compromise submissions, and installment agreements.

Recommendation: I strongly recommend that this legislation be passed. Thousands of IRS man hours are wasted each year when tax deniers try to raise frivolous issues that have repeatedly lost in the courts. The potential increased penalty has caused quite a bit of concern among the online tax denier groups who feel that while the IRS won't spend much time going after $500 to $1,500 in fines, they certainly have more incentive when the penalties total $5,000 to $15,000. Furthermore, by requiring the IRS to provide clear written guidance in advance on which arguments are frivolous, a tax denier who nonetheless continues to make such arguments can not claim later in court that he or she wasn't given notice that the scheme didn't work.

The Criminal Trials

There have been a number of high profile trials in recent years, resulting in long prison sentences for the promoters.

The following cases are a small sample of the most noteworthy cases:

- **Irwin Schiff:** Promoted the "Zero Return" scheme. Schiff was convicted in October 2005 and sentenced to 163 months in prison.
- **Lynne Meredith:** Promoted pure trust schemes, and in 2005 was sentenced to 121 months in prison.
- **Larken Rose:** Promoted the Section 861 Scheme, was convicted of 5 misdemeanors in 2005 and sentenced to 15 months in prison.
- **Institute of Global Prosperity:** Multiple convictions and prison sentences ranging from a few months to 20 years in prison.

Furthermore, some of the individuals featured in the We the People advertisements that were used as exhibits in the 2001 Committee Hearing have also been tapped for criminal prosecution:

- **Al Thompson:** California business owner who stopped withholding, was convicted in 2005, and sentenced to 6 years in prison.
- **Richard Simkanin:** Texas business owner who stopped withholding, was convicted in 2004, and was sentenced to 7 years in prison.

Unlike the civil injunction cases which tend to be quick and efficient, the criminal cases involving the tax scam industry are slow and problematic. The length of time from investigation to conviction can take years to complete, leaving the promoter plenty of time to recruit new members to the movement.

Furthermore, even though the tax denier industry is a national movement, the criminal investigations and prosecutions appear to be done on a regional or local basis. When there are only sufficient resources to bring a couple hundred tax denier cases to trial each year, it is imperative that the government agencies work together on a national level to ensure that those cases which have the biggest effect on the industry as a whole be given priority.

An Example

You may recall from the 2001 hearing that a tax-exempt charity called We the People Foundation took out full page advertisements (See links below) in USA Today advocating the non-payment of taxes. One advertisement featured five business owners who had stopped withholding taxes from their employees' paychecks. A second ad highlighted three former IRS employees who believed that income taxes were unconstitutional and therefore should not be paid.

http://www.givemeliberty.org/features/taxes/toto/totoad-03-02-01.pdf
http://www.givemeliberty.org/features/taxes/toto/totoad-02-16-01.pdf

Joseph Banister, a former IRS Criminal Investigator, was one of the people featured in that second advertisement. He was indicted in 2004 on one count of conspiring to defraud the US government and three counts of assisting his client Al Thompson (a business owner from the first advertisement) in the filing of false returns.

Even though Banister was national figure with clients spread out throughout the United States, and even though he has done numerous national advertisements and conferences with the We the People organization and the other two ex-IRS employees, when it came time to indict him, only the activities that occurred within the District where he was investigated were considered. In other words, this national figure was investigated only for local crimes.

In 2005, Mr. Banister was acquitted on all counts while his client Mr. Thompson is currently serving six years in prison. The man who brought them together and funded the advertisements and national conferences, Robert Schulz of the We the People Foundation, has never faced any criminal charges at all.

Recommendation: Thanks to the internet, it is now easy to market a tax scam to a national audience. I strongly recommend that the IRS and Justice Department put together a team to 1) investigate national level tax evaders and promoters, 2) bring them to trial, and 3) coordinate with the civil side on ongoing civil investigations. I strongly recommend that the overall prosecution strategy be looked at on a national scale. As mentioned earlier, if you only have the resources to prosecute a few cases each, those cases should be prioritized for maximum effectiveness.

Investigation Time Frame

The length of time from investigation to trial is an enormous concern when every year that a case is delayed means that the promoter is able to recruit hundreds of new people to the movement. Irwin Schiff, for example, has been actively and aggressively marketing his "Zero Income" scheme since he was last released from prison in 1993. In the twelve years that he operated his successful anti-tax business, his clients cost the government tens of millions of lost taxes and literally thousands of IRS and judiciary man hours.

Recommendation: It is fairly common for a case to take three to four years to come to the attention of the criminal investigators, another three or so for them to investigate, another year to indict, and another year to bring to trial. The investigation phase needs to be sped up considerably.

Other Criminal Trial Issues

In 2005, the largest "861 Scheme" promoter in the country, Larken Rose, was indicted and convicted on five counts of Willful Failure to File a Tax Return. Under current law, if you are found guilty of filing a false return, it is a felony subject to considerable potential prison time and fines. Failing to file at all, however, is only a misdemeanor.

Crime	Code Section	Level	Max Fine	Max Prison Term
Willful Failure to File a Tax Return	26 USC §7203	Misdemeanor	$100,000	1 year
Filing a False Return	26 USC §7206(1)	Felony	$250,000	3 years
Tax Evasion	26 USC §7201	Felony	$250,000	5 years
False Claims (Refund)	18 USC §287	Felony	$1,000,000	5 years

As a result, even though convicted on all five counts, Mr. Rose's prison time under Federal sentencing guidelines was only 15 months.

Recommendation: A few anti-tax promoters have noted the above disparity in the laws, and have recommended that their clients simply drop out of the tax system rather than risk the felony charges associated with the filing of false returns. Congress should consider bringing these crimes (and the potential punishments) into parity.

Furthermore, Congress should consider better defining the word "willful" as it applies to Federal income tax cases. The current standard is based on the 1991 Supreme Court case, United States v. Cheek (498 US 192), which states:

> A good-faith misunderstanding of the law or a good-faith belief that one is not violating the law negates willfulness, <u>whether or not the claimed belief or misunderstanding is objectively reasonable</u>. (underline added)

Our tax system relies on voluntary compliance to succeed: if too many people cheat, the system collapses. Requiring that the willfulness element of the various tax crimes would be based on a reasonable misunderstanding would significantly reduce the number of absurd theories and frivolous defenses that are clogging our court system now.

Publicizing Victories

When the government only has the resources to enjoin or convict a limited number of promoters and cheats, it is imperative that these cases are brought to the attention of the public. The civil side of the Justice Department Tax Division, for example, produces a steady stream of press releases involving civil injunction and related cases which remain archived on their website for anyone to see. They also provide these releases to tax trade publications that do an excellent job in keeping professional preparers up to speed.

http://www.usdoj.gov/tax/taxpress2006.htm

In comparison, the announcements and internet information for the criminal tax cases are irregular at best. Almost none are posted on the national DOJ website (www.usdoj.gov), those that are often don't get posted there for several days after conviction or sentencing, and others are placed only on Assistant US Attorney websites with little or no detail provided to pique the interest of either reporters or trade publications.

For example, until her conviction last year, Lynne Meredith was a nationally recognized anti-tax promoter of pure trust schemes. She had been featured on national television shows and in June, 2005 she was handed down a significant prison term. Her case should send a clear message to consumers who already have or who are considering getting involved in a pure trust scheme: these plans don't work and those who use them could go to prison. Her sentencing received almost no press, while there is a press release on the local AUSA website, there is nothing on the national website. Other cases, such as the recent conviction of police detective Patrick J. Dain, had no press release put out at all. Considering that a growing number of tax deniers are government employees (police officers, bailiffs, defense contractors, parole officers, and even an FBI agent) it shouldn't be difficult to generate press interest in such trials.

Recommendation: There needs to be a nationally coordinated effort to publicize important cases and current trends.

Identifying New Scams

As I tried to emphasize in my 2001 testimony, in addition to combing returns, matching documents, and analyzing internal data, the IRS needs to watch the tax industry itself to see what's being promoted. By looking at how various promoters pitch tax evasion schemes, refunds scams, for example, can be caught years earlier than they currently are.

An Example

Peter Hendrickson is a Michigan anti-tax promoter who has served time in prison for mailing a bomb to the IRS. As various promoters such as Irwin Schiff, Larken Rose, Lynne Meredith, and Thurston Bell have been enjoined and/or incarcerated, several of their followers are looking for a new leader and many have decided to join Hendrickson's program.

Hendrickson's plan relies on a tortured definition of the word "includes" and while his legal theories will eventually lose in the various courts, in the meantime, his followers are successfully getting full refunds of every tax dollar they've paid into the system in the past three years, including Social Security premiums.

It isn't difficult to locate who has received these erroneous refunds. On the contrary, Mr. Hendrickson scans in copies of the actual refund checks and statements and posts them on his website to better market his book.

http://www.losthorizons.com/tax/MoreVictories.htm

To date, Mr. Hendrickson brags that his clients have received at least $821,913 in refunds. Client George Baer for example, has received two refund checks totaling more than $50,000. Patrick Mooney would have received $2,045 but the IRS first subtracted $1,500 in frivolous filing penalties for the same tax years they are now issuing a refund, a rather ironic statement that the IRS was already aware that this taxpayer was a tax denier.

Matching W-2s to Form 1040s wouldn't catch these refunds in time since W-2 pass first to the Social Security Administration before being processed by the IRS, whereas refund requests are processed immediately.

Recommendation: As various promoters are shut down or incarcerated, the IRS should be watching where those clients go. Enabling the Service to once again label a tax denier as such should help considerably, but also setting up a task force to monitor the marketing efforts of the promoters would cut down the number of erroneous refunds and provide a more efficient list of promoters to be targeted for civil and criminal action.

In other cases, promoters market methods to get around current IRS reporting requirements. In one scheme, self employed individuals are advised to incorporate. If their clients pay them more than a minimum amount as individuals, the clients would be required to issue 1099s, and the IRS would therefore be notified of that income. If the individual incorporates, no 1099s are required and the self employed person is effectively under the radar screen.

In yet another case, a promoter who markets offshore investments claims that his product is arranged such that the taxpayer can answer "no" on the 1040 to the question regarding foreign accounts.

From http://www.newfuelnow.com/commentary/september2005/schiff0926.htm :

> *Anonymity -*
> *Part of the obvious attraction of the PMCP is the opportunity to move some capital off-shore. What investors may also be pleasantly surprised to learn is that the Mint does not report to any U.S. Government agency; additionally, it is our opinion that the purchase of gold, silver or platinum through the Mint does not constitute a foreign account that must be reported under current disclosure rules (please check this with your tax consultant).*

Recommendation: Promoters are getting more sophisticated regarding reporting and timing issues, and the IRS will not be able to identify such schemes through traditional matching programs. Instead, to supplement current inward looking analysis, the Service should set up teams who monitor the marketing promises made by promoters.

Other External Information That Should be Monitored

There is a wealth of information about the tax denier movement to be found in Tax Court cases, District Court cases, criminal cases, tax return attachments, and filings. These should be monitored for trends and easy fixes to some of the more common problems.

An Example

One common tax scheme involves Section 861 of the Tax Code. The proponents claim that only foreign source income is taxable to people living in the US. In literally dozens of tax court and criminal cases, the tax denier has pointed to the instructions for the Form 1040 which read as follows:

Income
Foreign-Source Income
You must report unearned income, such as interest, dividends, and pensions, from sources outside the United States unless exempt by law or a tax treaty. You must also report earned income, such as wages and tips, from sources outside the United States.

Many tax deniers point to this paragraph as proof that the 861 argument is valid, since no similar language appears in the instructions regarding domestic income.

To avoid this confusion, the IRS could simply add five words to the paragraph, "In addition to domestic income, you must report..."

Recommendation: This is just one example of literally hundreds of issues that have been raised in the various court cases. Like many similar problems, it is simple to fix once it is identified.

Violence in the Tax Denial Industry

Many of us who have been paying attention to the tax denier movement over the years are concerned. As leaders are shut down and incarcerated, the followers and remaining promoters are expressing increasingly strong threats of physical violence, especially towards judges. While domestic terrorism is not new to the anti-tax community, the anger and blind hatred towards the courts and federal employees is escalating.

An Example

There were at least a dozen threats of violence surrounding the Irwin Schiff criminal trial in Las Vegas last fall. Throughout the trial, Schiff would post audio messages and multi-page diatribes on the various websites and blogs, goading his followers to do something about the "criminal character" of the judge and prosecutors.

During the trial, his followers 1) shot out the windows in two cars - one belonging to a juror, another to a court employee, 2) poured acid on three federal employees' cars, 3) took shots at both the courthouse and the IRS building, 4) followed the judge into the hallways of his church, 5) posted detailed maps and instructions to the judge's home, 5) posted the home addresses and phone numbers of all the jurors in the case.

Recommendation: There needs to be an increased priority in tracking and preventing potential violence.

Summary

In conclusion, a tremendous amount of improvement has been made since 2001 in addressing the problems of the online tax denier industry. The civil injunctions have been remarkably effective, the IRS has done a very good job of publishing consumer education and detailed revenue rulings debunking the most popular schemes, and while the criminal cases could be better publicized, several of the top promoters have been brought to trial and convicted.

I recommend, however, that the IRS and DOJ put together a comprehensive national plan to better target key participants in the movement and to reduce the amount of time it takes to bring these promoters and cheats to trial.

In 2001, as an exercise to show how prevalent the tax scam industry was on the Web, I spent two hours browsing the various anti-tax websites and made a list of 24 fairly random tax denier promoters. I have reproduced that list in the Appendix of this letter, and have noted what has happened to each promoter in the last five years.

To summarize briefly, four of the 24 promoters have been criminally prosecuted, seven have been civilly enjoined and shut down, nine have shut down their websites voluntarily, and only four are still peddling scams. While this was a random group of promoters, and is certainly not a large enough pool to be considered an accurate analysis of what has happened in the last five years, it certainly shows a hint at the progress that has been made.

I would happy to answer any additional questions you may have.

Sincerely,

JJ MacNab
Bethesda, MD

APPENDIX A
Two Hour Research Project (Updated)

Website	Comments	Where are they now?
www.yourtaxfreedom.com www.incometaxfreedom.com The 4 Your Success Group (Minnesota)	"Many Americans have a very definite idea about how the Internal Revenue Service behaves. And in many respects, they are correct. Testimony before the Senate Committee in October of 1997 revealed, for the first time for many Americans, just how the IRS tries to intimidate and bully you."	**YourTaxFreedom.com was taken down.** IncomeTaxFreedom.com is still run by Jim Paulson of Minnesota, but has recently been **stripped of all product information.** The promoter currently has an outstanding federal tax lien exceeding $443,000.
landbusiness.safeshopper.com Land Business Systems (Pennsylvania)	Also sells mineral supplements on eBay.com, battery recovery systems, "Liberty Pure Trusts," and "Constitutional Products."	**Website was taken down.**
www.taxgate.com RBH and Associates (New Jersey)	"US Income Tax Law:" Very large Pure Trust and tax avoidance portal. Has more than 1,325 pages of data and articles. Not selling products, but charge $165 for membership / consultation. Website states that it has 345,000 hits per month.	Rick Haraka (aka Rick Bryan) was **permanently enjoined** from selling tax scams in 2003. The promoter currently has an outstanding federal tax lien exceeding $472,000.
www.buildfreedom.com/economic/eco_6.html Terra Libra Ventures (Arizona)	"Freedom" Portal. Offers books for sale, as well as free information such as "How to Stop Employers From Withholding Income Taxes."	Website is still active.
www.heritage-institute.com Heritage Institute for Estate Planning (California)	Offers Contractual Pure Trusts and Living Trusts. Explains that Pure Trusts are "safe" from Medicaid look-back rules. Displays the Better Business Bureau Reliability Seal.	They work with the "Heritage Institute for the Sovereign State Creation." Claims to be located in 47 states with 700 representatives. **Only vague references to pure or complex trusts remain on the website.**
www.solgroup.com www.puretrust.com www.no1040s.com !SOLUTIONS! Group (Ohio)	Offers the Liberty Pure Trust. Also sells web-hosting and offshore investments. Counter shows almost 39,000 "hits."	Dana C. Ewell was **permanently enjoined** from selling tax scams in 2005. All three websites were taken down. The promoter currently has outstanding federal tax liens exceeding $524,000.
www.cktrust.com Without Prejudice (Tennessee)	Run by a "barrister at law" named Austin Gary Cooper. Offers the "Clark Kent Trust," (a Pure Trust) for $578 and an expatriation / repatriation kit for $388.	Austin Gary Cooper and Martha Cooper were **permanently enjoined** from selling tax scams in 2003. The website is gone.

www.yelmtel.com/~trusts Family of Eagles Ltd. / American Beauty Rose (Washington)	Pure Trusts sold by private appointment only.	Raymond Leo Bell was **permanently enjoined** from selling tax scams in 2005. The website is gone.
www.webtrust.com Localink Information Services (California)	Sells Living Trusts and Irrevocable Pure Business Trusts. Offers sample documents for $9.95.	Website is still active.
www.iossbs.org Int'l Organization of Self Sufficient Benefit Societies (Nevada)	A "fraternal society". Also sells water purifiers, waste systems, pyramid greenhouses, offshore credit and ATM cards, offshore bank accounts and trusts.	**Website was taken down.**
www.i-f-c.com Innovative Financial Consultants (Arizona)	Also offers Pure Trust Organizations, offshore banking, foreign bank formation, and Limited Liability Companies. Counter indicates almost 67,000 "hits."	In 2004 and 2005, **eight promoters either pleaded guilty to or were convicted** of conspiracy to defraud the US government and/or willful failure to file tax returns.
www.f-f-a.com Financial Fortress Associates (El Cajon, CA)	Sells Pure Trust Organizations, Limited Liability Companies, conducts regular sales seminars, and claims 7,000 clients.	Website is still active.
www.puretrusts.com www.givemeliberty.net R&H Publishers (Oklahoma)	Offers books, packages, and "do-it-yourself" manuals to set up Pure Trusts.	**Both websites have been taken down.**
webf0126.ntx.net BizNet Equity Management Trust (Florida)	Sells Pure Common Law Trusts through a "Do-It-Yourself Trust System." "Authorized dealer of EHMT". Currently hiring new dealers.	**Website was taken down.**
www.ehmt.com Entrepreneur Holdings Management Trust (Florida)	No information. Just a one page site that says "International Strategies" with a phone number. Copyright information shows 1994-2001.	**Website was taken down.**
www.webyellowpages.com/pill www.pill.net Prosper International League Ltd. (Florida)	Claim 20,000 customers and seven years' experience setting up Pure Trusts. Multi-level marketing program. Also offers offshore credit cards, offshore banking, and Belize Trusts. "Start an account for only $200."	The company is still active, and was used extensively by Irwin Schiff and his clients. **Schiff was recently convicted on multiple tax charges.** PIL client and Global Prosperity affiliate **Dwayne Robare pleaded guilty** to tax evasion in 2005 and is awaiting sentencing.

www.joyfoundation.com The Joy Foundation (Florida)	The Joy Foundation. Earn an Associates Degree in avoiding income taxes. Multi level marketing program. Join for $1,680. Also sells books through Amazon.com.	Promoter Joseph Sweet was **permanently enjoined** in 2002.
www.wealth4freedom.com Capital Strategies (Florida)	Same website as The Joy Foundation. Presumably a dealer/associate.	No longer shows Joy Foundation info, but still publishes tax protest advice. The promoter, Janis E. Greehey was **permanently enjoined** in 2005 for marketing a different tax scam, the corporation sole.
www.pure-trust.com Lamb & Associates (California)	Recently merged with pre-paid legal services website.	**Website was taken down.**
home.swbell.net/ministry/ International Fellowship of Churches and Ministers (Texas)	"Education - Ordination - Church Charters - Irrevocable Pure Trusts and Snore-ends". Purchase a church charter for $300 and "Free your church, yourself, your business from undue tax burden."	**Website was taken down.**
www.freedomtrustgroup.com www.theawaregroup.com Freedom Trust Group (South Carolina)	Sells software so that buyer can produce an "unlimited number of all five different types of common-law irrevocable contracts of Pure Trusts." Also sells International Business Corporations.	The website is still selling pure trusts, was recently updated (2005), and no action appears to have been taken against the promoter, John Howard Alexander, who also heads The Aware Group.
www.trustenterprises.com Trust Enterprises (California)	The CPA who started the current movement by obtaining a letter from the IRS saying that a "Pure Trust Organization has no tax requirements."	**Website was taken down. The promoter, Greg P Karl was convicted** of conspiracy and four counts of mail fraud and was sentenced to 20 months in prison.
www.mysticbird.com The Phoenix Group (Oregon)	Sells "Contractual Business Entities." "The IRS is very aware of what a "pure common law trust" (CBE) is, and understands that they are exempt from statute."	**Website was taken down.**
www.successlinks.com Institute of Global Prosperity (Florida)	Audio tape and seminar package to set up offshore accounts, trusts, Internal Business Corporations, and Limited Liability Companies.	At least **21 individuals have either pleaded guilty or been convicted** of tax crimes related to Global Prosperity and Andersen Ark. Additional criminal trials are pending.

DEPARTMENT OF THE TREASURY
INTERNAL REVENUE SERVICE
WASHINGTON, D.C. 20224

COMMISSIONER

May 19, 2006

The Honorable Charles E. Grassley
Chairman, Committee on Finance
United States Senate
Washington, D.C. 20510

Dear Senator Grassley:

I am pleased to respond to your letter of March 8, 2006, on the most significant compliance issues within the responsibility of the Large and Mid-Size Business Division (LMSB). LMSB's taxpayer base consists of the largest businesses in the United States, including corporations, sub-chapter S corporations, and partnerships with assets greater than $10 million, including over 6,100 publicly traded companies. LMSB taxpayers file approximately 176,000 income tax returns annually, and while the population base remains relatively stable, we continue to see an increase in complex business structures and pass-through return filings. LMSB taxpayers, particularly public companies, are driven to show high after-tax profitability to shareholders in a very competitive and complex economic environment. They have the resources and willingness to aggressively defend and contest tax law positions.

As you requested, we have outlined below the top LMSB tax compliance concerns and matters that raise questions about whether the actions of taxpayers are keeping with the intent and spirit of the Internal Revenue Code (the Code). In addition, we have outlined certain tax policy issues that we believe are worthy of discussions among the IRS, the Treasury Department, and the Finance Committee.

Introduction

Our response is divided into three parts. First, we discuss the current environment of large and mid-size businesses, our challenges, and the focus of our compliance efforts. Second, we list current specific compliance issues and how we are addressing these issues. These compliance issues include complex international transactions, significant domestic issues, compliance issues resulting from or impacted by provisions in the American Jobs Creation Act (AJCA), and tax shelters. Finally, we identify focus areas for discussion of reform.

i. General Environmental Challenges Affecting Compliance

We face new and more challenging tax administration problems resulting from globalization, complexity of the Code, complexity of business transactions, and the growing book-tax gap.

Globalization: Tax administration is complicated by the rapid pace at which businesses are continuing to expand globally. A growing percentage of large and mid-size business tax filings are from multinational businesses that have a myriad of subsidiaries and partnerships operating within an enterprise structure where the ultimate parent is as likely to be foreign as domestic. A growing number of U.S. businesses acquire raw materials, inventory, financing, products and services from foreign businesses. These events are natural outcomes of an increasingly global economy and businesses have the right to optimize their global structures. Nonetheless, the complexities of globalization and cross-border activity continue to challenge the Code and U.S. tax administration. With multiple domestic and global tiered entities, it is often difficult to determine the full scope and resulting tax impact of a single transaction or series of transactions. Complexities of globalization and cross-border activity create opportunities for aggressive tax planning demonstrated in several of the international/global current compliance issues mentioned in this letter.

Complexity of the Internal Revenue Code: The Code continues to expand, becoming more complex and challenging to administer. Large businesses utilize every available resource to explore opportunities to reduce their tax liability by challenging the most intricate and complicated Code provisions. Every new tax law, even those that are simple on their face, creates additional complexity while providing taxpayers with further tax planning opportunities adding to our challenges to administer the Federal Tax System. These changes make it more difficult for us to treat similarly situated taxpayers in a consistent manner. Three of the current specific compliance issues mentioned in this letter arise from new Code provisions enacted by the AJCA.

Complexity of Transactions: Large businesses engage in sophisticated transactions that result in complex relationships with multiple filing requirements. Tax administration continues to be challenged by the increasing number of high value, sometimes cross-border, mergers, acquisitions and other multifaceted international and domestic tiered transactions. The increasing volume and complexity of these transactions make it difficult for us to identify them and to effectively address them in a timely manner.

Growing Book-Tax Differences: Companies strive to reflect the highest possible after-tax profits in their financial statements while at the same time being incentivized to report the lowest possible taxable income and tax liability. The difference between income reported by public companies to their shareholders and income reported on their tax returns to the IRS has grown dramatically in recent years, from $79.0 billion in 1995 to $203.8 billion in 2002.[1] The climb slowed in the period 2000-2002 when the economy cooled down and the equity markets declined. When post-2002 data becomes available, given that the economy returned to a period of expansion and the equity markets have recovered, we believe we will see the increase in book-tax differences pick up where it left off in 2000.

Research indicates that book-tax differences sometimes indicate significant compliance risk, as is the case in many of the issues discussed in Section II below. When the details of business transactions and book-tax differences are not visible, the accurate determination of shareholder value, the efficiency of capital markets and the correct determination of tax can be jeopardized. An extreme example was highlighted by the Congressional investigation of Enron. The company told its shareholders during the period 1995-2000 that it earned a robust $13 billion, whereas for the same 5-year period, the company's Federal Income Tax Returns reported only $76 million in taxable income.

The IRS Addresses These Challenges

We have taken a proactive approach to dealing with the challenges of effective tax administration in the environment described above. Overall, our strategy depends on making compliance checks as much as possible on a real-time or near-real-time basis, being as current in our examinations as possible, and having as much transparency to book-tax differences and other indicators of risk as possible. To that end, we have initiated several programs that foster transparency, currency, pre-filing compliance opportunities, and improved efficiencies in issue and risk identification.

We are looking at various methods to better address issues involving cross-border/multi-national enterprise activities as well as the domestic items that are a subject of this letter. In general, we have found Issue Management Teams (IMTs) to be successful when we employ them to provide executive oversight and focus upon areas of high risk. We have used IMTs to combat tax shelters, and have expanded their use to include other areas of high compliance risk. We have also used special teams of experienced personnel to assist with the examination of specific issues in the tax shelter arena, and plan to use similar teams to address other compliance issues. Additionally, we are working to enhance the use of internal web site information to better inform examiners of high risk areas and the steps they must take to ensure consistent application of the law.

Improving Transparency: To improve transparency of corporate taxpayers, we introduced a new Schedule M-3. The Schedule M-3 provides more detail on book-tax differences, enabling us to identify and focus more quickly and precisely

[1] See attached chart of Book-Tax Difference Trend.

on those tax returns and issues that present the highest potential compliance risk.

Improving Currency and Transparency: We introduced the Compliance Assurance Program (CAP), to improve both currency and transparency. The CAP is a real-time approach to compliance review that allows us, working in conjunction with the taxpayer, to determine tax return accuracy prior to filing. We believe the CAP is more efficient than a post-filing examination–we are currently piloting the model and will refine as necessary–as it provides corporations certainty about their tax liability for a given year within months, rather than years, of filing a tax return. This win-win program greatly reduces taxpayers' compliance burden and their need for contingent book tax reserves, while increasing currency and allowing for more efficient use of our resources.

Pre-Filing Compliance: We created the Pre-Filing Agreement (PFA) program to provide taxpayers an opportunity to request that revenue agents examine and resolve potential issues before tax returns are filed. We continue to explore ways to improve and create additional pre-filing compliance opportunities and are designing another pre-filing initiative to expand our ability to work with LMSB taxpayers on a pre-filing basis to address their federal tax liability compliance.

Improving Issue and Risk Identification: LMSB identifies emerging high risk issues as early as possible, issuing guidance to taxpayers and examiners on the proper treatment of these issues, and efficiently and vigorously examining those returns where taxpayers engage in that behavior. One additional method we are employing to improve issue identification and the selection for examination of high risk returns is electronic filing (*E-Filing*). Many corporations are now required to file their tax returns electronically and this mandate will expand in future tax years. *E-filing* will provide more consistent treatment and data analysis for efficient, near real time identification of high risk issues and taxpayers. *E-filing* and Schedule M-3 together also allow us to more efficiently identify and exclude lower risk taxpayers from consideration for examination.

The approaches described above better position us to more timely address the rapid change of business in the domestic and global arenas. The earlier we learn of emerging trends, the better positioned we will be to adjust resources to appropriately address compliance risks.

II. Current Specific Compliance Issues and Actions Taken

The most significant compliance problems facing LMSB are issues that include one, several, or all of the following factors: significant impact on one or more industries; a large number of taxpayers; significant dollar risk; substantial compliance risk; and/or high visibility. In addition to these general problem areas, LMSB also continues to combat tax shelters and other abusive tax avoidance schemes.

To address these tax compliance challenges, to dissuade promoters and others from initiating new ones, and to achieve our key goal of tax compliance through service and enforcement, we are working to make our examination resources more efficient, using tools to increase taxpayer disclosure and transparency, leveraging technology, and reengineering our processes to identify and resolve emerging issues and potentially abusive transactions.

The volume of return examinations has increased with a focus on returns where we have identified significant compliance issues. IMTs have been, or are in the process of being, established for all issues with significant compliance problems. We continue to work with Counsel to ensure written guidance is provided to examiners for addressing each of these significant compliance issues. Examiners are expected to consider penalties on all returns with examination adjustments and on promoters of tax avoidance schemes. Below is a summary of our most significant compliance problems and the actions we are taking to address these areas of non-compliance.

International/Global Transactions

Transfer of Intangibles Offshore/Cost Sharing: Tax issues associated with the transfer of intangibles outside the United States have been a high risk compliance concern for us and have seen a significant increase in recent years. Taxpayers, especially in the high technology and pharmaceutical industries, are shifting profits offshore through a variety of arrangements that result in the transfer of valuable intangibles to related foreign entities for inadequate consideration. Cost sharing arrangements are often the method of choice for this activity. The buy-in amount in cost sharing arrangements is particularly troublesome. It is often understated, resulting in the improper shifting of income offshore.

As part of our response to these issues, we proposed a comprehensive set of cost sharing regulations in August 2005, that seek to ensure such arrangements do not facilitate a disguised transfer of intangible assets outside the United States in a manner inconsistent with the arm's length standard. We intend to finalize these regulations this year.

We have also established a cost sharing IMT to improve Service-wide coordination in the identification, development, and resolution of cost sharing issues. The team issued a cost sharing audit checklist in 2005 that provides guidance to field examiners for developing potential cost sharing audit issues and ensuring consistency. The team has completed its efforts to identify and review cases with a cost sharing issue to determine the impact and compliance risk. The team is developing a coordinated issue paper that will provide the basis and support for examining issues and to assist with potential Appeals Settlement

Guidelines. In 2005, the LMSB Commissioner issued guidance to field examiners for requesting transfer pricing documentation.

Abusive Foreign Tax Credit Transactions

Taxpayers are manipulating the Code to create and claim foreign tax credits (FTCs) where the associated foreign-source income is not taxed in the United States. One type of transaction involves the inappropriate separation of the FTCs from related foreign-source income. These transactions typically involve the acquisition of assets that generate an income stream or built-in gain that is subject to foreign taxes but not U.S. taxes; or, the use of partnerships, foreign consolidated regimes, or "check the box" reverse hybrid entities to obtain FTCs before the related foreign income is subject to U.S. tax. In addition, cross-border financing transactions are being structured to generate abusive FTC results. In the case of U.S. lender transactions, a U.S. person makes a loan to a foreign person in a transaction structured to shift a portion of the borrower's foreign tax liability to the U.S. lender. In the case of U.S. borrower transactions, a U.S. person borrows from a foreign person in a manner that allows the U.S. person to pay creditable foreign taxes in lieu of deductible interest. In both types of cases, the FTCs are used to shelter unrelated foreign source income. These structured financing transactions often result in the duplication of tax benefits through the use of certain structures designed to exploit inconsistencies between U.S. and foreign laws. We are aware of 11 structured financing transactions with an estimated $3.5 billion at issue in these cases.

To address cross-border financing transactions that are designed to generate FTCs, LMSB has formed an IMT. The team will work to: identify and address all open cases with an abusive FTC issue; identify and explore all viable legal arguments to combat the abuses including the application of judicial doctrines, such as economic substance, and/or step transaction arguments; provide guidance to the field; and pursue possible legislative and/or regulatory modifications. Due to the global aspects of this issue, we must consider tools available under international treaties and exchange of information agreements. In addition, the IRS and Treasury have several major regulatory projects underway that will address numerous issues involving the inappropriate separation of FTCs from related foreign-source income.

Abusive Hybrid Instrument Transactions: Taxpayers can use hybrid instruments, hybrid entities, and similar structures to capitalize on differences between foreign and domestic tax laws because these structures are often treated differently for U.S. and foreign tax purposes. This kind of arbitrage can be the natural outgrowth of global economies and disparate tax systems. Concern exists, however, that in some cases, hybrid instruments or entities might be used to avoid U.S. tax rules. For example, inappropriate FTCs can be generated. The use of these hybrid instrument transactions by U.S. multinational domestic corporations and foreign controlled domestic subsidiaries is a common practice. Indications are the use of these types of transactions is on the rise.

In response, we recently formed an IMT to develop a Service-wide position on hybrid instruments. Due to the global aspects of this issue, we will consider international treaties and simultaneous examination processes. In addition, the IRS and Treasury have a number of guidance projects under way that would address some of the issues raised by hybrid instruments, hybrid entities, and similar structures.

Transfer Pricing: Taxpayers are continuing to shift significant profits offshore. Taxpayers often manipulate the price of related transactions so that the income of an economic group is ostensibly earned in low tax jurisdictions, or in no jurisdiction, rather than in the U.S., thus lowering the enterprise's worldwide tax burden. We apply the arms length principle to determine the appropriate allocation of income between related parties based upon the application of acceptable transfer pricing methodologies (section 482 of the Code).

In response to the significant compliance risks of transfer pricing issues, the LMSB Commissioner issued a Transfer Pricing Compliance Memorandum in January 2003 that provided instruction and guidance to all field examination personnel regarding potential transfer pricing issues. Additionally, the LMSB Commissioner issued a Transfer Pricing Documentation Memorandum that requires all field examination personnel to request and review taxpayer transfer pricing studies. As a subset of the transfer pricing issue category, a section 936 Termination Strategy issue has been identified for additional compliance coordination. Associated with the sunsetting of section 936, taxpayers have created structured transactions to transfer U.S. intangibles that were used in Puerto Rico to other low tax jurisdictions. An IMT has been established to identify, coordinate, and propose resolution alternatives for this issue. Field examiners and technical advisors will provide technical support to teams with the development of this tax issue.

Significant Domestic Issues

R & E Credit Claims: Taxpayers are filing refund claims, often marketed to them on a contingency fee basis, to claim additional research credit. These claims are frequently based on unsupportable amounts, nonqualified expenditures, or estimates for which the taxpayers do not have contemporaneous documentation. The Ogden Service Center has received 673 corporate tax year claims for more than $1.3 billion in additional credits since we released Notice 2002-44 (July 8, 2002). This notice provides a new filing address and guidance for the research credit or refund. The increase in the number of research credit refund claims, often filed late in the examination cycle, has placed an enormous resource burden on many examination teams. In addition to the administrative burden created by the filing of these research credit claims, other significant issues need to be resolved, such as identifying the business entity within a consolidated group that is claiming the credit, prototype issues, re-computation (or computation for the first time) of base period historical information for the years 1984 through 1988, and start-up company issues. Most of these issues are exacerbated by a lack of contemporaneous records to support the amounts claimed.

To address improper research credit claims, we have a number of administrative actions in process. These include conducting training and providing expert guidance to examiners to assist with examining the issue, the issuance of a Research Credit Audit Technique Guide (ATG), and the issuance of four Coordinated Issue Papers providing guidance on the research credit.

The difficulties we have encountered in administering this credit are exacerbated by the temporary nature of the credit. In addition, the credit's structure raises a number of technical issues – defining what constitutes "qualified research," determining the proper treatment of section 174 depreciation expenses, defining "supplies" and "gross receipts" (as well as determining the treatment of foreign gross receipts), and defining the effects of the section 280C(c) reduced credit election, to name a few. Although the Treasury Department and the IRS are working to address many of these issues through the administrative guidance process, substantial noncompliance will likely continue in this area.

Universal Service Fund (USF): Federal and state governments impose taxes on telecommunication service consumers to fund subsidies to the telecommunication carriers for universal service programs. The issue is whether amounts received by telecommunications carriers from federal and state universal service programs constitute non-shareholder contributions to capital under section 118, or are taxable income under section 61. The funds are paid to reduce rates and are charged to customers so that certain customers in high cost areas or rural areas are not charged more than customers in urban areas where costs are lower. The tax impact per year is about $2.5 billion for the federal USF payments alone. A complete dollar estimate for the state USF payments is not available now, but it is substantial. Approximately 1,500 carriers are receiving USF subsidies, and, combined with the expansion of the USF program, the number is likely to increase in the future along with the total amount of subsidies.

Some telecom taxpayers are receiving significant USF subsidies and not reporting them as income. The position of these carriers, that the USF subsidy is a non-shareholder capital contribution that is not taxable income under section 118, creates a competitive disadvantage for compliant taxpayers. Taxpayers are relying on the language in the Federal Telecommunication Act of 1996 that the funds are to be used for "the provision, maintenance, and upgrading of facilities and services for which the support is intended." The use of section 118 by businesses to exclude other governmental subsidies is spreading–benefits, such as local incentives for a business to relocate to or stay in its jurisdiction and for utility companies to continue to provide basic services, are being claimed as nontaxable under section 118, while related expenses are being fully deducted.

We believe these positions often are without merit, and we have challenged them on audit. We have issued a Coordinated Issue Paper directing examiners to take specific audit positions which was followed by an Appeals Settlement Guideline allowing for minimal litigation hazards. We believe the courts will sustain our position under the current statute. Nevertheless, we are working on guidance to address the USF issue.

Mixed Service Costs: Some electric and gas utility companies have changed their method of accounting to allow them to consider certain large self-constructed assets "routine and repetitive" under the simplified service cost method (SSCM), which allows a much faster (on occasion it has been immediate) write off. The impact of this issue is substantial.

Our position is that the classification as "routine and repetitive" is often flawed. We recently published a regulation that eliminates this issue as of August 2005. An IMT is currently examining 62 claims that pre-date the regulation changes. The IMT is partnering with other IRS functions and external stakeholders to develop a resolution strategy that will resolve open cases under Rev. Rule. 2005-53. No additional legislation or legal guidance is currently required. The new regulations remove the ambiguity for what qualifies as "self constructed assets" that led to the 62 taxpayer claims.

Issues Resulting From or Impacted by the American Jobs Creation Act

Section 199 Issues: This AJCA provision provides a deduction for certain manufacturing activities conducted in the United States. The section 199 deduction increases from 3% of qualified income during the first 2 years, to 6% for the next 3, and finally reaches 9% in 2010. Many difficult issues arise as a result of this complex section, some of which we are addressing in regulations that we will soon finalize. We are concerned, however, that mass-marketed, contingency fee-based refund claims will become a problem under section 199.

We have formed an IMT has been formed to address the many potential issues which may arise and are paying special attention to the potential challenges posed by different business types and industries in which taxpayers operate. We issued extensive guidance under section 199 : Notice 2005-14 in January 2005 and proposed regulations in October 2005. The IMT has regular communications with external stakeholder organizations and the Multi-State Tax Commission. It will use Information gathered on calendar year 2005 filings to determine audit selection and compliance risks and to create a Coordinated Issue Paper.

Foreign Earnings Repatriation (Sec. 965: This AJCA provision provides a limited window for companies to repatriate foreign earnings to the United States provided they satisfy certain requirements and conditions. Audit issues are likely to include compliance with board approved reinvestment plans, and the compliance of repatriated funds with regulatory requirements. Significant tax dollars are at stake. As of late 2005, 91 of the Standard and Poor's 500 had repatriated or planned to repatriate funds under this provision.

To address this issue, we have established a process to capture tax return information from 2005 tax returns filed by taxpayers claiming the benefits of this provision. The IMT formed for this issue has developed initial administrative guidance for field examiners to use for compliance checks of taxpayers claiming the benefit to ensure compliance. In 2005, we issued three pieces of published guidance regarding section 965d: Notice 2005-10; Notice 2005-38; and Notice 2005-64.

Executive Compensation (Sec. 409A): Section 409A was enacted as part of the AJCA. It provides that the executive or other service provider must include all deferred amounts under a nonqualified deferred compensation (NQDC) plan for all taxable years to the extent they are not subject to a substantial risk of forfeiture and not previously included in income, unless certain requirements are met. If the service provider does not meet these requirements, it will be taxed on the deferred amounts, and will owe an additional 20% tax and an additional tax based upon interest on the deferred tax. This issue crosses all industries. The "Estimated Budget Effects of the Conference Agreement for H.R. 4520" estimates the revenue impact for all taxpayers is approximately $1 billion for tax years 2005-2014. This issue is reflected on Schedule M-3.

While section 409A is effective for taxable years beginning on or after January 1, 2005, we have issued guidance that extends certain transition relief until December 31, 2006. Other transition relief provides that information reporting for 2005 will not be required until further guidance is issued. We have formed an IMT and most, if not all, of its activity is focused upon issuing final guidance for both the transition and post-transition periods. Guidance issued to date includes: Notice 2005-1 – December 20, 2004 (revised January 6, 2005); Proposed Regulations – September 30, 2004.

Tax Shelters and Other Abusive Tax Avoidance Transactions

One of the most significant compliance challenges facing us is the early identification of abusive transactions. In an effort to address this challenge, the Office of Tax Shelter Analysis (OTSA) continues its effort to identify and combat abusive tax shelters through analysis of Forms 8886 – Reportable Transaction Disclosure Statement filed by investors, and Forms 8264 – Application for Registration of a Tax Shelter filed by material advisors. We assigned for examination listed transactions identified on Form 8886s. We evaluate non-listed transactions identified on Form 8886s for emerging issues and other enforcement action as appropriate.

To effectively use the strengthened material advisor rules enacted in the AJCA, we are focusing more heavily on the Form 8264s in order to identify promoted transactions as early as possible. Analysis of transactions at the time of implementation better enables us to develop a position and take preemptive measures to address any abuse.

To address abusive transactions more quickly, we have implemented a new emerging issue process. The new process, while still under refinement, will expedite the assembly of an IMT to more effectively develop our position with the goal of getting ahead of abusive transactions before returns are filed claiming inappropriate benefits.

LMSB continues to allocate resources to abusive transactions as a top priority. LMSB initiatives such as settlement agreements or Appeals Settlement Guidelines have helped us address these transactions, resulting in billions of dollars in collected taxes, interest, and penalties. In addition to recapturing lost revenues, targeting abusive transactions produces favorable returns on investment relative to other populations of returns, and should reduce future non-compliance by deterring repetition. We do not believe this effort is over, and continue to look for ways to better leverage the enhanced reporting rules and penalties under AJCA to help us in identifying new transactions.

III. Tax Policy Issues and IRS Focus Areas for Discussion of Reform

To effectively address the compliance challenges of globalization, the complexity of the Code and modern business transactions, and the growing book-tax gap, we need support and perhaps new legislation that will improve our ability to effectively administer the Code. Several tax policy issues and focus areas are briefly described below.

Book-Tax Differences

We think the Senate Finance Committee should examine the increase in book-tax differences in greater depth in order to fully understand its impact on compliance. Such a review might reveal opportunities to eliminate some of the book-tax non-conformity.

We believe that some reduction in the number of book-tax differences could help to improve compliance. As is readily seen from the attached chart depicting the growth in book-tax differences, book-tax differences will require the use of a growing percentage our resources to enforce tax compliance. Efforts to address book-tax differences could eliminate many potential compliance issues that stem from the tension to increase reportable financial statement profits while decreasing taxable income and tax liabilities. There are many book-tax differences specifically established by the Code that are temporary differences by nature. A meaningful reduction in the number and size of temporary book-tax differences might reduce compliance risk overall and, to a large degree, the amount of resources we spend in policing those differences. Resources relieved could focus more effectively on compliance enforcement areas related to permanent loss of revenue.

Other Tax Policy Issues and IRS Focus Areas for Discussion of Reform

Tax Administration Support Needed for R&E Credit Claims: The R&E credit should be made permanent. Recordkeeping and substantiation requirements need to be more comprehensive to improve our ability to effectively administer the Code for R & E credit refund claims. These claims continue to have a substantial adverse effect on compliance and produce substantial administrative burdens. The temporary nature of the credit, its repeated renewals, and its incremental nature each contribute to these difficulties. In addition, the credit's structure raises a number of technical issues, such as, defining what is "qualified research" and the "costs" that qualify for the credit. While these problems may be alleviated to a degree by additional regulatory guidance or legislation to clarify or resolve some interpretative issues, we believe that absent substantial simplification in the structure of the credit itself and a targeted penalty provision aimed at frivolous or negligent assertions of qualified research expenditure credit claims, substantial non-compliance will continue in this area. Issues involving one aspect or another of the R&E credit constitute a high portion of chief counsel's significant case litigation inventory.

The IRS and Treasury are currently working on a number of guidance projects to improve application and administration of the R&E credit. These projects include: internal use software; gross receipts for purposes of the research credit computation; computation and allocation of the research credit for controlled groups; and section 174 depreciable property for purposes of the research credit.

Penalties are Needed for Improper Refund Claims: The accuracy related penalties in the Code apply only in the case of an underpayment of tax and provide no disincentive to taxpayers who file frivolous or negligent claims for refund. We believe this encourages promoters, including accounting firms, to market improper refund of claims schemes. The Finance Committee could consider how the accuracy-related penalty could be expanded to cover abusive refund claims.

Improved Summons Enforcement Process: Improved summons enforcement processes are needed to increase the effectiveness of summonses and reduce resources and time needed for enforcement. The current process requires us to issue a summons and, if it is not complied with, to seek to enforce it in the Federal District Court using the Court's contempt power. This is time consuming and expensive to the Government and puts a burden on the District Courts. The Finance Committee could consider addressing this problem through revisions to the rules imposing sanctions against taxpayers who make improper objections to, or fail to properly respond to a summons, or through enactment of a streamlined process in which to seek enforcement of a summons.

I would be happy to discuss the above concepts and policy issues with the Senate Finance Committee or members of its staff, at your convenience. Please call Floyd Williams at (202) 622-3720, if you would like to discuss these issues.

Thank you for the opportunity to highlight what we believe to be our greatest compliance challenges. We look forward to working with the Committee on problems in the Large and Mid-Size Business community and exploring ways to better equip us to deal with these problems. I am also writing to Senator Baucus.

If you have any questions, please contact me or call or Deborah Nolan, LMSB Commissioner, at (202) 283-8710.

Sincerely,

Mark W. Everson

Book-Tax Income Difference Measures

- Two Measures of Book Income
  - Worldwide Pre-Tax Income from Compustat (Net of State and Other Income Tax Expenses)
  - Pre-Tax Income from Form 1120, Schedule M-1 (Lines 1 + 2)
- Relative to Net Taxable Income (Form 1120, Line 28)

Worldwide Income Differences ($ Billions)

Category	1995	1996	1997	1998	1999	2000	2001	2002
Worldwide Income								
Total	79.0	94.2	98.1	134.4	194.0	214.1	121.3	203.8
LMSB Industry								
Financial Services	12.0	13.3	22.4	41.4	52.3	44.6	28.4	46.9
Natural Resources	7.8	16.6	16.7	8.1	20.6	32.0	41.8	24.9
Comm, Tech. & Media	13.3	18.7	16.2	21.7	64.8	76.7	5.0	42.7
Retail, Food, Pharm & Health	17.8	26.9	25.3	31.3	28.7	41.2	37.5	58.2
Heavy Manufact. & Transp.	27.8	17.9	16.5	30.6	26.1	17.7	6.1	27.7
Global Character								
Domestic	5.0	8.0	9.8	7.4	9.8	14.1	15.6	13.8
Multinational	74.0	86.2	88.3	127.1	184.3	200.0	105.7	189.9
Profitability								
Net Inc>0	66.5	75.7	71.1	103.7	149.7	155.8	141.5	159.1
Net Inc<=0	12.5	18.6	27.0	30.8	44.3	58.4	-20.1	44.7

Worldwide Book & Tax Income (All Firms)

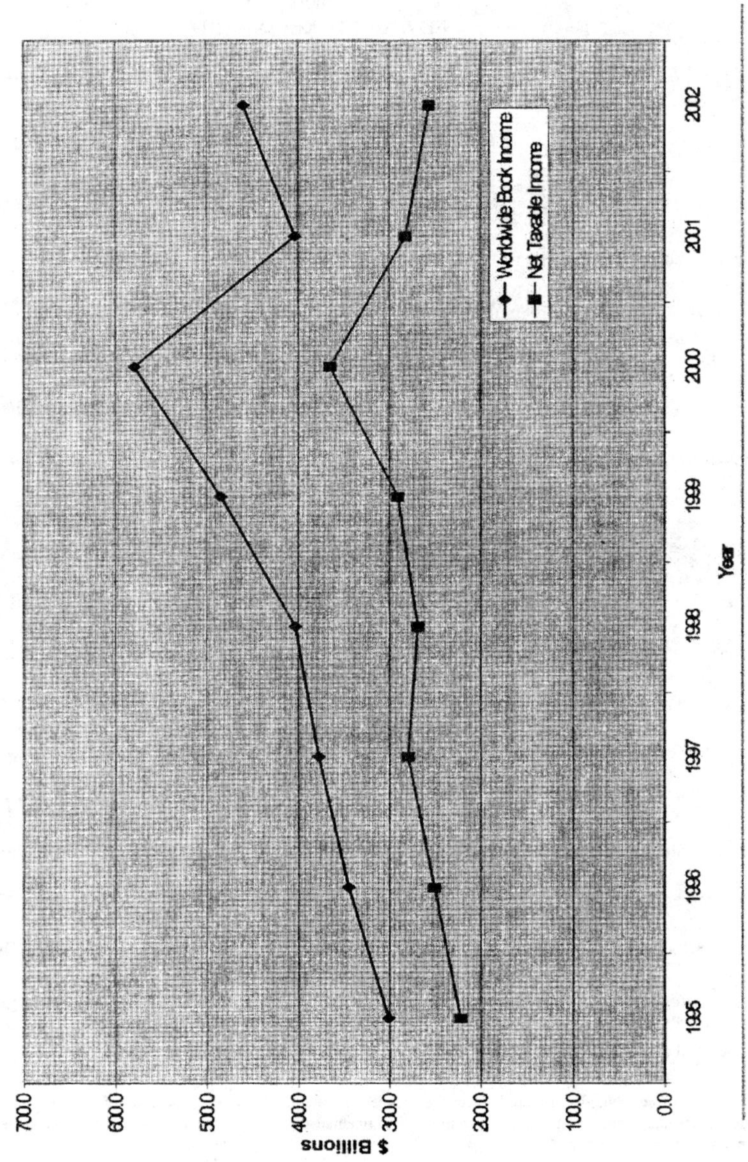

TESTIMONY OF
EDWARD D. KLEINBARD
CLEARY GOTTLIEB STEEN & HAMILTON LLP
BEFORE THE COMMITTEE ON FINANCE
UNITED STATES SENATE
JUNE 13, 2006

Chairman Grassley, Ranking Member Baucus, and members of the Committee, thank you for inviting me to testify on the advisability of public disclosure of U.S. corporate federal income tax returns. While I am a lawyer in private practice with the firm of Cleary Gottlieb Steen and Hamilton LLP, my testimony today grows out of my personal work in the public interest to improve our federal business tax system, and does not represent the views of my firm or its clients.

In brief, I believe that there are strong policy and practical reasons *not* to mandate the public disclosure of the entirety of corporate tax returns. On the other hand, I believe that there is a completely persuasive case for requiring public companies to release to the public their consolidated Schedule M-3's — a new IRS schedule first adopted for 2004 tax returns, the purpose of which is to reconcile a corporation's financial statement and taxable incomes.[1]

The M-3 can be understood as a relatively simple Rosetta Stone that maps the relationship between a corporation's financial statements, on the one hand, and its taxable income and tax balance sheet, on the other. The Schedule M-3 divides a corporation's income and deductions into 30 or so categories, and then requires the taxpayer to reconcile the amount in each category for tax purposes with the comparable amount attributable to that category for financial statement purposes.

---

1 For convenience, I include in my references to Schedule M-3 the revised Schedule L as well; the former is an income statement reconciliation, and the latter a balance sheet reconciliation that relies on the same basic reconciliation principles.

Don't Mandate the Release of the Entirety of Corporate Tax Returns.

A very recent IRS News Release describing its corporate tax return e-filing program revealed that General Electric's 2005 tax return was the electronic equivalent of a 24,000 page document.[2] I hope that the IRS knows what to do with those 24,000 pages; I am reasonably confident, by contrast, that no public investor, securities analyst or policy expert would. Making such a return public thus would sacrifice the confidentiality of a taxpayer's commercial information for very little benefit to the public. In fact, the only group that I can see that would benefit from the public release of tax returns of similar heft conceivably might be competitors; in theory, they could invest the resources required to develop systems to mine the data contained in such returns to discover important information relating to a corporation's strategic and budgetary decisions.

For these reasons, I believe that this Committee ought not to pursue the idea of requiring a corporation to release to the public all or substantially all of its federal income tax return. The Schedule M-3, however, is different, both in its size, in its lack of confidential commercial data, and in the utility of the information its public release would convey to investors and policymakers alike.

Investors Will Directly Benefit From Public M-3's

U.S. financial statement accounting principles and the Internal Revenue Code have similar objectives — to measure the changes in a corporation's financial results and condition from period to period — but operate largely independently of each other. As such, financial accounting principles and the federal income tax system are rival models that each

---

2 IR-2006-84 (May 31, 2006), reprinted 2006 TNT 105-5.

attempt to describe the entirety of private economic activity. Each model in turn is conditioned by decades of its own internal history and its responses to different external pressures.

Before the Schedule M-3, the IRS was accustomed to reviewing a corporation's financial results almost entirely through the prism of its federal income tax return.[3] Now that the Schedule M-3 has been developed, the IRS for the first time can see a corporation's financial performance with binocular vision. In other words, by pondering the sources of any differences between financial statement and taxable income, and the underlying transactions from which those differences spring, the IRS can more easily develop an accurate perception of the three-dimensional reality of a company's economic performance and tax profile, and thereby tailor its audit examination of the company accordingly.

Similarly, investors and policymakers today are conditioned to view the financial performance of publicly-held corporations solely through the prism of financial accounting conventions, and corporate managers of course manage with a view to achieving financial accounting targets. In the absence of any other viewpoint, investors and managers alike often confuse a corporation's financial statements with the underlying economic reality that those accounting principles seek to model: that is, they treat the model as if it were reality.

Investors deserve the same sort of stereoscopic insights into public companies' performances that the IRS now enjoys. The public disclosure of the Schedule M-3's of publicly-held companies would permit just that.[4] At the same time, the public release of a public

---

[3] I have previously described the inadequacies of the Schedule M-3's predecessor, the Schedule M-1, in "Disclosing Book-Tax Differences," 96 *Tax Notes* 999 (August 12, 2002).

[4] Technically, a corporation must file as part of its federal income tax return a separate Schedule M-3 for every subsidiary in its group. I envision, however, that public companies would be required to disclose only a single consolidated Schedule M-3 at the parent company level, because that consolidated schedule would correspond with the consolidated GAAP financial statements to which investors have access.

company's Schedule M-3 (which, after all, is just a set of relatively high level book-tax reconciliation information by category of income and expense) should not expose that company to the risk of revealing proprietary commercial information to competitors — especially when compared to the geographic and business segment information already available to the public in SEC filings. Similarly (and certainly with the development of appropriate headings), publicly-available Schedule M-3's should not cause investor confusion or reasonably be mistaken for some alternative means of reporting financial results. The public release of the consolidated Schedule M-3 thus would not expose material proprietary *commercial* information to public scrutiny, but would still have direct and material *financial* benefits for investors.

Investors today do not enjoy the more nuanced understanding of corporate financial results that the Schedule M-3 would provide. In addition, they know shockingly little about the cash tax liabilities of public corporations, because the financial statement "current" tax liability provision is not equivalent to cash taxes paid and payable in respect of that year. Corporations today often reflect in their financial statement tax provisions reserves for "contingent" tax liabilities — that is, the expected cost of resolving ongoing or anticipated disputes with tax authorities. The existence of these reserves, and the relatively subjective standards applicable to setting them (and releasing them), at least theoretically present a possible opportunity for earnings management. More generally, in the absence of any transparency on tax matters, investors have no ability to question how tax practices and behavior might affect the quality of corporate earnings.

To address these points, I recommend that the release of public corporations' Schedule M-3's be accompanied by a simple reconciliation of cash taxes paid to a company's tax provision.[5] The combined public disclosure of the consolidated Schedule M-3 and the accompanying reconciliation schedule of cash taxes paid to the financial statement current tax provision would permit investors to bring stereoscopic vision to bear on corporate financial performance, would reduce any potential for corporate earnings management through the timing of additions to, and releases from, tax reserves, and would permit a more pointed analysis of the quality of a company's tax expenses and appetite for tax risk.[6] These are powerful reasons to proceed with the idea.

<u>Public M-3's Will Modestly Help Tax Administration.</u>

The public release of Schedule M-3's also can be expected to have a modestly helpful impact on curbing corporate tax shelter activities. The development of the M-3 of course was an enormously important step forward for the administration of the corporate tax system. In fact, in my view, it was the most important innovation in corporate tax compliance in the last decade or more. But the direct beneficiary of this development — the IRS — does not need public disclosure in order to reap the benefits of using the Schedule M-3 to perform more targeted audit examinations of corporate taxpayers.

Nonetheless, at the margin, Schedule M-3 disclosure might dampen some corporate enthusiasm for tax shelter transactions. The Schedule M-3 in fact requires a corporate taxpayer to list each "Reportable Transaction" in which it has engaged. The public release of the consolidated Schedule M-3 thus might make plain to investors that the source of a company's enhanced after-tax earnings was the wholesale pursuit of aggressive tax trades, and managers in

---

5 The Schedule M-3 does not contain such a reconciliation table because the IRS already has the information: the IRS knows the cash taxes paid by a corporation from the face of its return.

6 I understand that FASB currently is considering requiring a similar reconciliation schedule that would show changes from period to period in a corporation's tax contingency reserve, to be effective as of 2007. My understanding, however, is that FASB has not yet adopted this proposal as a final rule.

turn might therefore become less interested in following such strategies. By the same token, the public release of the M-3 also should make more apparent those cases, like that of Enron, where corporations design complex structures to hold assets "off balance sheet" that they simultaneously view as owned by themselves for tax purposes. In practice, however, the principal importance of the M-3 in the battle against corporate tax shelters is the information that the M-3 already provides to the IRS, not the information its public release might offer investors.

Public M-3's Will Improve the Quality of Tax and Accounting Systems as a Whole.

The final reason to release the Schedule M-3's of publicly-held companies is the benefits that public release of the Schedule will have to the tax and financial accounting systems as a whole, and to citizens' understanding of the tax burdens that many corporations shoulder. Many policymakers today are troubled by the fact that the gap between corporate pre-tax financial statement income and taxable income as reported to the IRS exceeded $200 billion in 2002 (the most recent year for which data was available). Some of these policymakers believe that this gap can only be explained by substantial and as yet undetected corporate tax shelter activity (a belief that, I at least, do not share). Other observers, by contrast, are concerned that releasing the Schedule M-3's of publicly-held companies will create opportunities for random public flagellations of corporations that have done nothing wrong, because there are many logical and harmless reasons why taxable income can diverge from financial statement income.

These conflicting perspectives in fact coexist because of a single underlying fact, which is that *no one knows* all the sources of this $200 billion book-tax earnings gap.[7] If the Schedule M-3's of publicly-held companies were available to the public, the current collective

---

[7] Desai, "The Divergence Between Book and Tax Income," in J. Poterba, ed., *Tax Policy and the Economy* (17), 169-206 (MIT Press 2003).

uncertainty as to the reasons for the book-tax earnings gap would dissipate. We could replace wild suppositions about the source of book-tax earnings differences with actual facts, susceptible of being cataloged and analyzed, and citizens would have a fair picture of how and why corporate taxable incomes differ from financial statement earnings.

Armed with hard information, the designers and maintainers of each rival model (financial accounting and tax) in turn might learn something from the other. That is, there is nothing necessarily wrong with the financial statement income of any particular industry regularly exceeding its aggregate taxable income, but that fact might lead this Committee, for example, as one of the institutions responsible for maintaining the U.S. tax system, to review whether current tax law accurately captures the industry's annual economic results — or, just as legitimately, that fact might lead FASB to review whether current financial accounting standards might not be the model that is in need of an overhaul.

Good quality data derived from publicly-available Schedule M-3's about book-tax differences thus would enable academics and the maintainers of each system (financial statement and tax) to revisit whether one model or the other might require *recalibration*. Fresh vantage points will lead to increased perspective, and with that better vision will come greater insight into how to capture all the complexity of modern economic activity in both financial income statements and tax returns.

SCHEDULE M-3 (Form 1120)

Department of the Treasury
Internal Revenue Service

Net Income (Loss) Reconciliation for Corporations With Total Assets of $10 Million or More

▶ Attach to Form 1120.
▶ See separate instructions.

OMB No. 1545-0123

2005

Name of corporation (common parent, if consolidated return) | Employer identification number

Part I Financial Information and Net Income (Loss) Reconciliation

1a Did the corporation file SEC Form 10-K for its income statement period ending with or within this tax year?
☐ **Yes.** Skip lines 1b and 1c and complete lines 2a through 11 with respect to that SEC Form 10-K.
☐ **No.** Go to line 1b.
b Did the corporation prepare a certified audited income statement for that period?
☐ **Yes.** Skip line 1c and complete lines 2a through 11 with respect to that income statement.
☐ **No.** Go to line 1c.
c Did the corporation prepare an income statement for that period?
☐ **Yes.** Complete lines 2a through 11 with respect to that income statement.
☐ **No.** Skip lines 2a through 3c and enter the corporation's net income (loss) per its books and records on line 4.

2a Enter the income statement period: Beginning ____/____/____ Ending ____/____/____
b Has the corporation's income statement been restated for the income statement period on line 2a?
☐ **Yes.** (If "Yes," attach an explanation and the amount of each item restated.)
☐ **No.**
c Has the corporation's income statement been restated for any of the five income statement periods preceding the period on line 2a?
☐ **Yes.** (If "Yes," attach an explanation and the amount of each item restated.)
☐ **No.**
3a Is any of the corporation's voting common stock publicly traded?
☐ **Yes.**
☐ **No.** If "No," go to line 4.
b Enter the symbol of the corporation's primary U.S. publicly traded voting common stock . . . ☐☐☐☐☐
c Enter the nine-digit CUSIP number of the corporation's primary publicly traded voting common stock . . . ☐☐☐☐☐☐☐☐☐

4	Worldwide consolidated net income (loss) from income statement source identified in Part I, line 1	4	
5a	Net income from nonincludible foreign entities (attach schedule) . . .	5a	( )
b	Net loss from nonincludible foreign entities (attach schedule and enter as a positive amount) . .	5b	
6a	Net income from nonincludible U.S. entities (attach schedule) . . .	6a	( )
b	Net loss from nonincludible U.S. entities (attach schedule and enter as a positive amount) . . .	6b	
7a	Net income of other includible corporations (attach schedule) . . .	7a	
b	Net loss of other includible corporations (attach schedule) . . .	7b	( )
8	Adjustment to eliminations of transactions between includible corporations and nonincludible entities (attach schedule) . . .	8	
9	Adjustment to reconcile income statement period to tax year (attach schedule) . . .	9	
10	Other adjustments to reconcile to amount on line 11 (attach schedule) . . .	10	
11	**Net income (loss) per income statement of includible corporations.** Combine lines 4 through 10 . . .	11	

Schedule M-3 (Form 1120) 2005 Page **2**

Name of corporation (common parent, if consolidated return)	Employer identification number
If consolidated return, check applicable box: (1) ☐ Consolidated group (2) ☐ Parent corporation (3) ☐ Consolidated eliminations (4) ☐ Subsidiary corporation	
Name of subsidiary (if consolidated return)	Employer identification number

Part II **Reconciliation of Net Income (Loss) per Income Statement of Includible Corporations With Taxable Income per Return**

	Income (Loss) Items	(a) Income (Loss) per Income Statement	(b) Temporary Difference	(c) Permanent Difference	(d) Income (Loss) per Tax Return
1	Income (loss) from equity method foreign corporations				
2	Gross foreign dividends not previously taxed				
3	Subpart F, QEF, and similar income inclusions				
4	Section 78 gross-up				
5	Gross foreign distributions previously taxed				
6	Income (loss) from equity method U.S. corporations				
7	U.S. dividends not eliminated in tax consolidation				
8	Minority interest for includible corporations				
9	Income (loss) from U.S. partnerships (attach schedule)				
10	Income (loss) from foreign partnerships (attach schedule)				
11	Income (loss) from other pass-through entities (attach schedule)				
12	Items relating to reportable transactions (attach details)				
13	Interest income				
14	Total accrual to cash adjustment				
15	Hedging transactions				
16	Mark-to-market income (loss)				
17	Cost of goods sold				
18	Sale versus lease (for sellers and/or lessors)				
19	Section 481(a) adjustments				
20	Unearned/deferred revenue				
21	Income recognition from long-term contracts				
22	Original issue discount and other imputed interest				
23a	Income statement gain/loss on sale, exchange, abandonment, worthlessness, or other disposition of assets other than inventory and pass-through entities				
23b	Gross capital gains from Schedule D, excluding amounts from pass-through entities				
23c	Gross capital losses from Schedule D, excluding amounts from pass-through entities, abandonment losses, and worthless stock losses				
23d	Net gain/loss reported on Form 4797, line 17, excluding amounts from pass-through entities, abandonment losses, and worthless stock losses				
23e	Abandonment losses				
23f	Worthless stock losses (attach details)				
23g	Other gain/loss on disposition of assets other than inventory				
24	Disallowed capital loss in excess of capital gains				
25	Utilization of capital loss carryforward				
26	Other income (loss) items with differences (attach schedule)				
27	**Total income (loss) items.** Combine lines 1 through 26				
28	**Total expense/deduction items** (from Part III, line 36)				
29	Other income (loss) and expense/deduction items with no differences				
30	**Reconciliation totals.** Combine lines 27 through 29				

Note. Line 30, column (a), must equal the amount on Part I, line 11, and column (d) must equal Form 1120, page 1, line 28.

Name of corporation (common parent, if consolidated return) | Employer identification number

If consolidated return, check applicable box: (1) ☐ Consolidated group (2) ☐ Parent corporation (3) ☐ Consolidated eliminations (4) ☐ Subsidiary corporation

Name of subsidiary (if consolidated return) | Employer identification number

Part III **Reconciliation of Net Income (Loss) per Income Statement of Includible Corporations With Taxable Income per Return—Expense/Deduction Items**

	Expense/Deduction Items	(a) Expense per Income Statement	(b) Temporary Difference	(c) Permanent Difference	(d) Deduction per Tax Return
1	U.S. current income tax expense				
2	U.S. deferred income tax expense				
3	State and local current income tax expense				
4	State and local deferred income tax expense				
5	Foreign current income tax expense (other than foreign withholding taxes)				
6	Foreign deferred income tax expense				
7	Foreign withholding taxes				
8	Interest expense				
9	Stock option expense				
10	Other equity-based compensation				
11	Meals and entertainment				
12	Fines and penalties				
13	Judgments, damages, awards, and similar costs				
14	Parachute payments				
15	Compensation with section 162(m) limitation				
16	Pension and profit-sharing				
17	Other post-retirement benefits				
18	Deferred compensation				
19	Charitable contribution of cash and tangible property				
20	Charitable contribution of intangible property				
21	Charitable contribution limitation/carryforward				
22	Domestic production activities deduction				
23	Current year acquisition or reorganization investment banking fees				
24	Current year acquisition or reorganization legal and accounting fees				
25	Current year acquisition/reorganization other costs				
26	Amortization/impairment of goodwill				
27	Amortization of acquisition, reorganization, and start-up costs				
28	Other amortization or impairment write-offs				
29	Section 198 environmental remediation costs				
30	Depletion				
31	Depreciation				
32	Bad debt expense				
33	Corporate owned life insurance premiums				
34	Purchase versus lease (for purchasers and/or lessees)				
35	Other expense/deduction items with differences (attach schedule)				
36	**Total expense/deduction items.** Combine lines 1 through 35. Enter here and on Part II, line 28				

August 1, 2006

Responses to Written Questions for the Record Posed by Chairman Charles Grassley

On June 13, 2006, I testified before the Senate Committee on Finance at its hearing titled "A Tune-Up On Corporate Tax Issues: What's Going On Under the Hood?" This document contains my responses to written questions for the record posed to me by Chairman Grassley following that hearing.

Edward D. Kleinbard

I. QUESTIONS RELATING TO BOOK-TAX CONFORMITY.

1. *Are there any guideposts or factors that you would recommend that we keep in mind with respect to book-tax conformity as we begin discussions about tax reform? That is, are there clear guidelines for when conformity or non-conformity is the right answer?*

I cannot point to clear guidelines for determining when book-tax conformity is the right answer for our income tax system. The fundamental problem, as I discussed in my testimony, is that financial accounting standards and the Internal Revenue Code are two rival models for describing all of economic activity; we cannot simply take a module from one such model and import it to the other without careful consideration of that module's context and purpose in each model. Each model can usefully illuminate some of the express or unconscious assumptions of the other (that, after all, is one of the principal purposes of the Schedule M-3), but the fact that we gain useful perspective by viewing each model from the vantage point of the other does not necessarily mean that we will improve the tax model by the wholesale importation of financial accounting rules.

Nonetheless, there are a few small suggestions that can be made. First, in those circumstances in which the tax and financial accounting rules are attempting to accomplish precisely the same goal, there are significant advantages in terms of both tax compliance costs and tax administrative efficiency for the tax rules to piggyback on financial accounting standards. Second, as the sorry state of LIFO book-tax conformity demonstrates,[1] Congress should be very careful about using conformity with financial accounting principles as an artificial governor on taxpayers' willingness to adopt taxpayer-favorable rules. And finally, as demonstrated by the much happier story of "mark-to-market" accounting by securities dealers (and others) as required (or permitted) under section 475, "book-tax" conformity in fact can lead to positive reinforcement in taxpayer behavior and robust tax accounting standards in those cases where the underlying conformity is not simply an artificially imposed identity between "book" and "tax" accounting, but rather a conformity of both "book" and "tax" accounting to the accounting method employed in *non-tax commercial decisionmaking.* In this latter case, the

---

[1] See, in this regard, my answer to Question for the Record 6 posed to me by Senator Baucus, to which I responded in a memorandum dated July 14, 2006.

critical inquiry is to demonstrate that firm management in fact relies on the relevant accounting method to make purely commercial decisions.

II. QUESTIONS RELATING TO TRANSFER PRICING AND INTERNATIONAL TAX COMPLIANCE.

2. *Commissioner Everson identified tax issues associated with transfer pricing generally, and the transfer of intangible assets outside the United States in particular, as high-risk compliance concerns. Mr. Walker noted that the deferral of income of controlled foreign corporations is the second largest corporate tax expenditure in our tax code. The principle of deferral serves to enable U.S. multinationals to remain competitive with foreign-based multinationals, who are often subject to tax on a territorial basis.*

a. Do you agree that transfer pricing issues generally, and transfer pricing issues with respect to intangible property in particular, are at or near the top of the list of challenges to the administration of our tax system?

I agree that transfer pricing issues, in particular those associated with intangibles, are at the top of the list of challenges to the administration of the international tax provisions of the Code. That observation is consistent as an anecdotal matter with the issues that I see in private practice. More usefully to your Committee, that observation also is consistent with objective data.

In a very recent and sophisticated paper, Dr. Harry Grubert of the U.S. Treasury Department and Prof. Rosanne Altshuler of Rutgers University (and formerly on the staff of the President's Advisory Panel on Federal Tax Reform) considered in detail the role of intangibles in cross-border transfer pricing.[2] Paraphrasing the work of this academic study (hopefully without excessive violence to the authors' intent), Dr. Grubert and Prof. Altshuler concluded that:

- The exportation of intangible assets has been a "significant source" of foreign direct investment income; royalties and license fee income received by U.S. companies *tripled* from 1990 to 2004.[3]
- At the same time, and directly relevant to your inquiry, royalties paid by foreign subsidiaries to U.S. parent companies "represent *less than half* of the contribution that parent R&D makes to subsidiary income."[4]
- The data suggest that low-tax countries "are becoming much more important destinations for U.S. produced intangible assets;" in this connection, "the share of

---

2 Grubert & Altshuler, *Corporate Taxes in the World Economy: Reforming the Taxation of Cross-Border Income*, presented at the Baker Institute for Public Policy on Apr. 27, 2006, *available at* http://bakerinstitute.org/events/event01_27apr06.html (hereinafter "*Grubert and Altshuler*").

3 *Id.* at 9.

4 *Id.* at 10 (emphasis supplied).

total affiliate royalties accounted for by Ireland and Singapore doubled between 1994 and 1999."[5]

- "[P]re-tax profits in relation to sales are almost three times higher in Ireland on average than the group mean. These 'excess' profits presumably reflect the fact that very valuable intellectual property is located in Ireland and the royalties paid back to the United States, while significant, do not fully reflect its contribution."[6]

An important *Wall Street Journal* article from November 2005 gives life to these dry statistics by describing in detail Microsoft's use of "cost-sharing agreements" with an Irish subsidiary to develop and exploit Microsoft's core intellectual property.[7] According to that article, Round Island One, Microsoft's intellectual property holding company in Ireland, earned nearly $9 billion in gross profits in 2004, and roughly $2.4 billion in taxable income, by exploiting intangible assets to which it acquired ownership by virtue of its cost-sharing agreements with its U.S. parent.[8]

To be clear, I do not mean to suggest that Microsoft's arrangements with its Irish subsidiary violate the requirements of the extensive Treasury arm's-length transfer pricing regulations governing cost-sharing agreements. That is the purpose of the IRS examination process, to which I am a complete outsider. I do think it fair, however, to point to the *Wall Street Journal* article, and the academic paper discussed above, to illustrate the magnitude of the issue, and its importance to tax administration.

I also believe it fair to draw from all of the above the inference that the Internal Revenue Service is shouldering a near-impossible burden in this area, for two reasons. First, the accurate valuation by outsiders of intangible assets like Microsoft's proprietary "crown jewel" software is nearly impossible, because the assets themselves are incredibly complex, and because in practice genuinely comparable third-party transactions almost never exist. (That is, major software companies rarely enter into cost-sharing agreements with third parties to develop new versions of their crown jewel intangible assets.) Yet the Treasury arm's-length transfer pricing cost-sharing regulations require just such an inquiry.

Second, the entire premise of our transfer pricing rules — that related parties should deal with each other for tax purposes at the prices and on the terms at which third parties would engage in comparable transactions — is unachievable, particularly when applied to high-value intangible assets held by multinational enterprises. There is abundant literature to support the proposition that multinational enterprises thrive in the world economy precisely because the

---

5 *Id.* at 18.

6 *Id.* at 26.

7 Glenn R. Simpson, *Irish Subsidiary Lets Microsoft Slash Taxes in U.S. and Europe*, Wall Street Journal, Nov. 7, 2005, at A1.

8 I derived the latter figure by grossing up Round Island's reported tax liability to Ireland of $300 million at the Irish tax rate of 12.5 percent. I ignored in this calculation the $17 million that the *Wall Street Journal* reported that Round Hill paid in tax to other European countries (presumably through withholding taxes). If, as I believe to be the case, those payments were creditable in Ireland, Round Hill's taxable income actually would have slightly exceeded $2.5 billion in 2004.

economy is increasingly global, and because multinational enterprises can muster *tightly integrated* global resources to take advantage of that fact.[9] The paradigmatic example of the integrated global strategies of modern multinational enterprises, of course, is the worldwide exploitation of a common pool of high-value intangible assets.

"Arm's-length" transfer pricing tends to deny (or perhaps misallocate) the synergies that flow directly from the globally integrated activities that explain the success of multinational enterprises in the first place. As applied to intangible assets, arm's-length transfer pricing requires us to pretend that a multinational group does not in practice control a single common pool of intangible assets with worldwide application, but rather comprises essentially independent enterprises negotiating with each other as if trade barriers to the direct global exploitation of those intangible assets still existed.

As a result, the arm's-length transfer pricing principle at its core presupposes a business model that is fundamentally inconsistent with the business strategies of multinational enterprises that possess high-value and globally relevant intangible assets. When the tax model that we have created is so fundamentally agonistic to business realities, the administration of the tax system can never be wholly successful.

b. *How would changing to a territorial system affect (i) the prominence of transfer pricing issues in the U.S. tax system; and (ii) the competitiveness of U.S. multinationals?*

(i). I believe that changing to a territorial tax system would greatly exacerbate the importance of transfer pricing issues. The reason is simple. Under current law, the principal "reward" for successfully gaming our transfer pricing rules is the accumulation of profits in a foreign subsidiary, presumably located in a low-tax jurisdiction.[10] To collect this "reward," however, a U.S. firm must keep those earnings offshore. *Territorial tax systems, by contrast, reward successful transfer pricing gamers as "instant winners"* by enabling the successful U.S. firm immediately to recycle its offshore profits as tax-exempt dividends paid to the U.S. parent.[11]

---

9 See, in this regard, Impact of International Tax Reform on U.S. Competitiveness: Hearings Before the Subcomm. on Select Revenue Measures of the H. Comm. on Ways and Means, 109th Cong. (2006) (Testimony of Dean R. Glenn Hubbard) (hereinafter "*Hubbard Testimony*") ("Multinationals are an intrinsic part of global integration because they represent an alternative means by which nations conduct cross-border transactions. That is, the economic costs of production, transportation, distribution, and final sale may be lower [if] conducted within a single firm than via a series of market transactions. Accordingly, the rise in global integration carries along with [it] an increased volume of transactions for which multinationals have a particular advantage.").

10 In addition, a U.S. parent company can employ a related strategy, under which it shelters from U.S. tax the zero-taxed royalty income from foreign subsidiaries paid to the U.S. parent company (and thereby not subject to deferral) with foreign tax credits arising from repatriating very high-taxed operating income from other foreign subsidiaries. *Grubert and Altshuler* describes this strategy in detail; that paper estimates that in 2000, royalties received by U.S. parent companies amounted to roughly $45 billion, but that roughly $30 billion of this amount was sheltered from tax by these foreign tax credit-blending strategies. *Grubert and Altshuler*, *supra* note 2, at 9-10.

11 It is true, as *Grubert and Altshuler* points out, that territorial tax systems disable the popular current strategy of blending zero-taxed foreign source royalties paid to the U.S. parent by foreign subsidiaries with high-taxed dividend income, to shelter those royalties from tax. *Grubert and Altshuler*, *supra* note 2, at 28-30. Without

This concern is widely shared, and has been identified as a topic of concern by the Staff of the Joint Committee on Taxation and other authors who have described or proposed possible territorial tax systems.[12] The principal difference between my views and those of these other observers is that they typically conclude that the administration of our existing arm's-length transfer pricing rules simply will require greater vigilance in a territorial tax system.[13] By contrast, for the reasons summarized in my answer to the preceding question, I believe that it is unrealistic to expect that enhanced administration can ever adequately address the transfer pricing challenge that modern tightly integrated multinational enterprises possessing high-value intangible assets would pose to a territorial tax system.

(ii). Your question also asks me to address the effect of switching to a territorial tax system on the competitiveness of U.S. multinational firms. The answer is surprisingly complex, and not at all intuitive.

At the outset, let me identify myself as someone who strongly believes that one goal of our international tax system should be to provide an environment in which U.S.-based multinational enterprises can compete on fair terms with multinational firms domiciled in other countries. In recent years, many observers have described how the rapid evolution of the global economy has compelled U.S. tax policymakers to become increasingly sensitive to issues of international competitiveness. For example, Glenn Hubbard, the Dean of the Columbia Business School and former Chairman of the President's Council of Economic Advisers, recently testified before the House Ways and Means Committee on precisely this topic. Dean Hubbard identified several important themes relating to the changing competitive landscape in his testimony, including the increasingly integrated nature of the global economy, the enormous rise in

---

considering any possible dynamic responses by U.S. multinational firms, the effect of a territorial tax system thus would be to *raise* the effective rate on the exploitation of intangible assets from low-taxed jurisdictions. *Id.* at 29.

One probable dynamic response by taxpayers to a territorial system would be to attempt to understate royalty payments owed to the U.S. parent by foreign subsidiaries. *Id.* at 30. In addition, cost-sharing agreements, in particular, do not ordinarily generate royalty payments to the U.S. parent company beyond any "buy-in" payments required from the foreign subsidiary. This means that, for companies that employ cost-sharing agreements, royalty payments to the United States should decline in relation to the value of the intangible assets that the foreign subsidiary owns outright with the passage of time. As royalties paid to the United States decline (in absolute or relative terms), a foreign subsidiary will be able to capture more profits over time as exempt active foreign income.

12 Staff of the Joint Committee on Taxation, *Options to Improve Tax Compliance and Reform Tax Expenditures*, JCS-02-05, at 195, n. 431 (Jan. 2005) (hereinafter "*JCT Staff I*") (noting that an "exemption system may place somewhat more pressure on [transfer pricing rules], thus making it somewhat more important to remedy existing defects in the design and administration of those rules."); President's Advisory Panel on Federal Tax Reform, *Simple, Fair, and Pro-Growth: Proposals to Fix America's Tax System*, at 242 (Nov. 2005) (hereinafter "*Tax Reform Panel Report*") (stating that "because pressures" to use transfer pricing to minimize taxable income "are more pronounced in a territorial system, it would be necessary to continue to devote resources to transfer pricing enforcement."); Peter Merrill et al., *Restructuring Foreign-Source Income Taxation: U.S. Territorial Tax Proposals and the International Experience*, 111 *Tax Notes* 799, 810 (2006) (arguing that that the incentive for transfer pricing gaming will become greater under territoriality); Michel J. Graetz & Paul W. Oosterhuis, *Structuring an Exemption System for Foreign Income of U.S. Corporations*, 44 Nat'l Tax J. 771, 772, 775 (2001) ("A simpler system would no doubt result if the transfer pricing rules…rather than an exclusion from income, could be relied on to constrain tax avoidance [on passive /highly mobile income]").

13 See note 12, supra.

international capital flows (which include cross-border portfolio investments), and the shift over the last several decades from the United States' role as the world's largest exporter of capital to its current status as the world's largest capital importer.[14]

Dean Hubbard rightly draws from these facts the conclusion that U.S. international tax policy norms from, say, 1962, do not necessarily serve the interests of the United States in 2006. The following questions remain, however: what principles should we adopt as our international tax policy norms in the new world economy? And, how can we measure different tax proposals against those norms?

It is the traditional practice in discussions of international tax policy choices to begin to address these questions by laying out the principle of "Capital Export Neutrality" — the principle that a U.S. multinational firm should face the same tax burden on a new investment wherever in the world that investment might be made — and the principle of "Capital Import Neutrality" — the principle that a U.S. multinational firm should bear the same tax when competing in a foreign market as its local competitors face.[15] To these can be added at least two other widely discussed "neutralities" — "National Neutrality" and "Capital Ownership Neutrality."[16]

The traditional discussion then goes on to demonstrate that it is not possible fully to satisfy both Capital Export Neutrality and Capital Import Neutrality simultaneously in the real world.[17] At the same time, most analysts acknowledge that, all other things being equal, maintaining capital export neutrality would be desirable, and by the same token so would maintaining capital import neutrality. Finally, every traditional discussion concludes by asserting that whatever policy is being proposed represents a fair balancing between these two irreconcilable objectives, in every case based largely on the author's preexisting intentions. No wonder our international tax policy is in a muddle!

In a refreshing break from this familiar presentation, *Grubert and Altshuler* implicitly concludes that the traditional "Battle of the Neutralities" (as I term the process) is an essentially sterile exercise that by itself cannot usefully guide this Committee or other tax policymakers in shaping the international tax policy norms of the United States. Instead, the authors of that paper urge policymakers to focus on the *behavioral distortions* among taxpayers (and, to a lesser extent, governments) that flow from current law, and to evaluate reform proposals by reference to their success in mitigating these distortions:

---

14 *Hubbard Testimony*, *supra* note 9. *See also* Impact of International Tax Reform on U.S. Competitiveness: Hearings Before the Subcomm. on Select Revenue Measures of the H. Comm. on Ways and Means , 109th Cong. (2006) (Testimony of Prof. Michael J. Graetz) (hereinafter "*Graetz Testimony*") (recognizing "integration of the world economy").

15 Staff of the Joint Committee on Taxation, *The Impact of International Tax Reform: Background and Selected Issues Relating to U.S. International Tax Rules and the Competitiveness of U.S. Businesses*, JCX-22-06, at 3, 5, 57-61. (June 2006).

16 *See, e.g.*, Mihir A. Desai and James R. Hines, Jr., *Old Rules and New Realities: Corporate Tax Policy in a Global Setting*, 57 Nat'l Tax J. 937 (2004).

17 *See, e.g., Michael J. Graetz, Taxing International Income: Inadequate Principles, Outdated Concepts and Unsatisfactory Policies*, 54 Tax L. Rev. 261, 272 (2001).

> [W]hat reform within an income tax can hope to accomplish is to eliminate unnecessary waste and the possibility of extremely high or low tax burdens that are not justified under any standard. Then we can at least be sure that we are moving toward the optimum without overshooting it and running the risk of making things worse.
>
> [I]nternational tax systems can act on many behavioral margins in addition to the choice of location. The current tax system induces a number of behavioral responses that both waste resources and lead to inappropriate incentives to invest tangible and intangible capital in various locations. These include strategies to avoid the U.S. repatriation tax on dividends, to shift debt from high-tax to low-tax locations, and to shift income to low-tax locations by distorting transfer prices or paying inadequate royalties. Besides directly wasting resources, these strategies can lead to inefficient choices between related party and arms' length transaction and a distribution of tangible and intangible assets that cannot be justified on any conceptual basis.
>
> In our evaluation of the distortions that may be eliminated by some of the reform proposals, we focus on how the proposals affect (1) the location of tangible capital, (2) the location of intangible capital, (3) the repatriation decision, (4) financing decisions, (5) income shifting, (6) incentives to lower foreign tax burdens, (7) export decisions and (8) host government decisions regarding the taxation of U.S. companies.[18]

I submit that reviewing the impact of current law or any tax reform proposal on the eight criteria listed immediately above is a far more productive exercise than continuing the sterile "Battle of the Neutralities" that has dominated much of the policy discussion to date.

As a final preliminary matter, it unfortunately is absolutely necessary in evaluating any international tax reform proposal to wade into the technical details of how that proposal will be implemented. It turns out that an international tax reform proposal must be *specified* and *analyzed* in detail, if one is to predict with any degree of accuracy how the behaviors of differently situated taxpayers will be affected by the proposal, and therefore what distortions in economic activity might follow.[19]

This is one small area where lawyers in private practice actually are at something of a comparative advantage to many tax economists, because their work for clients gives them good intuitions as to the effect that new tax rules will have on taxpayer behavior, when measured by reference to the criteria listed above, or how differently situated taxpayers can be encouraged by any set of tax rules to respond in different manners. For example, extensive dealing with the real world consequences of tax rules has taught practicing lawyers the critical importance of expense

---

18 *Grubert and Altshuler, supra* note 2, at 16 (enumeration in the last paragraph supplied by this author).

19 This, in effect, is the major theme of *Grubert and Altshuler*.

allocation, or how an elegant structural solution for a client that is habitually in an excess foreign tax credit position would be disastrous for a client in an "excess limitation" position.

With these preliminary observations completed, it is possible to turn to your question on the effect of territorial tax systems on the international competitiveness of U.S. multinational firms. The usual intuition is that territorial tax systems are the paradigmatic implementation of Capital Import Neutrality themes, and as such would greatly improve the competitiveness of U.S. multinationals. In fact, as I observed at the outset, the analysis is more complex than that, and the results not always consistent with this common intuition.

A territorial tax system unquestionably would improve the competitiveness of U.S. firms — or, more consistently with the basic analytic framework summarized above, would reduce distortions inherent in the current system — in one important respect, which is that it would eliminate the barriers to repatriation that current law imposes. As I observed earlier, a U.S. firm today must "earn" the tax benefit of deferral through patiently deploying its active foreign profits outside the United States, even if the highest and best use of those funds would be in a domestic application.[20]

As a result, current law encourages the wasteful accumulation of profits abroad, and in some cases the wasteful investment of those profits in the expansion or acquisition of "active" businesses, solely to preserve the continuing benefits of deferral. A territorial tax system eliminates tax considerations from the repatriation decision, and therefore removes these significant economic distortions of current law.

At the same time, a territorial tax system can stimulate less desirable taxpayer impulses, or introduce new forms of economic distortions, than those that exist under current law. One important example of these adverse phenomena is the increased pressures that our tax administration would face under a territorial tax system in respect of transfer pricing issues (particularly relating to high value intangibles), as described in the immediately preceding answer. The remainder of this answer considers some other, less obvious, issues raised by territorial tax systems, beginning with perhaps the most surprising one, which is the probable effect of a territorial tax system on effective tax rates.

In January, 2005, the Staff of the Joint Committee on Taxation (the "JCT Staff") proposed a comprehensive territorial tax system, described as a "dividend exemption" system.[21] The JCT Staff estimated that its territorial system would *raise* $55 billion in tax revenues over ten years. It is difficult to describe this proposal as self-evidently enhancing the competitiveness of U.S.-based multinational firms, if by that phrase one means a *reduction* in total tax burdens imposed on the income of U.S. multinationals.

---

20 The 2005 experience with the one-year 5.25% repatriation tax afforded by section 965 illustrates the magnitude of the issue: current estimates put the size of the one-year repatriation flows triggered by that section as in the neighborhood of $200 billion. *Grubert & Altshuler*, *supra* note 2, at 19. Another $100 billion is expected to be repatriated by the end of 2006. American Shareholders Association, *ASA Repatriation Scorecard* (Mar. 20, 2006), http://www.americanshareholders.com/news/asa-repats-03-20-06.pdf.

21 *JCT Staff I*, *Supra* note 12, at 189. The JCT Staff proposal in turn was said to be modeled on that of Harry Grubert & John Mutti, Taxing International Business Income: Dividend Exemption versus the Current System (2001).

Later in 2005, the President's Advisory Panel on Federal Tax Reform proposed a system similar in broad outline to the JCT Staff proposal, although with some differences in detail (particularly with respect to expense allocation rules).[22] No official revenue estimate accompanied that proposal. Most recently, *Grubert and Altshuler* acknowledges that switching to a territorial system would generate a small revenue gain, but that the revenue estimate was critically sensitive to possible behavioral responses that are very difficult to model.[23] That paper also summarizes earlier work that concluded that a territorial tax system would significantly *increase* the tax burden on investments in low-taxed foreign subsidiaries.[24]

There are two principal factors at work behind these surprising effective tax rate results. First, every territorial tax system that has been seriously studied in the United States to date has included a provision to allocate interest expense incurred in the United States, and in some cases other classes of domestic expenses, against foreign "exempt" income (which of course is not necessarily exempt in a global sense, and which may in fact have borne foreign tax at rates as high or higher than the U.S. rate).[25]

Some sort of sensible interest expense allocation rule, or some comparable provision (e.g., an efficacious "thin capitalization" rule that would prevent the overleveraging of U.S. operations) unquestionably is required in the context of a territorial foreign tax system, in order to protect the *domestic* tax base. In the absence of such a rule, U.S. firms would overleverage their U.S. operations to the point where they "zeroed out" their U.S. tax liability on their domestic operations, and would service that debt with tax-exempt (from the perspective of the United States) foreign source income. Similar arguments have been made in respect of other U.S. domestic expenses (e.g., "head office" general and administrative expenses, or domestic R&D expenditures), but there is less of a consensus on how these expenses should be treated.

The second principal reason why a territorial tax system can actually raise effective tax rates in some cases is that it eliminates a taxpayer's ability under current law to average down high-taxed foreign income with zero-taxed foreign royalty income (or low-taxed affiliate income). I liken the process to a master distiller blending a perfect tax liqueur, in which the blended product bears tax at precisely 35 percent, so that no residual U.S. tax is due, and no excess credits are generated.

---

22 For a comparison of the two proposals, and a rough revenue estimate for the Advisory Panel's package, consult Merrill, *supra* note 12, at 808-09.

23 *Grubert and Altschuler*, *supra* note 2, at 12.

24 *Id.* at 29. This observation leads to the conclusion, to paraphrase the dry humor of academic articles, that when applied to the lowest-taxed foreign affiliates, a territorial system actually is a step towards Capital *Export* Neutrality.

25 The interest expense allocation proposals in particular typically apply "worldwide" fungibility principles (as developed in the American Jobs Creation Act of 2004), thereby avoiding the logical errors of prior law's "water's-edge" approach, Daniel N. Shaviro, *Does More Sophisticated Mean Better? A Critique of Alternative Approaches to Sourcing the Interest Expense of U.S. Multinationals*, 54 Tax L. Rev. 353 (2001), but even worldwide fungibility can be criticized as significantly imperfect, because it does not treat foreign currency translation losses as, in effect, a component of worldwide interest expense.

More specifically, every territorial tax system that has been seriously studied in the United States would *not* exempt from tax royalty or interest income paid by a foreign subsidiary to its U.S. parent, on the theory that those amounts were deductible abroad, and that exempting them from U.S. tax thus would result in those amounts bearing tax nowhere in the world. Under current law, a U.S. parent company's stream of royalty or interest receipts from its foreign subsidiaries nominally also constitutes taxable income, but in fact the actual tax liability on those amounts is largely sheltered by the tax "master blender" at each company, who brings up sufficient high-taxed income from other foreign operations to shelter those income streams.

In a territorial system, by contrast, the royalty and interest income would be fully includible in income without offset for any tax credits attributable to exempt income. As a result, a firm's cask of exempt high-taxed income could not be blended with liqueur from a low-taxed cask in a way that would reduce the effective tax rate on the former.

It is for these sorts of reasons, I believe, that Stephen Shay, in his recent testimony before the House Ways and Means Committee on the theme of international competitiveness, suggested that U.S. multinationals today actually enjoy the best of all worlds.[26] In a similar vein, the National Foreign Trade Council in 2002 undertook a comprehensive review of territorial tax proposals on behalf of a wide range of U.S. multinational firms. That study concluded that the evidence did *not* unambiguously support the claim that a territorial tax system would enhance competitiveness:

> While it is true that a territorial system could improve competitiveness and simplicity for some U.S.-based companies with substantial operations abroad, the accompanying reduction in foreign tax credits attributable to exempt income could more than offset that benefit for other such companies. Moreover, the benefit for any significant group of companies would be dependent on the adoption of a broad exemption a cut back on the existing subpart F rules, and reform of the current expense allocation rules.[27]

It is ironic that some proponents of territoriality may be unaware that the current system often can be used to optimize a U.S. firm's global tax liabilities in ways that a territorial system cannot.

The previous few paragraphs focused on the complex and ambiguous effects of a well-designed territorial tax system (i.e., one with proper expense allocations or other mechanisms to safeguard the domestic tax base) on a U.S. multinational firm's worldwide effective tax burden. There are other important aspects of a territorial system, however, that might be viewed as anti-

---

[26] Impact of International Tax Reform on U.S. Competitiveness: Hearings Before the Subcomm. on Select Revenue Measures of the H. Comm. on Ways and Means, 109th Cong. (2006) (Testimony of Stephen E. Shay) Hubbard). The JCT Staff made a similar point in 2005: "[I]n many cases, the present-law 'worldwide' system actually may yield results that are more favorable to the taxpayer than the results available in similar circumstances under the 'territorial' exemption systems used by many U.S. trading parties . . ." *JCT Staff I, supra* note 12, at 189.

[27] National Foreign Trade Council, *NFTC Territorial Tax Study Report*, at 24 (2002), *available at* http://www.nftc.org/default/tax/Territorial%20Report.pdf (hereinafter "*NFTC Territorial Report*").

competitive — or, more accurately, as increasing distortions in behavior when measured against one or more of the eight criteria described above.

First, a territorial system can be expected to impose radically different tax burdens across different U.S. industries, largely as a result of different industry norms for debt-to-equity ratios,[28] and different levels of reliance on separately-identifiable intangible assets (as opposed to goodwill and the like).

Second, one important criterion for identifying potential sources of distortion, not expressly identified in *Grubert and Altshuler's* list, is the relative attractiveness for U.S. (or foreign) investors of making portfolio investments in U.S. multinational firms, as compared to making such investments in foreign-domiciled multinationals—or, for that matter, investing in U.S. multinational firms as opposed to U.S. domestically-oriented businesses. In light of the enormous surge in global capital flows, the increased transparency and liquidity of many foreign capital markets, and the ease of global research through online tools, it is absolutely imperative that U.S. international tax policy consider any tax reform proposal's potential for distorting these portfolio investment decisions.[29]

As envisioned by the Staff of the Joint Committee on Taxation, a territorial tax system would not seem by its design to distort portfolio investment decisions, although of course the ultimate effective tax rates imposed on different firms or different industries in a particular implementation of territoriality might do so. The same cannot be said, however, of the territorial proposal made by the President's Advisory Panel on Federal Tax Reform, because of the peculiar way in which the Panel chose to combine its territorial tax proposal with domestic relief from the double taxation of dividends. Essentially, when viewed from the perspective of the ultimate owners of a business enterprise, the Panel's proposal would have dramatically preferred investment in domestically-oriented U.S. firms over U.S.-based multinational enterprises that bore precisely the same effective global tax rate.

More specifically, the Panel's "Simplified Income Tax," apparently following the (erroneous) logic in this respect of the U.S. Treasury's 1992 "Comprehensive Business Income Tax" ("CBIT"), would have imposed a sort of compensatory tax when a U.S. company paid dividends to its U.S. shareholders out of exempt foreign earnings.[30] The result would have been a significantly anti-competitive step backwards for U.S. multinationals in respect of their cost of

---

[28] Traditional industrial firms, for example, might have debt-to-equity ratios of 1:1, while in the financial services industries debt-to-equity ratios might be on the order of 30:1.

[29] *Cf.* National Foreign Trade Council, *NFTC Foreign Income Project: International Tax Policy for the 21st Century*, at 98-99 (2001), *available at* http://www.nftc.org/default/tax/Territorial%20Report.pdf (hereinafter "*NFTC Foreign Income Project*").

[30] See *Tax Reform Panel Report*, *supra* note 12, at 243-244 (stating that under its proposal, "shareholders of U.S. corporations could exclude from income 100 percent of the dividends paid from income of the corporation reported as taxable in the United States," implying that the exclusion would be limited in the case of a corporation that is not taxable in the United States).

equity capital.[31] In this respect, the Simplified Income Tax proposal would have introduced a distortive double tax on foreign income.

There is a third, more controversial, aspect to your competitiveness question that should be mentioned. At least some proponents of a territorial tax system use "competitiveness" as a code word for "the lowest possible tax on foreign income that can legally be devised." I acknowledge that the point is controversial, but one can at least fairly ask whether competitiveness in that sense is truly non-distortive, or whether instead a less distorting goal might be to design a tax system that would enable a U.S. firm to compete against local firms in their domestic markets at an effective tax burden that is directly comparable to that faced by those local firms.

These two thoughts are not identical. We all understand the importance of "check the box" disregarded entities, hybrid instruments and hybrid entities in U.S. international tax planning today. The difficult question that deserves more debate is whether, if a U.S. firm can employ these arrangements to drive its effective tax rate on its Freedonian operations *below* the rate imposed in law and in practice by Freedonia on its domestic companies, we should applaud that result as enhancing competitiveness, or instead decry the result as distorting investment decisions.

Finally, territorial tax systems are clearly distortive in one unassailable respect, which is that they would bring with them enormous deadweight losses in the form of compliance and similar costs. *A territorial tax system is simpler than current law only in the imaginations of those who have* never *immersed themselves in the detailed implementation of either.*

---

[31] CBIT's designers apparently believed that a compensatory tax was appropriate in this case because the Internal Revenue Code as then drafted (and, indeed, today) did not grant an indirect foreign tax credit to individuals. The Code does, however, grant the indirect credit to our principal vehicle for conducting business (the corporation). Since the whole purpose of CBIT and other integration proposals is to treat individual stakeholders as if they directly earned their share of business enterprise income, it is far more logical to assume in designing an integrated tax system that a tax credit that has always been available to prevent double taxation of business income should remain available when that business income is taxed only once, rather than twice. Otherwise, one simply substitutes one form of distortive double taxation for another.

The President's Advisory Panel on Federal Tax Reform followed the logic of CBIT in this respect in fashioning the international tax provisions of the Panel's "Simplified Income Tax." As a result, that proposal, like CBIT, would introduce a distortive double tax on foreign income.

For example, imagine two U.S. corporations, Domestico and Globalco. Domestico earns $100 pre-tax, entirely from U.S. operations; Globalco also earns $100 pre-tax, but entirely from operations in Freedonia. Both companies are entirely equity funded.

Under the Simplified Income Tax, Domestico pays $31.50 in tax on its $100 income. Domestico then can distribute the remaining $69.50 to its shareholders as an exempt dividend.

Globalco, by serendipity, also pays $31.50 in income tax on its $100 income, but Globalco makes out the check for its tax payment to the Internal Revenue Service of Freedonia. Globalco can repatriate its $69.50 of after-Freedonian tax profits to the United States, but when it distributes that amount to its U.S. shareholders, they will be subject to full ordinary income tax on the distribution, while their brethren who invested in Domestico keep the same $69.50 distribution free of any tax.

More specifically, every territorial tax system that has been seriously proposed in the United States would retain a "subpart F" construct for passive and/or mobile income.[32] This subpart F income in turn would be entitled to foreign tax credits, so that all the complexities of current law would be replicated, except that the new system would stimulate new taxpayer impulses, which in turn would require new anti-abuse rules[33].

Today, subpart F income means the unavailability of deferral; tomorrow, categorizing revenues as subpart F income would mean that those revenues would move from wholly exempt to immediately taxable status. The result would be even greater stress on the divide between active and subpart F income than exists under current law.[34] Similarly, the U.S. law of the "source" of income (and many losses or expenses) is relatively undeveloped, compared to other areas of the Internal Revenue Code. These concepts would become critical, however, in defining and policing the scope of a territorial tax system.

c. *How would repealing deferral affect (i) the prominence of transfer pricing issues in the U.S. tax system; and (ii) the competitiveness of U.S. multinationals? Under such a system, what, in your view, would the appropriate tax rate be so that the competitiveness of U.S. multinationals is not undermined? Please explain your reasoning. In addition, to what extent would you recommend altering the foreign tax credit rules in such a system?*

(i) In direct contrast to current law, or to a territorial tax system, a "full inclusion" U.S. tax system would greatly attenuate the role of transfer pricing strategies as an affirmative taxpayer device to minimize global tax liability, because all income earned by a U.S. multinational group would be taxed by the United States on a current basis. As a result, any remaining transfer pricing issues would relate primarily to conflicting positions that might be taken by different taxing jurisdictions. A U.S. multinational corporation ordinarily would be a disinterested bystander to any such disputes, except in the limited case where the foreign jurisdiction's tax rates greatly exceed those of the United States.[35]

For the reasons developed in my answers above, by attenuating the relevance of transfer pricing strategies to multinational corporations, a full inclusion tax system would remove significant tax-induced distortions in corporate behavior. The data marshaled in *Grubert and Altshuler* and other academic papers are just too powerful to ignore: it cannot simply be the luck of the Irish, for example, that explains the extraordinary and systematic profitability of Irish

---

32 *See, e.g., JCT Staff I, supra* note 12, at 191.

33 For example, under a territorial tax system a U.S. parent company might try to convert high-taxed *exempt* income into subpart F income, so that those high foreign tax credits could be utilized to shelter low-taxed subpart F income elsewhere in the system.

34 *See NFTC Territorial Report*, supra note 27, at 19 ("in light of the higher stakes presented by a territorial exemption…even greater pressure would be placed on the issues of whether and to what extent types of active business income now subject to subpart F (e.g., foreign base company sales and services income) would be eligible for exemption.").

35 The U.S. firm might hope to either maximize low-taxed foreign source income, or minimize high-taxed foreign income, but only for the purpose of averaging down that very high-taxed income to the U.S. rate, so as to be able to use all its foreign tax credits.

subsidiaries of U.S. firms. A full inclusion tax model is the only approach that directly addresses this critical problem.

(ii) "Repealing deferral" would enhance competitiveness directly in the same important respect that adopting a territorial tax system would, which is that, without deferral, U.S. firms' repatriation decisions would reflect the highest and best use of their cash surpluses, rather than tax rate arbitrage. Ironically, then, the most unambiguous pro-competitive consequence of adopting a territorial tax system — the elimination of tax considerations in firms' decisions as to whether to repatriate offshore profits — is a feature that territoriality shares with its mirror image, a full inclusion system.

Repealing deferral also would eliminate two important economic distortions found in current law, which territorial solutions exacerbate rather than resolve. First, as described above, simply "repealing deferral" would greatly attenuate current law's incentives for multinational corporations to embrace transfer pricing strategies with excessive enthusiasm.

Second, the territorial tax systems that have been proposed for the United States all suspend the availability of the foreign tax credit for exempt (active) income, but preserve the foreign tax credit, and all its attendant limitations, exceptions, and qualifications, for subpart F (passive) income. This requires drawing clear lines between the two categories of income, as well as even more elaborate mechanisms than exist under current law to ensure that uncreditable foreign taxes associated with exempt income do not, through advanced tax planning or accounting, migrate over to a taxpayer's subpart F income (where those taxes would become valuable as credits). By dispensing with the sharp demarcation between exempt (active) and subpart F (passive) income, full inclusion systems eliminate the need to police the border between uncreditable foreign taxes associated with exempt income and creditable foreign taxes associated with subpart F income.

Notwithstanding these attractive features of any full inclusion system, in my estimation, simply "repealing deferral" would be profoundly noncompetitive. First, corporate income tax rates are much too high relative to those of our important trading partners.[36] Second, without modification, our current foreign tax credit system, and in particular its interest expense allocation rules, would leave too many companies with "excess" foreign tax credits, which in this context means that their global effective tax burden would be even higher than the (too high) nominal U.S. corporate tax rate. Third, almost every proposal of which I am aware that proposes to "repeal deferral" has been inconsistent with the economic neutrality that the proposal purports to espouse, in that the repeal of deferral is not accompanied by an ability on the part of the U.S. parent to deduct losses incurred by foreign operations.

While it follows from the above that simply "repealing deferral" would be a profoundly anti-competitive idea, it remains the case that a full inclusion system, like a territorial system, would eliminate current law's important distorting effects on firms' repatriation decisions. Full inclusion systems also eliminate the incentives found in current law (which are *exacerbated* by territorial tax systems) for multinational corporations to engage in over-enthusiastic transfer

---

[36] *See* Martin Sullivan, *On Corporate Tax Reform, Europe Surpasses the U.S.*, 111 Tax Notes 992 (May 29, 2006).

pricing strategies, to game the boundary between exempt and subpart F income, and to cause the migration of high effective foreign tax rates to subpart F income, all for the purpose of minimizing their global tax liabilities.

In light of these attractive elements of a full inclusion system, the intriguing questions is, can a full inclusion system be designed that retains these desirable features, but is pro-competitive as well? I have been exploring exactly that question in my own research over the last two years, and I believe the answer to be "yes."

My research in this area has centered around a comprehensive package to reform the U.S. federal taxation of business enterprises, while retaining the familiar outlines of a recognizable income tax. I term this package of reforms the "Business Enterprise Income Tax," or "BEIT."[37]

The BEIT proposal is a tightly integrated package of ideas, and its international aspects therefore require a bit of background on the basic domestic rules. Very briefly, the BEIT system, as applied to large business enterprises (there are special rules for small businesses), contains the following key components:

1. Taxation of all business enterprises, regardless of form (e.g., partnerships as well as corporations), as separate taxable entities (thereby avoiding the tremendous complexity of getting tax concepts to work with a wide range of different kinds of tax-transparent and tax-opaque vehicles).

2. "True" tax consolidation (i.e., a system that would treat all subsidiaries as an indistinguishable part of the parent company, rather than the current consolidated tax return regulations' complex hodgepodge of rules, which in fact do not in the end embrace *consolidation* principles so much as a *combination* of separate company results). Consolidation would be measured at the 50% level, and would be measured by reference to all of a company's long-term financial instruments (with tie-breaker rules to prevent multiple consolidations).

3. Repeal of all tax-free organization/reorganization rules, and their replacement with a much simpler "tax neutral" acquisition system. Under the BEIT, all acquisitions, incorporations or the like — basically, any transfer of business assets from a nonbusiness user to a business enterprise, or the entry of a business enterprise into (or exit from) a "true" consolidated group — are treated as taxable asset acquisitions. The seller's tax rate, however, depends on the present value of the step-up to the buyer in the tax basis of the various assets acquired. The result actually is similar to making all acquisitions tax-free (because the seller's tax liability equals the present value of the buyer's tax benefits), but with important technical advantages.

---

37 I presented the bare-bones outline of the BEIT in *The Business Enterprise Income Tax: a Prospectus*, 106 Tax Notes 97 (2005). That outline was expanded in some respects in a presentation made to the President's Advisory Panel on Federal Tax Reform, available online at http://www.taxreformpanel.gov/meetings/meeting-05_11-12_2005.shtml. Finally, an explanation of the conceptual underpinnings of the BEIT, titled *Designing an Income Tax on Capital*, was presented at the Brookings Institution in September 2005, and is scheduled to appear in a volume to be published containing the papers from that conference.

4. The adoption of a comprehensive and consistent system for taxing time value of money returns to investors (and deducting the cost of capital to issuers), called the "Cost of Capital Allowance" (COCA). The fundamental theme of the COCA system (in conjunction with all the other rules described above) is to tax "economic rents" and risky returns at the business enterprise level, and to tax time value of money returns once (and only once) at the investor level. COCA thus achieves both *integration* (i.e., the elimination of the double taxation of corporate profits) and a consistent and accurate measure of the income generated by investments. To accomplish the latter, COCA taxes an expected time value of money return on *all* forms of capital invested in businesses, whether called debt or equity, *on a current basis*. The details get a little complex, but in the end it really is just arithmetic, not rocket science.[38]

5. Lower corporate (business enterprise) rates. My target is 28 percent, but 25 percent would make the BEIT proposal even more attractive to a wide spectrum of American businesses.

From an internationalist's perspective, the BEIT can be seen in large measure as the perfect mirror image of a territorial system. The international aspects of the BEIT begin with the "true" tax consolidation described above. This idea is intended to apply globally. As a result, the BEIT treats foreign subsidiaries as if they were branches. The most obvious consequence of this, of course, is the end of deferral (and with it, the need to maintain rules to distinguish between active income and subpart F income). Another immediate consequence is to vastly attenuate the relevance to the United States of transfer pricing issues for outbound investments, for the reasons already described. Global consolidation also means, of course, that foreign losses will be deductible in the United States as those losses are incurred, thereby restoring true neutrality in application to the usual call to "end deferral."

Without more, the international aspects of the BEIT could fairly be described as economically neutral in respect of transfer pricing, repatriation decisions and the location of risky investments, but probably on balance still anti-competitive. The BEIT contains two other critical design elements, however, that revise that calculus, to yield a system that fair-minded business people should agree is pro-competitive. The first, and most important, is *lower tax rates* — as mentioned above, 28 percent is my goal, but 25 percent (if affordable) would be even better — financed through systematic base broadening.[39] The second design element is the repeal of the allocation of domestic interest expense (now, COCA) deductions against foreign income for purposes of calculating a U.S. business enterprise's allowable foreign tax credit in respect of its international operations, for the reasons described below.

As previously described, sensible territorial tax proposals must incorporate an interest expense allocation system (or some equally painful alternative, such as an efficacious thin capitalization regime). The reason, of course, is that the failure to do so would mean that territoriality would quickly lead to a zeroing out of the U.S. *domestic* business tax base, by borrowing money (and deducting the resulting interest expense) domestically, and supporting the

---

38 The papers referenced in note 37, *supra*, describe the COCA component of the BEIT in great detail.

39 The COCA system, in particular, is carefully designed, based on 30 years of practice in the area, to be a robust system to capture the time value of money component of financial investments — the hallmark of an income tax — on a current basis. The BEIT includes other significant base-broadening components as well, which in many cases flow from the imposition of the "true" consolidation and acquisition rules described earlier.

attendant interest deductions with exempt cash flows from equity-financed foreign investments. The BEIT, by contrast, contemplates retaining in general the foreign tax credit system, but, in sharp contrast to current law (and to territorial tax systems), dispensing with any requirement that U.S. taxpayers allocate domestic interest expense (now COCA) deductions between U.S. and foreign sources.

The BEIT abandons interest expense (now COCA expense) allocations for two reasons. First, by virtue of the "true" consolidation of foreign income, there is no income that is exempt or indefinitely-deferred anywhere in the BEIT system. As a result, there is no urgent need to protect the U.S. tax base by ensuring that domestic interest expense is not ultimately serviced from deferred or exempt income. Admittedly, however, current inclusion of all income may not be sufficient by itself to support the conclusion that no expense allocation is required.

The second, and ultimately more powerful, reason why domestic COCA expense need not be allocated against foreign income under the BEIT is that the purpose of the COCA deduction in the BEIT is different from today's interest expense deduction. In the BEIT, the COCA deduction exists to achieve a form of business enterprise-investor *integration*, and applies across the board to all forms of financial capital invested in a business. As such, the COCA deduction is not an "expense;" it is an income allocation device. If one were to imagine that all business enterprises were 100 percent equity-funded, we would not spend very much time worrying about allocating (nonexistent) cost of capital deductions. The COCA result is the same in theory (but superior in many practical respects) to a world in which all interest expense is disallowed, or in which (to put things in today's perspective) all firms are 100 percent equity-funded. Accordingly, given that under the BEIT we have neither exempt nor deferred income, and that we also have implemented an integrated tax system, there is no convincing reason to treat the device by which we achieve that integration as if it were an old-fashioned interest expense deduction.[40]

I previously observed that portfolio investments have taken on a larger role in cross border financial flows in recent years. A tax system that produces radically different results for portfolio investments by U.S. investors in foreign companies as compared to portfolio

---

40 The absence of a COCA expense allocation deduction can create the misimpression that foreign tax credits are sheltering U.S. domestic business income, but this result is one of cosmetics, not substance. For example, assume that a company has $100 of invested capital (i.e. tax basis in its assets), and that the COCA rate (the company's deduction for its cost of capital) is 5%. Further assume that the company earns $12 before its COCA deduction, that 1/2 of that amount ($6) is treated by both the U.S. and Freedonia as income arising in Freedonia, and that this $6 accordingly is taxed in Freedonia. Finally, assume that both the Freedonian and the US tax rate is 30%.

The company will pay $1.80 in Freedonian income tax. All of that foreign tax will be creditable in the United States, because the company's pre-COCA foreign income = $6, and the Freedonian tax is no greater than the U.S. tax on that income. The net result will be that the company will have $7.00 of taxable income, and a tentative tax liability of $2.10, but will pay only $0.30 to the U.S. Government — or will it? The 'missing' US tax liability has not disappeared at all, but rather has migrated to investors, who will have Minimum Inclusions = the COCA rate multiplied by their aggregate tax bases in their investment. Assuming for convenience that their bases also = $100 (in fact of course this will not be true, but it is a useful simplifying assumption), they will include $5 of income in respect of their investments, and pay $1.50 in tax. So in total the U.S. fisc collects $1.80, and Freedonia collects $1.80, on the company's pre-COCA income of $12, which reflects a tax split that precisely mirrors the relative domestic and foreign pre-COCA taxable incomes of the company.

investments in U.S. business enterprises (which in turn make foreign direct investments) will prove not to be very stable. A related question is how to deal with foreign income when distributed by a U.S. business enterprise to its domestic investors.[41]

The BEIT addresses these issues differently than do other proposals. As noted above, full consolidation combined with the COCA deduction/inclusion system basically works to tax economic rents and risky returns at the business enterprise level, and time value returns at the investor level. The COCA component of the BEIT achieves neutrality between U.S. investors investing in either U.S.-based multinational firms or foreign-based firms — between, say, investing in Exxon or investing in British Petroleum — by the simple expedient of applying its investor "Minimum Inclusion" rules (current inclusion of time value of money returns, regardless of cash distributions) to portfolio investments in foreign companies, just as those new rules apply to domestic portfolio investments. Finally, the BEIT achieves source neutrality at the level of US portfolio investors in US firms with foreign income by not discriminating (through compensatory taxes, or otherwise) against different source of enterprise-level earnings when ultimately received by investors.

Grubert and Altshuler reviews the economic theory and revenue effect of the international aspects of the BEIT (which that paper – no doubt sensibly – renames the "burden neutral" international proposal). That paper concludes that the international component of the BEIT "seems to dominate" both current law and territorial tax proposals as a matter of theory.[42] The paper further estimates that tax rates could come down to 28 percent and the BEIT international provisions would still be revenue neutral compared to current law.[43]

The principal criticism that can be leveled against the international provisions of the BEIT — or, indeed, of any full inclusion system — is that the system can distort at the margin international investments by U.S. business enterprises. If foreign tax rates are materially lower than those of the United States, it is argued that U.S. firms would have no great incentive to minimize their foreign tax burden. Conversely, if tax rates are very high in a foreign jurisdiction, a U.S. firm at the margin would have an incentive to "average down" its effective foreign tax rate by making its next investment in a low-taxed jurisdiction.[44]

The first objection to a full inclusion system — the indifference to actual foreign tax liabilities, if the aggregate effective foreign tax rate is materially lower than that of the United States — is substantially undercut in a world where the U.S. corporate tax rate has been repositioned at the low end of the rates imposed by the major world economies. This, of course,

---

41 For example, the Treasury Department's 1992 Comprehensive Business Income Tax proposal contemplated imposing a compensatory tax on foreign source income earned by a U.S. firm when that income was distributed as a dividend to its domestic portfolio investors. *See* note 31, *supra*.

42 *Grubert and Altshuler*, *supra* note 2, at 31.

43 *Id.* at 33. ("the burden neutral rate based on 'static' calculations is about 28%") *Grubert and Altshuler* does not analyze the revenue impact of the domestic reforms contemplated by the BEIT, in particular its key COCA system.

44 *See, e.g.*, Impact of International Tax Reform on U.S. Competitiveness: Hearings Before the Subcomm. on Select Revenue Measures of the H. Comm. on Ways and Means, 109th Cong. (2006) (Testimony of Prof. James R. Hines, Jr.).

is a key component of the implementation of the BEIT. Moreover, we have today regulations in our foreign tax credit systems that prohibit the crediting of "voluntary" taxes, and, more important, so called "soak-up" taxes.[45] These rules in fact work reasonably well. As a result, the United States is largely the beneficiary of a "free rider" phenomenon, in which local firms can be expected to lobby for lower local tax rates, which local subsidiaries of U.S. firms also will enjoy.

The BEIT responds to the second objection to any full inclusion system — that, at the margin, a U.S. firm might have an incentive to invest in a very low-tax jurisdiction, to "average down" its overall foreign tax rate to the amount allowable as a credit in the United States — by eliminating the allocation of U.S. interest expense (now COCA) deductions against foreign income for foreign tax credit purposes, for the reasons described above. Current law's interest expense allocation rules are necessary in our deferral system, but are the principal source of "excess" foreign tax credit problems, and with them the incentive for U.S. firms to "average down" their foreign tax credit systems.

Notwithstanding the above rebuttals, I acknowledge that even a well-implemented full inclusion system brings with it the theoretical possibility of some distortions to investment behavior, particularly if U.S. tax rates are so low as to leave many U.S. firms in excess credit positions, even in a world without interest (COCA) expense allocation for foreign tax credit purposes.[46] Ultimately, policymakers will not be able to choose a perfect international tax system — that cannot exist in a world of many sovereign nations with different rates — but they can endeavor to adopt the least distortive practical design. A territorial tax system brings with it two problems that, for all the reasons described above, are insuperable at a practical level: the policing of transfer pricing, and the policing of the divide between active (exempt) and passive (currently taxable) income.[47] Against these overwhelming problems, the objection to a well-designed full inclusion system — that it might encourage a firm to invest real capital in a location that makes little business sense in order to "average down" its aggregate foreign tax rate to the U.S. rate — seems, to this practitioner at least, a remote and speculative concern.

Finally, territorial tax systems in practice inevitably bring with them another sort of distortion, which is the prospect of "Stateless" income — income that is taxed nowhere in the world (or, at least, taxed at extremely low rates in a country where the income is not earned). Stateless income is not simply an artifact of transfer pricing abuses, but also arises from decisions as to where to place financial capital within a multinational group (so as to generate interest expense in a high-tax country and offsetting income in a very-low tax jurisdiction), differences in implementation of different tax systems, hybrid instruments and hybrid entities.

---

45 Treas. Reg. § 1.901-2(e)(5) ("noncompulsory" taxes); § 1.901-2(c) ("soak up" taxes).

46 In practice, U.S.-based multinationals are likely to deal with the incentive to "average down" in a much more straightforward manner than by locating *physical* capital in a low-tax jurisdiction. Instead, U.S. firms will average down by financing high-taxed operations with deductible *financial* capital (in the form of loans paying deductible interest) provided by low-taxed affiliates.

47 To this can be added the practical and political problems in designing a satisfactory interest expense allocation system (or an alternative, like an efficacious thin capitalization solution), to protect the domestic tax base — and the associated problems of protecting that solution from erosion through years of taxpayer lobbying.

For example, if a territorial system permits a deductible payment paid by one foreign affiliate out of its exempt income to retain its exempt character, when paid to another foreign affiliate, that system will encourage — indeed, impel — taxpayers to use affiliate interest, rents and royalties to strip out earnings from the countries in which that income economically is earned. This leads directly to the phenomenon of "Stateless" income. Conversely, treating all such income as "passive" (and therefore as immediately taxable in the United States), will be criticized as undercutting the purpose of a territorial system. The conflict inevitably will lead both to difficult technical issues (e.g., layering rules for determining from which income a deductible interaffiliate expense is paid) and to a political tug-of-war identical to that which has bedeviled subpart F of the Code, as reflected in its various "same country" exceptions, the recent adoption of the temporary provisions of section 954(c)(6), and the even more recent passage by the House of Representatives of a Bill to scale back some of the provisions of section 954(c)(6).[48]

All territorial tax systems struggle with the issue of Stateless income.[49] This problem, which has become both more urgent and more obvious in recent years, in turn explains my response to another criticism that might be leveled against the particular implementation of a "full inclusion" system that I advocate, which is that it is different from the tax systems employed in the other major capital exporting countries. The major European capital exporting countries in particular can fairly be said to be in a state of crisis in respect of their own territorial tax systems, as a result of the European Court of Justice's approach to the intersection of EU Member State cross-border investment rules and EU constitutional concerns. This is an area where I believe the United States could lead by example. The result would be both conformity to a new norm and a sharp reduction in Stateless income, which is another way to get to a playing field that is fair as well as level.

---

[48] In light of the central importance of deductible inter-affiliate payments in determining the consequences and scope of a territorial tax system one would expect extensive discussion of the issue in the literature. Oddly, this does not appear to be the case.

[49] Organization for Economic Co-operation and Development, *Harmful Tax Competition: an Emerging Global Issue*, at 43 (1998). One popular solution, rejected by most, but not all, U.S. proposals, is to limit the benefits of exempt income status to income earned in jurisdictions with specified minimum tax rates, or jurisdictions on a "good" list, or jurisdictions not on a "black" list.

July 14, 2006

Responses to Written Questions for the Record Posed by Senator Max Baucus

On June 13, 2006, I testified before the Senate Committee on Finance at its hearing titled "A Tune-Up On Corporate Tax Issues: What's Going On Under the Hood?" This document contains my responses to written questions for the record posed to me by Senator Baucus following that hearing.

Edward D. Kleinbard

I. **QUESTIONS RELATING TO PUBLIC DISCLOSURE OF TAX RETURN DATA.**

1. *Mr. Kleinbard, you have been quoted to say that if WorldCom's tax return had been available to investors, "WorldCom's [incorrect] capitalization of expenses would have jumped out at everybody in the difference between financial and tax numbers."*

   a. *To what extent could the WorldCom scandal have been avoided if the tax return information had been publicly available? How could transparency have prevented the Enron scandal?*

It is difficult, even with the benefit of hindsight, to predict what might have happened in respect of the scandals to which you refer had each company's Schedule M-3 been available to the public. Nonetheless, I believe that, armed with the information contained therein, securities analysts might well have asked more focused questions that would have indicated the existence of larger issues. For example, Enron apparently relied heavily on highly-leveraged special purpose vehicles that were not consolidated with it for financial statement purposes, but were for tax purposes. The Schedule M-3 could well have led analysts to note the existence of many controlled entities not reflected on the face of its financial statements.

   b. *You state in your written testimony that the difference between corporate pre-tax financial statement income and taxable income in 2002 was $200 billion. You also state there is disagreement about what is behind this figure. In your opinion, what are the primary contributors to this huge book/tax gap?*

The $200 billion figure from 2002 that I offered in my written testimony came from commissioner Everson's testimony. Interestingly, on the day following this Committee's hearings at which I testified, the IRS held a Research Conference at which preliminary data from the 2004 Schedule M-3 (the first year to which Schedule M-3 applied) was presented. I was not invited to the Research Conference, but I have seen a copy of the presentation made by Ellen

Legel and Charles Boynton of the Internal Revenue Service and Portia DeFilippes of the Treasury Department, as well as the underlying preliminary data.

Very briefly, I believe that the preliminary data can be summarized as follows. Of course, the most appropriate individuals to present this material to your Committee would be authors of the report referred to above.

The aggregate amount by which book income exceeded taxable income in 2004 on the Schedule M-3's of those corporate taxpayers whose data was "reconcilable" was roughly $132 billion. This figure is significantly lower than the IRS's estimates for 2002 to which I referred in my testimony (approximately $200 billion).

Putting aside differences in the economy between the two years (which would argue, I believe, for a *larger* book-tax difference in 2004 than in 2002), I suspect that the lower aggregate book-tax differences recorded in 2004 reflected primarily (i) the difficulties that the IRS faced in earlier years (when there were no Schedule M-3's) in coming up with meaningful estimates, and (ii) in particular, the differences in starting points: the Schedule M-3 data look essentially to the book-tax differences in the U.S. tax consolidated group, not the (ordinarily larger) group of companies that are consolidated for financial statement purposes. Again, the authors of the study described above would be best situated to interpret the data.

The preliminary data show a number of categories where book income significantly exceeded taxable income, and a number where the converse was true. Given that the data are preliminary and that the authors of the study presumably will prepare a paper for publication, I do not think it appropriate for me to try to interpret their material in detail.

My understanding, however, is that the largest contributors to book income exceeding taxable income (excluding certain highly technical and uncontroversial items, like the elimination of "equity method" financial statement income inclusions for minority investments) — presumably the direction of greatest interest to this Committee — include the following:

<u>Largest Items Where Book Income Exceeded Taxable Income</u>
(In Descending Order of Importance)

- "Other" Items aggregated in the data
- Depreciation
- Items relating to reportable transactions
- Nonqualified stock options
- Pension and profit-sharing
- Interest income

To emphasize, there are other large items going in precisely the opposite direction: that is, cases where taxable income substantially exceeded book income. By way of example, the aggregate book-tax difference attributable to depreciation was roughly $113 million — almost 86% of the entire *net* book-tax difference of $132 million, but a significantly smaller percentage of only those items where book income exceeded taxable income.

The very large quantity of "other" adjustments probably reflects either first-year failures by taxpayers in properly preparing the Schedule M-3, or design issues in the M-3 form itself that can be addressed in coming years.[1] My understanding is that the IRS is working diligently at understanding the underlying components of this "other" category.

II. QUESTIONS RELATING TO THE LIFO METHOD OF ACCOUNTING.

2. *Do you consider repeal of LIFO to be a tax increase? Explain.*

I do not consider the repeal of LIFO (Last In, First Out) accounting for inventories to be a tax increase. To the contrary, repealing LIFO would "increase" a business enterprise's taxes only in the sense that eliminating any special-interest tax break is described as a "tax increase" by those firms threatened by the loss of their preferential treatment.

Under reasonable commercial assumptions and the economic conditions that have prevailed for many decades, *the purpose and effect of LIFO is to provide eligible taxpayers with a deduction for an expense that is never incurred.*[2] The author of the leading treatise on the taxation of inventories (and the author as well of the memorandum submitted to this Committee by the LIFO Coalition on June 26, 2006) acknowledged exactly this point at the beginning of his treatise's discussion of LIFO accounting:

> "The single most important factor that has influenced taxpayers to adopt the LIFO method is the tax savings that result from its use for tax purposes. Theoretically, use of the LIFO method results only in a deferral of taxes. However, as long as inflation continues and a taxpayer's LIFO inventories remain relatively constant or increase in size, the tax deferral is perpetuated and tends to become 'permanent.'"[3]

To see how LIFO works to accomplish this permanent deferral (that is, the equivalent of a deduction for an expense that is never incurred), it is helpful to review for a few paragraphs how LIFO and other inventory accounting methods operate.

Physical inventories generally are necessary to run a business that depends on the steady sale of similar goods to customers. The existence of physical inventories in turn means that a

---

[1] A very recent news article quotes an IRS official as saying that there was a "significant amount" of noncompliance by taxpayers in respect of their Schedule M-3 reporting obligations for 2004. That same article notes that "over 200" tax returns have been specifically selected for examination as a result of the information contained in those taxpayers' Schedule M-3s. Tandon, *More Than 200 Returns Targeted on Basis of Schedule M-3 Data, IRS Official Says*, 2006 Tax Notes Today 133-4.

[2] Those conditions are rising price levels for inventories attributable to inflation, and a continuation of a business's product lines such that, though those product lines change in all of their recognizable details, they can trace their history back to the taxpayer's original adoption of LIFO.

[3] Leslie Schneider, *Federal Income Taxation of Inventories*, at §10.01[1] (2006) (footnote omitted). Moreover, James Leisenring, an IASB board member and former FASB director, has publicly stated, "I don't think anybody thinks LIFO is a good inventory method for anything except tax purposes." Tim Reason, *On the Same Page: U.S. and International Standard Setters are Coordinating Their Efforts to Craft a Common Language for Business*, CFO, May 2002.

taxpayer typically is simultaneously selling its goods to the public and buying (or manufacturing) replacement goods — its inventories.

A taxpayer's net annual income from the sale of goods that it manufactures or purchases for resale simply equals its sales revenues minus its "cost of goods sold." The purpose of inventory accounting methods is to determine, in light of the fact that a taxpayer is selling its goods to customers and simultaneously buying (or spending money to manufacture) replacement goods, which of the taxpayer's total costs incurred during the year for the goods that it manufactures or purchases for resale relate to goods sold during the year, and which of such costs are attributable to the goods that remain on hand as inventory at the end of the year.

Every practical inventory accounting method makes this determination by adopting an arbitrary ordering rule that assigns in some mechanical fashion the costs incurred by the taxpayer during a year to manufacture or purchase for resale the goods that it sells to the public to (i) the goods that the taxpayer in fact sold during the year (i.e., to the "cost of goods sold") and (ii) to the taxpayer's goods remaining on hand (i.e., in inventory) at the end of the year. Allocating a greater proportion of the taxpayer's total costs for the year to the cost of goods sold during the year reduces current income, and simultaneously reduces the value assigned to the taxpayer's year-end inventories.

FIFO's (First In, First Out) arbitrary ordering rule for inventory costs is that the taxpayer's inventoriable goods are deemed to have been sold in the order purchased (or manufactured); the costs associated with acquiring those goods are tracked as prices change, and the first costs incurred during the year are assigned to the goods sold during the year. As a result, the taxpayer's ending inventory is deemed to comprise the taxpayer's most recently purchased or manufactured goods.

A collateral consequence of FIFO's ordering rule is that FIFO tends to value inventories on hand at year-end at their approximate market values (replacement cost).[4] This result is consistent with underlying income tax principles, because these principles seek to include in income net annual increases in a taxpayer's wealth, to the extent those increases are visible and quantifiable through "realization" events.

LIFO's arbitrary ordering rule is the opposite of FIFO's: it assumes that the taxpayer sells the most recently purchased (or manufactured) inventoriable goods first, so that the taxpayer's first-acquired inventories are deemed *never* to be sold (unless the taxpayer shrinks its inventories below historic levels).[5] As a result, a taxpayer that employs LIFO carries its year-end inventories at values that can relate back all the way to the taxpayer's adoption of LIFO — a date that often is decades in the past. For example, a taxpayer that adopted LIFO in 1976 and that has not shrunk its inventory levels since that date will carry its core inventories at values equal to their 1976 cost.

---

4 Of course, the degree to which FIFO succeeds in this depends on the velocity with which inventory turns over, and the rate of price increases. In situations where turnover is rapid, and price increases are moderate, FIFO's carrying values will more closely approximate current market values than will be the case with slow-moving inventory and very rapid price changes.

5 Average cost inventory methods, as the name implies, produce results that fall between FIFO and LIFO.

LIFO is described as achieving a better matching than does FIFO between current revenue and current expense, which in turn is said to further good tax policy, by "ameliorat[ing] the harmful effects of inflation on capital investment."[6] Thus, the memorandum submitted to this Committee by the LIFO Coalition on June 26, 2006, argued that LIFO should have fulfilled a function analogous to the purpose underlying the Code's accelerated depreciation methods for investments in productive machinery and equipment.[7]

The problem with this happy syllogism, however, is that it is inconsistent with larger income tax principles, in four fundamental respects. First, LIFO is not at all analogous to accelerated depreciation and similar timing benefits, because, as the author of the LIFO Coalition's memorandum himself has noted in the passage from his treatise quoted earlier in this answer, LIFO accounting for inventory typically yields a *permanent* deferral of tax – the equivalent of a deduction for a cost that is never incurred.[8]

Second, LIFO accounting's theme of "matching current revenues to current expenses" violates the principle that our income tax requires a taxpayer to account *annually* for the income (i.e., increases to the taxpayer's wealth, to the extent those increases are observable) that the taxpayer earns during the year. We honor that principle, for example, by requiring that tax be paid in the same year that income is "realized" (and recognized) by selling property. LIFO, by contrast, treats every sale of inventory property in effect as a tax-free exchange.[9] That is, the LIFO method suspends the application of the realization principle in the case of certain sales of property (LIFO inventories) for cash — and by doing so, deviates from a comprehensive effort to capture current increases in a taxpayer's wealth (including increases in the value of inventories, like any other property), as documented through actual realization events (sales of goods for cash) in the taxpayer's annual income. In short, in this fundamental respect LIFO accounting produces results directly in opposition to the purpose of an annual income tax.

LIFO's theme of "matching current revenues to current expense" also violates larger tax principles in a third fundamental respect, which is that it is a *selective* partial immunization from inflation — one that is not available to all taxpayers in a consistent manner. This is what I meant in my oral testimony when I referred to LIFO as an "*ersatz basis indexation scheme*." We could produce the same tax results as an idealized LIFO scheme by repealing it, and replacing that accounting method with FIFO inventory accounting coupled with indexing the basis of inventories — and no other class of property or investment — for inflation each period. (In fact, this system would be *superior* to LIFO in one critical respect, which is that it would properly include *only* inflationary gains in the deferral mechanism, and not the "value creep" that I describe two paragraphs below.) The result would be a tax deduction (the upwards indexation of the cost of goods sold) without any commensurate out of pocket cash expense.

---

6 Memorandum from LIFO Coalition to Sens. Charles E. Grassley and Max Baucus (June 26, 2006), *in LIFO Coalition Letter to Sens. Grassley, Baucus, With Memo Responding to Testimony on Last-In, First-Out Inventory Method*, BNA DAILY TAX REPORT, June 28, 2006 [hereinafter LIFO Coalition Memorandum].

7 *Id.*

8 See *supra* note 3, and accompanying text.

9 The memorandum recently submitted to this Committee by the LIFO Coalition acknowledges as much when it states that "when the proceeds of sale of an inventory item are reinvested in a corresponding replacement item of inventory, there has been no genuine economic realization event." LIFO Coalition Memorandum.

To be clear, inflation is a terribly important issue in the design of any income tax system. Our tax system today largely deals with inflation by ignoring it, at least explicitly (with the exception of certain tax bracket adjustments and the like.[10] My point in criticizing the argument that LIFO is a response to inflation concerns is not to trivialize the importance of inflation, but rather to explain that *ad hoc* and selective solutions like LIFO distort economic decisionmaking even more than not addressing the issue at all does.

Fourth, and as I explain in more detail in my answer to Question 8, below, the LIFO method permits taxpayers to defer much more than simple inflationary gains. Very generally, the LIFO method permits taxpayers to defer income attributable to *all* cost increases in their inventory, including not only cost increases due to inflation, but those due to years of incremental technological improvements to the inventoriable goods. LIFO is simply ineffective at distinguishing between pure inflationary increases in costs, and fundamental supply/demand imbalances, or engineering or other technological enhancements, that in either case increase both the *cost* of a taxpayer's inventory, *and* the *value* of these inventoriable goods – even in a hypothetical world of zero inflation. I term this phenomenon the "value creep" problem.

In summary, LIFO is a recognized accounting method, but that fact does not mean that its purpose or effect necessarily is consistent with the goals of our income tax system. As the Supreme Court explained in a case dealing directly with inventory valuation methods, appropriate (or at least permissible) financial accounting inventory methods sometimes conflict with the design and purpose of our income tax.[11] In those cases, the financial accounting method must be rejected for tax purposes.

Once one sees LIFO for what it is — an ersatz basis indexation scheme available only to some taxpayers in some businesses — it becomes apparent that LIFO functions as just another preferential tax break available only to certain taxpayers, but paid for by all, through the higher tax rates needed to raise the same aggregate revenues. And returning to my initial observation, just as true basis indexation for inflation of all inventories would give taxpayers in inventory-intensive industries a "free" deduction — one that requires no cash outlay to create tax basis in inventory — so too it becomes easy to see how the effect of LIFO is to give only those taxpayers eligible for that method an effective deduction for an expense that is never incurred.

Repealing LIFO thus is not a "tax increase," but rather the removal of a preferential tax break not available to all taxpayers. The repeal of LIFO would be one important step in the larger process to fund lower tax rates for *all* business enterprises in a neutral fashion by eliminating special interest provisions, thereby broadening the tax base.

---

10 Many tax economists view this as a failing, and would argue for systematic basis indexation for all assets. At the same time, however, those same economists would point out that our current system's reliance on the realization principle also is a failing, when compared to a comprehensive (and completely infeasible) marking to market of all of a taxpayer's assets, so as to capture on a current basis a taxpayer's true annual economic income (i.e., its accession to wealth in the period, whether "realized" or not).

11 See *Thor Power Tool Co. v. Comm'r of Internal Revenue,* 439 U.S. 522, 542-44 (1979).

3. *You estimated that the LIFO reserve for the Fortune 600 companies is $60 billion. What is your estimate of the cumulative LIFO reserve for all taxpayers, and the total amount of tax that is being deferred?*

I believe that the figures that you quote came from Professor Plesko's testimony, not mine. I have no independent estimate to offer of the cumulative amount of tax that has been deferred through the use of LIFO. I note, however, that the memorandum submitted to this Committee by the LIFO Coalition following this Committee's hearings acknowledges that the total amount of tax that has been deferred through the use of LIFO is "many times greater than the $60 billion that Professor Plesko estimates in his testimony."[12]

4. *What is the average number of years that a company defers taxes by using LIFO? Considering the time value of money, what is the present value of your estimate of the total amount of tax that is being deferred as a result of LIFO?*

I do not have any independent estimate of the average number of years that a company defers taxes by using LIFO. I note, however, that the memorandum submitted to this Committee by the LIFO Coalition following this Committee's hearings acknowledges that it would not be unusual for a company to have employed LIFO to defer its tax liability "for over 30 years."[13] More directly, the same author, in the quotation from his treatise on LIFO accounting set out in my answer to your Question 2, describes the practical effect of LIFO accounting as tending towards a "permanent" deferral of tax liability, which can alternatively be described as a deferral for an infinitely long period of time.

5. *What impact would the repeal of LIFO have on our nation's economy, competitiveness, employment levels and the financial markets?*

The repeal of LIFO by itself can be expected to present a cash flow issue for those companies that have employed LIFO for many decades. This cash flow problem is no different, however, than the cash crunch faced by individual tax shelter "junkies" in the 1970's, when the Internal Revenue Code was amended to foreclose most individual shelters, or the cash crunch faced by any other group of taxpayers that have enjoyed preferential tax treatment, when that preference is taken away.

The solution to this cash crunch issue is twofold. First, as implied at the end of my answer to your Question 2, I believe that LIFO repeal most appropriately should take place in the context of fundamental corporate income tax reform, in which the income tax base is broadened and rates lowered. In this context, the cash costs of LIFO repeal will be mitigated, although the extent of that mitigation will vary from firm to firm.

---

12 LIFO Coalition Memorandum.
13 *Id.*

Second, legislation to repeal LIFO also should permit taxpayers to pay their back taxes attributable to the LIFO tax deferral that they previously enjoyed over a period of years. For example, when Congress added section 475 to the Code in 1993 to require securities dealers to change to a "mark to market" system to account for their inventories of securities, the dealer community faced exactly the same sort of one-time cash crunch.[14] Congress recognized this problem by permitting securities dealers to pay the back taxes attributable to the deferral benefits they previously had enjoyed ratably over five years (without any interest charge). I recommend that a similar rule be adopted in connection with LIFO repeal.

I am not an accounting professional, but I am told that LIFO repeal should not adversely affect the balance sheets of business taxpayers, because the consequence of LIFO repeal would be that the carrying values of inventories would be written up to their current replacement cost values. As a result, businesses that employ LIFO will show a new cash payable (a liability) to the government in respect of the back taxes on their deferred income, but a commensurately higher value for their inventory assets. Since the new tax liability will equal only 35 percent of the step-up in carrying value of a business's inventories, it can be argued that balance sheets actually in general will look *stronger* after LIFO repeal.

LIFO repeal also should *not* affect international competitiveness, for the simple reason that LIFO is almost entirely a creature of U.S. accounting practice. Since most foreign countries do not permit LIFO accounting for inventories, foreign subsidiaries of U.S. firms will be in exactly the same competitive position after LIFO repeal as they were before. Moreover, the consolidated financial statements of U.S. firms attributable to the activities of those subsidiaries already reflects the inventories carried by those subsidiaries on a basis other than LIFO, and therefore would be completely unaffected to that extent by the repeal of LIFO.[15]

Finally, it has been suggested by the LIFO Coalition that, "if the LIFO method were repealed . . . , this would tend to cause businesses to try to increase the selling prices of their goods . . . , thus further exacerbating inflationary tendencies."[16] This argument plainly falls of its own weight. Businesses today do not gratuitously refrain from taking advantage of price increases out of gratitude for the government's continuing to make LIFO available to them. The laws of supply and demand drive prices today, and will tomorrow, regardless of the accounting methods employed by businesses for their inventories. More generally, by removing a tax subsidy for one form of capital investment, LIFO repeal will lead to a more efficient allocation of capital across the American economy.

---

[14] Prior to the adoption of section 475, most dealers had employed "lower of cost or market" accounting for their securities inventories.

[15] The LIFO Coalition's memorandum acknowledges as much: "Moreover, most large U.S. businesses have significant overseas operations carried on by foreign affiliates and the inventories held by these foreign affiliates are not eligible for the LIFO method. However, these inventories of foreign affiliates are required to be included in the businesses' consolidated U.S. financial statements along with the inventories associated with U.S. operations, even though these inventories of foreign affiliates are not ordinarily required to be reflected on U.S. consolidated tax returns since the foreign affiliates are not subject to U.S. income tax." LIFO Coalition Memorandum.

[16] *Id.*

6. *To what extent do you believe there is a benefit in the book/tax LIFO conformity rule? Since companies can use different LIFO "submethods" for book and tax, resulting in different LIFO reserve amounts for book and for tax, does the conformity rule serve its intended purpose?*

There is no real book/tax conformity in our tax system; it is illusory. First, as your question suggests, a taxpayer can satisfy the conformity requirement even if it uses different LIFO sub-methods for its financial statement and tax accounting statements.[17] Second, public corporations that use LIFO accounting methods for tax purposes almost invariably also disclose (in footnotes) what their profits would have been under a FIFO accounting method. These footnotes are both clearly written and closely read by securities analysts,[18] suggesting that those issuers perceive a great benefit in disclosing what they perceive to be their *real* book income, and in the process subverting the supposed conformity requirement.

The accounting literature agrees with this assessment, noting that "[t]he LIFO conformity rules set forth in IRS regulations permit numerous disclosures of financial information on a non-LIFO basis."[19] For example, while the taxpayer must prepare the face of its financial accounting income statement using a LIFO inventory method, it may supplement that statement with a note or appendix,[20] or publish news releases, hold press conferences, and pepper various sections of its Annual Report with alternative accounting methods.[21] A taxpayer may also use alternative measures in its forecasts,[22] and in reported income statements covering periods under one year in duration.[23] As a result, taxpayers can give shareholders and creditors clear signals as to what their profits would be under FIFO accounting and still satisfy the conformity requirement of section 472(c).

Most tellingly, a company that employs LIFO accounting for tax purposes need *not* use LIFO principles for internal capital allocations purpose, new project feasibility studies, management compensation, or any other genuinely commercial decisions.[24] For example, it appears to be the case that public companies that employ LIFO accounting for tax purposes often

---

17 The IRS permits a taxpayer to use a specific goods LIFO method for financial purposes and a dollar-value method for tax purposes without violating the conformity requirement. Rev. Rul. 85-129.

18 The accounting literature suggests that accounting changes between FIFO and LIFO, and the resulting changes in reported earnings, do not affect a public company's stock price. Donald E. Kieso et al., *Intermediate Accounting* 395 & n.26 (12th ed. 2005); *see* Shyam Sunder, *Stock Prices and Risk Related to Accounting Changes in Inventory*, 50 Acct. Rev. 305, 314 (1975); Rosalyn Mansour, Summary, *Sunder S. 2002. Management Control, Expectations, Common Knowledge, and Culture*, http://www.maaw.info/ArticleSummaries/ArtSumSunder2002.htm (2004); Rashad Abdel-Khalik, *The Effect of LIFO-Switching and Firm Ownership on Executives' Pay*, 23 J. Acct. Res. 427, 429 (1985); *see also* Douglas A. Shackleford & Terry Shevlin, *Empirical Tax Research in Accounting*, 31 J. Acct. & Econ. 321, 328-330 (2001).

19 Barry A. Tovig & Diane P. Herndon, *Inventories: General Principles; LIFO Method*, 578-3rd Tax Mgmt., at A-45 n.373 (2005); *see also* Donald E. Kieso et al., *Intermediate Accounting* 396 (12th ed. 2005).

20 IRS Reg. §1.472-2(e)(3)(ii)-(iii).

21 IRS Reg. §1.472-2(e)(3)(iv).

22 Rev. Rul. 88-84.

23 IRS Reg. §1.472-2(e)(1)(iv).

24 IRS Reg. §1.472-2(e)(1)(ii)-(iii); PLR 9029016 (amendments to profit-sharing and incentive stock option plans may use non-LIFO methods to determine book income, book value and book earnings); PLR 7824002 (management compensation); *see also* Tovig & Herndon, *supra* note 19, at A-131 (noting that the justification for an exception for internal management reports is that they are not reports to shareholders or other equity holders).

base their management compensation decisions on a business unit's non-LIFO accounting results.[25]

Given all of these exceptions and loopholes, it is clear that book-tax conformity as it is currently practiced does not in fact impose any material constraints on how public companies communicate their financial results to public investors or creditors. A larger question is, what purpose would be served by an efficacious book-tax conformity rule? The rule appears originally to have been grounded in a notion that LIFO's adoption for tax purposes should be artificially constrained by requiring companies to "put their money where their mouth is"[26] for financial statement purposes.[27] But this rationale in turn is an implicit acknowledgement that LIFO accounting produces results that are undesirable for tax purposes — why else would an artificial governor on its scope be required?

The *real* conformity that this Committee should employ as its lodestone is *conformity with non-tax commercial decisionmaking.*[28] The absence of consistent evidence that companies base management compensation or any other commercial decisions on LIFO financials again illumines LIFO's role as an artifice of pure tax avoidance.

7. *The International Accounting Standards Board (IASB) has proposed prohibiting the LIFO method of accounting for inventory. The U.S. Financial Accounting Standards Board (FASB) has entered into a Memorandum of Understanding with the IASB with the intention of achieving international convergence. To what extent should the tax code comport with accounting standards that prohibit LIFO. To what extent should other ideas from financial accounting be imported to the tax law?*

If it were the case that LIFO accounting for inventories promoted the goals of the U.S. income tax system, then a persuasive case could be made that LIFO accounting should be permitted for tax purposes, regardless of whether LIFO constituted a viable accounting method for financial statement purposes. For the reasons developed in my answer to your Question 2, however, LIFO in fact produces results directly in opposition to the goals of our income tax system. This is the best reason to repeal LIFO.

---

25 Donald E. Kieso et al., *Intermediate Accounting* 384-85 (12th ed. 2005); A. Rashad Abdel-Khalik, *The Effect of LIFO-Switching and Firm Ownership on Executives' Pay*, 23 J. Acct. Res. 427, 428 (1985).

26 LIFO Coalition Memorandum.

27 A participant in the three-member committee that originally advocated allowing LIFO tax accounting, Carmen Blough, originally acquiesced to allowing LIFO (and requiring LIFO conformity) "because he believed that few firms would actually adopt it." Blough had since reversed his opinion and lobbied against LIFO because his "prediction that usage would be limited proved to be incorrect." *FASB Suggests Eliminating LIFO Conformity Reg*, 2001 Tax Notes Today 86-34, ¶3 (2001) (quoting William D. Cooper et al., *Establishing the LIFO Conformity Rule*, CPA J., July 1996, *available at* http://www.nysscpa.org/cpajournal/1996/0796/newsviews/nv7.htm).

28 In 1993, when Congress required securities dealers to employ mark-to-market accounting for tax purposes, one of the principal rationales was that dealers consistently employed mark-to-market accounting for all important commercial purposes.

For the reasons developed in my answer to your Question 6, I do not believe that there is any practical significance to LIFO "book-tax conformity" as it is observed today. As I also discuss in that answer, it is not clear what purpose the "book-tax conformity" rule ever was thought to serve, other than implicitly to acknowledge that LIFO accounting for inventories was simply a preferential tax break for some businesses, and therefore had to be accompanied by some sort of artificial governor on its utilization. As a result, the best reason to look to the international convergence of financial accounting standards as supporting the repeal of LIFO is simply that it forces attention to be brought to bear on the issue (due to the nominal "book-tax conformity" rule). Substantively, international financial accounting convergence is the tail, and good income tax policy the dog. Both, however, point in the same direction.

Your larger question of the extent to which accounting concepts should be imported into the Internal Revenue Code is very difficult to answer in the abstract. As I indicated in my testimony, I see financial accounting standards and the Code as two rival models for describing all of economic activity; we cannot simply take a module from one such model and import it to the other without careful consideration of that module's context and purpose in each model.

Nonetheless, there are some aspects of the financial accounting model that I believe could profitably be imported to the tax system. For example, in the proposal for fundamental business tax reform that I presented to the President's Advisory Panel in Tax Reform, I proposed consolidated tax return rules that essentially follow financial accounting concepts, along with a consistent treatment of all acquisitions under "purchase" rather than "pooling" principles. The details of doing so, however, are complex, and it might be fairer to describe the result proposed therein as the adoption for tax purpose of principles similar to those employed in financial accounting, rather than the wholesale adoption of specific financial accounting rules.

8. *To what extent do existing LIFO methods accurately isolate cost increases due to inflation compared to other factors, including inventory mix, definition of an item, transportation costs, and productivity? How could LIFO be revised so that factors other than inflation are not included in the reserve? Would these revisions require legislative changes or could they be done administratively?*

Although the LIFO accounting method usually is described as a means to defer tax on inventory gains attributable solely to inflation, I do not believe that LIFO in fact isolates (and thereby permits deferral only of) cost increases due to inflation. One recent and dramatic example has been the steep run-up in crude oil prices over the last 24 months. That run-up is *not* commensurate with inflation rates, but rather reflects both global security issues and fundamental supply/demand imbalances. By one measure, the taxable income deferred by U.S. large integrated oil companies through LIFO accounting for 2005 alone through this "value creep" (that is, changes in the value of inventory that are not inflation-related) might have been on the order of $19 billion.[29]

---

29 I derived this number as follows. The Tax Relief Act of 2005, as considered by this Committee on November 15, 2005, contained a provision (not ultimately enacted) that would have required U.S. large integrated oil companies that employed LIFO accounting to include in income 75 percent of their 2005 increase in economic

LIFO – and in particular "dollar value" LIFO, as employed by many retailers and manufacturers – fails to account for "value creep" in other respects as well, particularly with respect to retailers. The reason is that one purpose of "dollar value" LIFO is to obviate the need to make distinctions between the nature of the goods that comprise closing inventories and those contained in beginning inventory, even though the goods in closing inventory "may, and generally do, differ considerably as to type, quality and price from those in the beginning inventory."[30] Technological improvements over time may reduce a manufacturer's costs of manufacturing an item of inventory, but by the same token new standard features can increase both the value and the cost of inventory for retailers, in particular, by amounts that exceed any reductions attributable to lower manufacturing costs. As these new high-value improvements accumulate in an item of inventory without it being redefined as a new "item" for LIFO purposes, then the taxpayer can defer ever increasing amounts of income, not simply because of inflation, but because the taxpayer is matching the *expense of selling state-of-the-art goods against the revenues from selling older inventory*.

To see this point more clearly, imagine an automobile retailer that maintains an inventory of cars, where LIFO accounting was adopted in 1976. Thirty years later, the engineering and build quality of cars have improved, standard features have been added, manufacturing has become more efficient, and there has also been inflation. For LIFO to isolate inflation, it must somehow separate all of these improvements and changes, even though they have occurred incrementally over time (such that each year's model is only a slight improvement over the prior year's).

In the absence of separating out these different components of changing cost (and value) – which current law does *not* require, and which would be unadministrable if one were to attempt to do so – "dollar value" LIFO permits deferral of income attributable to all of these factors, unless and until the differences in degree of the nature of an "item" become so extensive as to constitute a difference in kind.

The Tax Court wrestled with exactly this issue in a case involving a new car dealer at a time when automobiles were undergoing rapid technological evolution.[31] The Tax Court's opinion ultimately concluded that the issue must be resolved on a case-by-case basis – hardly a clear standard for future decisions – but that in this case the taxpayer should be permitted to treat the more feature-rich new model as the same kind ("item") of inventory as the old model. I discuss this case further in my answer to your Question 12, below.

In the leading treatise on the taxation of inventories, the author (who also was the author of the memorandum submitted to this Committee by the LIFO Coalition on June 26, 2006) expressly acknowledges that LIFO accounting permits a permanent tax deferral whose magnitude is affected by several factors in addition to inflation.[32] In particular, he notes that how

---

value of their crude oil inventories. That provision was scored as raising approximately $5 billion in tax. $5 billion ÷ 0.75 = $6.7 billion. $6.7 billion ÷ 0.35 = $19 billion.

30 *Hutzler Brothers Co. v. Commissioner*, 8 T.C. 14, 25 (1947); see also *Basse v. Commissioner*, 10 T.C. 328, 338 (1948).

31 *Wendle Ford Sales, Inc. v. Commissioner*, 72 T.C. 447 (1979).

32 Leslie Schneider, *Federal Income Taxation of Inventories*, at §10.01[1][b] (2006).

a company defines an "item," which I discuss in my answer to Question 12 below, can have a positive or negative impact on how well LIFO isolates inflation.

One possible way of rethinking the LIFO accounting method to isolate only inflationary adjustments to cost, rather than "value creep," would be to abandon LIFO and simply index the cost of inventory (determined presumably on a FIFO basis) to inflation.[33] This solution might address one of the four fundamental problems with LIFO accounting that I identified in my answer to your Question 2, but not the other ones.

9. *Do you think taxpayers generally calculate LIFO inventory accurately? What are the most frequent factors of noncompliance?*

I have no independent information to offer on the extent of taxpayer noncompliance with the detailed requirements of LIFO reporting. The Commissioner of the Internal Revenue Service would be in a better position to answer this question.

10. *Do you think the IRS does a good job of enforcing LIFO? Do you think IRS guidance accurately applies the law?*

I have no independent information to offer on the quality of the IRS's enforcement of the detailed requirements of LIFO.

11. *What is your opinion of the IRS "cut-off" method for voluntary changes in LIFO? Is it fair to allow taxpayers who stop using LIFO to avoid paying taxes on their LIFO deferrals when other taxpayers have paid taxes all along on their income?*

There are two ways a taxpayer can respond if it changes its accounting method from Accounting Method A to Accounting Method B. If a section 481(a) adjustment applies, the taxpayer records its income in the year after its accounting change as if it had been using method B all along. Because doing so ordinarily results in the duplication or omission of income or deductions, a section 481(a) adjustment will add or subtract an amount from the current year's income to avoid such results.[34]

Alternatively, a "cut-off" method applies in most situations if the taxpayer is switching from one LIFO method or sub-method to another.[35] The "cut-off" method allows the taxpayer to

---

33 In the context of a larger tax reform project, the U.S. Treasury Department made a similar proposal. *See* 1 U.S. Dep't of the Treasury, *Tax Reform for Fairness, Simplicity, and Economic Growth: The Treasury Department Report to the President* 111 (1984) (proposing both the repeal of LIFO conformity, and the adoption of inflation-indexed FIFO).

34 If the switch is voluntary, the adjustment can occur over a default period of four years, rather than immediately. Rev. Proc. 97-27 § 5.02(3)(a).

35 Rev. Proc. 97-27 § 5.02(3)(b). The term "change within the LIFO inventory method" is defined at § 3.09.

continue using LIFO Sub-Method A for all transactions arising before the method switch, and LIFO Sub-Method B for all subsequent transactions. The taxpayer will continue using both methods until, in the LIFO situation, all the original inventory accounted for under LIFO Sub-Method A is exhausted. This effectively allows the taxpayer to continue deferring income just as it had been under the original method A. Therefore, to the extent that the practices under method A understated the taxpayer's income in a given year, I do not believe that permitting the cut-off method is fair to those taxpayers who have not been using LIFO to defer income.

To be clear, the "cut-off" method only applies when a taxpayer switches between two LIFO methods or sub-methods, and would not apply if the taxpayer switches between LIFO and FIFO. Section 481(a), in combination with a subsequent IRS revenue procedure,[36] requires a taxpayer to recapture previously deferred income over a four-year period when the taxpayer voluntarily switches from LIFO to FIFO. As discussed in my answer to your Question 5, I recognize the substantial cash cost associated with this rule, and therefore advocate back taxes that become due in connection with the legislative repeal of LIFO.

12. *Do you consider the "definition of an item" to be a FIFO or a LIFO issue?*

The word "item" is sufficiently broad in meaning as to have relevance to both contexts, but I think of the phrase, when used as a term of art, as principally relevant to the detailed application of LIFO, and in particular the dollar-value LIFO method. The avowed purpose of LIFO is to permit taxpayers to defer inflation-related increases in inventory values.[37] To do so, one must compare the costs of producing (or buying) apples in one year to the cost of producing (or buying) apples – or at least other forms of hand fruit – in other years. The purpose of the word "item" is to make sure that the production or acquisition costs being compared relate to the same kind of good – and not, to continue the analogy, to apples in 1976 but to steak in 2006. If a taxpayer's inventory tax accounting methods define apples as the same "items" as steak (e.g. "foodstuffs"), then the increased acquisition cost of steak over apples would be caused by the substitution of goods, rather than inflation in the market for hand-fruit. Very generally, therefore, a narrower definition and interpretation of the word "item" leads to a better isolation of the inflationary component of increased inventory costs, and also the risk of imposing higher administrative burdens on taxpayers.[38]

Thus, in one famous case,[39] the taxpayer was an automobile dealer; its "items" of LIFO inventory comprised new cars and new trucks. The question was whether the introduction of catalytic converters and new solid state ignition systems in 1975 meant that 1975 new cars were not sufficiently similar to 1974 new cars as to be the same "item." As it happens, the Tax Court in this case concluded that these engineering developments were not sufficient to make 1975 cars different "items" from 1974 cars. The Tax Court also rejected the taxpayer's argument that a "car is a car," but declined to offer any further guidance, other than to hold that the issue of when

---

36 Rev. Proc. 97-27 § 5.02(3)(a).

37 *Amity Leather Products Co. v. Commissioner*, 82 T.C. 726, 732 (1984); *Hamilton Industries, Inc. v. Commissioner*, 97 T.C. 120, 130 (1991).

38 *Richardson v. Commissioner*, T.C. Memo 1996-368,at 48-49.

39 *Wendle Ford Sales, Inc. v. Commissioner*, 72 T.C. 447 (1979).

the point when an original "item" has evolved (through "value creep" or otherwise) into a new "item" must be determined on a case-by-case basis.

As this summary suggests, it is very difficult to decide where to draw the line: are 1976 new cars, for example, the same "item" as 2006 new cars in the hands of a new car dealer? The case-by-case approach used by the courts and the IRS in drawing this line is far too ambiguous in application to ensure that taxpayers will not use LIFO accounting to offset price increases unrelated to inflation.[40] The tremendous practical difficulties in policing this distinction argue in favor of repealing the LIFO method of inventory accounting.

---

[40] The IRS's own internal guidance to Revenue Agents hints at the practical difficulties they face in making these refined judgments. For example, in its manual on how to audit new car dealerships, after a brief discussion of *Wendle*, the IRS instructs its auditors that "[a] 1995 Ford Thunderbird does not even closely resemble a Thunderbird of the early sixties; for all practical purposes only the name remains the same . . . . Therefore, in lieu of everything else, most new vehicle inventory should be reclassified as new items periodically." Internal Revenue Service, *New Vehicle Dealership, Audit Technology Guide (ATG)* ch. 5, at 14 (2005). The guide notes that the judge in *Wendle* suggested that vehicles should "perhaps" be reclassified every 5, 10 or 15 years. *Id.* Lastly, the guide instructs auditors, when comparing vehicles, to "consider[] differences in make, year, model, body style, standard equipment, options, and other factors; appropriate adjustments should be made to the cost of the vehicles on hand at the end of the prior taxable year to account for as many of these factors as possible." *Id.* at ch. 5, 8. In light of all these administrative difficulties, the IRS has developed an alternative "simplified" LIFO method exclusively for new automobile dealers; taxpayers have the option to follow this method or not. Rev. Proc. 97-36.

Statement of
Eileen J. O'Connor
Assistant Attorney General
Tax Division
Before the
Committee on Finance
United States Senate

Concerning

"CORPORATE AND PARTNERSHIP ENFORCEMENT ISSUES"
June 13, 2006

Introduction

I thank the Committee for inviting me to discuss the work of the Tax Division of the United States Department of Justice. I last had an opportunity to come before the Committee a year ago, and there is much to report on our progress in addressing the challenges of improving the climate of tax compliance.

My remarks this morning will detail our recent experience in dealing with tax matters that affect taxpayers within the responsibility of the Large and Midsize Business Division of the IRS (LMSB) - - including corporations, sub-chapter S corporations, and partnerships with assets greater than $10 million. Due to the good work of our attorneys, there are many successes to report. I will also discuss the challenges we face in defending the fisc when we are up against large and well-financed legal opponents, as is often the case in tax shelter litigation. Following this, I will respond to your more specific questions concerning the Supreme Court's holding in *Cheek v. United States*, 498 U.S. 192 (1991), and the recommendations contained in letters by Ms. J.J. MacNab and Mr. Jay Adkisson. As you requested, I will also attempt to address issues that we view as limiting the ability of our office to effectively enforce the tax laws passed by the Congress or matters that we believe are frustrating the spirit or intent of law passed by the Congress.

The Tax Division

The primary mission of the Tax Division is to enforce the nation's tax laws fully, fairly, and consistently. The Tax Division enforces the nation's criminal tax laws. The Tax Division authorizes all grand jury investigations and prosecutions involving violations of the Internal Revenue Code and, in conjunction with the United States Attorneys, tries criminal tax cases in the federal courts and represents the United States in criminal appeals. The Tax Division represents the United States in federal civil tax trials in all state and federal courts, except the United States Tax Court, represents the United States in all appeals of cases involving or affecting the administration or enforcement of federal tax laws in the federal circuit courts of appeals and in the state appellate courts, and assists the Solicitor General of the United States in Supreme Court cases involving those matters.

At any given time, we have about 7,000 civil cases in progress and about 750 cases before the United States Courts of Appeal. This past fiscal year, we authorized the prosecution of more than 1,400 defendants, an increase of 2% from the prior year, which itself was an increase of 22% over the year before that. To accomplish all of this, the Tax Division employs about 500 people, of whom about 295 are attorneys.

The Tax Gap

The IRS estimates that the Tax Gap - the difference between taxes owed and taxes paid on a timely basis - was approximately $345 billion in 2001. This amount was reduced by late payments and enforced collection activity to a net tax gap of $290 billion in 2001. The two components of the Tax Gap most relevant to the focus of today's hearing are underreporting by large corporations and underreporting of business income by individuals. The IRS estimates that the first category -- large corporate underreporting -- accounts for about $25 billion of the Tax Gap. Underreporting of business income by individuals accounts for $109 billion of the Tax Gap, and a portion of this total includes underreporting by the high-net-worth individuals who have owned interests in the large passthrough entities - - partnerships, LLCs, or S Corporations -- that are believed to have engaged in improper tax shelter transactions.

President Bush has made tax enforcement a priority: IRS's enforcement funding for the current year is $442 million more than it was last year, and the President's Budget for the upcoming fiscal requests another $137 million increase. If Congress passes the FY 2007 increase the President has requested, IRS will have $579 million more devoted to enforcement in FY 2007 than it did in FY 2005.

The Tax Division's caseload is a direct result of IRS enforcement activity, and generally occurs about two years after it. For this reason, the President's budget request for FY 2007 includes increased funding for the Tax Division to enable it to follow through on the IRS's increased enforcement efforts.

The immediate results of the Administration's increased focus on closing the Tax Gap are clear to see. IRS has increased enforcement revenue from audits of corporations and individuals to $17.7 billion in 2005 compared to $10.7 billion in 2003. In all, from 2004 to 2005, collection from heightened enforcement efforts rose 10%, from $43.1 billion to $47.3 billion.[1]

The Tax Division's work on this mission has an immediate payoff. Over the last five years, Tax Division attorneys on average have returned 24 dollars to the Treasury for every dollar they cost to employ. Significant as the dollars are, they are but a fraction of taxes voluntarily paid by taxpayers because of the precedents set by the Division's cases and taxpayers' trust in the integrity of the tax system that results from them. Thus, the effects of the Division's litigation on tax administration extend well beyond the cases that it handles. Decisions in the Division's cases settle

---

[1] Source: "Testimony of Commissioner of Internal Revenue Mark Everson Before the Senate Committee on the budget on the Tax Gap and How to Solve It," February 15, 2006.

questions of law that frequently govern millions of taxpayers. One favorable decision can resonate far beyond the parties directly involved and lead to billions of dollars in additional tax collections. Similarly, as discussed in more detail later, criminal prosecutions brought or authorized by the Division deter many taxpayers who might consider evading taxes in ways large and small.

Additionally, the Division's independent review of the merits of cases to be brought or defended significantly improves the consistency of the Government's position with applicable law and policy. This balance of independence and, where appropriate, aggressive litigation, helps to ensure that taxpayers pay the taxes the law requires and at the same time helps to maintain their perception of the fairness of the law.

The Tax Division is a key player in efforts to close the Tax Gap. In addition to its work collecting taxes for the Government, a significant portion of the Division's time and resources is directed to stopping the spread of improper tax shelters, shutting down promoters of tax schemes and scams, and assisting the IRS in collecting the information necessary to identify persons marketing and using tax avoidance packages.

The work of the Tax Division has been and will continue to be directly and significant impacted by the increased level of IRS enforcement activity. For example, in addition to stepping up audits and investigations, the IRS has increased its use of "settlement initiatives" - - such as the multi-billion dollar Son of BOSS tax shelter settlement initiative - - under which the IRS publicly states the terms under which it will agree to resolve a dispute concerning the taxes, penalties, and interest owed as a result of a specific tax shelter. Tax Division litigation plays a major role in the success of IRS settlement initiatives. First, the Tax Division's vigorous litigation to obtain judicial enforcement of IRS summonses resulted in the identification of tax shelter participants who might otherwise have evaded detection. Secondly, the Tax Division's success in litigation challenging the merits of improper tax shelters creates the credible threat that shelter participants will lose in court, which encourages them to settle.

The IRS received full funding support of its FY 2006 budget request, which focuses primarily on enforcement initiatives. The Tax Division has been an integral part of the Administration's increased enforcement initiatives, resulting in ever-increasing workloads for the Division's attorneys. However, the additional resources being devoted in the IRS's FY 2006 and FY 2007 budget will push the Tax Division's workload for FY 2008 even higher, as the IRS develops even more civil and criminal cases the Tax Division will be called upon to litigate. The Congress' continued support of the President's resource requests for tax law enforcement for FY 2006 and FY 2007 and future years is very important. The chart below depicts the Tax Division's workload growth.

Increases in IRS Enforcement Drive Tax Division Caseloads Higher

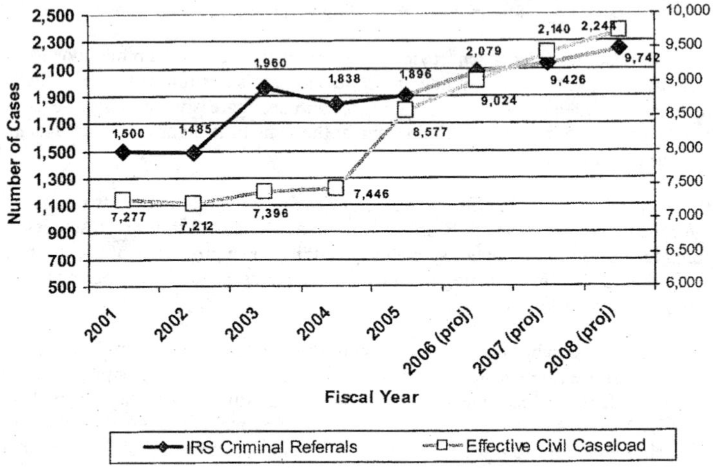

Civil Litigation

The Division's civil trial and appellate work covers a broad spectrum of litigation in the United States district courts, the United States Court of Federal Claims, United States bankruptcy courts, the United States Circuit Courts of Appeals (and working with the Office of the Solicitor General, the United States Supreme Court), and state courts. The Division's civil trial attorneys are responsible for assuring public compliance with the nation's internal revenue laws, while advocating fair and consistent positions.

The Tax Division's civil litigation has both a direct and an indirect impact on federal tax laws. In cases the Tax Division handles, billions of dollars are directly at stake, either defending against unjustified refund claims taxpayers have filed against the United States Treasury or through affirmative litigation that seeks to collect revenue to satisfy unpaid tax debts. Defensive litigation has averaged, since FY 2001, 75% (by hours) and 78% (by cases received), respectively, of the Tax Division's civil caseload. Equally important, the Tax Division's civil trial and appellate litigation results in precedents that control the disposition of thousands of cases pending administratively with the IRS, thus giving the Division's work an even more significant, indirect impact on tax administration.

For civil cases, the Tax Division measures cases successfully litigated, in total or in part, by the resolution of a claim through judgment or other court order. In FY 2005, the Division won the following percentages of cases decided:

Trial Courts – 96%
Taxpayer Appeals – 95%
Government and Cross Appeals - 70%

a. Civil Litigation Involving Large Taxpayers

i. Stopping the Spread of Tax Shelters

Abusive tax shelters cost the Government many billions of dollars each year. The IRS says that tax-shelter proliferation is one of the most significant problems confronting our tax system. A February 2005 GAO report concluded that 207 Fortune 500 companies engaged in tax-shelter transactions, costing the Federal Treasury as much as $56 billion. Sophisticated tax professionals promote these complicated transactions to corporations and wealthy individuals. Frequently, the individuals are key officers in these business entities. Tax shelters typically involve multiple, complex, and sometimes well-disguised transactions that have been structured to provide substantial tax benefits that were not intended by Congress or that otherwise lack economic substance independent of those tax benefits. Because these transactions involve enormous sums of money and often attract significant media attention, a coordinated and effective effort is essential to prevent substantial losses to the Treasury and to deter future use of such shelters by other taxpayers.

The Tax Division plays an important role in the Government's efforts to combat improper tax shelters by defending in the federal district courts, the Court of Federal Claims, and the appellate courts the IRS's determination that the tax shelter is abusive tax avoidance. The cases the Division defends involve millions of dollars in tax revenue, and affect potentially billions of dollars of tax revenue owed by other taxpayers.

The chart below shows how the number of tax shelter cases in litigation has been steadily increasing. As of March 31, 2006, the Division is handling 68 groups of related cases, involving over 200 taxpayers. The Division projects a total of 76 groups of shelter cases by the end of the Fiscal Year. Despite victories in significant cases, the number of tax shelter cases being handled by the Tax Division continues to increase substantially. As IRS continues to vigorously investigate tax shelters, the Tax division's litigation to support that effort – by litigating to enforce summonses and to defend tax shelter refund claims – will continue as well.

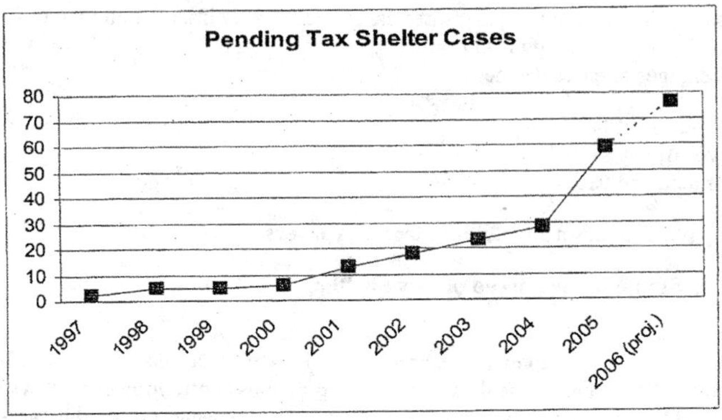

The Tax Division anticipates that over the next several years, tax shelters will continue to be hotly contested in the federal district courts and in the Court of Federal Claims. New significant cases are anticipated in the near future. Some of these transactions coming to the Tax Division involve complex leasing arrangements, known as "LILO" and "SILO" transactions, and were addressed in part on a prospective basis by Congress in 2004 (The 10-year revenue estimate provided for the legislative amendments was $26.56 billion[2]).

Many of tax shelters use structures partnership structures that introduce special considerations and particular problems into their resolution. For example, the partnership provisions of the Tax Equity and Fiscal Responsibility Act of 1982 ("TEFRA") did much to consolidate the resolution of partnership matters in a single proceeding, which matters previously had been subject to as many lawsuits as there were partners. More than two decades after enactment, many TEFRA procedural issues remain to be resolved. Distinguishing between partnership-level items and partner-level items, for example, continues to be problematic. We often must litigate the question whether a given issue is within the jurisdiction of the court hearing the TEFRA suit. There are three significant problems areas:

- First, disputes involving the proper character of items under TEFRA, which must be briefed and argued, and which are a tactical concern that must be handicapped and planned by the lawyers, are a drain on resources -- the Department's, the taxpayers,' and the courts.'
- Second, the line currently drawn between partner and partnership items leaves outside of the TEFRA suit some issues that, we believe, would be best resolved in that suit -- issues

[2] Staff of the Joint Committee on Taxation, "Estimated Budget Effects Of The Conference Agreement For H.R. 4520, The 'American Jobs Creation Act Of 2004,'" October 7, 2004.

that should be resolved in one setting for all the partners, but that, under the current regime, must instead be resolved in a plurality of post-TEFRA partner proceedings.

- Third, the distinction creates the possibility of a sport of whipsaw. An issue that *may* be resolved in the TEFRA suit *must* be resolved there. An issue that is eventually determined to have been a partner*ship*-level issue is untimely if asserted later at the partner level in the post-TEFRA proceeding. On the other hand, the statute of limitations to assess tax arising from an issue that is eventually determined to have been a *partner*-level issue will have run if the issue was wrongly characterized as a partnership-level issue. For that reason, either the Government may lose a defense by guessing wrong about its ultimate characterization, or else the Government takes protective action to maintain *both* possibilities, and proceedings are thereby multiplied.

More recent partnership litigation has arisen in a somewhat different procedural context than the controversies which gave rise to the original legislation. The original TEFRA procedures were designed primarily to address controversies involving large partnerships with dozens of unrelated partners. In those cases, efficient resolution of the controversies required limitation of the litigation to the handful of common issues involving all of the partners; resolution of issues unique to the individual partners would complicate the proceeding and delay resolution of the proceeding. In contrast, more recent controversies have involved partnerships with fewer partners, most of whom are related. In those instances, the presence of issues unique to the individual partners is less significant; indeed, issues previously thought unique to individual partners in the case of large partnerships are often common to many (if not all) of the individual partners in these cases. As a result, a broader definition of the issues which may be resolved at the partnership level would provide for the most efficient resolution of the controversy.

There are several other areas related to tax shelter litigation that are also worthy of consideration by the Committee.

ii. Summons Enforcement Litigation

When individual or business taxpayers do not comply with an IRS summons, the IRS can refer the matter to the Department of Justice to seek a judicial order compelling enforcement. These judicial proceedings not only provide the Government with an essential tool for obtaining information in appropriate cases, but also afford those affected by the summons important procedural and substantive rights.

The Tax Division's success in significant summons enforcement litigation was a key to the ability of the IRS to identify many tax-shelter participants. When prominent law firms and public accounting firms began marketing tax shelters to corporations and wealthy individuals, the IRS asked for information the firms were required by law to maintain and provide, and the firms shielded the identify of these customers with invalid claims of privilege. Subsequently, the Tax Division obtained judicial enforcement of IRS summonses issued to Jenkens & Gilchrist, Sidley Austin Brown & Wood, KPMG, BDO Seidman, and Arthur Andersen. Materials produced by these summoned parties were the catalyst for the IRS' ability to clamp down on Son-of-BOSS tax shelters and, ultimately, to collect billions of dollars. Of equal importance, this litigation sent a clear message to promoters and their customers that the Government would not allow them to hide in dark corners behind invalid, and sometimes bogus, claims of privilege. These victories produced important general deterrence, chilling the market for improper tax shelters.

The Tax Division's development of these cases before filing suit is essential to its success. Challenges to claims of privilege require that we review hundreds, sometimes thousands, of pages of documents and testimony to demonstrate that the communications are not privileged because the communications were not confidential, had been disclosed, were not made for the purpose of seeking or giving legal advice, or were made in connection with an on-going or contemplated crime or fraud.

On occasion, we may even need to identify and hire an expert witness. For example, in order to prepare the summons enforcement action for tax accrual workpapers which was recently filed in *United States v. Textron*, (D. R.I.), the Tax Division decided that to adequately explain the relationship of tax accrual workpapers to the audit process, an expert witness should be retained to inform the court about the nature of tax accrual workpapers, the manner in which they are prepared, and the reasons they are prepared. The expert's declaration anticipates many of the arguments that we expect will be made by taxpayers with respect to these documents, including claims of privilege and work-product.

The Division's reputation for tenacious and thorough litigation of summons cases on occasion permits us to obtain voluntary compliance even prior to filing a petition. Of course, these are cases where the IRS was unable to secure compliance on its own. In two tax accrual workpaper referrals, for example, Department attorneys met with taxpayers' counsel and persuaded them to comply (at least in substantial part) with the summonses, thereby obtaining information quickly and without litigation.

iii. Stopping the Promoters of Schemes and Scams

In addition to the complex and technical improper tax shelters used by corporations, large partnerships, and the wealthy persons that invest in them, there are a multitude of less sophisticated tax schemes and scams. Other recent schemes have included:

1. Claims that people are not required to pay taxes for frivolous reasons, such as that Section 861 of the Internal Revenue Code exempts U.S. citizens from paying taxes on income received in the U.S.; or that one can expatriate oneself from the tax system without leaving the U.S.

2. Filing large refund requests through the amended returns process to avoid extensive scrutiny.

3. Schemes setting up sham trusts to allow taxpayers to deduct personal expenses.

4. "Warehouse banks" to commingle and conceal assets.

5. Schemes advocating filing tax returns falsely reporting "zero" income.

6. Urging employers to fail to withhold, report, or pay payroll and income taxes.

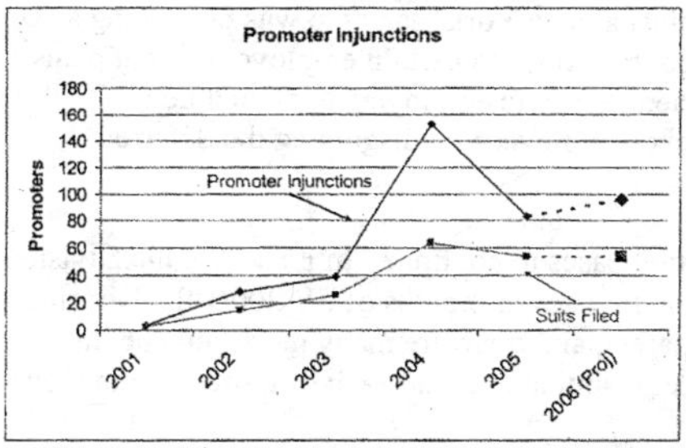

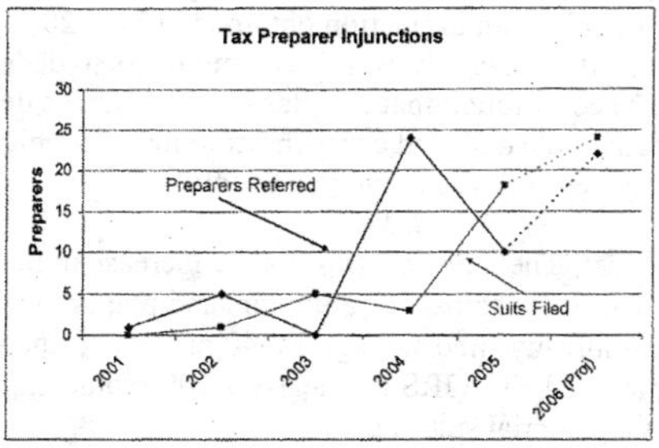

Note: The spike in FY 2004 reflects a single case involving 45 promoters. Referrals of tax scam promoters for injunction litigation are expected to continue at a high rate.

Typically marketed by persons who purport to be tax experts, these scams in reality are nothing more than false and fraudulent "do-it-yourself" tax-relief packages sold to individuals who are uninformed or willfully naïve. Tax Division efforts have led to over 180 injunctions entered against tax scam promoters and fraudulent tax return preparers, shutting down scams involving nearly 400,000 taxpayers and over one billion dollars.

Such schemes place an enormous burden on the IRS. Substantial audit, collection, and administrative resources must be devoted to detect, correct, and collect unpaid taxes that result from improper filings by purchasers of these illicit arrangements. The schemes undermine public confidence in the integrity of our tax system, if honest taxpayers see tax fraud scams being aggressively marketed and going unchallenged.

The Division has encouraged the IRS to target these schemes at their source, *i.e.*, the promoters, so they can be shut down before they result in the need for more IRS examination and collection activity. The Tax Division has developed an expedited referral process so that the cases are quickly and properly investigated. Division employees have helped to train hundreds of Internal Revenue Service agents and lawyers about developing injunction and penalty cases against tax scam promoters.

The Division has recently obtained several notable victories in this area. In April 2006, a federal judge granted the Division's request to permanently enjoin a large organization, ostensibly a charitable one, from falsely advising that its program of providing down payment assistance by home sellers gave rise to a charitable deduction. The IRS estimated that tens of millions of dollars in improper deductions had been claimed by taxpayers based on this erroneous advice.

In September 2005, a court in Florida ordered an individual to stop promoting a variety of tax fraud schemes that had cost the Treasury nearly $18 million and ordered the production of the addresses of hundreds of customers that were involved in filing these false returns. Another example is an injunction obtained in May 2005 against a New York man who was promoting a tax plan that allegedly permitted employers to deduct contributions to certain employee benefit plans. The court found that the plans were schemes designed to enable employers to deduct non-deductible deferred compensation for select high-level employees by disguising the deferred compensation as employee benefits.

The Division expects the increase in injunction cases to continue. In FY 2005, the Division filed suits against 72 promoters and preparers. In the first seven months of FY 2006, the Division has already filed suit against 40 promoters and preparers, and there are many more suits being prepared. The IRS has nearly 1,100 promoters under examination, and each of those examinations is a potential suit in the future.

b. Defending the United States

Suits brought against the United States comprise the majority of the Division's caseload, and the plaintiffs in many of these cases are large corporations or partnerships. The Division defends these lawsuits, which include requests for refund of taxes, challenges to federal tax liens, and allegations of wrongdoing by IRS agents. Overall, the Division's representation of the Government in refund litigation saves the Treasury many hundreds of millions of dollars annually -- *in Fiscal Year 2005 alone the direct savings totaled $1.02 billion.*

c. Civil Tax Appeals

The Tax Division represents the United States in all appeals involving federal tax statutes in the United States circuit courts and their state government equivalents (except for appeals from the Southern District of New York). During the past year, many of the Division's most important cases have involved corporate or large partnership tax shelters. The Division's appellate section attorneys also assist the Solicitor General of the United States by preparing initial drafts of pleadings and briefs in tax cases filed in the Supreme Court, and by preparing drafts of *amicus curiae* briefs when the Supreme Court has called for the Government's views in tax-related cases in which the United States is not a party. The Division also closely reviews all adverse decisions entered by the lower courts in tax cases to determine whether the Government should appeal, and prepares a recommendation to the Solicitor General. The appellate section generally recommends appeal only in those cases where there is a substantial likelihood the Government will ultimately prevail or where an important principle is at stake. Vigorous review of these cases not only secures the result that Department resources are spent wisely on only the most meritorious appeals, but also advances the Tax Division's mission of promoting the fair, correct, and uniform enforcement of the federal tax laws.

The Tax Division has established an impressive record in the appellate courts. For FY 2005, the Tax Division prevailed, in whole or in part, in 95 % of the appeals in which it was defending a favorable lower court decision, and in 70% of the appeals in which it was urging reversal. For FY 2006 (interim through March 31, 2006), the figures are 98% for taxpayer appeals and 87% for Government appeals.

The following cases illustrate the Division's appellate work with specific reference to cases involving corporations, large partnerships or the promoters of tax schemes:

Adverse summary judgment reversed and remanded in $270 million tax shelter case – *Black & Decker Corp. v. United States* (United States Court of Appeals for the Fourth Circuit)

In February, 2006, the Fourth Circuit remanded a $230 million tax shelter case involving an attempt by Black & Decker to deduct a $560 million contingent liability as a business loss. The court stated that the Tax Division had introduced "ample evidence" from which a reasonable trier of fact could conclude that the deductions were not authorized.

Government Victory in Corporate Owned Life Insurance Tax Shelter case– *Dow Chemical Co. v. United States* (Sixth Circuit)

Dow Chemical purchased life insurance policies on the lives of many of its employees, and it paid for the premiums, to a large extent, by borrowing from the insurers and using the cash value of the policies as collateral. For the years 1989 to 1991, Dow Chemical claimed tax deductions of more than $33 million for interest on the loans. The Sixth Circuit disallowed the deductions, determining that the life insurance plans were economic shams because without the benefit of the claimed interest deductions the plans would generate negative cash flows.

Courts of appeals affirm injunctions and enforce summonses against tax-shelter promoters– *U.S. v. Gleason* (Sixth Circuit); *U.S. v. Saladino* (Ninth Circuit); *U.S. v. Kahn* (Eleventh Circuit); *U.S. v. Hargis* (Ninth Circuit)

The Sixth, Ninth, and Eleventh Circuits affirmed lower-court injunctions against promoters of a variety of tax-avoidance schemes. Daniel Gleason assisted his customers in deducting their personal living expenses by setting up sham businesses in their homes. Joseph Saladino had his clients drop out of the tax system by becoming private churches or by invoking fictitious constitutional and common-law rights to exclude their compensation from income. Bryan Malatesta, a CPA and a participant in abusive tax schemes promoted by Eddie Ray Kahn, sent frivolous FOIA requests to the IRS on behalf of Kahn's customers and filed frivolous complaints against IRS employees. The Ninth Circuit affirmed a summons enforcement order against Anthony Hargis and his "warehouse bank," through which Hargis assisted his customers in hiding their income, assets, and identities from the IRS.

Tax Shelter "Investors" Owe Negligence Penalties – *Mortensen v. Commissioner* (Sixth Circuit); *Van Scoten v. Commissioner* (Tenth Circuit)

The Sixth and Tenth Circuits affirmed negligence penalties imposed on taxpayers who invested in sham cattle-breeding partnerships promoted by Walter J. Hoyt III. The courts rejected the taxpayers' claims that the penalties should not be imposed because they reasonably relied upon representations of Hoyt and others in his organization. Hundreds of other taxpayers are also facing negligence penalties on account of their Hoyt partnership investments.

Deliberative process privilege need not be invoked by agency head – *Marriott Int'l Resorts, L.P. v. United States* (Federal Circuit)

The Federal Circuit, reversing the Court of Federal Claims, held that the deliberative-process privilege permits delegation and does not need to be invoked by the agency head. During discovery, Marriott sought documents from the IRS that the Government claimed were protected by the privilege. The privilege had been invoked by a delegate of the Commissioner of Internal Revenue, rather than by the Commissioner himself. The court of appeals held that delegation is permissible if it is carefully undertaken, and the Commissioner's delegation order satisfied this test because it provided detailed criteria to his delegates for invoking the privilege.

Tax Court properly upheld $350 million in deficiencies – *Chrysler Corp. v. Commissioner* (Sixth Circuit)

In resolving all three litigated issues in favor of the Government, the Sixth Circuit disallowed Chrysler's claim for a deduction of $287 million for anticipated warranty liabilities, its claim for almost $62 million in foreign tax credit carryovers, and its claim for a deduction of $327 million for amounts paid to redeem its common stock held by a trust as part of an employee stock ownership plan.

Criminal Prosecution and Appeals

The Tax Division's criminal trial attorneys investigate and prosecute individuals and corporations that attempt to evade taxes, willfully fail to file returns, submit false tax forms, or otherwise violate the federal tax laws. They also investigate and prosecute tax violations committed with other criminal conduct, such as narcotics trafficking, securities fraud, bankruptcy fraud, health-care fraud, organized crime, and public corruption. In addition, Tax Division attorneys investigate and prosecute domestic tax crimes involving international conduct, such as the illegal use of offshore trusts and foreign bank accounts to conceal taxable income and evade taxes. They also conduct Organized Crime and Drug Enforcement Task Force (OCDETF) and terrorism-related criminal investigations, and prosecute organizers of Internet scams.

The Tax Division authorizes and either conducts or supervises all prosecutions under the federal tax laws. The Division's two-pronged mission is: to prosecute criminal tax violations; and to promote a uniform nationwide approach to criminal tax enforcement. In many cases, the Tax Division receives requests from the IRS to prosecute tax violations after the IRS has investigated them administratively. In other cases, the IRS asks the Tax Division to open grand jury investigations to determine whether prosecutable tax crimes have occurred. Tax Division lawyers review and analyze these referrals to assure that uniform standards of prosecution are employed and that criminal tax violations warranting prosecution are prosecuted. After the Division authorizes tax charges, the cases are handled either by the respective United States Attorney's Office (USAO) or, in complex cases or cases in which the USAO is recused or requests assistance, by the Tax Division's own experienced prosecutors. Tax Division prosecutors conduct training seminars for IRS criminal investigators and Assistant U.S. Attorneys, and often provide advice to other federal law enforcement personnel, including the DEA and FBI.

The Tax Division's Criminal Appeals and Tax Enforcement Policy Section (CATEPS) represents the United States in appeals in criminal tax cases prosecuted by Division attorneys, and supervises appeals in matters tried by the USAOs around the country. Similar to the initial review of tax cases by criminal trial attorneys, the appellate review plays a vital role in promoting the fair, correct and uniform enforcement of the internal revenue laws. CATEPS also assists in the negotiation of international tax assistance treaties and policy issues, such as the application of the sentencing guidelines.

Although many such cases are difficult to prosecute, the Division has maintained a conviction rate at or greater than 95%. In FY 2005, the Division's conviction rate was 98% in tax cases. During the first half of FY 2006, the conviction rate was 100%. While the Tax Division is very proud of its conviction rate, the emphasis is on uniform and fair enforcement of the tax laws.

a. Prosecutions of "Pure Tax" Crimes

Many of the cases reviewed, investigated and prosecuted by the Tax Division involve so-called "legal source income." As the name implies, these cases encompass tax crimes involving unpaid taxes on income earned legally (*e.g.*, a restaurateur who skims cash receipts; or a dentist who inflates deductible expenses.) The Division also prosecutes many return preparers who fraudulently inflate deductions or underreport income to obtain unwarranted refunds for their customers. The defendants frequently include return preparers, non-filers and individuals engaging in illegal protest activities.

Evasion of taxes on income from legal sources significantly erodes the federal tax base, so the Division works hard to maintain a strong deterrent. Failure of the Government to vigorously prosecute such cases would undermine the confidence of law-abiding taxpayers and jeopardize in the Government's ability to operate a revenue collection system that depends upon voluntary compliance.

When these cases involve difficult issues of tax law or complex methods of proof, USAOs often call upon the special skills that Tax Division prosecutors bring to the Justice Department's goal of reducing white-collar crime. Prosecutions in these cases often receive substantial local press and media coverage and assure law-abiding citizens who pay their taxes that those who don't aren't getting away with it. During the past year, Division attorneys investigated and prosecuted cases involving tax crimes committed by individuals from all walks of life, including corporate executives, business owners, attorneys, doctors, dentists, an artist and others. A few examples:

In ***United States v. Thomas Mower, et al.*** (D. Utah), a jury convicted Thomas and Leslie Mower, the owners of Neways, Inc., a multilevel marketing company, of conspiracy and evading income taxes for six years. The indictment charged that the Mowers, with the assistance of their corporate counsel, James Thompson, devised a scheme to conceal from the IRS in excess of $1 million in Neways, Inc.'s overseas gross receipts and in excess of $3 million in commission income the Mowers received from Neways. The defendants will be sentenced in September 2006.

In December 2005, in ***United States v. Ronald Bailey*** (E.D. Va.), a former manager of a nursing home in Northern Virginia was sentenced to 51 months in prison and ordered to pay $1.4 million in restitution to the IRS, for committing tax evasion and filing false tax returns. From 1991 through 2000, Bailey withheld taxes from the nursing home employees' wages, but he failed to pay over those taxes to the IRS. In addition, he filed false returns for 1992 through 1995, on which he understated his income and falsely claimed that taxes had been withheld from his income, and he evaded his income taxes for the years 1997 through 2000.

On April 27, 2006, in ***United States v. James Delfino and Jeaniene Delfino*** (E.D. Va.), husband and wife business owners were sentenced to 78 months in prison and 63 months in prison, respectively, for conspiring to impede the IRS and evading the payment of more than $2 million in income tax. The defendants own and operate a successful computer consulting business, but have not paid personal income tax since 1993. The Government proved at trial that the defendants concealed their income and assets from the IRS using sham trusts.

In ***United States v. Walter Anderson*** (D.D.C.), a telecommunications entrepreneur was charged in a 12-count indictment with tax evasion, obstructing the Internal Revenue Service, and defrauding the District of Columbia government by failing to pay well in excess of $200 million in taxes owed to the federal and District of Columbia governments. Anderson is in federal custody pending his trial, which is currently scheduled for January 2007.

The Tax Division and the IRS have encouraged the entry of restitution orders in criminal tax cases in order to facilitate collection of the related civil tax liability. But, while a restitution order can be entered as an independent element of a sentence after conviction for any Title 18 offense, *see* 18 U.S.C. 3663(a)(1)(A), under current law, a restitution order can only be entered as an independent part of a sentence for a Title 26 offense if the defendant consents to paying restitution in a plea agreement. Otherwise, a court may order restitution for such an offense only as a condition of probation or supervised release. *See* 18 U.S.C. 3663(a). In the case of supervised release, collection of restitution is delayed: the restitution requirement does not go into effect until the defendant begins serving the supervised release. The tax loss suffered by the United States is currently treated differently from other kinds of pecuniary loss suffered by the Government or private citizens. There are also issues presented when the Service attempts to collect tax ordered to be paid as restitution. In order for the Service to collect a tax, it must first assess the tax. At present, it appears that the Service may assess amounts of restitution actually paid by a taxpayer with respect to his tax obligation, *see* 26 U.S.C. 6213(b)(4), but there is some question as to whether the Service may assess unpaid amounts of tax ordered to be paid as restitution.

b. Promotions of Improper Tax Shelters

The Division also prosecutes persons who promote or use fraudulent tax shelters and other schemes to evade taxes and hide assets. The number of taxpayers who use these schemes to improperly reduce, or totally evade, their federal income tax liabilities has increased significantly in recent years. One type of scheme involves the use of domestic or foreign trusts to evade taxes. Promoters of these schemes, often using the Internet, aggressively market trusts by employing strained, if not demonstrably false, interpretations of the tax laws. Employing what they often call "asset protection trusts" (ostensibly designed to guard an individual's assets from creditors, including the IRS), these promoters are in fact helping taxpayers to fraudulently assign income and conceal their ownership of income-producing assets in order to evade paying taxes.

In ***United States v. KPMG.*** (S.D.N.Y.), the Government entered into a deferred prosecution agreement with KPMG that charges KPMG with conspiracy to defraud the IRS by developing, implementing and marketing numerous illegal tax shelters. KPMG admitted that its personnel took deliberate steps to conceal the existence of the tax shelters from the IRS. The agreement provides that prosecution against KPMG will be deferred until December 31, 2006, if specified conditions, including payment of the $456 million in fines, restitution, and penalties, are met.

In ***United States v. Jeffrey Stein, et al.*** (S.D.N.Y.), eighteen former officers and associates of the Big-Four accounting firm KPMG and a former tax partner of a national law firm were charged with conspiracy to defraud the IRS, tax evasion and obstruction of the internal revenue laws arising out of illegal tax shelters that KPMG and others designed, marketed and implemented. The shelters allegedly generated at least $11 billion in fraudulent tax losses and resulted in at least $2.5 billion in tax evaded by wealthy individuals. In late March 2006, former KPMG partner David Rivkin pleaded guilty to conspiracy and tax evasion charges. Trial against the remaining defendants is currently scheduled for September 2006.

In February 2006, in ***United States v. HVB*** (S.D.N.Y.), Germany's second largest bank, entered a deferred prosecution agreement with the United States in connection with its role in facilitating tax shelters marketed by KPMG. According to the agreement, HVB will pay nearly $30 million to the United States in fines, penalties and restitution stemming from its work on four questionable tax shelters, and will implement substantial compliance improvements to its operations.

In ***United States v. Michael A. Vallone, et al.*** (N.D. Ill.), nine defendants were charged with participating in a nearly decade-long conspiracy to market and sell sham domestic and foreign trusts through "The Aegis Company." The defendants marketed the scheme to more than 600 wealthy taxpayer clients throughout the United States to hide hundreds of millions of dollars in income, resulting in a tax loss to the United States of at least $68 million. Trial is scheduled to begin in November 2006.

In ***United States v. Graham, et al.*** (S.D. Ohio), six defendants are charged with promoting sham Aegis Company trusts to 220 clients that resulted in a $20 million tax loss to the Federal Treasury. During the course of the scheme, the defendants prepared fraudulent tax returns that concealed clients' income from the IRS. Trial of these defendants is scheduled to begin in Spring 2007.

c. Return-Preparer Fraud

Corrupt accountants and unscrupulous tax return preparers are a major concern of the Tax Division and IRS. Some accountants and return preparers financially benefit by duping unwitting clients into filing fraudulent returns and then take a significant portion of the unwarranted refund as a fee. Other corrupt accountants and unscrupulous return preparers serve as willing "enablers," providing a veneer of legitimacy for clients predisposed to cheat. In either kind of case, the professionals often commit a large number of frauds, and their status, as "professionals," may be perceived as legitimizing tax evasion thereby promoting disrespect for the rule of law. Tax Division attorneys continue to aggressively investigate and prosecute such cases, including the following:

On January 27, 2006, in ***United States v. Jerome H. Harris*** (S.D. Tex.), a Federal judge sentenced the defendant, a full-time City of Houston employee and the owner and operator of a bookkeeping and tax service, to 57 months in prison for preparing hundreds of false tax returns for tax years 1995 through 2000. The false returns the defendant prepared resulted in claims for fraudulent refunds by his clients totaling almost $1.3 million. The Tax Division's Criminal Appeals and Tax Enforcement Section is now handling the defendant's appeal to the United States Court of Appeals for the Fifth Circuit.

On May 2, 2006, in ***United States v. Susan O'Brien, et al.*** (S.D. Cal.), after an eleven-week trial, a Federal jury convicted a professional tax return preparer and two associates of tax fraud. The defendants were charged with promoting a $1 million tax fraud scheme involving sham trusts and the fraudulent preparation of income tax returns. Five other defendants pleaded guilty to felony tax charges before trial.

In ***United States v. Michael Craig Cooper, et al.*** (D. Kan.), four individuals and the organization "Renaissance, the Tax People, Inc.," are charged with conspiracy to impede the IRS, mail fraud and wire fraud in connection with an $84 million tax scheme. From June 1997 though April 2002, the defendants marketed a fraudulent home-based business package through which was offered purportedly legitimate tax return preparation, tax advice and audit protections. Trial of the defendants is scheduled for November 2006.

d. Tax Fraud Promotion

Another Tax Division initiative focuses on active promotion of tax fraud. Tax schemes in this category include claims that an individual is a "sovereign citizen" not subject to U.S. laws, the U.S. income tax is unconstitutional. Other related conduct may include taxpayers taking sham "vows of poverty" and harassing Government employees and judges.

On February 24, 2006, in ***United States v. Irwin Schiff, et al.*** (D. Nev.), a federal judge sentenced high profile tax scam promoter Irwin Schiff to 151 months in prison for tax fraud, an additional 12 months for contempt of court and ordered Schiff to pay $4.2 million in restitution to the IRS. Schiff's two associates, Lawrence Cohen and Cynthia Neun were sentenced to prison terms of 33 months and 68 months, respectively. The defendants were convicted by a federal jury in October 2005, after a six-week trial. Schiff, a nationally recognized tax-protest organizer, and his associates encouraged taxpayers to impede the IRS by filing tax returns with zeroes on each income and expense line, resulting in fraudulent claims for refunds of taxes paid. As a result of the heavily-marketed scheme, taxpayers filed nearly 5,000 fraudulent "zero returns" during a three-year period. The Tax Division's Criminal Appeals and Tax Enforcement Section is currently handling appeals arising out of the convictions.

On February 21, 2006, in ***United States v. David Carroll Stephenson*** (W.D. Wash.), a federal jury convicted the defendant of conspiring to defraud the United States and willful failure to file income tax returns for 1998 through 2000, in connection with his promotion of a tax evasion scheme using "pure equity trust" organizations. Co-conspirator Michael Joseph Shanahan pleaded guilty to the conspiracy charge and failing to file an income tax return for 1999. They falsely advised more than 400 clients that they could avoid paying income tax if they placed their income and assets in "pure equity trusts," while continuing to maintain control over such income and assets. The defendants received more than $2 million in revenue from the scheme. In May, 2006, Stephenson was sentenced to 96 months in prison.

On November 22, 2005, in ***United States v. Larken Rose*** (E.D. Pa.), a federal judge sentenced the defendant to 15 months in prison. A jury convicted Rose, the owner of a medical transcription business, of five counts of willfully failing to file tax returns. Rose is a leading proponent of the so-called 861 position, which incorrectly claims that wages earned by Americans working for domestic companies are not taxable. The federal courts have consistently denounced the 861 position as frivolous.

e. Scams by Prison Inmates

On June 29, 2005, the House Ways and Means Committee, Subcommittee on Oversight held a hearing "to examine tax fraud by inmates." During the past decade, there has been a significant problem with false tax refund claims schemes organized and perpetrated by incarcerated persons, usually in state facilities, often with the assistance of friends and relatives on the outside. While organizers have been prosecuted for criminal tax violations, such prosecutions are time consuming and we found that often, the perpetrators were already serving terms of imprisonment more lengthy than those received for the tax crimes. Also, periodic prisoner transfers spread "know-how" concerning such schemes to other prisons.

Particularly in light of the increasing demands on scarce prosecutorial and judicial resources, the disclosure of information about these schemes to prison officials would facilitate application of administrative punishments, such as isolation and loss of other privileges, which would be more prompt and effective in halting the spread of the schemes than federal criminal prosecutions. The tax "privacy" act, 26 U.S.C. 6103, does not currently authorize disclosure of tax information to state and local prison officials for use in imposing administrative sanctions against prisoners perpetrating federal tax fraud schemes.

On December 15, 2005, the Honorable Jim Ramstad introduced H.R. 4549 to permit the IRS to disclose information about prison inmates to the heads of federal and state correctional agencies for use in preventing the filing of false tax returns, including imposing punishments for violating administrative rules of the prison facility. The principal focus of H.R. 4549 is the filing of false refund claims. However, we have also encountered other fraudulent filing by inmates that did not involve refund claims. The Department has sent a letter to the Subcommittee on Oversight of the House Ways and Means Committee supporting efforts to deal with these problems. Fraudulent actions of inmates are a significant tax enforcement problem that deserves the attention of this Committee.

f. Enforcing the United States' Tax Laws in Today's Global Economy

Americans' abuse of foreign tax havens is on the rise, and abusive tax shelters often make use of tax haven domiciles for the partnerships or other business entities. Increased technical sophistication of financial instruments and the widespread use of the internet have made it easy to instantly move money in and out of the United States, around the world, irrespective of national borders. Usage of tax havens facilitates evasion of United States taxes and the commission of related financial crimes.

Offshore tax schemes are often difficult to detect and prosecute. The countries whose banks are used in such schemes usually have strict bank secrecy laws and will not, or cannot, provide assistance to investigators for the United States. Sophisticated criminals may also use jurisdictions other than traditional tax haven countries, such as Latvia or Germany, in attempting to confuse the U.S. Government and hide their crimes. Some examples of Tax Division efforts follow:

In ***United States v. Daniel P. Andersen, et al.*** (W.D. Wash.), five defendants were charged with operating a multi-level marketing program through an entity named "The Institute for Global Prosperity" that promoted tax evasion schemes to thousands of customers through audio tapes and offshore seminars. The defendants concealed more than $40 million in revenue from the scheme using offshore nominee entities and offshore bank accounts. Four defendants have pleaded guilty to felony tax charges, including the two co-founders of Global Prosperity. The remaining defendant in this case, Global Prosperity co-founder David Struckman, fled to Panama. In early 2006, after months of searching, Panamanian officials arrested Struckman, expelled him from Panama, and accompanied him to the United States. Struckman has been arraigned and is being detained in Seattle pending trial, which is scheduled for January 2007.

In December 2005, in ***United States v. John J. Rizzo*** (D. Ariz.), the defendant, a former state municipal judge, was sentenced to 43 months in prison for promoting a tax fraud scheme at offshore seminars hosted by "The Institute of Global Prosperity." At the seminars, Rizzo marketed written materials that he called the "Millennium 2000 Reliance Defense Program," which were designed to provide taxpayers a good faith reliance defense against potential criminal tax prosecutions. The tax loss for this case is estimated at $200,000.

In ***United States v. Paul Harris, et al.*** (D. Colo.), after a five-week trial, a jury convicted Paul Harris and Lester Retherford of conspiracy and aiding and assisting in the preparation of fraudulent tax returns. The defendants used trusts, offshore debit cards, false invoices, and false option agreements to surreptitiously move clients' money offshore, primarily to the Turks & Caicos Islands, to avoid the scrutiny of the IRS. In December 2005 and January 2006, respectively, a federal judge sentenced Retherford to four years in prison, and Harris to more than five years in prison, for their roles in the scheme. The court found that the tax loss in the case was between $2.5 million and $7 million, but the Judge departed downward from the Sentencing Guidelines for Retherford because of his age and health.

In ***United States v. Evanson, et al.*** (D. Utah), six professionals (two attorneys, two CPAs, an accountant and an investment broker) were charged with conspiracy, fraud and tax charges in connection with promoting a tax fraud scheme that cost the Federal Treasury over $20 million in taxes. The defendants' scheme used, among other things, offshore entities, offshore bank accounts and the services of offshore nominees to create bogus expense and capital loss deductions for their clients. The court has not scheduled a trial date for this case.

Our existing money laundering laws reach domestic laundering of the proceeds of specified unlawful activity with intent to evade tax, *see* 18 U.S.C. § 1956 (a)(1)(A)(ii), but there is no corresponding money laundering offense addressing the international movement of funds with the intent to commit a tax offense. Section 1956(a)(2)(A) criminalizes the international movement of funds with the intent to promote the carrying on of "specified unlawful activity," a defined term that does not include tax offenses. Section 1956(a)(2)(B) also does not apply because the funds involved in the offense must represent the proceeds of some form of unlawful activity; and the transportation of such funds must be intended either to conceal or disguise the proceeds of specified unlawful activity or to avoid a transaction reporting requirement under State or Federal law.

An increasing number of criminal tax trials require the use of evidence obtained from overseas. One problem we face when dealing with evidence obtained from overseas is admissibility of the evidence. Most of the countries with which we exchange information for use in criminal tax trials have systems that differ significantly from our own. Under 18 U.S.C. § 3505, we can use foreign business records as evidence at a criminal trial, if the records are accompanied by a certificate signed by the custodian of the records. For purposes of section 3505, a "foreign certification" means "a written declaration made and signed in a foreign country by the custodian of a foreign record of regularly conducted activity or another qualified person that, if falsely made, would subject the maker to criminal penalty under the laws of that country." 18 U.S.C. § 3505(c)(2). The systems of some countries (for example the Netherlands) however, simply do not provide for such certifications by custodians of records.

h. International Cooperation to Investigate Evasion of U.S. Taxes

Tax Division attorneys provide advice and assistance to Government attorneys and agents seeking information and assistance from other countries for both civil and criminal investigations and cases. Recently, the Division provided advice and assistance to attorneys and agents seeking information from numerous countries including Sweden, Germany, Israel, Canada, the Cayman Islands, the Netherlands Antilles, Brazil, Panama, Venezuela, and Switzerland.

Tax Division attorneys also advise and assist in efforts to secure increased cooperation with foreign nations. The Division recently assisted the Department of State deciding what countries to put on the Treaty Priority List for the current year. The Division also helped the Treasury Department in its negotiations on tax treaties with Belgium, Bulgaria, and other countries. The Division also assisted in negotiating important Tax Information Exchange Agreements that recently went into effect in the Cayman Islands, Jersey, Guernsey, and the British Virgin Islands.

The Division also provided significant assistance to the IRS in drafting a démarche to be sent to U.S. Embassies located in countries that are members of the Organization of American States (OAS). The démarche urges the Embassies to encourage the countries in which they are located to sign a protocol to the OAS Mutual Legal Assistance Treaty (MLAT). The protocol requires member states to exchange information in criminal tax cases. The current OAS MLAT allows member states receiving a request for information to refuse to provide the information if the offense is a tax offense, unless the offense involves laundering of proceeds of an offense covered by the agreement. The State Department expects to issue the démarche soon.

The Division also consults with and provides advice to the Financial Action Task Force (FATF) to combat money laundering and the financing of terrorism. The Tax Division also helps teach international training programs to improve other countries' tax administration and enforcement programs, and seeks to foster international cooperation in tax, money laundering, and counter terrorist financing matters.

Cheek Defense

The Chairman's letter of June 1, 2006, asked us to comment on the impact of the Supreme Court's holding in *Cheek v. United States* (498 U.S. 192, 112 L. Ed. 2d 617, 111 S. Ct. 604 (1991)) that a good-faith defense does not need to be objectively reasonable to negate "willfulness"– the state of mind that the Government must establish in order to prove a tax crime. In her March 15, 2006, letter to the Committee, J.J. McNabb recommends that the Congress enact legislation requiring that willfulness be based on a reasonable misunderstanding of the law.

As the Supreme Court explained in *Cheek*, the tax laws are complex, and Congress did not intend that a taxpayer's *bona fide* misunderstanding of the tax law should be penalized as a criminal violation. The courts typically exclude as irrelevant or confusing defendants' efforts to show that there are others who agree with their outrageous claims about the state of the tax law. The more outrageous the alleged belief, of course, the easier it is for the Government to prove that the taxpayer violated a known legal duty. In our view, changing the standard from subjective reasonableness to objective reasonableness would not be particularly helpful.

Furthermore, we doubt that the availability of the so-called *Cheek* defense is responsible for the proliferation of "absurd theories" Our continuing success in prosecuting the peddlers of those theories, both before and after *Cheek*, has shown that *Cheek* in fact offers the scam artists no real shelter. We see frivolous defenses now for the same reasons we always have: the scammers are greedy and think they can get away with it.

Comments on Points Raised by J.J. MacNab and Jay D. Adkisson

The Tax Division appreciates the focus, determination, and energy Ms. MacNab and Mr. Adkisson bring to putting a halt to tax scams. And we share it. The Tax Division has obtained more than 180 injunctions against tax scam promoters and fraudulent tax return preparers. These scams involved nearly 400,000 taxpayers and more than a billion dollars. This stands in stark contrast to the mere handful of injunctions obtained during the preceding eight years.

Complementing our civil efforts to stop promoters of tax-fraud schemes and scams are our criminal prosecutions. During the past five years, more than 120 tax fraud promoters have been convicted. Many had nationwide reach and visibility. They include well-known tax scammers mentioned by Ms. MacNab—Irwin Schiff, Lynne Meredith, Larken Rose, Anderson's Ark Associates, and the Institute for Global Prosperity—as well as many others.

We appreciate Ms. MacNab's and Mr. Adkisson's positive feedback and compliments on the work of the Tax Division and the assistance they have provided to the Department on several occasions in identifying individuals who defied injunction orders or whose illegal conduct otherwise merited our attention.

Publicity

In our view, justice must not only be done, it must be seen to be done. We all know that the tax system would not work if, believing that the tax system was not fairly administered, people did not voluntarily comply with their tax obligations. An IRS three or four times its present size could not compel payment of a fraction of the trillions of tax dollars paid into the Treasury each year, if compulsion were the only means for getting payment. For our system of voluntary compliance to succeed, it must be seen to be fairly enforced.

For this reason, when I took office, the Tax Division began issuing press releases on our civil injunctions and criminal prosecutions, and posting them on our website. Our website at http://www.usdoj.gov/tax/taxpress2006.htm publicizes our enforcement actions, and our cases have garnered substantial favorable press coverage in major local and national media outlets over the past five years. We continue to improve our website to ensure that those who might otherwise be tempted by the latest tax scam will easily be able to find information about our law-enforcement efforts against scam promoters and participants.

Coordination

The Tax Division and the Internal Revenue Service work hand-in-glove on all matters that could involve litigation, including tax fraud schemes. Our executives meet regularly to discuss emerging challenges and to establish priorities. As appropriate, our personnel engage in cross-training. One challenge unique to tax enforcement, of course, is the privacy necessarily accorded return information.

Other Technical Issues That Affect Enforcement

The Committee asked us to identify issues that make tax enforcement difficult or that are not in keeping with the spirit or intent of the tax law. Here are a few:

- The budget President Bush submitted to congress for the upcoming fiscal year recommends legislation giving the United States Tax Court jurisdiction over all collection due process (CDP) cases and providing for post-levy review of levies relating to unpaid employment taxes. These proposals would significantly improve the CDP procedures, and deserve the Committee's prompt attention. The Honorable James S. Halpern made a similar suggestion last year, when he testified at a confirmation hearing regarding his reappointment to the United States Tax Court.

- Under current law, the offense of willful failure to file a tax return is a misdemeanor punishable by imprisonment for no more than one year. As a result, the sentence for this offense is limited to one year. On several occasions, most recently in S. 2020, the Tax Relief Act of 2005, this Committee has approved legislation creating a new felony offense for an aggravated failure to file–the failure to file a tax return for three or more consecutive years.

- We have successfully enjoined many cases of abusive conduct on the authority of IRC §§ 7407 and 7408. We are studying whether changes to the injunction provisions would be helpful, and may have proposals at a later date.

- Congress has enacted numerous penalties to crack down on tax shelter promoters and to ensure that "reportable transactions" are disclosed to the IRS. As with all other tax penalties, these new penalties are subject to discharge in a bankruptcy proceeding that is commenced more than three years after the penalty transaction occurs. Nontax penalties generally cannot be discharged.

Conclusion

The dedicated men and women of the Tax Division are fully committed to the fair and uniform enforcement of the internal revenue laws, and to restoring and maintaining the integrity of the federal tax system. Since I last had the opportunity to address the Committee, we have made significant progress. And, as then, considerable challenges remain.

Thank you, Mr. Chairman and Members of the Committee. I will be pleased to respond to any questions you might have.

Eileen J. O'Connor
Assistant Attorney General
Tax Division
United States Department of Justice
Statement before the Senate Finance Committee
Hearing on Corporate Tax Issues
June 13, 2006

Stock options give employees the right to purchase shares later at the price of the stock on the date of the grant. The issue to which you refer is the highly suspicious award of stock options to executives at a low point of stock value.

In several districts around the country, the Department of Justice is investigating allegations that:

(1) certain stock option grants were backdated to provide the executive a lower price at which to exercise the option, and/or

(2) other unfair (and perhaps illegal) practices were employed to price the options at a low dollar amount, like awarding options based on "inside" information about a pending event that would send the stock price upwards.

Such conduct would be a fraud on the market: it would boost executive's compensation at the expense of other investors. If the investigations reveal criminal behavior, charges that might be brought would include securities fraud, mail fraud, wire fraud, and various tax charges against both the individuals and the corporations.

Information more detailed than that I am not at liberty to disclose. I can tell you, however, that the Department considers allegations of this nature to be very serious. The criminal penalties (if the crime occurred after July 30, 2002):

- Mail (18 USC 1341) and wire (18 USC 1343) fraud - 20 years incarceration and $250,000 fine
- Securities fraud (18 USC 1348) - 25 years incarceration and $250,000 fine
- Tax evasion (26 USC 7201) - 5 years incarceration and $250,000 fine
- Filing a false tax return - 3 years incarceration and $250,000
- Penalties under the Securities Act of 1934 (15 USC 78ff) 20 years incarceration and a $5,000,000 fine

Successful prosecutions will require careful and detailed investigations. Until those investigations have concluded, it is difficult to assess whether, or which charges will be prosecuted.

Questions for the Record for
Eileen J. O'Connor
Assistant Attorney General for the Tax Division
United States Department of Justice
Senate Finance Committee
June 13, 2006 hearing
"A Tune-Up On Corporate Tax Issues: What's Going On Under the Hood?"

From Senator Grassley:

1. **I would like your views on the matter of forum shopping, particularly by corporations.**

   The Committee is hearing more and more that corporations are aggressively using forum shopping for purposes of litigation. I'm concerned about the impact this is having on efforts to fight tax shelters and also the difficulties in tax administration of having so many courts having different opinions on tax questions.

   I would like your views on this problem and specifically, should Congress look at providing taxpayers one forum, the tax court, for civil tax matters?

A taxpayer can challenge an Internal Revenue Service (IRS) deficiency determination by filing a petition in the United States Tax Court or by paying the tax and commencing a refund suit in a United States District Court or in the United States Court of Federal Claims. Similarly, in a case subject to the Tax Equity and Fiscal Responsibility Act of 1982 (TEFRA) unified partnership audit procedures, the tax matters partner or another partner can file a Tax Court petition to obtain judicial review or, after making deposit in the amount of the tax, can file suit in the district court or the Court of Federal Claims. Decisions of the Tax Court and district courts are reviewed by the United States Court of Appeals for the taxpayer's home circuit. Court of Federal Claims decisions are reviewed by the Court of Appeals for the Federal Circuit.

In choosing whether to petition the Tax Court or to instead bring suit in a district court or the Court of Federal Claims, taxpayers take a variety of factors into consideration. The existence of favorable precedent in one court or unfavorable precedent in another court can be a significant factor, as can differences in the courts' procedures. While district courts and the Court of Federal Claims allow broad discovery, for example, discovery in the Tax Court is limited.

In district courts, but not in the Court of Federal Claims or in Tax Court, a jury trial can be had. This is the case in all refund suits against the United States, including those involving tax shelters, unless TEFRA requires unified partnership proceedings. A taxpayer might have more confidence in a jury of peers than in an unknown single judge. Certainly, tax issues are equal in importance to other issues where citizens have a right to a jury trial. When a judge is to be the decision-maker, a taxpayer may analyze the pros and cons of a tax specialist judge over a judge exposed daily to a broad range of alleged legal violations. Access to a local federal district court provides taxpayers with an opportunity to have their disputes resolved by generalist judges at the local level. In large complex cases, the willingness of the Court of Federal Claims to conduct the trial at multiple locations for the convenience of the parties and witnesses may be an important consideration. The Tax Court provides a pre-payment forum before tax specialist judges. The fact of a pre-payment forum is frequently determinative but a taxpayer may be willing to make payment in order to deal with Department of Justice attorneys who will give an independent evaluation of the issues raised.

The availability of three trial courts for challenging an IRS audit determination provides taxpayers with alternative forums in which to challenge audit determinations. Allowing a choice of forum gives taxpayers more confidence in the fairness of the judicial results they receive and in tax administration generally. The fact that significant legal issues affecting the taxpaying public are analyzed and considered by judges who specialize in tax cases, as well as by generalist and local judges who bring insights from other disciplines, helps ensure that a correct interpretation of the law ultimately occurs. The litigation of the same or similar issues in multiple courts provides an opportunity for issues to percolate. Multiple decisions from different legal minds and perspectives are likely to achieve a better result for tax administration. Moreover, regardless of the trial forum, all appeals from trial court decisions will be heard by generalist judges. All sophisticated litigants, including corporations, partnerships, and individuals, engage in some level of forum shopping. It is safe to assume that this is a reason for the increase in the Justice Department's inventory of tax shelter cases in recent years. Regardless of the court in which a taxpayer challenges an IRS determination on the merits of a tax shelter transaction, however, the Government should be able to prevail if the IRS position is correct. In sum, the current system for litigating civil tax cases works well and does not warrant change.

2. **Ms. O'Connor, I would like you to give a general overview of Department of Justice efforts to deal with tax shelter and tax scheme promoters. I'm concerned that this remain a top priority for Justice. In addition, I would also ask that you touch on two issues.**

   The first issue, related mostly to Justice and action against KPMG is that critics are stating that Justice has failed to prove that the tax products were tax shelters.

   The second issue is from a tax protestor case where the defendant cited the Paperwork Reduction Act as a justification for not paying taxes. This recent court decision has been burning up the internet.

General Overview of Tax Division's Enforcement Efforts

The Department of Justice is vigorously engaged in the Government's efforts to stop the promotion and use of tax scams and abusive tax shelters. As I'm sure you are aware, the Tax Division of the Department of Justice has no investigating agents of its own. Any investigation of violations of the tax laws must be initiated and undertaken by agents of the IRS, the federal agency charged with administering the tax laws.

Tax Division attorneys, however, whether civil or criminal, trial or appellate, are dedicated to the fair and uniform enforcement of our nation's tax laws. This is why the Tax Division encourages the IRS to develop and refer to us cases we can bring to, and win in, court.

Since 2001, the Department of Justice has successfully prosecuted hundreds of tax cheats and promoters of abusive tax schemes; it has sought and obtained civil injunctions to stop the promotion of tax scams and the preparation of false and fraudulent tax returns; and it has continued to identify and pursue those who used abusive tax shelters to avoid tax on their income. At the same time, the Department has pursued the professionals who designed, facilitated, or accommodated the underlying tax shelter transactions.

I can assure you that continuing the efforts I describe below to address tax enforcement challenges - ranging from the sophisticated and high dollar schemes promoted to and used by thousands of corporations and wealthy individuals, to the simpler low dollar schemes promoted to and used by hundreds of thousands of individuals and smaller businesses – is a very high priority of this Administration, including the Tax Division of the United States Department of Justice. That is why IRS enforcement has increased by more than a third over the last four years as a result of increased appropriations, and why the President's budget request for the Tax Division for FY 2007 includes increased resources for the Tax Division to follow through on enforcement efforts the IRS has begun, but which its administrative tools alone cannot bring to fruition.

Tax Shelter Enforcement

During the past several years, the Justice Department and the IRS have significantly increased their enforcement efforts against the promoters and facilitators of abusive tax shelters. Some have estimated that abusive shelters for large corporations and high-income individuals have cost the federal treasury more than $10 billion annually. The Tax Division also had notable successes in federal court defending the federal Treasury against tax shelter-related claims of large companies and individual investors. Among the successes in this area are the following:

- KPMG, one of the world's largest accounting firms, entered into a deferred prosecution agreement for conspiracy to commit tax fraud. The agreement calls for KPMG to cease marketing and promoting abusive tax shelters and to pay $456 million in fines, restitution, and penalties;
- HVB, Germany's second largest bank, entered into a deferred prosecution agreement for its role in facilitating tax shelters marketed by KPMG. The agreement requires HVB to implement substantial changes in its operations and pay nearly $30 million to the United States in fines, penalties, and restitution;

- Donald Rivkin, a former senior KPMG partner, pleaded guilty to income tax evasion and conspiracy to commit tax fraud;
- Dominick DeGeorgio, an HVB principal, pleaded guilty to conspiracy and tax evasion charges;
- In September 2005, the United States Court of Appeals for the Second Circuit upheld a 40 percent penalty with respect to Long Term Capital Holdings' "lease stripping" tax shelter, *Long-Term Capital Holdings, LP v. United States,* 150 Fed.Appx. 40, 2005 WL 2365336, (2d Cir., September 27, 2005), *aff'g* 330 F.Supp.2d 122, 142 (D.Conn.2004)
- In January 2006, the Tax Division won a significant appellate victory in defense of the IRS's position on Dow Chemical's corporate owned life insurance (COLI) tax shelter, *Dow Chemical Co. v. United States*, 435 F.3d 594 (6th Cir. 2006);
- In February 2006, the Tax Division largely prevailed before the United States Court of Appeals for the Fourth Circuit, winning a remand for trial in Black & Decker's contingent liability tax shelter, *Black & Decker Corp., v. United States*, 436 F.3d 431 (4th Cir. 2006);
- In March 2006, following a trial in the United States District Court for the Western District of Texas, the Tax Division prevailed in a major tax shelter case involving the so-called "lease stripping" tax shelter that TransCapital Corp. marketed to the International Bank of Commerce of Laredo, Texas, *Transcapital Leasing Associates 1990-II, L.P. v. United States,* 2006 WL 897723 (W.D.Tex., March 31, 2006)
- In July 2006, the Tax Division won a resounding victory in *Coltec,* an important contingent liability tax shelter case in the Federal Circuit, where, in a strongly worded opinion, the Court accepted the Tax Division's articulation of the economic substance doctrine, *Coltec Industries, Inc. v. United States*, 454 F.3d 1340 (Fed. Cir. 2006)
- In August 2006, the Second Circuit held that General Electric Credit Corporation's tax shelter involving a purported partnership with foreign banks was ineffective so that the IRS properly reallocated the income to the taxpayer, *TIFD III-E, Inc. v. United States*, 459 F.3d 220 (2d Cir. 2006).

The Department of Justice has likewise been very successful in its summons enforcement actions, securing information to help the Internal Revenue Service identify and locate people and businesses that use offshore accounts to hide their income and assets from the IRS.

Tax Scheme Promoters

The Tax Division brings both its civil and its criminal tools to bear in the fight against tax fraud. An ongoing tax scam causes continuing harm to the federal Treasury and it leaves participants owing taxes, interest and, often, penalties. It would often be too costly to the Federal Treasury for us to wait until a criminal case has been developed to take action to stop the scam. Rather, the Justice Department brings injunction suits to stop the promotion of tax scams and the preparation of false or fraudulent returns. Additionally, in appropriate cases, the Justice Department brings criminal charges against the promoters, preparers, and scam participants. By taking fast action, we minimize the number of people who get caught up in these schemes and help to assure that everyone abides by this essential duty of citizenship — the duty to pay tax.

Since January 2001, the Justice Department has sought and obtained injunctions against more than 200 tax scam promoters and fraudulent return preparers. The IRS continues to investigate these violations of law, and to refer cases to the Tax Division, where we develop them and bring suit where appropriate. Schemes we have enjoined include:

- Filing tax returns that falsely report "zero income;"
- Failing to withhold, report and pay payroll and income taxes;
- Claiming personal living expenses as business expenses;
- Purporting to pay employees in commodities such as milk;
- Using trusts to conceal ownership or control of assets;
- Claiming that only income from a foreign source is taxable; and
- Forming a "corporation sole" for the improper purpose of avoiding tax.

The Department of Justice also has obtained injunctions against employers who fail to withhold, account for and pay over employment and withholding taxes, and against return preparers who prepare false returns.

The Tax Division's criminal enforcement priorities include investigating and prosecuting schemes that involve:

- Using trusts or other entities to conceal control over income and assets;
- Shifting assets and income to hidden offshore accounts;
- Claiming fictitious deductions and losses;
- Using frivolous justifications for not filing truthful tax returns;
- Failing to withhold, report and pay payroll and income taxes;
- Failing to report income; and
- Failing to file tax returns.

Action Against KPMG

You note that critics have charged that the Justice Department's "action against KPMG" relates to "tax products" the Department has yet to prove are "tax shelters." It is Department policy to not comment on pending litigation beyond what appears in the public record. As a general matter, however, the Department would like to note that the

Tax Division's litigation, whether civil or criminal, affirmative or defensive, does not turn on whether a transaction or series of transactions is a "tax shelter." The filing, preparation, or facilitation of a false tax return — one that omits income or claims fabricated or overstated deductions or losses — is the nub, not whether the reason for the false return was something someone might label a "tax shelter."

As the Government noted in its response to pretrial motions in *United States v. Stein, et al.*, case no. S1-05 Crim. 0888 (LAK), pending in the Southern District of New York:

> [T]he defendants here repeatedly claim that no court has invalidated the fraudulent shelters they peddled. As an initial matter, it is important to reiterate that the defendants are charged with committing a fraud by means of various false and misleading statements and documents that (a) misrepresented the tax shelter transactions, and (b) concealed the true facts regarding those transactions. To say that no court has ruled on such a theory is preposterous — every false deductions case stands for the proposition that tax positions based on lies do not work. Second, *Ingredient Technology* plainly states that "it is immaterial that 'there is no litigated fact pattern precisely on point.'" (citation omitted)

Government's Memoranda in Opposition to Defendants' Pretrial Motions, *Stein* at 12.

The *Stein* court addressed the issue of whether a court must find the transactions marketed by KPMG to be illegal tax shelters before the Government can prosecute KPMG and its partners for promoting such transactions. In denying the defendants' pre-trial motions to dismiss the indictment on this basis, the court wrote:

> [A]ccording to the government, defendants developed a series of fraudulent transactions designed solely to produce tax losses and then drafted opinion letters intended to disguise the true nature of the transactions and to mislead the IRS. The government intends to prove, for example, that the BLIPS transactions — which defendants claim involved nonrecourse premium loans to tax shelter clients to finance seven-year, multi-stage investments in emerging market currencies — actually were "designed to be terminated before year-end for tax purposes" and to involve "no real loan premium, no realistic possibility of making a reasonable pre-tax profit, no contingency to the obligation to repay the loan premium, and no purpose for the purported borrowing except to generate a tax loss." Given this theory, the question whether the transactions described in the allegedly phony opinion letters were lawful is immaterial. Defendants' motions therefore are denied.

United States v. Stein, 429 F.Supp.2d 633, 638 (S.D.N.Y. 2006).

As a general matter, separate from the *Stein* case, the Department of Justice only commences a prosecution when the evidence establishes that an individual or entity deliberately violated the tax laws.

Tax Protester Case Involving the Paperwork Reduction Act Argument

Your inquiry concerning a tax protester case where the defendant cited the Paperwork Reduction Act (PRA) as a justification for not paying taxes pertains to the prosecution of Robert Lawrence in the Central District of Illinois.

In *United States v. Lawrence,* Case No. 06-10019 (C.D. IL), defendant Robert Lawrence was charged with three counts of tax evasion and three counts of failure to file tax returns stemming from his participation in a scheme that promoted the false notion that wages are not income. The indictment alleged that, as an employee at the Mitsubishi Motors plant in Normal, Illinois, Lawrence submitted Forms W-4 to his employer claiming to be exempt from withholdings. According to the indictment, Lawrence also stopped filing income tax returns for tax years 1999, 2000, and 2001.

Three days before trial, the Government moved to dismiss the indictment against Lawrence with prejudice after it discovered errors in its tax calculations relative to the tax evasion charges. As articulated in its recent submission to the district court setting forth the basis for the dismissal, the IRS recommended dismissing the case and the Government believed the tax calculation errors might undermine the prosecution. (*See,* United States' Response to Defendant's Motion for Attorney Fees and Costs, Dkt. #31, pg. 7) The Government's pleading makes clear that "the basis for the dismissal of the case against the defendant had nothing to do with the PRA or any other legal theory advanced by the defendant." (*Id.* at pg. 11). These errors were discovered on May 11, 2006, four days before the scheduled trial. The Government moved to dismiss the case the following day, May 12, 2006.

After the case was dismissed, the taxpayer filed a motion to recover attorney's fees and costs. The court denied the motion finding no reasons to doubt the Government's explanation of the reasons for the dismissal.

3. **Ms. O'Connor, as we have heard from several witnesses, a significant portion of corporate income tax noncompliance involves multinational corporations. I would like your thoughts on a few points.**

   Please describe the degree of interaction you have with law enforcement offices from other nations.

   Are there any changes in U.S. law that would facilitate your work with other nations' law enforcement officers?

   Are there any holes in our legal sanctions that are needed to ensure that noncompliance that spans more than just the U.S. is properly punished?

Interaction With Law Enforcement Offices From Other Nations

Tax Division Attorneys have substantial interaction with law enforcement officials from other nations. The contacts fall into two distinct categories. First, attorneys make requests and obtain information pursuant to existing mutual legal assistance treaties, tax treaties and tax information agreements. These requests are made through the Office of

International Affairs or the Internal Revenue Service - Director International, to the appropriate designated authority of the foreign nation.

Second, the Tax Division's Counsel for International Tax Matters participates in the negotiation of mutual legal assistance treaties, tax treaties, and tax information exchange agreements. Through these negotiations, the Counsel for International Tax Matters interacts with representatives of the Ministries of Treasury and Justice, as well as representatives of law enforcement agencies in other countries.

The Tax Division has recently begun to participate in the International Law Enforcement Academy (ILEA) for Latin America. The ILEAs provide a network throughout the world to combat transnational crime, international drug trafficking, and terrorism through strengthened international cooperation. Over the past several years, the United States and participating nations have established ILEAs to serve four regions: Europe, Asia, Africa, and Latin America.

In June 2006, the Tax Division made a presentation to the participants at the Core Law Enforcement Management Development Program at the ILEA Latin America in El Salvador (the Core program). Several times each year, the ILEA Latin America presents its Core program. The ILEA attempts to reach the representatives before they are promoted to the higher managerial level and to provide them with important information that they will need upon their promotions. The participants in the June 2006, Core program represented Costa Rica, Ecuador, El Salvador, and Panamá.

The subject of the Tax Division's presentation was international cooperation in investigating serious financial crime. The Tax Division representative discussed methods available to obtain evidence and assets from other countries, and the process of extradition.

The Tax Division and the Internal Revenue Service view the Tax Division's participation in the ILEA Latin America as particularly important given the fact that the United States has very few tax treaties or tax information exchange agreements with countries in Latin America. In the absence of such treaties or agreements, tax information cannot be exchanged. In view of the porousness of our borders and the growing interdependence of the countries in North, Central, and South America, increased cooperation in fighting serious transnational crime is of critical importance.

Suggested Legislative Changes

There are two legislative changes that would facilitate the Tax Division's work in the international arena: a change in the statute governing certification of foreign records and an amendment to the international money laundering statue. Each change is discussed in more detail below.

1) Foreign Evidence

With the recent technological advances in the financial industry, the increased sophistication of those violating the tax laws, the explosion of the Internet, and the increasing porousness of national borders has come an increased use of traditional tax haven countries, as well as other countries, by American citizens trying to evade taxes and commit other tax-related offenses. The use of other countries to commit tax and tax-related crimes poses unique challenges for prosecutors and investigators. Recent criminal tax trials have depended on use of evidence obtained from overseas.

One problem we face when dealing with evidence obtained from overseas is its admissibility. Most of the countries with which we exchange information for use in criminal tax trials have legal systems that differ significantly from our own. Under 18 U.S.C. § 3505, we can use foreign business records as evidence at a criminal trial, if the records are accompanied by a certificate signed by the custodian of the records. Section 3505(a)(1) provides that:

> In a criminal proceeding in a court of the United States, a foreign record of regularly conducted activity, or a copy of such record, shall not be excluded as evidence by the hearsay rule if a foreign certification attests that —
>
> (A) such record was made, at or near the time of the occurrence of the matters set forth, by (or from information transmitted by) a person with knowledge of those matters;
>
> (B) such record was kept in the course of a regularly conducted business activity;
>
> (C) the business activity made such a record as a regular practice; and
>
> (D) if such record is not the original, such record is a duplicate of the original;
>
> unless the source of information or the method or circumstances of preparation indicate lack of trustworthiness.

Id. For purposes of § 3505, a "foreign certification" means "a written declaration made and signed in a foreign country by the custodian of a foreign record of regularly conducted activity or another qualified person that, if falsely made, would subject the maker to criminal penalty under the laws of that country." 18 U.S.C. § 3505(c)(2). The systems of some countries (for example, the Netherlands) do not provide for such certifications by custodians of records. It would be very helpful if § 3505 could be amended to allow the use of certifications signed by an official of the competent authority or central authority of the foreign government that the records are business records of the company that the competent authority properly acquired through the domestic laws of the foreign government.

2) International Money Laundering

Existing money laundering laws reach domestic laundering of the proceeds of specified unlawful activity with intent to evade tax (*see* 18 U.S.C. § 1956 (a)(1)(A)(ii)), but there is no corresponding money laundering offense addressing the international movement of funds with the intent to commit a tax offense. Section 1956(a)(2)(A) criminalizes the international movement of funds with the intent to promote the carrying on of "specified unlawful activity," a defined term that does not include tax offenses. Section 1956(a)(2)(B) also does not apply because the funds involved in the offense must represent the proceeds of some form of unlawful activity; and the transportation of such funds must be intended either to conceal or disguise the proceeds of specified unlawful activity or to avoid a transaction reporting requirement under State or Federal law.

Congress should amend the offense of international money laundering in § 1956(a)(2) to include the movement of funds with the intent to engage in conduct constituting a violation of sections 7201 or 7206 of the Internal Revenue Code.

4. **Ms. O'Connor, in your testimony you discuss the Tax Division's role in the investigating and prosecuting tax violations committed with other criminal conduct, such as narcotics trafficking, securities fraud, bankruptcy fraud, health-care fraud, organized crime, and public corruption. I notice that sex trafficking was not listed among these crimes. The Senate Finance Committee is very interested in understanding the amount of enforcement that is being conducted in this area and addressing tax issues relating to crimes involving the enslaving of humans for commercial sex purposes. Could you please provide a detailed description of the types of criminal sex trafficking cases that the Department of Justice's Tax Division has pursued over the past five years? Also, please provide an analysis of the number of criminal sex trafficking cases that the Tax Division has pursued over the past five years. Included in this analysis should be a notation of the number of referrals the Tax Division has received from the IRS and other agencies and how many of these cases were independently generated within the Department of Justice. What were the results of the actions pursued by the Tax Division? Please also discuss the difficulties that the Tax Division faces in prosecuting these types of cases.**

All criminal tax cases referred to the Tax Division for prosecution are initiated and investigated by either the Criminal Investigation Division of the Internal Revenue Service or the United States Attorney's Offices. A search of the Division's database of criminal tax cases received in the last five years revealed no tax prosecutions associated with violations of 18 U.S.C. §§ 2421- 2425, the specific criminal statutes that outlaw the trafficking of persons and juveniles for the purpose of sexual activity.

The difficulties in prosecuting a tax case associated with human sex trafficking are similar to those in prosecuting any cash-intensive illegal enterprise. In most cases, proving the amount of income generated by the criminal activity can only be accomplished through the use of an indirect method of proof, such as a net worth analysis. This is a resource-intensive analysis that takes a significant period of time to complete. When time is of the essence to stop the illegal activity, prosecutors often will forgo adding a tax crime to the prosecution. Other complicating factors include locating the victims and the reluctance of such victims to testify as witnesses against the pimps.

From Senator Hatch:

What effect would simplifying the tax code have on tax compliance?

Tax simplification would have a positive impact on tax compliance. The complexity of the Internal Revenue Code results in confusion, and confusion has an adverse impact on tax compliance. Complexity not only causes innocent mistakes or errors but also creates unintended opportunities for aggressive and abusive actions by promoters and taxpayers.

From Senator Baucus:

1. **Recently, three tax shelter cases have been lost in the courts - *Castle Harbor, Coltec* and *Black and Decker.* Each shelter case that is lost in the courts weakens the IRS's ability to prevail at the examination level and could encourage new tax shelters.**

a. **Why do you think the government did not prevail in each of these cases? What lessons were learned?**

In *Coltec,* the Court of Appeals for the Federal Circuit in a resounding win for the Government reversed the decision of the Court of Federal Claims, held that the contingent liability tax shelter at issue lacked economic substance, and remanded the case for the limited purpose of determining whether the taxpayer was entitled to a partial refund on account of a capital loss. *Coltec Industries, Inc. v. United States*, 454 F.3d 1340 (Fed. Cir., 2006). In *Black & Decker*, another contingent liability case, the Fourth Circuit reversed and remanded the adverse decision of the district court, and we are preparing to try the economic substance issue. *Black & Decker Corp. v. United States*, 436 F.3d 431 (4th Cir. 2006). In the *Castle Harbor* case, the Second Circuit reversed the adverse trial court ruling and held that General Electric Credit Corporation's tax shelter involving a purported partnership with foreign banks was ineffective for tax purposes, *TIFD III-E, Inc. v. United States*, 459 F.3d 220 (2d Cir. 2006). Our briefs in these cases explain the Government's legal position in some detail, and we would be pleased to provide the briefs to the Committee. The lesson learned from these cases is that the Judiciary understands the economic substance doctrine and knows how to apply it. Codification of the doctrine is neither necessary nor desirable.

b. **How does the Department of Justice (DOJ) decide which cases to take to court? What criteria does the DOJ use when deciding whether to ask for summary judgment? To what extent does the DOJ consult with the IRS prior to making these decisions?**

The Department of Justice defends the United States in tax refund suits and TEFRA partnership suits (and is a respondent in bankruptcy suits), so that we initiate virtually none of our tax shelter litigation other than summons enforcement cases.

We have filed motions for summary judgment (in whole or in part) in only a few tax shelter cases, and in most of those cases our motion was in fact a cross-motion that we filed only after the taxpayer first moved for summary judgment in whole or in part–a circumstance in which the tactical decision is less delicate. The criteria that we use (in addition to the requirements of Rule 56) are the same criteria that we use in any case, including the fact-intensive nature of the case, the likelihood of success of the proposed legal argument, the savings in time and money that summary judgment might effect, and the utility of the precedent that might result under Rule 56 as opposed to a fact-based decision after trial, except that the large dollar value or precedential value of the tax shelter cases may change the dynamic. We consult with IRS in making that tactical decision, typically discussing whether to file a summary judgment motion in general terms and then requesting comments on a proposed brief. If the IRS expresses concerns about a proposed motion, then the issue is discussed at the Deputy Assistant Attorney General level or higher.

c. How does the DOJ prepare for a complex tax shelter case? Are there procedures in place to coordinate with IRS attorneys and technical staff?

In general our procedure is that when a case is recognized as involving a tax shelter, the chief of the section in which the case is pending notifies the Deputy Assistant Attorney General for Civil Matters and the Tax Shelter Coordinators. The Deputy Assistant Attorney General then consults with the section chief and the coordinators to determine which attorneys (in that section, or borrowed from other sections) should staff the case. The attorneys assigned to the case prepare a case plan (with a proposed budget for expert witnesses and other special needs), describing the nature of the case and its issues. This report is shared with the Deputy Assistant Attorney General and the shelter coordinators. An attorney in the Appellate Section is assigned to serve as a consultant on the case. (Usually, an Appellate attorney serves as the liaison for all the cases involving a given type or sub-type of shelter.)

Tax shelter cases are subject to the usual coordination with IRS that takes place in every case (*i.e.*, preparation of the defense letter, consultation when new issues or arguments are raised, and consultation when settlement is considered), and are also subject to special high level coordination. A principal function of the shelter coordinators is coordination with the IRS. They consult frequently with the IRS for the purposes of obtaining information (and sources of information) relevant to our cases and discussing the issues and appropriate legal theories arising in our cases, with a particular interest in identifying common issues and ensuring consistency in positions taken. One of the most important occasions for such coordination is when substantive briefs are being prepared (either pre-trial or post-trial briefs, or briefs filed in support of motions for summary judgment, or briefs on significant discovery issues). The IRS appoints a team to review and provide comment on the Division's brief. The team includes LMSB or SBSE attorneys as well as subject-matter experts in the various divisions of the Office of Chief Counsel.

2. Three courts have jurisdiction over tax cases, the Tax Court, the District Court, and the Court of Claims. This choice may encourage taxpayers to "shop" for

venues and it may contribute to disparate court decisions that create uncertainties about the underlying law.

a. **What are the pros and cons associated with having three venues for taxpayers to choose from?**

b. **In your opinion, do you think this should be changed? Please explain your answer.**

Please see the response to Senator Grassley's Question 1.

3. **As we have heard from several witnesses, a significant portion of corporate income tax noncompliance involves multinational corporations.**

a. **Please describe the degree of interaction you have with law enforcement offices from other nations**

b. **Are there any changes in U.S. law that would facilitate your work with other nations' law enforcement officers?**

c. **Are there any holes in our legal sanctions that are needed to ensure that noncompliance that spans more than just the U.S. is properly punished?**

Please see the response to Senator Grassley's Question 3.

4. **In light of the court's ruling in the Cheek case, that a good-faith misunderstanding and belief submission, whether or not the claimed belief or misunderstanding is objectively reasonable, negates willfulness, how does the DOJ plan to prosecute future violators of criminal tax laws?**

Tax Division prosecutors and Assistant United States Attorneys rarely have difficulty proving the willfulness element in their prosecution of tax crimes. In *Cheek v. United States*, 498 U.S. 192 (1991), the Supreme Court held, among other things, that a defendant's good-faith mistaken belief as to the requirements of the tax laws, even if not objectively reasonable, could negate willfulness. Even before that decision, however, every United States court of appeals to address the issue, with the exception of the Seventh Circuit, had already reached the same conclusion. *See, e.g., United States v. Whiteside,* 810 F.2d 1306, 1310-1311 (CA5 1987); *United States v. Phillips*, 775 F.2d 262, 263-264 (CA10 1985); *United States v. Aitken*, 755 F.2d 188, 191-193 (CA1 1985).

In the more than 15 years since *Cheek* was decided, the Government has successfully prosecuted hundreds of tax protesters who claimed to have relied on objectively unreasonable interpretations of the tax laws. While objective unreasonableness of a defendant's alleged belief does not automatically preclude a good-faith defense, under *Cheek*, the unreasonableness of a claimed belief is a matter a jury may consider in deciding whether a defendant actually held the belief in good faith. The Government prosecutes tax violators now — as it did before *Cheek* — by inviting juries to reject claims of reliance on frivolous tax theories. Significantly, *Cheek* distinguished between a good-faith mistake of law and a good-faith disagreement with the law. The Court held that the latter does not negate willfulness. Many protester cases have involved disagreements with the law, and *Cheek* has been helpful in those cases.

5. Recently, President Bush pardoned eleven individuals for crimes dating back to 1980. Four of the eleven individuals were pardoned for tax crimes. Please explain in detail why each of the individuals mentioned below was pardoned. Who initiated each pardon? What criteria were considered in order to determine whether a pardon should be granted?

(1) Mr. Anthony Americo Franchi, income tax evasion. Sentenced February 9, 1983.

(2) Mr. Kenneth Ward Hill, attempted tax evasion. Sentenced June 4, 1992.

(3) Mrs. Margaret Ann Leggett, conspiracy to defraud the United States by making false claims for income tax refunds. Sentenced May 8, 1981.

(4) Mr. Carl Manar White, conspiracy to defraud the United States and Pittsburg County, Oklahoma by tax evasion and mail fraud. Sentenced July 27, 1983.

In addition, please provide the following documents for each of the cases: the pre-sentencing report; the brief filed by the Assistant United States Attorney who handled the case; the IRS special agent's prosecution report; and the judgment and committed order generated by the court.

A. The Tax Division is not responsible for processing pardon requests. The Division consulted, however, with the Office of the Pardon Attorney, which provided the following information:

The decision to grant or deny a pardon belongs exclusively to the President, and the Department does not disclose the information and advice it provides the President in connection with a clemency matter. The Department can acknowledge, however, that each of the persons mentioned in your letter submitted a formal petition for pardon to the Office of the Pardon Attorney in accordance with § 1.1 of the Rules Governing Petitions for Executive Clemency (28 CFR §§ 1.1 – 1.11).

The criteria applied in the Department's consideration of pardon petitions generally are set forth in § 1-2.112 of the United States Attorneys' Manual (http://www.usdoj.gov/usao/eousa/foia_reading_room/usam/index.html). Although the factors considered are discussed in more detail in the Manual, the following are the principal factors considered: (1) post-conviction conduct, character, and reputation; (2) seriousness and relative recentness of the offense; (3) acceptance of responsibility, remorse, and atonement; (4) need for relief; and (5) official recommendations and reports.

B. Of the various documents relating to the four pardon recipients that Senator

Baucus has requested, we are able to provide only copies of the judgment order in each case, which is considered a public record document. Copies of the judgment orders are attached. Although the Office of the Pardon Attorney (OPA) has informed me that it requested and received the presentence report in each of the four cases mentioned above,[1] we cannot release these documents to you. As you are no doubt aware, a presentence report is a confidential document prepared by the probation office to assist the court at a sentencing proceeding and typically contains a host of sensitive personal information about the defendant, including facts about his family, medical, psychological, financial, and employment history. Although a presentence report is an official document that must be made available to the defendant prior to sentencing, it is not made available to the public upon request, *see United States Department of Justice v. Julian*, 486 U.S. 1 (1988), and OPA obtains these reports from the probation offices on the condition that it will maintain their confidentiality. Because the information gleaned form these reports is crucial to the Department's ability to adequately advise the President, it is a matter of considerable importance that the Pardon Attorney honor this commitment.

[1] In one of the four cases, the presentence report was returned to the U.S. Probation Office, in accordance with that office's instructions, after the President made his decision in the case. Accordingly, OPA currently has possession of only three of the requested presentence reports.

AO 245 (Rev. 7/90) Judgment in a Criminal Case

FILED

United States District Court

JUN 10 1992

Northern District of Mississippi

NORMAN L. GILLESPIE, Cl
By D. Adams
Dep

UNITED STATES OF AMERICA
V.
KENNETH W. HILL
(Name of Defendant)

JUDGMENT IN A CRIMINAL CASE
(For Offenses Committed Prior to November 1, 1987)

Case Number: 3:92CR051-S

Robert Elliott/Charles Brocato
Defendant's Attorney

THE DEFENDANT:

☒ pleaded guilty to count(s) one (1).
☐ was found guilty on count(s) ______ after a plea of not guilty.

Accordingly, the defendant is adjudged guilty of such count(s), which involve the following offenses:

Title & Section	Nature of Offense	Date Offense Concluded	Count Number(s)
26:7201	Attempt to Evade and Defeat Tax	April 15, 1986	1

☐ The defendant has been found not guilty on count(s) ______, and is discharged as to such count(s).

☐ Count(s) ______ (is)(are) dismissed on the motion of the United States.

IT IS THE JUDGMENT OF THIS COURT THAT:
The defendant shall be placed on probation for two (2) years with the following special conditions:
1) You shall reside for a period of 60 days at a community corrections cent and shall abide by the regulations of that facility.
2) You shall perform 50 hours of non-compensated community service work und the direction of the probation officer.
3) You are allowed to travel outside of the Northern District of Mississipp in connection with your employment.

The Court is amenable to any modification of conditions of probation.

The defendant shall pay a fine of $20,000 to the U. S. District Court Clerk, ND/MS.

In addition to any conditions of probation imposed above, IT IS ORDERED that the conditions of probation set out on the reverse of this judgment are imposed.

J/C BK # 28 123 Entered 06-10-92

AO 245 (Reverse)

CONDITIONS OF PROBATION

While the defendant is on probation pursuant to this judgment, the defendant:

1) shall not commit another federal, state or local crime.
2) shall not leave the judicial district without the permission of the court or probation officer;
3) shall report to the probation officer as directed by the court or probation officer and shall submit a truthful and complete written report within the first five days of each month;
4) shall answer truthfully all inquiries by the probation officer and follow the instructions of the probation officer;
5) shall support his or her dependents and meet other family responsibilities;
6) shall work regularly at a lawful occupation unless excused by the probation officer for schooling, training, or other acceptable reasons;
7) shall notify the probation officer within seventy-two hours of any change in residence or employment;
8) shall refrain from excessive use of alcohol and shall not purchase, possess, use, distribute, or administer any narcotic or other controlled substance, or any paraphernalia related to such substances, except as prescribed by a physician;
9) shall not frequent places where controlled substances are illegally sold, used, distributed, or administered;
10) shall not associate with any persons engaged in criminal activity, and shall not associate with any person convicted of a felony unless granted permission to do so by the probation officer;
11) shall permit a probation officer to visit him or her at any time at home or elsewhere and shall permit confiscation of any contraband observed in plain view by the probation officer;
12) shall notify the probation officer within seventy-two hours of being arrested or questioned by a law enforcement officer;
13) shall not enter into any agreement to act as an informer or a special agent of a law enforcement agency without the permission of the court;
14) as directed by the probation officer, shall notify third parties of risks that may be occasioned by defendant's criminal record or personal history or characteristics, and shall permit the probation officer to make such notifications and to confirm the defendant's compliance with such notification requirement.
15) shall pay any fine or obligation imposed by this judgment.
16) shall not possess a firearm or destructive device.

☒ IT IS FURTHER ORDERED that the defendant shall pay a special assessment of $ 50.00 , for count(s) one (1) , which shall be due ☒ immediately ☐ as follows:

IT IS FURTHER ORDERED that the defendant shall notify the United States attorney for this district within 30 days of any change of name, residence, or mailing address until all fines, restitution, costs, and special assessments imposed by this judgment are fully paid.

☐ The court orders commitment to the custody of the Attorney General and recommends:

Defendant's Soc. Sec. No.: [redacted]
Defendant's Date of Birth: [redacted]
Defendant's Mailing Address:
[redacted]
Falkner, MS [redacted]

Defendant's Residence Address:
[redacted]
Falkner, MS [redacted]

June 4, 1992
Date of Imposition of Sentence

[signature]
Signature of Judicial Officer

L. T. Senter, Jr., Chief
U. S. District Judge
Name & Title of Judicial Officer

June 4, 1992
Date

DATING STAMP
I hereby certify that the foregoing is a true copy of the original thereof now in my office.
Attest 6/10/92
Norman L. Gillespie, Clerk
By M. Adams
Deputy Clerk

RETURN

I have executed this judgment as follows:

Defendant delivered on ______ to ______ at ______ with a certified copy of this judgment.

United States Marshal

By ______
Deputy Marshal

...ted States of America vs.

United States District Court for

D[redacted]RICT OF MASSACHUSETTS

FENDANT: ANTHONY [redacted] FRANCHI

CRIMINAL INDEX

DOCKET NO. CR 82-00317-01-MA

JUDGMENT AND PROBATION/COMMITMENT ORDER

In the presence of the attorney for the government the defendant appeared in person on this date → MONTH DAY YEAR: February 9, 1983

COUNSEL

[ ] WITHOUT COUNSEL — However the court advised defendant of right to counsel and asked whether defendant desired to have counsel appointed by the court and the defendant thereupon waived assistance of counsel.

[X] WITH COUNSEL — James DeGiacomo, Esq. (Name of Counsel)

PLEA

[X] GUILTY, and the court being satisfied that there is a factual basis for the plea, [ ] NOLO CONTENDERE, [ ] NOT GUILTY

There being a finding/verdict of
[ ] NOT GUILTY. Defendant is discharged
[X] GUILTY.

NDINGS & DGMENT

Defendant has been convicted as charged of the offense(s) of willfully and knowingly attempting to evade and defeat a large part of the income tax due and owing to the U.S. for the calendar years 1976 and 1978 by preparing and causing to be prepared, by signing and causing to be signed, by mailing and causing to be mailed in the District of Massachusetts, false and fraudulent income tax returns, which were filed with the Internal Revenue Service, in violation of Section 7201, Internal Revenue Code; Title 26, U.S.C. §7201 as charged in Counts 1 and 3.

NTENCE OR BATION RDER

The court asked whether defendant had anything to say why judgment should not be pronounced. Because no sufficient cause to the contrary was shown, or appeared to the court, the court adjudged the defendant guilty as charged and convicted and ordered that: The defendant is hereby committed to the custody of the Attorney General or his authorized representative for imprisonment for a period of six (6) months on each of Counts 1 and 3 to be served concurrently with each other; execution of said sentence is suspended and the defendant is placed on probation for a period of two (2) years.

The Court further orders that the defendant pay a fine in the amount of $10,000.00 on each of Counts 1 and 3 for a total fine of $20,000.00 to be paid within two (2) weeks.

ECIAL DITIONS OF BATION

The Court further orders that it shall be a special condition of probation that the defendant will perform voluntary community service for eight (8) hours per week under the direction of the Chief United States Probation Officer.

TIONAL DITIONS OF BATION

In addition to the special conditions of probation imposed above, it is hereby ordered that the general conditions of probation set out on the reverse side of this judgment be imposed. The Court may change the conditions of probation, reduce or extend the period of probation, and at any time during the probation period or within a maximum probation period of five years permitted by law, may issue a warrant and revoke probation for a violation occurring during the probation period.

ITMENT MMEN-TION

The court orders commitment to the custody of the Attorney General and recommends,

It is ordered that the Clerk deliver a certified copy of this judgment and commitment to the U.S. Marshal or other qualified officer.

D BY
[ ] U.S. District Judge
[ ] U.S. Magistrate

A. David Mazzone

37

nited States of America vs.	Unite States District Court for
DEFENDANT: CARL W[illegible]E	EASTE[illegible] DISTRICT OF OKLAHOMA
	DOCKET NO. 82-7-1-CR

JUDGMENT AND PROBATION/COMMITMENT ORDER

AO 245 (8/82)

In the presence of the attorney for the government the defendant appeared in person on this date — MONTH July DAY 27, YEAR 1983

COUNSEL

[ ] WITHOUT COUNSEL However the court advised defendant of right to counsel and asked whether defendant desired to have counsel appointed by the court and the defendant thereupon waived assistance of counsel.

[X] WITH COUNSEL Eddie Harper (Name of Counsel)

PLEA

[X] GUILTY, and the court being satisfied that there is a factual basis for the plea, [ ] NOLO CONTENDERE, [ ] NOT GUILTY

FINDING & JUDGMENT

There being a finding [ ] NOT GUILTY. Defendant is discharged
[X] GUILTY.

Defendant has been convicted as charged of the offense(s) of on or about January 1978, and continuing thereafter to on or about Dec. 31, 1980, deft. did conspire to impede lawful functions of Internal Revenue Service in collection of personal income taxes and conspired to devise a scheme to defraud the citizens of Pittsburg County, Oklahoma, in violation of 18 U.S.C., Section 371.

SENTENCE OR PROBATION ORDER

The court asked whether defendant had anything to say why judgment should not be pronounced. Because no sufficient cause to the contrary was shown, or appeared to the court, the court adjudged the defendant guilty as charged and convicted and ordered that: The defendant is hereby committed to the custody of the Attorney General or his authorized representative for imprisonment for a period of two (2) years.

FILED
JUL 27 1983
LEWIS L. VAUGHN
CLERK, U. S. DISTRICT COURT
BY........ DEPUTY CLERK

SPECIAL CONDITIONS OF PROBATION

Defendant shall report to designated institution on or before Monday, August 15, 1983, by 2:00 P.M.

ADDITIONAL CONDITIONS OF PROBATION

In addition to the special conditions of probation imposed above, it is hereby ordered that the general conditions of probation set out on the reverse side of this judgment be imposed. The Court may change the conditions of probation, reduce or extend the period of probation, and at any time during the probation period or within a maximum probation period of five years permitted by law, may issue a warrant and revoke probation for a violation occurring during the probation period.

COMMITMENT RECOMMENDATION

The court orders commitment to the custody of the Attorney General and recommends,

It is ordered that the Clerk deliver a certified copy of this judgment and commitment to the U.S. Marshal or other qualified officer.

SIGNED BY
[ ] U.S. District Judge
[ ] U.S. Magistrate

[signature] X July 27, 1983

(6/76)

United States of America vs. *Please Return*

United States District Court for the Eastern District of Arkansas

DEFENDANT: MARGARET ANN LEGGETT

DOCKET NO. LR-CR-81-15 (2)

JUDGMENT AND PROBATION/COMMITMENT ORDER

In the presence of the attorney for the government the defendant appeared in person on this date — MONTH: May DAY: 8, YEAR: 1981

COUNSEL

[ ] WITHOUT COUNSEL — However the court advised defendant of right to counsel and asked whether defendant desired to have counsel appointed by the court and the defendant thereupon waived assistance of counsel.

[X] WITH COUNSEL — Robert Fussell (Name of counsel)

FILED
U.S. DISTRICT COURT
EASTERN DISTRICT ARKANSAS
JUL 7 1981
CARL R. BRENTS, CLERK
By: ______ DEP. CLERK

PLEA

[X] GUILTY, and the court being satisfied that there is a factual basis for the plea.
[ ] NOLO CONTENDERE,
[ ] NOT GUILTY

FINDING & JUDGMENT

There being a finding/[redacted] of
[ ] NOT GUILTY. Defendant is discharged
[X] GUILTY.

Defendant has been convicted as charged of the offense(s) of knowingly and wilfully conspiring to defraud the United States by presenting claims for payment of income tax refunds knowing such claims to be false, fictitious and fraudulent in violation of 18 USC 28

SENTENCE OR PROBATION ORDER

The court asked whether defendant had anything to say why judgment should not be pronounced. Because no sufficient cause to the contrary was shown, or appeared to the court, the court adjudged the defendant guilty as charged and convicted and ordered that: The defendant is hereby committed to the custody of the Attorney General or his authorized representative for imprisonment for a period of (3) three years; and on condition the defendant be confined in a jail type institution for a period of (3) three months, the execution of the remainder of the sentence of imprisonment is hereby suspended, and the defendant is placed on probation with supervision for the remaining period, to commence upon the defendants release from confinement, and is to be on the following terms and conditions:

SPECIAL CONDITIONS OF PROBATION

1. That she obey all local, state and federal laws.
2. That she comply with the rules and regulations of the probation office.
3. That she shall not enter into any agreement to act as an "informer" or special agent for any law enforcement agency without permission of the probation office.
4. That she shall not have firearms or other dangerous weapons in her possession

Execution of the sentence of imprisonment is hereby stayed until noon, Monday, May 18, 1981, at which time defendant shall report to, or at the direction of the United States Marshal at Little Rock, Arkansas.

Defendant will remain on the same bond until that date.

ADDITIONAL CONDITIONS OF PROBATION

In addition to the special conditions of probation imposed above, it is hereby ordered that the general conditions of probation set out on the reverse side of this judgment be imposed. The Court may change the conditions of probation, reduce or extend the period of probation, and at any time during the probation period or within a maximum probation period of five years permitted by law, may issue a warrant and revoke probation for a violation occurring during the probation period.

FILED
MAY 8 1981
CARL R. BRENTS, CLERK
By ______ DEP. CLERK

COMMITMENT RECOMMENDATION

The court orders commitment to the custody of the Attorney General and recommends,

It is ordered that the Clerk deliver a certified copy of this judgment and commitment to the U.S. Marshal or other qualified officer.

CERTIFIED AS A TRUE COPY ON
THIS DATE 5/8/81
BY Marge Higginbotham
[ ] CLERK
[X] DEPUTY

SIGNED BY
[X] U.S. District Judge
[ ] U.S. Magistrate

Date 5/8/81

16

RECEIVED
MAY 11 10 35 AM '81
U.S. MARSHAL'S OFFICE
LITTLE ROCK, ARK.

FILED
U.S. DISTRICT COURT
EASTERN DISTRICT ARKANSAS
JUL 7 1981
CARL R. BRENTS, CLERK
BY: DEP CLERK

GENERAL CONDITIONS OF PROBATION

Where probation has been ordered the defendant shall, during the period of probation, conduct himself as a law-abiding, industrious citizen and observe all conditions of probation prescribed by the court. TO THE DEFENDANT — You shall:
(1) refrain from violation of any law (federal, state, and local) and get in touch immediately with your probation officer if arrested or questioned by a law-enforcement officer;
(2) associate only with law-abiding persons and maintain reasonable hours;
(3) work regularly at a lawful occupation and support your legal dependents, if any, to the best of your ability. (When out of work notify your probation officer at once, and consult him prior to job changes);
(4) not leave the judicial district without permission of the probation officer;
(5) notify your probation officer immediately of any change in your place of residence;
(6) follow the probation officer's instructions and report as directed.
The Court may change the conditions of probation, reduce or extend the period of probation, and at any time during the probation period or within the maximum probation period of 5 years permitted by law, may issue a warrant and revoke probation for a violation occurring during the probation period.

Appeared on Criminal Summons 03-24-81, released on PR Bond 03-24-81.

Dani Howard
Dani Howard
Criminal Clerk USMS E/AR

RETURN

I have executed the within Judgment and Commitment as follows:

Defendant delivered on ________________ to ________________

Defendant noted appeal on ________________

Defendant released on ________________

Mandate issued on ________________

Defendant's appeal determined on ________________

Defendant ~~released~~ surrendered on 5-15-81 to FCI

Fort Worth Tex, the institution designated by the Attorney General, with a certified copy of the within Judgment and Commitment.

FILED
U.S. DISTRICT COURT
EASTERN DISTRICT ARKANSAS
MAY 28 1981
CARL R. BRENTS, CLERK
BY: ________________

Dudley Blevins Warden
~~United States Marshal~~

By Gary E Helfer
~~Deputy Marshal~~
R&D Officer

15

17

TESTIMONY OF
GEORGE A. PLESKO
UNIVERSITY OF CONNECTICUT SCHOOL OF BUSINESS
BEFORE THE COMMITTEE ON FINANCE
UNITED STATES SENATE
JUNE 13, 2006

Chairman Grassley, Ranking Member Baucus, members of the Committee, thank you for inviting me to testify at today's hearing on current issues in corporate taxation. My testimony will primarily deal with the last-in, first-out (LIFO) inventory method, but I will also briefly address two additional issues: the possibility of increased conformity in financial and tax accounting, and the effectiveness of current disclosures of tax information by publicly-traded corporations.

Inventory accounting

An important thing to keep in mind about inventory accounting is that it may have little or no relation to the underlying physical flow of goods. Inventory accounting methods are *cost-flow assumptions*, and, with some exceptions, will have no direct relation to the underlying management of physical inventory. Rather, the purpose of an inventory accounting method is to provide an appropriate measure of costs to match to a period's revenues in order to determine profit.

Consider three basic inventory accounting methods typically described in an accounting textbook: specific identification, first-in first-out (FIFO), and last-in first-out (LIFO). Under specific identification, each item in inventory has a cost associated with it, and when a particular item is sold, the firm reports the costs associated with the purchase or manufacture of that particular item. This method seems intuitive because it generates cost-flows that match physical flows, but this method creates other problems. First, depending on the number of items a business carries, record keeping could be quite burdensome. Second, if identical items in inventory were purchased at different times and at different costs, management can manipulate the amount of profit on each sale by choosing à higher or lower priced inventory item to deliver to the customer.

The FIFO method eliminates the ability to pick and choose costs associated with each sale; items are assumed to be sold in the order in which they were purchased. In other words, the oldest item in inventory is always the next one sold. While this description implies that the oldest items *physically* in inventory are sold first, the FIFO method merely allocates the oldest inventory *costs* to the item sold. Businesses with perishable inventories may also physically manage items on a FIFO basis (for example, placing milk with the earliest expiration date in the front), but for businesses with nonperishable inventories (e.g., a gravel pile) the order of physical delivery is irrelevant.

LIFO recognizes costs in the reverse order of FIFO: the most recent purchases are assumed to be the items sold first. If prices are rising over time, firms using LIFO will report higher cost of sales, and correspondingly lower profit, relative to firms using FIFO.

The difference in the amounts of income reported using FIFO or LIFO is offset in the value of inventory a business reports on its balance sheet. Since a firm that uses FIFO expenses its oldest costs first, the value of inventory at the end of the year will be closer to current replacement cost. By contrast, since LIFO assumes that the most recent purchases are sold first, the inventory on a firm's books will be understated (assuming inflation) compared to its current replacement cost. To provide better information about the value of LIFO inventories to shareholders, financial statements provide supplemental disclosures on the difference between the LIFO cost of inventory as reported on the balance sheet and what its value would be under FIFO or current cost. This difference is referred to as the *LIFO reserve* or *inventory valuation allowance*. The value of the LIFO reserve represents the cumulative amount of additional costs that have been expensed by the firm because of the choice of LIFO over its alternatives.

To maximize reported profit, the choice of an inventory method seems rather straightforward: choose the method that allows the firm to recognize the least amount of cost in each period. If firms face increased costs over time, FIFO is the obvious choice because the oldest (smallest) costs will be subtracted from current sales in order to determine profit. However, this inventory decision is complicated by the tax code's allowance of LIFO for tax reporting purposes, provided that the firm also uses LIFO for financial reporting purposes.[1] Given the choice to choose an inventory accounting method that reduces tax liabilities, even with the consequences of reporting lower earnings to shareholders, many firms find the tax benefits dominate.

Use of LIFO

The choice of an inventory accounting method need not be the same for all inventory that a firm has - some of a company's inventory could be valued using LIFO while the remainder is valued using FIFO or another method. Figure 1 shows the trend in the use of LIFO among the largest publicly-traded firms over the past 40 years. The solid line in Figure 1 shows that the use

---

[1]The use of LIFO for income tax purposes goes back to the Revenue Act of 1938, when LIFO was allowed for a small number of narrowly defined industries, and some type of book-tax accounting conformity rule has existed since the Revenue Act of 1939 expanded LIFO's availability. A brief history can be found in W.B. Johnson and D.S. Dhaliwal, 1998, "LIFO Abandonment," *Journal of Accounting Research* 26: 236-272.

of LIFO by these large firms for at least part of their inventory rose dramatically during the mid 1970s (a period of high inflation) and peaked in the early 1980s at just under 70 percent. Since then, the use of LIFO has steadily declined, and at the end of 2004 about 40 percent of the largest firms use LIFO for some of their inventory.

The dashed line in Figure 1 reports the percentage of these largest firms that use LIFO for a majority of their inventory. Similar to the use of LIFO for any portion of inventory, the use of LIFO by firms for a majority of inventory increased throughout the 1970s and early 1980s, reaching a peak of 43 percent in 1985. As seen in the trend for companies with any LIFO usage, the percentage of firms using LIFO for a majority of their inventories has also steadily declined, and was 21 percent of the sample at the end of 2004.

Table 1 provides an industry breakdown of LIFO use for the years 2003 and 2004 (corresponding to the top line in Figure 1). For 2004, 16 of the 49 industry groups reported no LIFO inventories. At the other extreme, four industries reported more than 80 percent of sample companies using LIFO for some portion of their inventories: chemicals (85 percent of companies), furniture (80 percent), general merchandisers (90 percent), and metals (80 percent).

These numbers on the use of LIFO in Figure 1 and Table 1 are based on reviews of the financial statements of 600 of the largest 1,000 publicly-traded corporations and may not be representative of the corporate sector as a whole. An analysis of an electronic database of the financial statements of publicly traded firms found approximately 5,000 companies with inventories. Of those 5,000, only 8.7 percent reported a LIFO-reserve, suggesting that even among publicly-traded, inventory-holding firms, the use of LIFO is not widespread.

While publicly-traded firms represent the vast majority of economic activity, they are only a small fraction of all corporations: approximately 9,000 firms are publicly-traded, compared to more than 5 million corporate tax returns filed in 2002. Because of limited data on the characteristics of non-public firms, the use of LIFO by the rest of the corporate sector is hard to estimate, but it is believed to be fairly small. Treasury's 1984 tax reform study ("Treasury I") reported that 95 percent of taxpayers use FIFO.

The advantages and disadvantages of LIFO

Financial reporting advantages

The reporting advantage LIFO provides is its matching of current inventory costs to the current sales of a firm. As a result, the information provided to investors in a firm's income statement allows for the evaluation of a firm's current performance on the basis of both current sales prices and the current economic cost to the firm of generating those sales. While this creates the problem of understating the value of inventory on a firm's balance sheet, the disclosure of the LIFO reserve allows investors to adjust inventory numbers to what they would be under an alternative cost-flow assumption. This disclosure is particularly important when investors and other financial statement users want to compare LIFO firms to non-LIFO firms. Such comparisons are both common and necessary, given that the majority of firms do not use LIFO. Because of its importance, the method to convert LIFO-valued costs and inventories to FIFO is universally covered in accounting classes and textbooks (the information necessary to convert FIFO or other inventory costs to LIFO is not available). However, both the need to covert LIFO-based numbers to alternative bases, and the common use of inventory methods other than LIFO, suggest that the advantage of LIFO-based measures of current cost in an income statement may not be large.

Tax advantages

The primary advantage of LIFO, however, is the tax benefit that LIFO provides firms experiencing increasing input prices. By allowing firms to deduct current rather than historic costs to determine their profits, firms that benefit will elect to use LIFO, while others will use another inventory method. For electing firms, LIFO provides an indefinite deferral of profits that would otherwise be reported. Indeed, since the effect of LIFO-conformity is to require companies to report *lower* earnings to their shareholders, the tax benefits to the firms that use LIFO must be larger than the sum of the administrative cost incurred to maintain LIFO inventory records and any costs they might incur through lower reported profits. Given that analysts and other sophisticated users of financial statements can "undo' the LIFO cost assumption, it is not clear that the financial markets are necessarily worse-off, and some evidence suggests that LIFO earnings may be perceived as having higher quality.[2]

Figure 2 provides information on the magnitude of the tax benefits of deferral generated by LIFO, based on a tabulation of data of publicly-traded firms from 1975 to 2004. The LIFO reserve, which represents the cumulative dollar amount of the difference between the cost of sales under LIFO and the costs under an alternative inventory method, is shown by the gray bars and corresponds to the left axis of the graph. Similar to the pattern in Figure 1, the dollar value of the LIFO reserve peaked in the early 1980s and has generally fallen since. For the last year for which data is readily available, 2004, the aggregate value of the reserve is nearly $60 billion. This $60 billion represents the cumulative amount of additional tax deductions that firms have claimed relative to what their deductions would have been if they had not used LIFO.

---

[2]See L. Revsine, D.W. Collins, and W.B.Johnson, Financial Reporting and Analysis 3rd edition, 2002 (Pearson Prentice Hall, 2002), especially pp 470 - 472.

The solid line in Figure 2 shows the amount of the LIFO reserve as a percentage of the inventories reported by LIFO firms and corresponds to the right axis of the graph. Similar to the LIFO reserve, this percentage peaked in the early 1980s, and has declined over the past 20 years. At the end of 2004, the aggregate LIFO reserve equaled approximately 15 percent of the value of inventories. In other words, for the average firm, the reported value of inventories was 15 percent lower than it would have been if the firm had used current cost. The LIFO reserve as a percentage of the reported value of inventories can vary substantially by firm and industry. For example, in its FY2005 10-K filing, Exxon reported inventories of $7.8 billion, but noted that the replacement cost of the inventory was an additional $15.4 billion. In other words, the balance sheet value of inventory was only about 1/3 of its market value, and the LIFO reserve was approximately 200% of the value of reported inventories.

With respect to LIFO repeal, the $60 billion aggregate LIFO reserve reported in Figure 2 represents the amount of additional net income publicly-traded firms would report on their tax returns if a tax change required them to recognize this reserve as income. This amount would be reduced to the extent firms had net operating loss carry forwards. Assuming that this income would be taxed at an average rate of 30 percent, this implies a potential revenue gain of approximately $18 billion before credits. By contrast, the JCT estimated the revenue effect of the LIFO provision in H.R. 4297, affecting only oil companies, to be $4.3 billion.

Financial reporting disadvantages

While use of LIFO may create some benefits to financial markets by providing an income statement based on current costs, the use of LIFO raises other concerns related to inventory management.[3] Because a firm knows both the current cost of purchasing or producing items for inventory and the (presumably) lower cost of selling an item out of existing inventory, firms have a greater opportunity to manage the earnings they report to their shareholders. If a firm wants to report higher earnings, it can choose to sell from existing (lower cost) inventory rather than acquire or produce new inventory. The LIFO conformity requirement may be a deterrent in this instance, because reporting higher earnings to shareholders will also result in higher taxable income.

Alternatively, the use of LIFO has raised concerns that firms may have an incentive to hold more inventory than is optimal because of the tax costs of reducing their inventory levels. Firms may have an incentive to purchase unneeded inventory to avoid recognizing the additional taxable income that would result from selling inventories valued at less than the current market price.

If the financial reporting benefits of LIFO were perceived as significant, that is, having current costs in the income statement were superior to costs generated by other available inventory methods, then we would expect to see more widespread use of LIFO by U.S. firms than revealed in Figures 1 and 2 and Table 1. Further, if there were significant financial reporting benefits from LIFO, we would also expect to see it used in other countries. However, the U.S. is clearly in the minority in allowing LIFO for financial reporting purposes. In contrast to U.S. generally accepted accounting procedures (GAAP), International Accounting Standards (IAS) generally prohibit the use of LIFO. Given the trend to harmonize international accounting

---

[3]For a review of the literature on the effects of taxes on financial reporting and other decisions see D. A. Shackelford, and T. Shevlin, "Empirical tax research in accounting," *Journal of Accounting and Economics* 31: 321-387.

standards, it is not clear that LIFO will remain an acceptable method for U.S. financial reporting purposes, and, given the requirement of LIFO conformity, for tax reporting purposes. In these circumstances Congress could repeal the LIFO conformity requirement and allow firms to use LIFO for tax reporting only, but doing so would create additional administrative complexity, as well as increased book-tax reporting differences. Since many companies that use LIFO for external reporting purposes do not use it for internal decision making (such as pricing or compensation), allowing LIFO for tax purposes in the absence of LIFO-conformity would appear to generate no benefit other than the deferral of income taxes by LIFO firms.

An analysis of the process leading up to the IAS position on LIFO reveals a number of important factors.[4] First, contrary to arguments that LIFO provides a better matching of cost in the income statement, the only public comment letters supporting LIFO came from countries in which the method was allowed for tax purposes. Further, with the exception of firms receiving a tax benefit from LIFO, none of the response letters argued that LIFO provided any financial reporting benefit. Second, contrary to the assumption that the U.S. delegation would oppose any limitation on LIFO, the U.S. delegation supported its elimination.

Book-Tax Conformity

Since the 1999 Treasury report on tax shelters, the disparity in both the levels and growth rates of book and taxable income has been looked at as possible evidence of the growth in tax shelters. One approach that has been suggested to deter the use of tax sheltering behavior, and

---

[4]See D.A. Guenther and M. Hussein, 1995, "Accounting standards and national tax laws: the IASC and the ban on LIFO," *Journal of Accounting and Public Policy* 14, 115-141.

enhance compliance generally, is to increase the extent to which book and taxable income conform, if not converge to one accounting system.

I do not agree that more book-tax conformity is always more desirable, and I advise caution in considering these proposals. Tax and financial accounting serve related, but distinct, functions, and the measure of income for one cannot be assumed to be the appropriate measure for the other. LIFO, as discussed above, has book-tax conformity, but it is not clear that there is much of a financial reporting benefit gained by it, or, alternatively, that, in the absence of a tax benefit, any firm would adopt LIFO for financial reporting purposes. Such a conclusion goes to the heart of an economic analysis of the tax system: if a tax system were neutral, firms would make the same decisions in the presence of the tax as they do in its absence. Given that few firms might use LIFO in the absence of the tax benefit, the economic benefits of LIFO need to be very large to justify its presence in the tax code. The additional conformity requirement only increases the distortions that LIFO may cause.

Some aspects of the tax code, such as depreciation, have objectives that are clearly at odds with financial reporting objectives and should not conform. Others, such as the cost of exercised stock options, were correctly recognized as an expense to a firm for tax purposes, and should have been recognized as an expense for book purposes years ago. Traditionally, the development of tax policy has not fully considered the financial reporting aspects of tax changes. This is clearly no longer true. Going forward, I think it will be useful for all those involved in developing business tax policy to consider the effects of proposed tax changes on firms' financial statements, and in particular, to identify situations where the benefits of a particular activity should only be allowed when there is conformity, as well as those situations when conformity is not desirable. In cases where conformity is not desirable there may still be benefits to greater disclosure. Balancing the financial markets' needs for information with any potential benefits and costs of conformity is not an easy task, but the financial reporting effects of tax changes may be as important as any tax effect.

Disclosure

An important factor in being able to understand the role of taxes on a firm's operations is knowing the amount of taxes paid and the other tax attributes of a firm. I had the honor of testifying before this committee on the release of the Joint Committee on Taxation's Investigative Report on Enron, and I stated at that time that I was not convinced full public disclosure of corporate tax returns is warranted. I am still not convinced. However, I remain convinced that more and better disclosure of tax information could be achieved with little, or no, additional administrative or economic cost to the firm.

The new Schedule M-3, with its reconciliation of financial statement income to taxable income, and a detailed accounting of temporary and permanent differences, will provide important information to the IRS, and I commend the Commissioner and the IRS and Treasury staff for their efforts. Financial accounting reports, however, have not provided significant new information about the tax characteristics of firms to their investors. I still believe that more detailed information about taxes needs to be included in corporate financial reports.

At the time of the Enron hearing, I suggested that any debate on the public disclosure of corporate tax return information should begin with the idea of disclosing the information on what has now become the M-3. Although the final version of the M-3 contains a level of detail far beyond what I considered likely to be required, public disclosure is still worth considering. From a competitive perspective, any concern that these disclosures would harm a company should be considered only to the extent to which new information goes beyond the detail a firm should be providing under GAAP.

Thank you, again, for the opportunity to be here today. I look forward to the further discussion of these issues.

Table 1
Companies Reporting Use of LIFO, by Industry

	2004		2003	
	No.	%	No.	%
Advertising marketing	-	-	-	-
Aerospace	5	29	5	29
Apparel	7	47	7	50
Beverages	4	40	4	40
Building materials, glass	5	63	6	75
Chemicals	23	85	24	83
Computer and data services	-	-	-	-
Computer peripherals	-	-	-	-
Computer software	-	-	-	-
Computers, office equipment	1	9	1	9
Diversified outsourcing services	-	-	-	-
Electronics, electrical equipment	13	31	12	29
Engineering, construction	1	8	1	9
Entertainment	-	-	-	-
Food	12	52	12	50
Food and drug stores	13	81	11	73
Food services	-	-	-	-
Forest and paper products	14	70	16	80
Furniture	8	80	8	67
General merchandisers	9	90	9	82
Health care	-	-	-	-
Homebuilders	-	-	-	-
Hotels, casinos, resorts	-	-	-	-
Industrial and farm equipment	25	69	26	74
Medical products and equipment	3	23	4	31
Metal products	15	79	17	81
Metals	12	80	12	86
Mining, crude-oil production	2	14	3	23
Miscellaneous	1	17	2	22
Motor vehicles and parts	9	60	10	59
Network communications	-	-	-	-
Petroleum refining	11	79	12	92
Pharmaceuticals	4	40	4	40
Publishing, printing	9	43	11	55
Rubber and plastic products	4	57	5	83
Scientific, photographic, and control equipment	5	26	5	25
Semiconductors	-	-	-	-
Soaps, cosmetics	3	43	3	38
Specialty retailers	6	33	5	29
Telecommunications	-	-	-	-
Temporary help	-	-	-	-
Textiles	3	75	3	60
Tobacco	3	50	3	50
Toys, sporting goods	-	-	-	-
Transportation equipment	2	50	2	50
Trucking, truck leasing	-	-	-	-
Waste management	-	-	-	-
Wholesalers	7	44	8	42
Total companies	**239**	**40**	**251**	**42**

These totals are based on a review of the financial statements of 600 companies selected from the Fortune 1000. For each year, the first column gives the number of companies reporting some use of LIFO, and the second column expresses that as a percentage of reviewed companies in that industry. Source: Iofe., Y. And M.C. Calderisi, eds, 2005, *Accounting Trends & Techniques, 59th Edition*, (New York, NY: AICPA), pp. 169-170.

Figure 1
Use of LIFO by the 600 Largest Firms as Reviewed by *Accounting Trends*

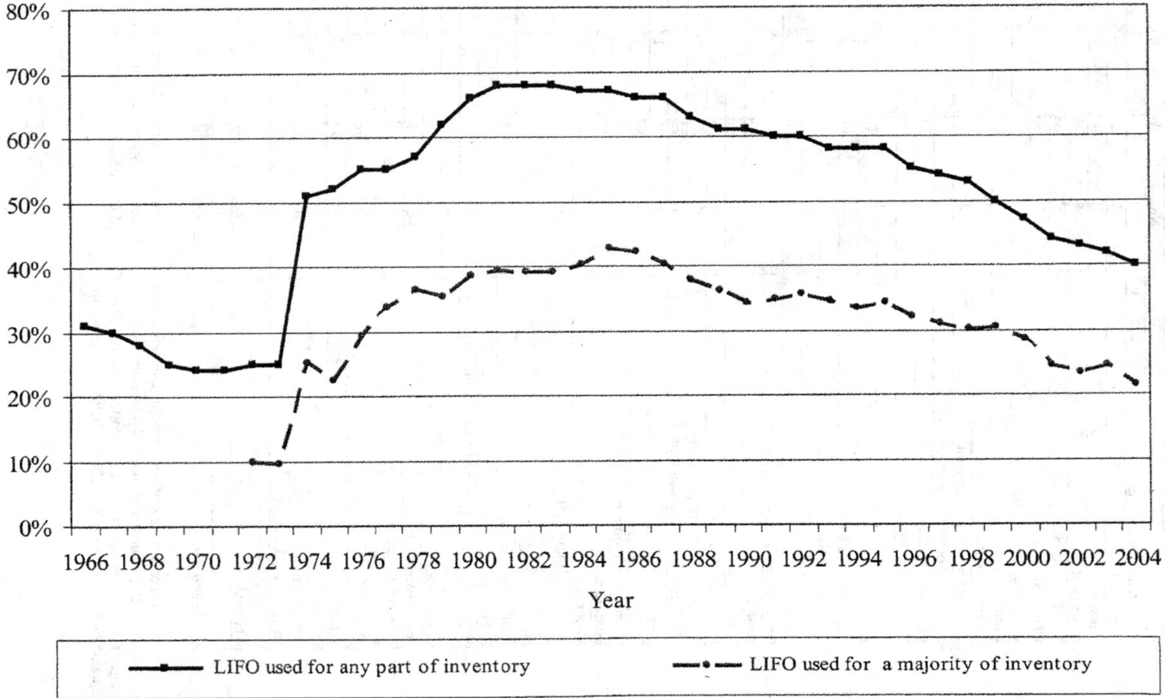

Source: *Accounting Trends & Techniques,* various years.

Figure 2
Significance of LIFO Reserves

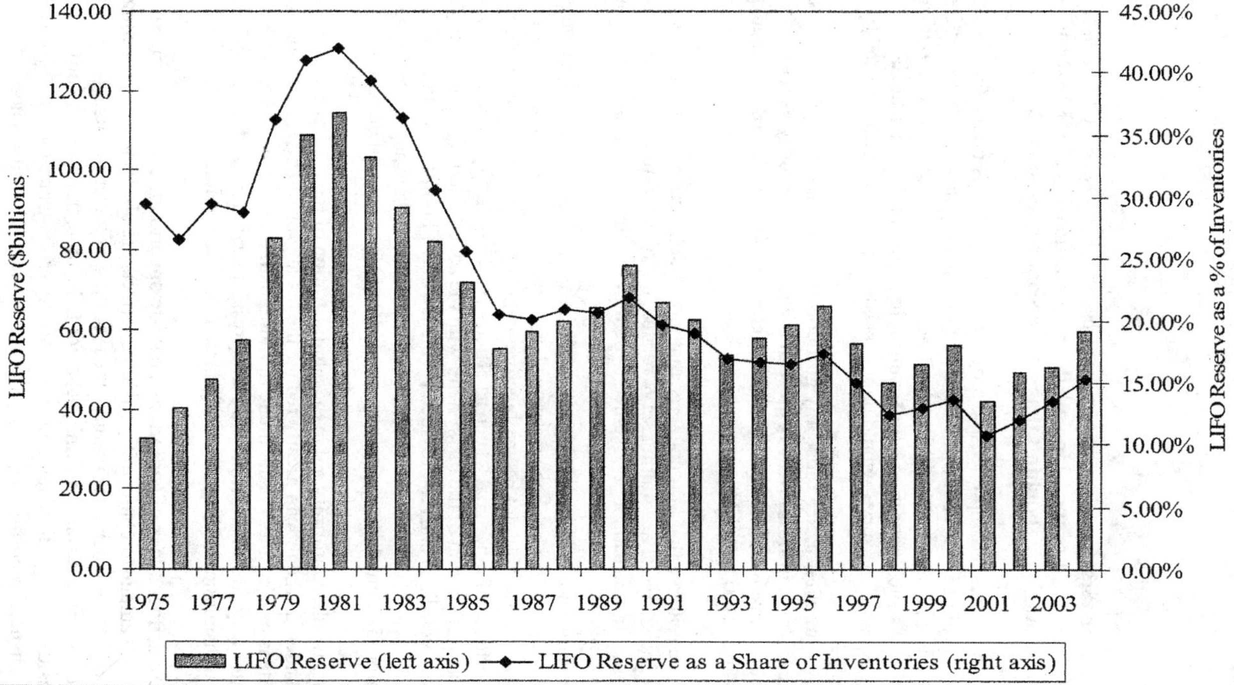

Source: author's calculations.

Questions for the Record for Dr. George A. Plesko
June 13, 2006

From Senator Grassley:

1. Doctor Plesko, you refer to data presented in "Treasury I" in your testimony. The Treasury I proposal included a recommendation that LIFO conformity be eliminated. Why shouldn't that same recommendation hold now?

Treasury I was a comprehensive proposal with numerous inter-related recommendations. The repeal of LIFO conformity was part of general plan to index the entire tax system and was designed to ensure economic neutrality with respect to other newly indexed assets. As such, repealing LIFO conformity, without the other fundamental changes suggested in Treasury I, would only exacerbate any distortions created by LIFO.

2. Doctor Plesko, are there any guideposts or factors that you would recommend that we keep in mind with respect to book-tax conformity as we begin discussions about tax reform? That is, are there clear guidelines for when conformity or non-conformity is the right answer?

Let me reiterate that I do not agree that more book-tax conformity is always desirable. Tax and financial accounting serve related, but distinct, functions, and the measure of income for one cannot be assumed to be the appropriate measure for the other.

While questions of book-tax conformity have been around as long as the corporate income tax, there has been a renewed and growing focus on these issues in recent years. Conformity should not be an objective in and of itself, and certainly should not rise to the importance of other goals, such as efficiency. Conformity should be thought of as aiding the administration of the tax system, with the added feature of potentially reinforcing the incentives/disincentives provided by the tax code. I don't think that we have yet reached a point where there is a consensus on the principles that should govern book-tax conformity, but there are some general questions to help guide policy.

First, would conformity aid in the administration of the tax law? Conformity should be considered when it can greatly reduce the tax and/or financial reporting compliance burdens of a business or facilitate the administration of the tax system, so long as the conformity does not compromise Congress' intended goal of the tax provision or inhibit the transmission of important information to shareholders.

Second, does a lack of conformity generate opportunities for avoidance or manipulation? One advantage to conformity is that tax effects are also financial reporting effects, and tax minimizing behavior requires the reporting of lower profits. Therefore, in situations where Congress wants a firm's behavior to be most transparent, conformity should be considered. The disadvantage to conformity arises when the tax objective is at odds with the financial reporting objective. In cases when conformity is not desirable, improved disclosure to both the IRS and investors may be able to achieve many of the same objectives.

For additional information on book-tax conformity please refer to my previous testimony before this Committee on February 13, 2003 during hearings on *Enron: The Joint Committee on Taxation's Investigative Report* (S. Hrg. 108-117), and recent testimony by Professor Douglas Shackelford before the Subcommittee on Select Revenue Measures of the House Committee on Ways and Means , May 9, 2006.

From Senator Bunning:

1. In your discussion regarding the use of LIFO in corporate America, your written testimony cites numbers suggesting over 40% of large corporations use LIFO for some or all of their inventory accounting. Later, you assert that an analysis of the 5000 publicly traded companies with inventory shows only 8.7% of firms with inventories use LIFO. Could you explain the difference in these numbers?

Differences in the percentages are due to differences in the groups of firms analyzed. The "40% of large corporations" is based on an analysis of inventory choices of only the largest 600 publicly-traded corporations, as surveyed in *Accounting Trends & Techniques*. This is not a representative sample of all publicly-traded firms, as the same 600 firms are not analyzed in each year of the publication. For example, if several non-inventory firms were to become large enough to be in the sample, and they displaced the same number of firms using LIFO for their inventories, then it would (correctly) show the use of LIFO among the largest firms had declined, but, as stated in my testimony, "may not be representative of the corporate sector as a whole" (p. 4).

To better measure the extent of LIFO use I examined the inventory choices of all publicly-traded firms, and found the use of LIFO among firms with inventories to be substantially less than implied in *Accounting Trends & Techniques*. The 8.7% figure in my testimony was for 2004. Over the 1975 to 2004 period, the percentage peaked at 26% in 1980, and has steadily declined. As a result, the use of LIFO appears to be less prevalent than indicated by analyzing just the largest firms, and the use of LIFO appears to have declined regardless of what sample of firms are examined.

2. Your testimony implies that only about 5% of all companies use LIFO to account for their inventory. Treasury estimates that in 2003 there were more than 2 million C corporations, 3.2 million S corporations, and more than 2 million LLC's and partnerships. Assuming your estimate is correct, approximately 350,000 businesses would be adversely affected by the repeal of LIFO. Your analysis also suggests these businesses are concentrated in manufacturing, steel and chemical production, and retail. How would repeal of LIFO affect these businesses and industries?

The 5% figure was taken from *Tax Reform for Fairness, Simplicity, and Economic Growth: The Treasury Department Report to the President*, Volume 1, page 111

(November 1984), and the citation in my testimony inadvertently overstated the use of LIFO. In my testimony I stated that "Treasury's 1984 tax reform study ("Treasury I") reported that 95 percent of taxpayers use FIFO." (page 5). However, the Treasury I study reads, "Roughly 95 percent of firms *with inventories* use FIFO accounting for tax purposes." (page 111, emphasis added.) As a result, the 5 percent number cannot be multiplied by the 5.4 million corporate returns filed in 2003 to determine the number that use LIFO, but should be multiplied by the (smaller) number of firms *with inventories*. I do not think the number of corporate tax returns reporting inventories can be determined from the published IRS data, and therefore an estimate of the number of affected companies cannot be made with publicly-available data. However, the number of companies with inventories will be substantially smaller than the total number of companies.

Absent a more recent analysis of tax return data by the Joint Committee on Taxation or the Treasury Department, the Treasury I statistic of 5 percent is the most definitive estimate available. There is, however, evidence to suggest that the percentage will be lower, rather than higher, today. The percentage of publicly-traded firms that used LIFO for any portion of their inventories peaked in the early 1980s, and their use of LIFO is now only about one-third of those levels. It seems likely that the use of LIFO among privately-held firms would also have declined.

As for the sectors, the data presented in my testimony only represents the concentration of LIFO use among the 600 largest publicly-traded corporations as surveyed by *Accounting Trends & Techniques.* This may or may not be representative of the entire population of businesses, be they publicly-traded or privately-held, or whether they are corporations or pass through entities.

How LIFO repeal would affect any firm will depend on many firm-specific characteristics and the details of the specific provision, including what inventory methods would be permitted and the phase-in period. If LIFO repeal were an element of a tax reform proposal that both broadened the base and lowered the rate, the net effect on any firm will depend on the interrelationship of all of the provisions.

3. Your testimony notes that the LIFO reserves reported on the financial statements of publicly traded companies has declined since 1984 and now is around $60 billion dollars. The implication is that LIFO is less frequently used and that repealing LIFO would result in new tax revenues of around $18 billion. Given that your estimate does not include the LIFO reserves of the vast majority of companies that are not publicly traded, isn't it likely that the actual tax increase incurred by hundreds of thousands of small and large businesses would be several times your estimate?

The $18 billion figure cited in my testimony was not intended as a revenue estimate of any action the Committee might take, but merely to provide guidance about the magnitude of the cumulative amount of income deferred, and an idea of the tax revenue that might be generated, by changes to LIFO. First, as stated in my oral testimony, that figure was based on 2004 data, and I expect that the aggregate value of LIFO reserves has increased. Second, the data examined only publicly-traded firms, and, as your question points out, excluded privately-held entities. Third, there are other differences in how tax and financial accounting treat inventoried costs that would affect the estimate. Fourth, by looking only at the effect of taxing past deferrals the number explicitly ignored any future changes in the taxable income of firms no longer using LIFO.

However, were Congress to restrict or repeal the use of LIFO, the effect on revenue over the budget period would also be affected by the legislative language, which would likely mitigate some of the effects through transition rules. Among issues the language would likely address are: (1) the alternative methods of inventory accounting that would be permitted, and (2) the number of years allowed for firms to pay any liability.

The fact that the total number of companies using LIFO may be many times larger than the number of publicly-traded firms using LIFO does not imply that the revenue effects of changing LIFO would be many times the amount inferred from data available from publicly-traded firms. While there are a large number of businesses subject to the corporation income tax, aggregate economic activity is concentrated among the very largest firms.

IRS data for 2003 shows that 5.4 million corporate tax returns were filed, and that these businesses reported a total of $53.6 trillion in assets. Of these 5.4 million returns, only 2,018 returns (0.0004 of the total, or four one-hundredths of a percent) reported assets in excess of $2.5 billion, yet these same 2,018 returns reported more than 75 percent of all assets and were responsible for 67 percent of the total amount of net income (less deficit). If the size threshold is lowered to returns with at least $100 million in assets, there were 20,477 returns filed (0.38 percent of the total), and they reported 93 percent of all corporate assets and 85 percent of net income (less deficit).

With respect to inventories, the 2,018 largest returns reported 34 percent of all inventories, and the 20,477 largest returns reported 60 percent of all inventories. But these percentages are likely understated because the balance sheets of firms using LIFO understate the value of inventory relative to other inventory methods (e.g., FIFO). As described above, the understatement is likely greatest among the largest, publicly-traded, firms.

Further, even among publicly-traded firms using LIFO, the effect of changes in LIFO will be concentrated among a relatively small number of firms. Based on 2004 financial statements, 50 percent of the total LIFO reserve is attributable to 15 companies, and 80 percent is attributable to 53 companies.

In short, as with many corporate tax changes, changes in revenue are likely concentrated among the largest, publicly-traded, firms.

4. Your written testimony indicates that LIFO reserves reported by publicly traded companies has declined since 1984. Is that trend necessarily due to a lower use of LIFO or could part of the decline be due to lower overall inventory levels in the U.S. due to increased use of just-in-time inventory management techniques?

Declines in the aggregate LIFO reserves can be caused by many factors, of which the decline in the use of LIFO documented above is only one. The textbook cited in my testimony provides a detailed description of how different factors may affect the interpretation of the LIFO reserve (L. Revsine, D.W. Collins, and W.B. Johnson, Financial Reporting and Analysis, 3rd edition, (Pearson Prentice Hall, 2004), chapter 9.)

Interestingly, recent research provides evidence that for some firms the adoption of just-in-time (JIT) inventory methods can be facilitated by the presence of LIFO reserves as increases in reported income resulting from LIFO liquidations offset the additional reported costs incurred in the same period to implement JIT. However, taxable firms with large LIFO reserves are found to be less likely to adopt JIT because of the tax consequences of LIFO liquidations. Further, the evidence suggests that firms with a history of managing their reported earnings were also less likely to adopt JIT. As a result, it appears that the adoption of new inventory management may actually be hampered by the use of LIFO. (M.R. Kinney and W.F. Wempe, "JIT Adoption: The Effects of LIFO Reserves and Financial Reporting and Tax Incentives," *Contemporary Accounting Research* 21:3 (Fall 2004) pp. 603-638.)

5. Your analysis of inventory manipulation is particularly interesting. For example, you assert that a company may purchase more inventory than it needs at the end of the tax year in order to reduce its tax obligation. Have there been real-world situations where you are aware of such inventory manipulation? How likely do you think such manipulation is in light of the incremental costs of purchasing and storing additional inventory to the business? If such manipulation did take place, what would be the resulting tax implications for the second tax year of this manipulation, when the company now has more inventory than it needs?

The incentives that LIFO provides for year-end purchasing is well-understood in the accounting literature and the results of academic studies are widely referenced or summarized in textbooks. For example, D.E. Kieso, J.J. Weygandt, and T.D. Warfield, *Intermediate Accounting*, 11th Edition (Hoboken: Wiley, 2005) state:

> Because of the liquidation problem, LIFO may cause poor buying habits. A company may simply purchase more goods and match these goods against revenue to ensure that the old costs are not charged to expense. Furthermore, the possibility always exists with LIFO that a company will attempt to manipulate its net income at the end of the year simply by altering its pattern of purchases. (page 393)

For firms to purchase additional inventory despite the incremental costs shows how significant the tax benefits can be, and further demonstrates the distortion in firm behavior LIFO can cause. Frankel and Trezevant (1994), for example, examine the year-end purchasing decisions of firms as a function of their inventory accounting methods and tax status and report (1) high-tax LIFO firms are more likely to purchase extra inventory at year-end than low-tax LIFO firms, (2) LIFO firms are more likely to purchase extra inventory than FIFO firms, and, by contrast, (3) FIFO firms do not show differences in purchasing that are related to their tax status. The authors conclude that their finding "that additional year-end LIFO inventory purchases appear to be made for tax reasons suggests that permitting the LIFO method to be used for tax purposes leads to inventory management inefficiencies." (M. Frankel and R. Trezevant, "The Year-End LIFO Inventory Purchasing Decision: An Empirical Test," *The Accounting Review* 69, No. 2. (April 1994), pp. 382-398.)

As for the "second year" effect" of such purchases, Frankel and Trezevant's results suggest that if the firm remains in a high tax rate position inventory can continue to (inefficiently) build. Another alternative, described by Revsine, Collins, and Johnson in their textbook, shows how firms can use LIFO to manipulate multiple year's earnings (both up and down) to meet targeted levels through year-end purchases or liquidations (L. Revsine, D.W. Collins, and W.B. Johnson, *Financial Reporting and Analysis,* 3rd edition, (Pearson Prentice Hall, 2004) pp. 469-470).

A comprehensive summary of research on the tax-motivated effects of LIFO can be found in D.A. Shackelford, and T. Shevlin, "Empirical tax research in accounting," *Journal of Accounting and Economics* 31: 321-387 (2001).

6. Your testimony argues that the only reason a company would use LIFO is to reduce their tax liability. However, isn't it true that companies have used LIFO to hedge against inflation? Absent the use of LIFO, how would you ensure the Federal Treasury does not profit from inflated nominal earnings resulting from inflation?

Companies have many ways to hedge against the possibility of increasing prices for inputs, such as through the use of futures contracts. Note that the primary reason a firm would want to do this is to reduce its cost of sales relative to what they would be in an unhedged position, exactly the opposite of the result that LIFO yields in calculating earnings. LIFO is not a hedge in the traditional use of the term unless one explicitly acknowledges it as a tool to manage both tax liability and reported earnings.

The value of a business's inventory can go up for many reasons, not all of which can be generically attributed to inflation, yet LIFO can be used to reduce the tax liability of a firm regardless of the source of the change. As pointed out in Treasury I, there may well be strong arguments for mitigating the effects of inflation *throughout* the tax code, but to address inflation selectively leads to distortions in behavior. Interestingly, inflation does not appear to have been part of the original justification for the existence of LIFO, which at its inception was only narrowly permitted as a replacement for the base stock method disallowed in the 1920s. (A history and analysis of the development of inventory methods can be found in H.G. Barden, *The Accounting Basis of Inventory* Accounting Research Study No. 13 (New York: AICPA) 1973.)

If the use of LIFO was primarily motivated by management rather than tax considerations, then we would expect LIFO to be an integral part of firms' operations, but this does not appear to be the case:

> Many companies use LIFO for tax and external reporting purposes but maintain a FIFO, average cost, or standard cost system for internal reporting purposes. There are several reasons to do so: (1) Companies often base their pricing decisions on a FIFO, average, or standard cost assumption, rather than on a LIFO basis. (2) Record keeping on some other basis is easier because the LIFO assumption usually does not approximate the physical flow of the product. (3) Profit-sharing and other bonus arrangements are often not based on a LIFO inventory assumption. Finally, (4) the use of a pure LIFO system is troublesome for interim periods, for which estimates must be made of year-end quantities and prices. (Kieso, Weygandt, and Warfield *Intermediate Accounting*, 11th Edition, (Hoboken: Wiley, 2005), page 384).

Note in particular that if profit-sharing and management bonuses are not based on LIFO the implication is that the company does not consider LIFO to be a cost assumption appropriate in measuring a firm's performance.

If proponents of LIFO believe its use is necessary to ensure that income is properly reported, it seems they should advocate a requirement that *all* firms use LIFO for tax and financial accounting purposes, or, at a minimum, that an electing firm be required to use LIFO *exclusively,* rather than permit a business to use LIFO for a portion of inventories and another method (or methods) for their remaining inventory.

From Senator Baucus:

LIFO

1. Do you consider repeal of LIFO to be a tax increase? Explain.

In and of itself, repealing LIFO will increase revenues during the budget window. Over time, LIFO seems to have been intended to help mitigate the effects of changes in input prices. In practice, LIFO seems to have created a large indefinite deferral of income, in many cases resulting in a permanent rather than temporary loss of revenue. Unless the intent of LIFO is to allow businesses to permanently exclude inventory holding gains from taxation, the elimination of LIFO would only change the timing, not the overall amount, of revenue to be collected from these firms. If the use of LIFO has created an opportunity to permanently defer recognition of this income, then LIFO repeal will increase revenues relative to any baseline.

Given the tone of the hearing, it seems that the Committee is considering the possibility of numerous tax changes that would result in a more efficient tax system. At the heart of such a system, as discussed by Dr. Sullivan, is the goal of having a broader base and lower tax rates for all corporations. Any analysis of options to broaden the base of the corporate tax systems will need to examine the role of LIFO in greater detail.

2. You estimated that the LIFO reserve for the Fortune 600 companies is $60 billion. What is your estimate of the cumulative LIFO reserve for all taxpayers, and the total amount of tax that is being deferred?

The $60 billion figure is based on the LIFO reserve reported by all publicly-traded firms, not just the largest 600 firms.

It is difficult to estimate the full extent of LIFO usage without access to confidential tax return information. However, similar to other corporate tax changes, the preponderance of the revenue is likely to come from the largest, publicly-traded, firms. Please see my answer to Senator Bunning's Question 3.

3. What is the average number of years that a company defers taxes by using LIFO? Considering the time value of money, what is the present value of your estimate of the total amount of tax that is being deferred as a result of LIFO?

It is impossible to determine the number of years that a company has deferred taxes based upon their published information. As pointed out in my testimony, one of the reporting issues with LIFO is that inventory values on the balance sheet reflect "old" costs. Comparisons of a LIFO company to another LIFO company, or to a FIFO company, are difficult because companies may implement LIFO in different ways.

As I state in my reply to Question 3 from Senator Bunning, the $18 billion figure cited in my testimony was not intended as a revenue estimate and ignores a number of factors. However, with respect to an estimate of the present value of deferral, the number would be larger than $18 billion because I did not have data on privately-held firms, and I ignored all future benefits that firms would receive if LIFO continued into the future.

Given that LIFO may be creating a permanent, rather than temporary, deferral of income, knowing the average, and maximum, length of companies' reserves would help to inform the debate. If the average number of years is relatively short, then we could conclude that the benefits of LIFO are to smooth, rather than eliminate, tax liabilities. If the evidence shows the existence of very old LIFO layers then LIFO would be more accurately described as exempting, rather than just deferring, income from taxation.

4. What impact would the repeal of LIFO have on our nation's economy, competitiveness, employment levels and the financial markets?

The effect of LIFO repeal is hard to assess without knowing the specifics of what would replace it, especially if it were part of a comprehensive plan for base-broadening and rate reduction.

The relative effect of LIFO repeal for tax purposes depends not just on whether other countries allow it (some do) but also its particular implementation, and the extent of its use, in those countries. For example, if another country allows LIFO, but restricted it to situations where it matched physical flow, that country's experience would not be comparable to the U.S. If LIFO is, as financial data suggests, primarily a U.S. phenomenon, then it is difficult to imagine that U.S. firms that currently use LIFO would be at a disadvantage were they required to use the same accounting as their competitors. Further, as my reply to Senator Bunning's Question 6 points out, firms using LIFO do not appear to use LIFO costs for pricing or other businesses decisions, implying that the ability of a U.S. firm to compete is already independent of the availability of LIFO.

From a financial reporting perspective, we know that LIFO is generally a U.S. phenomenon and that at worst LIFO repeal would force U.S. companies to use the same financial accounting methods that companies in other countries use. Given that only a minority of publicly-traded firms with inventories appear to currently use LIFO for any portion of their inventories, it is difficult to imagine that there would be any significant effect on financial markets, especially since the LIFO conformity rule has been substantially weakened over time – a subject I address in Question 5, below.

Any inherent superiority LIFO may have over FIFO for financial reporting is also at odds with some firms' own disclosures. Consider the 2000 *Annual Report of The Goodyear Tire & Rubber Company*, which changed from LIFO to FIFO to *improve* its reporting:

> During the fourth quarter of 2000, the Company changed its method of inventory costing from last-in first-out (LIFO) to first-in first-out (FIFO) for domestic inventories. Prior periods have been restated to reflect this change. The method was changed in part to achieve a better matching of revenues and expenses. The change increased net income in 2000 by $44.4 million ($.28 per basic and diluted share), and increased retained earnings for years prior to 1998 by $218.2 million. (page 42)

Goodyear received a clean audit report from its auditor, PricewaterhouseCoopers, with the auditors appropriately noting that the change took place:

> As discussed in Note 7 to the consolidated financial statements, the Company changed its method of accounting for domestic inventories in 2000. (Page 61).

5. To what extent do you believe there is a benefit in the book/tax LIFO conformity rule? Since companies can use different LIFO "submethods" for book and tax, resulting in different LIFO reserve amounts for book and for tax, does the conformity rule serve its intended purpose?

The phrase "LIFO conformity" is a general one that implies (or assumes for simplicity) that inventory accounting is identical for tax and financial reporting purposes if a firm elects LIFO. This is an oversimplification, and observers suggest that firms are able to take advantage of LIFO for tax purposes without having to report LIFO costs to shareholders.

In an April 13, 2001 letter to Secretary Paul H. O'Neill, Edmund Jenkins, then serving on the Financial Accounting Standards Board, argued for repealing LIFO conformity because conformity was not, in practice, taking place. Specifically, Mr. Jenkins stated

> The level of conformity that is in fact achieved may well be illusory. The background section of Accounting Series Release (ASR 293) reports the following:
>
> "On January 13, 1981, the IRS published amended regulations[2] concerning the LIFO conformity rule. For many years, the IRS strictly enforced the conformity rule and required companies to apply LIFO in most cases identically for books and tax purposes and did not permit companies to disclose supplemental information about alternative methods of inventory pricing.[3] The Commission considers two aspects of the IRS amendments to be significant: (1) companies may apply LIFO differently for book purposes than for tax purposes as long as they use an acceptable form of LIFO; and (2) companies may provide supplemental non-LIFO disclosures if they are not presented on the face of the income statement."
>
> [2] Treasury Decision 7756, Title 26 CFR 1.472.2(e).
> [3] There have be exceptions to this rule, e.g. the IRS issued annual waivers to permit companies in [*sic*] comply with ASR 190, involving replacement cost, without violating the conformity rule.
>
> Source: Tax Notes Today (2001 TNT 86-34).

Mr. Jenkins further argued that the existence of the rule was "an impediment to improving international accounting standards."

6. The International Accounting Standards Board (IASB) has proposed prohibiting the LIFO method of accounting for inventory. The U.S. Financial Accounting Standards Board (FASB) has entered into a Memorandum of Understanding with the IASB with the intention of achieving international convergence. To what extent should the tax code comport with accounting standards that prohibit LIFO? To what extent should other ideas from financial accounting be imported to the tax law?

Tax and financial accounting rules serve different, but related, purposes. Some level of conformity, even if it is only conceptual, will reduce the administrative and compliance burdens of the two systems. Regarding LIFO, the tax system seems to encourage financial reporting that is different from what firms would otherwise choose. To the extent that the conformity requirement is not binding, LIFO provides only a tax benefit that evidence suggests may interfere with other business decisions.

As for the broader question of book-tax conformity, please see my response to Senator Grassley's Question 2.

7. To what extent do existing LIFO methods accurately isolate cost increases due to inflation compared to other factors, including inventory mix, definition of an item, transportation costs, and productivity? How could LIFO be revised so that factors other than inflation are not included in the reserve? Would these revisions require legislative changes or could they be done administratively?

Isolating the effects of inflation from other sources of price changes is always difficult, and incorporating such adjustments into the tax code adds complexity. The use of "dollar-value LIFO," which further separates LIFO costs from physical flows by allowing the pooling of different items into a single LIFO pool, makes it even more difficult to isolate inflation from other factors that increase the value of inventories.

As part of its goal to address indexing throughout the tax code, Treasury I proposed firms be given the option to use indexed FIFO, which would adjust for the effect of inflation on the value of inventory since it was acquired, while removing the ability to manage reported earnings through end of year purchases / liquidations.

8. Do you think taxpayers generally calculate LIFO inventory accurately? What are the most frequent factors of noncompliance?

See answer to question 9 below.

9. Do you think the IRS does a good job of enforcing LIFO? Do you think IRS guidance accurately applies the law?

With respect to Questions 8 and 9, I have no basis to suggest that taxpayers are unable to effectively comply with the LIFO regulations, nor can I comment on the IRS's enforcement efforts. However, as the IRS has worked to make compliance with the LIFO rules easier it appears to have also created opportunities for more inventory gains to be permanently deferred, and compromised the original intent of the book-tax conformity requirement.

Further, the lack of substantial numbers of IRS challenges to current LIFO practices is separate from the issue of whether firms are able to manipulate their reported income through the use of LIFO. The academic evidence is clear that LIFO is a mechanism used by firms to manage both their financial and tax reporting results.

10. What is your opinion of the IRS "cut-off" method for voluntary changes in LIFO? Is it fair to allow taxpayers who stop using LIFO to avoid paying taxes on their LIFO deferrals when other taxpayers have paid taxes all along on their income?

The fundamental problem with allowing any recognition of LIFO deferrals without subjecting them to tax is that it converts what should be a deferral to an exemption. While I cannot directly attest to "fairness," allowing selective exemption from taxation clearly violates principles of horizontal equity.

11. Do you consider the "definition of an item" to be a FIFO or a LIFO issue?

The "definition of an item" is a legal issue beyond the scope of my testimony. However, I will note that the need to define an item is necessitated by inventory accounting rules that separate cost flows from physical flows, and therefore a more important issue under LIFO.

PUBLIC DISCLOSURE OF TAX RETURN INFORMATION

1. Do you think the tax return information of companies who are not required to file Schedule M-3 should be public? If so, please explain what forms and schedules should be released, and why.

I do not think that the case has been made that the complete tax return of any company, regardless of whether it files an M-3, should be made public. Further, there is a distinction between requiring disclosures from public companies, which are already required to provide substantial information through regulatory filings, and private companies, which generally have no such requirement. The case for better disclosure of tax information, at this point at least, relates to public companies.

2. How do you respond to concerns about protecting a company's confidentiality if tax return information is disclosed?

Confidentiality of taxpayer information, even of publicly-traded firms, is an important factor when considering additional disclosures. Unrestricted disclosure has the potential of both revealing confidential information to competitors and may jeopardize or complicate our system of voluntary compliance.

However, with respect to public companies, financial reporting already requires disclosure of many aspects of a firm's operations, including various tax attributes. Empirical evidence, as well as the observations of financial market practitioners, suggests that current disclosures are often inadequate in providing the intended information, and make the inference of tax attributes difficult, if not impossible, for users of financial statements.

In this regard, the Schedule M-3 is unique. In the absence of new financial reporting requirements the release of the Schedule M-3, or a version of the Schedule M-3 consolidated to match the published financial statements, would seem to provide the same type of information that current financial accounting rules require, but supply it in a format and level of detail that would be of greater use to investors.

3. What impact would the disclosure of tax return information have on the foreign and domestic competitive position of US companies?

As stated above, unrestricted disclosure of tax return information has the potential to reveal important confidential information to competitors, either domestic or foreign. The exact effect on U.S. companies is difficult to estimate, but in the absence of compelling evidence that the disclosures are both necessary, and cannot be met through less invasive means (such as the Schedule M-3 and / or better financial statement disclosures) disclosure is not warranted.

However, it should also be noted that foreign companies that file their financial statements in countries that have greater book-tax conformity than the U.S already provide greater information about their tax attributes than do U.S. firms.

Statement of Senator Gordon H. Smith
U.S. Senate Committee on Finance Hearing
"A Tune-Up on Corporate Tax Issues: What's Going on Under the Hood?"
June 13, 2006

I applaud Chairman Grassley and Ranking Member Baucus for holding this important hearing.

In 2004, Congress passed the Jobs Act, which included the most extensive corporate tax cuts in years. For example, the bill included a tax deduction for domestic production. When fully phased in, this deduction will effectively reduce the maximum tax rate on domestic manufacturing from 35 percent to about 32 percent.

However, much more needs to be done. American companies today compete in a global market. In the 1960s, trade in goods to and from the U.S. represented just over six percent of GDP. Today, it represents over 20 percent of GDP, a three-fold increase. The U.S. role in the global economy also is quite different. Forty years ago, the U.S. was dominant, accounting for over half of all multinational investment in the world. Yet, today the U.S. economy represents about 30 percent of global GDP and accounts for only about 20 percent of multinational investment.

Our tax code has not kept up with the globalization of the U.S. economy. The rules are outdated and penalize U.S. economic interests by hindering American businesses' ability to effectively compete in our global economy.

For example, the corporate tax rate in the U.S. is higher than the rate in all EU countries. These countries have been lowering their corporate tax rates for years. The average top statutory corporate tax rate for EU countries has fallen from about 43 percent in 1996 to about 32 percent in 2006. But the U.S. rate has not dropped. In fact, the last time Congress acted on the corporate tax rate, we actually raised it.

A high corporate tax rate is not good for American businesses – or our economy. A high rate deters corporate investment in the U.S. It also incentivizes companies to shifts their profits to lower tax jurisdictions. To attract businesses and profits to America, we need to lower our corporate tax rate.

We must reform the corporate tax rules – but we can't do so in a vacuum. Today America participates in a global economy. For our businesses to remain competitive, we must update our corporate tax rules to reflect globalization.

Thank you.

A New Era in Corporate Taxation

Testimony before the Committee on Finance,
United States Senate
June 13, 2006

Martin A. Sullivan
Contributing Editor
Tax Analysts
www.tax.org

Mr. Chairman, Ranking Member Baucus, and members of the Committee, thank you for the opportunity to appear before your committee. Today I would like to share with you some developments in international corporate taxation. I think these changes are so striking that they represent a "New Era of Corporate Taxation." After laying out the facts, I will briefly explain the underlying causes of these changes and then suggest some ways the United States should respond.

PART I. THE FACTS

Like everything else, corporate taxes around the world are being fundamentally reshaped by the forces of globalization.[1] Let's take a quick look at Europe, home of five of the world's ten largest economies.

Fact Number 1: Statutory corporate tax rates in Europe have declined dramatically over the last decade.

In Figure 1 we see that the average top statutory corporate tax rate for the 25 countries of the European Union has dropped from 43.2% in 1996 to 32.6% in 2006--a drop of more than 10 percentage points.[2]

---

[1] This section is based on two recent articles: "On Corporate Tax Reform, Europe Surpasses the U.S." *Tax Notes*, May 29, 2006, p. 992; and "A New Era in Corporate Taxation, *Tax Notes*, Jan. 30, 2006, p. 440.

[2] All the corporate tax rates referred to in this testimony are statutory rates paid by the largest corporations. They all include both national and sub-national taxes. EU average tax rates are weighted by national GDP so the effect of a country's tax rate on the average tax rate depends on the size of its economy.

FIGURE 1
While European Corporate Tax Rates are Declining US Rate Has Not Moved

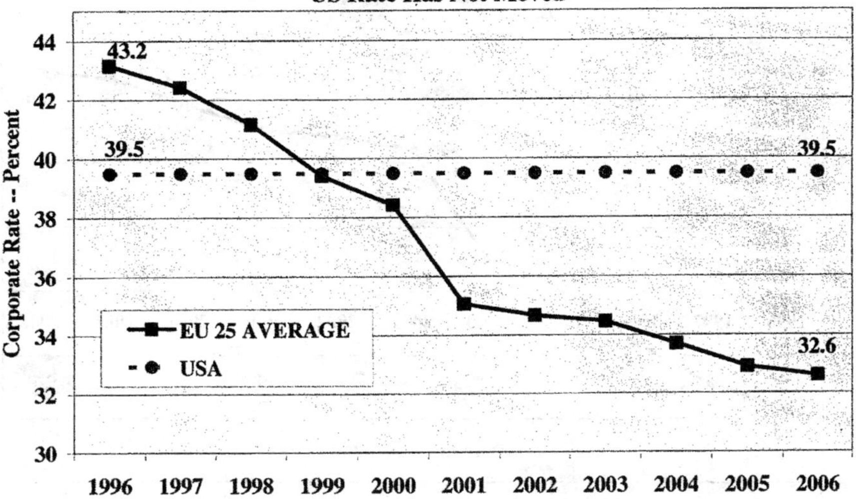

FIGURE 2
Corporate Rate Are Falling in Both Large and Small European Countries

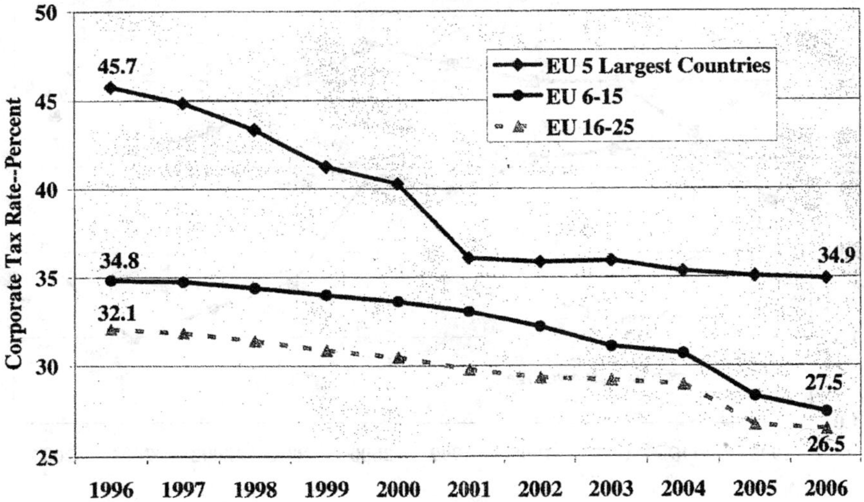

FIGURE 3
By Standing Still We are Moving Backward: Difference Between U.S. Corporate Rate and Average European Rate

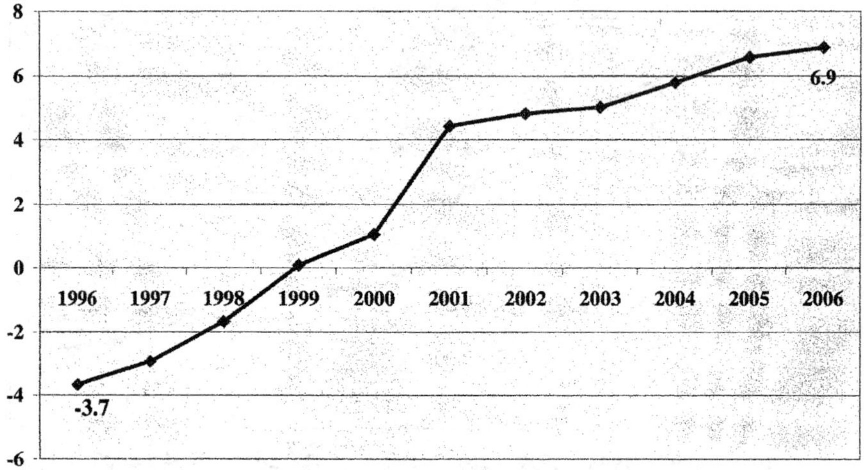

FIGURE 4
EU Corporate Tax Revenue is Rising, US Corporate Tax Revenue is Falling

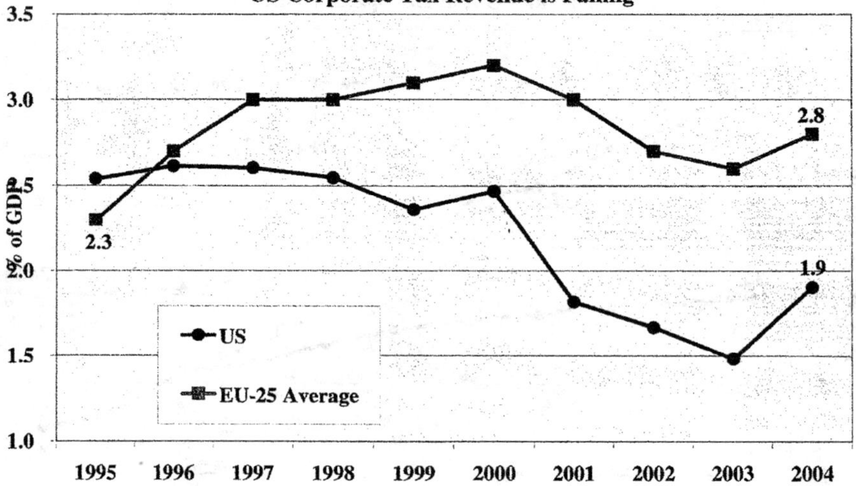

There has been a lot of publicity about flat taxes and low tax rates in the former communist countries of Eastern Europe. But it would be a mistake to think that all, or even most, of the decline in statutory rates shown in Figure 1 is attributable to smaller Eastern European countries. Figure 2 breaks down the EU average into three categories: the five largest economies, the other 10 EU countries that were part of the EU before 2003, and the 10 new—primarily eastern European countries—that joined the EU in 2003. It's true that the rates are higher for the large countries than for the new entrants. But the *decline* in corporate rates in the five largest countries (10.8 percentage points) has actually been greater than the decline of rates in the new EU countries (6.6 percentage points).

Over the last decade, 22 out of the 25 countries that now compose the European Union have cut their corporate tax rates. In the United Kingdom, Conservatives lowered the corporate tax rate from 40% to 33% in the early 1990s. When Britain's Labor Party took over it lowered the corporate rate to the current level of 30%. France reduced its rate from 41.7% in 1998 to its current rate of 33%. Italy's corporate tax rate was 53.2% in 1996; it is now 37.3%. And Spain has announced it will reduce its rate from 35% to 30% in the near future.

Meanwhile, the U.S. corporate tax rate has not budged. The last time the United States changed its top corporate tax rate that rate *increased* from 34% to 35% in 1993. Taking into account state taxes (to be consistent with the EU data that include sub-national taxes), the combined state-federal rate for the United States is 39.5%.

The end result of all this is that the current U.S. corporate tax rate is higher than the corporate tax rate in *all* 25 EU countries. There is only one country in the world with a higher tax rate, Japan. And that rate is only a fraction above the U.S. rate.

Figure 3 shows that by doing nothing we have fallen behind. In 1996 the U.S. corporate tax rate was 3.7% *below* the EU average. By the end of 2004 the U.S. rate was 6.9% *above* the EU average.

Fact Number 2. Despite large rate cuts, European corporate tax revenue has not declined.

There are two reasons to expect that European corporate tax revenues should have declined over the last decade. First, of course, there are the lower tax rates. Second, we know there has been a fair amount of profit shifting from high-tax to low-tax countries—through adjustment of transfer prices and the use of cross-border intra-company loans. Yet, despite these trends, the drops in revenue one might have expected have not materialized.

You can see this in Figure 4. It shows corporate tax revenues as a percentage of GDP in the EU and in the United States. Corporate revenues jump around a lot over the business cycle so the pattern isn't crystal clear. But certainly there has been no decline in the EU. There, corporate tax revenues increased slightly from 2.8% of GDP during the five years from 1995 to 1999 to an average 2.9% of GDP during the years 2000 through 2004. In contrast, the trend for the United States is down. The U.S. five-year average for 1995-99 was 2.5% of GDP; for 2000-04 the average dropped to 1.9% of GDP.

Fact Number 3. To offset the cost of rate cuts, European governments broadened their corporate tax bases.

Part of the surprising strength of European corporate tax revenues is probably due to increases in profits. As to the amount, we cannot be sure because of the difficultly economists have in measuring profits on a consistent basis across countries.

But we do know for sure that part of the strength in revenue is attributable to actions taken by European governments to reduce tax benefits and increase their corporate tax bases. In a summary description of tax developments, a May 17 report[3] from the European Union notes that corporate rate cuts in Austria, Belgium, Cyprus, France, Germany, Hungary, Portugal, Slovakia and the United Kingdom coincided with cutbacks in corporate tax breaks. The report concludes that rates cuts and "reductions in the scale of deductions and exemptions" were the two dominant trends in EU corporate taxation over the last decade.

Economic research supports this view. According to calculations by a team of British economists, depreciation schedules across Europe have become less generous.[4] Two notable examples are the United Kingdom and Ireland, which both eliminated expensing.

I'd like to close this "facts" section with a summary of the recent history of the corporate tax in Germany, Europe's largest economy. In 2000 the government, under the control of Social Democrats, reduced the top corporate tax rate from 54% to 39%. But this was not the end of the Social Democrats ambitious plans for rate cuts. Before his loss at the polls in September 2005, then-Chancellor Gerhard Schroeder had proposed a further reduction in the corporate rate from 39% to 33%. How did the German government propose to finance the rate cut? Germany's former Finance Minister Hans Eichel explained at the time: "As there is no room for tax giveaways in public budgets, we will have to offset the rate cut by broadening the tax base. This is the only way we can finance all the necessary measures without taking on new debt."

PART II. WHY REFORM NOW?

Rate cutting and base broadening—the kind we see taking place across Europe--is the essence of tax reform. Few economists doubt that rate-cutting, base-broadening tax reform is a big plus for competitiveness. It's a major step toward reducing government's role in the economy. By reducing distortions, it increases efficiency, productivity, and—

---

[3] *Structures of the Taxation Systems in the European Union - Data 1995-2004*, May 17, 2006.
[4] Michael Devereux, Rachel Griffith, and Alexander Klemm, "Corporate Income Tax Reforms and International Tax Competition," *Economic Policy*, October 2002.

ultimately—wages. It also makes taxation simpler, removes the incentive to bend the rules, and appeals to people's sense of fairness.

That's always been the case. But now, there is more reason than ever to reform corporate taxes. In this new era of corporate taxation, it is not accelerated depreciation and tax credits that are the big draw for corporate investment. It's the reduction of corporate tax rates.

Why the change? There are several reasons.

First, as economies move away from manufacturing—as intangible assets become more important than plant and equipment, as the rate of profitability per dollar of physical capital increases—it is a straightforward matter of arithmetic that rates play a larger roll than conventional incentives in determining the after-tax profit of investment decisions.

Second, as transportation and communications costs have dropped, and trade barriers and currency controls have also declined, there is more cross-border investment than ever. In the old days—say, before 1995—economists were thinking about how to use taxes to get a *domestic* firm to boost its *domestic* investment on the margin, for example, by 3 or 4%. In that case—that is, in the case of investment of borderline profitability—traditional incentives can mean a lot. And because this was the type of investment governments were trying to encourage, using tax credits and depreciation was a revenue-efficient way for governments to provide investment incentives.

But with increased capital mobility, economists have changed their thinking about how taxes motivate investment. Under the new paradigm, governments are trying to influence location decisions of multinationals. Because these decisions involve large chunks of investment—not just those marginally profitable—tax rates matter more than tax credits.

Finally, as mobile as capital may be, profits are more mobile. In deciding where to channel profits, tax rate differentials are all important, and conventional incentives don't matter at all.

What does all this mean? It means that without increasing the deficit and without changing the overall tax burden on the corporate sector, a government can protect its revenue base, increase investment, and increase competitiveness. As the figures above show, that's exactly what EU countries are doing.

PART III. WHAT ABOUT THE UNITED STATES?

In order to return to the competitive position held in the mid-1990s, the U.S. corporation tax rate would have to be reduced significantly.

Proposal: Cut the federal corporate tax rate from 35% to 25%. Offset the revenue loss by broadening the corporate tax base.

I am not one who puts much stock in claims that tax cuts pay for themselves. But if ever there was a case that a tax policy could change behavior and those changes in turn would yield revenue offsets, this is it. With corporate tax reform, there would be some increase in overall economic growth (increasing revenues from all sources, not just the corporate income tax). There would be some shifting of real investment into the United States—as plant closings would decline and inbound investment increased. Finally, artificial profit shifting out of the United States would slow down and there would be incentive to begin shifting profits *into* the United States.

But these changes would only partially offset the costs of lower tax rates. To finish the job there would still need to be some major cutbacks in corporate tax breaks. To help get you started I'll give you a list of base broadening proposals that could pay for a big reduction in the corporate tax rate. These types of proposals, which ordinarily would be nonstarters in most tax bills, become possible in the context of tax reform. How do we know this? We saw it happen in this very room 20 years ago.[5]

- ***Reduce depreciation allowances.***

The Treasury Department estimates that accelerated depreciation is one of largest tax expenditures. Treasury figures show that bringing tax depreciation into conformity with true economic depreciation could raise tens of billions of dollars annually.[6] In Tax Reform Act of 1986 Congress reduced depreciation allowances to help pay for corporate tax rate cuts.

- ***Eliminate the deduction for domestic production activities.***

This is almost like a rate cut for a big part of the corporate sector. It should be repealed to pay for a real rate cut for the whole corporate sector. The revenue saving from repealing this provision would be over $10 billion annually.[7]

- ***Tighten transfer pricing rules—particularly those pertaining to cost sharing arrangements.***

There are no official estimates for revenue saving from tightening transfer pricing rules. I have estimated that profit-shifting out of the United State to a single country, Ireland, cost

[5] After 17 days of markup, the Senate Finance Committee on May 6, 1986 ordered (by a 20-0 vote) that tax reform legislation (H.R.3838) be favorably reported. The final version of the bill reduced the top corporate tax rate from 46% to 34%. It also lengthened depreciation lives and repealed the investment tax credit.

[6] Office of Management and Budget, *Budget of the United States Government, Fiscal Year 2007, Analytical Perspectives*, Chapter 19, "Tax Expenditures," Table 19.2.

[7] Office of Management and Budget, *Budget of the United States Government, Fiscal Year 2007, Analytical Perspectives*, Chapter 19, "Tax Expenditures," Table 19.2.

the U.S. Treasury at least $2 billion in 2002.[8] The revenue gains from an overhaul of these rules could be enormous.

I commend this committee's efforts to investigate the fairness and the appropriateness of results under Advanced Pricing Agreements. Unlike private letter rulings provided by the IRS, APAs are not disclosed to the public, so it is hard for us ordinary citizens to know the details. IRS officials may tell you the APA program is a success because they are "moving cases," but from what I can see in the data, the APA program is not protecting U.S. revenue. I look forward to public disclosure of the committee's findings.

To prevent inappropriate profit shifting and to raise revenue, the rules for cost sharing arrangements should be significantly tightened. I do not believe the regulations proposed by the Treasury Department, if finalized, would cause anything more than a temporary disruption to tax planners' efforts to transfer U.S. developed intangibles to tax havens.[9] I would suggest the starting point for effective rules should be to deny intangible holding companies in tax havens the privilege of entering into cost-sharing arrangements.

- ***Prevent income shifting to low-tax countries through related-party loans.***

Related-party loans are not like real loans, but the tax code treats them that way. Multinational corporations take advantage of this and the lack of restrictions on hybrid entities under the infamous "check-the-box rules.[10] I would suggest a good starting point for putting a lid on these manipulations is that all deduction-generating interest payments on interest from related party loans be disregarded for tax purposes. I can't put a figure on the revenue pick-up from this type of change, but this loophole is a favorite among tax planners, there is undoubtedly big money involved.

- ***Eliminate or reduce tax credits.***

Some of our tax credits are, simply, abominations.

On the top of my list is the section 29 nonconventional-source fuel tax credit as it applies to chemically modified coal. Take perfectly good coal; spray it with kerosene or some patented magic formula; get huge tax benefits.[11] It should be repealed without a second thought.

---

[8] "The IRS Multibillion-Dollar Subsidy for Ireland," *Tax Notes*, July 18, 2005, p. 287.

[9] "Half the Profits for None of the Work," *Tax Notes*, Sept. 12, 2005, p. 1243.

[10] "International Tax Planning: A Guide for Journalists," *Tax Notes*, Oct. 4, 2004, p. 32.

[11] "Former JCT Chief Turns Loser into a 'Winner'," *Tax Notes*, Mar. 13, 2006, p. 1126; and "Multibillion Dollar Coal Credit: Lots of Form, Little Substance," *Tax Notes*, Oct. 6, 2003, p. 34.

Most tax credits are simply well-intentioned but ineffective.[12] Energy credits generally and employment credits, like the work opportunity tax credit, fall into this category. They could be eliminated and there would be no major setbacks to the national well-being.

Even the venerable research credit could use a good trimming.[13] When it was first enacted in 1981, it was lean and mean. Because research is good for society as well as the company that performs it, there was excellent economic justification for subsidizing it. And because of its incremental design, the research credit could pack its incentive effect where it would do the most good—on *increases* in research. But the research credit of 2006 is no longer lean and mean. Instead of challenging taxpayers, it coddles them. In the recent decade the annual revenue loss from the credit has skyrocketed. And for all this cost, it is doubtful the credit has any significant effect on actually increasing research--especially for the billions of dollars of credit refunded as a result of research credit studies by accountants years after research is performed.

* * *

That concludes my remarks. Thank you for your attention. I welcome your questions today or anytime.

[12] "Tax Incentives and Economists," *Tax Notes*, Apr. 3, 2006, p. 20.

[13] "Research Credit Hits New Heights, No End in Sight," *Tax Notes*, Feb. 18, 2002, p. 801.

Questions for the Record for Dr. Martin Sullivan
June 13, 2006

From Senator Grassley:

1. Dr. Sullivan, you identify certain base broadening measures in your written testimony that would be characterized as tax expenditures. What is your view of how tax expenditures should be evaluated, and what do you think a Congressional review would entail?

There are at least three reasons for Congress to re-invigorate its scrutiny of tax expenditures.

First, most tax expenditures damage our competitiveness by picking winners and losers and moving the economy away from the efficiency of a free market. By narrowing the U.S. tax base, tax expenditures are the antithesis of tax reform.

Second, a great deal of the information Congress has about tax expenditures comes directly from—or is strongly influenced by--paid lobbyists devoted to establishing, expanding, and extending tax breaks.

Third, despite all the talk about tax reform and tax simplification, Congress in fact continues to increase the size of the tax expenditure budget.

To help remedy this lamentable situation I believe Congress would benefit from the establishment of a small permanent independent agency of tax professionals whose sole purpose would be the analysis and public scrutiny of *existing* and *proposed* tax expenditures.

Analysis should include the effect of each tax expenditure on compliance costs, on administrative costs, on the fairness to similarly situated taxpayers that do not get a benefit, on the integrity of the tax system, on the ability of taxpayers to "game" the benefit through accounting changes, on the effect on the deficit, on the effect (if any) on reducing damaging economic "externalities," on the effect (if any) in reducing existing tax or regulatory distortions, and--in the case of tax incentives—on the effect (in any) on the targeted activity.

The agency staff should be full-time tax specialists because of the complexity of issues involved. It should by multi-disciplinary, including economists, attorneys, and accountants. And it should be non-partisan.

Let me elaborate on some key features essential to the success of this new agency.

- ***Independence***. The director of this agency should be appointed for a five- to ten-year term. Its budget should be largely pre-determined and not subject to targeted cuts.

- *Access*. The agency staff should have unfettered access to tax legislative process. If it is be effective in its evaluation of proposed incentives, agency staff needs to know of their existence as early as possible. Their access should roughly equivalent to that of a member of the staff of the tax-writing committees. So it should have access to all committee mark-ups, official and unofficial. The committee staffs should urge lobbyists and advocates to share all their information and analysis with the new agency's staff. The new agency's staff should receive copies of all official revenue requests to the Joint Committee on Taxation. The staff should have access to taxpayer information (as do the JCT and the Treasury staff), and the IRS should be required to provide detailed information and background on request.

- ***Publication.*** The agency should be required to produce an annual report evaluating all existing and proposed tax expenditures. The tax-writing committees should hold annual hearings on these reports. In addition, the agency should be encouraged to distribute any other information for publication that it sees fit. All incoming and outgoing correspondence should be publicly available. And it should be encouraged, rather than discouraged, to respond to press inquiries.

This is not intended as a criticism of the tax analysis conducted by the staff of existing government agencies. Here I am thinking of the Joint Committee of Taxation, the Office of Tax Policy at the Treasury Department, the Congressional Budget Office, the Congressional Research Service and General Accountability Office. In fact, I suspect most of the staff of the new agency would be drawn from members currently working at these existing agencies.

Little of the new agency's task would substitute for or "compete with" existing efforts. Indeed, one of its tasks would be to utilize and publicize other agencies' work.

Existing efforts are thwarted mostly by institutional constraints. For example, the JCT has a multitude of day-to-day responsibilities that often only allow analysis when and if more pressing tasks can be completed. The CBO does not (to my knowledge) employ even a single tax attorney or accountant, and it is kept at arm's length from the tax legislative process.

Under the leadership of David Walker, the GAO has admirably increased its surveillance of tax expenditures, but its tax staff too is bogged down by specific legislative requests, and like CBO, is kept at too great a distance from the legislative process. The CRS produces an excellent and systematic review of existing tax expenditures, but this gets no publicity and any analysis it does of proposed tax expenditures is unavailable to the public.

Treasury and the JCT produce annual tax expenditures budgets, but they get very little press or congressional attention. (Similarly, the JCT annually produces an excellent review of the presidential proposal's that gets next to no attention. It should be allowed to make available to the public the same detailed scrutiny of *congressional* proposals). Unfortunately, Treasury staff tax analysis is too overwhelmed by political influences to provide a publicly available comprehensive critique.

2. Dr. Sullivan, corporate income tax receipts were a record $278.3 billion dollars in 2005, up 47 percent over the prior year and representing 2.3 percent of GDP – the highest percentage since 1980. The first 8 months of fiscal year 2006 show the trend continuing with corporate tax receipts up 30 percent over last year. This upward trend is particularly noticeable since 2003, when corporate tax revenues amounted to only 1.6 percent of GDP.

Dr. Sullivan, in your written statement, you compare corporate tax receipt trends in the U.S. with those in the EU, finding US receipts declining as a percentage of GDP, while the EU has experienced an increase. Your data does not include the recent uptick in corporate tax receipts in 2005 and 2006. While I don't doubt your conclusion that lowering tax rates and broadening the tax base can lead to an increase in tax revenues, I am curious about what you think is behind the recent surge in corporate tax receipts?

The chart below shows the rollercoaster ride that corporate tax receipts have been on over the last decade. As you noted, the rapid rise since 2003 is particularly striking.

Corporate Tax Receipts, 1996-2006

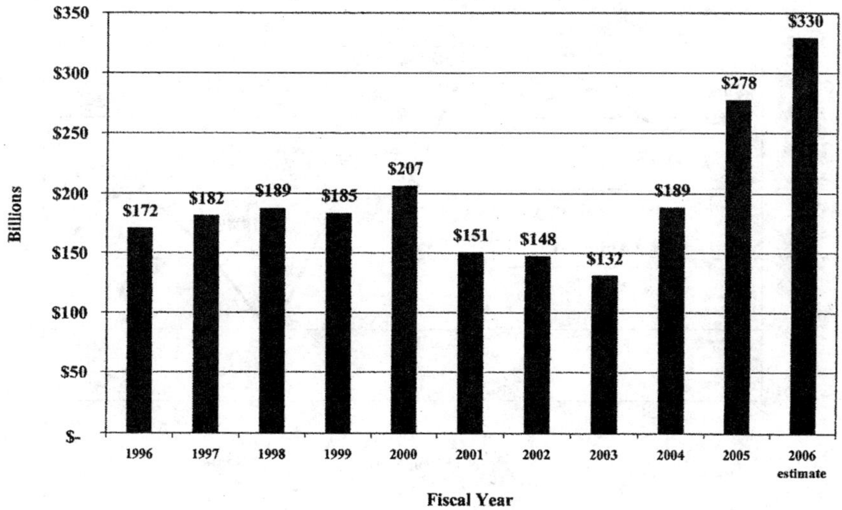

Your inquiry has prompted me to update my February 10, 2003 analysis in *Tax Notes* ("Is the Corporate Tax Withering Away?") At that time, you will recall, corporate tax receipts were unusually low. That analysis included years up through 2002. My conclusion for that article was: "Shelters may be damaging the corporate tax but the recent rapid decline in receipts cannot be used to support that conclusion."

In light of new developments (discussed below) that conclusion is turned on its head: *Despite their recent rapid rise, corporate tax receipts are in fact weaker than expected, and this may indicate an increase in avoidance activity.*

Pre-2003 data revised by the Department of Commerce and new data for 2003 through 2005 have yielded some surprising results. Although corporate tax receipts have surged, my calculations show that the increase is more than explained by increased profitability and changes in tax law. In other words, profits are lower that what we might expect given previous trends. This yet-to-be explained shortfall leaves open the possibility that tax avoidance has actually increased over the last few years.

The chart below illustrates my findings. The solid line is the ratio of actual corporate tax receipts (collected by the Treasury) to corporate profits ("profits before tax," as measured by the Department of Commerce). If all of the increase in receipts was due to a rising profits, the line would be flat. But there is still a dip and rise in receipts since 2000.

Ratio of Corporate Tax Receipts (Treasury) to Profits Before Taxes (Commerce Department)

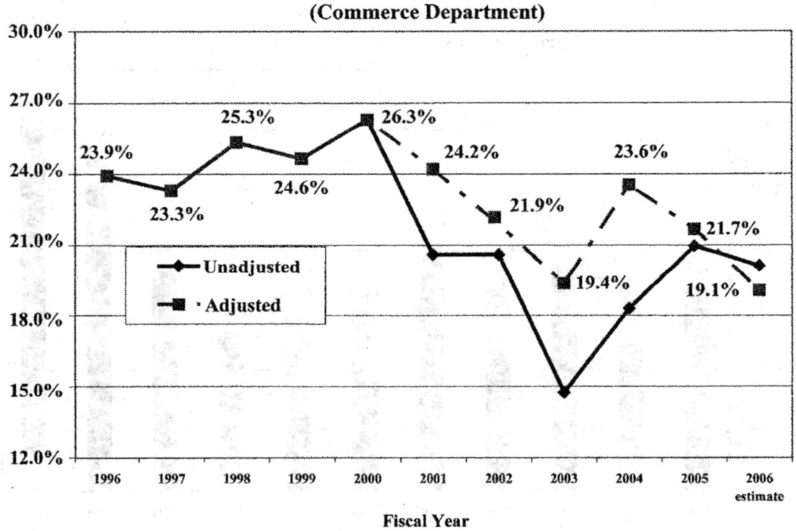

Of course, there have been major changes in tax law since 2001. In particular, there were large changes in the timing of corporate tax receipts due to the temporary enactment of bonus depreciation provisions in 2002 and 2003. Using JCT estimates of those changes (and making some minor adjustments for a technical matter and for 2004 legislation), the dotted line shows what the rate of tax receipts to profits would have been in the absence of legislation.

Its generally downward slope indicates that after controlling for profitability and major changes in tax law corporate profits are lower than we would otherwise have expected. This leads me to conclude that the recent rapid rise in corporate profits should give us no comfort that corporate tax avoidance is declining.

This analysis is preliminary. I expect I will be presenting my completed work in an upcoming issue of *Tax Notes*.

3. Are there any guideposts or factors that you would recommend that we keep in mind with respect to book-tax conformity as we begin discussions about tax reform? That is, are there clear guidelines for when conformity or non-conformity is the right answer?

Because of nature and complexity of the topic, analysis of book-tax conformity has been primarily from the accounting and legal perspectives. There is nothing wrong with this, but I believe economic analysis of the idea can also be useful to Congress. As an economist, let me offer some of that perspective.

Complete Conformity

For purposes of discussion, let's first suppose Congress goes to the extreme of requiring publicly-traded corporations to scrap the current corporate tax and instead pay tax equal to a tax rate multiplied by unadjusted book income reported to their shareholders and to the SEC. The three major benefits of this approach are:

(1) **A reduction of tax shelters.** With book income serving as the tax base, any attempt at tax sheltering or tax avoidance activity, by definition, would also reduce income reported to shareholders. Because corporations almost never want to do that, the new system would severely reduce corporations' willingness to engage in conventional tax planning.
(2) **Simplification.** Under the new law, corporations would simply look at their reported income and apply the tax rate. That would eliminate tens of billions of dollars corporations spend complying with current law. And it would also probably save the IRS a billion dollars or so.
(3) **Automatic tax reform.** In general book income is broader than taxable income so the switch would broaden the tax base and—assuming the switch is legislated to be revenue-neutral--allow a significant reduction in corporate tax rates. Estimates of the magnitude of the difference between book and tax income suggest a

reduction in the corporate tax rate to something in the neighborhood of 20 percent would be possible.

Economists are primarily concerned with promoting efficiency through tax neutrality. If there must be a corporate tax, the best would be one with the lowest rates and a tax base that taxed all corporate capital income evenly. Putting aside the issue of debt vs. equity, the best way to achieve this is by taxing pure *economic* income.

In general, book income is closer to economic income than taxable income. For example, book depreciation is generally closer to true economic depreciation than depreciation used for tax purposes. So, in general, using book income instead of taxable income would promote economic efficiency.

But book income has its own flaws. There are deviations between book income and economic income. A few of the reasons for the disparity are: lack of inflation adjustment, limited use of mark-to-market methods, and the accountant profession's predispositions to conservatism and to flexibility. If the disparity between book and economic income were uniform across industries and across corporations within industries, economic neutrality would still prevail.

But this is highly unlikely. I don't know enough accounting to describe these differences in detail, but I imagine the non-neutrality in taxation across and within industries could result in considerable economic distortion.

Of course, current law has its own economic distortions, but most of these have been legislated for a purpose and we understand and have adapted to them.

In summary a corporate tax base on book income overall would probably have smaller economic distortions than current law but the new ones would be haphazard and not consistent with current policies goals.

The system also has the potential to create new and different types of economic distortions. For example, if only publicly traded corporations are required to adopt the new rules, there would likely be a large disparity in the tax treatment of public vs. nonpublic corporations. (Whether than disparity was positive or negative would depend on the new tax rate chosen for the book-income system.) This would create two unwanted effects. First, one sector would be more favorably taxed than the other, creating distortions in investment. Second, corporations would have new tax motivations to move between public and private ownership.

Finally, economic theory predicts that eventually shareholders will develop information systems to let them see around reported book income and thus allow corporations to minimize taxes without hurting their standing with shareholders. For example, one could imagine a prestigious reporting service developing an "unofficial" profit measure for every publicly traded company. This new statistic would mimic the book income measure as we know it now. The company would officially report, and the IRS would collect tax on, "official" book income. But, with a collective nod and wink, everybody would know the real profitability of companies was reflected in the unofficial profit measure. Under this system, companies would be able to minimize tax even more easily than they do under current law and suffer no adverse consequence from shareholders.

Partial Conformity

For a variety of policy and political reasons it is likely Congress would make many adjustments to book income if it were to be used as the basis for corporate income taxation. There are no doubt dozens of controversial issues that would be stirred up with book-tax conformity. These would include:

(1) **Deferral of foreign source income**. Under accounting rules, foreign source income is booked as it accrues. Under tax rules, most foreign source income does not accrue until it is repatriated. If adjustments were not made to book income to account for this change, the Congress would be making the most sweeping change in international taxation since the inception of the income tax.
(2) **Exemption for interest on state and local bonds**. Interest on state and local bonds is not included in taxable income, but it is included in book income. About a third of these bonds are held by taxable corporations. Subjecting this interest to corporate tax would dry up a major source of funds for state and local governments and almost surely drive up their interest costs.
(3) **Accelerated depreciation**. Generous depreciation has been a mainstay of tax relief for business for decades. It would disappear with strict book-tax conformity.
(4) **Energy incentives**. A lot of U.S. energy policy is conducted through the tax code. A lot of that would be obliterated with book-tax conformity.
(5) **Research credit**. Although as a matter of mechanics, the research credit (and other tax credits) would not be repealed with book-tax conformity, it raises the same issues as any disparity between book and tax income. If a tax credit is not treated like other tax benefits in the form of deductions, two things will happen: (a) it will add complexity, it will provide and maneuvering room for tax avoidance, and it will lose revenue just like any other non-credit tax benefit would, thereby undermining the benefits of book-tax conformity and (b) advocates of every benefit currently in the form of a deduction will seek to convert the benefit to a credit in order to be exempt from the effects of a book-tax conformity requirement.

It does not seem unreasonable to assume that Congress does not want to tackle all these issues simultaneously as a by-product of their efforts to eliminate shelters and simplify the code. So, should Congress should just go ahead and make all the necessary adjustments and modifications to make it an easier pill to swallow?

It certainly could, and likely it would, but if Congress does that, all three benefits of book-tax conformity mentioned at the outset—reductions in tax shelters, simplification, and lowering of tax rates—are diminished.

How to Proceed

Any realistic book-tax conformity proposal will only be partial. Given that premise, I think the next critical question is whether it would be better to start with book income and make adjustments—a top-down approach—or stay with taxable income and adopt conformity on an issue-by-issue basis—a bottom-up approach.

The top-down approach is bolder and it is far more likely to reduce tax sheltering. But without a lot of careful study it is likely to entail a lot of unintended consequences. A bottom-up approach might be the wiser course initially if—as I hope and expect—the new M-3 reporting requirements on the differences between book and tax income reduce tax shelters by making them easier for the IRS to detect.

Before either approach is adopted I believe Congress needs to undertake a lot of study comparable in scale and scope to the hearings and analysis done in preparation for the Tax Reform Act of 1986. For starters, I would suggest topics for hearings would include: (1) the effect of book-tax conformity on manufacturing; (2) the effect of book-tax conformity on high-tech; (3) the effect of book-tax conformity on the energy sector; (4) the effect of book-tax conformity on financial business; (5) our experience with 1987-89 book income adjustment used in the corporate alternative minimum tax; and (6) foreign experience with book-tax conformity. I know that Germany, for example, has this basis it corporate taxable income on book income.

Finally, there is more to book-tax conformity than the effects that work through the tax system. Many analysts are worried that the tail might wag the dog—that is, that book-tax conformity could have adverse or unexpected impacts on financial reporting. As a tax person I don't think about these things, but that is a luxury the U.S. Senate cannot afford.

4. Commissioner Everson identified tax issues associated with transfer pricing generally, and the transfer of intangible assets outside the United States in particular, as high risk compliance concerns. Mr. Walker noted that the deferral of income of controlled foreign corporations as the second largest corporate tax expenditure in our tax code. The principle of deferral serves to enable U.S. multinationals to remain competitive with foreign-based multinationals, who are often subject to tax on a territorial basis.

Do you agree that transfer pricing issues generally, and transfer pricing issues with respect to intangible property in particular, are at or near the top of the list of challenges to the administration of our tax system?

How would changing to a territorial system affect (i) the prominence of transfer pricing issues in the U.S. tax system; and (ii) the competitiveness of U.S. multinationals?

How would repealing deferral affect (i) the prominence of transfer pricing issues in the U.S. tax system; and (ii) the competitiveness of U.S. multinationals? Under such a system, what, in your view, would the appropriate tax rate be so that the competitiveness of U.S. multinationals is not undermined? Please explain your

reasoning. In addition, to what extent would you recommend altering the foreign tax credit rules in such a system?

Magnitude of transfer pricing problem

Although it may sound like a detail to the layperson, aggressive transfer pricing is undoubtedly one of largest problem areas for the I.R.S. There is a wide variety of empirical evidence to support this. We know that many U.S. multinationals are increasing foreign profits without a corresponding increase in real business activity. We know that profit levels in tax havens and low-tax countries are much higher than they are in high-tax countries. I have estimated that inappropriate transfer pricing practices in a single year, 2002, in a single country, Ireland, cost the U.S. Treasury approximately $2 billion.

Because of the magnitude and complexity of transactions between affiliates, and because of the lack of comparable third-party transactions to use as benchmarks for transfer prices, the situation is nearly intractable for the IRS.

The problem is particularly acute for transfers of intangibles (and rights to use intangibles) because they are highly mobile, high-profit and--by their nature—unique, so comparables rarely exist. All of this would be bad enough, but the ability to transfer intangibles through favorable "qualified cost sharing arrangements" makes matters worse. IRS-proposed revisions to the regulations governing cost sharing arrangements will be an improvement, but they don't go far enough.

Transfer pricing—territorial system

A territorial system would increase incentives to engage in aggressive transfer pricing practices because the disparity in taxation between U.S. and foreign source income would increase. Although much foreign source income is effectively exempt from U.S. tax because earnings are retained offshore indefinitely, the benefits of profit shifting out of the United States for corporations that do not, or do not want to, defer repatriation indefinitely would increase substantially.

Competitiveness--territorial system

A territorial system would undoubtedly improve "the competitiveness of multinationals," that is, it would put investment by U.S.-based multinationals in foreign locations on level tax playing field with investment by foreign companies in those same foreign locations. But what is best for U.S. multinationals is not always what is best for U.S. citizens. The most obvious, direct effect of a tax advantage for, say, a new factory in China over a new factory in California is an increase in Chinese employment and reduction in U.S. employment.

Proponents of territoriality usually ignore or discount this uncomplicated conclusion and instead stress possible indirect benefits of a territorial system. The first of these is that foreign investment by U.S. multinationals increases U.S. exports. According to this view, subsidiaries of U.S. companies in foreign locations act as conduits for U.S. products into foreign markets.

The second argument is that foreign investment increases U.S. research and development. According to this view, a greater international presence gives U.S. multinationals a larger return on their research and development.

A third argument is that territoriality is an incentive for multinationals to keep their headquarters in the United States.

Although there is some truth to all of points, the magnitude of tax effects on exports, research, and location decisions for headquarters is a matter of speculation. I suspect they are small. Rather than review the inconclusive empirical evidence, let me instead make the following observations on the suitability of a territorial regime for achieving these benefits.

A fundamental precept of economics is that the most effective subsidy is a direct subsidy. In other words, if you want to subsidize, say, the production of bread, it would be nice to subsidize bread ovens or schools where bakers are trained, but the most cost-effective subsidy would be simply a subsidy for each loaf of bread produced.

If we want more exports (and there are strong economic arguments to not do this), we should subsidize exports *directly*. Moreover, there is no reason I know of to provide a subsidy only to exports by multinationals to low-tax countries.

If we want more research expenditure, we should subsidize research directly. Moreover, we do not want to subsidize research performed anywhere in the world (as a territorial regime might) but restrict tax benefits to domestic research and development.

Finally, if we want corporations to keep their headquarters in the United States, why not provide a direct subsidy to for corporations that locate front-office services in the United States. But then we must ask why jobs at a corporate headquarters deserve more of a subsidy then a job created at a hardware store or research laboratory.

There is one large and undeniable advantage of moving from our current system to a territorial system: the elimination of the "lock-out effect" on foreign earnings. Current law defers taxation of active foreign income until it is repatriated as a dividend to the U.S. parent. This gives U.S. corporations a large incentive to keep funds that could be used for domestic investment outside the United States.

But as explained below, there is a solution superior to territoriality that also eliminates the "lock-in" problem and does not tilt the playing field against U.S. workers.

Repeal deferral—effect on transfer pricing

If deferral were repealed the tax rate on income from foreign would never be less that the tax rate on income from domestic investment. And so the tax motivation to shift profits out of the United States through adjustment of transfer prices and other profit shifting methods would be largely eliminated.

Repeal deferral—effect on competitiveness

The elimination of deferral would end the incentive under current law for U.S. corporations to invest abroad. It would also eliminate the incentive to shift profit abroad and would thereby eliminate costly transfer pricing disputes. It would also remove the incentive for U.S. corporations to keep funds bottled up in foreign subsidiaries.

The revenue gains from the repeal of deferral should be used to reduce the corporate tax rate. The rate reduction would provide large additional benefits. It would increase the competitiveness of *all* U.S. corporations on *all* their business activities.

Both the elimination of the domestic-foreign rate differential and the lowering of the U.S. corporate would increase domestic investment. The larger domestic capital stock would increase employment and productivity. Higher productivity would ultimately lead to high wages and a higher standard of living for U.S. residents.

Appropriate corporate rate if deferral is repealed

There is no magic number for a competitive rate reduction. The lower, the better. But I would suggest that a rate reduction of at least 10 percentage points is justified by the 10 percentage point average reduction in the European Union over the last decade.

Some experts, like Professor Michael Graetz of Yale, have advocated for a lower rate. Graetz in particular has a plan for a 15-percent corporate rate paid for by the imposition of a new U.S. value-added tax. The Graetz proposal has a lot of merit, but because of the scope of his reform, he opens up a host of issues not related to reform of corporate taxation.

A rate reduction to 25 percent could realistically be paid for by broadening the corporate tax. Of course, such a base broadening would be ambitious. But it is not unprecedented. A reform of approximately the same scale—a 12 percentage point reduction in rates, from 46 to 34 percent--was accomplished in 1986. And, unlike 1986 when net corporate tax increases were used pay for cuts in the individual income tax, the corporate sector this time would not be subject to a tax increase.

Change to foreign tax credit rules if deferral is repealed

The ability to average low-tax foreign income with high-tax foreign income—so called "cross crediting"—could undermine benefits from the repeal of deferral.

Example: Suppose the U.S. has a tax rate of 30 percent. And suppose a U.S. multinational has $100 of U.S. income and $100 of foreign income all from a country with a 40-percent corporate tax rate. The foreign tax credit limit would leave $10 of foreign tax uncredited.

Now suppose the U.S. multinational is considering an investment that will yield an additional $100 of income. And suppose there are two possible locations for this investment: the United States or a country with a tax rate of 20 percent.

If the investment is made in the United States, there is no change in foreign tax and additional tax U.S. tax of $30. If, however, the investment is made in the low-tax country, there is no change in U.S. tax and additional foreign tax of $20. The table below has all the calculations.

	WW Income	US Tax Before Credit	FTC	US Tax After Credit	Foreign Tax	Total Tax
Before New Investment	200	60	30	30	40	70
Investment in US	300	90	30	60	40	100
Invest in Low-Tax	300	90	60	30	60	90

Conclusion: Unless cross-crediting is limited, the tax incentive to invest and shift income from the United State to low-tax countries will remain even if deferral is repealed.

From Senator Hatch:

1. Dr. Sullivan, I have heard some suggest that we could make our corporate tax system much simpler by having publicly-traded corporations merely use the income they report to shareholders as the base for paying federal income taxes rather than having income defined by the Internal Revenue Code. Why would this be a good or a not so good idea? Wouldn't this have the potential to save billions in tax compliance costs?

Not only would book-tax conformity save billions in compliance and administrative costs, it would greatly reduce the incentive for using tax shelters, and in a single stroke achieve many of the benefits of a comprehensive reform. Still, whether or not it is a good idea is a tricky question. There are three general problems.

First, for many good policy reasons, and for some purely political reasons, Congress would make many adjustments to reported book income it was used as the tax base for the corporate tax. Each of these adjustments would diminish the benefits described above. Namely, the gains in simplicity, the reduction in tax avoidance, and the benefits to the economy would all be reduced.

Second, even if Congress made numerous adjustments, the changes are so large and sweeping—like a mandate that the U.S. auto industry convert from gasoline to electric engines—that there are likely to be many unintended consequences—some bad, some good. The uncertainty and the consequent need for significant follow-up legislation further diminish economic benefits.

Finally, many accounting experts believe that book-tax conformity would lead to distortions in financial reporting to shareholders.

On net it is hard to say whether the potential benefits outweigh the potential costs. The idea certainly deserves more attention. If Congress decides to further investigate the possibility I would suggest the following pursuing the following:

(1) To get an idea of the political repercussions of the proposal, ask individual corporations at what rate of tax under the new system they would break even with the current system? I expect there would be wide variations, and so there would be big winners and big losers.
(2) Learn form real-world experience with the issue by investigating the U.S. experience of using book income in the corporate alternative minimum tax in the years 1987 through 1989 and the experience of several foreign countries that use book income in their corporation taxes.
(3) Closely monitor the benefits of the expanded book-tax reporting requirements (Schedule M-3). This will provide a lot of information about book-tax differences. More importantly, if it has a major impact on diminishing corporate shelters, there would be less need for change to book income. If, on the other hand, M-3 reporting does not help reduce shelters, or for whatever reason sheltering activity still is unacceptably large, the potential benefits of requiring book-tax conformity would be larger.

2. What would be the economic consequences of such a change? Do you think it might be a good idea? Since income reported to shareholders is very often higher than that reported to the IRS, might such a change allow us to lower the tax rate?

In general book income is broader than taxable income so the switch would broaden the tax base and—assuming the switch is legislated to be revenue-neutral--allow a significant reduction in corporate tax rates. Estimates of the magnitude of the difference between book and tax income suggest a reduction in the corporate tax rate to something in the neighborhood of 20 percent would be possible.

Economists are primarily concerned with promoting efficiency through tax neutrality. If there must be a corporate tax the best would be one with the lowest rates and a tax base that taxed all corporate capital income evenly. Putting aside the issue of debt vs. equity, the best way to achieve this is by taxing pure *economic* income.

In general, book income is closer to economic income than taxable income. For example, book depreciation is generally closer to true economic depreciation than depreciation used for tax purposes. So, in general, using book income instead of taxable income would better promote economic efficiency.

But there are deviations between book income and economic income. A few of the reasons for the disparity are: lack of inflation adjustment, limited use of mark-to-market methods, accountants' predisposition to conservatism and to flexibility. If the disparity between book and economic income were uniform across industries and across corporations within industries, economic neutrality would still prevail.

But this is highly unlikely. I don't know enough accounting to describe these differences in detail, but I imagine the non-neutrality in taxation across and within industries could result in considerable economic distortion.

Of course, current law has its own economic distortions, but most of these have been legislated for a purpose and we understand and have adapted to them.

In summary a corporate tax base on book income overall would probably have smaller economic distortions than current law but the new ones would be haphazard and not consistent with current policies goals.

The system also has the potential to create new economic distortions. For example, if only publicly traded corporation must adopt the new system, there would likely be a large disparity in the tax treatment of public vs. nonpublic corporations. (Whether than disparity was positive or negative would depend on the new tax rate chosen for the book-income system.) This would create two unwanted effects. First, one sector would be more favorably taxed than the other creating distortions in investment. Second, corporations would have new tax motivations to move between public and private ownership.

Finally, economic theory predicts that eventually shareholders will develop information systems to let them see around reported book income and thus allow corporations to minimize taxes without hurting their standing with shareholders. For example, one could imagine a prestigious reporting service developing an "unofficial" profit measure for every publicly traded company that mimicked the book income measure as we know it know. The company would officially report and the IRS would collect tax on the "official" book income but with a collective nod and wink everybody would know the real profitability of companies was reflected in the unofficial profit measure. Under this system, companies would be able to minimize tax even more easily than they do under current law and suffer no adverse consequence from shareholders.

3. Dr. Sullivan, do you believe the U.S. should consider switching to a territorial tax system? Why or why not?

Because deferral of active foreign source income is now so widely available under current tax rules, a switch to a territorial system in many respects would not be as large a change as it once was. The major benefit of the switch would be the elimination of the current tax incentive to keep profits out of the Unite States (because they are not subject to U.S. tax until they are repatriate as dividends back to the United States). A minor benefit of the change would be modest simplification to U.S. international tax rules. So, if the choice is between current law and a territorial system, Congress should seriously consider territoriality. The detailed 2004 proposal by the Joint Committee on Taxation is the obvious starting point.

There is, however, a better option: repeal of deferral accompanied by a revenue-neutral reduction of corporate tax rates. This would remove the incentive under current-law and a territorial system for U.S. corporations to invest abroad. It would improve the competitiveness of all U.S. corporations—not just multinationals. Like a territorial system, it would remove the current tax benefit of keeping funds offshore. Finally, it would eliminate—rather than increase under a territorial system—the hugely costly problem of transfer pricing.

From Senator Kerry:

In your testimony, you focus on broadening the corporate tax base and lowering the rate. Do you think that deferral should be repealed?

I believe deferral should be repealed and the associated revenue gains should be used to reduce the corporate tax rate. The rate reduction would have the benefit of increasing the competitiveness of *all* U.S. corporations on *all* their business activities. The elimination of deferral would end the incentive under current law for U.S. corporations to invest abroad. It would eliminate costly transfer pricing disputes. And it would remove the incentive for U.S. corporations to keep funds bottled up in foreign subsidiaries.

United States Government Accountability Office

GAO

Testimony

Before the Committee on Finance, U.S. Senate

For Release on Delivery
Expected at 10:00 a.m. EDT
Tuesday, June 13, 2006

TAX COMPLIANCE

Challenges to Corporate Tax Enforcement and Options to Improve Securities Basis Reporting

Statement of David M. Walker
Comptroler General of the United States

This testimony was amended on July 7, 2006 to correct the graphic on the highlights page and the labeling of the graphs on page 6. Wording was also changed on pages 1 and 4 to clarify that $277 billion is the amount of corporate income taxes OMB estimates will be collected in fiscal year 2006.

G A O
Accountability ★ Integrity ★ Reliability

GAO-06-851T

GAO
Accountability-Integrity-Reliability

Highlights

Highlights of GAO-06-851T, a Testimony to Committee on Finance, U.S. Senate

Why GAO Did This Study

Corporate income taxes are expected to bring in about $277 billion in 2006 to help fund the activities of the federal government. Besides raising revenue, the tax alters investment decisions and raises concerns about competitiveness in an environment of increasing global interdependency. The complexity of the tax breeds tax avoidance, including an estimated $32 billion of noncompliance detected by the Internal Revenue Service (IRS).

This testimony provides information on trends in corporate taxes and opportunities to improve corporate tax compliance.

The committee also asked that GAO discuss recent work on the misreporting of capital gains income from securities sales and options to improve compliance.

This statement is based largely on previously published GAO work.

www.gao.gov/cgi-bin/getrpt?GAO-06-851T.

To view the full product, including the scope and methodology, click on the link above. For more information, contact Michael Brostek at (202) 512-9110 or brostekm@gao.gov.

June 13, 2006

TAX COMPLIANCE

Challenges to Corporate Tax Enforcement and Options to Improve Securities Basis Reporting

What GAO Found

The corporate income tax is an important source of federal revenue and must be considered in dealing with the nation's long-term fiscal imbalance. Reexamining both federal spending and revenues, including corporate tax policy, corporate tax expenditures and corporate tax enforcement must be part of a multi-pronged approach to address the imbalance.

Corporate Income Tax Revenues as a Share of Federal Taxes, 1962-2005

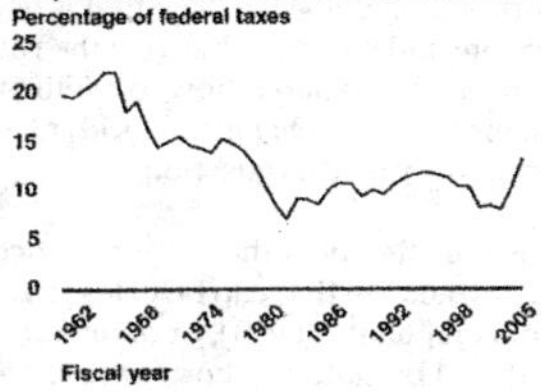

Source: GAO Analysis of OMB Data.

The total amount of corporate tax avoidance, which includes the $32 billion in noncompliance estimated by IRS, is unknown. A complex tax code, complex business transactions, and often multinational corporate structures make determining corporate tax liabilities and the extent of corporate tax avoidance a challenge. Opportunities exist to improve corporate tax compliance and include simplifying the tax code, obtaining better data on noncompliance, continuing to oversee the effectiveness of IRS enforcement, leveraging technology, and sending sound compliance signals through increased collections of taxes owed.

In a companion report issued today, GAO found that many taxpayers misreport capital gains or losses, sometimes inappropriately underpaying their taxes and sometimes overpaying them. IRS has efforts in place to help ensure proper reporting of capital gains and losses, but these efforts face several obstacles. GAO found that expanding third-party information reporting on the cost basis of capital assets could help mitigate this problem if related problems are addressed. GAO suggested that Congress consider requiring brokers to report adjusted basis to taxpayers and IRS and requiring IRS to work with the securities industry to develop cost-effective ways to mitigate reporting challenges. GAO also recommended that IRS clarify its guidance on reporting capital gains and losses.

Mr. Chairman and Members of the Committee:

I appreciate the opportunity to discuss the corporate income tax with you as well as our work on options for improving taxpayers' voluntary compliance in reporting their capital gains or losses from the sales of securities. As the Committee is well aware, the U.S. position in the worldwide economy has fundamentally changed and the structure and composition of our economy has shifted. U.S. workers and firms must now succeed in a world of fast-paced technological change and constantly evolving global competition. This raises two sets of questions about the corporate income tax. The first is about reforming the overall U.S. tax system and perhaps changing the role of corporate taxes. The second set of questions is about how to administer and enforce the existing corporate income tax in a changing world. As per your request, my statement focuses principally on this question.

The complexity of the corporate income tax generates opportunities for tax avoidance that can be categorized as clearly legal, clearly noncompliant (illegal), or of uncertain legality. Corporate tax base is reduced by statutory corporate tax expenditures, legal and illegal tax avoidance, and deliberate underreporting of income. The overall amount of tax base reduction is unknown but the Internal Revenue Service (IRS) has estimated the amount of clear noncompliance to total $32 billion for tax year 2001. Corporate tax avoidance in its various forms reduces overall federal revenue or, for the government to take in the same revenue, means that other taxpayers pay more.

My statement today makes the following points:

- Although less of a revenue source than it once was, the corporate income tax is one of the pillars of the federal tax system.[1] The $277 billion in corporate tax revenues that the Office of Management and Budget (OMB) estimates will be paid in fiscal year 2006 must be part of overall considerations for dealing with the nation's long-term fiscal imbalance. More specifically, corporate tax policy, corporate tax expenditures and corporate tax enforcement all must be part of a multi-pronged approach that reexamines both federal spending and revenues.

[1] For purposes of this statement, when we refer to the corporate income tax or corporations, we are excluding S-corporations, which are pass-through entities whose income or losses are generally not taxed at the corporate level, but are passed through to their owners.

- Determining corporate income tax liabilities and the extent of corporate tax avoidance is a challenge because of the complex tax code, complex business transactions and often multinational corporate structures. Opportunities exist to improve corporate tax compliance, such as simplifying the tax code, obtaining better data to the extent feasible on noncompliance, continuing to oversee the effectiveness of IRS's efforts, continuing to leverage technology, and sending sound compliance signals through such things as increased effectiveness in collecting taxes owed.

Also, at your request, I have included a section in this statement that discusses our findings in the area of capital gains basis reporting. In summary, we found that many taxpayers misreport capital gains or losses, sometimes inappropriately underpaying their taxes and sometimes overpaying them. IRS has efforts in place to help ensure proper reporting of capital gains and losses, but these efforts face several obstacles. Finally, we found that expanding third-party information reporting on the cost basis of capital assets could help mitigate this problem if related problems are addressed.

My statement today is largely drawn from previous GAO reports and testimonies, which were done in accordance with generally accepted government auditing standards. We also relied on other published information for the sections of this statement dealing with corporate taxation. The latter part of this statement discusses capital gains basis reporting and is drawn from the report on that subject we are releasing today.

Background

The base of the federal corporate income tax includes net income from business operations (receipts, minus the costs of purchased goods, labor, interest, and other expenses). It also includes net income that corporations earn in the form of interest, dividends, rent, royalties, and realized capital gains. The statutory rate of tax on net corporate income ranges from 15 to 35 percent, depending on the amount of income earned.[2]

[2] In addition, present law imposes an alternative minimum tax (AMT) on corporations to the extent that their minimum tax liability exceeds their regular tax liability. In general, the AMT applies a lower tax rate to a broader tax base. Specifically, the regular tax base is increased for AMT purposes by adding back certain items treated as tax preferences and disallowing certain deductions and credits. Also, marginal rates are higher over limited income ranges to recapture the benefits of the rates below 35 percent.

The United States taxes the worldwide income of domestic corporations, regardless of where the income is earned, with a foreign tax credit for certain taxes paid to other countries. However, the timing of the tax liability depends on several factors, including whether the income is from a U.S. or foreign source and, if it is from a foreign source, whether it is earned through direct operations or through a subsidiary.[3]

Statutory and effective tax rates are not necessarily the same. An effective tax rate, which is often lower—even substantially lower—than the statutory rate, measures the amount of tax that a corporation actually pays on a dollar of its economic income, when all aspects of the tax (deductions, credits, deferrals, etc.) are taken into account. Statutory and effective rates may differ, for example, because depreciation allowances for specific types of capital investments exceed (or fall short of) the true (economic) depreciation. Other differences arise because income from foreign subsidiaries is generally not taxed until it is repatriated to the United States. Special incentives, such as the research tax credit, that are designed to encourage certain behavior, also cause the effective rate of the tax to differ from its statutory rate. A recent Congressional Budget Office (CBO) study found that the United States' statutory corporate tax rates are high relative to Organization for Economic Cooperation and Development (OECD) countries but comparable with the rates for what were then the G-7 countries.[4] Comparisons of effective rates depend on the type of investment and the type of financing. According to CBO, U.S. effective corporate tax rates in 2003 were the G-7 median for equity-financed investments in machinery, second lowest for debt-financed investment in

[3] Very generally, corporations first calculate their taxable income. Taxable income is total income, including taxable income from foreign sources, minus deductions such as for salaries and wages, depreciation, and net operating loss carryovers. The next step is to calculate the tentative tax owed (taxable income times the applicable rate). The last step is to subtract any tax credits, including the foreign tax credit, to get the taxes owed.

[4] OECD consists of 30 market democracies and its purpose is to provides member countries a setting where governments can compare policy experiences, seek answers to common problems, and coordinate domestic and international policies. At the time of the CBO study, the G-7 consisted of Canada, France, Germany, Italy, Japan, the United Kingdom, and the United States. The G-7's purpose is to provide a forum for the leaders of the largest industrialized democracies to discuss major economic and political issues. When the Russian Federation participates at the meetings, the group is known as the G-8.

machinery, and second highest for equity-financed investment in industrial structures.[5]

Differences in effective tax rates across types and sources of income are pervasive, reflecting the complexity of the tax code. The corporate income tax (1) reduces the after tax return on capital income and, therefore, affects the incentive individuals have to save and invest; (2) taxes corporations differently than partnerships and sole proprietorships; (3) taxes U.S. corporations operating in foreign countries differently than those operating domestically and differently than foreign governments tax corporations; (4) taxes different types of corporate investments, such as machinery or structures, unevenly; and (5) taxes debt-financed investment at lower rates than equity-financed investment. These differences in effective tax rates alter both investment decisions and the reporting of corporate income as firms try to minimize their taxes. Such tax avoidance, much of it legal but some illegal, reduces tax revenue. Guiding investments to lightly taxed activities rather than those with high before tax productivity may reduce economic growth, further reducing tax revenue from what it otherwise would have been.

Corporate Income Taxes Are a Significant Source of Federal Revenue and Must Be Part of the Overall Considerations for Fiscal Reform

At about $277 billion, corporate income taxes are far smaller than the $841 billion in social insurance taxes and $998 billion in individual income taxes that OMB estimates will be paid in fiscal year 2006 to fund the federal government.[6] Figure 1 shows the relative importance of federal taxes.

[5] Congressional Budget Office, *Corporate Income Tax Rates: International Comparisons*, (Washington, D.C.: November 2005). The study focuses on how corporate income taxes affect incentives for investment by calculating marginal effective tax rates in different countries. The calculations include differences across countries in statutory tax rates and depreciation rules.

[6] Office of Management and Budget. *Historical Tables, Budget of the United States Government, Fiscal Year 2007*. (Washington, D.C.: Feb. 2006).

Figure 1: Trend in Federal Taxes, 1962-2005

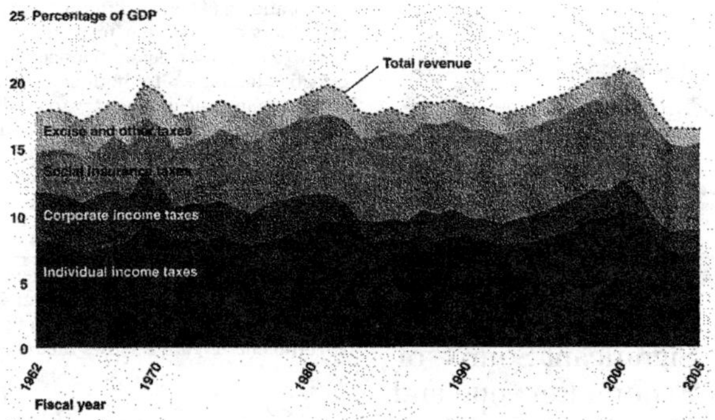

Source: GAO representation of OMB data.

Figures 1 and 2 show the trend in corporate tax revenues since 1962. Tax experts have written that corporate tax revenues fell from the 1960s to the early 1980s for several reasons. For example, corporate income became a smaller share of national income during these years, partly due to the fact that corporate debt, and therefore deductible interest payments, increased relative to corporate equity, reducing the tax base. In addition, tax expenditures, such as more generous depreciation rules and corporate tax rate reductions lowered corporate taxes.[7] Since the early 1980s corporate

[7] Steuerle, C. Eugene, *Contemporary U.S. Tax Policy*. Washington, D.C.: The Urban Institute Press, 2004.

Gravelle, Jane G., "The Corporate Tax: Where Has It Been and Where Is It Going?" *National Tax Journal*, vol. 57, no. 4 (2004): 903-23.

tax revenues have fluctuated in a narrower range, reflecting changes in corporate profits, tax laws, and other factors.

Since the early 1980s the corporate tax has accounted for from about 6 to 13 percent of federal revenue, as shown in figure 2. Consequently, although not the largest, it remains an important source of federal revenue. Relative to the gross domestic product (GDP), the corporate tax has ranged from a little over 1 percent to just under 2.5 percent during those same years. CBO has recently projected that despite the recent uptick, corporate tax revenue for the next 10 years as a percentage of GDP is expected to stay within this same range.

Figure 2: Corporate Income Tax Revenues as a Share of Federal Taxes and as a Share of GDP, 1962-2005

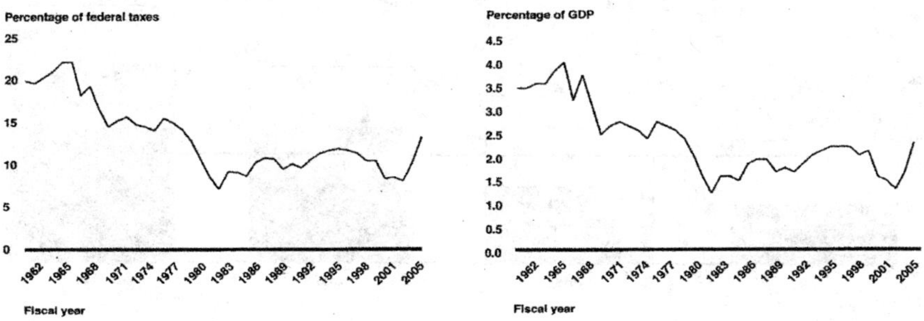

Source: GAO analysis of OMB data.

Corporate tax revenues of the magnitude shown in figure 2 make them relevant to considerations about how to address the nation's long-term fiscal imbalance. Over the long term, the United States faces a large and growing structural budget deficit primarily caused by demographic trends and rising health care costs as shown in figure 3, and exacerbated over time by growing interest on the ever larger federal debt. Continuing on this imprudent and unsustainable fiscal path will gradually erode, if not suddenly damage, our economy, our standard of living, and ultimately our national security.

Figure 3: Composition of Federal Spending as a Share of GDP, Assuming Discretionary Spending Grows with GDP after 2006 and That Expiring Tax Provisions Are Extended

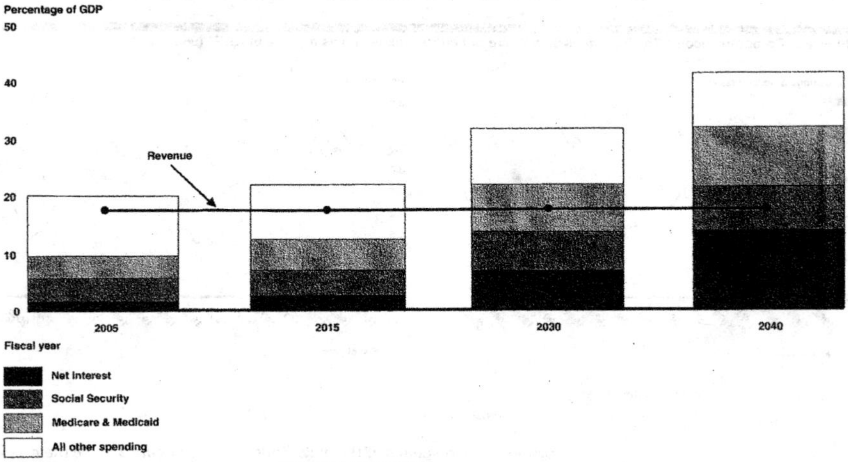

Source: GAO's May 2006 analysis.

Note: This includes certain tax provisions that expired at the end of 2005, such as the increased alternative minimum tax exemption amount.

We cannot grow our way out of this long-term fiscal challenge because the imbalance between spending and revenue is so large. We will need to make tough choices using a multipronged approach: (1) revise budget processes and financial reporting requirements; (2) restructure entitlement programs; (3) reexamine the base of discretionary spending and other spending; and (4) review and revise tax policy, including tax expenditures, and tax enforcement programs. Corporate tax policy, corporate tax expenditures, and corporate tax enforcement need to be part of the overall tax review because of the amount of revenue at stake.

Corporate tax expenditures reduce the revenue that would otherwise be raised from the corporate income tax. As already noted, to reduce their tax liabilities, corporations can take advantage of preferential provisions in the tax code, such as exclusions, exemptions, deductions, credits, preferential rates, and deferral of tax liability. Tax preferences—which are legally known as tax expenditures—are often aimed at policy goals similar to those of federal spending programs. For example, there are different tax expenditures intended to encourage economic development in disadvantaged areas and stimulate research and development, while there are also federal spending programs that have similar purposes. Also, by narrowing the tax base, corporate tax expenditures have the effect of raising either corporate tax rates or the rates on other taxpayers in order to generate a given amount of revenue.

The sum of estimated forgone revenue for the federal government because of corporate tax expenditures was $80 billion for fiscal year 2005.[8] In its most recent report, the Department of the Treasury (Treasury) listed 27 tax expenditures for corporate taxpayers only and another 52 provisions available to both corporations and other businesses. As of fiscal year 2005, the two largest tax expenditures used by corporations were the accelerated depreciation of machinery and equipment ($15.9 billion) and the deferral of income of controlled foreign corporations ($10.5 billion); these two accounted for a third of the sum of corporate revenue losses estimated by Treasury.

We reported in September 2005[9] that the effectiveness of many tax expenditures is not subject to a level of review similar to that of programs

[8]Summing the individual tax expenditure estimates is useful for gauging the general magnitude of the federal revenue involved, but it does not take into account possible interactions between individual provisions. See GAO, *Government Performance and Accountability: Tax Expenditures Represent a Substantial Federal Commitment and Need to Be Reexamined*, GAO-05-690 (Washington, D.C.: Sept. 23, 2005).

[9] GAO, *Government Performance and Accountability: Tax Expenditures Represent a Substantial Federal Commitment and Need to Be Reexamined*, GAO-05-690 (Washington, D.C.: Sept. 23, 2005).

that spend money directly. Although some corporate income tax expenditures are reviewed by government agencies, academics, and others, all should be reviewed periodically to ensure they have not outlived their usefulness, are not redundant, or are not inefficient in accomplishing their intended purpose. In that report, we recommended that the OMB and Treasury take steps to ensure regular reexamination of tax expenditures, including the corporate provisions. OMB disagreed with the recommendations, citing methodological and conceptual issues. Our report discusses in detail the issues that OMB raised and why we continue to believe that our recommendations are valid. Also, as far back as 1994, we have suggested that Congress should review these tax expenditures, considering such things as how well the corporate tax expenditures are achieving their purposes and whether they should remain, given the potential benefits of a simpler corporate tax code, possibly with reduced tax rates.[10]

Opportunities Exist to Improve Corporate Tax Compliance

Ensuring corporate income tax compliance is challenging because much corporate tax avoidance is legal and the true tax liability for large corporations is difficult to determine. A wide variety of strategies will undoubtedly be needed to address corporate tax compliance. Opportunities to pursue include simplifying the tax code, obtaining better data to the extent feasible on noncompliance, continuing to oversee the effectiveness of IRS's efforts, continuing to leverage technology, and sending sound compliance signals through such things as increased effectiveness in collecting taxes owed.

Corporate Tax Avoidance Is Bred in Part by Complexity

The amount of corporate tax avoidance is unknown. A complex tax code, complicated business transactions, and often multinational corporate structures make determining corporate tax liabilities and the extent of corporate tax avoidance a challenge. Tax avoidance has become such a concern that some tax experts say corporate tax departments have become "profit centers" as corporations seek to take advantage of the tax laws in order to maximize shareholder value. Some corporate tax avoidance is clearly legal, some falls in gray areas of the tax code, and some is clearly noncompliance or illegal. Tax code simplification has the potential to reduce at least some of this avoidance.

[10] GAO, *Tax Policy: Tax Expenditures Deserve More Scrutiny*, GAO-GGD/AIMD-94-122 (Washington, D.C.: June 3, 1994).

Often corporate tax avoidance is legal. For example, multinational corporations can locate active trade or business operations in jurisdictions that have lower effective tax rates than does the United States and, unless and until they repatriate the income, defer taxation in the United States on that income, thus reducing their effective tax rate. Similarly, making investments that qualify for accelerated depreciation can lower a corporation's current effective tax rate, although in the future its rate would be higher.[11]

Corporate tax planners may find legal ways to exploit tax code complexity to play one provision of the code off another in ways that Congress never intended. In response, Congress has sometimes acted to address what it considered to be abusive tax shelters. For example, the American Jobs Creation Act of 2004[12] limited the tax benefits of leasing transactions involving tax-exempt entities, such as transit authorities. One type of transaction the act limited was the sale-in/lease-out (SILO) arrangement, which involved a taxable entity buying assets, such as railcars, from a tax-exempt entity, for example, a metropolitan transit system, and leasing them back to the tax-exempt entity. The estimated revenue gain from the 2004 act's provision covering leasing transactions with tax-indifferent parties was about $26.6 billion for 2005 through 2014.

Complicating corporate tax compliance is the fact that in many cases the law is unclear or subject to differing interpretations. In fact, some have postulated that major corporations' tax returns are actually just the opening bid in an extended negotiation with IRS to determine a corporation's tax liability. An illustration is transfer pricing. Transfer pricing involves setting the appropriate price for such things as goods, services, or intangible property (such as patents, trademarks, copyrights, technology, or "know-how") that is transferred between the U.S.-based operations of a multinational company and a foreign affiliate. If the price paid by the affiliate to the U.S. operation is understated, the profits of the U.S. operation are reduced and U.S. taxable income is inappropriately reduced or eliminated. The standard for judging the correct price is the price that would have been paid between independent enterprises acting at "arm's length." However, it can be extremely difficult to establish what an arm's length price would be. Given the global economy and the number

[11] Accelerated depreciation lowers a corporation's marginal effective tax rate on investments by increasing the present value of these deductions.

[12] Pub. L. No. 108-357 (2004).

of multinational firms with some U.S.-based operations, opportunities for transfer pricing disputes are likely to grow.

Tax shelters are one example of how tax avoidance, including corporate tax avoidance, can shade into the illegal. Some tax shelters are legal though perhaps aggressive interpretations of the law, but others cross the line. In a 2003 testimony, we reported that IRS had identified 27 kinds of abusive shelter transactions—called listed transactions—promoted to corporations and others. As of June 2006, IRS's web site lists 31 such listed transactions. IRS also had a number of other transactions that had to be reported to IRS and may have had some characteristics of abusive shelters but were not, and possibly never would be, listed.

Abusive shelters often are complex transactions that manipulate many parts of the tax code or regulations and are typically buried among legitimate transactions reported on tax returns. Because these transactions are often composed of many pieces located in several parts of a complex tax return, they are essentially hidden from plain sight, which contributes to the difficulty of determining the scope of the abusive shelter problem. Often lacking economic substance or a business purpose other than generating tax benefits, abusive shelters have been promoted by some tax professionals, often in confidence, for significant fees, sometimes with the participation of tax-indifferent parties, such as foreign or tax-exempt entities. These shelters may involve unnecessary steps and flow-through entities, such as partnerships, which make detection of these transactions more difficult.

For example, a company had a sizable gain from the sale of a subsidiary and wanted to avoid or minimize paying tax on the gain. An investment bank proposed forming an offshore partnership with a foreign corporation (a tax-indifferent party) for the express purpose of sheltering the capital gains of its corporate client. The partnership purchased and quickly resold notes in a contingent installment sale transaction. The partnership earned a large capital gain, most of which it allocated to the foreign corporate partner. Later, related losses were allocated to the U.S. corporation, generating approximately $100 million in capital loss for the investment bank's client. The corporation used this capital loss to shelter its U.S.-based capital gains. Both the Tax Court and the Third Circuit Court of Appeals ruled that the transaction lacked economic substance. The Third Circuit, in addition to requiring economic substance, held that a transaction must have a subjective nontax business motive to be respected for tax purposes.[13] For this transaction, the investment bank was to earn a fee of $2 million.

In part because tax shelters are intentionally hidden, IRS has not been able to produce a reliable estimate of the revenues lost because of shelters. As we reported in October 2003, one estimate, which had a number of methodological limitations, suggested an average annual tax gap because of tax shelters (both corporate and individual) that could have been from about $11.6 billion to about $15.1 billion for the years 1993 through 1999.[14] Because the methodological limitations were serious, the true amount of the revenue loss could be lower or higher than this range. Furthermore, this estimate does not cover non-abusive tax shelters.

Establishing a presence in a low-tax country is another technique for avoiding corporate income tax. Some low-tax countries are called tax havens. The company's presence in a tax haven in some cases may be nominal, nothing more than a file in an office. Use of a tax haven can be questionable when combined with abusive transfer pricing or techniques, such as interest stripping, to artificially shift income to the tax haven. In several reports since 2002, we reported on federal contractors' use of tax havens. We reported that 4 of the top 100 federal contractors that were publicly traded corporations in 2001 were located in tax havens and that 3 of these were originally U.S.-headquartered corporations. Later, we reported that large tax haven contractors in both 2000 and 2001 had a tax cost advantage compared to large domestic contractors.[15]

[13] *ACM Partnership v. Commissioner*, 157 F. 3d 231 (3d Cir. 1998), aff'g, 73 T.C.M. 2189 (1997), cert. denied, 526 U.S. 1017 (1999).

[14] GAO, *Internal Revenue Service: Challenges Remain in Combating Abusive Tax Shelters*, GAO-04-104T, (Washington, D.C.: Oct. 21, 2003).

[15] GAO, *Information on Federal Contractors That Are Incorporated Offshore*, GAO-03-194R (Washington, D.C.: Oct. 1, 2002) and *International Taxation: Tax Haven Companies Were More Likely to Have a Tax Cost Advantage in Federal Contracting*, GAO-04-856 (Washington, D.C.: June 30, 2004).

IRS's Incomplete and Dated Estimates of Corporate Tax Noncompliance Can Be Improved

In large part because of the complexity and uncertainty in the application of tax laws, the actual level of corporate income tax noncompliance (illegal tax avoidance) is poorly understood. IRS estimates a corporate tax gap in the tens of billions of dollars, but also acknowledges that this estimate is not based on robust, recent, and reliable research.[16]

As noted above, IRS's published estimate of the corporate tax gap—the difference between what corporations pay voluntarily and on time in taxes and what they are required to pay under the law—is $32 billion for tax year 2001. This is out of an overall gross tax gap of $345 billion for that year. Underreporting of income was the largest component of the corporate tax gap, contributing an estimated $30 billion. The IRS estimate included both small corporations (those reporting assets of $10 million or less) and large corporations (those reporting assets of over $10 million). Underpayment of taxes due accounted for $2 billion of the corporate tax gap for tax year 2001. IRS has no estimate for nonfiling of corporate income tax returns for tax year 2001.

However, the available tax gap estimates are highly uncertain and incomplete. IRS has not systematically measured the level of compliance for large corporations, and the last measure of noncompliance for small corporations was from the 1980s. IRS's level of certainty with regard to the accuracy of the corporate tax gap estimate is low for reasons such as use of incomplete and old data, interpretation of complex laws, and resource constraints. The 2001 estimate used data from the 1970s and 1980s to estimate underreporting of corporate income taxes. For large corporate income tax underreporting, IRS based its estimate on the amount of tax recommended from operational examinations. As we reported in July 2005,[17] according to IRS officials, IRS relies on the amount of tax recommended because it is difficult to determine the true tax liability of large corporations because of complex and ambiguous tax laws that create opportunities for differing interpretations and that complicate the determination. Because these examinations do not cover all firms and do not test all items on a tax return, the estimate produced from the

[16] The tax gap estimate is an aggregate of estimates for three primary types of noncompliance: underreporting of tax liabilities on tax returns; underpaying of taxes due from filed returns; and nonfiling, which refers to the failure to file a required tax return altogether or on time.

[17] GAO, *Tax Compliance: Better Compliance Data and Long-term Goals Would Support a More Strategic IRS Approach to Reducing the Tax Gap*, GAO-05-753 (Washington, D.C. July 18, 2005).

examinations is incomplete. IRS officials also explained that because of these complexities and the costs and burdens of collecting complete and accurate data, IRS has not systematically measured large corporation tax compliance through statistically valid studies.

As of June of this year, IRS did not have approved plans to update the corporate tax gap estimate. Although measuring corporate tax compliance can be challenging and costly, such compliance data aid in identifying new or growing types of noncompliance, identifying changes in tax laws and regulations that may improve compliance, more effectively targeting examinations of tax returns, understanding the effectiveness of its programs to promote and enforce compliance, and properly determining its resource needs and allocations. In order to improve efforts to reduce the tax gap, we have recommended that IRS develop plans to periodically measure tax compliance for areas that have been measured, and study ways to cost effectively measure compliance for other components of the tax gap that have not been measured, such as excise taxes and corporate taxes. IRS agreed with our recommendations.[18]

IRS Has Strengthened Corporate Tax Compliance Efforts, but Continued Oversight Will Be Warranted

IRS has recently increased the number of corporate audits and recommended tax assessments. These trends are promising. However, given the lack of a reliable measure of the extent of corporate noncompliance and other factors, continued oversight of these efforts will be warranted to make informed judgments about their overall effectiveness.

As shown in figure 4, the number of corporate income tax returns that IRS examined rose from its recent low of 0.71 percent in fiscal year 2004 to 1.25 percent in fiscal year 2005. This number includes examinations of 20 percent of large corporations in fiscal year 2005 as well as audits of all 1,100 of the nation's largest corporations with assets of more than $250 million.

[18] GAO, *Tax Administration: Better Compliance Data and Long-term Goals Would Support a More Strategic IRS Approach to Reducing the Tax Gap*, GAO-05-753 (Washington, D.C.: July 18, 2005).

Figure 4: Percentage of Corporate Tax Returns IRS Examined, Fiscal Years 2001-2005

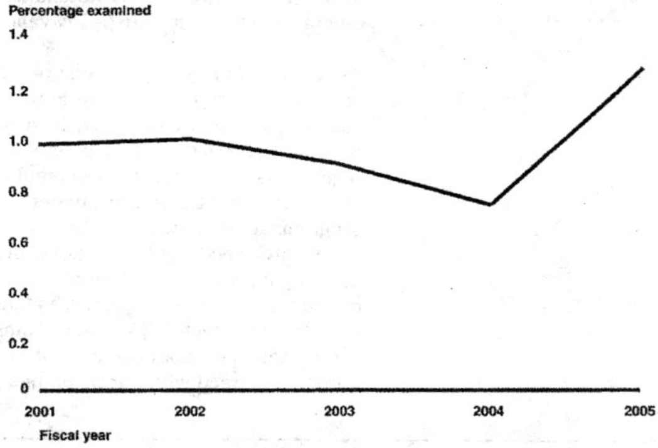

Source: IRS.

Figure 5 shows that the amount of taxes that IRS recommended as a result of examinations performed grew from its recent low of $13.5 billion in fiscal year 2003 to $32 billion in fiscal year 2005.

Figure 5: Amount of Taxes Recommended from Examinations of Corporations in Billions of Dollars, Fiscal Years 2001-2005

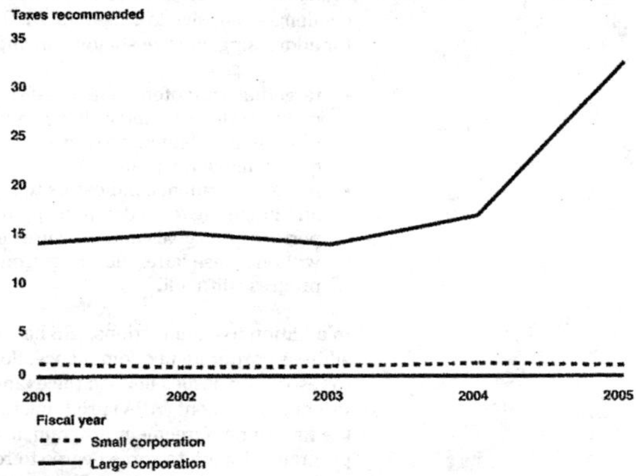

Source: IRS.

According to IRS, about a third of the increase in recommended assessments comes from tax shelter examinations, and nearly all of the increase comes from examinations of the largest corporations. IRS notes, not surprisingly, that a large portion of the recommended taxes were not agreed to by the corporations. In the past, we found that under IRS's examination program of the nation's largest corporations, the amount of taxes IRS actually assessed has been about 20 percent of the amount initially recommended during examinations.[10] Further, the amounts assessed often are not ultimately collected after cases are reviewed in IRS's Appeals function or in the courts. Because the various review and appeal options can be time consuming, it may be a number of years before actual collection occurs on some cases.

[10] GAO, *Tax Administration: IRS Measures Could Provide a More Balanced Picture of Audit Results and Costs*, GAO/GGD-98-128 (Washington D.C.: June 23, 1998).

The shelter-related results come from IRS's multiyear effort to attack tax shelters. In 2003 we reported that IRS had shifted resources to create a broad-based strategy to combat what it considered to be a high priority challenge—abusive tax shelters. IRS had adopted a broad-based strategy for addressing abusive shelters, including

- targeting promoters to head off the proliferation of shelters;
- making efforts to deter, detect, and resolve abuse;
- offering inducements to businesses to disclose their use of questionable tax practices; and
- using performance indicators to measure outputs and some outcomes and intending to go down the path it had started and develop long-term performance goals and measures linked to those goals. We said that without these latter elements, Congress would find gauging IRS's progress difficult.

In addition to examinations, IRS has undertaken a number of initiatives to address corporate tax compliance. Some of these initiatives are intended to resolve tax issues beyond the examination process. The Advance Pricing Agreement (APA) program, the Fast Track Settlement program, the Pre-Filing Agreement program, and the Industry Issue Resolution program all work to some degree to resolve contentious tax issues outside of the examination process. For example, the APA program is intended to address transfer pricing issues up front so that they do not arise during subsequent examinations.

IRS has also been revising the corporate tax examination process. For instance, IRS reports that it has shortened the cycle time of examinations. According to IRS, reducing cycle time allows IRS to examine additional taxpayers and reduces administrative burdens on taxpayers. Similarly, IRS's Limited Issue Focused Examination process seeks to have IRS and corporations reach a formal agreement to govern key aspects of the examination.

Future success in following through on these initiatives will require replenishment of IRS's staff, which could be challenging given the increasing numbers of key employees who are eligible for retirement or who are otherwise leaving key occupations. The Large and Mid-Size Business Division (LMSB), which is responsible for the compliance of the largest corporations, reported in its fiscal year 2006 strategic assessment that it will continue to lose substantial experience as revenue agents leave. The Small Business and Self Employed Division, which covers the rest of corporations, also has growing numbers of employees eligible for retirement or leaving their enforcement positions. Although hiring to fill positions is occurring, past experience suggests that training these new employees and giving them on-the-job experience will take time and likely adversely affect the divisions' overall productivity to some extent. The Treasury Inspector General for Tax Administration has designated managing human capital a management and performance challenge for IRS.

In part because IRS does not have a reliable measure of corporate tax compliance, it will be challenged to demonstrate the effectiveness of the increased audits and the various initiatives it has undertaken. The effectiveness of IRS's efforts will depend on the extent to which the taxes recommended are actually collected given past data showing that a relatively small portion of recommended assessments is ultimately collected. For these reasons, as well as human capital management challenges, IRS's increased compliance efforts will warrant continued oversight.

Continuing to Leverage Technology

Judicious use of technology has already helped IRS improve its productivity, and continued, well-managed technology initiatives have the potential to further improve the use of its resources. According to IRS, electronic filing of individuals' tax returns has enabled it to reduce the amount of staffing devoted to processing paper tax returns and to transfer staffing allocations to other endeavors, including compliance work. Further, because of the software used in electronically preparing and filing returns, these returns have fewer errors, thus saving IRS and taxpayers needless time and effort to correct avoidable errors.

Starting in 2006, many larger corporations are now required to file their tax returns electronically. This is no small undertaking, and some transition issues are likely to occur. However, electronic returns offer the potential to speed examinations—if for no other reason than often very voluminous corporate tax returns can be moved to appropriate locations for review immediately. IRS believes electronically filed returns will also speed analysis of corporate tax returns and the identification of issues and taxpayers most in need of examination or other resolution of potential compliance issues. IRS plans to gradually expand the number of firms required to electronically file. This and other opportunities to leverage modern technology can serve to help IRS deal with the complex tax issues in corporate tax returns.

Improving the Collection of Delinquent Taxes Would Send a Compliance Signal

When any taxpayer has been found to owe taxes and those amounts are no longer in dispute, failure to collect the taxes sends an adverse compliance signal. While not collecting these debts may send a message to corporations that IRS is not serious about enforcing the tax law, developing and exploiting opportunities to improve collections sends the opposite signal and can contribute to reducing corporate noncompliance. In February 2004, we reported that some Department of Defense (DOD) contractors abuse the federal tax system with little consequence.[20] We reported that based on our analysis of a limited number of DOD disbursement systems, more than 27,000 DOD contractors owed nearly $3 billion in unpaid federal taxes. In June 2005, we reported that many contractors of civilian agencies throughout the federal government also abuse the federal tax system.[21] Our analysis showed that about 33,000 contractors that received substantial federal payments from civilian agencies during fiscal year 2004 owed a total of more than $3 billion in unpaid taxes. The unpaid taxes owed by DOD and civilian agency contractors included corporate income, excise, unemployment, individual income, and payroll taxes.[22] We also found evidence of abusive and potentially criminal activities on the part of both DOD and civilian agency contractors.[23]

In our reports on this issue, we made numerous recommendations intended to improve the Federal Payment Levy Program by expanding the amount and type of tax debt eligible for inclusion in the program, expanding the volume of federal payments subject to levy, and correcting process and control deficiencies that hindered the program's ability to

[20] GAO, *Financial Management: Some DOD Contractors Abuse the Federal Tax System with Little Consequence*, GAO-04-95 (Washington, D.C.: Feb. 12, 2004). Although some of the contractors were corporations, we did not estimate how many were corporations.

[21] GAO, *Financial Management: Thousands of Civilian Agency Contractors Abuse the Federal Tax System with Little Consequence*, GAO-05-637 (Washington, D.C.: June 16, 2005).

[22] Payroll taxes are amounts that businesses withheld from employees' wages for federal income taxes, Social Security, and Medicare but failed to remit to IRS, as well as the related employer matching contributions for Social Security and Medicare taxes.

[23] We considered activity to be abusive when a contractor's actions or inactions, though not illegal, took advantage of the existing tax enforcement and administration system to avoid fulfilling federal tax obligations and were deficient or improper when compared with behavior that a prudent person would consider reasonable. We characterized as potentially criminal any activity related to federal tax liability that may be a crime under a specific provision of the Internal Revenue Code.

maximize the amount levied from payments to contractors with unpaid federal taxes. In our 2004 report, we also recommended that OMB develop options for prohibiting federal contract awards to businesses and individuals that abuse the federal tax system, including designating such tax abuse as a cause for government wide debarment or suspension. The agencies involved did not agree with all of our recommendations. We discuss their views and our responses in detail in our reports, as well as our continued belief that our recommendations are valid. Consistent with our recommendation to OMB, I believe Congress should consider suspending government business with contractors who are delinquent on their taxes as of a specific and prospective effective date, with a provision for limited waivers if necessary in unique circumstances.

Capital Gains Basis Reporting

Finally, you also asked us to testify on a report—done at your request—that we are issuing today on individual taxpayers' compliance in reporting capital gains' income from the sale of securities.[24] Misreporting such income[25] contributes to the annual tax gap, which is the gap between tax amounts that taxpayers should pay under the law and do pay voluntarily and on time. For tax year 2001, the IRS estimated a gross tax gap of $345 billion, of which at least $11 billion is attributed to individual taxpayers who misreported their income from capital gains or losses.[26] Taxpayers are to determine their capital gains or losses by subtracting the "basis" amount, which is generally the cost for an asset, from the gross proceeds amount when selling the asset.

[24] GAO, *Capital Gains Tax Gap: Requiring Brokers to Report Securities Cost Basis Would Improve Compliance if Related Challenges Are Addressed*, GAO-06-603 (Washington, D.C.: June 13, 2006).

[25] Taxpayers are to report gains or losses from selling securities on Schedule D of the federal income tax returns as well as the purchase and sale dates, adjusted cost basis, and gross proceeds from the sale.

[26] The overall capital gains tax gap could be larger than $11 billion if IRS had estimated the portion of the $48 billion tax gap for unfiled tax returns or unpaid taxes that is related to capital gains. According to an IRS research official, in mid-2006, IRS plans to publish its final report on the 2001 tax gap that will include an updated tax gap estimate based on a refined methodology. It is possible that the updated tax gap figures could differ from the current estimates.

In summary:

- For tax year 2001, an estimated[27] 36 percent (over 7 million) of individual taxpayers who sold securities misreported capital gains or losses. Using the wrong cost basis for the securities was a primary type of noncompliance leading to this misreported income. About two-thirds of the misreporting taxpayers understated gains or overstated losses, while about one-third overstated gains or understated losses. Additionally, a few taxpayers with securities sales misreported whether their gains or losses were short-term or long-term.[28]
- IRS attempts to address misreported securities sales' income through enforcement and taxpayer service programs, which are to find noncompliance or help taxpayers comply voluntarily. Various challenges limit the impact of these programs, such as that IRS enforcement programs contact relatively few taxpayers and the lack of cost basis information impedes efficient use of IRS's enforcement resources. IRS also faces difficulties in ensuring that taxpayers understand their obligations for determining and reporting their capital gains and losses.
- Expanding information reporting[29] to taxpayers and IRS on securities sales to include cost basis has potential to improve taxpayer voluntary compliance and help IRS verify securities gains or losses. Basis reporting would raise challenges, many of which can be mitigated to some extent. For example, broker costs would increase but could be constrained by limiting the scope of any reporting requirement and by building on the basis reporting to taxpayers that many brokers already do. For example, reporting basis for only future purchases would

[27] Our estimates are based on a review of a probability sample of IRS examinations selected from the nearly 46,000 randomly selected individual tax returns for tax year 2001 in its National Research Program, IRS's most recent study of individual tax compliance. We express our confidence in our estimates as a 95 percent confidence interval, plus or minus the margin of error. Our estimate for the percentage of misreporting taxpayers has a sampling error of (+/-) 7 percent or less, and we are 95 percent confident that from 6.2 million to 8.3 million taxpayers misreported securities sales.

[28] Securities assets sold after being held for 1 year or less are considered short-term while others sold are considered to be long-term and are generally taxed at lower tax rates.

[29] Information reporting involves third parties filing returns with IRS and taxpayers to report certain income. Brokers are required to file Form 1099-B with IRS and the taxpayer to report such information for securities sales as the dates, number of shares, and gross proceeds of the sale, but not the cost basis.

mitigate challenges when brokers do not know the basis for securities purchased in the past. To the extent that actions to mitigate the challenges to basis reporting delay its implementation or limit coverage to only certain types of securities, the resulting improvements to taxpayers' voluntary reporting compliance would be somewhat constrained. IRS's broad authority to require information reporting for securities sales may not be enough to require all the actions necessary to implement cost basis reporting and mitigate the challenges.

Based on these results, our report includes matters that Congress may want to consider, including requiring brokers to report to both taxpayers and IRS the adjusted basis of sold securities and ensuring that IRS has sufficient authority to implement the requirement. Congress could also require brokers to report whether the securities sold were short- or long-term and IRS to work with brokers to develop rules that mitigate the challenges. Further, we recommend that IRS modify the instructions for the individual tax return to (1) clarify the appropriate use of capital losses to offset capital gains or other income and (2) provide guidance on resources available to taxpayers to determine basis. IRS agreed with our recommendations.

Mr. Chairman, this concludes my prepared statement. I would be happy to respond to any questions you or other Members of the Committee may have at this time.

Contacts and Acknowledgments

For further information on this testimony, please contact Michael Brostek at (202) 512-9110 or brostekm@gao.gov. David Lewis, Assistant Director; Jeffrey Arkin; Kevin Daly; Amy Friedheim; Thomas Gilbert; Lawrence Korb; Signora May; Edward Nannenhorn; Cheryl Peterson; Michael Rose; Marylynn Sergent; Thomas Short; Michael Volpe; James White, Jennifer Wong; and James Wozny made key contributions to this testimony.

United States Government Accountability Office

GAO

Report to the Committee on Finance, U.S. Senate

June 2006

CAPITAL GAINS TAX GAP

Requiring Brokers to Report Securities Cost Basis Would Improve Compliance if Related Challenges Are Addressed

GAO
Accountability * Integrity * Reliability

GAO-06-603

GAO
Accountability·Integrity·Reliability

Highlights

Highlights of GAO-06-603, a report to the Committee on Finance, U.S. Senate

June 2006

CAPITAL GAINS TAX GAP

Requiring Brokers to Report Securities Cost Basis Would Improve Compliance if Related Challenges Are Addressed

Why GAO Did This Study

For tax year 2001, the Internal Revenue Service (IRS) estimated a tax gap of at least $11 billion from individual taxpayers misreporting income from capital assets (generally those owned for investment or personal purposes). IRS did not estimate the portion of this gap from securities (e.g., stocks, bonds, and mutual fund capital gains distributions).

GAO was asked for information on (1) the extent and types of noncompliance for individual taxpayers that misreport securities capital gains, (2) actions IRS takes to reduce the securities tax gap, and (3) options with the potential to improve taxpayer voluntary compliance and IRS's ability to address noncompliant taxpayers. For estimates of noncompliance, GAO analyzed a probability sample of examination cases for tax year 2001 from the most recent IRS study of individual tax compliance.

What GAO Recommends

To reduce securities capital gains noncompliance, GAO suggests that Congress consider requiring brokers to report adjusted basis to taxpayers and IRS and requiring IRS to work with the industry to develop cost effective ways to mitigate reporting challenges. GAO also recommends that IRS clarify its guidance on reporting capital gains and losses.

In commenting on a draft of this report, IRS agreed with our recommendations.

www.gao.gov/cgi-bin/getrpt?GAO-06-603.

To view the full product, including the scope and methodology, click on the link above. For more information, contact Michael Brostek at (202) 512-9110 or brostekm@gao.gov.

What GAO Found

GAO estimates that 38 percent of individual taxpayers with securities transactions misreported their capital gains or losses in tax year 2001. A greater estimated percentage of taxpayers misreported gains or losses from securities sales (36 percent) than capital gain distributions from mutual funds (13 percent). This may be because taxpayers must determine the taxable portion of securities sales' income whereas they need only add up their capital gain distributions. Among individual taxpayers who misreported securities sales, roughly two-thirds underreported and roughly one-third overreported. Furthermore, about half of these taxpayers who misreported failed to accurately report the securities' cost, or basis, sometimes because they did not know the basis or failed to adjust the basis appropriately.

IRS attempts to reduce the securities' tax gap through enforcement and taxpayer service programs, but challenges limit their impact. Through enforcement programs, IRS contacts taxpayers who may have misreported capital gains or losses and seeks to secure the correct tax amount. IRS also offers services to help taxpayers comply with capital gains tax obligations, such as guidance on how to determine securities' gains and losses. Challenges that limit these programs' impact include the lack of information on basis, which IRS needs to verify most gains and losses, and uncertainty as to whether taxpayers use or understand the guidance.

Expanding the information brokers report on securities sales to include adjusted cost basis has the potential to improve taxpayers' compliance and help IRS find noncompliant taxpayers. IRS research shows that taxpayers report their income much more accurately when it is reported to them and IRS. Basis reporting also would reduce taxpayers' burden. For IRS, basis reporting would provide information to verify securities gains or losses and to better target enforcement resources on noncompliant taxpayers. However, basis reporting would raise challenges that would need to be addressed. For instance, brokers would incur costs and burdens—even as taxpayers' costs and burdens decrease somewhat—and many issues would arise about how to calculate adjusted basis, which securities would be covered, and how information would be transferred among brokers. However, industry representatives said that many brokers already provide some basis information to many of their clients and some use an existing system to track and transfer basis and other information about securities. Many of the challenges to implementing basis reporting also could be mitigated. For example, many of the challenges could be addressed by only requiring adjusted basis reporting for future purchases, and by developing consistent rules to be used by all brokers. To the extent that actions to mitigate the challenges to basis reporting delay its implementation or limit coverage to only certain types of securities, the resulting improvements to taxpayers' voluntary reporting compliance would be somewhat constrained.

Contents

Letter

Appendixes

Related GAO Products

Tables

Figures

GAO
Accountability * Integrity * Reliability

United States Government Accountability Office
Washington, D.C. 20548

June 13, 2006

The Honorable Charles Grassley
Chairman
The Honorable Max Baucus
Ranking Minority Member
Committee on Finance
United States Senate

Every year, a gap arises between the tax amount that taxpayers pay voluntarily and on time and the amount they should pay under the law. For tax year 2001, the Internal Revenue Service (IRS) estimated a gross tax gap of $345 billion.[1] IRS estimated that it would eventually recover $55 billion of the gross tax gap through late payments and IRS enforcement efforts, leaving a net tax gap of $290 billion.[2] The tax gap arises when taxpayers fail to comply with the tax laws, whether intentionally or unintentionally. Because of their noncompliance, the burden of funding the nation's commitments falls more heavily on taxpayers who voluntarily and accurately pay their taxes. In light of the size of the tax gap and the nation's budget deficit, Congress has held several hearings seeking to identify how the gap can be reduced. Given its size, even small or moderate reductions in the net tax gap could yield substantial returns.

One type of noncompliance that contributes to the tax gap occurs when individual taxpayers do not accurately report gains or losses from transactions involving capital assets, which generally refers to property owned for investment or personal purposes, on their tax returns. Taxpayers generally determine their capital gains or losses by subtracting the basis, which is generally the price they paid for an asset, from the gross amount of proceeds they received from its sale. IRS estimated that for 2001, individual taxpayers' failure to accurately report their capital gains income

[1]According to an IRS research official, in mid-2006, IRS plans to publish its final report on the 2001 tax gap that will include an updated tax gap estimate based on a refined methodology. It is possible that the updated tax gap figures could differ from the current estimates.

[2]Unless otherwise noted, references to the tax gap refer to the gross tax gap.

accounted for at least $11 billion of the gross tax gap for that year.[3] This amount is due to taxpayers understating their capital gains or overstating their capital losses, both of which reduced the amount of taxable income they reported. Although IRS has not estimated the amount of the capital gains tax gap attributed to specific types of capital assets, it has estimated that in recent years, securities transactions have accounted for the majority of individuals' capital gains and losses.[4] Securities transactions include the sale of securities—stocks, mutual funds, bonds, and options—and capital gain distributions from mutual funds.[5] Securities transactions may be executed through third parties, such as brokers.

To address your long-standing concerns about the tax gap, and particular concern about the tax gap from individual capital gains tax noncompliance for securities, this report responds to your request for information on (1) the extent of and primary types of noncompliance that cause individual taxpayers to misreport capital gains from securities, (2) actions IRS takes in attempting to reduce the individual capital gains tax gap for securities and any challenges that IRS faces with these actions, and (3) options with the potential to improve taxpayers' voluntary compliance for reporting securities gains and losses and IRS's ability to find noncompliance related to the individual capital gains tax gap for securities.

To provide information on the extent of and primary types of noncompliance that cause individual taxpayers to misreport capital gains from securities, we reviewed a probability sample of case files selected from the nearly 46,000 randomly selected individual tax returns from tax year 2001 that IRS reviewed or examined through the National Research Program (NRP), IRS's most recent study of individual taxpayer compliance. We used the results of our case file review along with data from IRS's

[3]The overall capital gains tax gap could be larger than $11 billion because IRS did not estimate the portion of the combined $48 billion tax gap attributable to capital gains for individual taxpayers who did not file tax returns or did not pay the taxes they reported on filed returns.

[4]IRS's most recent published studies of capital asset transactions were for tax years 1997 through 1999. See IRS Statistics of Income Bulletin, *Sales of Capital Assets Reported on Individual Tax Returns, 1999*, Summer 2003, Publication 1136 (Rev. 09-2003), and *Sales of Capital Assets Reported on Individual Tax Returns, 1998 and 1997*, Summer 2002, Publication 1136 (Rev. 08-2002).

[5]Options are contracts giving the purchaser the right to buy or sell a security at a fixed price within a specific period of time. Mutual funds pay capital gain distributions from their net realized long-term capital gains.

examinations of the tax returns from NRP to make estimates for the entire population of individual taxpayers. We present information on the extent of noncompliance by estimating the percent of noncompliant taxpayers. We did not estimate the portion of the capital gains tax gap specific to securities. We could not provide a meaningful estimate of the tax gap for securities because (1) of the 1,017 cases in our sample, we only received 849 complete cases by the time we completed our review, (2) the cases we received included too few taxpayers who misreported securities transactions (when selecting our sample, we could not determine which cases included misreported gains and losses from securities as compared to other types of capital assets), and (3) taxpayers misreported a wide range of dollar amounts from the transactions. Since our estimates are based on a sample, we express our confidence in our estimates as a 95 percent confidence interval, plus or minus the margin of error indicated along with each estimate in the report, which is the interval that would contain the actual population value for 95 percent of the samples we could have selected. To address the question of what actions IRS takes in attempting to reduce the individual capital gains tax gap for securities and related challenges, we reviewed documents from IRS's enforcement programs and IRS publications that address capital gains. We also interviewed IRS officials knowledgeable about the subject. To identify options with the potential to improve taxpayers' voluntary compliance for reporting securities gains and losses and IRS's ability to find noncompliance related to the individual capital gains tax gap for securities, we reviewed our prior reports, documents from IRS's enforcement programs, IRS publications that address capital gains, and industry reports on securities holdings and information reporting.[6] We also spoke with IRS officials and representatives related to the securities industry. For further discussion of our scope and methodology, see appendix I. We conducted our review from June 2005 through May 2006 in accordance with generally accepted government auditing standards.

Results in Brief

For tax year 2001, an estimated 38 percent of individual taxpayers who had securities transactions failed to accurately report their capital gains or losses from the transactions (8.4 million out of 21.9 million taxpayers), often because they misreported the securities' cost basis. A greater

[6]Information reporting involves the filing of returns with IRS and taxpayers that contain information on certain transactions, such as information on gross proceeds that brokers report from securities sales.

percentage of taxpayers are estimated to have misreported gains or losses from their securities sales (36 percent) than misreported their capital gain distributions from mutual funds (13 percent). One reason for this difference could be because taxpayers must determine what portion of income from securities sales is taxable whereas taxpayers need only add up their capital gain distributions and enter the amounts on their tax returns. We were not able to determine the total amount of capital gains income from securities that taxpayers misreported or the securities tax gap because the cases we reviewed included too few misreported securities transactions and we did not receive other cases in time to include them in our review. However, we found that around half of taxpayers who did not accurately report their securities sales were estimated to have misreported at least $1,000 of capital gains or losses. Also, around half of the taxpayers who misreported their gains or losses from securities sales did so because they failed to accurately report the securities' basis, sometimes because they did not know the securities' basis or failed to take certain events into account that required them to adjust the basis of their securities. Additionally, around 9 percent of taxpayers with securities sales misreported whether their gains or losses were short-term or long-term.

IRS attempts to reduce the individual capital gains tax gap for securities through enforcement and taxpayer service programs; however, various challenges limit the impact these programs have on reducing this tax gap. IRS uses enforcement programs to contact selected taxpayers it believes may have inaccurately reported capital gains or losses. IRS's automated enforcement programs largely rely on matching tax returns filed by taxpayers to information returns provided by brokers that report taxpayers' gross proceeds from securities sales. IRS also examines tax returns by reviewing taxpayers' records of their securities transactions. Additionally, IRS offers various taxpayer services intended to help taxpayers comply with capital gains tax obligations, such as publications describing how to determine tax liabilities from selling securities. The challenges that limit the impact these programs have on reducing the tax gap for securities include the relatively small portion of taxpayers with securities transactions that IRS contacts through its enforcement programs and the lack of information on the basis of securities sold, which IRS needs to verify most gains or losses, and the difficulty in communicating capital gains tax reporting requirements. Although IRS assesses additional taxes through its enforcement programs, neither IRS nor we know the extent to which these assessments reduced the 2001 capital gains tax gap for securities, in part because the gap itself is not known.

Expanding information reporting on securities sales to include cost basis has potential to improve taxpayers' voluntary compliance and help IRS find noncompliance related to the capital gains tax gap for securities. On one hand, some of this potential exists if IRS were to change its enforcement and taxpayer service programs, such as by examining more tax returns or enhancing guidance related to securities gains or losses. However, examinations can be costly, and taxpayers may not know about or use the guidance. On the other hand, basis reporting to taxpayers and IRS would help taxpayers to voluntarily comply and would reduce their burden in computing capital gains or losses. IRS research has repeatedly shown that taxpayers' compliance is strongly related to the extent to which their income is subject to information reporting. Basis reporting also would provide information to help IRS verify securities gains or losses and target enforcement resources to noncompliant taxpayers. However, such basis reporting would raise challenges and trade-offs. Many of the challenges can be mitigated to some extent. For example, tracking and reporting basis would increase brokers' costs, but decisions about the scope and details of the reporting could constrain the increase. Further, taxpayers' costs would be reduced, and many brokers already provide some form of basis information to taxpayers. The challenges arising when brokers do not know the basis for securities purchased in the past could be mitigated by only reporting basis for future purchases, which would somewhat delay the full impact that basis reporting would have on reducing the capital gains tax gap. Although IRS has broad authority to require information reporting for securities sales, it may not have the authority to require all of the actions that would be needed to implement cost basis information reporting.

This report includes matters Congress may want to consider to reduce the capital gains tax gap for securities. Specifically, Congress could require brokers to report to both taxpayers and IRS the adjusted basis of securities that taxpayers sell and whether the gains or losses were short- or long-term, and direct IRS to work with brokers and related parties to develop rules that seek to cost effectively mitigate some of the challenges associated with requiring basis reporting. We are also making recommendations to IRS on clarifying guidance related to reporting capital gains and losses. In commenting on a draft of this report, the Commissioner of Internal Revenue agreed with our recommendations.

Background

Individual taxpayers generally realize gains or losses when they sell capital assets, which are generally defined as properties owned for investment or personal purposes and outside the normal course of a taxpayer's trade or business. In recent years, IRS studies show that the majority of capital asset transactions and capital gains and losses were for securities transactions, including sales of corporate stock, mutual funds, bonds, options,[7] and capital gain distributions from mutual funds.[8] For example, in 1999, the latest year for which IRS published data on capital assets sales, an estimated 91 percent of capital asset transactions, 62 percent of capital gains, and 79 percent of capital losses were from securities transactions.[9] Also, over the past two decades, individual ownership of securities assets held outside of retirement accounts has increased.[10] According to the Federal Reserve Board, the percentage of families that own stock, mutual funds, and bonds outside of retirement accounts increased from 25 percent in 1983 to a high of 42 percent in 2001, before falling to 38 percent in 2004.[11]

When taxpayers sell or otherwise receive income from securities, they must report the transactions on their federal income tax returns. For securities sales, taxpayers are to report the dates they acquired and sold the asset; sales price, or gross proceeds from the sale; cost or other basis of the sold asset; and resulting gains or losses on Schedule D to the individual

[7]Although by statute, futures contracts are not considered securities, we include them as securities for the purposes of this report because futures transactions are generally reported by brokers to IRS and we found 2 taxpayers through our file review who misreported such transactions. A futures contract is an agreement to buy or sell a specific quantity of a commodity or financial instrument at a specified price on a particular date in the future.

[8]Other types of capital assets include personal residences and other personal-use property; real property held for investment; collectibles, such as art, coins or precious metals; and interest in a partnership, S corporation, estate, or trust. Capital gains and losses for assets sold by partnerships, S corporations, estates, or trusts are generally taxed at the partner, shareholder, or beneficiary level. Non-business bad debts are treated as capital losses. All or part of the net gains from certain other transactions may be treated as capital gains, including involuntary conversions from destruction, theft, condemnation, or eminent domain; other depreciable real property or personal property used in a business; land used in a business, including farmland; timber; livestock; patents; and copyrights.

[9]Includes futures transactions.

[10]References to capital assets in this report refer to assets held outside of retirement accounts.

[11]The Federal Reserve Board surveys U.S. families' holdings of financial assets in its triennial Surveys of Consumer Finances. See Robert B. Avery, Glenn B. Canner, Gregory E. Elliehausen, and Thomas A. Gustafson, *Survey of Consumer Finances, 1983*, Federal Reserve Bulletin, vol. 70 (September 1984), and Brian K. Bucks, Arthur B. Kennickell, and Kevin B. Moore, *Recent Changes in U.S. Family Finances: Evidence from the 2001 and 2004 Survey of Consumer Finances*, Federal Reserve Bulletin, vol. 92 (February 2006).

tax return—Form 1040. Taxpayers are to report this information separately for short-term transactions and long-term transactions. Taxpayers also are to report the total amount of their capital gain distributions from mutual funds, which are always considered to be long-term transactions. Taxpayers are to report their overall gains or losses from securities sales, capital gain distributions, and other capital gains on the Form 1040 tax return itself.

Generally, a taxpayer's gain or loss from a securities sale is simply the difference between the gross proceeds from the sale and the original purchase price, or original cost basis.[12] However, before taxpayers can determine any gains or losses from securities sales, they must determine if and how the original cost basis of the securities must be adjusted to reflect certain events, such as stock splits, nontaxable dividends, or nondividend distributions. For example, figure 1 shows how a taxpayer would need to adjust the basis of a stock following a stock split to accurately determine the resulting capital gain or loss when the stock is sold. In this example, if the taxpayer fails to properly adjust the basis of the stock to account for the split, he or she will incorrectly report a capital loss from the sale.

[12]The original cost basis of a security can also include costs of purchase, such as sales commissions.

Figure 1: Example of How Failure to Adjust Basis Can Lead to Misreporting a Capital Gain or Loss from a Securities Transaction

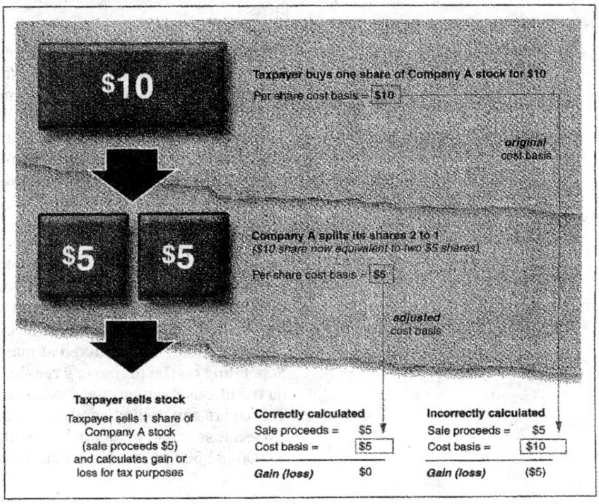

Source: GAO.

Taxpayers who buy and sell the same stock or mutual fund shares at various times can determine basis in a number of ways. Taxpayers can specifically identify the groups of shares they want to sell. For example, if a taxpayer buys a group of 10 shares of stock in one year for $1 per share and another group of 10 shares of the same stock in the next year for $2 per share, and then sells 10 shares of the stock, the taxpayer can choose to sell the stocks with either the $1 or $2 cost basis.[13] If taxpayers cannot identify which shares they sold among many they bought on varying occasions,

[13]Taxpayers who specifically identify groups of shares sold among multiple groups held must inform their brokers which shares to sell, and brokers are to provide written confirmation of taxpayers' decisions.

they must report the basis of the securities they purchased first as the basis of the sold shares. Except for mutual fund shares, taxpayers cannot use the average cost of securities they purchased at various times to determine basis.

When taxpayers sell securities through a broker, that broker is required to file Form 1099-B with IRS and the taxpayers to report a description of the security, sales date, number of shares sold, and gross proceeds from the sale, along with other information.[14] Brokers are not required to report the cost or other basis of the sold security or, with the exception of regulated futures contracts, the resulting gain or loss from a security sale. Capital gain distributions from mutual funds are to be reported on Form 1099-DIV.[15]

The rate at which income from securities is taxed depends on how long taxpayers held a security before sale and taxpayers' regular income tax rates. Securities assets sold after being held for 1 year or less are considered short-term and taxed at the taxpayers' regular income tax rates. Assets sold after being held for more than 1 year are considered to be long-term and are generally taxed at maximum rates of 5 percent or 15 percent, depending on the taxpayer's regular income tax rates.[16] Capital gain distributions from mutual funds are always taxed as long-term gains. Taxpayers can deduct capital losses against their capital gains, and any excess losses can be deducted against ordinary income up to a limit of $3,000 ($1,500 for married taxpayers filing separately), beyond which the

[14]Congress established the requirement that brokers report proceeds in the Tax Equity and Fiscal Responsibility Act of 1982—Pub. L. No. 97-248 (1982). Other information that can be reported on Form 1099-B includes the security's Committee on Uniform Security Identification Procedures number; gross amounts received through bartering; federal income tax withheld; classes of stock exchanged, such as preferred or common stock; and profit or loss for regulated futures contracts. Brokers may send a substitute for Form 1099-B if it meets IRS requirements for substitutes.

[15]A number of other dividends and distributions are also reported on Form 1099-DIV.

[16]The Jobs and Growth Tax Relief Reconciliation Act of 2003—Pub. L. No. 108-27 (2003)—established maximum tax rates for long-term gains at 5 percent for income otherwise taxed in the 10 percent and 15 percent marginal income tax brackets and 15 percent for income otherwise taxed at higher rates, effective for assets sold or exchanged on or after May 6, 2003, and before January 1, 2009. These rates were extended for assets sold or exchanged before January 1, 2011 in the Tax Increase Prevention and Reconciliation Act of 2005—Pub. L. No. 109-222 (2006).

losses can be carried over to offset capital gains or ordinary income in future tax years.

Individual Taxpayers Frequently Misreported Their Capital Gains or Losses from Securities Sales, Often Because They Misreported the Securities' Basis

Thirty-eight percent of individual taxpayers who had securities transactions misreported their securities gains or losses for tax year 2001. A greater percentage of taxpayers misreported their securities sales (36 percent) than misreported their capital gain distributions (13 percent), and most of the misreported securities transactions exceeded $1,000 of capital gain or loss. Taxpayers often misreported their capital gains or losses from securities sales because they failed to accurately report the securities' basis.

Individual Taxpayers Frequently Misreported Their Capital Gains or Losses from Securities Sales

For tax year 2001, individual taxpayers frequently misreported their capital gains or losses from the securities they sold. Overall, an estimated 8.4 million of the estimated 21.9 million taxpayers with securities transactions misreported their gains or losses.[17] Table 1 shows the estimated percentages of taxpayers who misreported their securities sales and capital gain distributions, overall and by the securities' holding period.

[17]We are 95 percent confident that from 7.3 million to 9.5 million taxpayers misreported securities transactions and from 20.3 million to 23.5 million taxpayers had securities transactions.

Table 1: Estimated Percentage of Individual Taxpayers with Securities Transactions Who Misreported the Gain or Loss from One or More Transaction, Tax Year 2001

	Estimated percentage of taxpayers who misreported their transactions		
Type of transaction	Short-term transactions	Long-term transactions	All transactions[a]
Securities sales	28	31	36
Capital gain distributions	N/A[b]	13	13
All securities[c]	28	32	38

Source: GAO analysis of IRS data and examination case files.

Note: Percentage estimates have sampling errors of (+/-) 7 percent or less.

[a]For securities sales, "all transactions" includes those for which we could not determine whether the holding period was short-term or long-term.

[b]Capital gain distributions are always considered long-term transactions.

[c]"All securities" includes taxpayers who misreported both securities sales and capital gain distributions.

Table 1 shows that a higher estimated percentage of taxpayers misreported a securities sale than a capital gains distribution. Overall, an estimated 7.3 million out of an estimated 20.3 million taxpayers misreported their securities sales compared to the estimated 1.2 million out of an estimated 9.1 million taxpayers who misreported their capital gain distributions.[18] One reason taxpayers may misreport securities sales more frequently is that taxpayers must compute the portion of their sales proceeds that constitutes a gain or loss, whereas taxpayers need only add up their capital gain distributions from information returns they receive and enter the amounts on their tax returns. Table 1 also shows that individual taxpayers are estimated to have misreported their short-term securities sales about as often as their long-term sales. In addition, our analyses showed the following:

- Of those taxpayers who misreported securities sales, an estimated 97 percent misreported gains or losses from the sales of stocks and mutual funds while an estimated 5 percent misreported bonds, options, or futures.[19]

[18]We are 95 percent confident that from 6.2 million to 8.3 million taxpayers misreported securities sales, from 18.7 million to 21.9 million taxpayers sold securities, from 0.66 million to 1.7 million taxpayers misreported capital gain distributions, and from 7.8 million to 10.4 million taxpayers had capital gain distributions.

[19]Some taxpayers misreported both stocks and mutual funds and bonds, options or futures. Estimates have sampling errors of (+/-) 5 percent or less.

- Individual taxpayers misreported securities sales more frequently than other types of income, such as wages and salary, dividend income, and interest income. Respectively, an estimated 10 percent, 17 percent, and 22 percent of taxpayers with these types of income misreported the income.[20]

We were not able to estimate the capital gains tax gap for securities because the cases we reviewed included too few misreported securities transactions and taxpayers misreported a wide range of dollar amounts from the transactions, among other reasons (see app. I). However, we were able to determine the direction of the misreporting. For securities sales, an estimated 64 percent of taxpayers underreported their income from securities (i.e., they understated gains or overstated losses) compared to an estimated 33 percent of taxpayers who overreported income (i.e., they overstated gains or understated losses).[21] For both underreported and overreported income, some taxpayers misreported over $400,000 in gains or losses. Also, as shown in table 2, around half of taxpayers who did not accurately report their securities sales were estimated to have misreported at least $1,000 of capital gains or losses (that is, taxpayers not in the less than $1,000 categories).[22]

[20]Estimates have sampling errors of (+/-) 2 percent or less.

[21]Figures do not sum to 100 percent because some taxpayers misreported securities sales in a way that had no effect on the amount of income from the sales, for example, in cases where taxpayers only misreported the securities' holding periods. Estimates have sampling errors of (+/-) 9 percent or less.

[22]By comparison, from 49 percent to 96 percent of taxpayers that misreported their capital gain distributions were estimated to have misreported between $0 and $1,000 of income.

Table 2: Distribution of the Estimated Amount of Net Misreported Capital Gains Income From Securities Sales by Misreporting Taxpayers, Tax Year 2001

Net misreported amount	Percentage of misreporting taxpayers
Overreporting taxpayers	
Less than $1,000[a]	19
$1,000 to $9,999	15
$10,000 and greater	5
Underreporting taxpayers	
Less than $1,000	27
$1,000 to $9,999	19
$10,000 and greater	14

Source: GAO analysis of IRS data and examination case files.

Notes: Percentage figures do not sum to 100 because of rounding. Percentage estimates have sampling errors of (+/-) 8 percent or less.

[a]Category includes taxpayers that misreported securities sales in a way that had no effect on the gain or loss from the sales.

In terms of income levels, the distribution of taxpayers who misreported gains or losses from securities sales and capital gain distributions did not vary greatly from the income level for all individual taxpayers for tax year 2001, as shown in table 3.

Table 3: Estimated Distribution of Individual Taxpayers Who Misreported Capital Gains or Losses from Securities Transactions and All Individual Taxpayers by Adjusted Gross Income, Tax Year 2001

Adjusted gross income	Percentage of misreporting taxpayers	Percentage of all individual taxpayers
Less than $25,000	51	46
$25,000 to $49,999	20	25
$50,000 to $99,999	20	20
$100,000 or greater	9	9

Source: GAO analysis of IRS data and examination case files.

Notes: For misreporting taxpayers, estimates have sampling errors of (+/-) 8 percent or less. For all individual taxpayers, estimates have sampling errors of (+/-) 0.3 percent or less.

Misreported Basis Was a Primary Type of Noncompliance That Caused Taxpayers to Inaccurately Report Their Capital Gains or Losses from Securities Sales

Based on information in the files we reviewed, a primary type of noncompliance that caused taxpayers to inaccurately report their capital gains or losses from securities sales in tax year 2001 was misreporting the basis of the securities they sold. Table 4 shows the estimated frequency of the types of noncompliance that caused taxpayers to misreport capital gains or losses from their securities sales.[23]

Table 4: Estimated Frequency of Types of Noncompliance That Caused Individual Taxpayers to Misreport Capital Gains or Losses from Securities Sales, Tax Year 2001

Type of noncompliance	Estimated percentage of misreporting taxpayers
Misreported basis of security sold	49
Failed to report sale	44
Misreported sale proceeds	12
Misclassified holding period	9
Other	9

Source: GAO analysis of IRS data and examination case files.

Notes: Estimates in this table do not include the results of our review for four cases where we could not determine the type of noncompliance that caused taxpayers to misreport securities sales. The "Other" category includes taxpayers who misclassified capital income as other types of income or vice versa or made mathematical errors. Some taxpayers misreported more than one security sale or misreported a sale because of more than one type of noncompliance. Percentage estimates have sampling errors of (+/-) 9 percent or less.

For taxpayers who misreported basis, a greater percentage failed to accurately report basis for long-term securities holdings (35 percent of taxpayers who misreported securities sales) than for short-term holdings (21 percent).[24] Taxpayers who failed to report securities sales altogether did not report short-term and long-term securities sales at a similar rate (20 percent and 22 percent, respectively, of taxpayers who misreported securities sales).[25]

Although we were able to determine the percentage of taxpayers who failed to accurately report their securities sales because they misreported

[23]For taxpayers who misreported capital gains distributions, from 48 percent to 89 percent were estimated to have failed to report the distributions altogether.

[24]Estimates have sampling errors of (+/-) 8 percent or less.

[25]Estimates have sampling errors of (+/-) 8 percent or less.

basis (49 percent), we could not develop reliable estimates on the reasons for this type of misreporting because most of the NRP examination case files did not provide sufficiently descriptive information. However, of the 133 taxpayers who misreported basis from the 849 case files we reviewed, we were able to determine that 32 taxpayers misreported basis for the following reasons:

- Taxpayers did not have records of their securities purchases (16 taxpayers). Although during examinations, IRS was able to obtain basis records for some of these taxpayers from their brokers, for 9 taxpayers, basis records could not be obtained. For these taxpayers, IRS examiners considered basis to be zero and treated all gross proceeds amounts as capital gains.
- Taxpayers used original cost basis instead of adjusted cost basis (6 taxpayers).
- Taxpayers did not understand how to determine basis (5 taxpayers).
- Taxpayers reported basis information that was incorrectly determined by a tax return preparer (4 taxpayers).[26]
- One taxpayer reported inaccurate basis information provided by a broker.

Of taxpayers who failed to report their securities sales altogether, an estimated 28 percent were estimated to have failed to report capital losses.[27] By not reporting losses, these taxpayers potentially failed to offset other capital gains or deduct their losses against other types of income they reported. Likewise, some of these taxpayers who failed to report capital losses exceeding $3,000 did not carry over these losses to offset capital gains or other income in future tax years. Although in most cases we could not determine why taxpayers did not report these losses, some taxpayers

[26]Of all taxpayers who misreported a securities transaction, an estimated 52 percent used a tax return preparer with a sampling error of (+/-) 9 percent or less. Of all individual taxpayers, an estimated 56 percent used a tax return preparer for tax year 2001 with a sampling error of (+/-) 0.4 percent or less. We recently reported that some tax return preparers make serious errors when completing returns. See GAO, *Paid Tax Return Preparers: In a Limited Study, Chain Preparers Made Serious Errors*, GAO-06-563T (Washington, D.C.: Apr. 4, 2006).

[27]Estimate has a sampling error of (+/-) 13 percent or less.

told IRS examiners that they did not know they had to report losses. In addition, IRS officials said some taxpayers might not report their capital losses because they worry that their returns will be examined if they overstate their losses. Also, the officials told us that taxpayers might want to avoid the burden of filing a Schedule D or the cost of paying someone to prepare their returns in cases where filing Schedule D would make the difference between self preparing and using a paid preparer.

As also shown in table 4, taxpayers failed to accurately report their securities sales because they misreported the amount of their sale proceeds (12 percent) or misclassified the securities' holding period (9 percent). However, the case files did not contain enough information to explain why taxpayers made these errors. Also, the responsible officials we interviewed at IRS could not provide explanations for why taxpayers might have made these errors.

IRS Attempts to Reduce the Individual Capital Gains Tax Gap for Securities through Enforcement and Taxpayer Service Programs, but Various Challenges Limit Their Impact

IRS uses both enforcement and taxpayer service programs in attempting to reduce the individual capital gains tax gap for securities. IRS checks the accuracy of tax returns through its enforcement programs and contacts taxpayers who may have inaccurately reported their securities gains or losses. IRS also offers service programs to provide taxpayers with assistance in fulfilling their capital gains tax obligations. However, these programs face challenges that limit their impact on reducing the capital gains tax gap for securities. Although IRS assesses additional taxes for securities income through its enforcement efforts, neither IRS nor we know the extent to which these assessments reduced the 2001 capital gains tax gap for securities.

IRS Attempts to Reduce the Individual Capital Gains Tax Gap for Securities through Enforcement and Taxpayer Service Programs

Consistent with its overarching philosophy that a combination of enforcement and service efforts are essential to tax compliance, IRS attempts to reduce the individual capital gains tax gap for securities through its programs that enforce the tax laws and that seek to help taxpayers voluntarily comply with the laws. IRS uses its enforcement programs to check the accuracy of filed tax returns and contacts taxpayers who have potentially made errors or inaccurately reported capital gains information on their returns.[28] Aspects of IRS's enforcement programs related to capital gains income for securities appear in table 5.[29]

Table 5: IRS Enforcement Programs and Types of Securities Capital Gains Tax Noncompliance They Can Detect

IRS program	Capable of detecting
Math Error	Data reported inconsistently between Schedule D and Form 1040
Automated Underreporter (AUR)	Inaccurately reported gross proceeds from securities sales and capital gain distributions
Automated Substitute for Return (ASFR)	Taxpayers who received proceeds from securities sales but did not file tax returns
Examination	All forms of capital gains noncompliance for securities

Source: IRS.

Math Error, AUR, and ASFR are automated enforcement programs. IRS uses the Math Error program to check filed tax returns for internal inconsistencies or mathematical errors, and contacts taxpayers, including when the errors result in a tax change. Through AUR, IRS computers match the amounts of capital gains proceeds that taxpayers report on their tax returns and that brokers report on information returns. If this matching indicates that taxpayers may have underreported their sale proceeds for securities and IRS cannot resolve the discrepancies based on available information, IRS may send notices asking taxpayers to explain the discrepancies or pay any taxes assessed. When IRS determines through ASFR that taxpayers for whom IRS received information returns on the sale proceeds for securities failed to file tax returns, it may create tax returns for the taxpayers and assess tax liabilities.

During examinations, IRS uses information from third parties as well as from taxpayers to determine if taxpayers have accurately reported their

[28]Taxpayers can appeal additional taxes that IRS assesses.

[29]For a more complete discussion of these programs, see GAO, *Tax Administration: IRS Should Continue to Expand Reporting on Its Enforcement Efforts*, GAO-03-378 (Washington, D.C.: Jan. 31, 2003).

capital gains or losses.[30] Examiners also may use other resources, such as online services, to help them determine the basis of taxpayers' securities. IRS assesses additional taxes if it determines that taxpayers have underreported their capital gains income from securities.

IRS's taxpayer service programs provide taxpayers with information, support, and assistance to help them understand and fulfill their capital gains tax obligations for securities. For example, IRS produces publications that explain how to report capital gains or losses and provide examples of how to determine adjusted basis.[31] IRS also provides Web-based information and telephone, written, or face-to-face assistance at Taxpayer Assistance Centers on how to accurately report capital gains and losses.

Various Challenges Limit the Impact IRS Programs Have on Reducing the Individual Capital Gains Tax Gap for Securities

IRS's enforcement and taxpayer service programs face limitations in reducing the individual capital gains tax gap for securities. In addition to resource constraints that limit how many cases of potential noncompliance are pursued, table 6 summarizes the main limitations each program faces.

[30]IRS performs some examinations through correspondence and others through face-to-face meetings with taxpayers.

[31]IRS publications related to capital gains or losses from securities include Publication 544, *Sales and Other Dispositions of Assets*, Publication 550, *Investment Income and Expenses*; Publication 551, *Basis of Assets*, and Publication 564, *Mutual Fund Distributions*.

Table 6: IRS Enforcement and Taxpayer Service Programs and Their Principle Limitations on Reducing the Individual Capital Gains Tax Gap for Securities

IRS program	Principle limitations
Math Error	Not intended to verify if taxpayers have accurately reported their capital gains tax liabilities for securities
AUR	Lack of basis information from brokers prevents AUR from verifying the accuracy of reported capital gains or losses from securities sales
ASFR	Lack of basis information from brokers prevents AFSR from accurately determining how much of taxpayers' gross proceeds from securities sales is taxable
Examination	Capital gains are too complex and time consuming to examine through correspondence Face-to-face examinations are resource intensive and cover a small percentage of taxpayers with capital gains
Taxpayer services	Taxpayers may not use the services Taxpayers may not understand information IRS provides

Source: IRS.

As table 6 shows, IRS cannot use its automated programs to fully verify the reported capital gains or losses from securities sales because it does not receive basis information from brokers. Also, according to IRS officials, a lack of basis information reduces productivity because IRS spends resources contacting taxpayers for whom it ultimately does not assess additional taxes. For example, for tax year 2002, the latest year for which IRS has complete data, IRS did not assess additional taxes for around 46 percent of the taxpayers it contacted through AUR to address potentially misreported securities sales.[32] By comparison, this "no tax change" percentage was around 20 percent for AUR contacts for all other types of income for 2002.[33] For ASFR, IRS officials said that the lack of basis

[32]For some taxpayers, IRS did not assess additional taxes when it identified underreported income from securities sales because the changes to reported income only reduced taxpayers' capital loss carryovers.

[33]Through AUR, IRS contacted around 190,000 taxpayers who potentially misreported securities sales out of a total of over 2.3 million taxpayers it contacted for all types of misreported income for tax year 2002. IRS does not collect information on the number of taxpayers it contacts through Math Error and ASFR programs who potentially misreported capital gains.

information hampers IRS's ability to determine which taxpayers with gross proceeds from securities sales should have filed tax returns and to productively pursue those taxpayers who did not file.

Given that IRS does not receive basis information from brokers, it can only verify the accuracy of the basis and gains and losses that taxpayers report for their securities sales by examining these individuals' tax returns. IRS does not examine these taxpayers' returns through correspondence because it believes the returns are too difficult and would take too much time to examine. IRS can only verify the accuracy of the reported basis and gains and losses from securities sales through face-to-face examinations. However, these examinations are resource intensive and only cover a small percentage of individual taxpayers. For example, in fiscal year 2004, IRS conducted approximately 200,000 face-to-face examinations[34] for the 130 million individual taxpayers that filed tax returns in 2003, including the estimated 22.7 million taxpayers that filed a Schedule D with their tax returns.[35] Even when IRS selects individual taxpayers to examine face-to-face, IRS often places a greater focus on issues it believes are more productive than securities sales, such as business income or the sale of personal or business real property, according to an IRS official responsible for examination planning.

In providing taxpayer services, IRS faces challenges in communicating information to taxpayers on complying with capital gains reporting requirements. Taxpayers may not use the services IRS offers or may not understand the information that IRS provides. For example, IRS recently changed the instructions for filing Schedule D to include language that specifies taxpayers must include the details of all their capital gains transactions when filing their tax returns. Although IRS included this language to clarify an existing reporting requirement, some taxpayers and tax practitioners perceived that the instructions required taxpayers to report each capital asset transaction on Schedule D itself and not on attached brokerage statements, as otherwise allowed. This misconception required IRS to clarify on its Web site that taxpayers could continue to

[34]By comparison, IRS examined through correspondence approximately 800,000 individual tax returns in fiscal year 2004. Approximate examination figures are given because, according to IRS, in general, examination activity may be associated with returns filed in the previous calendar year.

[35]We are 95 percent confident that the number of taxpayers who reported capital gains or losses was from 22.4 million to 22.9 million.

report the details of their transactions on attached statements as long as all transactions were included and they reported aggregate information on Schedule D.

The Extent to Which IRS Enforcement Programs Have Reduced the 2001 Capital Gains Tax Gap for Securities Is Not Known

Through its enforcement programs, IRS assessed additional taxes for taxpayers who misreported their securities gains and losses for tax year 2001; however, neither IRS nor we know the extent to which these assessments reduced the securities tax gap for that year. IRS has not estimated the portion of the capital gains tax gap attributed to securities for tax year 2001, and we were not able to estimate this portion of the tax gap from our review of NRP case files. Likewise, IRS does not have complete information on the amount of additional taxes it assessed for taxpayers who underreported their income from securities sales for 2001.

Through AUR for tax year 2001, IRS assessed around $190 million in additional taxes for securities sales and around another $5 million for capital gain distributions, and refunded over $8 million to taxpayers who overreported securities income.[36] For tax year 2001 examinations, IRS does not have complete data for the amount of taxes it assessed for misreported capital gains or losses. IRS maintains a database that tracks examination results by the type of issue examined, such as capital gains or losses. However, prior to October 2004, the database only captured examination results for around 60 percent of individual examinations, according to IRS officials.[37] As such, the database does not include all capital gains noncompliance that IRS identified in tax year 2001 examinations. Even when it includes such noncompliance, the database does not distinguish between misreported capital gains income from securities versus other capital assets. Likewise, the database does not specify the portion of additional tax assessments that is attributable to misreported capital gains

[36] For tax year 2002, IRS increased the number of taxpayers contacted for potentially misreported securities sales to around 190,000, assessing over $550 million in additional taxes.

[37] As previously reported, IRS had not been entering all examination cases into this database, and started implementing improvements in October 2004 to case processing and data capture. See GAO, *Tax Compliance: Better Compliance Data and Long-term Goals Would Support a More Strategic IRS Approach to Reducing the Tax Gap*, GAO-05-753 (Washington, D.C.: July 18, 2005).

income versus other types of noncompliance.[38] Finally, IRS does not maintain data on additional taxes assessed and collected because of capital gains noncompliance through the Math Error or ASFR programs.

Reporting of Cost Basis Could Reduce the Individual Capital Gains Tax Gap for Securities, but Implementation Challenges Would Need to Be Addressed

Expanded reporting of cost basis information has the potential to reduce the individual capital gains tax gap for securities. Making administrative changes to IRS's compliance programs that address capital gains also has some potential to reduce the tax gap, but enforcement programs can be resource intensive and taxpayers do not always use IRS's taxpayer service programs. With such limitations, these changes likely would not significantly boost taxpayers' voluntary compliance involving securities sales. Information reporting of adjusted cost basis to taxpayers and IRS would likely help reduce the tax gap from securities sales by improving taxpayers' voluntary compliance and IRS's ability to cost effectively address noncompliant taxpayers. Consistent reporting of basis information would involve challenges that would need to be, and to some extent can be, mitigated.

Increasing Examinations of Taxpayers with Securities Sales Could Reduce That Portion of the Tax Gap but at the Expense of Not Covering Other Areas of Noncompliance

IRS could seek to reduce the capital gains tax gap for securities by increasing examination coverage of taxpayers with gains or losses from securities, either by considering them when selecting taxpayers to examine through correspondence or by increasing face-to-face examinations of these taxpayers. Conducting more of each type of examination could increase the amount of taxes assessed for misreporting securities income. However, absent an increase in resources or access to basis information, which would help IRS better target its resources toward truly noncompliant taxpayers, focusing on taxpayers with securities gains or losses would divert IRS's examination resources away from other productive areas of noncompliance, according to IRS officials. An increased focus on securities sales could reduce the capital gains tax gap, but a diversion of resources could result in greater noncompliance for other types of income. Moreover, although increasing examination coverage could induce taxpayers who are misreporting willfully to voluntarily comply, expanded coverage would not significantly affect voluntary compliance for taxpayers who make mistakes while trying to

[38]If the data were complete, according to IRS it would be possible to estimate the portion of additional taxes IRS assessed that could be attributed to capital gains.

comply, such as taxpayers who made errors calculating basis, according to an IRS research official who has studied the impact of enforcement on taxpayer compliance.

Enhanced Taxpayer Services Might Improve Taxpayers' Voluntary Compliance, but the Impact of Any Changes Would Be Hard to Gauge

Addressing capital gains tax noncompliance for securities sales by enhancing IRS's taxpayer service efforts might improve taxpayers' voluntary compliance by helping them to better understand and fulfill their capital gains tax obligations for securities. However, the effects of any additional guidance that IRS might develop, for example on reporting losses or on resources for determining basis, would be tempered by challenges similar to those previously discussed, such as taxpayers not using or understanding information IRS provides. Although IRS attempts to generally ensure tax compliance through its service efforts, IRS researchers have found it difficult to determine the extent to which taxpayer services improve compliance among taxpayers who want to comply. As such, it is hard to know if these improvements to IRS's service efforts would have a substantial impact on taxpayer's reporting compliance for securities sales.

Regardless, IRS's instructions for reporting capital gains and losses and related guidance do not contain some information related to the causes for taxpayers misreporting the basis of securities they sold or failing to report sales at all—the leading types of noncompliance when taxpayers erred in reporting capital gains and losses. In many cases, we could not determine and IRS did not know exactly why taxpayers made these errors. However, some taxpayers did not know they had to report gains or losses and others did not understand how to determine basis. One counterintuitive situation existed among the cases we reviewed, that is some taxpayers did not report losses, which generally help them by lowering their tax liabilities. IRS's instructions for filing Schedule D direct taxpayers to report their capital gains or losses but the instructions do not clarify the appropriate use of capital losses to offset capital gains or other income. Further, although IRS provides guidance on how to calculate basis for a variety of securities transactions, the instructions to Schedule D do not contain guidance on resources available to taxpayers and tax practitioners to determine basis for securities. Some examples of resources taxpayers might use to determine the basis of their securities holdings include brokers, tax preparers, or Web sites for companies that issue stocks or other information. Providing taxpayers more information on the benefits of reporting losses and resources available to them on calculating basis would be consistent with IRS's responsibility to ensure that taxpayers pay the right amount of tax. Further, compared to other steps such as enforcement actions, providing additional guidance to taxpayers would be a low cost option to potentially increase their capital gains reporting compliance. Finally, any improvement in taxpayers' compliance due to better guidance would reduce IRS's enforcement expenses related to capital gains.

Information Reporting of Adjusted Basis Could Reduce the Capital Gains Tax Gap for Securities

According to IRS officials and some representatives related to the securities industry, taxpayers would likely report their gains or losses from securities sales more accurately and at a reduced burden if brokers consistently provided them with the adjusted basis of the securities they sold. Likewise, basis reporting would allow IRS to verify taxpayers' securities gains and losses through its automated enforcement programs and take more efficient enforcement actions to address noncompliant taxpayers, according to IRS compliance officials. The likely increase in taxpayers' voluntary compliance and in the productiveness of IRS enforcement actions resulting from basis reporting would likely substantially reduce the capital gains tax gap for securities.

Taxpayers would benefit from basis reporting because, in many cases, they would not have to track and compute the adjusted basis of the securities they sold. Therefore, basis reporting would likely reduce the chance that taxpayers who had not been tracking their adjusted basis would misreport it for securities they sold. Also, if taxpayers received basis information from their brokers for the securities they sold, they would enjoy a reduced burden in filing Schedule D with their tax returns because, in many cases, they would not need to make basis calculations on their own.

For taxpayers, the greater accuracy and reduced burden of reporting basis that would result from basis reporting would likely improve their voluntary compliance. As shown in figure 2, taxpayers tend to accurately report income that third parties report on information returns because the income is transparent to taxpayers as well as to IRS. For example, individual taxpayers misreport nearly twice the percentage of their income from sources subject only to some information reporting, which is the case with income from securities sales now, compared to income subject to substantial information reporting, such as income from dividends and interest, and which would be close to the case for securities sales if basis were consistently reported, according to an IRS research official. Also, as discussed previously, based on our file review, taxpayers were much less likely to misreport capital gain distributions (13 percent), which are similar to dividends and are subject to substantial information reporting, compared to income from securities sales (36 percent), for which information reporting only covers gross proceeds but not cost basis. The smallest percentage of misreporting is for wage and salary income, for which substantial information reporting exists and taxes are withheld by taxpayers' employers.

Figure 2: Individual Net Income Misreporting Categorized by the Extent of Income Subject to Information Reporting, Tax Year 2001

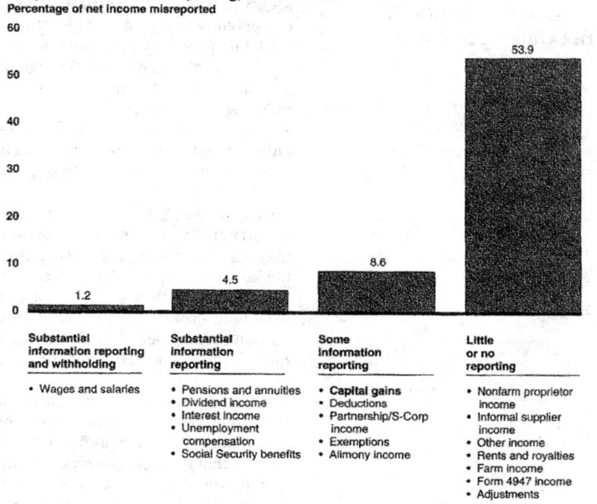

Source: IRS.

Cost basis reporting would also benefit IRS, to the extent the reporting was complete and accurate. IRS could use basis information to verify securities gains and losses through its automated enforcement programs and could more effectively allocate its enforcement resources to focus on the most noncompliant taxpayers. For AUR and ASFR, IRS officials told us that basis information would allow it to more precisely determine taxpayers' income for securities sales and would allow it to identify which taxpayers who misreported securities income have the greatest potential for additional tax assessments. IRS's examination program could similarly benefit. Specifically, IRS officials told us that receiving cost basis information might enable IRS to examine noncompliant taxpayers through correspondence because it could productively select tax returns to examine. Also, having cost basis information could help IRS identify the best cases to examine face-to-face, making the examinations more productive while simultaneously reducing the burden imposed on compliant taxpayers who otherwise would be selected for examination. As a result of all these benefits, basis reporting would allow IRS to better allocate its resources that focus on securities misreporting across its enforcement programs.

IRS has endorsed the concept of matching information returns to tax returns for the purpose of identifying unreported income since the 1960s and Congress has created a number of statutes requiring information reporting for various types of income or taxpayer information.[39] The related GAO products section at the end of this report provides references to selected GAO reports related to information reporting.

We previously discussed the notion of basis reporting to help reduce capital gains tax noncompliance in our May 1994 report on the tax gap.[40] Also, based on discussions we had with officials from IRS's Taxpayer Advocate Service when we initiated our review, the National Taxpayer Advocate recommended that brokers be required to track and report cost basis for stocks and mutual funds in her *2005 Annual Report to Congress*.[41] In March 2006 a bill was introduced in the U.S. Senate and in April and May 2006 bills were introduced in the House of Representatives that would require brokers to report taxpayers' basis for their securities transactions.[42]

[39]For a list of major legislation affecting IRS's information returns program, see GAO-03-378.

[40]GAO, *Tax Gap: Many Actions Taken, But a Cohesive Compliance Strategy Needed*, GAO/GGD-94-123 (Washington, D.C.: May 11, 1994).

[41]Internal Revenue Service, Taxpayer Advocate Service, *National Taxpayer Advocate 2005 Annual Report to Congress* (Washington, D.C.: Dec. 31, 2005).

[42]S. 2414, 109th Cong. §2 (2006), H.R. 5176, 109th Cong. §206 (2006), and H.R. 5367, 109th Cong. §2 (2006).

Expanding Basis Reporting Involves Implementation Challenges That Would Need to Be Addressed

Expanding information reporting on securities sales to include basis information would involve challenges for brokers and IRS. There are various ways to mitigate each challenge. Tables 7 and 8 list some major challenges for brokers and IRS, respectively, as well as some ways to start mitigating the challenges. Discussion after the tables covers some issues to consider when evaluating these mitigation strategies.

Table 7: Challenges to Brokers Associated with Basis Reporting and How the Challenges Could Be Mitigated

Challenges to brokers	Ways to mitigate challenges
Implementing systems to track and report basis involves monetary costs	• Although the following do not directly mitigate costs for all brokers, • Many brokers and mutual funds already track and report basis to many taxpayers, which could help form a foundation for expanded basis reporting • Brokers could leverage existing systems that track and report gross proceeds to taxpayers and IRS • Congress or IRS could provide an appropriate effective date that would allow brokers that lack such systems to develop them
Brokers may not be able to determine basis for some securities transactions because of complex tax laws	• Brokers could report on those securities transactions not affected by complex tax laws • Tax laws on selling securities could be simplified[a] • Absent tax law changes, IRS could develop consistent reporting rules in concert with those who report
Brokers may not know basis for securities purchased through another broker	• Brokers could use an existing system that allows them to transfer basis information when taxpayers move their securities holdings from one broker to another
Brokers may not know basis for securities purchased through companies that directly issue stock (e.g., employee stock purchase plans)	• Companies that directly issue stock could track and report basis and use the basis transfer system
Brokers may not know basis for older securities	• Brokers could track and report basis prospectively (i.e., only for securities purchased after a particular date)
Brokers that do not know the basis may rely on taxpayers to provide basis without any verification (e.g., for stocks received as gifts)	• Prospective reporting would likely produce fewer cases in which the broker does not know the basis • Brokers could indicate on the information return if the basis information came from taxpayers

(Continued From Previous Page)

Challenges to brokers	Ways to mitigate challenges
Brokers cannot always obtain timely adjusted basis information from companies that issue stock and engage in corporate events (e.g., mergers, acquisitions)	• These companies and the securities industry in concert with IRS could develop a system to timely make such information available on corporate events that affect basis

Source: GAO.

[a]Tax code simplification is a method through which some believe tax compliance could be enhanced. See GAO, *Understanding the Tax Reform Debate: Background, Criteria, & Questions*, GAO-05-1009SP (Washington, D.C.: September 2005).

Table 8: Challenges to IRS Associated with Basis Reporting and How the Challenges Could Be Mitigated

Challenges to IRS	Ways to mitigate challenges
Expanding IRS's computer system capacity to store and use additional data on basis involves monetary costs	• Cost to implement system would be outweighed by increased tax revenue resulting from higher voluntary reporting compliance (although such funds would not be IRS's to directly use) • Funds could be budgeted to cover these costs
IRS systems may not be able to process and match basis for each securities sale reported on information returns and on Schedule D of the Form 1040 (including any attachments on the securities sold)	• Brokers could report aggregate adjusted basis for all securities sold for a taxpayer on the information return while reporting adjusted basis for all sales on annual statements provided to taxpayers
IRS may still encounter taxpayers that misclassify the holding period for their securities sales	• Brokers could report aggregate basis and gross proceeds for short-term and long-term transactions separately on the information return
Taxpayers may improperly report basis when they sell portions of their holdings in a security that they purchased on multiple occasions	• Allow taxpayers to use the average costs of their securities holdings to determine basis for securities beyond mutual funds • Taxpayers could indicate the method they will use to determine basis when their security is sold and brokers then would report the method selected and the related basis amount on the information return

Source: GAO.

Although not all inclusive, the strategies discussed above could help mitigate many of the challenges facing brokers and IRS if information reporting were expanded to include cost basis. However, the strategies also involve a number of trade-offs that would need to be considered in terms of the costs and burdens associated with basis reporting for taxpayers, IRS, and brokers, and the impact on reducing the capital gains tax gap for securities.

Representatives from the securities industry we interviewed said that brokers would incur additional costs to develop and maintain systems to track and report basis, although they did not provide precise costs. However, we were also told that almost all of the largest brokers directly provide basis information to a significant portion of their clients, and many smaller brokers provide basis to a significant portion of their clients through outsourcing. Also, representatives of the mutual fund industry estimated that 80 to 90 percent of mutual funds provide average cost basis information to their shareholders. Likewise, from a societal perspective, the cost that brokers would incur in reporting basis information would be offset to some extent by the reduced costs to taxpayers in researching, calculating, and reporting basis, or paying a return preparer to perform such services. However, some brokers may pass on the costs of reporting basis information to their customers. Further, decisions about the scope and details of basis reporting, as further discussed below, could constrain how much brokers' costs would increase.[43]

Also, representatives from the securities industry told us that their ability to provide taxpayers and IRS with accurate basis information would be challenged when taxpayers move their securities holdings from one broker to another. Some brokers use a system to transfer basis among one another, but the system is not used by all brokers. In addition, brokers do not always track and transfer basis in a consistent manner; that is, some track original cost basis while others track adjusted cost basis. Without a system through which all brokers transfer standardized basis information, the effectiveness of basis reporting would be limited.

Additionally, brokers do not always know or may be challenged in determining the basis of taxpayers' holdings. For example, some taxpayers may hold securities that they purchased long ago or received as a gift, for which neither they nor their brokers know the original purchase dates. In these cases, brokers cannot know the basis of the securities. However, this challenge could be mitigated to a large extent if brokers were to track and

[43]Although IRS has not estimated the costs to taxpayers of filing Schedule D, taxpayers spend billions of dollars every year in complying with their tax obligations. See GAO, *Tax Policy: Summary of Estimates of the Costs of the Federal Tax System*, GAO-05-878 (Washington, D.C.: Aug. 26, 2005).

report basis prospectively, that is, only for securities purchased after a specified future date. The trade-off to prospective basis reporting, however, is that it would not help some taxpayers report basis for securities they owned before brokers began to report basis, which for a period of time would limit the impact basis reporting would have on reducing the tax gap. Also, prospective reporting would be complicated in cases where a taxpayer held a security prior to the specified date and then purchased additional shares of the same security after the specified date. Brokers would likely incur some additional costs to separately account for shares of stock purchased before and after the specified date for prospective reporting on information returns.

Likewise, it is difficult for brokers to determine basis for some complicated securities transactions, according to representatives of the securities industry. For example, when taxpayers sell stock for a loss and then buy shares of the same stock within 30 days, they are prohibited from claiming a loss on the original sale. For these sales, known as wash sales, basis is difficult for the broker to determine because the taxpayer is required to add the disallowed loss from the wash sale to the basis of the subsequently purchased stock. The difficulty in determining basis for wash sales is compounded when taxpayers sell a stock at a loss through one broker and then buy the same stock within 30 days from another broker. In this case, the second broker would not know of the wash sale the taxpayer executed through the first broker and would not know to adjust the taxpayer's basis accordingly. We only found two cases through our file review where taxpayers had misreported basis because of wash sales. Regardless, transactions such as wash sales may be too complex for brokers to feasibly report basis. Excluding these transactions from basis reporting, however, would further reduce the impact of basis reporting on closing the securities tax gap.

For IRS, having basis information, along with gross proceeds information, for each of a taxpayer's securities sales would best enable the agency to check whether taxpayers properly reported their capital gains and losses. However, storing and making use of such information would be challenging because of the costs and difficulty involved in storing and computer matching the large volume of information that transactional reporting would entail. However, if brokers were to report only aggregate basis amounts to IRS for all of a taxpayer's transactions, the costs and difficulties of storing and using the information for matching would be reduced. Aggregate reporting would also reduce the costs to brokers of reporting basis to IRS, although they could still report basis for all transactions to taxpayers.

Another complication for IRS and brokers is that taxpayers can choose among various methods for reporting basis in cases where they sell some of their shares of a security they purchased on multiple occasions. Taxpayers may choose to report basis in a different way than brokers would otherwise choose because taxpayers can (1) specifically identify which shares they sell among many they hold and report basis for those shares; (2) use the basis of the first shares they bought; or (3) in the case of mutual funds, use the average cost of the shares they own.[44] Taxpayers could indicate the method they chose to determine basis when they sell their securities, and brokers then could report the method selected and the related basis amount on information returns. However, this additional layer of tracking would likely add to costs to taxpayers, brokers, and IRS. Although this challenge could be alleviated if taxpayers were required to report basis in a consistent manner, this requirement would end taxpayers' ability to determine basis in the most advantageous manner for their particular tax situations.

Given the number of decisions that would need to be made in conjunction with basis reporting, IRS may not be able to require such reporting given its current authority. Although IRS has long had the authority to require information reporting related to securities, an official from IRS's Office of Chief Counsel told us that IRS may not have the authority to require all of the actions that would be needed to implement cost basis information reporting, such as regulating a system through which brokers transfer standardized basis information. Therefore, it may be difficult for IRS to implement cost basis information reporting without further statutory authority.

Representatives from the securities industry told us that in order to implement basis reporting, a set of rules would need to be developed to clearly establish, for example, what types of securities transactions would be covered by any requirement and how a system to transfer basis would

[44]Taxpayers who own mutual funds face similar choices through reinvested dividends. However, tracking and computing cost basis for dividend reinvestments may not be as challenging to track because mutual funds shareholders can use the average costs of their holdings to determine basis, a method that cannot be used for stocks or other securities.

be standardized. These representatives thought their input could be helpful in designing any set of rules.

Conclusion

Although neither IRS nor we know the size of the tax gap related to securities sales, tens of millions of taxpayers hold securities outside of their retirement accounts and, according to our analysis of IRS data, an estimated 36 percent of taxpayers who sold securities in 2001 erred in reporting their gains and losses (an estimated 7.3 million out of an estimated 20.3 million taxpayers). Of those erring, an estimated 64 percent underreported their income and 33 percent overreported income. Also, an estimated 9 percent of individual taxpayers who sold securities misclassified their holding periods, either reporting short-term holdings as long-term, or vice versa. Enhancing IRS's current enforcement and service efforts is an option for addressing these compliance problems, but the most effective tool for improving taxpayers' compliance levels has long been information reporting and tax withholding. Individual taxpayers misreport nearly twice the percentage of their income from sources subject only to some information reporting—which is the case for securities income now—compared to income subject to substantial information reporting. Also, given that the tax consequences associated with the holding period of securities are significant, broker reporting on this specific issue, whether as part of basis reporting or separately, would help taxpayers apply the proper tax rules to their gains or losses and help IRS in identifying compliance problems.

Extending information reporting for securities sales to include basis information is not a simple and straightforward proposition. The manner in which basis reporting is designed would affect how the costs of basis reporting are distributed among taxpayers, brokers, and IRS, and the extent to which basis reporting would close the securities-related tax gap. In addition, although IRS has the general authority to require basis reporting, IRS officials were not certain the agency had sufficient authority to regulate how such reporting is implemented, such as regulating a system through which brokers transfer standardized basis information.

In the event that brokers were required to report basis for securities purchased as of a specific future date, some taxpayers may continue to misreport their gains and losses from the securities holdings they currently hold. For these taxpayers, additional guidance on reporting basis and gains or losses for securities sales could be a low cost way to help them voluntarily comply with their tax obligations. For example, an estimated 28 percent of taxpayers who failed to report their securities sales had losses. Clarification of IRS's instructions for Schedule D on the appropriate use of capital losses to offset capital gains or other income could be a means to help ensure that taxpayers do not disadvantage themselves when they experience losses from their investments. Also, given the complexity involved in determining some securities' basis because of events such as stock splits, guidance on the resources available to taxpayers on determining basis, such as utilizing brokers, or services offered by companies that issue stocks or other information available on Web sites, could help improve taxpayers' ability to determine their securities' basis.

Matters for Congressional Consideration

In order to reduce the capital gains tax gap for securities, Congress may want to consider requiring brokers to report to both taxpayers and IRS the adjusted basis of securities that taxpayers sell and ensuring that IRS has sufficient regulatory authority to implement the requirement. Either in connection with requiring basis reporting or separately, Congress could also require brokers to report to taxpayers and IRS whether the securities sold were short-term or long-term holdings. Additionally, Congress could direct IRS to work with brokers and related parties to develop rules that seek to mitigate some of the challenges associated with requiring basis reporting.

Recommendations for Executive Action

To assist taxpayers in accurately reporting their capital gains and losses from securities, in the instructions to Schedule D the Commissioner of Internal Revenue should (1) clarify the appropriate use of capital losses to offset capital gains or other income and (2) provide guidance on resources available to taxpayers to determine their basis.

Agency Comments and Our Evaluation

In written comments on a draft of this report, which are reprinted in appendix II, the Commissioner of Internal Revenue agreed with our recommendations. He also concurred that for some securities, basis reporting involves unique challenges and noted that IRS is committed to working with industry stakeholders to develop cost effective methods to mitigate such reporting challenges. IRS also provided comments on several technical issues, which we incorporated in this report where appropriate.

As agreed with your offices, unless you publicly announce its contents earlier, we plan no further distribution of this report until 30 days from its issue date. At that time, we will send copies to the Chairman and Ranking Minority Member, House Committee on Ways and Means; the Secretary of the Treasury; the Commissioner of Internal Revenue; and other interested parties. Copies will be made available to others upon request. This report will also be available at no charge on GAO's Web site at http://www.gao.gov.

If you or your staff have any questions, please contact me at (202) 512-9110 or brostekm@gao.gov. Contact points for our Offices of Congressional Relations and Public Affairs may be found on the last page of this report. Key contributors to this report are listed in appendix III.

Michael Brostek
Director, Tax Issues
Strategic Issues Team

Scope and Methodology

To provide information on the extent of and primary types of noncompliance that cause individual taxpayers to misreport capital gains from securities, we performed a number of activities that relied on data from IRS's National Research Program (NRP). Through NRP, IRS selected and reviewed a stratified random sample of 45,925 individual income tax returns from tax year 2001. The NRP sample is divided across 30 strata by the type of individual tax return filed and income levels. IRS accepted as filed some of the NRP returns, accepted others with minor adjustments, and examined the remainder of returns either through correspondence or face-to-face meetings with taxpayers. If IRS examiners determined that taxpayers misreported income for any aspect of the selected tax returns, they adjusted the taxpayers' income accordingly and assessed additional taxes.

IRS captured data from taxpayer returns and examination results in the NRP database, including capital gains income. However, the data on capital gains do not indicate the type of capital asset for which taxpayers reported gains or losses or for which examiners made income adjustments. Therefore, to obtain information on the extent and primary types of capital gains tax noncompliance specific to securities, we selected a statistical sample of NRP examination files to review.

The sample we selected contained 1,017 cases spread across 90 substrata, defined by replicating each of the 30 NRP strata across 3 GAO substrata. The first GAO substratum consisted of examination cases for which the adjustments to capital gain income the examiners made had the largest impact on the total amount of these adjustments for all taxpayers when weighted for the entire population of individual taxpayers. We focused on cases with the largest adjustments, in weighted terms, because including these cases would improve the level of confidence of any estimates of the total amount of capital gains income adjustments for securities. Because our sample is a subsample of the NRP sample and is subject to sampling error, we added cases, when applicable, to ensure that each of the 30 NRP strata in this GAO substratum contained a minimum of 5 cases. In total, we selected 290 cases for the first GAO substratum, and these cases accounted for around 75 percent of the total capital gains adjustments in NRP when weighted for the population of individual taxpayers.

The second substratum consisted of 187 cases for which IRS did not identify misreported capital gains income when it reviewed or examined the tax returns. We included these returns as part of our sample to verify that the NRP examinations had correctly recorded when taxpayers were compliant with respect to reporting capital gains and losses. We selected these cases at random and in proportion to the NRP sample through an iterative process, ensuring that a minimum of 5 cases and a maximum of 15 cases was included in each of the 30 NRP strata.

The remaining 540 cases that constitute the third GAO substratum were selected from cases for which IRS examined taxpayers' capital gain income. We selected these cases at random and in proportion to the number of NRP returns for which IRS examined capital gains income, ensuring that we selected a minimum of 5 cases for each NRP stratum. For one stratum, we only included 2 cases because they were the only cases in the corresponding NRP stratum.

Of the 1,017 cases we selected for our sample, we reviewed 849 cases. We did not review the remaining 168 cases because either IRS did not provide the files in time to include in our review (164 cases) or the files did not contain examination workpapers essential to determining if examiners made adjustments to taxpayers income from securities (4 cases).[1] Based on an analysis of the response rates by the 90 GAO substrata, we concluded that the missing cases did not bias our analyses. We requested the cases at two points, in late-December 2005 and late-January 2006, and periodically checked on the status of our requests with IRS. We were only able to review cases that arrived by April 21, 2006 in order to meet our agreed upon issue date for the report.

We reviewed each selected case file to determine if the taxpayers reported securities transactions on their returns or if examiners discovered any misreported securities transactions. For returns where examiners discovered misreported income from securities transactions, we determined, when possible, the related security type, holding period, adjustment amount, and reason for the adjustment, along with other information. We recorded all determinations on a data collection instrument (DCI) that we developed.

To ensure that our data collection efforts conformed to GAO's data quality standards, each DCI that a GAO analyst completed was reviewed by another GAO analyst. The reviewers compared the data recorded on the DCI to the data in the corresponding case file to determine whether they

[1]IRS could not provide one of these cases that was not yet closed because it was with IRS's Appeals function.

concurred with how the data were recorded. When the analysts differed on how the data were recorded, they met to reconcile any differences.

We input the data we recorded on the DCIs into a computer data collection program. To ensure the accuracy of the transcribed data, each electronic DCI entry was compared to its corresponding paper DCI by analysts other that those that electronically entered the data. If the reviewers found any errors, changes were made to the electronic entries, and the entries were reviewed again to ensure that all data were transcribed accurately.

The estimates we included in this report were based on the NRP database and the data we collected through our file review and were generated using statistical software. All computer programming for the resulting statistical analyses were checked by a second, independent analyst. Our final sample size was large enough to generalize the results of our review or had margins of error small enough to produce meaningful estimates in terms of percentages of taxpayers who were noncompliant in reporting capital gains from securities transactions. However, we could not produce meaningful estimates of the total amount of net misreported capital gain income from securities or determine the securities tax gap, in part because (1) in selecting our sample, we could not distinguish which cases included misreported securities transactions as opposed to misreported transactions for other types of capital assets, (2) some cases with large amounts of misreported capital gains or losses were due to noncompliance for assets other than securities, (3) 53 of the cases we requested from IRS from our first substratum, which represented a large percentage of the total amounts of misreported capital gains or losses, were not provided in time to include in our review, and (4) taxpayers misreported a wide range of dollar amounts from the transactions.[2] We discussed our estimates with IRS officials to obtain their perspectives on the results of our analysis.

Because we followed a probability procedure based on random selection, our sample is only one of a large number of samples that we might have selected. Since each sample could have resulted in different estimates, we express our confidence in the precision of our particular sample's results as a 95 percent confidence interval, plus or minus the margin of error indicated along with each estimate in the report. This interval would

[2]IRS could not provide one of these cases that was not yet closed because it was with IRS's Appeals function.

contain the actual population value for 95 percent of the samples we could have selected.

We assessed whether the examination results and data contained in the NRP database were sufficiently reliable for the purposes of our review. For this assessment, we interviewed IRS officials about the data, collected and reviewed documentation about the data and the system used to capture the data, and performed electronic testing of relevant data fields for obvious errors in accuracy and completeness. We compared the information we collected through our case file review to corresponding information in the NRP database to identify inconsistencies. Based on our assessment, we determined that the NRP database was sufficiently reliable for the purposes of our review.

We also used IRS's Statistics of Income (SOI) file for individual taxpayers, which relies on a stratified probability sample of individual income tax returns, to develop estimates for categories of individual taxpayers on adjusted gross income, the percentage of individual taxpayers that used paid tax preparers, and the number of taxpayers that filed a Schedule D with their tax returns for tax year 2003. We compared our analyses against published IRS data to determine that the SOI database was sufficiently reliable for the purposes of our review.

To provide information on actions IRS takes in attempting to reduce the individual capital gains tax gap for securities and on challenges that IRS faces with these actions, we reviewed documents from IRS compliance programs as they related to capital gains and interviewed IRS officials knowledgeable about the subject. We reviewed documentation for IRS's enforcement programs that address capital gains and reviewed IRS publications and other documents that provided information on how to accurately report capital gains and losses. To provide additional information on IRS's compliance programs and identify challenges IRS faces in using these programs to reduce the individual capital gains tax gap for securities, we interviewed IRS officials from various areas of the agency, including the enforcement, taxpayer service, and research functions.

To identify options with the potential to improve taxpayers' voluntary compliance for reporting securities gains and losses and IRS's ability to find noncompliance related to the individual capital gains tax gap for securities, we reviewed prior GAO reports and other documents on capital gains reporting and compliance such as those from IRS compliance programs and industry reports on securities holdings and information reporting. We also spoke with IRS officials and numerous representatives from, and related to, the securities industry. At IRS, we spoke with officials from various areas of the agency, including the enforcement, taxpayer service, and research functions. Additionally, we spoke with officials from the Taxpayer Advocate Service and members of IRS's Information Return Program Advisory Committee (IRPAC).[3] We also spoke with representatives of the Securities Industry Association; Investment Company Institute, which represents the mutual fund industry; Bond Market Association; American Banking Association Securities Association; American Institute of Certified Public Accountants; and the American Bar Association to get their perspectives on capital gains tax noncompliance, ways to reduce noncompliance, and any challenges related to reducing noncompliance and how those challenges could be mitigated.

[3]IRPAC advises IRS on information reporting issues of mutual concern to the private sector and federal government. It is composed of 17 members who represent various private and public sector organizations with an interest in, or responsibility for, information reporting.

Appendix II

Comments from the Internal Revenue Service

DEPARTMENT OF THE TREASURY
INTERNAL REVENUE SERVICE
WASHINGTON, D.C. 20224

COMMISSIONER

June 5, 2006

Mr. Michael Brostek
Director, Tax Issues
U.S. Government Accountability Office
441 G Street, N.W.
Washington, D.C. 20548

Dear Mr. Brostek:

I have reviewed the draft Government Accountability Office (GAO) report titled "Capital Gains Tax Gap: Requiring Brokers to Report Securities Cost Basis Would Improve Compliance if Related Challenges Are Addressed" (GAO-06-603). We agree with the recommendation contained in the report and would like to offer several comments.

Accurate reporting of capital gains and losses related to securities is an important component of the tax gap. Determining cost calculations for stocks or mutual funds is complex especially when purchased over a long time span, and where dividends and other distributions are automatically reinvested. Calculations may also be complicated by the taxpayer's choice of accounting methods, stock splits, mergers and corporate reorganizations.

This report suggests that Congress consider requiring brokers to report the adjusted basis of securities sold and identify whether gains and losses are short or long-term. IRS research shows that taxpayer's reporting compliance is strongly related to the extent of third party reporting, however, basis reporting would raise unique challenges in the area of burden on brokers and taxpayers when reporting unique situations such as wash sales and options. The report discusses that a solution would be to exclude wash sale transactions from basis reporting. To exclude these transactions from basis reporting, a broker must be able to distinguish them from non-wash sale transactions. Because of the way wash sale transactions are defined under current law, however, in many cases brokers would not be able to identify the transactions by the time reporting would be required, so excluding them may not be possible in all situations.

In the short term, the IRS will continue to clarify guidance related to the accurate reporting of capital gains and losses. We will revise the instructions for Schedule D, "Capital Gains and Losses," to clarify the appropriate use of capital losses and provide guidance on resources available to taxpayers to determine their basis. A previous example of our efforts is the 2005 revision of instructions for Schedule D. The revision provides taxpayers with references to IRS publications and applicable Internal Revenue Code sections, and reminds taxpayers to report information critical to evaluating the accuracy of the capital gain or loss claimed.

2

I am pleased to inform you that the IRS Office of Taxpayer Burden Reduction is leading an effort to address the capital gains tax gap and related tax burden. We are committed to working with industry stakeholders to develop cost effective methods to mitigate reporting challenges that impact taxpayers, tax practitioners, financial institutions and tax software vendors.

I appreciate your continued support and the valuable assistance and guidance from your staff. Our response to your recommendation is enclosed. If you have any questions please contact Floyd Williams, Director, Legislative Affairs, at (202) 622-4725.

Sincerely,

Mark W. Everson

Enclosure

Enclosure

GAO Draft Report – Capital Gains Tax Gap: Requiring Brokers to Report Securities Cost Basis Would Improve Compliance if Related Challenges Are Addressed (GAO-06-603)

GAO Recommendation: To assist taxpayers in accurately reporting their capital gains and losses from securities, in the instructions to Schedule D the Commissioner of Internal Revenue should (1) clarify the appropriate use of capital losses to offset capital gains and (2) provide guidance on resources available to taxpayers to determine their basis.

IRS Response: We agree with the recommendation and will revise the instructions for Schedule D to clarify the appropriate use of capital losses and provide guidance on resources available to taxpayers to determine their basis.

GAO Contact and Staff Acknowledgments

GAO Contact

Michael Brostek, (202) 512-9110 or brostekm@gao.gov

Acknowledgments

In addition to the contact named above, Wes Phillips and Tom Short, Assistant Directors; Jeff Arkin; Susan Baker; Candace Carpenter; Keira Dembowski; Fred Jimenez; Matthew Keeler; Donna Miller; John Mingus; Franklin Ng; Karen O'Conor; Cheryl Peterson; Sam Scrutchins; Jay Smale; and Jennifer Li Wong made key contributions to this report.

Related GAO Products

Tax Gap: Making Significant Progress in Improving Tax Compliance Rests on Enhancing Current IRS Techniques and Adopting New Legislative Actions. GAO-06-453T. Washington, D.C.: February 15, 2006.

Tax Gap: Multiple Strategies, Better Compliance Data, and Long-term Goals Are Needed to Improve Taxpayer Compliance. GAO-06-208T. Washington, D.C.: October 26, 2005.

Tax Compliance: Better Compliance Data and Long-term Goals Would Support a More Strategic IRS Approach to Reducing the Tax Gap. GAO-05-753. Washington, D.C.: July 18, 2005.

Tax Compliance: Reducing the Tax Gap Can Contribute to Fiscal Sustainability but Will Require a Variety of Strategies. GAO-05-527T. Washington, D.C.: April 14, 2005.

Tax Administration: More Can Be Done to Ensure Federal Agencies File Accurate Information Returns. GAO-04-74. Washington, D.C.: December 5, 2003.

Tax Administration: IRS Should Continue to Expand Reporting on Its Enforcement Efforts. GAO-03-378. Washington, D.C.: January 31, 2003.

Tax Administration: IRS Can Improve Information Reporting for Original Issue Discount Bonds. GAO/GGD-96-70. Washington, D.C.: March 15, 1996.

Reducing the Tax Gap: Results of a GAO-Sponsored Symposium. GAO/GGD-95-157. Washington, D.C.: June 2, 1995.

Options Reporting to IRS. GAO/GGD-95-145R. Washington, D.C.: May 5, 1995.

Tax Gap: Many Actions Taken, But a Cohesive Compliance Strategy Needed. GAO/GGD-94-123. Washington, D.C.: May 11, 1994.

Tax Administration: Computer Matching Could Identify Overstated Business Deductions. GAO/GGD-93-133. Washington, D.C.: August 13, 1993.

Information Reporting. GAO/GGD-93-55R. Washington, D.C.: July 22, 1993.

Tax Administration: Information Returns Can Improve Reporting of Forgiven Debts. GAO/GGD-93-42. Washington, D.C.: February 17, 1993.

Tax Administration: Overstated Real Estate Tax Deductions Need to Be Reduced. GAO/GGD-93-43. Washington, D.C.: January 19, 1993.

Tax Administration: Federal Agencies Should Report Service Payments Made to Corporations. GAO/GGD-92-130. Washington, D.C.: September 22, 1992.

Tax Administration: Approaches for Improving Independent Contractor Compliance. GAO/GGD-92-108. Washington, D.C.: July 23, 1992.

Tax Administration: Benefits of a Corporate Document Matching Program Exceed the Costs. GAO/GGD-91-118. Washington, D.C.: September 27, 1991.

IRS Needs to Implement a Corporate Document Matching Program. GAO/T-GGD-91-40. Washington, D.C.: June 10, 1991.

Tax Administration IRS Can Improve Its Program to Find Taxpayers Who Underreport Their Income. GAO/GGD-91-49. Washington, D.C.: March 13, 1991.

Tax Administration: Expanded Reporting on Seller-financed Mortgages Can Spur Tax Compliance. GAO/GGD-91-38. Washington, D.C.: March 29, 1991.

IRS' Compliance Programs to Reduce the Tax Gap. GAO/T-GGD-91-11. Washington, D.C.: March 13, 1991.

IRS Can Use Tax Gap Data to Improve Its Programs for Reducing Noncompliance. GAO/T-GGD-90-32. Washington, D.C.: April 19, 1990.

Tax Administration: Information Returns Can Be Used to Identify Employers Who Misclassify Workers. GAO/GGD-89-107. Washington, D.C.: September 25, 1989.

Tax Administration: Missing Independent Contractors' Information Returns Not Always Detected. GAO/GGD-89-110. Washington, D.C.: September 8, 1989.

Tax Administration: IRS' Efforts to Establish a Business Information Returns Program. GAO/GGD-88-102. Washington, D.C.: July 22, 1988.

The Merits of Establishing a Business Information Returns Program. GAO/T-GGD-87-4. Washington, D.C.: March 17, 1987.

Questions for the Record for Hon. David Walker
June 13, 2006

From Senator Grassley:

1. Mr. Walker, in your written testimony you estimate that, in 2005, corporate tax expenditures accounted for $80 billion of foregone revenue. The GAO has noted that, unlike direct spending programs, the effectiveness of many tax expenditures is not subject to review. You recommend that corporate tax expenditures "should be reviewed periodically to ensure they have not outlived their usefulness, are not redundant, or are not inefficient in accomplishing their intended purpose."

Mr. Walker, what would a congressional review of corporate tax expenditures, as suggested in your testimony, entail?

GAO has urged a more comprehensive, consistent, and integrated approach to evaluating all programs relevant to specific areas and desired outcomes—encompassing spending, tax expenditures, and regulatory programs—using a common framework. Such an analysis is necessary to capture whether a program complements and supports other related programs, whether it is duplicative and redundant, or whether it actually works at cross-purposes to other initiatives. It is also necessary to understand what outcomes are being achieved in key areas.

Comprehensive congressional review of tax expenditures would require more complete information on the intended and actual effects of major tax expenditures. Such information could be included in agency performance and accountability reports and the government's consolidated financial statements. A framework for conducting performance reviews of tax expenditures would also be necessary, and in our 2005 report on tax expenditures,[1] one of our recommendations was that OMB, in consultation with Treasury, develop and implement such a framework. We also recommended that OMB require that tax expenditures be included in the PART process and any future such budget and performance review processes so that tax expenditures are considered along with related outlay programs in determining the adequacy of federal efforts to achieve national objectives. OMB disagreed with our recommendations and stated that it has no current plans to implement any of them, but stated that other tax expenditures may be evaluated with the PART in the future. We continue to believe our recommendations are valid. We also believe that the Congress needs to subject all major tax preferences to periodic oversight and possible reauthorization.

---

[1] GAO, *Government Performance and Accountability: Tax Expenditures Represent a Substantial Federal Commitment and Need to Be Reexamined*, GAO-05-690 (Washington, D.C.: Sept. 23, 2005).

2. Mr. Walker. According to the Congressional Budget Office, corporate income tax receipts were a record $278.3 billion dollars in 2005, up 47 percent over the prior year and representing 2.3 percent of GDP – the highest percentage since 1980. The first 8 months of fiscal year 2006 show the trend continuing with corporate tax receipts up 30 percent over last year. This upward trend is particularly noticeable since 2003, when corporate tax revenues amounted to only 1.6 percent of GDP.

Mr. Walker, your statement says that the revenues from the corporate income tax should be considered in light of our long-term fiscal challenges. Could you please tell us what you think is behind the recent surge in corporate tax receipts, and tell us what you mean by taking the corporate tax revenues into account?

According to CBO, the recent growth in corporate tax receipts is largely attributable to the economic recovery from the 2001 recession. Tax law changes, such as the partial expensing provisions enacted by Job Creation and Workers Assistance Act (JCWAA) of 2002 and the Jobs and Growth Tax Relief Reconciliation Act of 2003 (JGTRRA) constrained the growth of corporate tax receipts between September 2001 and December 2004, but have contributed to increased corporate tax receipts following the expiration of these provisions at the beginning of 2005.[2] Finally, other factors, such as pension contributions to defined-benefit pension plans, which can vary significantly from year to year, also affect the level of corporate tax receipts.

As noted in my statement, corporate taxes are not the largest source of federal revenue, but they are still relevant to considerations about how to address the nation's long-term fiscal imbalance. Over the long term, the United States faces a large and growing structural budget deficit and continuing on this imprudent and unsustainable fiscal path will gradually erode, if not suddenly damage, our economy, our standard of living, and ultimately our national security. Any consideration of changes to corporate income tax policies should be done in light of the impacts of those changes on the nation's long-term fiscal imbalance. At a minimum, if corporate income tax revenues are reduced, revenues must be raised elsewhere or spending must be reduced so that our fiscal imbalance is not exacerbated. Ultimately, we will need to reform entitlement programs, reduce spending, and enhance revenues in order to close our large long-term fiscal gap.

[2] According to CBO, partial expensing allowed corporations to immediately deduct from taxable income between 30 percent and 50 percent of any investment in equipment made between September 11, 2001 and December 31, 2004.

3. Mr. Walker, as you know, the Tax Increase Prevention and Reconciliation Act of 2005, that was signed into law in May of this year, imposed a new withholding structure on certain government payments made after December 31, 2010. In your testimony today, you recommend that federal contractors with delinquent tax debt should be prohibited from receiving future federal contracts. Can you expand on this recommendation and its interaction with the new withholding structure?

As I testified at the hearing, I believe Congress should consider suspending government business with contractors who abuse the federal tax system. Allowing such contractors to continue to do business with the federal government without consequence creates an unfair competitive advantage for them over the vast majority of contractors who pay their fair share of taxes. In our view, this provision could be implemented at some prospective effective date and applicable to any contractors with delinquent tax debts who have not entered into a payment agreement with the IRS as of that date or who are not current on their payment agreement. Congress could allow for limited waivers in unique circumstances, such as where national security could be compromised. In general, withholding has been shown to increase tax compliance, so the withholding provisions of TIPRA could assist in preventing more contractors from getting into a delinquent tax debt situation.

4. Mr. Walker, Commissioner Everson has raised compliance concerns about the complexity of the tax code and the complexity of business activity in today's global economy. Simplification of the tax code is always held up as something we ought to do. Congress has enacted some simplification measures, particularly with respect to our international tax regime. Yet, on the whole, as Commissioner Everson notes, "the Code continues to expand, becoming more complex and challenging to administer."

Mr. Walker, would you please comment on why our business tax rules need to be simplified, and how we should consider accomplishing it.

Tax code complexity adds to the compliance burden and creates opportunities for tax evasion or for hiding such evasion. Simplification could take the form of broadening the tax base while reducing tax rates. Simplification would also be advanced by undertaking an examination of all major tax expenditures and making sure that they are achieving their intended results at a reasonable cost in lost revenue and added burden.

5. Are there any guideposts or factors that you would recommend that we keep in mind with respect to book-tax conformity as we begin discussions about tax reform? That is, are there clear guidelines for when conformity or non-conformity is the right answer?

While GAO has not done the work to offer any guidelines, literature on the topic indicates that that this is not a simple issue as accounting rules and tax rules are designed for different purposes. Consequently, changes should be made only after careful scrutiny. One place to start would be to examine data from the new schedule M-3 to identify the areas that account for the biggest differences in book and tax income. Ideally, changes should simplify the tax code as well as improve economic efficiency and tax compliance.

From Senator Baucus

1. Mr. Walker, is it feasible and possible for the Administration to develop a comprehensive plan of action to close the tax gap? What are the key criteria that should be considered in developing such a plan? Does the IRS have existing strategic plans that could be consolidated into one master plan?

A comprehensive plan to reduce but not eliminate the tax gap is feasible to develop and IRS is making progress in this regard. We recently reported that IRS's 2007 budget request,[3] for the first time, sets long-term goals aimed at reducing the tax gap. IRS established two agencywide, long-term performance goals; one to improve voluntary compliance from 83 percent in 2005 to 85 percent by 2009, and another to reduce the number of taxpayers who think it is acceptable to cheat on their taxes from 10 percent in 2005 to less than 9 percent in 2010. According to IRS, these are the first in a series of quantitative goals that are to link to its three strategic goals—improve taxpayer service, enhance tax law enforcement, and modernize IRS through technology and processes.

These goals will be challenging to meet, because for three decades, IRS has consistently reported a persistent, relatively stable tax gap. Because of a lack of quantitative estimates of how changes to its service and enforcement programs affect compliance, quantifying the impact of IRS's service and enforcement programs on compliance or cheating is very challenging. Consequently, IRS is unable to show in a data-based plan how it will use those programs to reach the two long-term goals. The type of data needed to make such a link does not currently exist, and will not be easy to collect.

Lacking such quantitative estimates, IRS must take a more qualitative approach in its plans for increasing compliance, which would likely also involve changing attitudes towards cheating. IRS's overall approach to reducing the tax gap consists of improving service to taxpayers and enhancing enforcement of the tax laws. We have also reported that IRS has taken a number of steps that may improve its ability to reduce the tax gap—favorable trends in staffing of IRS enforcement personnel; examinations performed through correspondence, as opposed to more complex face-to-face examinations; and the use of some enforcement sanctions such as liens and levies are encouraging.[4] Also, IRS has made progress with respect to abusive tax shelters through a number of initiatives and recent

[3] GAO, *Internal Revenue Service: Assessment of the Interim Results of the 2006 Filing Season and Fiscal Year 2007 Budget Request*, GAO-06-499T (Washington, D.C.: April 27, 2006).
[4] GAO, *Tax Gap: Making Significant Progress in Improving Tax Compliance Rests on Enhancing Current IRS Techniques and Adopting New Legislative Actions*, GAO-06-453T (Washington, D.C.: Feb. 15, 2006).

settlement offers that have resulted in billions of dollars in collected taxes, interest, and penalties. Finally, IRS has continually improved taxpayer service by increasing, for example, the accuracy of responses to tax law questions.

2. Some of the "most significant" issues that the IRS identified to the Committee have been under consideration for years, including cost sharing, transfer pricing and the universal service fund.

a) These are tough issues, but once the facts patterns have been determined, does the passage of time make it any easier for the government to take a legal position?
b) To what extent do you think it takes the IRS too long to decide its position on an issue?
c) What impact does the lack of guidance have on corporate compliance and the tax gap?

These would generally be case-by-case decisions, but there may be times when there is a greater compliance risk posed by the absence of guidance than the compliance risk created by putting out imperfect guidance more quickly. In areas where corporations or other taxpayers are trying to be compliant but the rules are unclear, they may find themselves out of compliance despite their best intentions. When the government needs more time to finalize a position, interim guidance in advance of a final determination can help taxpayers in their efforts to comply with the tax laws.

3. To leverage its resources and to become more current in its examinations, the IRS uses several expedited or abbreviated audit techniques, including the limited scope audit and the LIFE (limited issue focused exam) audit.

a. Do you think that audits designed to pick the "low hanging fruit" are good policy? How effective is the IRS at finding Enron-type situations that aren't readily apparent when you look at the return?

b. What impact do you think limited audits have on the tax gap? Has quality been sacrificed for currency?

c. Are there alternative ways the IRS could conduct fast, efficient audits that would not sacrifice quality?

It is important that IRS have a balanced approach to enforcement. Innovation is necessary, but IRS also needs to evaluate its new initiatives to ensure that they are working as intended and IRS must continually reevaluate the balance it must strike among its different enforcement initiatives. As implied in your questions, some of the most egregious noncompliance can be well disguised. IRS needs a strategy to ensure that emerging areas of noncompliance are not overlooked. Research on corporate tax compliance similar to the National Research Program studies of individual taxpayers and subchapter S corporations would help IRS identify noncompliance in the corporate area.

4. What is your opinion about the public disclosure of tax return information?
5. How would you respond to concerns about protecting the confidentiality of tax return information?
6. What impact would the disclosure of tax return information have on the foreign and domestic competitive position of US companies?

Tax return confidentiality is an important element of voluntary compliance—taxpayers are likely to be more willing to provide proprietary or other tax return information to IRS if they are assured it will remain confidential. Publicly disclosing tax return information could also leave some companies at a competitive disadvantage. However, some have argued that making schedule M-3 data public would not threaten confidentiality, so we believe that this proposal is worth considering.

7. Your statement says that the revenues from the corporate income tax should be considered in light of our long-term fiscal challenges. Could you expand on what you mean by taking the corporate tax revenues into account?

As noted in my statement, corporate taxes are not the largest source of federal revenue, but they are still relevant to considerations about how to address the nation's long-term fiscal imbalance. Over the long term, the United States faces a large and growing structural budget deficit and continuing on this imprudent and unsustainable fiscal path will gradually erode, if not suddenly damage, our economy, our standard of living, and ultimately our national security. Any consideration of changes to corporate income tax policies should be done in light of the impacts of those changes on the nation's long-term fiscal imbalance. At a minimum, if corporate income tax revenues are reduced, revenues must be raised elsewhere or spending must be reduced so that our fiscal imbalance is not exacerbated. Ultimately, we will need to reform entitlement programs, reduce spending, and enhance revenues in order to close our large long-term fiscal gap.

8. What would a congressional review of corporate tax expenditures as suggested in your testimony statement entail?

GAO has urged a more comprehensive, consistent, and integrated approach to evaluating all programs relevant to specific areas and desired outcomes—encompassing spending, tax expenditures, and regulatory programs—using a common framework. Such an analysis is necessary to capture whether a program complements and supports other related programs, whether it is duplicative and redundant, or whether it actually works at cross-purposes to other initiatives. It is also necessary to understand what outcomes are being achieved in key areas.

Comprehensive congressional review of tax expenditures would require more complete information on the intended and actual effects of major tax expenditures. Such information could be included in agency performance and accountability reports and the government's consolidated financial statements. A framework for conducting performance reviews of tax expenditures would also be necessary, and in our 2005 report on tax expenditures,[5] one of our recommendations was that OMB, in consultation with Treasury, develop and implement such a framework. We also recommended that OMB require that tax expenditures be included in the PART process and any future such budget and performance review processes so that tax expenditures are considered along with related outlay programs in determining the adequacy of federal efforts to achieve national objectives. OMB disagreed with our recommendations and stated that it has no current plans to implement any of them, but stated that other tax expenditures may be evaluated with the PART in the future. We continue to believe our recommendations are valid. We also believe that the Congress needs to subject all major tax preferences to periodic oversight and possible reauthorization.

9. Could you please discuss other options for dealing with the long-term fiscal challenge?

Our nation's large, growing, and structural fiscal imbalance will require a multi-pronged approach:

- restructuring existing entitlement programs,
- reexamining the base of discretionary and other spending,
- reviewing and revising existing tax policy, including tax expenditures, which can operate like mandatory spending programs,
- re-imposing past budget controls as well as adding some new ones, and
- improving budget & legislative processes and improving transparency of financial and budget reporting.

In our report entitled 21st Century Challenges: Reexamining the Base of the Federal Government (GAO-05-325SP) we presented illustrative questions for policy makers to consider as they carry out their responsibilities. These questions look across major areas of the budget and federal operations including discretionary and mandatory spending, and tax policies and programs. We hope that this report, among other things, will be used by various congressional committees as they consider which areas of government need particular attention and legislative reconsideration.

Addressing the nation's long-term fiscal imbalances constitutes a major transformational challenge that may take a generation to resolve. Given the size of our projected deficit we will not be able to grow our way out of this problem—tough choices will be required. As such, traditional incremental approaches to budgeting will need to give way to more fundamental and periodic reexaminations of the base of government, ultimately covering discretionary and

[5] GAO, *Government Performance and Accountability: Tax Expenditures Represent a Substantial Federal Commitment and Need to Be Reexamined*, GAO-05-690 (Washington, D.C.: Sept. 23, 2005).

mandatory programs as well as the revenue side of the budget. An important step towards this goal would be a capable, credible, and bipartisan commission to study tax and entitlement reform.

The nature and magnitude of the fiscal, security, and economic and other adjustments that need to be considered are not amenable to "quick fixes;" rather they will likely require an iterative, thoughtful process of disciplined changes and reforms over many years. Nonetheless, the magnitude of and potential disruption from related changes can be mitigated if the necessary policy changes are made sooner rather than later.

10. Why is simplification needed?
11. How can we simplify the tax code? (combined answer to both questions)

Tax code complexity adds to the compliance burden and creates opportunities for tax evasion or for hiding such evasion. Simplification could take the form of broadening the tax base while reducing tax rates. Simplification would also be advanced by undertaking an examination of all major tax expenditures and making sure that they are achieving their intended results at a reasonable cost in lost revenue and added burden.

12. In your testimony, you cited a CBO study finding that the U.S. corporate tax rate was high among OECD countries, but was comparable among the G7 industrialized countries. Mr. Sullivan testified similarly that compared to the EU average, the U.S. tax rate was high, but just compared to the five largest EU countries, the rate was much closer. Can you explain why the CBO and others have argued that such comparisons should only include other large industrialized countries?

The CBO report we cited notes that an analysis of tax-rate differentials should recognize the ways in which countries vary and that countries' economies may differ and interact in ways that affect how those countries tax systems should be compared. The report includes comparisons with both the large industrialized nations of the G-7 and with the larger group of OECD countries.

From Senator Kerry:

1. Comptroller General Walker mentioned that $11 billion of the tax gap can be attributed to individual taxpayers who misreported their income from capital gains or losses. I am cosponsor of S. 2556 legislation introduced by Senator Bayh that would require investment brokers to report the adjusted basis of securities of their customers. Do you think this legislation will help narrow the tax gap? Do you recommend other reporting requirements that would help reduce the tax gap?

As we recently reported, requiring brokers to report the adjusted basis of securities that taxpayers sell could improve tax compliance and narrow the capital gains tax gap.[6] About 36 percent of taxpayers with securities transactions in 2001 misreported their gains or losses from their securities sales, and around half of those taxpayers misreported because they did not accurately report the basis of the securities they sold. Basis reporting could help taxpayers to accurately report the basis and gains or losses of securities they sell and help IRS identify taxpayers that misreport. However, basis reporting involves a number of challenges that would need to be addressed, such as determining how to standardize the transfer of basis information among brokers and developing rules related to securities for which basis would be reported. Also, the impact of a basis reporting requirement would depend on whether the requirement would apply only to future securities purchases as opposed to the securities that taxpayers currently hold.

As for information reporting, in general, having third parties file information returns with IRS and taxpayers has been shown to lead to high levels of tax compliance. In the past, we have identified a few areas where additional information reporting requirements could serve to improve compliance, such as requirements related to payments made to independent contractors (lowering the $600 threshold for requiring information returns and requiring businesses to separately report on their tax returns the total amount of payments to independent contractors) and requiring information return reporting on payments made to corporations.

2. In your testimony, you discussed how many federal contractors have unpaid federal taxes. Is legislation needed rather than an executive order to require that only those who have paid taxes are eligible for federal contracts?

Legislative changes are not the only possible approach to the problem of federal contractors with delinquent tax debts. In our 2004 report on Department of Defense contractors that abuse the federal tax system,[7] we recommended that the Director of Office of Management and Budget (OMB) develop and pursue policy options for prohibiting federal contract awards to contractors in cases in which abuse to the federal tax system has occurred and the tax owed is not contested. In this recommendation, we stated that options could include designating such tax abuse as a cause for governmentwide debarment and suspension or, if allowed by statute, authorizing IRS to declare such businesses and individuals ineligible for government contracts. However, OMB has not implemented this recommendation. Currently, the Federal Acquisition Regulation (FAR) does not specifically require contracting officers to take into account a contractor's tax debt when assessing whether a prospective contractor is a responsible party and therefore should be awarded a contract. As a result, neither GSA nor other federal agencies perform reviews to determine whether prospective contractors have unpaid taxes at the time a contract is awarded.

---

[6] GAO, *Capital Gains Tax Gap: Requiring Brokers to Report Securities Cost Basis Would Improve Compliance if Related Challenges Are Addressed*, GAO-06-603 (Washington, D.C.: June 13, 2006).

[7] GAO, *Financial Management: Some DOD Contractors Abuse the Federal Tax System with Little Consequence*, GAO-04-95 (Washington, D.C.: Feb. 12, 2004).

Another policy option is to change federal law, as implemented by the FAR, and require the contracting officer's responsibility review to include an assessment of contractor tax delinquency before issuance of a contract. In addition to the general concerns about the federal government doing business with delinquent taxpayers, allowing these contractors to do business with the federal government creates an unfair competitive advantage over the vast majority of contractors who pay their taxes. This causes a disincentive to contractors to pay their fair share of taxes, and could lead to further erosion in compliance with the nation's tax system. However, certain issues would need to be considered in implementing such a provision, including ensuring the accuracy of taxpayer information, timely communication of the tax status of a prospective contractor to the contracting officer, and the legal barriers that currently prevent IRS from disclosing taxpayer information. This latter issue could be addressed through a requirement that prospective contractors certify that they do not owe any tax debts and provide consent to IRS to provide information on their tax status to the contracting officer. In addition, other issues would need to be addressed, such as developing a standard on what constitutes abuse of the federal tax system and the ability to expedite the negotiation of contracts as quickly as possible.[8]

At the June 13, 2006, Committee on Finance hearing, Senator Bingaman asked Mr. Walker about the need for legislative changes to deal with the problem of federal contractors with delinquent tax debts. Mr. Walker's reply included a statement that he would provide additional information in writing.

Legislative changes are not the only possible approach to the problem of federal contractors with delinquent tax debts. In our 2004 report on Department of Defense contractors that abuse the federal tax system,[9] we recommended that the Director of Office of Management and Budget (OMB) develop and pursue policy options for prohibiting federal contract awards to contractors in cases in which abuse to the federal tax system has occurred and the tax owed is not contested. In this recommendation, we stated that options could include designating such tax abuse as a cause for governmentwide debarment and suspension or, if allowed by statute, authorizing IRS to declare such businesses and individuals ineligible for government contracts. However, OMB has not implemented this recommendation. Currently, the Federal Acquisition Regulation (FAR) does not specifically require contracting officers to take into account a contractor's tax debt when assessing whether a prospective contractor is a responsible party and therefore should be awarded a contract. As a result, neither GSA nor other federal agencies perform reviews to determine whether prospective contractors have unpaid taxes at the time a contract is awarded.

---

[8] We considered activity to be abusive when a contractor's actions or inactions, though not illegal, took advantage of the existing tax enforcement and administration system to avoid fulfilling federal tax obligations and were deficient or improper when compared with behavior that a prudent person would consider reasonable.

[9] GAO, *Financial Management: Some DOD Contractors Abuse the Federal Tax System with Little Consequence*, GAO-04-95 (Washington, D.C.: Feb. 12, 2004).

Another policy option is to change federal law, as implemented by the FAR, and require the contracting officer's responsibility review to include an assessment of contractor tax delinquency before issuance of a contract. In addition to the general concerns about the federal government doing business with delinquent taxpayers, allowing these contractors to do business with the federal government creates an unfair competitive advantage over the vast majority of contractors who pay their taxes. This causes a disincentive to contractors to pay their fair share of taxes, and could lead to further erosion in compliance with the nation's tax system. However, certain issues would need to be considered in implementing such a provision, including ensuring the accuracy of taxpayer information, timely communication of the tax status of a prospective contractor to the contracting officer, and the legal barriers that currently prevent IRS from disclosing taxpayer information. This latter issue could be addressed through a requirement that prospective contractors certify that they do not owe any tax debts and provide consent to IRS to provide information on their tax status to the contracting officer. In addition, other issues would need to be addressed, such as developing a standard on what constitutes abuse of the federal tax system and the ability to expedite the negotiation of contracts as quickly as possible.[10]

[10] We considered activity to be abusive when a contractor's actions or inactions, though not illegal, took advantage of the existing tax enforcement and administration system to avoid fulfilling federal tax obligations and were deficient or improper when compared with behavior that a prudent person would consider reasonable.

COMMUNICATIONS

ACLI AMERICAN COUNCIL OF LIFE INSURERS FINANCIAL SECURITY FOR LIFE

Statement

of the

American Council of Life Insurers

on

"A Tune-Up on Corporate Tax Issues: What's Going on Under the Hood?"

before the

Committee on Finance

of the

United States Senate

June 13, 2006

I. INTRODUCTION

The American Council of Life Insurers (ACLI) welcomes the opportunity to place this statement into the record of the United States Senate Committee on Finance hearing entitled: *A Tune-Up On Corporate Tax Issues: What's Going On Under The Hood?* The 377 member companies of the ACLI account for 90% of all life insurance premiums and 95% of all annuity considerations and have assets representing 91% of all U.S. legal reserve life insurance companies. When you pop the hood on the topic we wish to address, you will find a complicated mass of wires and hoses much in need of streamlining through elimination.

In 1999, Congress took major steps forward in rewriting the regulatory structure of the financial services industry in the United States.[1] This realignment has had a positive impact on the way life insurance companies serve their customers, conduct their operations and structure their businesses. Unfortunately, the complex, outdated restrictions on filing consolidated income tax returns by affiliated groups containing life insurance company members present barriers to the life insurance industry's integration with other sectors of the fast moving global financial services marketplace.

These restrictions[2] do not apply to any other financial or non-financial companies and date back to a tax regime that no longer exists and serves no justifiable purpose. The unjustified complexity and anti-competitive nature of the consolidated tax restrictions is exacerbated under the current regulatory structure for financial services companies.

Prior to 1984, life insurance companies were subject to a federal tax regime that differed significantly from other corporations. The resulting arcane, complicated rules for life insurance taxation were justified on the basis that life insurers are under-taxed or not taxed on their full income. Primarily as a result of these restrictions, today and for many years, life insurance companies have been paying very significant federal income taxes at a rate that far exceeds that for all U.S. corporations.[3]

Finally, to the extent there is concern about the ability of corporate groups with life insurance company affiliates to shelter income through the acquisition of loss companies, since enactment of the Tax Reform Act of 1986, IRC section 382 rules have operated to severely limit the use of such previously incurred or "built-in" losses. Section 382's limitations apply to all corporate acquisitions, whether or not a life company is involved. In addition, consolidated return regulations also provide significant limitations against the use of pre-acquisition NOL carry-forwards against income generated from other members within the affiliated group.

---

[1] Gramm-Leach-Bliley Act of 1999 ("1999 Act"), Pub. L. No. 106-102, 113 Stat. 1341.

[2] Internal Revenue Code §§ 1503(c) and 1504(c).

[3] A Coopers & Lybrand study shows that life insurers paid $57.6 billion in federal corporate income taxes from 1991-1997. In the last year of that period, 1997, the life insurance industry paid over $9 billion in federal taxes. The average effective tax rate of U.S. life insurers over that seven-year period was 35.4%, significantly higher than the 28.3% average effective rate for all U.S. corporations.

For the reasons detailed below, the ACLI advocates repeal of these provisions of current tax law as part of any corporate tax reform effort.

II. LIFE/NON-LIFE CONSOLIDATED RETURN PENALTIES – SECTIONS 1503(C) AND 1504(C)

Background

In general, tax law permits members of an affiliated group of corporations to file consolidated tax returns so that the entire economic income of the group may be taxed as a whole (as if the included corporations were divisions of a single company). General exceptions to this treatment exist to account for non-taxed corporations and pass-through entities (such as IRC § 501 entities, regulated investment companies, and real estate investment trusts), as well as foreign corporations. In addition, current tax law includes a number of restrictions on the ability of a group of affiliated companies to file a consolidated federal income tax return if the group includes a company that is taxed as a life insurance company under IRC § 801. The consolidation rules applicable to other corporations, including other financial intermediaries, contain no such restrictions. While such restrictions may have had justification at a time when life insurance companies were subject to a tax regime that differed from other corporations, this is no longer the case.

From 1918 to 1927, insurance companies were permitted to file consolidated returns on the same basis as other companies. This continued even after 1921 tax law changes made life insurers taxable only on their investment income. Starting in 1928, life companies were not permitted to file consolidated returns with non-life affiliates because of this different tax base. With passage of the Tax Reform Act of 1976 (the "1976 Act")[4], beginning in 1981, life companies were able again to consolidate with non-life companies, but they faced severe tax restrictions. These limits were intended to ensure that life companies that owned or purchased property and casualty companies still paid taxes despite potential large losses in the property and casualty company. These rules still exist today, even though in 1984 the tax treatment of life insurance companies and property and casualty companies were brought more closely in line with that of other corporate taxpayers. Today, insurance companies (life and property and casualty) are taxed on an income base equivalent to that of other corporate taxpayers.

Nature of the Restrictions

<u>Five-Year Rules</u>

Under Section 1504(c), a life insurance company cannot be included in a consolidated tax return with other non-life companies until the life company has been part of the affiliated group for five years. Moreover, net operating losses of a non-life member cannot be used to offset life subgroup income if the non-life member has not been part of the affiliated

[4] Pub. L. No. 94-455 (1976).

group for five years. Losses of non-life subgroup members that have been part of the affiliated group for less than five years are considered "ineligible losses" and can only be used to offset non-life subgroup taxable income.[5]

35% Loss Limitation Rules

Under Section 1503(c), if a life company is part of the consolidated group, the consolidated group is divided into a life subgroup and a non-life subgroup. Each subgroup must separately compute and keep track of its taxable income as well as its capital and ordinary losses. The losses of the non-life subgroup may be used to reduce life subgroup income, but only to the extent of the lesser of (i) 35% of the non-life subgroup losses or (ii) 35% of the life subgroup taxable income.

Restrictions are based on a tax regime for life insurers that no longer exists and serve no justifiable purpose

The prohibition on life insurance companies joining in a consolidated return dates back to 1928[6]. From 1921 through 1957, life insurance companies were taxed only on their "free" investment income: the amount of investment income not considered necessary to fund current and projected policyholder liabilities as required by state law. Various adjustments were made to the formula for determining the portion of investment income that was "free" between 1921 and 1957, but during this period, neither underwriting income nor capital gains from life insurance business were taxed[7].

The Life Insurance Company Income Tax Act of 1959 (the "1959 Act")[8] expanded the calculation of a life insurance company's taxes to include underwriting income in a complex "three phase" formula that remained in effect until 1984. With the passage of the 1959 Act, the tax base of life insurers began to resemble more closely that of other corporate taxpayers. The Deficit Reduction Act of 1984[9] sought to tax life insurance companies on gross income from all sources (investment and underwriting), reduced by ordinary and necessary business expenses plus reserve deductions for amounts put aside to fund current and projected liabilities to policyholders. Therefore, from 1984 forward, life insurance companies, like other taxpayers, have been subject to tax on all income:

---

[5] To guard against "incubating" a shell company for five years, Treas. Reg. Sec. 1.1502-47(d)(12) has rules such as requiring the conduct of an active trade or business, prohibiting a change in tax character and not allowing disproportionate asset acquisitions.

[6] Revenue Act of 1928, Pub. L. No. 562, sec. 141(e), Conference Committee Report Amendment No. 91, H.R. Rep. No 1882, 70th Cong., 1st Sess. 17 (1928).

[7] An extensive summary of the tax laws applicable to life insurance companies can be found in "AICPA Communication on Consolidate Returns and Life Insurance Companies", in *Insurance Tax Review* (March 1993), at 344 *et seq.*

[8] Pub. L. No. 86-69, sec. 4 (1959).

[9] Pub. L. No. 98-369, 98 Stat. 434 (1984)

investment, operating, and capital gain income. Passage of the Tax Reform Act of 1986[10], while not directed specifically at insurance companies, lowered corporate tax rates generally and eliminated special 20 percent deductions that life insurance and property casualty companies had received in the 1984 Act. So, from 1986 through the present, insurers have been taxed at the same 35% rate as other corporations.

Nonetheless, the limitations of Sections 1503(c) and 1504(c) remain in the tax code and continue to unfairly penalize any group containing a life insurance company member. Corporations in other industries can consolidate the income from various businesses into a single tax return by operating them as divisions of a single corporation. This avenue is generally not available to insurance companies because of both state insurance law and other non-tax business considerations that mandate operating through separate corporate entities.

Restrictions cause enormous administrative complexities

Consolidated return rules for all corporations (general business as well as insurance) are a complicated area without adding the limitations of Sections 1504(c), 1503(c) and Treas. Reg. §1.1502-47. Together these provisions create a level of complexity that makes little sense given the current system of taxing life insurance companies. The staff of the Joint Committee on Taxation in its 2001 study on tax simplification[11] noted:

> The treatment of affiliated groups of corporations that include both life insurance companies and other types of companies is more complicated than other types of affiliated groups that wish to file consolidated returns. The two five-year rules require substantial additional record-keeping and calculations by taxpayers, as well as creating complexity in structuring business transactions.[12]

Joint Committee staff recommended that the two five-year rules relating to consolidated returns of affiliated groups including life insurance and non-life insurance companies should be eliminated. They pointed to reductions in complexity associated with filing consolidated returns for affiliated groups including both life and non-life companies and also to reduction in complexity for both acquired corporations and existing members of affiliated groups in corporate acquisitions involving life and non-life companies with respect to record-keeping and calculation of tax liability.[13]

The complications caused by the five-year rules pale in comparison to the 35% limitation rules. To comply with the 35% rules, each year, two separate "subgroups" must be

---

[10] Pub. L. No. 99-514 (1986).

[11] *Study of the Overall State of the Federal Tax System and Recommendations for Simplification Pursuant to Section 8022(3)(B0 of the Internal Revenue Code of 1986,* JCS-3-01 April 2001.

[12] *Id.*, Vol. II at 382.

[13] *Id.*

created and maintained for tax accounting purposes – a life subgroup, and a non-life subgroup. The sole reason for establishing these subgroups is to keep the income and losses of each subgroup separate for purposes of applying the 35% limitations on loss utilization. Complex ordering rules are required that mandate loss carrybacks and carryforwards being applied within each subgroup before the net result can be combined with the other subgroup, if eligible. Losses carried back to any year guarantee the necessity of filing an amended return for the carryback year, as well as amended returns for subsequent years according to a set of complex "bumping" rules that determine from which subgroup losses are deemed to be utilized. While carrybacks and carryovers can always cause complications, the level of difficulty increases exponentially when the subgroup and ordering rules of the regulations are layered in[14].

One of our members, a large multi-line insurance company, provided us with the following real-life example of a recent acquisition. Both the acquiring company X and the acquired Company Y were primarily life insurance companies, but also have non-life subgroups in their consolidated returns. Each group filed a life/non-life consolidated return prior to the acquisition as did other companies acquired within the last five years. Here are some of the consequences:

- **Acquisition Triggers Five-Year Deconsolidation:** Instead of full consolidation to a single tax return as allowed with other corporations, the acquiring Company X must now file multiple (17) tax returns (see Appendix I)) including:
    - o the basic life/non-life return for the old Company X consolidated return (one return) and,
    - o life/life returns for life companies acquired in the Company Y acquisition (seven separate returns),
    - o non-life/non-life returns for non-life companies acquired in the Company Y acquisitions (nine separate returns), and
    - o various separate company (either life or non-life) returns for other companies acquired as part of the Y Company acquisition.
    - o Company X would also file multiple consolidated and separate returns with respect to other companies acquired within the last five years.

These multiple returns are required because the life/non-life limits require life insurers to wait five years to consolidate returns on newly acquired companies and further breaks up the existing life/non-life return of the acquired company into multiple separate and consolidated groups based upon the placement of non-life companies in the organization

[14] Treas. Reg. Sec. 1.1502-47 sets out a four step computation of income for each subgroup. First, separate consolidated life insurance company taxable income (LICTI) and non-life consolidated income are computed. Second, the subgroup results are carried back to prior years in each subgroup with the possibility of "bumping" a prior consolidated calculation. Third, after the carryback computation, a "bottom line" offset is calculated for the current year. Ordinary losses of one subgroup may offset ordinary income of the other subgroup (limited by the 35% restriction on non-life losses). Fourth, unused ordinary and capital losses carried forward from the current year must first offset the income of the subgroup that created the carryforward.

chart. *An acquisition that closed in 2005 will prevent the parent company from fully consolidating its return until 2011.*

- **Logical Business Operation Unnaturally Affected:** These artificial tax limits prevent the full integration of business operations after an acquisition. While business operations are usually integrated soon after an acquisition, the legal entities in some instances cannot be merged or consolidated until full tax consolidation is allowed. Due to the five-year rules, Company X must retain separate corporate status for many more subgroup members than normally are needed, while these companies are consolidated for business and GAAP reporting purposes. This adds unnecessary costs and complexity even where it doesn't increase the overall tax costs.

- **Non-Life Losses Artificially Segmented and Limited:** Even before the acquisition, Company X was subject to the 35 percent limit on consolidation of non-life insurance company losses. This limit, which was originally enacted to limit the use of property and casualty insurance losses to offset life insurance, applies to any loss from a company that is not a life company. Ironically, Company X has a consistently profitable property and casualty subsidiary that produces non-life taxable income. However, Company X's holding company has debt, most of which has been incurred to provide regulatory capital to life companies (the substantial portion of the consolidated groups business operations) or to acquire other businesses including the profitable life company business of Company Y. This holding company debt produces interest deductions (which are treated as non-life losses) while the life company capital produced by the borrowing produces life company income including the taxable income of the life companies in the Company Y group, which can not be fully offset by the deductions (i.e. subject to the 35% limitation).

Restrictions discriminate against life insurers

The life/non-life consolidated return penalties come into play only when a life insurance company enters the equation. If a general business corporation (or another financial services company), with no life insurance members in its consolidated group acquires an unprofitable property/casualty insurance company, there are no prohibitions or limitations on immediate utilization of the insurer's post-acquisition losses by the new consolidated return group. At a time when legislative initiatives have been taken to modernize financial services regulation and make it easier for banks, insurance companies and securities firms to combine to provide better services to customers and compete in the global marketplace, this puts life insurance companies at a particular and unjustifiable disadvantage. For these competitive reasons, in addition to providing a great reduction in the complexity of this portion of the Tax Code, sections 1503(c) and 1504(c) should be repealed.

As an example, one of our member companies reports that a major source of its non-life losses is generated by interest expense that stems from indebtedness incurred to finance strategic acquisitions. Their's is not a unique situation since state insurance laws and regulations effectively prohibit life insurance companies from bearing substantial debt.

This leads to issuance of debt by an affiliated non-life company. However, the consolidated return rules restrict offsetting the interest expense against what is often the sole source of income in the group: that of the life insurance companies. While these disallowed losses carry forward and can usually be utilized, there is a substantial risk that some of the losses will expire unused.

In addition to the deferral or possible loss of interest deductions on debt solely incurred to acquire a profitable life insurance company, the rules lead to other inequities. For example, multiple tax return filing groups create the potential for taxes on inter-company dividends, resulting in three levels of tax: a shareholder level of tax as well as two corporate levels of tax. (Corporate tax policy contemplates two levels of tax, but has traditionally avoided taxing the same income more than twice.) This triple taxation occurs because reallocating capital within the group can trigger a tax as if the affiliated units were unrelated and assets had changed ultimate ownership.

The result of these life/non-life consolidated return rules is to impose an unfair "surtax" on life insurers by effectively taxing more than their full, economic incomes. Member companies echo the concerns we have raised above concerning the complexity of these rules. One company estimates that the extra work required by the life/non-life consolidated return restrictions requires the equivalent of 12 professional employees to complete.

III. Conclusion

The consolidated return restrictions are remnants of a past era in the taxation of life insurance companies that are no longer relevant under current law. In today's world, life insurers are fully taxed on their total income and eager to fully benefit from modernization of financial services laws intended to allow them to compete equally in the new global market with other financial institutions. As has been shown, the justifications for these life insurance-only tax provisions no longer exist and they create enormous administrative burdens for the companies and the IRS. They also hinder the ability of life insurance companies to plan for the future, both in their core businesses and in any attempts to expand to other areas. For these reasons, ACLI urges the repeal of sections 1503(c) and 1504(c).

Appendix I

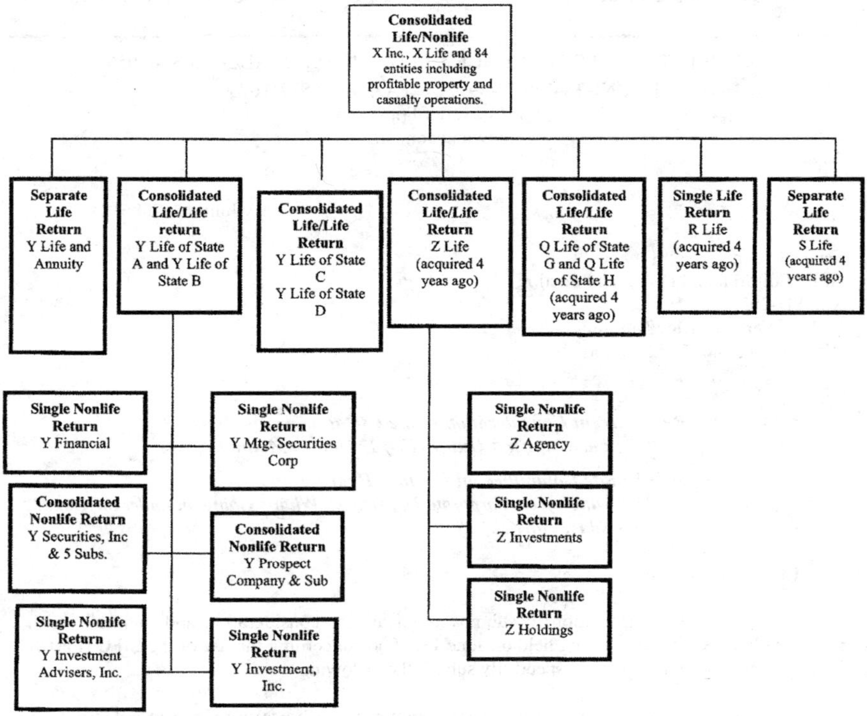

Color Key: Totals for Year
Black: 1 Life/Nonlife Tax Return
Red: 7 Life Insurance Tax Returns
Blue: 9 Nonlife Insurance Tax Returns

If full consolidation were allowed, one single and consolidated return would be filed and many of the life insurance companies acquired would be merged and the legal entities eliminated.

Willard J. De Filipps, CPA, P.C.

317 WEST PROSPECT AVENUE MT. PROSPECT, ILLINOIS 60056
PHONE (847) 577-3977 FAX (847) 577-1073
http://www.defilipps.com
cpawjd@aol.com

June 16, 2006

Senate Committee on Finance
Attn: Editorial and Document Section
Rm. SD-203
Dirksen Senate Office Building
Washington, D.C. 20510-6200

Re: Current Consideration of the Use of the Last-In, First-Out (LIFO) Inventory Method

Senate Committee on Finance Hearing
"A Tune-up on Corporate Tax Issues: What's Going on under the Hood?"
Tuesday, June 13, 2006

Dear Chairman Grassley:

In response to the invitation to submit comments for consideration and inclusion in the record with respect to the hearing held on June 13, 2006 concerning the use of the LIFO (Last-In, First-Out) inventory method, I respectfully submit the following.

My primary concern in submitting these comments is to raise my voice in defense of the many closely-held businesses that are currently using the LIFO method. I believe that the Senate Finance Committee should not overlook the vital role that LIFO has played in sustaining these businesses over the years. Although some may argue that consistency with international accounting standards is an important consideration, the economic well-being of a broad base of U.S. taxpayers - to the extent that it can be enhanced by the use of the LIFO method - should, in my opinion, be given greater attention and precedence over other considerations.

Don't Overlook Reliance on the LIFO Method by Closely-Held Businesses

In the real world, thousands of non-publicly-held businesses (i.e., closely-held businesses) are using the LIFO method, with all of its limitations and complexities. Consideration of "the LIFO issue" solely on the basis of financial statement reporting merits and/or a desire to reduce "complexity in the tax code" could severely penalize the many businesses who depend, in part, upon the continued use of the LIFO method to survive in a competitive, inflation-threatened economy.

(Continued)

At the June 13th hearing, Professor George A. Plesko mentioned the so-called incentives to use LIFO to manage earnings reported by publicly-held companies. This is far less a real factor in the decisions of the closely-held businesses using LIFO that I have been involved with for over 40 years. Rather than trying to "manage earnings," these businesses rely upon LIFO to provide additional cash (resulting from paying lower taxes on lower reported profits) so they can use the money not paid in taxes to purchase new inventory (which costs more as a result of inflation) to replace the goods that were sold.

Often, these businesses have used the "tax savings from LIFO" to finance the cost of constructing new and/or enlarged facilities, to meet payroll needs and to address other pressing working capital needs. And, most of these closely-held or non-publicly-held businesses, operating in their own best interests, provide jobs and growth here in the United States, rather than abroad.

Professor Plesko states that, in theory, firms using LIFO may have a greater opportunity to manage the earnings that they report to their shareholders. However, it has been my consistent experience over the years that the vast majority of decision-makers that I have worked with would rather sell a product/inventory immediately (notwithstanding its LIFO valuation) than hold on to it for "tax purposes" and thereby lose the opportunity to make the sale.

According to Prof. Plesko, again in theory, "firms may have an incentive to purchase unneeded inventory to avoid recognizing the additional taxable income." However, the more practical business considerations of the costs of financing and insuring the ***additional*** or ***unneeded*** inventory, not to mention the risk of loss by other means, far outweigh any other advantage that may theoretically exist. Also, effective measures exist by which the IRS can police such alleged tax-avoidance practices if they are suspected in the course of an audit examination.

More Useful Information Is Readily Available

I would urge the Committee to significantly question and to not rely entirely upon some of the inferences that otherwise might be drawn from Professor Plesko's comments about the use of LIFO by publicly-held companies. I believe that decisions about the continued viability of LIFO as part of the Internal Revenue Code should not be based on limited information drawn from the Fortune 1,000 (Prof. Plesko's Table 1).

The decline of the use of LIFO by "the 600 largest firms as reviewed by *Accounting Trends*" (Prof. Plesko's Figure 1) may be explained by many factors other than discontent over its impact on financial reporting. Perhaps there is a strong correlation between the inferred decline in the use of the LIFO method and the desire of publicly-held companies to manage and increase their reported earnings by discontinuing the use of a LIFO election.

In his comments, Professor Plesko refers to the findings reported in "Treasury I" that 95% of taxpayers use the FIFO (First-In, First-Out) cost-flow assumption/method. If I am not mistaken, "Treasury I" is now over 20 years old, and the years to which it referred in reporting on the use of LIFO further pre-date that 1984 report. ***This data is too far out of date to suggest anything meaningful.***

A much more useful statistic is readily available and would shed a far more informative light on the reliance on LIFO by non-publicly-held businesses.

Every business income tax return requires the completion of a few questions regarding inventory methods. On the second page, Question 9(d) in Schedule A of the current corporate income tax Form 1120 asks, simply, if the taxpayer used the LIFO inventory method in its calculation of taxable income for the year. Check the box, "Yes" or "No." If the answer is "Yes," then the taxpayer is required to report either (1) the percentage or (2) the dollar amounts of inventory computed by the use of the LIFO method. Comparable income tax returns for partnerships, electing S corporations and other businesses contain similar questions.

Is it not possible for Commissioner Everson to direct the IRS to collect this information for the Joint Committee? This ***current*** information on the use of LIFO by closely-held (i.e., non-publicly-held) businesses should be considered by the Committee in evaluating the potential impact of whatever action it may consider regarding the continuation of the use of the LIFO method. Given the remarkable strides that the IRS has reported in processing tax return information lately, the effort to collect this information about the use of LIFO in income tax returns should be minimal.

At the very least, I believe that the IRS should conduct a survey of the responses to these LIFO questions on the U.S. Income tax returns filed by all of the publicly-held companies. Either or both of these suggested surveys would provide the Committee with far more useful information than inferences from outdated *Accounting Trends* and/or Fortune 1,000 compilations.

An Alternative Proposal ... A LIFO User Surtax

It appears that the Committee may be considering only the two extreme alternatives of either (1) allowing LIFO to continue as is or (2) terminating or phasing out the use of LIFO entirely. I submit for your Committee's consideration a third alternative... Namely, ***a surtax or surcharge on the use of LIFO***.

Some twenty years ago, I submitted similar views in proposing a LIFO user surtax to the drafters of the Tax Reform Act of 1986. Reflecting on this surtax proposal today, in June, 2006, and under the current circumstances, I have even more reason to believe that this proposal has merit as a possible solution to avoid either extreme. A copy of this proposal is attached as Exhibit I.

There are many possibilities for adapting both the degree of impact and the calculation effect of any surtax on the use of the LIFO method. These variations should enable the Committee to fashion an approach that would permit at least closely-held businesses to continue to retain the benefits afforded by the use of the LIFO method.

While implementing the proposed surtax or surcharge on the use of LIFO may slightly increase the "complexity" of just one section of the Internal Revenue Code, a surtax, in my opinion, provides a better resolution of the matter than would adoption of either of the two extreme alternatives.

Furthermore, if a surtax or surcharge on the use of LIFO were implemented, taxpayers continuing to use the LIFO method would simply have to regard the additional computations and cost as (modest) offsets against the overall benefits that the use of the LIFO method provides. No taxpayer is required to elect LIFO … Therefore, any taxpayer that might consider the added burden or cost of the "surtax" on the use of LIFO to be excessive or unjust could simply elect to discontinue using the method.

LIFO Financial Statement Conformity Requirements

One of the aspects of the LIFO financial statement conformity requirements that Prof. Plesko did not address was the fact that taxpayers who use the LIFO method are permitted to report greater earnings for financial statement purposes than for income tax purposes by using different LIFO methods. In many cases, this is a common practice which achieves the desired results.

Many years ago, an AICPA Task Force studied what might be generally accepted and/or alternative practices for disclosing the use of LIFO in financial statements. The conclusions of this Task Force provide minimal guidance and permit many publicly-held companies to provide little useful information in their so-called LIFO-related disclosures.

I have enclosed, as Exhibit II, a discussion of the special challenges presented by the LIFO conformity requirements as they relate to the use of the LIFO method by closely-held businesses. This article may be useful in helping to understand the more practical impact of these requirements on the vast majority of companies that are outside of the publicly-held domain.

Finally, attached (Exhibit III) is an article that, despite being written long ago, demonstrates two significant points that are relevant to today's discussions of the use of LIFO.

First, not much has changed over the years in connection with the basic requirements and principles by which taxpayers must abide if they want to use the LIFO method for valuing their inventories for income tax purposes. (The article was written long before the IRS promulgated in 1992 a safe-harbor calculation approach for automobile dealers' new vehicle inventories on LIFO.)

Second, and more importantly, by its specific industry application, this article identifies just one of the many broad U.S. industries which the Committee might otherwise overlook if its consideration of this issue is not broadened to include the significant, beneficial impact that the use of LIFO has for non-publicly-held (i.e., closely-held) businesses.

In Conclusion

I believe that the Committee's consideration of the continued use of LIFO should not be limited, as it appeared to be in the June 13, 2006 hearing, to information on the use of the LIFO method by publicly-held corporations, or by the acceptance (or disfavor) of LIFO among the academic and international communities.

I would urge the Committee to give careful consideration to the articulate writings of some of the advocates of the use of the LIFO method in its emerging years (and particularly, with regard to the development and ultimate acceptability of the dollar-value LIFO method by the Tax Court). These discussions of sound accounting theory should not be ignored at this time in an effort to arrive at a simple, one-size-fits-all solution.

Also, I believe that a surtax on the use of LIFO should be considered as an alternative to its complete elimination or its retention in the Internal Revenue Code without change.

Since beginning practice as a CPA over 40 years ago, I have seen LIFO used as an important business and income tax strategy by countless closely-held businesses. I cannot help but protest as much as possible the one-sided and oversimplified attention that is focused on the use of the LIFO method when it is considered only in the context of publicly-held and/or international companies.

In addition to teaching seminars on the use of LIFO all over the country and consulting with closely-held businesses and CPA firms, I have written extensively on LIFO issues in my publication, the *LIFO Lookout*. For a comprehensive, topical index listing all articles from 1991 to Dec. 2005, see www.defilipps.com (follow the "Publication" and "Index of Articles" links).

Thank you for the opportunity to present my views and proposal for a LIFO user surtax. I would be pleased to expand on these comments and suggestions if you would like further information.

Sincerely,

Willard J. De Filipps

Willard J. De Filipps, CPA

Willard J. De Filipps, CPA, P.C.

317 WEST PROSPECT AVENUE MT. PROSPECT, ILLINOIS 60056
PHONE (847) 577-3977 FAX (847) 577-1073
http://www.defilipps.com
cpawjd@aol.com

June 16, 2006

Senate Committee on Finance
Attn: Editorial and Document Section
Rm. SD-203
Dirksen Senate Office Building
Washington, D.C. 20510-6200

Re:* *Current Consideration of the Use of the Last-In, First-Out (LIFO) Inventory Method

Senate Committee on Finance Hearing
"A Tune-up on Corporate Tax Issues: What's Going on under the Hood?"
Tuesday, June 13, 2006

EXHIBIT I*

SURTAX ON THE USE OF THE LIFO (LAST-IN, FIRST-OUT) INVENTORY METHOD

A Proposal Originally Submitted July 29, 1986
To the Department of the Treasury, Deputy Assistant Secretary (Tax Analysis)

* Attachment to Comment Letter dated June 16, 2006

guest editorial

TAX ANALYSTS

LIFO-USER SURTAX

by Willard J. De Filipps

Willard J. De Filipps is a CPA from Mt. Prospect, Illinois. His editorial on a LIFO-user surtax is based on a proposal he made to the drafters of the Tax Reform Act of 1986. The views expressed in guest editorials do not reflect the views of Tax Analysts.

The guest editorial page is open to any person who wishes to express an opinion on tax or fiscal policy. It is our hope that the views expressed in our guest editorials will contribute to the development of a sound and administrable system of taxation. Please address proposed guest editorials to Tim Vettel on our Special Reports and Articles staff.

If it is necessary to raise business taxes, all corporations should share that burden as fairly as possible. Under the Tax Reform Act of 1986 (TRA 1986), corporations with large investments in depreciable properties lost investment credits and depreciation advantages, but many inventory-intensive businesses using the LIFO (last-in, first-out) inventory method were relatively untouched. This disparity was not addressed in TRA 1986, even though it seems less than equitable.

LIFO inventory tax deferrals may be built up and grow steadily for decades, thus affording the inventory-intensive business a tax-timing deferral that...spans the entire corporate existence.

I suggest a "LIFO-user surtax." This could be imposed on a short-term basis as a percentage of the *addition* each year to a LIFO inventory reserve account. The actual rate of the LIFO-user surtax could be adjusted based on the overall revenue needs and phased out or terminated at a future date.

Major depreciation adjustments, considered only as tax deferrals, tend to self-correct over the depreciable life of the asset or the period it is actually owned. On the other hand, LIFO inventory tax deferrals may be built up and grow steadily for decades, thus affording the inventory-intensive business a tax-timing deferral that in some cases spans the entire corporate existence!

Knowledgeable advisors avoid discussing the enormous revenue potential or distract attention from the issue by showing how 'complex' or 'burdensome' the LIFO rules are.

It seems a major group of taxpayers (LIFO users) is just hoping it can remain unnoticed a little longer, so its ox is not gored. Knowledgeable advisors avoid discussing the enormous revenue potential or distract attention from the issue by showing how "complex" or "burdensome" the LIFO rules are. All the more reason for a tax on LIFO's use—for within its subjective boundaries many corporations have been able to provide significantly lower effective rates for themselves over the years.

Basic Mechanics of the Proposal: A Modest Tax Tradeoff

Under the proposal, any business now using the LIFO inventory method or electing to use it in the future would simply pay a surtax in years when its LIFO reserve increased. The surtax could be a flat percentage of the current year's addition, collected as part of the regular income tax. In the interests of simplicity and revenue-preservation, there would be no refund of the surtax in years when the LIFO reserve decreased. Applied in this way, it would be a "one way" (or nonrefundable) surtax paid for the privilege of obtaining an indefinite tax deferral arising from the impact of inflation on inventory costs. The LIFO-user surtax would be part of the net cost to be considered in using LIFO after the enactment of TRA 1986. It would be similar to emergency excise taxes levied by some states on ACRS accelerated depreciation deductions.

The LIFO-user surtax would not tax existing LIFO reserve balances: it would tax LIFO deferrals only as they are being built up and prevent such increases from avoiding a preference tax obligation because of *other* (non-LIFO) offsetting factors. Such an approach avoids more detailed accounting or classification problems that could arise if LIFO reserve additions were to be treated as separate tax preference items.

Also, LIFO reserves already built up under the former, higher rates will be taxed at lower post-1986 corporate rates as they are taken into income. Thus, a LIFO-user surtax would partially offset the overall loss in Federal tax revenues by acting as a tax on this eventual "windfall" for LIFO users.

Further Practical Justification for a LIFO-User Surtax

A LIFO-user surtax has even more practical justification: It would indirectly address some of the problems the IRS faces due to the increasing use of LIFO by many companies and its own limited manpower. These problems result where factors *other than inflation* are not removed from the computation of an addition to the LIFO reserve. In such cases, exaggerated indexes that do not reflect only inflation are produced.

The position of the Internal Revenue Service and the Tax Court is simply that if factors other than inflation enter into the LIFO inventory computations, the result does not clearly reflect income. In many cases where these other factors, such as technological change or improved product performance, have not been removed, the tax deferral gained under LIFO is not the legitimate deferral it should be under Code section 472.

Many LIFO-using companies and advisors know this, but simply wait for the IRS to challenge their calculations. In some instances, the Service rarely—or ineffectually—makes the challenge. If you ask them, IRS and Treasury officials will readily admit that examining agents are poorly trained or unprepared to audit many LIFO inventory applications. Agent competence, familiarity, and interpretation of LIFO inventory "rules" is less than uniform—to say the least.

In other instances, taxpayers naturally resolve subjective or "gray area" issues in their own favor. This results in significant increases in LIFO reserves which simply prolong or increase LIFO deferral benefits within legitimate bounds. In these circumstances, the proposed LIFO-user surtax would represent a *modest* lessening of the overall benefit from unchallenged interpretations of the rules.

A portion of the funds collected from the proposed LIFO-user surtax might even be earmarked for further training of IRS agents in this complex area, which might result in even greater yields in audit situations.

Willard J. De Filipps, CPA, P.C.

317 WEST PROSPECT AVENUE MT. PROSPECT, ILLINOIS 60056
PHONE (847) 577-3977 FAX (847) 577-1073
http://www.defilipps.com
cpawjd@aol.com

June 16, 2006

Senate Committee on Finance
Attn: Editorial and Document Section
Rm. SD-203
Dirksen Senate Office Building
Washington, D.C. 20510-6200

Re: Current Consideration of the Use of the Last-In, First-Out (LIFO) Inventory Method

Senate Committee on Finance Hearing
"A Tune-up on Corporate Tax Issues: What's Going on under the Hood?"
Tuesday, June 13, 2006

*EXHIBIT II**

SPECIAL LIFO CHALLENGES: CONFORMITY REPORTING REQUIREMENTS AND PROJECTIONS FOR YEAR-END PLANNING

***De Filipps'* LIFO Lookout**
December 2005

* Attachment to Comment Letter dated June 16, 2006

SPECIAL LIFO CHALLENGES: CONFORMITY REPORTING REQUIREMENTS AND PROJECTIONS FOR YEAR-END PLANNING

YEAR END ALERT

Taxpayers using Last-In, First-Out (LIFO) for valuing their inventories are often under great pressure to issue their financial statements as quickly after the year-end as possible. Whether under great time pressure or not, any taxpayer using LIFO must be sure that all year-end statements satisfy all of the LIFO conformity requirements. If they do not, the taxpayer risks the loss of its LIFO election.

There are many year-end LIFO conformity requirements, and there are many kinds of businesses using LIFO. All taxpayers using LIFO must comply with all of the year-end financial statement conformity reporting requirements in order to remain eligible to use the method.

As emphasized throughout the discussions on the following pages of the special rules and IRS guidance for auto dealerships, taxpayers outside the scope of that guidance should be careful ***not*** to rely on that guidance as if the IRS had generalized or intended it to be applicable in their own different situations or industries. Similarly, auto dealerships - although benefiting from some clarification by the IRS

see **CONFORMITY REPORTING REQUIREMENTS**, page 6

SPECIAL YEAR-END CHALLENGES FOR LIFO USERS

CONFORMITY REPORTING REQUIREMENTS

YEAR-END PROJECTIONS FOR PLANNING PURPOSES

(Continued from page 5)

on certain reporting issues - should be careful ***not*** to rely on that guidance as if the IRS had generalized or intended it to be applicable beyond the carefully worded "scope" sections in Revenue Ruling 97-42 and in Revenue Procedure 97-44.

BASIC LIFO ELIGIBILITY REQUIREMENTS: "CONFORMITY" IS ONLY ONE

First: the bigger picture, of which conformity is only a part. The IRS can disallow a taxpayer's LIFO election if it finds a violation of any one of four eligibility requirements. The four requirements involve cost, conformity, consent, and the maintenance of adequate books and records.

TERMINATION SITUATIONS

1. Failure to value LIFO inventory at cost for tax purposes for the year preceding the year of LIFO election, the election year, and in all subsequent years ***(Cost).***
2. Violation of the financial statement reporting conformity requirements for the election year and all subsequent years ***(Conformity).***
3. Failure to properly elect LIFO, including the failure to file Form 970 ***(Consent).***
4. Failure to maintain adequate books and records with respect to the LIFO inventory and all computations related to it ***(Adequate Books & Records).***

In 1999, in *Mountain State Ford Truck Sales v. Commissioner*, the Tax Court held that the taxpayer's use of replacement cost for valuing parts inventories could not be employed as a substitute for actual cost in connection with LIFO inventories ... nor for any other non-LIFO inventories. Although the IRS subsequently issued Revenue Procedure 2002-17, effectively negating the Tax Court's holding in *Mountain State*, this case serves as a warning that whenever the IRS chooses, it can take a very aggressive position, threatening the very existence of a long-standing LIFO election.

If a violation of any one of the four eligibility requirements occurs, the Internal Revenue Service has the discretionary power to allow the LIFO election - if it can be persuaded to exercise that power in the taxpayer's favor. For example, Revenue Procedure 79-23 reflects the position of the Service that a LIFO election can be disallowed if the taxpayer fails to maintain adequate books and records with respect to the LIFO inventory and computations related to it.

However, if a taxpayer is able to reconstruct the information necessary to calculate the LIFO inventory amount properly, it ***may*** be possible to avoid termination of the LIFO election for a violation of the "books and records" requirement.

Revenue Procedure 79-23 (1979-1 C.B. 564) states that in other circumstances where disputes with the IRS arise over computational errors, incorrect pool selection or item determination, or differences in the levels of costing inventories between financial statements and tax returns - the IRS is not authorized to terminate the taxpayer's LIFO election.

However, where the LIFO violations involve cost, conformity, Form 970 consent matters or "inadequate books and records," the Service usually looks to invoke this more dramatic measure. In *Mountain State Ford Truck Sales*, the Tax Court expressed the position that the list of four "termination situations" in Rev. Proc. 79-23 was not an exclusive listing ... In other words, other circumstances or situations might support the Service taking the position that a LIFO election should be terminated.

Revenue Procedure 97-44, which allowed certain taxpayers (automobile dealerships) with conformity violations to avoid termination of their LIFO elections by paying a 4.7% penalty amount, should also be regarded as a very limited exception to the IRS general approach of terminating a LIFO election whenever it uncovers an eligibility violation.

FORM 970 QUESTIONS REGARDING CONFORMITY

Form 970 is the LIFO election form which is required to be included with the tax return for the first LIFO year. One of the significant traps for the unwary is that Form 970 asks only whether the year-end financial statements *for the election year* have satisfied certain conformity requirements.

On its face, Form 970 does not warn taxpayers that these conformity requirements must be satisfied for every year-end financial statement for as long as the LIFO method is being used. This requirement is spelled out in Reg. Sec. 1.472-2(e)(1).

Worse yet, the relatively limited Form 970 instructions give no hint of the many troublesome interpretations that can arise under the Regulations. As evidenced by the debacle that auto dealers and their CPAs floundered through for nearly a decade (and that resulted in Rev. Proc. 97-44), it would seem that many practitioners have never even looked at, much less attempted to study in detail, the Regulations dealing with this critical issue.

→

CONFORMITY REQUIREMENTS... THERE ARE MANY

There are many conformity requirements. They exist as restrictions on a taxpayer's general desire to pay lower taxes using a LIFO method for valuing inventories, while reporting more income to shareholders or banks and other creditors using a non-LIFO method. To prevent this from happening, the Treasury says that LIFO must be used in all reports covering a full year to insure that the use of LIFO for tax purposes conforms as nearly as possible with the best accounting practice in the trade or business in order to provide a clear reflection of income.

It is often stated that LIFO must be used to compute income in the year-end ***financial statements***. However, it is more technically correct to state that the IRS only requires LIFO to be used in the primary presentation of income (i.e., in the Income Statement). For most taxpayers, the LIFO conformity requirements pose at least two general sets of requirements:

TWO SETS OF REQUIREMENTS

FIRST, they require that any year-end financial statements ***issued in the traditional report form*** by the business to creditors, shareholders, partners or other users must reflect the year-end results on LIFO.

SECOND, they also require all year-end ***manufacturer-formatted financial statements*** sent by certain dealers to a manufacturer/supplier/creditor (12th, 13th and any other fiscal year-end statements) to reflect LIFO results.

A taxpayer may adopt LIFO only if it has used no other procedure than LIFO in preparing an Income Statement or a profit or loss statement covering the first taxable year of adoption. As noted previously, for subsequent taxable years, similar restrictions are imposed. However, the Commissioner has the discretion to allow a taxpayer to continue to use the LIFO method even though conformity violations might have occurred.

Accordingly, a LIFO reserve, no matter how large, can be completely and abruptly lost if careful attention is not paid to the conformity requirements in year-end, manufacturer-formatted financial statements sent to the Factory/Manufacturer/Supplier...as well as in the more conventional year-end statements issued in report form by CPAs.

EVERY YEAR, ALL OF THE CONFORMITY REQUIREMENTS MUST BE MET

To remain eligible to use LIFO, ***every year***, the last monthly statement for the year sent to the manufacturer and/or any other credit source must reflect an estimate of the year-end change in the LIFO reserve if the actual change cannot be computed before the statement has to be released.

If a taxpayer is thinking about making a LIFO election for the year, then it should place an estimate of the year-end LIFO reserve ...or the actual amount if it has been calculated... in the year-end statements (including those issued to the Factory/Manufacturer or issued to any other party) in order to preserve its ability to elect LIFO when it files Form 970 as part of its Federal income tax return for the year at a later date.

Also, the expansion of the conformity requirements to other classes of goods should not be overlooked if a taxpayer is already on LIFO for one class of inventory (such as new vehicles or equipment) and is considering extending LIFO to another class of inventory (such as used vehicles, equipment or parts). In this situation, the year-end Income Statements should also reflect an estimate of the LIFO reserve expected to be produced by extending the LIFO election(s) to the additional classes of goods under consideration.

TRADITIONAL FINANCIAL STATEMENTS IN ANNUAL REPORTS ISSUED BY CPAs

This section deals with reports issued by CPAs, where the CPA controls the release, content and format of the financial statements, notes and supplementary information. These are unlike monthly statements which may be prepared internally by the taxpayer's accounting department or controller and sent out to a manufacturer, supplier or other creditor without direct CPA involvement or review.

The LIFO conformity requirement as it relates to reports issued by CPAs requires that in the primary presentation of income (i.e., the Income Statement), the results disclosed must only be the net-of-LIFO results. The primary Income Statement *cannot* show results before LIFO, followed by either an addition or subtraction for the net LIFO change, coming down to a final net income or loss after-LIFO figure. This means that during a period of rising prices, a business using LIFO will usually be reporting lower operating results in order to comply with the conformity requirements. Very strict disclosure limitations existed with no room for deviation for many years.

The Regulations were liberalized in 1981 and they now allow LIFO taxpayers to disclose non-LIFO operating results in *supplementary financial statements*, as long as those supplementary non-LIFO financial statements satisfy two tests: ***First***, they must be issued as part of a report which includes the

see **CONFORMITY REPORTING REQUIREMENTS**, page 8

Conformity Reporting Requirements (Continued from page 7)

primary presentation of income on a LIFO basis. ***Second***, each non-LIFO financial statement must contain on its face a warning or statement to the reader that the non-LIFO results are supplementary to the primary presentation of income which is on a LIFO basis. Accordingly, in CPA-prepared year-end financial statements, a LIFO taxpayer's results on a non-LIFO basis can be fully disclosed as supplementary information if both of these requirements are met.

Alternatively, the Regulations permit disclosure of non-LIFO results in a footnote to the regular year-end financial statements, as long as the Statement of Income itself does not disclose this information parenthetically or otherwise on its face, and the notes are all presented together and accompany the Income Statement in a single report.

As a result of these "liberalizations" in the Regulations in 1981, these LIFO conformity requirements should not present any major reporting problems for reports issued by CPAs.

DEALERSHIP YEAR-END STATEMENTS SENT TO MANUFACTURER/SUPPLIER/CREDITORS

Many CPAs serving automobile dealerships are now aware that the Regulations contain several year-end LIFO reporting restrictions which apply to the specially formatted financial statements sent by auto dealerships and other businesses immediately after year-end to the Manufacturer/Supplier/Creditors. Some of those CPAs who were not had a rude awakening when their (former) dealer clients - through their attorneys - asked them to reimburse the dealers for their payments of the 4.7% penalty "settlement amounts" due under Revenue Procedure 97-44.

For automobile dealerships, and for any other LIFO users who have similar year-end reporting fact patterns or requirements, these restrictions on year-end dealership-issued statements pose fatal LIFO traps that are much harder to deal with than those for year-end reports issued by CPAs.

The Regulations provide that any Income Statement that reflects a full year's operations must report on a LIFO basis. This requirement applies regardless of whether the Income Statement is the last in a series of interim statements, or a December statement which shows two columns, one for the current month results and another for the year-to-date cumulative results.

The Regulations further provide that a series of credit statements or financial reports is considered a single statement or report covering a period of operations if the statements or reports in the series are prepared using a single inventory method and can be combined to disclose the income, profit, or loss for the period. See Reg. Sec. 1.472-2(e)(6). If one can combine or "aggregate" a series of interim or partial-year statements to disclose the results of operations for a full year, then the last Income Statement must reflect income computed using LIFO to value the inventory.

Literally interpreted, this wording applies to all franchised auto dealers' 12th statements (i.e., December unadjusted) as well as to their 13th statements. The 12th statement is usually issued on a preliminary basis, before accruals and estimates are refined by detailed adjusting entries. The 13th statement is usually issued several weeks after the 12th statement, and it reflects year-end accrual adjustments and other computations not otherwise completed within the tight time frame for the issuance of the December or 12th statement (usually by the 10th day of the following month).

The IRS National Office confirmed dealers' worst fears during 1995 in LTR 9535010. In this Letter Ruling, a calendar year dealership raised the conformity question in the context of what happens when the monthly statements, including the December year-end statement, are not on LIFO but the CPA prepares annual audited financial statements for the dealership which do reflect LIFO.

Here, the taxpayer's argument was that the CPA's audited statements reflecting LIFO were the primary financial statements, while the monthly statements sent by the dealership to the manufacturer and to the credit corporation were "supplementary statements." The IRS concluded that the dealer in LTR 9535010 had violated the LIFO conformity requirement because:

IRS TESTS

1. The dealership used an inventory method other than LIFO in ascertaining its income in the monthly financial statements,
2. The financial statements ascertained income for the "taxable year,"
3. The financial statements were "for credit purposes," and
4. The financial statements were not within any of the exceptions to the LIFO conformity requirements that are provided in the Regulations.

With respect to the use of the financial statements "for credit purposes," the IRS found that a debtor-creditor relationship did exist between the dealership and the manufacturer and the credit corporation. The IRS stated that if the taxpayer's "operations began to deteriorate, it is doubtful that Corp. X (the manufacturer) and Corp. Y (the Credit Corporation) would ignore these reports and continue to →

extend credit to T (the taxpayer) as though nothing has changed." The IRS noted that the taxpayer was unable to provide any explanation of what purpose other than credit evaluation the credit subsidiary might have for requesting the dealer's financial statements.

In a companion letter ruling, LTR 9535009, the IRS "officially" restated its position with respect to a dealer who reported for tax purposes using a fiscal year. The IRS employed the same four-step analysis as above to determine whether the fiscal year dealership had violated the LIFO conformity requirements. In connection with the second "test" related to whether the dealership's financial statement to the Factory ascertained the taxpayer's income for the taxable year, the IRS noted that the year-to-date column information readily provides this computation for the reader. Even without year-to-date accumulations on the face of the monthly Income Statement, any series of months could simply be added together to reflect a complete 12-month period of anyone's choice.

LTR 9535009 states that the fiscal year dealer taxpayer issued a financial statement (in January, 19xx) that ascertained its income for the entire prior calendar year, and that calendar year statement is considered a statement covering the "taxable year" because it covers a 1-year period that both begins and ends in a taxable year or years for which the taxpayer used the LIFO method. This is the IRS' interpretation of Reg. Sec. 1.472-2(e)(2) which covers *one-year periods other than a taxable year.*

WARNING

- This would seem to be the position of the IRS for all taxpayers whose fact patterns fall under the Regulation.
- Only the special and limited relief afforded to certain dealers in Revenue Ruling 97-42 and Revenue Procedure 97-44 (discussed next) saved some taxpayers from the consequences of this narrow and harsh interpretation.

REV. RUL. 97-42: DISCLOSURE GUIDELINES FOR CERTAIN DEALERS

On September 25, 1997, the IRS issued Revenue Ruling 97-42 which provides special interpretations allowing auto dealers to satisfy the LIFO conformity requirements. ***These special interpretations apply only to a year-end financial statement prepared in a format required by an automobile manufacturer on preprinted forms supplied by the automobile manufacturer.***

Placement in the Income Statement. LIFO adjustments must appear in the twelfth month Income Statement. However, they do ***not*** have to be reflected in the Cost of Goods Sold section through the inventory valuation accounts. As long as the LIFO adjustments are reflected somewhere in the determination of net income on the Income Statement, that conformity requirement will be satisfied.

Revenue Ruling 97-42 makes it clear that if a LIFO reserve adjustment is posted directly to the retained earnings account and reflected on the dealership's Balance Sheet, that treatment of the LIFO reserve change will ***not*** satisfy the conformity requirement. For years ending after October 14, 1997, it is thus imperative that the LIFO adjustment be properly reflected in the Income Statement prepared for the last month of the year.

Use of estimates. A "reasonable estimate" of the change in the LIFO reserve for the year may be reflected instead of the actual change..., as long as that "reasonable estimate" is reflected somewhere in the year-end Statement of Income.

No one knows what the IRS will accept as a "reasonable estimate." Similarly, no one knows what procedures the IRS will accept as being "reasonable" in the preparation of an estimate of the change of the LIFO reserve for the year.

Fiscal year taxpayers. If an auto dealer employs a fiscal taxable year, and reflects the LIFO change in Cost of Goods Sold or anywhere else in the Income Statement, the LIFO conformity requirements can be satisfied in either of two ways: ***First***, the dealer may make an adjustment for the change in the LIFO reserve that occurred during the calendar year in the month and year-to-date column of the ***December*** Income Statement.

Alternatively, the dealer may make an adjustment for the change in the LIFO reserve that occurred during the fiscal year in the month and year-to-date columns of the Income Statements provided for the ***last month of the fiscal year.***

In other words, the IRS does not require the change in the LIFO reserve to be updated twice in the fiscal year-end... calendar year-end sequence. The IRS will permit a timing mismatch under these limited circumstances. For example, in a situation where a dealer has a September fiscal year-end and December (calendar) reporting year to the manufacturer: If the dealer reflects the (reasonable estimate) change in the LIFO reserve in the September monthly and year-end statement, that dealer does not need to recompute and update a LIFO change for the three month period from October 1 through December 31 and reflect a 3-month change in the December statement.

The dealer may simply carry through the annual LIFO reserve change effect reflected in the Septem-

see **CONFORMITY REPORTING REQUIREMENTS**, page 10

Conformity Reporting Requirements

(Continued from page 9)

ber fiscal year-end Income Statement without modification in the December Income Statement. Note that the December Income Statement must reflect the charge against income for the prior fiscal year-end LIFO reserve change and that prior September fiscal year-end LIFO reserve change should ***not*** be reversed so that the December Statement of Income does not reflect any LIFO reserve charge for the twelve month period ending December 31.

REV. PROC. 97-44: LIMITED RELIEF FOR CERTAIN DEALERS

Revenue Procedure 97-44 provided "relief" to auto dealers whose year-end Factory statements failed to satisfy the conformity requirements at any time during a six-year "look-back" period. These dealers were allowed to keep their LIFO elections if they paid a 4.7% penalty/settlement tax based on the amount of their LIFO reserves as of the last taxable year ended on or before October 14, 1997 (i.e., as of December 31, 1996 for most calendar-year auto dealers). These dealers were also required to satisfy certain other conditions as terms of the settlement.

In Revenue Procedure 98-46, the IRS extended this relief for similar conformity violations to all medium and heavy-duty truck dealers, providing them with a slightly different series of payments dates.

One of the major traps that practitioners and auto dealers now face is in the lack of synchronization between the language in Revenue Ruling 97-42 and the language in Revenue Procedure 97-44. Revenue Ruling 97-42 applies to the issuance of statements to a "credit subsidiary." In contrast, Revenue Procedure 97-44 contains broader language in its scope (Section 3) referring to the providing "for credit purposes" ... of an Income Statement in the format required by the franchisor.

See the analyses of Revenue Procedure 97-44 in the September, 1997 and December, 1997 issues of the *LIFO Lookout* for discussions of the settlement amount 4.7% penalty payment and many questions that still remain unanswered.

SPECIAL INTERPRETATIONS CLARIFIED ONLY FOR AUTO DEALERS ... ALL OTHER LIFO USERS BEWARE

Different year-ends for book and tax purposes (fiscal years). LIFO conformity problems are multiplied where a taxpayer has a different year-end for reporting to a manufacturer, supplier, or creditor (calendar year-Dec. 31) than the fiscal year it uses to report for income tax return purposes and for other financial statement reporting purposes.

For these fiscal year taxpayers... other than auto dealers and light, medium & heavy-duty truck dealers... in order to satisfy another strict conformity requirement, the full-year Income Statements must reflect LIFO at the end of *both* twelve month annual reporting periods or years (Reg. Sec. 1.472-2(e)(2)).

This Regulation states that the conformity rules also apply to (1) the determination of income, profit, or loss for a one-year period other than a taxable year, and to (2) credit statements or financial reports that cover a one-year period other than a taxable year, but only if the one-year period both begins and ends in a taxable year or years for which the taxpayer uses the LIFO method for Federal income tax purposes. For example,...in the case of a calendar year taxpayer, the requirements...apply to the taxpayer's determination of income for purposes of a credit statement that covers the period October 1, 1981, through September 30, 1982, if the taxpayer uses the LIFO method for Federal income tax purposes in taxable years 1981 and 1982.

Placement of LIFO change in the year-end Statement of Income. In fighting with auto dealers over conformity, in 1994 the IRS informally indicated that on the last monthly (i.e., twelfth) statement, the LIFO adjustment had to be run through the Cost of Goods Sold section (via the beginning-of-the-year and the end-of-the-year inventory valuations), rather than through an other income/deductions account...or else dealers would not be in compliance with the LIFO year-end conformity requirement. The IRS subsequently retreated on this "placement" issue in Revenue Ruling 97-42.

For LIFO taxpayers other than those dealers indicated above, where and how the year-end LIFO adjustment is placed on the Income Statement is still critical. The IRS "only-through-Cost-of-Goods-Sold" interpretation could result in countless LIFO election terminations in situations where the (projected) change in the LIFO reserve at year-end was placed in some other section of the Income Statement, such as with an *Other Income* or *Other Deductions*. Fortunately, in Revenue Ruling 97-42, the IRS said (to certain dealers only) that the LIFO adjustment could be placed anywhere on the Income Statement.

Unfortunately, the IRS "guidance" for franchised auto dealers in Revenue Ruling 97-42 and the "relief" for prior conformity violations under Revenue Procedures 97-44 and 98-46 ***do not apply*** to any other types of taxpayers issuing what might be "similar" statements under "similar circumstances" to other manufacturers, suppliers or credit sources. No one can be sure what these other businesses with LIFO

→

violations should do in light of what is now understood to be the IRS interpretation of these Regulations.

> **WARNING**
> All taxpayers ... other than automobile and truck dealerships ... using LIFO who issue monthly statements to manufacturers, suppliers or creditors are not protected by the special rules in Revenue Ruling 97-42 which modify the Regulations only for special reporting situations faced by auto dealers.

What should these businesses/taxpayers be told about their LIFO elections? Are they subject to retroactive termination of their LIFO elections at any time, literally at will, by the IRS? What responsibility does the CPA practitioner have as preparer of the tax return now that the IRS position has been more clearly set forth in Revenue Ruling 97-42? These are the questions that (should) haunt practitioners and their clients today.

CONFORMITY VIOLATIONS CANNOT BE CORRECTED ONCE THE YEAR-END FINANCIAL STATEMENTS HAVE BEEN RELEASED

What if year-end financial statements are issued (in a hurry) and the conformity requirements have been overlooked?

The position of the IRS is that once a year-end Income Statement has been issued or released on a non-LIFO basis, that statement cannot be recalled and corrected to reflect LIFO by the re-issuance of statements satisfying the conformity requirement. Furthermore, it then becomes discretionary with the IRS Commissioner as to whether or not the Commissioner chooses to terminate the taxpayer's LIFO election as a penalty for the violation.

The *William Powell Company* decision (81-1 USTC ¶ 9449) illustrates one taxpayer's success (or possibly good fortune) in avoiding termination of its LIFO election when it came down to "all-or-nothing" on this issue. This case, decided in 1981, involved what would have been the termination of a LIFO election made in 1973 because at the end of the first LIFO year, the taxpayer had issued non-LIFO statements and then later made a LIFO election when it filed its tax return.

In that case, the taxpayer recalled its previous non-LIFO statements and replaced/reissued LIFO statements to all the banks, creditors and shareholders before the income tax return for the first year was filed. The taxpayer probably would have lost its LIFO election if it had litigated the issue in the Tax Court, but the taxpayer chose to litigate this issue in the District Court in Ohio.

The taxpayer took the position that it had not "used" FIFO within the meaning of Section 472(c). Its position with respect to Section 472(c)(2) was that non-LIFO "worksheets" were not used for "credit purposes," since the credit had been extended prior to the delivery of the worksheets. The District Court accepted the taxpayer's arguments. With respect to Section 472(c)(1), Powell contended that *use* is determined at the time of the LIFO election and that this election need not be made until the taxpayer files its return. At the time Powell elected LIFO, it was no longer *using* the FIFO statements, inasmuch as they had been recalled prior to the election and LIFO statements had been reissued.

The District Court, while agreeing that Powell's activities seemed to violate the plain language of Section 472(c)(2), was hesitant to strictly apply the "plain meaning rule" in this case. The Court said that it is the general rule that the words of a revenue statute are interpreted "in their ordinary, everyday senses," and a rigid application of this rule would not be consistent with the Commissioner's ongoing interpretation of the conformity requirement.

HOW SOME BUSINESSES GET AROUND THE LIFO CONFORMITY LIMITATIONS

Many businesses using LIFO - especially publicly-held companies reporting to the SEC - would like to reduce taxes by reporting lower taxable income/earnings in tax returns while at the same time reporting higher earnings/more income to their shareholders and creditors for financial and market valuation purposes. This can be done easily, thanks to loopholes conveniently provided in the Regulations. But one has to know they are there.

The Regulations allow taxpayers to legitimately avoid the intent of the conformity requirement by allowing them to use LIFO methods and sub-elections in their financial statements that are different from those LIFO sub-elections and methods that are used in their income tax return computations. That's right: ***Different LIFO methods may be used for book and for tax purposes***. It is not necessary for the year-end financial statements to use the same exact LIFO sub-elections that are used in the tax return LIFO calculations. The Regulations simply require that both sets of financial statements (i.e., those included in the financial reports and those inherent in the income tax returns) must report using LIFO methods.

This allows some companies to use more pools ...in one case, several hundred more pools... for financial reporting purposes than for income tax purposes. Others use link-chain or link-chain, index

see CONFORMITY REPORTING REQUIREMENTS, page 12

Conformity Reporting Requirements (Continued from page 11)

(dollar-value) methods to lower LIFO income for tax purposes, while they use double-extension (dollar-value) LIFO methods for financial reports. Still others reconstruct long distant base prices for new items in their tax return LIFO calculations while they price new items at current cost in their financial statements. These companies enjoy the best of both worlds without violating the fine print of the "conformity" requirements.

Based on the foregoing, we continue to question the wisdom of the *advice* given by Wall Street to dealer groups going public in connection with terminating their LIFO elections. How many millions of dollars of LIFO deferral tax savings have been thrown away needlessly in exchange for the perceived benefit of higher earnings per share and hopefully higher market valuations? The significant - if not Draconian - penalties the investing marketplace exacts from businesses that miss their earnings per share projections by even a penny suggest that sacrificing real millions of LIFO tax deferral dollars "just for show" can be costly, if not almost unnecessary.

INTERIM REPORTS

Interim reports covering a period of operations that is less than the whole of a taxable year may be issued on a non-LIFO basis without violating the LIFO conformity requirement for tax purposes. The Regulations are completely clear and unambiguous on this point. Although generally accepted accounting principles may present some difficulties in this regard, the Income Tax Regulations clearly do not.

OTHER CONCERNS: *INSILCO* & SEC. 472(g)

For another example of how seriously the Treasury/IRS polices the LIFO conformity requirement, consider the origin of Code Section 472(g). This subsection was added because the IRS lost the *Insilco* decision in the Tax Court. This case involved a subsidiary using LIFO who reported to its parent corporation using LIFO, but the parent corporation reported its consolidated earnings (which included those of the LIFO-user subsidiary) to its own shareholders on a non-LIFO basis.

In upholding the taxpayer in *Insilco*, the Tax Court told the IRS that if it didn't like the result, it should get Congress to change the law. And that's exactly what the IRS/ Treasury did! After its loss, the Treasury persuaded Congress to change the law (which it did by adding subsection (g) to Section 472) so that taxpayers in the future couldn't get around the conformity requirement the way Insilco had.

Section 472(g) provides that all members of the same group of financially related corporations shall be treated as one taxpayer for purposes of the conformity provisions of the Internal Revenue Code. For purposes of these provisions, affiliated groups are determined by using a lower 50% ownership threshold (than 80%). Furthermore, Section 472(g)(2)(B) provides that any other group of corporations which consolidate or combine for purposes of financial statements...shall be treated as one taxpayer for purposes of the conformity provisions.

"CONFORMITY" ... WHERE FOREIGN CORPORATIONS ARE INVOLVED

As we have seen, collectively, Sections 472(c) and (e)(2) require that in the first year on LIFO ... and in all subsequent years ... financial statements must reflect the use of the LIFO method for valuing inventories. These requirements affect all financial statements covering a full year's operations that are issued to shareholders, partners, or other proprietors, or to beneficiaries, or for credit purposes.
The taxpayer may be required to discontinue the use of the LIFO inventory method if this requirement is violated.

Compliance with these requirements becomes more complicated when ***affiliated and/or consolidated groups*** exist. Section 472(g) provides that all members of the same group of financially related corporations are treated as a single taxpayer for purposes of the LIFO conformity requirements. The term "group of financially related corporations" means any affiliated group as defined in Section 1504(a), determined by substituting 50% for 80% each place where it appears, and any group of corporations that consolidate or combine for purposes of financial statements.

When ***foreign corporations*** are mixed in with U.S. corporations in various parent-subsidiary arrangements, compliance with these conformity rules and with Revenue Ruling 78-246 becomes even more complicated.

In Letter Ruling 200540005, dated June 20, 2005, the IRS addressed a situation involving the LIFO conformity requirement application to consolidated financial statements and foreign operations and subsidiaries.

A summary of Rev. Rul. 78-246 (1978-1 C.B. 146) and more details on LTR 200540005 appear on the facing page.

In this Ruling, the Service held that ...

1. For the parent's fiscal year in issue, the parent had substantial foreign operations within the meaning of Revenue Ruling 78-246, and

see **CONFORMITY REPORTING REQUIREMENTS**, page 14

Rev. Rul. 78-246	**Foreign Corporations & Foreign Operations** **Financial Statement Conformity Requirements & the 30% Test or Threshold**
Background	• The LIFO financial statement reporting requirements were enacted to ensure that the LIFO method "conforms as nearly as may be to the best accounting practice in the trade or business. ..." (H. Rep. No. 2330, 75th Cong., 3d Sess. 34 (1938)). • The legislative history of Section 472 indicates that the conformance "to the best accounting practice" is to be made on the basis of United States standards of accounting practice. • Congress was concerned solely with domestic accounting practice. Therefore, the conformity requirements of Section 472 should not be extended to determine what is the "best accounting practice" in foreign countries.
Are Operating Assets of "Substantial Value" Used in the Foreign Operations?	• If a foreign parent owns ***operating assets of substantial value which are used in foreign operations,*** the LIFO financial statement conformity requirements ***do not apply*** to the consolidated financial statements. ◆ This applies to ownership by the parent either directly or indirectly through members of its group. • Operating assets are considered to be used in foreign operations if they are owned by, and used in the business of, corporations that ... (1) are members of the consolidated group, (2) are ***foreign*** corporations, (3) ***do not use the LIFO method*** of accounting for Federal income tax purposes, and (4) ***engage in a business outside the United States.*** • For purposes of this test, operating assets are all the assets necessary for the conduct of an active operating company.
30% or More Threshold	• The foreign parent corporation will be considered as owning substantial foreign assets if the total value of such assets constitutes ***30% or more*** of the total operating assets of the consolidated group. • This determination will be made annually. • This determination ***will normally be made on the basis of the asset valuation*** reflected in the consolidated financial statements of the group for the year.
Facts & Circumstances	• ***If the consolidated group does not satisfy the 30% test,*** the IRS may waive the 30% test and make a determination on the basis of all of the ***facts and circumstances*** presented.
	LTR 200540005 ... Dated June 20, 2005
LTR Summary	• In LTR 200540004, the IRS was dealing with a foreign parent corporation that had to issue consolidated financial statements to its shareholders and creditors in which it was reporting its own operations and the operations of subsidiaries acquired by its own wholly-owned U.S. subsidiary. • The taxpayer persuaded the IRS that, although it failed to have operating assets in excess of the 30% threshold, it should be considered to have satisfied the alternative "facts and circumstances" test. • As a result, the parent was permitted to issue consolidated financial statements on a non-LIFO basis without violating the LIFO financial statement conformity requirements ... ***but only for the one year in question.***
LTR Facts	• The parent (a foreign corporation, not reporting under U.S. GAAP) made an agreement whereby the taxpayer (its wholly-owned U.S. subsidiary) would acquire all of the outstanding stock of a group of new subsidiaries. ◆ Prior to the acquisition, the taxpayer also had other wholly-owned U.S. subsidiaries ("old subs"). ◆ Following the acquisition, the activities of the parent, the taxpayer, and the taxpayer's subsidiaries (old subs and new subs) would be reported in the consolidated financial statements of the Parent. • Prior to the acquisition, the new subs used LIFO for valuing their inventories. The parent and the taxpayer used a non-LIFO method for valuing inventory for U.S. and for the parent's foreign country tax purposes.
LTR Discussion	• The taxpayer conceded that it did not meet the more than 30% test for establishing substantial foreign operations under Rev. Rul. 78-246. However, it said that it should be allowed to make certain distinctions in order to qualify under the alternative "facts and circumstances" test. • The taxpayer argued that as a result of the stepped-up basis in the assets involved in the acquisition, financial statement comparisons did not fairly represent its situation. The assets of the new subsidiaries reflected current value because the acquisition was recorded as a purchase pursuant to U.S. GAAP. • Accordingly, the taxpayer argued that it should be allowed to compare the higher ***market values*** (i.e., instead of the lower asset book values) of the foreign operations to its total operations. ◆ In determining the market value of new subsidiaries, the taxpayer proposed to use the purchase price of the new subsidiaries. ◆ For the market value of the remainder of the Group, the taxpayer proposed to use EBITDA (earnings before interest, taxes, depreciation and amortization) as a basis for allocating the Group's market value, prior to the acquisition, between its foreign and domestic operations. • As a result of this alternative analysis, the computed percentage of assets used in foreign operations (to total operations) would only be slightly less than the 30% minimum threshold set forth in Rev. Rul. 78-246.

2. Consequently, for the fiscal year in question, the issuance of consolidated financial statements by the parent reporting the new subsidiaries' operations on a non-LIFO basis would not violate the LIFO conformity requirements.

This Ruling did not come without several limitations and restrictions. It applied only to the ***one*** taxable year in issue. ***It did not apply to any subsequent taxable year.*** In addition, the IRS expressed no opinion as to whether the parent might have substantial foreign operations for subsequent years, or whether the parent may issue consolidated financial statements for subsequent years reporting new subsidiaries' operations on a non-LIFO basis without violating the LIFO conformity requirements. Finally, this PLR was not to be construed as approving the use of the taxpayer's market value analysis for subsequent years (in connection with determining its compliance with the 30% threshold of Rev. Rul. 78-246).

CONCLUDING CONFORMITY WARNINGS

The *William Powell Company* and the *Insilco* decisions are the only recorded cases where taxpayers contested the IRS termination of their LIFO elections in court. The bottom line is that the IRS takes all of these conformity requirements seriously. On many audits, instead of assuming that the taxpayer has complied, the IRS asks for proof that financial statements at year-end were not in violation of the LIFO conformity requirements.

The first year of the LIFO election is very often the easiest one for the IRS to find a conformity violation in. This is because by the time the election is "officially" made in the tax return many months after year-end, the financial statements for the year are long gone out the door.

In these situations, the IRS asserts that there is no statute of limitations preventing it from inquiring as to a taxpayer's compliance with the conformity requirement ... and that the Service can look into this as far back as the initial LIFO election year. Furthermore, the burden of proof is on the taxpayer - not on the IRS - in these inquiries.

The IRS position is that there is no limit on its ability to go back to ***any*** prior year...no matter how far distant...to terminate a LIFO election because of a violation of any one of the many conformity requirements discussed above. The IRS supports its argument by reminding taxpayers that they have explicitly agreed to this result right on the Form 970 that they included in their tax returns when they elected LIFO!

(Continued from page 12)

The only exception to this is the IRS' uncharacteristic and somewhat voluntary self-imposed limitation in 1997 for certain retail auto and truck dealers. Consequently, LIFO users cannot be too cautious or careful in dealing with conformity matters.

YEAR-END PROJECTIONS FOR STATEMENT CONFORMITY OR FOR INCOME TAX PLANNING PURPOSES

Projections for statement conformity purposes. Revenue Ruling 97-42 states explicitly that, when the pressure is great to issue the financial statements before detailed LIFO computations can be made, the conformity requirement should be satisfied by using a reasonable estimate of the change in the LIFO reserve in lieu of the actual amount.

As mentioned previously, another alternative might be to use a different LIFO computation methodology for the financial statements than the one used for tax purposes.

Projections for income tax planning purposes. It is unrealistic to attempt any serious planning for a business that uses LIFO without first projecting the change in the LIFO reserves for year-end.

Make projections early. These projections should be made early enough so that management can consider not only the financial impact of what is likely to happen, but also whether legitimate steps, motivated by sound business reasons, can be undertaken to produce a result different from that shown by the projections.

One thing is certain: After year-end, it will be too late to change the results that might have been avoided by proper planning with adequate timing.

Even if it is concluded that nothing can be done to avoid the LIFO reserve payback consequences, it is far better to know the extent of the impending "hit" so that other buffering actions can be taken, than it is to be caught entirely off-guard or without any idea of how large the LIFO reserve recapture is going to be.

PROJECTION MECHANICS, STEP-BY-STEP

Projecting year-end changes in LIFO reserves need not be too difficult nor time-consuming.

Making these LIFO reserve change projections involves ***only two estimates:***

1. The ending inventory level, and
2. The overall inflation percentage for the year.

All other necessary factors are known at the time the projections are made because they are ***four facts related to the beginning of the year:***

→

Conformity Reporting Requirements (Continued)

1. Beginning-of-the-year inventory expressed in total dollars and in base dollars,
2. Beginning-of-the-year LIFO valuation of the inventory,
3. Method used for valuing current year increments, and
4. Cumulative inflation index as of the beginning-of-the-year.

The computation of the projected change in a LIFO reserve is made by plugging in the estimates of (1) the year-end inventory level and (2) the current year's rate of inflation or inflation index ... and then "working backwards." These eight steps are detailed in the table below.

UNDERSTANDING WHY (PROJECTED) LIFO RESERVES GO UP OR DOWN

Taxpayers using LIFO are often surprised when they find out that even though their year-end inventory levels are projected to be lower than they were at the beginning-of-the-year, their LIFO reserves are expected to increase. And often these increases are very large. The *Practice Guide* on the following page explains why LIFO reserves change the way they do.

WORKING OUT OF ANTICIPATED YEAR-END LIQUIDATION OR DECREMENT SITUATIONS

When a liquidation or decrement situation is anticipated, the starting point is to calculate the payback potential from a series of reduced inventory levels. In other words, as the year-end inventory drops, how much more (or less) is the LIFO reserve going to change? These calculations determine what the real LIFO recapture vulnerability will be as the anticipated current-year's decrement is carried-back on a LIFO basis against the prior LIFO layers that have been built up over the years.

This recapture potential will be different for every pool, since each pool has its own history and characteristics. For auto dealers, this recapture impact will be different for the new auto pool compared to what it will be for the new light-duty truck pool. The LIFO reserve repayment potential impact should be computed for ***each*** LIFO pool and expressed as a readily understandable dollar amount. For an example of this type of successive calculation, see "GM Dealers

PROJECTIONS STEP-BY-STEP

1. ***Determine*** the cumulative index as of the end-of-the-year—this is the estimated current year inflation index times (i.e., multiplied by) the beginning-of-the-year cumulative index,
2. ***Divide*** the end-of-the-year estimated (or, if known, actual) inventory dollars by the year-end cumulative index—to determine the end-of-the-year inventory stated or expressed in base dollars,
3. ***Compare*** the end-of-the-year inventory expressed in base dollars with the beginning-of-the-year inventory stated in base dollars to determine whether there is an increment or a decrement projected for the year,
4. ***Value*** the projected increment under the method already selected for valuing increments on Form 970.

   Alternatively, if a decrement is projected for the year, carry back the decrement (expressed in base dollars) against prior years' incr³ments (also expressed in base dollars) on a LIFO or reverse-chronological-order basis. This means that the most recent/last layer built up is the first one eliminated, and then prior years' layers are eliminated in reverse-chronological order. In other words, a decrement in 1999 is carried back first against any 1998 increment, then against 1997, then against 1996, then against 1995, etc. until the entire amount of the 1999 decrement (expressed in base dollars) has been fully accounted for. In some instances, a decrement may end up being carried all the way back to the original first LIFO year base layer.
5. ***Add*** all the resulting layers of inventory at their respective LIFO valuations to get the end-of-the-year inventory stated at its LIFO valuation,
6. ***Subtract*** the ending inventory at its LIFO valuation from the ending inventory at its actual or estimated current non-LIFO cost to determine the projected LIFO reserve as of the end-of-the-year,
7. ***Subtract*** the *actual* LIFO reserve as of the beginning-of-the-year from the projected LIFO reserve as of the end-of-the-year. The result determined in this final step is the estimate of the change in the LIFO reserve for the year.
8. ***Reconcile and prove out*** the projected changes to understand why the reserve is going up or down. See accompanying *Practice Guide:* ***Why LIFO Reserves Change the Way They Do.***

see **CONFORMITY REPORTING REQUIREMENTS**, page 17

Practice Guide	WHY LIFO RESERVES CHANGE THE WAY THEY DO
Background	• Taxpayers using LIFO are often surprised when they find out that even though their year-end inventory levels are (*projected to be*) lower than they were at the beginning-of-the-year, their LIFO reserves (*are expected to*) increase. ♦ Often these (*projected*) increases in LIFO reserves are very large.
Change Factors	• The *net amount of change* in the LIFO reserve for any year is the result of two complementing and/or offsetting factors. • This ***variation analysis*** simply involves ... ♦ ***Price changes***, i.e., inflation or deflation ... prices either increased or decreased, and ♦ ***Quantity changes***, i.e., changes in the dollar amount of the inventory investment levels.
Upward influences **... causing increases (i.e., factors causing the LIFO reserve to go up) ...**	
Upward ... Increases	• ***Price increases*** ...inflation. • ***Quantity increases***, if a dual index LIFO methodology/approach is used for valuing increments. • ***Certain decreases in inventory investment levels*** - To the extent that a current-year quantity decrease (referred to as a "decrement") is carried back against an increment built up in a prior year or years, any pay-back of the previously built-up LIFO increment and its related contribution to the LIFO reserve will ***increase*** the current year's LIFO reserve if ... ♦ There was deflation in the prior year(s)'s layers that are now being invaded, and ♦ The layers being invaded are/were contributing "negatively" or negative amounts to the LIFO reserve at the end of the preceding year. ♦ ***Stated another way ...*** The layers of inventory being invaded by the carryback of a decrement (expressed in base dollars) are contributing negative amounts toward the overall LIFO reserve balance; Accordingly, to the extent that any carryback of the current-year's decrement eliminates these negative effects, that leaves only inventory layers contributing positive amounts toward the overall LIFO reserve balance ... or fewer inventory layers still contributing negatively toward the overall LIFO reserve balance.
Downward influences **... causing decreases (i.e., factors causing the LIFO reserve to go down) ...**	
Downward ... Decreases	• ***Price decreases*** ...deflation. • ***Decreases in inventory investment levels*** - i.e., pay-backs of previously built-up LIFO reserves to the extent resulting from the carryback of a current-year inventory quantity decrease (referred to as "decrements") against increases ("increments") built up in prior years. • ***Decreases in inventory investment levels ... But not always ... Sometimes no payback.*** ♦ An inventory decrease/decrement may not necessarily cause, or result in, any pay-back of some or any of the LIFO reserve at the beginning of the year. Whether or not there is a "pay-back" depends the order in which the prior year layers were built up over time and how they were valued for LIFO purposes.
No Effect	• If the decrement in the current year is less than the amount of the increment in the immediately preceding year, there will be no dollar change in the LIFO reserve due to the carryback of that decrement against that prior year's increment. • This result will occur under any LIFO method that values a current-year increment by using the cumulative inflation index (factor) at the end of the year. ♦ Alternative LIFO Methods for New and/or Used Vehicles
Articles Analyzing Changes in LIFO Reserves	• "*Why Do Some LIFO Reserves Go Up Even Though Inventory Levels Go Down?*" in the March 1992 *LIFO Lookout* • "*Another Rebasing Example - With Proofs: Why LIFO Reserves Go Up Even Though Inventory Levels Go Down and Despite Rebasing Indexes to 1.000 in Between*" in the June 1993 *LIFO Lookout.* • "*Strange ... But Explainable ... Results from the Wacky World of Negative LIFO Reserves,*" in the December 1998 *LIFO Lookout.* This article, with supporting schedules, analyzes pay-back mechanics where negative LIFO reserves are involved. • "*Dealers Who've Remained on LIFO Through a Few Years of Deflation Are Finally Rewarded by Inflation & Big LIFO Reserve Increases*" in the June 2004 *LIFO Lookout.* ♦ This article, with supporting schedules, analyzes LIFO reserve changes where some of the more recent years' LIFO layers reflect general price deflation, but not to the point where overall negative LIFO reserve balances have been created.

Conformity Reporting Requirements

(Continued from page 15)

Low on LIFO Inventory May Face Stiff Recapture ... Planning May Lessen the Blow," in the June 1998 *Dealer Tax Watch.*

Armed with this diagnostic information, taxpayers anticipating a liquidation may be able to lessen the anticipated LIFO recapture in at least three ways. The second and third considerations below are discussed in the June 1998, *Dealer Tax Watch* article referenced above.

ALTERNATIVES

1. ***Manage inventory levels.*** Attempt to increase or "manage" the inventory level through transactions that might not otherwise have been considered, but which still have some degree of business justification (other than solely attempting to minimize the impact of LIFO layer liquidations).
2. ***Year-end change.*** If eligible, change to a fiscal year-end that is prior to the year-end expected to be adversely affected by the significant inventory reduction.
3. ***Switch to the IPIC/BLS method.*** Consider changing to the IPIC/BLS method under the recent changes...and expeditious consent procedure ... available in Section 10.04 of the Appendix to Revenue Procedure 2002-9.

   The IPIC Method LIFO Regulations (Reg. Sec. 1.472-8(e)(3)) were finalized in January, 2002, and contain several taxpayer-friendly changes that make use of the IPIC method more attractive in several situations. (See *Highlights of the Final IPIC LIFO Regulations*, pages 8-10 in the December, 2002 issue of the *LIFO Lookout.*)

If a business using LIFO is trying to avoid a significant year-end reserve reduction, steps to increase the inventory level should be completed and documented before year-end. These actions should be considered only if they make sense from a business standpoint, after considering carrying costs, insurance, expected ability to sell the additional inventory and the possibility of challenge by the IRS.

Despite cautions that inventory purchasing decisions should be based on sound business judgment and not solely on the desire to reduce projected LIFO pay-backs, some taxpayers may still wish to pursue more aggressive strategies and to take their chances in this regard.

As discussed in the next section, the IRS has been successful in challenging transactions that appeared to be motivated by the desire to avoid LIFO recapture impact. In these cases, the IRS ignored the last-ditch efforts that resulted in inventory on hand at year-end which was not "intended to be sold or placed in the normal inventory channels."

Ideas dealers might consider if faced with significant projected decrements. A dealer might attempt to increase or "manage" the year-end inventory level by considering some transactions that otherwise would not have entered his mind. These may be rationalized under the "Nothing ventured, nothing gained" generalization. However, they may not necessarily be justified ***if*** the IRS digs deeply into them and sees them as motivated solely by liquidation-avoidance. Therefore, these strategies should be regarded by dealers and their advisors as aggressive and not without the likelihood of challenge by the IRS. They are only generalized here, and they should be carefully and more fully evaluated by the dealer's advisors before any further action is taken.

1. After determining which pool (new automobiles or new light-duty trucks) has the greater LIFO repayment potential, a dealer may simply try to have more inventory dollars in the pool with the greater repayment potential.

   In other words, if the dealer can have only $2,000,000 worth of inventory, if the LIFO repayment payback potential is 30% on the dollar in the new automobile pool and 60% on the dollar in the new light-duty truck pool, the dealer should try to have more inventory dollars at year-end in the new light-duty truck pool than in the new automobile pool.

2. Attempt to purchase new vehicles of other makes (for resale to retail customers) to put into inventory.

   Under the Alternative LIFO Method, all new automobiles, regardless of manufacturer, including those used as demonstrators, must be included in a dollar-value LIFO pool, and all new light-duty trucks regardless of manufacturer, must be included in another separate LIFO pool. Thus, the Alternative LIFO Method would appear to contemplate all new automobiles being placed in one pool, regardless of manufacturer. Accordingly, a GM dealer who has other non-GM franchises in the same selling entity as the GM franchise(s) might try to stock up on the non-GM new vehicles to the extent possible.

3. Similarly, a dealer might simply attempt to purchase (for retail sale) some very expensive makes (Lamborghini or Rolls Royce) and put them in the new automobiles pool. ("A few will do.") Does a dealer have to have that franchise to sell those vehicles? What about creating a special joint venture, or flow-through type entity with another *franchised* dealer?

see **CONFORMITY REPORTING REQUIREMENTS**, page 18

Conformity Reporting Requirements

How far can the "retail resale" aspect be pushed? Will this pass muster with the IRS? One cannot be sure.

Caution: Section 4.02 of Revenue Procedure 97-36 does contain some troublesome language relating to LIFO pools. It states that *"for each separate trade or business,"* all autos, regardless of manufacturer, must be placed in one pool. No one really knows what *"for each separate trade or business"* really means, and the IRS has yet to define or explain it. If these words don't mean anything, why are they there? Might the IRS assert some specialized interpretation for this term under these circumstances?

In TAM 199911044, the IRS gave some indication of its interpretation of the "for each separate trade or business" language. In this TAM, the National Office allowed an auto dealer to keep all new autos in one pool and all new light-duty trucks in a separate pool, even though that dealer was involved with two manufacturers, five franchises and three locations, all of which were in the same city. For more on this TAM, see "Automobile Dealer with Multiple Franchises & Locations Can Use One Pool for all New Cars," *LIFO Lookout*, June 1999.

4. A dealer might actively seek out another dealer with less of a LIFO recapture impact potential and attempt to purchase inventory from that dealer, perhaps paying a "premium" or offering that dealer some other considerations for that inventory that makes the transaction economically attractive to both parties.

5. Dealers with multiple franchises in different entities should make similar LIFO recapture impact calculations for all their LIFO pools in all entities... to determine whether a shifting of inventory from one entity to another, if feasible, might create a favorable recapture-avoidance result.

6. Finally, although it may seem heresy, a dealer might consider not closing sales until after the end of the year. For some dealers, what they hope to realize in gross profit and potential customer loyalty may be smaller than the real dollar outflow that *definitely* will result from the reduction of inventory by sales which will *definitely* trigger the LIFO recapture. Some dealers may simply be unable to make the right decision on this.

SOMETIMES THE IRS REVERSES YEAR-END LIQUIDATION AVOIDANCE MEASURES

In 1996, the Tax Court observed that taxpayers often "desire a higher base-year cost of ending inventory in a given year to avoid liquidating a LIFO layer, causing a match of historical costs against current revenues" (see *E. W. Richardson*, Tax Court Memo Decision 1996-368).

(Continued from page 17)

The Court's observation was made in the context of three other cases and Revenue Ruling 79-188. All of these collectively stand for the proposition that the IRS may successfully overturn and even penalize year-end inventory transactions that are solely LIFO-benefit motivated.

1. ***Ingredient Technology Corporation*** (Su Crest Corporation, 83-1 USTC 9140, January 5, 1983). Tax fraud convictions by means of LIFO inventory overstatements.

2. ***Illinois Cereal Mills***, (86-1 USTC 9371 affirming T.C. Memo 1983-469, Dec. 40,342(M), 46 TCM 1001, August, 1983). Legal ownership of the goods did not justify inclusion in the taxpayer's inventory because the taxpayer did not intend to use the corn in its milling business.

3. ***Ballou and Company, Inc.***, (85-1 USTC 9290, U.S. Claims Court, No. 247-82T; March 29, 1985). The Court upheld the IRS' removal of year-end gold purchases from LIFO inventory calculations because the IRS adjustments removed only the amounts of gold that the taxpayer had purchased in order to temporarily inflate inventory levels solely for income tax/LIFO purposes at year end.

Revenue Ruling 79-188 can be given a positive spin and interpreted to indirectly suggest some planning considerations:

PLANNING CHECKLIST

1. Attempt to document that sales during the year are at levels that justify the purchase of year-end inventory levels in the ordinary course of business.
2. It helps if the inventory acquired at year-end can be sold to regular customers in due course or to a third party, rather than back to original supplier. This helps to avoid the "cast" as a resale.
3. The inventory acquired at year-end should be paid for before its subsequent sale, again in an effort to demonstrate an intent to receive and use the goods in the ordinary course of the business.
4. The specific mechanics of taking possession and title prior to reselling the inventory should also be considered. But note, even doing all this legally did not stop the IRS in *Illinois Cereal Mills*.

TAM 9847003 provides evidence of how closely the IRS scrutinizes year-end inventory levels and transactions. In this case, the IRS concluded that an affiliated group had engaged in inventory-level manipulation stating: "The Group simply used Y (one →

affiliated member) as a purchasing and holding company so that it could manipulate the quantity of goods in X's (another affiliated member) ending inventory, thereby artificially inflating X's cost of good sold ... This purchasing arrangement was designed to artificially reduce the Group's taxable income and avoid taxes; it had no independent purpose ... Although papers were drawn up to place formal ownership with Y, the ***objective economic realities*** indicate that X had effective command over the Y purchases."

Accordingly, the IRS National Office concluded that X was the owner of the Y purchases and should have included them in its inventory.

In this TAM, the IRS pursued the adjustment to correct the year-end inventory levels through the Group's corporate restructuring, holding that

1. X's method of accounting for the Y purchases carried over to the taxpayer created in the merger process,

2. the treatment of the purchases in inventory constituted an unauthorized change in method of accounting, and

3. corrections could be made by changing the new taxpayer's method of accounting and making adjustments pursuant to Section 481(a).

A WARNING ABOUT AGGRESSIVE YEAR-END INVENTORY PLANNING

Any LIFO taxpayer aggressively planning to avoid year-end LIFO layer liquidations should realize that even satisfying the apparent "boundaries" set forth in Revenue Ruling 79-188 and these other cases may not be enough. Taxpayers' year-end transactions may not prevail if year-end purchases are structured to involve subsequent re-sales back to the same source shortly after year-end or just to otherwise look good on paper.

Other practical considerations should be weighed in the balance if aggressive year-end planning techniques are going to be discussed with LIFO clients. The Internal Revenue Service may seek to impose penalties, or higher statutory interest rates, if it considers the actions taken to avoid LIFO layer invasions and recapture to be without any support or merit.

Circular 230...? Furthermore, consideration needs to be given to Treasury Department Circular 230 which regulates written communications about Federal tax matters between tax advisors and their clients. Practitioners need to be extremely careful in how they go about discussing various layer-invasion minimization techniques with their clients and how they document or formalize their recommendations in this regard.

Correspondence with clients may or may not be intended to constitute written tax advice communications, and it may or may not constitute what Circular 230 defines as a full "covered opinion." Other issues under Circular 230 may be raised if the client is asking the advisor to reach a conclusion involving confidence levels regarding the success of the actions under consideration.

Accordingly, where appropriate, LIFO taxpayers may need to be told - in writing - that planning advice (regarding avoidance of LIFO layer invasions) is not intended and cannot be used for the purpose of avoiding penalties that may be imposed by the Internal Revenue Service.

Willard J. De Filipps, CPA, P.C.

317 WEST PROSPECT AVENUE MT. PROSPECT, ILLINOIS 60056
PHONE (847) 577-3977 FAX (847) 577-1073
http://www.defilipps.com
cpawjd@aol.com

June 16, 2006

Senate Committee on Finance
Attn: Editorial and Document Section
Rm. SD-203
Dirksen Senate Office Building
Washington, D.C. 20510-6200

Re: ***Current Consideration of the Use of the Last-In, First-Out (LIFO) Inventory Method***

Senate Committee on Finance Hearing
"A Tune-up on Corporate Tax Issues: What's Going on under the Hood?"
Tuesday, June 13, 2006

*EXHIBIT III**

HOW LIFO WORKS

Originally Published in
The National Automobile Dealers Association's
Cars & Trucks
February 1975

* Attachment to Comment Letter dated June 16, 2006

CARS&TRUCKS
PUBLISHED BY THE NATIONAL AUTOMOBILE DEALERS ASSOCIATION

February 1975 VOL. 47 NO. 2

How LIFO Works

By Willard J. De Filipps
Partner, Wolf and Co.

The "last in, first out" inventory costing practice is one of the hottest issues on the business scene today. This two-part series should help the dealer decide whether LIFO will work for his business and, if so, how to best utilize it.

The following article is a practical survey of how the last in, first out method of inventory costing can be applied to the franchised new car or truck dealership. It was written by Willard J. De Filipps who is a partner in the Chicago office of Wolf and Co., Certified Public Accountants, a distinguished firm with considerable experience in the dealership field. Mr. De Filipps' article is a product of his sound theoretical knowledge of LIFO and his years of practical experience in the audit of dealerships. Next month, two partners of a firm of similar distinction and experience in the automotive field, A.M. Pullen & Co., will discuss the pros and cons of making the LIFO election.

MANY GENERAL discussions on the subject of LIFO can be found in intermediate textbooks and current financial literature. However, little is available on how an automobile dealer can convert to LIFO. This may be due to the relatively recent emergence of the severe conditions now focusing attention on LIFO in situations where previously it was ignored. Perhaps another reason is that a LIFO conversion requires choices among numerous alternatives and sub-elections, and the appropriate

(page 1 of 7 of article)

HOW LIFO WORKS
Willard J. De Filipps, CPA - Cars & Trucks, February, 1975

choices vary from case to case. This tends to invalidate any one approach as a "uniform" or "standardized" method applicable to all dealerships.

In considering the computational aspects of LIFO for automobile dealers, there seems to be a definite combination of choices which generally are more favorable for the dealer, regardless of the type of dealership. This article discusses these choices, and explains one approach for actually "putting a pencil to it." Although any category of an automotive inventory is adaptable to LIFO, this article discusses only the LIFO conversion of new cars, demonstrators, and light trucks carried by automobile dealers.

The application of LIFO to heavy truck and/or implement inventories would probably deviate somewhat from the basic approach suggested herein. This might happen because there may be a relatively smaller number of units in inventory. Also, there may be more significant variations between the percentage of total cost consisting of chassis costs and of attachment costs, combined with differing price increase rates.

A dealer's LIFO computations should satisfy three essential conditions. They should be *practical*, they should *prolong* the LIFO benefits as much as possible, and they should *promote* IRS acceptance by being logical and realistic. This will be discussed more fully after some background comment.

A dealer must first decide whether or not to adpt LIFO. Once made, this decision cannot be revoked without considerable complication. And there is relatively little time in which to decide. As discussed in many other articles, there are many advantages, disadvantages, and considerations which make the initial decision difficult. This article assumes a decision to convert, and discusses the application of LIFO to new car, demonstrator, and small truck inventories. The challenge at hand—for the dealer and his accountant—is to someway, somehow evaluate or estimate the effect of inflation on that inventory.

LIFO stands for "last in-first out." It is permitted by Section 472 of the tax law, and it is an accountant's short-hand way of describing an assumption used in calculating inventory values that treats the flow of cost as if the last goods purchased were the first ones sold. This assumption can be used for tax purposes even though it is possible to trace and identify the purchase of the actual goods in the ending inventory.

When prices rise, as they did at unprecendented rates during 1974, the LIFO inventory method produces lower income taxes by including the effect of inflation to some degree as an expense in the cost of goods sold. A taxpayer adopting LIFO computes a "personalized" index or estimated measure of the effect of inflation on his own ending inventory.

This is done by valuing his actual ending inventory in at least two ways, and comparing the results. It takes two of anything to make a comparison. Similarly, the ending inventory has to be valued at least twice to "compare" or estimate inflation's impact.

For LIFO purposes, the ending inventory must be valued at "base" prices and at "current" prices. Although there are many ways to make such a determination, the income tax regulations offer limited guidance on how to approach this task. The regulations do not contain specific procedural guidance for automobile dealers. Instead, they provide that LIFO computations are subject to review and approval by the Internal Revenue Service, and that the computations must "clearly reflect income"—whatever that means.

Against this background, the prerequisites for LIFO calculations center around practicality, preservation or prolongation of LIFO advantages, and prevention of IRS reversal upon audit. The consequences of decisions and sub-elections to be made in the course of working through a LIFO application must be synchronized with the nature of the automobile dealer's inventory and his business. In other words, they must be practical.

The combination of these methods should shortcut the overall clerical processes as much as possible. In addition, they should have the likelihood of preserving in succeeding years, as much as possible, the advantages initially sought by the adoption of LIFO. Everyone knows that LIFO is attractive when prices are rising. But if inventory levels are not maintained, or if price levels fall in future years, LIFO will report higher taxable income in those years and reduce some of the benefits initially secured. It is possible to minimize this reduction in future years by initially selecting the alternatives expected to boomerang least.

Under the combination of procedures suggested herein, the LIFO deferral is practical because it does not terminate each year with the introduction of new models. Under the dollar-value method, one pool would be established for all models and all model-year units. This pool combines all new cars, demonstrators, and light (smaller) trucks. Thus, 1974 and 1975 new car models all go into the same pool, and the introduction of 1975 models does not result in the recapture of the reserve established in connection with 1974 models, provided they have been replaced with 1975 models.

If the December 31, 1974, ending inventory consists of only 1975 models, it is still possible to establish a reserve for calendar year 1974 even though the inventory at January 1, 1974, consisted of 1973 and 1974 models. As will be seen, this is done by repricing the 1975 models at the prices of comparable models on hand at the beginning of the year (i.e., at January 1, 1974).

Assuming stable or slightly increasing future inventory quantities and prices, the LIFO deferral for 1974 would carry over indefinitely from year to year. The LIFO deferral might even grow in future years if inventory quantities remained about the same and prices continued to rise. If prices declined, the initial deferral would be reduced, but this would not be detrimental overall unless the prices declined below those in effect at January 1, 1974.

The careful combination of pooling and dollar-value techniques results in better chances of preserving the LIFO benefit, despite changes in model mix in future years. Over the lifetime of the business, the same aggregate income will be reported regardless of whether the dealer uses LIFO, FIFO, or specific identification methods.

Needless to say, the preservation of documentation to support each step through the LIFO computations is mandatory. The logic, realism, and completeness of the steps and computations should withstand reversal upon eventual examination by the Internal Revenue Service.

In any given dealership, the extent of the LIFO computations will vary depending on many factors, including:

1. The adequacy and availability of dealership cost records, invoice files, and factory price information;
2. The model mix;
3. The presence of certain price relationships suggesting shortcuts to reduce clerical work without materially changing the end result;
4. The willingness of the dealer to do a little more "homework" now, and to assemble and retain the supporting data which the Internal Revenue Service may eventually request and audit;
5. Whether the computations will be done manually or computerized for greater detail; and,
6. Whether the CPA is to render an opinion on the financial statements or merely "adjust the books and prepare a tax return."

This article contains the following discussions:

1. Suggestions for Sub-Elections;
2. The Dollar-Value Method of Applying LIFO;
3. Inventory Pools: A Single Broad Pool for All New Vehicles and Demonstrators;
4. Computing the LIFO Inflation Index: Steps Common to Automotive LIFO Conversions;
5. Valuing the Ending Inventory at "Current" Costs;
6. Link-Chain is the LIFO Valuation Technique Best Suited for Dealers;
7. Making the LIFO Election; and,

(page 2 of 7 of article)

HOW LIFO WORKS

Willard J. De Filipps, CPA - Cars & Trucks, February, 1975

8. Related Tax Forms and Cash Flow Improvement from the LIFO Election.

Sub-Elections. There are several sub-elections and decisions to be made in a LIFO conversion. The major ones are summarized below.

As to these sub-elections, it is suggested that:

1. A dealer should elect to use the dollar-value method for pricing LIFO inventories;

2. A dealer should elect LIFO only for certain parts of his inventory, not for the inventory as a whole. Although other separate LIFO pools might be considered for parts and accessories, and for used vehicles, a discussion of these is beyond the scope of this article;

3. New vehicles and demonstrators should be combined into a single broad pool. When a dealer also sells small trucks (for example, a Ford dealer selling Rancheros and Broncos), these should also be included in the single pool to maximize results. There should be no sub-pools within the single broad pool suggested above. To simplify and better organize the underlying computations, it would be logical to list and/or summarize the beginning and ending inventories by make and model. These workpaper groupings for underlying computational purposes are not, by themselves, indicative of sub-pools—they merely better assist in keeping track of the inventory changes and model mix;

4. A dealer should elect to use the link-chain index method for computing the LIFO value of his dollar-value pool for new vehicles and demonstrators. This method is *not* the one preferred by the regulations, and a separate informational filing requirement is imposed upon taxpayers adopting any link-chain and/or index method; and,

5. For purposes of valuing the ending inventory at "current cost" to determine the numerator in the current year's price index, the field of realistic alternatives narrows down to two. Consequently, current cost should be determined either by (a) using the earliest purchases method or (b) by specific identification of the actual ending inventory invoices which should approximate the "most recent purchases" method. The selection of the preferable alternative depends on many factors (see above), and no general recommendation can be made.

Dollar-Vaue Method. The LIFO cost method may be applied in either of two basic ways: (a) the unit (specific goods) method or (b) the dollar-value method. The latter is suggested because it treats the inventory as representing an investment of dollars rather than an aggregate of individual items.

The dollar-value method uses "base year" costs expressed in terms of total dollars invested in the inventory as its unit of measurement. This unit of measurement is applied to groupings, or categories, of inventory referred to as "pools." The term "base year cost" is the aggregate of the cost of all items in a pool determined as of the beginning of the year when the LIFO method is first adopted. The taxable year in which LIFO is first adopted is the "base year." The inventory at the beginning of that first year is the "base inventory."

An increment in a dollar-value LIFO pool occurs when the year-end inventory for the pool, expressed in terms of base year cost, exceeds the beginning of the year inventory for that pool, also expressed in base year cost. To determine the ending inventory LIFO value for a pool, any increment is adjusted for changing unit costs by reference to a percentage, relative to base year cost, determined for the pool *as a whole.*

Liquidations and increments of specific items contained within the pool are ignored; what counts is whether there is a net liquidation or increment for the pool *as a whole.* Thus, fluctuations may occur in quantities of various items within the pool. New items which properly fall within the pool may be added (i.e., 1975 models), and old items may disappear from the pool (i.e., 1973 and 1974 models) without necessarily changing the dollar value of the pool *as a whole.*

The dollar-value method is therefore preferable to the unit or specific goods method since it permits the partial or complete liquidation of one type of item in the pool (1974 models) to be offset by an increase in investment in another type (1975 models). It also copes with the situation presented when certain models are not continued in succeeding years (for example, Ford dropped its 1974 model Custom 500s and Galaxie 500s) or when "new" 1975 models are introduced (Ford, again, introducing Elites and Granadas).

Inventory Pools. As mentioned above, under the dollar-value method, goods contained in the inventory for which LIFO is elected are grouped into a pool or pools. The categorization or "pooling" is very important because the dollar-value calculations applied to a pool *as a whole* are separately applied to each pool. The more pools there are, the greater the likelihood that even though the dollar amount of inventory investment might remain constant, some items within the inventory will be completely liquidated from some pools while different and new items are added to other pools.

The regulations state that retailers shall place their inventory into pools by major lines, types, or classes of goods. In determining such groupings, the retailer's customary business classifications are an important consideration. The regulations cite the department in the department store as an example of customary business classification. In

(page 3 of 7 of article)

HOW LIFO WORKS
Willard J. De Filipps, CPA - Cars & Trucks, February, 1975

such cases, practices are relatively uniform throughout the trade, and departmental grouping is peculiarly adapted to the customs and needs of the business.

The Internal Revenue Service has issued pronouncements applicable only to retail department stores and certain specialty stores that price their inventories using the "retail" method. No detailed pronouncements have been issued for other types of retailers.

Consequently, taxpayers usually want to use as few inventory pools as possible where the primary purpose of LIFO is to minimize income tax. A single broad pool for all new vehicles and demonstrators is suggested. The inclusion of demonstrators in this pool seems logical, but there is no formal indication by the IRS that demonstrators must be included in the pool.

As far as pooling is concerned, the options and accessories included on any automobile should not have to be given any special treatment. Options and accessories certainly do make a difference in physical appearance and comfort in driving a car. However, the general requirement in the regulations is that pools be set up to represent "customary business classifications of the particular trade in which the taxpayer is engaged.

Since dealers do not separately report or account for options or accessories sold as part of new cars and demonstrators, this seems to support ignoring the net difference that the cost of options actually makes in the car for pooling purposes. Options usually account for between 10 and 20 percent of a new car's price, and recent price bulletins list dozens of options available on 1975 models.

This multiplicity suggests that as a matter of expediency, the options can be lumped in with vehicles without any significant distortion. Also, the Price and Profit Margin Regulations issued under the Economic Stabilization Program would support the general appropriateness of pooling all new vehicles and demonstrators without further regard for model and/or option differences.

For automobile dealers, a major question is whether this pooling arrangement will eventually be acceptable to the Internal Revenue Service or possibly upheld in court. If each model-year or model were treated as a separate pool, there would be a continuous series of partial or complete liquidations of multiple model-year pools while the total inventory at base year cost might remain relatively constant. However, as each model or model-year pool were liquidated, the removal of lower cost from inventory would result in increased taxable income.

Consequently, the use of a single broad pool for new vehicles and demonstrators is important to the long-range prolongation of benefits from a LIFO election. We believe this to be a practical arrangement, consistent with the concept of considering the inventory as representing an investment of dollars. We understand that, in certain areas, the Internal Revenue Service has accepted upon audit the concept of a single pool for new cars and demonstrators. Should the Internal Revenue Service formally rule that separate pools by model-years, by models, or other categories were required, this formal ruling would be a matter of interest to all dealers.

Computing The LIFO Index. If the computations are to be done manually, it is suggested that a listing first be prepared from the factory model introduction price lists showing all of the possible model variations. Two-door models should be listed separately from four-door models. If this listing is overlaid on columnar workpaper and photocopied several times, this will eliminate the need to recopy the same information onto several other schedules and thereby standardize the format of the workpapers.

Working upon this standardized listing or format, the following should be prepared:

1. A detailed analysis of all units in each model category in the beginning inventory—in quantities and in dollars;

2. A detailed analysis of all units in each model category in the ending inventory—in quantities and in dollars;

3. A schedule showing the base vehicle prices at which the models were purchased during the year. Although the introductory prices for 1974 and for 1975 models are probably most significant, other interim price increase information may also be posted to provide a more complete analysis of price changes; and,

4. A schedule showing by model an estimate of the adjustments necessary to reflect the costs attributable to options on 1974 models that became standard equipment on 1975 models. On other models (for example, certain Buick models) some options or equipment that were standard on 1974 models became optional on 1975 models. An estimate of the cost attributable to these changes should be posted to this workpaper, so that the net change can be added to the beginning of the year cost determined for each model. The presence of catalytic converters, high-energy ignition systems, steel-belted radial tires, and other changes on 1975 models should be quantified or approximated so that comparing the price of a 1975 model will be meaningful when compared to the "adjusted" price of the same 1974 model. Hopefully, these adjustments can be determined from factory price lists for options and accessories, delete option data and other information provided by the factory, or from knowledgeable people in the dealership or in the factory.

It is advisable to separately save one copy of the factory invoice underlying each unit in the beginning and in the ending inventory. These invoices will show the prices paid for the units in inventory; the respective option mixes and the costs of the options; changes in transportation charges; and, other relevant data.

The detailed analysis of the beginning inventory will indicate the dollars affected by changes in the model mix when compared with a similar analysis of the ending inventory. Also, this beginning inventory analysis will help *where or if* a weighted average base period (beginning of the year) price will be used.

In the process of reviewing and comparing the model mix in the beginning and ending inventory analyses, decisions and assumptions will have to be made to deal with the changes between the 1974 and the 1975 model line offerings. Here, using "body type" information may provide a reliable continuity. The Internal Revenue Service will have to be satisfied as to the propriety of these assumptions upon audit.

The dollar-value method allows the taxpayer to compute the LIFO value of the current year's physical increase or decrease in the inventory investment in terms of base date (i.e., constant purchasing power) dollars. Therefore, the next step is to compute the change, by valuing the year-end inventory twice: once at base cost and a second time at current cost. There are several alternative ways of computing the current year cost valuation of the ending inventory, as will be discussed later in the next section. However, for the time being it will be assumed that the current year "cost" is determined from the actual invoices for the units making up the ending inventory.

This double valuation or "double-extension" process to compute the price increase ratio is necessary in order:

1. To determine the ratio of total current year costs to total base period cost;

2. To determine the physical increase in the current year's inventory in terms of dollars of constant purchasing power (i.e., base period cost); and,

3. To value the current year's inventory layer—the physical increase or decrease—by multiplying the change computed in terms of base period cost by the ratio of total current year cost to total base year cost.

After the ending inventory has been extended at current and at base costs, the current year price index or ratio is determined by dividing the "current" valuation by the "base" valuation. This ratio or index can then be applied to the total dollars in the ending inventory pool in order to restate the ending inventory at base date cost.

(page 4 of 7 of article)

HOW LIFO WORKS

Willard J. De Filipps, CPA - Cars & Trucks, February, 1975

Under this procedure, the index has been developed by reference only to the change in base vehicle costs. The total dollars reflected in the ending inventory pool consists not only of that cost component, but also of the dollars attributable to the options and accessories on the vehicles and to destination and preparation charges. If the overall index developed by double-extending all of the base vehicle prices is then applied to the total dollars in inventory, this implies a similar rate increase for option prices and transportation charges.

Either of these assumptions can be independently tested by using the actual price list for options and accessories and other factory information. This can be an alternative to double-extending some or all of the (significantly large) optional equipment items.

The above approach represents in essence an "index" approach because each unit in inventory has been evaluated through its base vehicle cost component, rather than more perfectly through a repricing of all of the possible options and accessories as well. Hence, this approach of working principally with the base vehicle costs accounts for substantially all of the dollars tied up in the new vehicle pool without actually testing in detail every possible option and accessory on the units in ending inventory. With a computer programmed with the appropriate price lists, a complete repricing of all options, as well as base vehicle prices, would be possible.

The steps after determining the index are as follows: By dividing the end of the year inventory by the current year index or ratio, the end of the year inventory priced at base date cost is determined. This lower amount when compared with the beginning of the year inventory shows whether there has been an increase or decrease during the current year in terms of base date inventory dollars. As stated earlier, an increase or increment in the dollar value LIFO pool occurs when the end of the year inventory expressed in terms of base year cost exceeds the beginning of the year inventory expressed at base period cost.

To determine the inventory value for LIFO purposes of that pool, the current year increment is adjusted by multiplying the actual increase by the current year index or ratio. For example, if the increment were computed to be $100,000 and the current year index were 125 percent, the increment would be valued for LIFO purposes at $125,000. This valuation of the current year's increment, when added to the base inventory (i.e., the beginning of the year inventory), would result in the LIFO valuation of the ending inventory. The LIFO "reserve" would be the difference between this LIFO valuation and the valuation if LIFO had not been adopted (i.e., by specifically identifying and totalling all of the invoices underlying the units in ending inventory).

Valuing The Ending Inventory. As indicated above, in calculating the LIFO inflation index there is yet another subelection to be made. This has to do with the calculation of the numerator of the index or ratio fraction. However, the regulations provide that the current year cost of items making up a pool may be determined under one of four methods. These methods are:

1. By reference to the actual cost of the goods purchased during the taxable year in order of acquisition (earliest purchases method);

2. By reference to the actual cost of goods most recently purchased (most recent purchases method);

3. By application of an average unit cost; or,

4. Pursuant to any other proper method which, in the opinion of the Commissioner of the Internal Revenue Service, clearly reflects income.

The use of the earliest purchase method is most consistent with the overall LIFO concept. For automobile dealers reporting a calendar year basis, this would probably avoid the new model introduction price increases and produce a lower increment and valuation of that current year increment than would be determined under the other methods.

There may be situations where the alternative of determining current cost on a LIFO basis—that is, using the earliest purchases or order of acquisition method would provide greater tax benefits. This would be the case where it is anticipated that the inventory will increase over a period of years. In many situations, the earliest purchase method may be preferable because it maximizes the LIFO reserve in the year of adoption.

However, in other situations it may be preferable (where a dealer may not necessarily want to show the largest possible LIFO reserve) or necessary (because of inadequate records or time pressures) to select a method using the actual invoices underlying the ending inventory units to determine the "current cost" of the ending inventory. This would be very similar but not necessarily exactly the same as the most recent purchases method.

Although this would be theoretically inconsistent with the LIFO concept, this approach does tie the development of the index back to the actual ending inventory cost records on a specific identification basis. Also, it involves less clerical work since the information is readily available and avoids the "third" extension of the inventory otherwise necessary under the earliest purchases method. However, the additional work involved in the "third" extension might well be worth the effort if it results in a much larger LIFO reserve.

This choice has to be evaluated

(page 5 of 7 of article)

HOW LIFO WORKS
Willard J. De Filipps, CPA - Cars & Trucks, February, 1975

separately in each specific situation. It is not possible to determine which alternative for computing current cost would be preferable in the majority of cases.

Link-Chain Technique. Still another sub-election to be made involves selecting the method to be used in computing the LIFO value of the dollar-value pool. Again, there are several ways to make this computation. However, the choice usually narrows down to using either (a) the method preferred by the tax regulations and referred to therein as the "double-extension" method or (b) using the "link-chain" method. Either method produces the same results in the first year LIFO is adopted. However, after the first year, the procedures are different for treating new items coming into inventory. For the reasons indicated below, the link-chain method is suggested for dealers because it is better suited for dealing with the continuing technological changes evident in new car models every year and expected in the future.

Whenever a *new* item that was not in the initial LIFO year inventory enters the pool in a subsequent year, its price as of the base date must be either determined or reconstructed in order to develop the current year's price index or ratio. Under the "double-extension method" preferred by the regulations, new items usually are repriced or price reconstructed as of the first day of the composition of the pools used, the 1, 1974, for calendar taxpayers adopting LIFO in 1974. Over time, this date recedes farther into the past and will probably result in a greater amount of guesswork in future years when it is necessary to reprice subsequent models at equivalent base date (i.e., January 1, 1974) cost.

On the other hand, under the link-chain method, the base date reference point for costing new items in a pool in subsequent years would not be January 1, 1974. Instead, under the link-chain method, that base date each year would be updated to January 1 of that subsequent year. This automatic updating of the base date reference should be a real advantage in that it would be necessary to identify costs changes over only the span of a single model year.

Thus, for 1974, the base date would be the same under either method—that is, it would be January 1, 1974. However, in calendar 1975, the base date under the "double-extension" method would be January 1, 1974; although under the link-chain method, that base date would become January 1, 1975.

Looking to some future year, for example 1978, it would probably be easier, then, to determine the increase in 1978 by comparing the prices of 1979 models with the prices of 1978 models, rather than by repricing 1979 models at prices developed in 1974 and carried forward and adjusted each year through model-year 1975, 1976, 1977, and 1978 model changes.

Under the link-chain method, the ending inventory (priced at current costs) is repriced at beginning of the year costs rather than base date costs. The repricing may be accomplished for all items in the inventory or for a representative portion of the items constituting an acceptable sample. The aggregate end-of-year and beginning-of-year costs are compared and a ratio of price level movement from the beginning of the year to the end of the year is calculated. The procedure is repeated each year so that an index of current year price level movement is available for the year of election and subsequent years.

A cumulative index of price level movement for two consecutive years is obtained by multiplying the indices for each of the two years. A cumulative index from the beginning of the year of the LIFO election to the end of every following year can be obtained by multiplying each year's index of current year price level movement by the prior year's cumulative index. The derived cumulative index is then applied to the total ending inventory at current costs to restate the inventory at base-dollar costs and to price the current year's inventory increment.

Despite its obvious practical advantages, the regulations state that the link-chain method will be approved by the IRS only in those cases where the taxpayer can satisfactorily demonstrate that the use of either a direct-index method or the double-extension method would be "impractical or unsuitable in view of the nature of the pool."

Satisfying the Internal Revenue Service on this point may not be easy. However, anticipated technological change will make it almost impossible or at least impractical to determine a base year price for any given make or model many years from now. Economic and environmental pressures on automobile manufacturers are already evident in many ways. Catalytic converters, other emission control and pollution control changes—changes because of safety standards—and fuel conserving changes are but a few.

The construction of the price change link on a year-by-year basis under the link-chain method seems to be a better practical way to deal with the technological changes expected to occur in the future. Thus, the link-chain method seems justified because of anticipated technological changes and because the price pattern of items presently within the inventory pool are similar. Price patterns of items expected to be added to the pool in future years should also be similar.

The income tax regulations impose a very important extra filing requirement on taxpayers who elect to apply the link-chain method. The regulations re-

(page 6 of 7 of article)

HOW LIFO WORKS

Willard J. De Filipps, CPA - Cars & Trucks, February, 1975

quire a taxpayer using either an index or the link-chain method to file a complete statement detailing the particular method used in determining the index. This statement must be filed separately with the Commissioner of Internal Revenue, Attention: P:R:Washington 25, D.C. This special requirement is apparently intended to highlight the election of this method for review by the LIFO specialists in the Washington, D.C., National Office.

Making The LIFO Election. In order to elect the LIFO method, it is necessary to file a statement of election as part of the (corporate) income tax return filed for the election year. This statement of election is made on Form 970, and the form is entitled "Application to Use LIFO Inventory Method." Form 970 must be filed in duplicate and signed by the corporation and an officer.

This form and the instructions should be reviewed thoroughly by the dealer and his tax advisor. The form states, and the taxpayer agrees upon executing the form to be bound by the following statement: "The taxpayer hereby agrees to such adjustments incident to the change to (or from) the LIFO method, or to the use of such method in the inventories of prior taxable years or otherwise, as the District Director of Internal Revenue upon examination of the taxpayer's return for the years involved may deem necessary in order to clearly reflect income."

This binds the taxpayer to any adjustments necessary to state his beginning inventory *at cost*, as well as other adjustments which may be successfully contended by the IRS upon examination.

In connection with filing the Form 970, it is also necessary to submit analyses of the inventory as of the end of the initial year of change and the two preceding years. Thus, for a calendar year taxpayer, inventory analyses would be required for December 31, 1972, 1973, and 1974.

The IRS has the further authority to require the extension of LIFO to inventory categories not initially selected or necessarily desired under the circumstances where the extended application is necessary "in order to more clearly reflect income."

As indicated throughout this article, regulations do not tell an automobile dealer specifically how to apply LIFO to his inventories. Consequently, the initiative lies with the dealer and his tax advisor, subject to eventual review by the Internal Revenue Service. Regulations do state that the number and the composition of the pools used, the appropriateness of such pools; the propriety of all computations incidental to the use of the pools; and, all other aspects relating to the LIFO conversion are subject to examination and must be approved by the Internal Revenue Service. Adequate records must be maintained to support all computations.

Once the LIFO election has been approved by the Internal Revenue Service, the numerous computational elections or alternatives selected must be followed in subsequent years unless permission to change is granted by the Commissioner. Consequently, once a taxpayer elects LIFO, he is "locked in" to continue the procedures until he gets permission to change. All of this underscores the need for initial careful consideration of the sub-elections and computational alternatives *and* the significance of properly completing Form 970.

Tax Forms And Cash Flow. Usually the basic reason for considering LIFO is that it will reduce the dealership's (corporate) taxes for the year of change.

There are a few ramifications that follow from this. First, the corporation may have significantly overpaid its 1974 estimated income tax once the LIFO adjustment is taken into account. Where this occurs, the excess 1974 estimated tax payments are refundable, and the refund process can be speeded up. Where a corporation has overpaid its 1974 estimated tax payments for whatever reason, it should consider filing Form 4466 ("Corporate Application for a Quick Refund of Overpayment of Estimated Tax").

This form must be filed within two and one-half months after the end of the taxable year and before the corporation files its income tax return. For a calendar year dealership corporation, this form must be filed by March 15, 1975. This form can be filed by any corporation that has overpaid its estimated tax if the overpayment is (a) at least 10 percent of the expected tax liability *and* (b) at least $500. This form has instructions printed on its reverse side, and it should be filed with the Internal Revenue Service Center where the corporation files its tax return.

In many situations, the election of LIFO may create or increase a net operating loss for 1974. The net operating loss may be carried back to the three preceding taxable years and forward to the five succeeding years. The order of application is that a 1974 operating loss first goes back against 1971 income tax, then forward next to 1972, and then to 1973 before it is carried forward to 1975 through 1979.

Where the dealership has paid corporate taxes in 1971-2-3, Form 1139 can be prepared to speed up the refund of those prior years' corporate tax payments. Form 1139 is entitled "Corporate Application for Tentative Refund from Carryback of Net Operating Loss. . . ." This form can be filed within one year after the year in which the net operating loss occurs. In other words, it can be filed anytime before December 31, 1975, by a 1974 calendar year taxpayer. The usual practice is that it is prepared and filed when the corporate return is filed; however, it should be filed *separately* from the income tax return to expedite processing by the Internal Revenue Service.

Finally, LIFO provides a "breather" in terms of 1975 quarterly estimated tax payments. A corporation may base its 1975 estimated tax payments on the amount of tax shown to be due on its 1974 tax return. Consequently, to the extent LIFO reduces the 1974 tax liability, it correspondingly reduces the amount of quarterly estimated tax payments during 1975 of 1975 expected tax liability.

Conclusion. This article has discussed the major procedural aspects and the importance of carefully selecting alternatives to reflect the adoption of LIFO. Many factors affect the overall decision of whether to adopt LIFO. Some of these factors involve subjective considerations, the impact of which varies according to personalities and anticipated attitudes.

The results of the computations discussed in this article must be considered against the various basic considerations and front-end costs of switching to LIFO. The considerations are summarized briefly below:

1. Amended returns for the year prior to the change are required if inventory write-downs from cost were made;
2. Executive and other bonuses, profit sharing plan contributions, buy-sell agreements, and other contracts may be affected;
3. Complete information concerning inventories has to be submitted to the Internal Revenue Service;
4. Overall exposure before the Internal Revenue Service is increased and not necessarily limited to inventory matters;
5. All reports covering the full taxable year, whether they are annual reports to shareholders, to banks, to the factory for credit purposes, or to any other financing source, must be reported on the LIFO basis. This reporting consistency is a requirement in the tax law;
6. Considerable time and expense may be involved in explaining and justifying the LIFO application to the Internal Revenue Service and to the factory; and,
7. Overall price levels and/or inventory levels may go down, thereby requiring a repayment of some (or all) of the cumulative tax savings.

These and other factors all interrelate with each other to complicate arriving at a decision. For the dealer who has evaluated these with his tax advisor and decided to go ahead with LIFO, LIFO can present a Legitimate Inventory Financial Opportunity. It is hoped this article will help those who have decided to go ahead with LIFO for 1974.

(page 7 of 7 of article)

A Tune-Up on Corporate Tax Issues: What's Going on Under the Hood?

Senate Committee on Finance
June 13, 2006

Statement Submitted by
J. Michael Keeling
President, CAE
The ESOP Association
1726 M Street, NW Suite 501
Washington, DC 20036
202/293-2971 (p) 202/293-7568 (f)
Michael@esopassociation.org
www.esopassociation.org

Chair Grassley, ranking member Baucus and members of the Senate Committee on Finance.

My name is J. Michael Keeling, President of The ESOP Association, a national 501(c)(6) trade association with over 2400 members that represents corporations that sponsor employee ownership through Employee Stock Ownership Plans, or ESOPs.

You may feel it is out of place for the trade association representing ESOP companies to submit testimony to a hearing on Corporate Tax Reform.

The Senate Committee on Finance has a long and positive record in support of employee ownership in general, and ESOPs specifically. Those Senators with at least 20 years of service remember the concept of employee ownership through ESOPs originated in the Senate under the leadership of former Senator Russell B. Long.

Now, today, the Senate Committee on Finance is focused on Corporate Tax Reform; this focus is partially driven by the report released November 1, 2005, by the Presidential Panel on Federal Tax Reform recommendations for massive changes in how business and individuals are taxed under our Federal income tax system.

The ESOP community is very disappointed with the Panel's recommendations. Why? It is not just because of a recommendation it makes with regard to savings plans that would eliminate ESOPs, but because the Panel failed to recognize anything about ESOPs, and did not take notice of what ESOPs can do for American business, American employees, and American competitiveness.

For you see, the law is clear. ESOPs serve a dual purpose. Let us quote for the members 90 Stat. 1590. P.L. 94-455:

"(h) Intent of Congress Concerning Employee Stock Ownership Plans. – The Congress, in a series of laws (the Regional Rail Reorganization Act of 1973, the Employee Retirement Income Security Act of 1974, and the Tax Reduction act of 1975) and this Act has made clear its interest in encouraging employee stock ownership plans as a bold and innovative method of strengthening the free private enterprise system which will solve the dual problems of securing capital funds for necessary capital growth and of bringing about stock ownership by all corporate employees. The Congress is deeply concerned that the objectives sought by this series of laws will be made unattainable by regulations and rulings which treat employee stock ownership plans as conventional retirement plans, which reduce the freedom of the employee trust and employers to take the necessary steps to implement the plans, and which otherwise block the establishment and success of these plans."

As noted, this is the law; it is not a sense of the Congress resolution.

Our nation's courts have taken note of this law in law suits involving ESOPs since 1975, citing the law as the primary reason that ESOPs are to be judged by standards that are different from the traditional ERISA plan. A typical phrase used by courts is "ESOPs are intended by

Congress to be tools of corporate finance as well as retirement savings plans". Often courts add, "ESOPs are to be ownership plans as well as retirement savings plans.". See *Moensch v. Robertson et al*, Federal, 3rd Circuit, 1995.

Keeping in mind the purpose of ESOPs, let us not abandoned the wonderful concept that America should have more owners, or a true ownership society. We ESOP advocates were thrilled to hear President Bush say on January 20, 2005,

"*To give every American a stake in the promise and future…we will …build an ownership society. We will widen the ownership of homes and businesses, retirement savings, and health insurance—preparing our people for the challenges of life in a free society.*

By making every citizen an agenda of his or her own destiny, we will give our fellow Americans greater freedom from want and fear and make our society more prosperous and just and equal."

These very words resonate well with the Vision of The ESOP Association which provides,

"*We believe that employee ownership improves American competitiveness…that it increases productivity through greater employee participation in the workplace…that it strengthens our free enterprise economy and creates a broader distribution of wealth…and that it maximizes human potential by enhancing the self-worth, dignity, and well-being of our people.*

Therefore, we envision an America where employee ownership is widely recognized as a catalyst for economic prosperity…where the great majority of employees own stock in the companies where they work…and where employee ownership enables employees to share in the wealth they help create…"

So what is our purpose in submitting this testimony to a hearing on corporate tax reform?

We respectfully request that as the Committee reviews details of how to make taxes on businesses more fair, and more simple, that the Committee not overlook that we have a set of laws to make the tax on business more fair by encouraging businesses to be broadly owned by more people, their employees.

It may be that the changes you decide to make, if you do, will rearrange those ESOP laws that encourage current business owners to share their wealth by letting employees become what we like to say, "players" in the best economic system ever devised. If that is the case, then let us consider new ways, new approaches that encourage a more fair, more effective, and more productive pattern of ownership by continuing the Ways and Means' long standing posture of supporting broadened ownership of our nation's productive assets through ESOPs.

The ESOP community, as always, will stand ready to work constructively with the Committee and Committee staff to ensure laws promoting employee ownership are crafted in a manner to accomplish the goals of broad-based employee ownership.

On behalf of the ESOP community, I thank you for taking note of this testimony.

○